2018 EDITION

Greenberg's GUIDES

LIONEL® TRAINS

POCKET PRICE GUIDE

Edited by Roger Carp

D1521793

KALMBACH BOOKS

WAUKESHA, WI

688
CARP   REF.

Kalmbach Books
21027 Crossroads Circle
Waukesha, Wisconsin 53186
www.KalmbachHobbyStore.com

Published in 2017
Thirty-eighth Edition

Manufactured in the United States of America

ISBN: 978-1-62700-476-3

Front cover photo: 2383 Santa Fe F3 Diesel A Unit,
model courtesy Joe Algozzini

Back cover photo: 455 Operating Oil Derrick

We constantly strive to improve Greenberg's Pocket Price Guides. If
you find missing items or detect misinformation, please contact us.
Send your comments, new information, or corrections via e-mail
to books@kalmbach.com or by mail to Lionel Pocket Price Guide
Editor at the address above.

Library of Congress Control Number: 2017934275

CONTENTS

INTRODUCTION

Whether you are a longtime Lionel enthusiast or a newcomer to the toy train hobby, this guide contains the information you need to identify and evaluate thousands of items made by Lionel since 1901. Most of all, you'll have at your fingertips the most up-to-date prices for locomotives, freight cars, passenger cars, stations, tunnels, signals, track sections, transformers, and other items.

What is listed
Almost every Lionel O gauge toy train produced over the years is listed in the pages that follow.

This edition of the *Lionel Pocket Price Guide* contains information about new additions to the product line as described in Lionel catalogs, press releases, and other sources. Any additions that Lionel makes to its line after this book is printed will be reported in the next edition.

In addition, the *Lionel Pocket Price Guide* provides information about items associated with Lionel yet not mentioned in its catalogs. These uncataloged or promotional items include unique models and specially decorated locomotives and cars that Lionel produces for national and regional toy train collecting and operating groups, museums, local railroad clubs, and other customers.

When to consult this guide
Many readers of the *Lionel Pocket Price Guide* use it after the fact. They already have some trains and accessories and now want to identify and evaluate those items. Maybe someone lucked upon a bridge at a garage sale and wants to know whether it's a 300 Hellgate or a 314 deck girder type. Somebody else needs to provide his or her insurance agent with a complete list of O gauge locomotives that includes their conditions and current values. This guide contains the information needed to identify that bridge as well as determining present values for that engine roster.

In addition, the *Lionel Pocket Price Guide* can help you think about what to acquire in the future. That's really when the fun begins! You just have to spend some time considering how you want to approach the hobby. Collect, operate, or both? Prewar, postwar, or modern? Particular types of locomotives or cars? Favorite railroads? Promotional items?

Once you have a general idea of how to enjoy this hobby, you can make informed decisions about which trains you want.

UNDERSTANDING VALUES

The values presented here are an averaged reflection of prices for items bought and sold across the country during the year prior to the publication of this edition. These values are offered as guidelines and should be viewed as starting points that buyers and sellers can use to begin informed and reasonable negotiations.

In a listing for a steam locomotive, the value includes a tender, even if the tender is not listed in the description. The value of steam locomotives, particularly prewar items, may be affected significantly by the type of tender included.

Values for individual items may differ from what is listed in this price guide due to a few key factors. Where collectible trains are scarce and demand outruns supply, actual values may exceed what is shown. Values may also rise where certain items are especially popular, often because of their road names. And as with all collectibles, national and local economic conditions will impact values, which tend to drop when times are tough and demand falls.

Original packaging

Items in Like New or better condition require their original packaging to maintain their high level of value. The values given for items in Good and Excellent condition are not based on the expectation that a box and other associated items are present.

Items that do have their original packaging, especially if it is complete and undamaged, command a premium among collectors of prewar and postwar trains. No hard-and-fast rules can be stated as to how much higher their value is over the same items in Excellent condition. Generally speaking, though, boxed items in Like New condition are valued about 50 percent above the same item without a box.

Using the values

The values listed are what a consumer would pay—more or less—to get a particular item in a specific condition. One collector selling that item to another would probably ask the stated value and expect to get something close to it.

However, someone selling that same item to a person or business that intends to resell it (a train dealer) is unlikely to receive the stated value. Experience shows that sellers get about half the amount. Dealers offer less so they can earn a profit when reselling an item.

When buying or selling a toy train, you should learn more about it. Start by consulting this price guide and then look for more about it in a reference guide or website on toy trains. You can also ask more experienced hobbyists for their opinion about the item's condition and value.

FINDING A PRODUCT

The *Lionel Pocket Price Guide* has been divided into seven major sections.

Section 1: Prewar 1901–1942

Section 1 of the *Lionel Pocket Price Guide* is devoted to the prewar period. The entries cover just about every train, accessory, and transformer associated with Lionel's line during its first 42 years.

The only outfits (sets) listed are those of articulated streamlined trains that consist of a powered unit and attached unpowered cars.

In an item's listing, the basic description specifies its gauge (the distance between the inside of the outermost rails). During this time, Lionel catalogued models in four sizes. It is noted in parentheses whether an item is 2⅞-inch, Standard (2⅛ inches), O (1¼ inches), or OO (¾ inches). O gauge models intended to run on tighter 27-inch-diameter track belong to Lionel's O27 gauge line and are identified as such.

Transformers, rheostats, and many accessories were not limited to a single gauge, so their descriptions do not specify a gauge.

Section 2: Postwar 1945–1969

Section 2 concentrates on the postwar period. Nearly every train and accessory (except outfits) that Lionel cataloged between 1945 and 1969 has its own listing. By this time, Lionel no longer made trains in 2⅞-inch, Standard, or OO gauge. Instead, it offered trains that ran on track that had a diameter of either 31 inches (O gauge) or 27 inches (O27 gauge). However, the entries in this section do not distinguish between O and O27 since only a handful of locomotives and cars could operate solely on the wider curves.

Section 3: Modern Era 1970–2018

Section 3 shows the trains, accessories, transformers, and other items that Lionel has cataloged since 1970. The modern era encompasses the products of three companies: Model Products Corp. (MPC, a division of General Mills), 1970–85; Lionel Trains Inc. (LTI), 1986–95; and Lionel LLC (LLC), 1996–2018.

These incarnations of Lionel are responsible for an enormous inventory of trains, rolling stock, transformers, and accessories. Cataloged and uncataloged O gauge items (ranging from the near-scale Standard O to the toy-like O27) can be found within the pages of this section.

All items in Section 3 are arranged according to their Lionel catalog number (omitting the numeral 6 used as a prefix). The descriptions of products made during the modern era may include information that relates to where in the product line a particular item belongs. Models derived from MPC designs have been described as *traditional*. Rolling stock whose dimensions and features approach scale realism may be designated as Standard O (abbreviated as std O). Locomotives equipped with TrainMaster Command Control or its successor, Legacy, are identified with the abbreviation CC.

Section 4: Lionel Corporation Tinplate

Section 4 features 800 products developed jointly by Lionel and MTH Electric Trains since 2009. These Lionel Corporation trains and accessories are reproductions of Lionel (and some American Flyer) tinplate items from the prewar era. You'll find trains here that operate as tinplate trains did prior to 1942 as well as others that have been updated with modern features and technology, such as Proto-Sound. The retail prices are listed for these products.

Section 5: Club Cars and Special Production

Section 5 gathers the various items, principally locomotives and rolling stock, that Lionel has made or sponsored for different hobby organizations, museums, and businesses since the 1970s. These uncataloged club cars and special production items are arranged according to the groups that offered them for sale. Those groups are listed alphabetically; regional divisions of national organizations follow the parent organization's listing. Within each subordinate section, items are listed in numerical (not chronological) order, with a basic description similar to that used for cataloged entries.

Section 6: Boxes

Over the past 25 years, original boxes and other forms of packaging have assumed significance for some collectors. These hobbyists insist that the trains they buy come in the boxes and have the paperwork and ancillary pieces (inserts, instruction sheets, and envelopes) that the manufacturer packed with them before offering them for sale.

Cardboard boxes, inserts, and assorted sheets of paper are more fragile than die-cast metal or plastic trains. They were also deemed to be less important to the children playing with toy trains long ago and so were not treated with the same care. Instruction sheets were lost, and boxes were discarded. As a result, fewer boxes and instruction sheets have survived than have the trains and accessories that went with them. In some cases, the box that a particular locomotive, car, or even set came in is now valued more than the item itself.

Boxes are evaluated according to standards and conditions established by the Train Collectors Association, similar to those developed for toy trains and accessories:

P-10 **Mint:** Brand new, complete, all original as manufactured, and unused. Flaps appear to never have been opened, and edges are crisp. No tears, fading, or wear marks. Contains original contents and all applicable sealing tape, wrap, and staples.

P-9 **Store New:** Complete, all original, and unused. Box may have merchant additions such as store stamps and price tags. Must have appropriate inner liners.

P-8 **Like New:** Complete and all original. There is evidence of light use and aging. Box may have notations (discrete) added since leaving the manufacturer.

P-7 **Excellent:** Complete and all original. Box shows moderate signs of being opened and closed including edge and corner wear. All flaps must be intact.

P-6 **Very Good:** Complete and all original. Box shows signs of usage such as minor abrasions, small tears, color changes, and minor soiling. Inner liners may be missing, and inner flaps may require strengthening. The box can still safely store its original contents.

P-5 **Good:** Box shows substantial wear, and edges may be damaged. Box may have extensive color fading but no evident water damage or cardboard deterioration. Exterior flaps are present, but their connection to the box may require repair. Inner liners may be missing. With care, the box can still store contents. (Any box that has been repaired cannot be graded above P-5.)

P-4 **Fair:** Box shows heavy damage and may have been repaired. Inner flaps may be missing. Box cannot store its original contents. Water damage may be present.

Values for postwar boxes in this section are shown for Good (P-5) and Excellent (P-7) conditions.

Lionel used these box types during the postwar years:

Art Deco: Original postwar box with bold orange and blue design and lettering. It was used in 1946 and 1947.

Classic: More understated design than Art Deco. It was the main component box from 1948 through 1958. Boxes can be divided into Early (1948–49), Middle (1949–55), and Late (1956–58) Classic designs, which are marked by minor lettering changes.

Orange Perforated: This was a significant change from the Classic design. The solid orange box features white lettering and a tear-out perforated front panel. It was used in 1959 and 1960.

Orange Picture: Instead of a perforated panel, this version of the Orange Perforated box features an illustration of a steam locomotive and an F3 diesel on the front. It was used from 1961 to 1964.

Hillside Orange Picture: Similar to an Orange Picture box, it is labeled with Hillside, N.J., where Lionel's plant was located. It was used in 1965.

Cellophane: Used in 1966, this box features a clear cellophane window on the front.

Hagerstown Checkerboard: It has a Lionel checkerboard pattern and Hagerstown, Maryland, printed on end flap bottoms. The box was used in 1968.

Hillside Checkerboard: This 1969 box is the same as the Hagerstown Checkerboard box, but with Hillside, New Jersey, printed on it.

Lionel also used brown corrugated and plain white boxes.

Section 7: Sets

This section lists boxed train sets catalogued by Lionel during the postwar years, 1945–1969. When collecting sets, it is important that the sets, or outfits, contain all the items, including ancillary ones, that Lionel packed with them. These items include the locomotive (and tender if a steam engine) rolling stock, any accessories, track, transformer, instructions and other paper pieces, component boxes, and the set box.

The listings include the set's catalog number, a short description, and product numbers for the locomotives, rolling stock, and any major accessories. Sets came with O27 gauge, O gauge, or Super O track. O27 and Super O track are listed in the set's description. If no track is listed, the set came with O gauge.

Set values are listed for Excellent (C-7) condition. The presence and condition of original component boxes, set boxes, inserts and other packaging materials can have a significant effect on a set's value. The values reflect the inclusion of these materials. Values of individual set and component boxes can be found in Section 6.

Due to space constraints, not every item found in a set is listed in the description. You can find more complete information on a set's contents on various websites and in *Greenberg's Guide to Lionel Trains 1945–1969 Volume III: Catalogued Sets* by Paul Ambrose. (Although the book is out of print, it is available from booksellers on the Internet.)

USING THE GUIDE

Number	Description	Condition ——— Good	Exc	Cond/$
2561	Vista Valley Observation Car, *59–61* *	75	230	___
X6454	NYC Boxcar, *48*			
	(A) Brown body	15	35	___
	(B) Orange body	50	140	___
	(C) Tan body	20	60	___
6475	Libby's Crushed Pineapple Vat Car, *63 u*	35	90	___

Identifying a catalog number

A Lionel catalog number is usually stamped, printed, or painted on an item. However, some products do not contain a catalog number. In these cases, you can match the product with its catalog number using a comprehensive reference book or website, including Lionel.com, which contains past and current catalogs.

Two-, three-, and four-digit numbers predominated during the prewar (1901–42) and postwar (1945–69) periods. Four- and five-digit numbers have been most common during the modern era (1970–2018).

On the models, catalog numbers often double as road numbers, although sometimes separate road numbers were added.

Locating an item

Sections are arranged in numerical order of catalog numbers. Items having one or more zeroes as placeholders are listed before those without placeholders. For example, a 004 4-6-4 Locomotive is listed before a 4 Electric Locomotive.

In the prewar and postwar sections, some items such as transformers and track pieces, are identified by a letter. These products follow the numbered items.

Reading an entry

Every entry begins with the product's catalog number assigned by Lionel. (Club and special production cars may have numbers that were assigned by the group.)

A basic description of the model follows. It gives the type of product, lists the name of any railroad identified with it, and includes identifying characteristics, such as color or lettering. If the item has a road number that differs from its catalog number, that number is shown in quotation marks. (Most of these are seen in Section 3). Abbreviations used in the descriptions, including those of railroad names, are listed at the back of the price guide.

Next, you'll find the year or years during which that item was part of Lionel's cataloged product line. The years are shown in italics. If a year is followed by a *u*, this item is considered to be uncataloged. It was not part of the cataloged line but a promotional item that Lionel made or sponsored for an outside business or group.

Entries that show an asterisk (*) after the year have had one or more reissues of the item made.

Many entries feature variations, each indicated by a separate letter (A, B, and so forth). Variations amount to slight yet noteworthy differences in appearance that distinguish models that otherwise seem identical. These differences can relate to color, lettering, and details that were added or deleted. For items having many variations, an entry may not include every variation.

An entry concludes with an indication of the value of the item for several common conditions.

Condition

Lionel enthusiasts should be familiar with the condition and grading standards established by the Train Collectors Association, which are used as the basis for evaluating the condition of toy trains and accessories:

C-10 Mint: Brand new—all original, unused, and unblemished.

C-9 Factory New: Same condition as Mint but with evidence of factory rubs or slight signs of handling, shipping, and being test run at the factory.

C-8 Like New: Complete and all original with no rust or no missing parts; may show effects of being displayed or signs of age and may have been run.

C-7 Excellent: All original and may have minute scratches and paint nicks; no rust, no missing parts, and no distortion of component parts.

C-6 Very Good: Has minor scratches, paint nicks, or minor spots of surface rust; is free of dents and may have minor parts replaced.

C-5 Good: Shows evidence of heavy use and signs of play wear—small dents, scratches, minor paint loss, and minor surface rust.

C-4 Fair: Shows evidence of heavy use—scratches and dents, moderate paint loss, missing parts, and surface rust.

C-3 Poor: Requires major body repair and is a candidate for restoration; major rust, missing parts, and heavily scratched.

C-2 Restoration: Needs to be restored.

C-1 Junk: Parts value only.

Values are listed for prewar and postwar trains in Good (C-5) and Excellent (C-7) conditions. For modern-era trains, including special production and club cars, the values for Excellent (C-7) and Mint (C-10) are shown.

You may also see NRS listed as a value. NRS (No Reported Sales) refers to an item with limited pricing data since only a handful of these scarce items may have been reported.

Determining a model's condition

Look over a model carefully to see whether it has suffered serious damage, including warping and breaking. Then note whether any parts are missing. Feel for dents in metal and cracks in plastic. Check for areas marred by rust, mildew, or chipped paint.

The TCA condition standards will assist you in evaluating your model, such as deciding whether a prewar or postwar model falls below Good or above Excellent.

The assessment of a toy train's value is based on the expectations that it has not been modified and that all parts are present and original to it. Repainting or relettering a model seriously undermines a train's value, regardless of how beat-up and scratched it may have been before undergoing modification. Any model that has been altered should be labeled as a restoration; potential buyers deserve to be informed about how it has been modified, so they do not mistake it for an original.

A model that is missing some parts should be sold *as is* or have those parts replaced by identical originals. A tank car cataloged in 1935 that needs a brake wheel must have a part from 1935 put on it to be considered a true original. Adding a brake wheel from 1936 undermines the car's legitimacy as much as adding one from 2017 does.

The same rule applies to the ancillary items that came with various models. The value of a flatcar may depend largely on the miniature airplane or rocket packed with it; therefore, having a load that is a genuine original is essential to maintaining the value of that flatcar. Similarly, freight loaders must have whatever cargo came with them (coal, logs, trailers, and so forth). Reproductions should be identified as such.

		Good	Exc	
001	4-6-4 Locomotive (OO), *38–42*	195	360	____
1	Bild-A-Motor (O), *28–31*	60	140	____
1	Trolley (std), *06–14*			
	(A) Cream body, orange band and roof	1900	4750	____
	(B) White body, blue band and roof	1750	4750	____
	(C) Cream body, blue band and roof	1300	3150	____
	(D) Cream body, blue band and roof, Curtis Bay	2150	5550	____
	(E) Blue, cream band, blue roof	1450	3150	____
1/111	Trolley Trailer (std), *06–14*	1000	2700	____
002	4-6-4 Locomotive (OO), *39–42*	160	285	____
2	Bild-A-Motor (std), *28–31*	100	180	____
2	Trolley (std), *06–16**			
	(A) Yellow, red band	1200	3575	____
	(B) Red, yellow band	1200	2250	____
2/200	Trolley Trailer (std), *06–16*	1000	1800	____
003	4-6-4 Locomotive (OO), *39–42*			
	(A) 003W whistling Tender	190	395	____
	(B) 003T nonwhistling Tender	175	355	____
3	Trolley (std), *06–13*			
	(A) Cream, orange band	1400	3100	____
	(B) Cream, dark olive green band	1400	3100	____
	(C) Orange, dark olive green band	1400	3100	____
	(D) Dark green, cream windows	1400	3100	____
	(E) Green, cream windows, Bay Shore	1650	3700	____
3/300	Trolley Trailer (std), *06–13*	1500	3500	____
004	4-6-4 Locomotive (OO), *39–42*			
	(A) 004W whistling Tender	210	350	____
	(B) 004T nonwhistling Tender	190	310	____
4	Electric Locomotive 0-4-0 (O), *28–32**			
	(A) Orange, black frame	550	875	____
	(B) Gray, apple green stripe	580	1050	____
4	Trolley (std), *06–12*			
	(A) Cream, dark olive green band	3000	4950	____
	(B) Green or olive green, cream roof	3000	4950	____
4U	No. 4 Kit Form (O), *28–29*	1150	1600	____
5	0-4-0 Locomotive, no tender, early (std), *06–07*			
	(A) NYC & HRR	1000	1450	____
	(B) Pennsylvania	1400	2300	____
	(C) NYC & HRRR (3 Rs)	1250	2050	____
	(D) B&O RR	1500	2400	____
5	0-4-0 Locomotive, tender, early Special (std), *06–09*	980	1300	____

		Good	Exc
___ 5	0-4-0 Locomotive, no tender, later (std), *10–11*	750	1150
5 ___	0-4-0 Locomotive, tender, later Special (std), *10–11*	920	1200
___ 5/51	0-4-0 Locomotive, tender, latest (std), *12–23*	800	1100
___ 6	4-4-0 Locomotive (std), *06–23*	860	1250
___ 6	0-4-0 Locomotive Special (std), *08–09*	2050	2950
___ 7	Steam 4-4-0 Locomotive (std), *10–23**	1850	2300
8	Electric Locomotive 0-4-0 (std), *25–32*		
___	(A) Maroon or mojave, brass windows and trim	130	250
___	(B) Olive green, brass windows	155	205
___	(C) Red, brass or cream windows	195	250
___	(D) Peacock, orange windows	520	750
8	Trolley (std), *08–14**		
___	(A) Cream, orange band and roof	3000	5400
___	(B) Dark green, cream windows	3000	5400
8E	Electric Locomotive 0-4-0 (std), *26–32*		
___	(A) Mojave, brass windows and trim	175	250
___	(B) Red, brass or cream windows	150	225
___	(C) Peacock, orange windows	370	590
___	(D) Pea green, cream stripe	465	670
___ 9	Electric Locomotive 0-4-0 (std), *29**	1200	2150
___ 9	Motor Car (std), *09–12*		NRS
___ 9	Trolley (std), *09*	3000	5400
9E	Electric Locomotive (std), *28–35**		
___	(A) 0-4-0, orange	700	1250
___	(B) 2-4-2, two-tone green	880	1600
___	(C) 2-4-2, gunmetal gray	860	1100
___ 9U	Electric Locomotive 0-4-0 Kit (std), *28–29*	975	1975
10	Electric Locomotive 0-4-0 (std), *25–29**		
___	(A) Mojave, brass trim	145	215
___	(B) Gray, brass trim	125	205
___	(C) Peacock, brass inserts	145	205
___	(D) Red, cream stripe	580	880
10	Interurban (std), *10–16*		
___	(A) Maroon	3000	5750
___	(B) Dark olive green	1200	2150
___ 10E	Electric Locomotive 0-4-0 (std), *26–30*		
___	(A) Olive green, black frame		NRS
___	(B) Peacock, dark green or black frame	245	400
___	(C) State brown, dark green frame	435	630
___	(D) Gray, black frame	165	220
___	(E) Red, cream stripe	620	890
___ 011	Switches, pair (O), *33–37*	18	38
___ 11	Flatcar, early (std), *06–08*	150	360
___ 11	Flatcar, later (std), *09–15*	45	90

		Good	Exc	
11	Flatcar, latest (std), *16–18*	50	90	____
11	Flatcar, Lionel Corp. (std), *18–26*	50	80	____
012	Switches, pair (0), *27–33*	20	40	____
12	Gondola, early (std), *06–08*	150	360	____
12	Gondola, later (std), *09–15*	50	100	____
12	Gondola, latest (std), *16–18*	35	70	____
12	Gondola, Lionel Corp. (std), *18–26*	50	70	____
013	012 Switches and 439 panel board, *27–33*	120	190	____
13	Cattle Car, early (std), *06–08*	300	450	____
13	Cattle Car, later (std), *09–15*	150	225	____
13	Cattle Car, latest (std), *16–18*	65	115	____
13	Cattle Car, Lionel Corp. (std), *18–26*	65	115	____
0014	Boxcar (OO), *38–42*			
	(A) Yellow, Lionel Lines	80	155	____
	(B) Tuscan, Pennsylvania	40	75	____
14	Boxcar, early (std), *06–08*	195	435	____
14	Boxcar, later (std), *09–15*	80	105	____
14	Boxcar, latest (std), *16–18*	75	105	____
14	Boxcar, Lionel Corp. (std), *18–26*	80	105	____
0015	Tank Car (OO), *38–42*			
	(A) Silver, Sun Oil	40	90	____
	(B) Black, Shell	50	85	____
15	Oil Car, early (std), *06–08*	200	360	____
15	Oil Car, later (std), *09–15*	75	115	____
15	Oil Car, latest (std), *16–18*	75	115	____
15	Oil Car, Lionel Corp. (std), *18–26*	75	115	____
0016	Hopper Car (OO), *38–42*			
	(A) Gray	75	160	____
	(B) Black	60	115	____
16	Ballast Dump Car, early (std), *06–11*	400	700	____
16	Ballast Dump Car, later (std), *09–15*	95	175	____
16	Ballast Dump Car, latest (std), *16–18*	95	175	____
16	Ballast Dump Car, Lionel Corp. (std), *18–26*	95	175	____
0017	Caboose (OO), *38–42*	40	90	____
17	Caboose, early (std), *06–08*	220	440	____
17	Caboose, later (std), *09–15*	70	135	____
17	Caboose, latest (std), *16–18*	75	135	____
17	Caboose, Lionel Corp. (std), *18–26*	50	90	____
18	Pullman Car (std), *08*			
	(A) Dark olive green, nonremovable roof	700	2150	____
	(B) Dark olive green, removable roof	90	215	____
	(C) Yellow-orange, removable roof	315	870	____
	(D) Orange, removable roof	90	205	____
	(E) Mojave, removable roof	305	890	____
18	Pullman Car (std), *11–13*	600	900	____

			Good	Exc
____ 18	Pullman Car (std), *13–15*		150	270
____ 18	Pullman Car (std), *15–18*		150	270
____ 18	Pullman Car (std), *18–22*		90	155
____ 18	Pullman Car (std), *23–26*		270	530
19	Combine Car (std), *08*			
____	(A) Dark olive green, nonremovable roof		1100	2600
____	(B) Dark olive green, removable roof		80	145
____	(C) Yellow-orange, removable roof		260	430
____	(D) Orange, removable roof		115	205
____	(E) Mojave, removable roof		305	890
____ 19	Combine Car (std), *11–13*		600	900
____ 19	Combine Car (std), *13–15*		200	270
____ 19	Combine Car (std), *15–18*		200	270
____ 19	Combine Car (std), *18–22*		90	155
____ 19	Combine Car (std), *23–26*		265	520
____ 020	90-degree Crossover (O), *15–42*		4	15
____ 020X	45-degree Crossover (O), *17–42*		3	10
____ 20	90-degree Crossover (std), *09–32*		4	10
____ 20	Direct Current Reducer, *06*		95	195
____ 20X	45-degree Crossover (std), *28–32*		5	10
____ 021	Switches, pair (O), *15–37*		20	50
____ 21	90-degree Crossover (std), *06*		10	20
____ 21	Switches, pair (std), *15–25*		35	70
____ 022	Remote Control Switches, pair (O), *38–42*		40	70
____ 22	Manual Switches, pair (std), *06–25*		45	75
____ 023	Bumper (O), *15–33*		15	35
____ 23	Bumper (std), *06–23*		15	40
____ 0024	Pennsylvania Boxcar (OO), *39–42*		45	75
____ 24	Railway Station (std), *06*			NRS
____ 025	Bumper (O), *28–42*		15	40
0025	Tank Car (OO), *39–42*			
____	(A) Black, Shell		40	90
____	(B) Silver, Sunoco		40	80
____ 25	Open Station (std), *06*			NRS
____ 25	Bumper (std), *27–42*		25	45
____ 26	Passenger Bridge (std), *06*		15	40
____ 0027	Caboose (OO), *39–42*		40	70
____ 27	Lighting Set, *11–23*		15	40
____ 27	Station (std), *09–12*			NRS
____ 28	Double Station with dome, *09–12*			NRS

		Good	Exc	
29	Day Coach (std), *07–22*			
	(A) Dark olive green, 9 windows	1500	3000	___
	(B) Maroon, 10 windows	1200	1500	___
	(C) Dark green, 10 windows	3000	4500	___
	(D) Dark olive green, 10 windows	680	1000	___
	(E) Dark green, 10 windows	450	900	___
0031	2-rail 13" Curve Track (OO), *39–42*	5	10	___
31	Combine Car (std), *21–25*			
	(A) Maroon	70	90	___
	(B) Orange	125	195	___
	(C) Dark olive green	65	90	___
	(D) Brown	75	95	___
0032	2-rail 12" Straight Track (OO), *39–42*	10	15	___
32	Mail Car (std), *21–25*			
	(A) Maroon	85	125	___
	(B) Orange	120	185	___
	(C) Dark olive green	65	85	___
	(D) Brown	70	90	___
32	Miniature Figures, *09–18*	95	250	___
33	Electric Locomotive 0-6-0, early (std), *13*			
	(A) Dark olive green, NYC in oval	105	190	___
	(B) Black, NYC	320	950	___
	(C) Dark olive green, NYC	440	950	___
	(D) Pennsylvania RR	580	1250	___
33	Electric Locomotive 0-4-0, later (std), *13–24*			___
	(A) Dark olive green or black, NYC	105	170	___
	(B) Black, lettered C&O	395	720	___
	(C) Maroon, red, or peacock	340	620	___
0034	2-rail 13" Curve Track, electrical connectors (OO), *39–42*	10	15	___
34	Electric Locomotive 0-6-0, early (std), *12*	520	860	___
34	Electric Locomotive 0-4-0 (std), *13*	200	385	___
35	Pullman Car (std), *12–13*			
	(A) Dark blue	470	900	___
	(B) Dark olive green	170	235	___
35	Pullman Car (std), *14–16*			
	(A) Dark olive green, maroon windows	35	70	___
	(B) Maroon, green windows	75	105	___
	(C) Orange, maroon windows	125	195	___
35	Pullman Car (std), *15–18*	40	70	___

			Good	Exc
35		Pullman Car (std), *18–23*		
___		(A) Dark olive green, maroon windows	30	50
___		(B) Maroon, green windows	25	45
___		(C) Orange, maroon windows	120	210
___		(D) Brown, green windows	30	50
___	**35**	Boulevard Street Lamp, 6⅛" high, *40–42*	25	50
___	**35**	Pullman Car (std), *24*	40	55
___	**35**	Pullman Car (std), *25–26*	40	55
	36	Observation Car (std), *12–13*		
___		(A) Dark blue	315	810
___		(B) Dark olive green	145	205
	36	Observation Car (std), *14–16*		
___		(A) Dark olive green, maroon windows	60	95
___		(B) Maroon, green windows	50	70
___		(C) Orange, maroon windows	180	290
___		(D) Brown, green windows	50	75
___	**36**	Observation Car (std), *15–18*	60	80
	36	Observation Car (std), *18–23*		
___		(A) Dark olive green, maroon windows	40	55
___		(B) Maroon, green windows	40	55
___		(C) Orange, maroon windows	130	215
___		(D) Brown, green windows	40	55
___	**36**	Observation Car (std), *24*	40	55
___	**36**	Observation Car (std), *25–26*	40	55
	38	Electric Locomotive 0-4-0 (std), *13–24*		
___		(A) Black	100	135
___		(B) Red	475	680
___		(C) Mojave or pea green	405	540
___		(D) Dark green	270	360
___		(E) Brown	270	315
___		(F) Red, cream trim	405	540
___		(G) Maroon	170	270
___		(H) Gray	70	125
___	**41**	Accessory Contactor, *37–42*	3	7
___	**042**	Switches, pair (O), *38–42*	15	40
	42	Electric Locomotive 0-4-4-0, square hood, early (std), *12**		
___			760	1650
	42	Electric Locomotive 0-4-4-0 , round hood, later (std), *13–23*		
___		(A) Black or gray	300	510
___		(B) Maroon	1250	2050
___		(C) Dark gray	375	600
___		(D) Dark green or mojave	500	800
___		(E) Peacock	1100	1800
___		(F) Olive or dark olive green	750	1200

		Good	Exc	
043/43	Bild-A-Motor Gear Set, *29*	40	85	___
0044	Boxcar (OO), *39–42*	40	80	___
0044K	Boxcar Kit (OO), *39–42*	75	120	___
0045	Gateman, *35–36*	15	35	___
0045	Tank Car (OO), *39–42*			
	(A) Black, Shell	40	95	___
	(B) Silver, Sunoco	40	80	___
45	Gateman, *35–36*	10	25	___
0045K	Tank Car Kit (OO), *39–42*	75	120	___
45N	Automatic Gateman (std O), *37–42*	40	85	___
0046	Hopper Car (OO), *39–42*	50	90	___
0046K	Hopper Car Kit (OO), *39–42*			
	(A) Southern Pacific	75	135	___
	(B) Reading		NRS	___
46	Crossing Gate, *39–42*	75	120	___
0047	Caboose (OO), *39–42*	30	60	___
0047K	Caboose Kit (OO), *39–42*	75	135	___
47	Crossing Gate, *39–42*	70	140	___
48W	Whistle Station, *37–42*	20	65	___
50	Electric Locomotive 0-4-0 (std), *24*			
	(A) Dark green or dark gray	135	250	___
	(B) Maroon	315	600	___
	(C) Mojave	175	345	___
50	Cardboard Train, Cars, Accessory (O), *43**	200	360	___
0051	7" Curve Track (OO), *39–42*	5	15	___
51	0-4-0 Locomotive, late, 8-wheel (std), *12–23*	800	1150	___
0052	7" Straight Track (OO), *39–42*	10	15	___
52	Lamp Post, *33–41*	45	95	___
53	Electric Locomotive 0-4-4-0, early (std), *12–14*	1200	2450	___
53	Electric Locomotive 0-4-0, later (std), *15–19*			
	(A) Maroon	550	950	___
	(B) Mojave	670	1350	___
	(C) Dark olive green	560	1150	___
53	Electric Locomotive 0-4-0, latest (std), *20–21*	200	450	___
53	Electric Locomotive 0-6-6-0, early (std), *11*		NRS	___
53	Lamp Post, *31–42*	30	50	___
0054	7" Curve Track, electrical connectors (OO), *39–42*	10	15	___
54	Electric Locomotive 0-4-4-0, early (std), *12**	2500	4050	___
54	Electric Locomotive 0-4-4-0, late (std), *13–23*	1800	2700	___
54	Lamp Post, *29–35*	60	110	___

		Good	Exc
56	Lamp Post, removable lens and cap, *24–42*		
____	(A) Mojave	85	185
____	(B) Dark gray	50	110
____	(C) 45N green	25	45
____	(D) Pea green	30	50
____	(E) Aluminum	30	45
____	(F) Copper	60	160
____	(G) Dark green	30	45
57	Lamp Post with street names, *22–42*		
____	(A) Orange post, Main St. & Broadway	35	55
____	(B) Orange post, Fifth Ave. & 42nd St.	40	95
____	(C) Orange post, Broadway & 21st St.	45	90
____	(D) Orange post, Broadway, 42nd St., Fifth Ave. & 21st St.	70	120
____	(E) Yellow post, Main St. & Broadway	35	75
58	Lamp Post, 7⅜" high, *22–42*		
____	(A) Cream	30	60
____	(B) Peacock	30	60
____	(C) Silver	30	60
____	(D) Maroon	35	85
____	(E) Dark green	30	50
____	(F) Orange	30	60
____ **59**	Lamp Post, 8¾" high, *20–36*	40	100
____ **060**	Telegraph Post (O), *29–42*	10	25
____ **60**	Telegraph Post (std), *20–28*	10	25
60	Electric Locomotive 0-4-0, FAO Schwartz (std), *15 u*		NRS
____ **0061**	7" Curve Track, tubular (OO), *38*	3	10
____ **61**	Lamp Post, one globe, *14–36*	35	65
61	Electric Locomotive 0-4-4-0, FAO Schwartz (std), *15 u*		NRS
____ **0062**	7" Straight Track, tubular (OO), *38*	5	10
____ **62**	Semaphore, *20–32*	30	50
62	Electric Locomotive 0-4-0, FAO Schwartz (std), *24–32 u*		NRS
____ **0063**	Half Curve Track, tubular (OO), *38–42*	8	15
____ **63**	Semaphore, single arm, *15–21*	25	50
____ **63**	Lamp Post, two globes, *33–42*	135	265
____ **0064**	7" Curve Track, tubular, electrical connectors (OO), *38*	8	15
____ **64**	Lamp Post, *40–42*	35	70
____ **64**	Semaphore, double arm, *15–21*	30	60
____ **0065**	Half Straight Track, tubular (OO), *38–42*	10	15
____ **65**	Semaphore, one-arm, *15–26*	30	60
____ **65**	Whistle Controller, *35*	8	15
____ **0066**	5⅝" Straight Track (OO), *38–42*	10	15

		Good	Exc	
66	Semaphore, two-arm, *15–26*	35	70	___
66	Whistle Controller, *36–39*	5	10	___
67	Lamp Post, *15–32*	85	145	___
67	Whistle Controller, *36–39*	10	30	___
068	Warning Signal (0), *25–42*	10	25	___
69N	Electric Warning Signal (std 0), *36–42*	35	70	___
0070	90-degree Crossing, *38–42*	5	10	___
70	Outfit: 62 (2), 59 (1), 68 (1), *21–32*	60	130	___
071	060 Telegraph Poles, 6 pieces (std), *24–42*	70	160	___
71	60 Telegraph Post Set, 6 pieces, *21–31*	70	160	___
0072	Remote Control Switches, pair (OO), *38–42*	155	290	___
0072L	Remote Control Switch, left hand (OO), *38–42*	50	95	___
0072R	Remote Control Switch, right hand (OO)	50	95	___
0074	Boxcar (OO), *39–42*	35	85	___
0075	Tank Car (OO), *39–42*	50	145	___
076	Block Signal (0), *23–28*	35	105	___
76	Warning Bell and Shack, *39–42*	55	180	___
0077	Caboose (OO), *39–42*	30	60	___
77/077	Automatic Crossing Gate, *23–35*	25	50	___
78/078	Train Signal, *24–32*	40	100	___
79	Flashing Signal, *28–42*	85	150	___
80/080	Semaphore, *26–35*	50	120	___
81	Controlling Rheostat, *27–33*	5	10	___
82/082	Semaphore, *27–35*	40	120	___
83	Flashing Traffic Signal, *27–42*	65	195	___
084	Semaphore, *28–32*	60	100	___
84	Semaphore, *27–32*	45	85	___
85	Telegraph Pole (std), *29–42*	15	30	___
86	Telegraph Poles, 6 pieces, *29–42*	60	120	___
87	Flashing Crossing Signal, *27–42*	85	300	___
88	Rheostat, *15–27*	3	10	___
88	Direction Controller, *33–42*	4	10	___
89	Flagpole, *23–34*	40	75	___
90	Flagpole, *27–42*	40	95	___
91	Circuit Breaker, *30–42*	30	50	___
092	Signal Tower, *23–27*	85	190	___
92	Floodlight Tower, *31–42**	150	215	___
93	Water Tower, *31–42*	60	110	___
94	High Tension Tower, *32–42**	150	290	___
95	Controlling Rheostat, *34–42*	5	15	___
96	Coal Elevator, manual, *38–40*	165	220	___
097	Telegraph Set (0)	45	75	___
97	Coal Elevator, *38–42*	125	240	___
98	Coal Bunker, *38–40*	160	320	___
99N	Train Control Block Signal, *36–42*	45	180	___

PREWAR 1901-1942

			Good	Exc
____	**100**	Wooden Gondola (2⅞"), *01*		NRS
____	**100**	Bridge Approaches, 2 ramps (std), *20–31*	20	40
____	**100**	Electric Locomotive (2⅞"), *03–05**	2900	5200
	100	Trolley (std), *10–16*		
____		(A) Blue, white windows	1300	2700
____		(B) Blue, cream windows	1850	3600
____		(C) Red, cream windows	1300	2700
____	**101**	Bridge, span (104) and 2 approaches (100), *20–31*	65	120
____	**101**	Summer Trolley (std), *10–13*	1300	2700
____	**102**	Bridge, 2 spans (104) and 2 approaches (100), *20–31*	70	175
____	**103**	Bridge (std), *13–16*	40	75
____	**103**	Bridge, 3 spans (104) and 2 approaches (100), *20–31*	60	145
____	**104**	Bridge Center Span (std), *20–31*	20	45
____	**104**	Tunnel, papier mache (std), *09–14*	50	135
____	**105**	Bridge (std), *11–14*	40	70
____	**105**	Bridge Approaches, 2 ramps (O), *20–31*	50	70
____	**106**	Bridge, span (110) and 2 approaches (105), *20–31*	30	65
____	**106**	Rheostat, *11–14*	3	10
____	**107**	DC Reducer, 110V, *23–32*		NRS
____	**108**	Bridge, 2 spans (110) and 2 approaches (105), *20–31*	50	90
____	**109**	Bridge, 3 spans, (110) and 2 approaches (105), *20–32*	50	115
____	**109**	Tunnel, papier mache (std), *13–14*	30	70
____	**110**	Bridge Center Span (O), *20–31*	10	25
____	**111**	Box of 50 Bulbs, *20–31*	55	105
____	**112**	Gondola, early (std), *10–12*	225	400
____	**112**	Gondola, later (std), *12–16*	40	65
____	**112**	Gondola, latest (std), *16–18*	40	65
____	**112**	Gondola, Lionel Corp. (std), *18–26*	40	65
____	**112**	Station, *31–35*	145	270
____	**113**	Cattle Car, later (std), *12–16*	50	70
____	**113**	Cattle Car, latest (std), *16–18*	50	70
____	**113**	Cattle Car, Lionel Corp. (std), *18–26*	30	55
____	**113**	Station with light fixtures, *31–34*	150	310
____	**114**	Boxcar, later (std), *12–16*	50	90
____	**114**	Boxcar, latest (std), *16–18*	40	70
____	**114**	Boxcar, Lionel Corp. (std), *18–26*	40	70
____	**114**	Station with light fixtures, *31–34*	530	1200
____	**115**	Station with train control, *35–42**	185	370
____	**116**	Ballast Car, early and later (std), *10–16*	85	115
____	**116**	Ballast Car, latest (std), *16–18*	65	105
____	**116**	Ballast Car, Lionel Corp. (std), *18–26*	55	95

		Good	Exc	
116	Station with train control, *35–42**	640	920	____
117	Caboose, early (std), *12*	40	75	____
117	Caboose, later (std), *12–16*	40	75	____
117	Caboose, latest (std), *16–18*	40	75	____
117	Caboose, Lionel Corp. (std), *18–26*	30	60	____
117	Station, *36–42*	125	235	____
118	Tunnel, metal, 8" long (O), *20–32*	23	60	____
118L	Tunnel, metal, lighted, 8" long, *27*	20	55	____
119	Tunnel, metal, 12" long, *20–42*	25	60	____
119L	Tunnel, metal, lighted, 12" long, *27–33*	20	55	____
120	Tunnel, metal, 17" long, *22–27*	30	75	____
120L	Tunnel, metal, lighted, 17" long, *27–42*	75	140	____
121	Station, lighted (std), *09–16*			
	(A) 14" x 10" x 9"		NRS	____
	(B) 13" x 9" x 13"	150	300	____
121	Station (std), *20–26*	75	165	____
121X	Station (std), *17–19*	110	255	____
122	Station (std), *20–30*	80	190	____
123	Station (std), *20–23*	75	210	____
123	Tunnel, paperboard base, 18½" long (O), *33–42*	105	235	____
124	Lionel City Station, *20–36**			
	(A) Tan or gray base, pea green roof	90	240	____
	(B) Pea green base, red roof	200	360	____
125	Lionelville Station, *23–25*	80	185	____
125	Track Template, *38*	1	5	____
126	Lionelville Station, *23–36*	95	205	____
127	Lionel Town Station, *23–36*	80	160	____
128	115 Station and 129 Terrace, *35–42**	900	1900	____
128	124 Station and 129 Terrace, *31–34**	900	1900	____
129	Terrace, *28–42**	600	1100	____
130	Tunnel, 26" long (O), *20–36*	100	415	____
130L	Tunnel, lighted, 26" long, *27–33*	150	450	____
131	Corner Display, *24–28*	125	295	____
132	Corner Grass Plot, *24–28*	125	295	____
133	Heart-shaped Plot, *24–28*	125	295	____
134	Lionel City Station with stop, *37–42*	230	445	____
134	Oval-shaped Plot, *24–28*	125	300	____
135	Circular Plot, *24–28*	125	295	____
136	Large Elevation, *24–28*		NRS	____
136	Lionelville Station with stop, *37–42*	85	180	____
137	Station with stop, *37–42*	80	160	____
140L	Tunnel, lighted, 37" long, *27–32*	460	1050	____
150	Electric Locomotive 0-4-0, early (O), *17*	95	180	____

			Good	Exc
150	Electric Locomotive 0-4-0, late (O), *18–25*			
____	(A) Brown, brown or olive windows		95	150
____	(B) Maroon, dark olive windows		90	135
152	Electric Locomotive 0-4-0 (O), *17–27*			
____	(A) Dark green		90	135
____	(B) Gray		100	160
____	(C) Mojave		340	680
____	(D) Peacock		340	680
____ **152**	Crossing Gate, *40–42*		20	40
____ **153**	Block Signal, *40–42*		25	45
153	Electric Locomotive 0-4-0 (O), *24–25*			
____	(A) Dark green		100	160
____	(B) Gray		100	160
____	(C) Mojave		100	160
____ **154**	Electric Locomotive 0-4-0 (O), *17–23*		100	180
154	Highway Signal, *40–42*			
____	(A) Black base		25	50
____	(B) Orange base		95	220
155	Freight Shed, *30–42**			
____	(A) Cream base, terra cotta floor		180	320
____	(B) Ivory base, red floor		240	400
____ **156**	Electric Locomotive 0-4-0 (O), *17–23*		400	720
____ **156**	Station Platform, *39–42*		85	115
156	Electric Locomotive 4-4-4 (O), *17–23*			
____	(A) Dark green		475	810
____	(B) Maroon		540	890
____	(C) Olive green		600	1050
____	(D) Gray		670	1200
156X	Electric Locomotive 0-4-0 (O), *23–24*			
____	(A) Maroon		330	495
____	(B) Olive green		200	400
____	(C) Gray		530	710
____	(D) Brown		420	600
____ **157**	Hand Truck, *30–32*		20	40
158	Electric Locomotive 0-4-0 (O), *19–23*			
____	(A) Gray or red windows		75	205
____	(B) Black		95	250
____ **158**	Station Set: 136 Station and 2 platforms (156), *40–42*		120	280
____ **159**	Block Actuator, *40*		10	30
____ **161**	Baggage Truck, *30–32**		40	80
____ **162**	Dump Truck, *30–32**		40	80
____ **163**	Freight Accessory Set: 2 hand trucks (157), baggage truck (161), and dump truck (162), *30–42**		220	360
____ **164**	Log Loader, *40–42*		160	225

		Good	Exc	
165	Magnetic Crane, *40–42*	175	340	___
165-22	Scrap Steel with bag, *40–42*	50	125	___
165-83	Steel Blanks with bag, *40–42*	50	110	___
166	Whistle Controller, *40–42*	3	10	___
167	Whistle Controller, *40–42*	8	25	___
167X	Whistle Controller (OO), *40–42*	5	15	___
168	Magic Electrol Controller, *40–42*	25	50	___
169	Controller, *40–42*	4	20	___
170	DC Reducer, 220V, *14–38*	5	10	___
171	DC to AC Inverter, 110V, *36–42*	5	15	___
172	DC to AC Inverter, 229V, *39–42*	3	7	___
180	Pullman Car (std), *11–13*			
	(A) Maroon body and roof	145	205	___
	(B) Brown body and roof	145	255	___
180	Pullman Car (std), *13–15*	80	160	___
180	Pullman Car (std), *15–18*	80	160	___
180	Pullman Car (std), *18–22*	80	135	___
181	Combine Car (std), *11–13*			
	(A) Maroon, dark olive doors	145	205	___
	(B) Brown, dark olive doors	145	205	___
	(C) Yellow-orange, orange doors	350	495	___
181	Combine Car (std), *13–15*	80	160	___
181	Combine Car (std), *15–18*	80	160	___
181	Combine Car (std), *18–22*	80	135	___
182	Observation Car (std), *11–13*			
	(A) Maroon, dark olive doors	145	205	___
	(B) Brown, dark olive doors	145	205	___
	(C) Yellow-orange, orange doors	300	495	___
182	Observation Car (std), *13–15*	80	160	___
182	Observation Car (std), *15–18*	80	160	___
182	Observation Car (std), *18–22*	80	135	___
184	Bungalow, illuminated, *23–32**	65	85	___
185	Bungalow, *23–24*	50	115	___
186	184 Bungalows, set of 5, *23–32*	195	610	___
186	Log Loader Outfit, *40–41*	130	340	___
187	185 Bungalows, set of 5, *23–24*	170	590	___
188	Elevator and Car Set, *38–41*	115	370	___
189	Villa, illuminated, *23–32**	133	225	___
190	Observation Car (std), *08*			
	(A) Dark olive green, nonremovable roof	1150	2600	___
	(B) Dark olive green, removable roof	115	205	___
	(C) Yellow-orange, removable roof	320	620	___
	(D) Orange, removable roof	115	205	___
	(E) Mojave, removable roof	345	870	___

		Good	Exc
190	Observation Car (std), *11–13*	600	900
190	Observation Car (std), *13–15*	200	295
190	Observation Car (std), *15–18*	200	295
190	Observation Car (std), *18–22*	80	135
190	Observation Car (std), *23–26*	230	475
191	Villa, illuminated, *23–32**	125	325
192	Illuminated Villa Set: 189, 191, 184 (2), *27–32*	400	800
193	Automatic Accessory Set (O), *27–29*	150	325
194	Automatic Accessory Set (std), *27–29*	100	325
195	Terrace, *27–30*	350	740
196	Accessory Set, *27*	200	335
200	Electric Express (2⅞"), *03–05**	4000	6300
200	Trailer, matches No. 2 Trolley (std), *11–16*	1200	2400
200	Turntable (std), *28–33**	85	190
201	0-6-0 Locomotive (O), *40–42*		
	(A) 2201B Tender, bell	375	760
	(B) 2201T Tender, no bell	345	690
202	Summer Trolley (std), *10–13*		
	(A) Electric Rapid Transit	1300	2700
	(B) Preston St.	3250	4500
203	Armored 0-4-0 (O), *17–21*	1100	1800
203	0-6-0 Locomotive (O), *40–42*		
	(A) 2203B Tender, bell	400	495
	(B) 2203T Tender, no bell	375	550
204	2-4-2 Locomotive (O), *40–42 u*		
	(A) Black	55	105
	(B) Gunmetal gray	80	165
205	Merchandise Containers, 3 pieces, *30–38**	130	320
206	Sack of Coal, *38–42*	5	20
208	Tool Set: 6 assorted tools, *34–42**	65	150
0209	Barrels, wooden, 6 pieces (O), *34–42*		
	(A) Solid barrels	10	25
	(B) 2-piece barrels	53	145
209	Barrels, wooden, 4 pieces (std), *34–42*	10	25
210	Switches, pair (std), *26, 34–42*	40	75
211	Flatcar (std), *26–40**	125	195
212	Gondola (std), *26–40**		
	(A) Gray or light green	100	205
	(B) Maroon	75	135
213	Cattle Car (std), *26–40**		
	(A) Mojave, maroon roof	160	365
	(B) Terra-cotta, pea green roof	130	290
	(C) Cream, maroon roof	300	650

		Good	Exc	
214	Boxcar (std), *26–40**			
	(A) Terra-cotta, dark green roof	195	390	____
	(B) Cream body, orange roof	150	270	____
	(C) Yellow, brown roof	300	495	____
214R	Refrigerator Car (std), *29–40**			
	(A) Ivory or white, peacock roof	325	495	____
	(B) White, light blue roof	435	790	____
215	Tank Car (std), *26–40**			
	(A) Pea green	150	215	____
	(B) Ivory	220	360	____
	(C) Aluminum	315	720	____
216	Hopper Car (std), *26–38**			
	(A) Dark green, brass plates	195	335	____
	(B) Dark green, nickel plates	445	1100	____
217	Caboose (std), *26–40**			
	(A) Orange, maroon roof	250	510	____
	(B) Red, peacock roof	120	235	____
	(C) Red body and roof, ivory doors	150	320	____
217	Lighting Set, *14–23*		NRS	____
218	Dump Car (std), *26–38**	220	365	____
219	Crane Car (std), *26–40**			
	(A) Peacock, red boom	135	255	____
	(B) Yellow, light green or red boom	270	440	____
	(C) Ivory, light green boom	270	520	____
220	Floodlight Car (std), *31–40**			
	(A) Terra-cotta base	225	385	____
	(B) Green base	340	485	____
220	Switches, pair (std), *26**	25	90	____
222	Switches, pair (std), *26–32*	40	100	____
223	Switches, pair (std), *32–42*	35	120	____
224/224E	2-6-2 Locomotive (O), *38–42*			
	(A) Black, die-cast 2224 Tender	140	255	____
	(B) Black, plastic 2224 Tender	110	195	____
	(C) Gunmetal, die-cast 2224 Tender	385	950	____
	(D) Gunmetal, sheet-metal 2689 Tender	120	210	____
225	222 Switches and 439 Panel, *29–32*	115	260	____
225/225E	2-6-2 Locomotive (O), *38–42*			
	(A) Black, 2235 or 2245 Tender	210	370	____
	(B) Black, 2235 plastic Tender	185	320	____
	(C) Gunmetal, 2225 or 2265 Tender	210	360	____
	(D) Gunmetal, 2235 die-cast Tender	285	730	____
226/226E	2-6-4 Locomotive (O), *38–41*	275	630	____
227	0-6-0 Locomotive (O), *39–42*			
	(A) 2227B Tender, bell	600	1250	____
	(B) 2227T Tender, no bell	600	1150	____

		Good	Exc
228	0-6-0 Locomotive (O), *39–42*		
____	(A) 2228B Tender, bell	600	1250
____	(B) 2228T Tender, no bell	600	1150
229	2-4-2 Locomotive (O), *39–42*		
____	(A) Black or gunmetal, 2689W Tender	155	240
____	(B) Black or gunmetal, 2689T Tender	120	200
____	(C) Black, 2666W whistle Tender	155	280
____	(D) Black, 2666T nonwhistling Tender	120	200
____ **230**	0-6-0 Locomotive (O), *39–42*	1100	2050
____ **231**	0-6-0 Locomotive (O), *39*	1000	1800
____ **232**	0-6-0 Locomotive (O), *40–42*	1000	1800
____ **233**	0-6-0 Locomotive (O), *40–42*	1000	1800
____ **238**	4-4-2 Locomotive (O), *39–40 u*	430	710
238E	4-4-2 Locomotive (O), *36–38*		
____	(A) 265W or 2225W whistle Tender	280	345
____	(B) 265 or 2225T nonwhistling Tender	275	360
____ **248**	Electric Locomotive 0-4-0 (O), *27–32*	150	240
249/249E	2-4-2 Locomotive (O), *36–39*		
____	(A) Gunmetal, 265T or 265W Tender	100	270
____	(B) Black, 265W Tender	110	210
____ **250**	Electric Locomotive 0-4-0, early (O), *26*	125	220
250	Electric Locomotive 0-4-0, late (O), *34*		
____	(A) Yellow-orange body, terra-cotta frame	145	245
____	(B) Terra-cotta body, maroon frame	160	270
____ **250E**	4-4-2 Hiawatha Locomotive (O), *35–42**	400	1100
____ **250W**	Hiawatha Tender (O), *35–42**	125	250
251	Electric Locomotive 0-4-0 (O), *25–32*		
____	(A) Gray body, red windows	190	340
____	(B) Red body, ivory stripe	215	410
____	(C) Red body, no ivory stripe	200	380
251E	Electric Locomotive 0-4-0 (O), *27–32*		
____	(A) Red body, ivory stripe	225	425
____	(B) Red body, no ivory stripe	215	395
____	(C) Gray, red trim	195	350
252	Electric Locomotive 0-4-0 (O), *26–32*		
____	(A) Peacock or olive green	85	130
____	(B) Terra-cotta or yellow-orange	115	220
252E	Electric Locomotive 0-4-0 (O), *33–35*		
____	(A) Terra-cotta	145	250
____	(B) Yellow-orange	125	205

		Good	Exc
253	Electric Locomotive 0-4-0 (O), *24–32*		
	(A) Maroon	180	430 ___
	(B) Dark green	105	250 ___
	(C) Mojave	105	235 ___
	(D) Terra-cotta	180	430 ___
	(E) Peacock	95	195 ___
	(F) Red	210	475 ___
253E	Electric Locomotive 0-4-0 (O), *31–36*		
	(A) Green	150	205 ___
	(B) Terra-cotta	190	305 ___
254	Electric Locomotive 0-4-0 (O), *24–32*	240	340 ___
254E	Electric Locomotive 0-4-0 (O), *27–34*	180	270 ___
255E	2-4-2 Locomotive (O), *35–36*	485	1000 ___
256	Electric Locomotive 0-4-4-0 (O), *24–30**		
	(A) Rubber-stamped lettering	470	1175 ___
	(B) no outline around Lionel	425	770 ___
	(C) Lionel Lines and No. 256 on brass	450	1050 ___
257	2-4-0 Locomotive (O), *30–35 u*		
	(A) Black tender	145	300 ___
	(B) Black crackle-finish tender	240	435 ___
258	2-4-0 Locomotive, early (O), *30–35 u*		
	(A) 4-wheel 257 Tender	85	170 ___
	(B) 8-wheel 258 Tender	100	195 ___
258	2-4-2 Locomotive, late (O), *41 u*		
	(A) Black	60	100 ___
	(B) Gunmetal	85	135 ___
259	2-4-2 Locomotive (O), *32*	70	135 ___
259E	2-4-2 Locomotive (O), *33–42*	80	165 ___
259T	Tender	15	30 ___
260E	2-4-2 Locomotive (O), *30–35**		
	(A) Black body, green or black frame	385	475 ___
	(B) Dark gunmetal body and frame	440	640 ___
261	2-4-2 Locomotive (O), *31*	125	210 ___
261E	2-4-2 Locomotive (O), *35*	190	285 ___
262	2-4-2 Locomotive (O), *31–32*	185	320 ___
262E	2-4-2 Locomotive (O), *33–36*		
	(A) Gloss black, copper and brass trim	110	210 ___
	(B) Satin black, nickel trim	125	260 ___
263E	2-4-2 Locomotive (O), *36–39**		
	(A) Gunmetal gray	315	610 ___
	(B) 2-tone blue, from Blue Comet	415	950 ___
263W	Tender, gunmetal	90	200 ___

		Good	Exc
264E	2-4-2 Locomotive (O), *35–36*		
___	(A) Red, Red Comet	135	295
___	(B) Black	220	380
265E	2-4-2 Locomotive (O), *35–40*		
___	(A) Black or gunmetal	170	330
___	(B) Light blue, Blue Streak	460	800
___	(B) Tender	30	55
___ **267E/W**	Set: 616, 617 (2), 618, *35–41*	275	560
___ **270**	Bridge, 10" long (O), *31–42*	20	50
___ **270**	Lighting Set, *15–23*		NRS
___ **271**	270 Bridges, set of 2, *31–33, 35–40*	65	150
___ **271**	Lighting Set, *15–23*		NRS
___ **272**	270 Bridges, set of 3, *31–33, 35–40*	60	165
___ **280**	Bridge, 14" long (std), *31–42*	50	115
___ **281**	280 Bridges, set of 2, *31–33, 35–40*	90	205
___ **282**	280 Bridges, set of 3, *31–33, 35–40*	105	265
___ **289E**	2-4-2 Locomotive (O), *37 u*	120	305
___ **300**	Electric Trolley Car (2⅞"), *01–05*	2000	3600
300	Hellgate Bridge (std), *28–42**		
___	(A) Cream towers, green truss	800	1350
___	(B) Ivory towers, aluminum truss	765	1600
___ **303**	Summer Trolley, *10–13*	1500	3150
___ **308**	Signs, set of 5 (O), *40–42*	30	70
___ **309**	Electric Trolley Trailer (2⅞"), *01–05*	2500	4050
309	Pullman Car (std), *26–39*		
___	(A) Maroon body and roof, mojave windows	100	160
___	(B) Mojave body and roof, maroon windows	100	160
___	(C) Light brown body, dark brown roof	120	190
___	(D) Medium blue body, dark blue roof	170	280
___	(E) Apple green body, dark green roof	170	280
___	(F) Pale blue body, silver roof	100	185
___	(G) Maroon body, terra-cotta roof	130	195
___ **310**	Rails and Ties, complete section (2⅞"), *01–02*	5	15
310	Baggage Car (std), *26–39*		
___	(A) Maroon body and roof, mojave windows	100	160
___	(B) Mojave body and roof, maroon windows	85	160
___	(C) Light brown body, dark brown roof	115	185
___	(D) Medium blue body, dark blue roof	170	280
___	(E) Apple green body, dark green roof	170	280
___	(F) Pale blue body, silver roof	100	175

		Good	Exc
312	Observation Car (std), *24–39*		
	(A) Maroon body and roof, mojave windows	100	160
	(B) Mojave body and roof, maroon windows	85	160
	(C) Light brown body, dark brown roof	120	185
	(D) Medium blue body, dark blue roof	170	280
	(E) Apple green body, dark green roof	170	280
	(F) Pale blue body, silver roof	100	175
	(G) Maroon body, terra-cotta roof	130	195
313	Bascule Bridge (O), *40–42*		
	(A) Silver bridge	235	500
	(B) Gray bridge	250	590
314	Girder Bridge (O), *40–42*	20	40
315	Illuminated Trestle Bridge (O), *40–42*	30	80
316	Trestle Bridge (O), *40–42*	25	50
318	Electric Locomotive 0-4-0 (std), *24–32*		
	(A) Gray, dark gray, or mojave	150	250
	(B) Pea green	150	250
	(C) State brown	250	395
318E	Electric Locomotive 0-4-0, *26–35*		
	(A) Gray, mojave, or pea green	150	250
	(B) State brown	275	440
	(C) Black	550	1275
319	Pullman Car (std), *24–27*	105	175
320	Baggage Car (std), *25–27*	100	175
320	Switch and Signal (2⅞"), *02–05*		NRS
322	Observation Car (std), *24–27, 29–30 u*	100	175
330	90-degree Crossing (2⅞"), *02–05*		NRS
332	Baggage Car (std), *26–33*		
	(A) Red body and roof, cream doors	80	120
	(B) Peacock body and roof, orange doors	75	115
	(C) Gray body and roof, maroon doors	75	115
	(D) Olive green body and roof, red doors	90	145
	(E) State brown body, dark brown roof	190	430
337	Pullman Car (std), *25–32*		
	(A) Red body and roof, cream doors	95	190
	(B) Mojave body and roof, maroon doors	95	190
	(C) Olive green body and roof, red doors	105	225
	(D) Olive green body and roof, maroon doors	95	190
	(E) Pea green body and roof, cream doors	210	500
338	Observation Car (std), *25–32*		
	(A) Red body and roof, cream doors	95	190
	(B) Mojave body and roof, maroon doors	95	190
	(C) Olive green body and roof, red doors	105	225
	(D) Olive green body and roof, maroon doors	95	190

		Good	Exc
339	Pullman Car (std), *25–33*		
___	(A) Peacock body and roof, orange doors	55	90
___	(B) Gray body and roof, maroon doors	55	100
___	(C) State brown body, dark brown roof	135	380
___	(D) Peacock body, dark green roof	75	130
___	(E) Mojave body, maroon roof and doors	145	230
___ **340**	Suspension Bridge (2⅞"), *02–05**		NRS
341	Observation Car (std), *25–33*		
___	(A) Peacock body and roof, orange doors	50	70
___	(B) Gray body and roof, maroon doors	50	70
___	(C) State brown body, dark brown roof	75	160
___	(D) Peacock body, dark green roof	65	95
___	(E) Mojave body, maroon roof and doors	135	165
___ **350**	Track Bumper (2⅞"), *02–05*	225	550
___ **380**	Elevated Pillars (2⅞"), *04–05**	30	70
___ **380**	Electric Locomotive 0-4-0 (std), *23–27*	310	440
380E	Electric Locomotive 0-4-0 (std), *26–29*		
___	(A) Mojave	445	630
___	(B) Maroon	295	400
___	(C) Dark green	370	460
___ **381**	Electric Locomotive 4-4-4 (std), *28–29**	1600	2100
381E	Electric Locomotive 4-4-4 (std), *28–36**		
___	(A) State green, apple green subframe	1500	2500
___	(B) State green, red subframe	1900	3250
___ **381U**	Electric Locomotive 4-4-4 Kit (std), *28–29*	1600	4100
___ **384**	2-4-0 Locomotive (std), *30–32**	415	730
___ **384E**	2-4-0 Locomotive (std), *30–32**	425	650
___ **385E**	2-4-2 Locomotive (std), *33–39**	370	670
___ **390**	2-4-2 Locomotive (std), *29**	460	820
390E	2-4-2 Locomotive (std), *29–31**		
___	(A) Black, with or without orange stripe	460	690
___	(B) 2-tone blue, cream-orange stripe	650	1050
___	(C) 2-tone green, orange or green stripe	990	2050
392E	4-4-2 Locomotive (std), *32–39**		
___	(A) Black, 384 Tender	750	1250
___	(B) Black, large 12-wheel tender	1050	1850
___	(C) Gunmetal gray	1000	1800
___ **400**	Express Trail Car (2⅞"), *03–05**	3500	5850
400E	4-4-4 Locomotive (std), *31–39**		
___	(A) Black	1400	2150
___	(B) Blue	1550	2350
___	(C) Gunmetal or light blue	1650	2800
___	(D) Black crackle finish	1600	3500

PREWAR 1901-1942

		Good	Exc
402	Electric Locomotive 0-4-4-0 (std), *23–27*	365	570 ____
402E	Electric Locomotive 0-4-4-0 (std), *26–29*	345	550 ____
404	Summer Trolley (std), *10*		NRS ____
408E	Electric Locomotive 0-4-4-0 (std), *27–36**		
	(A) Apple green or mojave, red pilots	770	980 ____
	(B) State brown, brown pilots	2000	3000 ____
	(C) State green, red pilots	2000	3800 ____
412	California Pullman Car (std), *29–35**		
	(A) Light green body, dark green roof	590	1750 ____
	(B) Light brown body, dark brown roof	620	2100 ____
413	Colorado Pullman Car (std), *29–35**		
	(A) Light green body, dark green roof	590	1750 ____
	(B) Light brown body, dark brown roof	620	2100 ____
414	Illinois Pullman Car (std), *29–35**		
	(A) Light green body, dark green roof	590	1750 ____
	(B) Light brown body, dark brown roof	620	2050 ____
416	New York Observation Car (std), *29–35**		
	(A) Light green body, dark green roof	590	1750 ____
	(B) Light brown body, dark brown roof	620	2100 ____
418	Pullman Car (std), *23–32**	225	320 ____
419	Combination (std), *23–32**	190	280 ____
420	Faye Pullman Car (std), *30–40**		
	(A) Brass trim	485	900 ____
	(B) Nickel trim	500	1200 ____
421	Westphal Pullman Car (std), *30–40**		
	(A) Brass trim	500	900 ____
	(B) Nickel trim	500	1200 ____
422	Tempel Observation Car (std), *30–40**		
	(A) Brass trim	485	900 ____
	(B) Nickel trim	500	1200 ____
424	Liberty Bell Pullman Car (std), *31–40**		
	(A) Brass trim	350	530 ____
	(B) Nickel trim	385	650 ____
425	Stephen Girard Pullman Car (std), *31–40**		
	(A) Brass trim	350	530 ____
	(B) Nickel trim	385	650 ____
426	Coral Isle Observation Car (std), *31–40**		
	(A) Brass trim	350	530 ____
	(B) Nickel trim	385	650 ____
428	Pullman Car (std), *26–30**		
	(A) Dark green body and roof	250	385 ____
	(B) Orange body and roof, apple green windows	390	890 ____

		Good	Exc
429	Combine Car (std), *26–30**		
____	(A) Dark green body and roof	250	385
____	(B) Orange body and roof, apple green windows	390	890
430	Observation Car (std), *26–30**		
____	(A) Dark green body and roof	250	385
____	(B) Orange body and roof, apple green windows	390	890
431	Diner (std), *27–32**		
____	(A) Mojave body, screw-mounted roof	350	540
____	(B) Mojave body, hinged roof	465	720
____	(C) Dark green body, orange windows	410	720
____	(D) Orange body, apple green windows	410	720
____	(E) Apple green body, red windows	410	720
____ **435**	Power Station, *26–38**	215	400
436	Power Station, *26–37**		
____	(A) Power Station plate	135	265
____	(B) Edison Service plate	270	610
____ **437**	Switch Signal Tower, *26–37**	190	430
438	Signal Tower, *27–39**		
____	(A) Mojave base, orange house	185	325
____	(B) Black base, white house	325	640
____ **439**	Panel Board, *28–42**	85	145
____ **440/0440**	Signal Bridge, *32–35**	180	470
____ **440C**	Panel Board, *32–42*	90	145
____ **441**	Weighing Station (std), *32–36*	495	1325
____ **442**	Landscaped Diner, *38–42*	120	215
____ **444**	Roundhouse (std), *32–35**	1350	2850
____ **444-18**	Roundhouse Clip, *33*		NRS
450	Electric Locomotive 0-4-0, Macy's (O), *30 u*		
____	(A) Red, black frame	295	700
____	(B) Apple green, dark green frame	415	880
____ **450**	Set: 450, matching 605, 606 (2), *30 u*	750	1800
____ **490**	Observation Car (std), *23–32**	190	255
____ **500**	Electric Derrick Car (2⅞"), *03–04**	5000	6750
511	Flatcar (std), *27–40*		
____	(A) Dark green	65	95
____	(B) Medium green	75	165
512	Gondola (std), *27–39*		
____	(A) Peacock	35	60
____	(B) Light green	50	95
513	Cattle Car (std), *27–38*		
____	(A) Olive green, orange roof	70	165
____	(B) Orange, pea green roof	60	110
____	(C) Cream, maroon roof	90	250

		Good	Exc	
514	Boxcar (std), *29–40*			
	(A) Cream, orange roof	90	155	___
	(B) Yellow, brown roof	115	285	___
514	Refrigerator Car, ivory or white, peacock roof, (std), *27–28*	240	400	___
514R	Refrigerator Car (std), *29–40*			
	(A) Ivory, peacock roof	140	190	___
	(B) White, light blue roof	350	540	___
515	Tank Car (std), *27–40*			
	(A) Terra-cotta	90	145	___
	(B) Ivory	105	185	___
	(C) Aluminum	90	175	___
	(D) Orange, red Shell decal	340	750	___
516	Hopper Car (std), *28–40*			
	(A) Red	170	240	___
	(B) Red, rubber-stamped data	200	300	___
	(C) Light red, nickel trim	200	325	___
517	Caboose (std), *27–40*			
	(A) Pea green body, red roof	50	85	___
	(B) Red body and roof	105	155	___
	(C) Red body, black roof, orange windows	355	640	___
520	Floodlight Car (std), *31–40*			
	(A) Terra-cotta base	110	210	___
	(B) Green base	110	240	___
529	Pullman Car (O), *26–32*			
	(A) Olive green body and roof	25	45	___
	(B) Terra-cotta body and roof	25	60	___
530	Observation Car (O), *26–32*			
	(A) Olive green body and roof	25	45	___
	(B) Terra-cotta body and roof	25	60	___
550	Miniature Figures, boxed (std), *32–36**	175	455	___
551	Engineer (std), *32*	25	45	___
552	Conductor (std), *32*	20	40	___
553	Porter with stool (std), *32*	25	50	___
554	Male Passenger (std), *32*	25	45	___
555	Female Passenger (std), *32*	25	45	___
556	Red Cap with suitcase (std), *32*	25	65	___
600	Derrick Trailer (2⅞"), *03–04**	5000	8550	___
600	Pullman Car, early (O), *15–23*			
	(A) Dark green	65	170	___
	(B) Maroon or brown	45	85	___
600	Pullman Car, late (O), *33–42*			
	(A) Light red or gray, red roof	50	90	___
	(B) Light blue, aluminum roof	70	120	___

			Good	Exc
601		Observation Car, late (O), *33–42*		
___		(A) Light red body and roof	50	85
___		(B) Light gray, red roof	50	90
___		(C) Light blue body, aluminum roof	70	120
___	**601**	Pullman Car, early (O), *15–23*	50	70
	602	Lionel Lines Baggage Car, late (O), *33–42*		
___		(A) Light red or gray, red roof	60	110
___		(B) Light blue, aluminum roof	90	150
___	**602**	NYC Baggage Car (O), *15–23*	30	45
___	**602**	Observation Car (O), *22 u*	30	45
___	**603**	Pullman Car, early (O), *22 u*	40	70
___	**603**	Pullman Car, later (O), *20–25*	20	45
	603	Pullman Car, latest (O), *31–36*		
___		(A) Light red body and roof	45	85
___		(B) Red body, black roof	35	60
___		(C) Stephen Girard green body, dark green roof	35	60
___		(D) Maroon body and roof, Macy Special	60	125
___	**604**	Observation Car, later (O), *20–25*	35	60
	604	Observation Car, latest (O), *31–36*		
___		(A) Light red body and roof	45	85
___		(B) Red body, black roof	35	60
___		(C) Yellow-orange body, terra-cotta roof	35	60
___		(D) Stephen Girard green body, dark green roof	35	60
___		(E) Maroon body and roof	70	150
	605	Pullman Car (O), *25–32*		
___		(A) Gray, Lionel Lines	85	170
___		(B) Gray, Illinois Central	85	170
___		(C) Red, Lionel Lines	170	255
___		(D) Red, Illinois Central	255	340
___		(E) Orange, Lionel Lines	170	255
___		(F) Orange, Illinois Central	300	430
___		(G) Olive green, Lionel Lines	255	340
	606	Observation Car (O), *25–32*		
___		(A) Gray, Lionel Lines	130	215
___		(B) Gray, Illinois Central	90	170
___		(C) Red, Lionel Lines	170	255
___		(D) Red, Illinois Central	255	340
___		(E) Orange, Lionel Lines	170	255
___		(F) Orange, Illinois Central	170	255
___		(G) Olive green, Lionel Lines	255	340
	607	Pullman Car (O), *26–27*		
___		(A) Peacock, Lionel Lines	50	70
___		(B) Peacock, Illinois Central	75	115
___		(C) 2-tone green, Lionel Lines	50	75
___		(D) Red, Lionel Lines	75	110

		Good	Exc	
608	Observation Car (O), _26–37_			
	(A) Peacock, Lionel Lines	50	70	___
	(B) Peacock, Illinois Central	75	115	___
	(C) 2-tone green, Lionel Lines	50	75	___
	(D) Red, Lionel Lines	75	110	___
609	Pullman Car (O), _37_	60	85	___
610	Pullman Car, early (O), _15–25_			
	(A) Dark green body and roof	50	65	___
	(B) Maroon body and roof	60	95	___
	(C) Mojave body and roof	60	95	___
610	Pullman Car, late (O), _26–30_			
	(A) Olive green body and roof	65	80	___
	(B) Mojave body and roof	55	80	___
	(C) Terra-cotta body, maroon roof	100	155	___
	(D) Pea green body and roof	70	115	___
	(E) Light blue body, aluminum roof	130	260	___
	(F) Light red body, aluminum-painted roof	100	155	___
611	Observation Car (O), _37_	55	80	___
612	Observation Car, early (O), _15–25_			
	(A) Dark green body and roof	40	60	___
	(B) Maroon body and roof	70	90	___
	(C) Mojave body and roof	70	90	___
612	Observation Car, late (O), _26–30_			
	(A) Olive green body and roof	55	80	___
	(B) Mojave body and roof	55	80	___
	(C) Terra-cotta body, maroon roof	100	155	___
	(D) Pea green body and roof	70	115	___
	(E) Light blue body, aluminum roof	130	260	___
	(F) Light red body, aluminum-painted roof	100	155	___
613	Pullman Car (O), _31–40*_			
	(A) Terra-cotta body, maroon/terra-cotta roof	85	195	___
	(B) Light red body, light red/aluminum roof	175	350	___
	(C) Blue, two-tone blue roof	115	225	___
614	Observation Car (O), _31–40*_			
	(A) Terra-cotta body, maroon/terra-cotta roof	100	190	___
	(B) Light red body, light red/aluminum roof	175	350	___
	(C) Blue, two-tone blue roof	115	225	___
615	Baggage Car (O), _33–40*_	150	260	___
616E/W	Diesel only (O), _35–41_	90	215	___
616E/W	Set: 616, 617 (2), 618	225	570	___
617	Coach (O), _35–41_			
	(A) Blue and white	55	85	___
	(B) Chrome, gunmetal skirts	55	85	___
	(C) Chrome, chrome skirts	55	85	___
	(D) Silver-painted	55	85	___

		Good	Exc
618	Observation Car (0), *35–41*		
___	(A) Blue and white	55	85
___	(B) Chrome, gunmetal skirts	55	85
___	(C) Chrome, chrome skirts	55	85
___	(D) Silver-painted	55	85
619	Combine Car (0), *36–38*		
___	(A) Blue, white windows band	100	205
___	(B) Chrome, chrome skirts	100	205
___ **620**	Floodlight Car (0), *37–42*	50	85
629	Pullman Car (0), *24–32*		
___	(A) Dark green body and roof	25	40
___	(B) Orange body and roof	25	40
___	(C) Red body and roof	20	35
___	(D) Light red body and roof	30	55
630	Observation Car, *24–32*		
___	(A) Dark green body and roof	25	40
___	(B) Orange body and roof	25	40
___	(C) Red body and roof	20	35
___	(D) Light red body and roof	30	55
___ **636W**	Diesel only (0), *36–39*	90	175
___ **636W**	Set: 636W, 637 (2), 638, *36–39*	375	640
___ **637**	Coach (0), *36–39*	70	105
___ **638**	Observation Car (0), *36–39*	70	105
___ **651**	Flatcar (0), *35–40*	30	65
___ **652**	Gondola (0), *35–40*	30	55
___ **653**	Hopper Car (0), *34–40*	35	65
654	Tank Car (0), *34–42*		
___	(A) Orange or aluminum	35	60
___	(B) Gray	40	75
655	Boxcar (0), *34–42*		
___	(A) Cream, maroon roof	35	60
___	(B) Cream, tuscan roof	45	75
656	Cattle Car (0), *35–40*		
___	(A) Light gray, vermilion roof	40	100
___	(B) Burnt orange, tuscan roof	70	125
657	Caboose (0), *34–42*		
___	(A) Red body and roof	20	35
___	(B) Red body, tuscan roof	25	40
___ **659**	Dump Car (0), *35–42*	40	90
___ **700**	Electric Locomotive 0-4-0 (0), *15–16*	360	690
___ **700E**	4-6-4 NYC Hudson "5344," scale (0), *37–42**	1400	2950
___ **700K**	4-6-4 Locomotive, unbuilt gray primer (0), *38–42*	4400	5950
___ **701**	0-6-0 PRR Locomotive "8976", *41*	900	2100

		Good	Exc	
701	Electric Locomotive 0-4-0 (O), *15–16*	390	660	____
702	Baggage Car (O), *17–21*	115	305	____
703	Electric Locomotive 4-4-4 (O), *15–16*	1400	2350	____
706	Electric Locomotive 0-4-0 (O), *15–16*	375	630	____
708	0-6-0 PRR Locomotive "8976" (O), *39–42**	1450	2850	____
710	Pullman Car (O), *24–34*			
	(A) Red, Lionel Lines	200	300	____
	(B) Orange, Lionel Lines	150	225	____
	(C) Orange, New York Central	175	225	____
	(D) Orange, Illinois Central	300	450	____
	(E) 2-tone blue, Lionel Lines	300	415	____
	(F) Orange, New York Central	200	260	____
711	Remote Control Switches, pair (O72), *35–42*	80	190	____
712	Observation Car (O), *24–34*			
	(A) Red, Lionel Lines	185	355	____
	(B) Orange, Lionel Lines	140	265	____
	(C) Orange, New York Central	160	310	____
	(D) Orange, Illinois Central	280	530	____
	(E) 2-tone blue, Lionel Lines	280	485	____
714	Boxcar (O), *40–42**	350	610	____
714K	Boxcar, unbuilt (O), *40–42*	220	480	____
715	Tank Car (O), *40–42**			
	(A) SEPS 8124 decal	340	610	____
	(B) SUNX 715 decal	435	880	____
715K	Tank Car, unbuilt (O), *40–42*	250	530	____
716	Hopper Car (O), *40–42**	290	400	____
716K	Hopper Car, unbuilt (O), *40–42*	350	730	____
717	Caboose (O), *40–42**	340	510	____
717K	Caboose, unbuilt (O), *40–42*	275	590	____
720	90-degree Crossing (O72), *35–42*	20	40	____
721	Manual Switches, pair (O72), *35–42*	50	105	____
730	90-degree Crossing (O72), *35–42*	20	40	____
731	Remote Control Switches, pair, T-rail (O72), *35–42*	80	135	____
751E/W	Set: 752, 753 (2), 754 (O), *34–41**	640	1050	____
752E	Diesel only (O), *34–41**			
	(A) Yellow and brown	170	355	____
	(B) Aluminum	145	340	____
753	Coach (O), *36–41*			
	(A) Yellow and brown	85	185	____
	(B) Aluminum	75	180	____
754	Observation Car (O), *36–41*			
	(A) Yellow and brown	80	185	____
	(B) Aluminum	75	180	____

			Good	Exc
____	760	Curved Track, 16 pieces, (072), _35–42_	40	80
____	761	Curved Track (072), _34–42_	1	2
____	762	Straight Track (072), _34–42_	1	2
____	762S	Insulated Straight Track (072), _34–42_	2	5
	763E	4-6-4 Locomotive (0), _37–42_		
____		(A) Gunmetal, 263 or 2263W Tender	1000	2125
____		(B) Gunmetal, 2226X or 2226WX Tender	1150	2950
____		(C) Black, 2226WX Tender	965	2650
____	771	Curved Track, T-rail (072), _35–42_	3	10
____	772	Straight Track, T-rail (072), _35–42_	5	20
____	772S	Insulated Straight Track, T-rail (072), _35–42_	15	30
____	773	Fishplate Set, 50 plates (072), _36–42_	15	30
____	782	Hiawatha Combine Car (0), _35–41*_	230	380
____	783	Hiawatha Coach (0), _35–41*_	140	290
____	784	Hiawatha Observation Car (0), _35–41*_	205	445
____	792	Rail Chief Combine Car (0), _37–41*_	215	580
____	793	Rail Chief Coach (0), _37–41*_	290	800
____	794	Rail Chief Observation Car (0), _37–41*_	250	800
____	800	Boxcar (2⅞"), _04–05*_	2500	4050
	800	Boxcar (0), _15–26_		
____		(A) Light orange body, brown-maroon roof	45	70
____		(B) Orange body and roof, PRR	25	45
____	801	Caboose (0), _15–26_	30	50
____	802	Stock Car (0), _15–26_	40	60
____	803	Hopper Car, early (0), _23–28_	25	55
____	803	Hopper Car, late (0), _29–34_	30	55
____	804	Tank Car (0), _23–28_	20	45
	805	Boxcar (0), _27–34_		
____		(A) Pea green, terra-cotta roof	35	55
____		(B) Pea green, maroon roof	45	115
____		(C) Orange, maroon roof	45	95
	806	Stock Car (0), _27–34_		
____		(A) Pea green, terra-cotta roof	40	75
____		(B) Orange, various color roofs	35	50
	807	Caboose (0), _27–40_		
____		(A) Peacock body, dark green roof	20	35
____		(B) Red body, peacock roof	20	40
____		(C) Light red body and roof	20	40
	809	Dump Car (0), _31–41_		
____		(A) Orange bin	40	55
____		(B) Green bin	40	85
	810	Crane Car (0), _30–42_		
____		(A) Terra-cotta cab, maroon roof	170	270
____		(B) Cream cab, vermilion roof	130	205

		Good	Exc	
811	Flatcar (O), *26–40*			
	(A) Maroon	40	70	___
	(B) Aluminum	50	100	___
812	Gondola (O), *26–42*	40	70	___
812T	Tool Set: pick, shovel, hammer, *30–41*	40	105	___
813	Stock Car (O), *26–42*			
	(A) Orange body, pea green roof	65	145	___
	(B) Orange body, maroon roof	55	135	___
	(C) Cream body, maroon roof	100	225	___
	(D) Tuscan body and roof	800	1600	___
814	Boxcar (O), *26–42*			
	(A) Cream, orange roof	50	145	___
	(B) Cream, maroon roof	115	140	___
	(C) Yellow, brown roof	110	120	___
814R	Refrigerator Car (O), *29–42*			
	(A) Ivory, peacock roof	100	200	___
	(B) White, light blue roof	105	230	___
	(C) Flat white, brown roof	600	900	___
815	Tank Car (O), *26–42*			
	(A) Pea green, maroon frame	250	510	___
	(B) Pea green, black frame	70	155	___
	(C) Aluminum, black frame	50	100	___
	(D) Orange-yellow, black frame	150	255	___
816	Hopper Car (O), *27–42*			
	(A) Olive green	85	155	___
	(B) Red body	65	140	___
	(C) Black body	370	680	___
817	Caboose (O), *26–42*			
	(A) Peacock body, dark green roof	45	70	___
	(B) Red body, peacock roof	45	80	___
	(C) Light red body and roof	45	80	___
820	Boxcar (O), *15–26*			
	(A) Orange, Illinois Central	40	80	___
	(B) Orange, Union Pacific	50	105	___
820	Floodlight Car (O), *31–42*			
	(A) Terra-cotta	100	180	___
	(B) Green	100	175	___
	(C) Light green	105	180	___
821	Stock Car (O), *15–16, 25–26*	45	85	___
822	Caboose (O), *15–26*	35	65	___
831	Flatcar (O), *27–34*	20	45	___
840	Industrial Power Station, *28–40**	1200	3050	___
900	Ammunition Car (O), *17–21*	120	340	___
900	Box Trail Car (2⅞"), *04–05**	2000	3600	___
901	Gondola (O), *19–27*	25	50	___

			Good	Exc
_____	902	Gondola (0), *27–34*	25	45
_____	910	Grove of Trees, *32–42*	70	180
_____	911	Country Estate, *32–42*	195	440
_____	912	Suburban Home	300	620
_____	913	Landscaped Bungalow, *40–42*	140	285
_____	914	Park Landscape, *32–35*	90	205
_____	915	Tunnel, 65" or 60" long, *32–33, 35*	160	435
_____	916	Tunnel, 29" long, *35*	95	180
_____	917	Scenic Hillside, 34" x 15", *32–36*	90	205
_____	918	Scenic Hillside, 30" x 10", *32–36*	90	205
_____	919	Park Grass, cloth bag, *32–42*	10	20
_____	920	Village, *32–33*	600	1600
_____	921	Scenic Park, 3 pieces, *32–33*	980	2600
_____	921C	Park Center, *32–33*	400	1050
_____	922	Terrace, *32–36*	90	255
_____	923	Tunnel, 40" long, *33–42*	125	225
_____	924	Tunnel, 30" long (072), *35–42*	50	135
_____	925	Lubricant, *35–42*	25	120
_____	927	Flag Plot, *37–42*	70	135
_____	1000	Passenger Car (2⅞"), *05**	4500	6750
_____	1000	Trolley Trailer (std), *10–16*	1400	2250
	1010	Electric Locomotive 0-4-0, Winner Lines (0), *31–32*		
_____			90	160
_____	1010	Interurban Trailer (std), *10–16*	1000	1800
_____	1011	Pullman Car, Winner Lines (0), *31–32*	45	75
_____	1012	Station, *32*	40	70
_____	1015	0-4-0 Locomotive (0), *31–32*	100	205
_____	1017	Winner Station, *33*	25	70
_____	1019	Observation Car (0), *31–32*	50	70
_____	1020	Baggage Car (0), *31–32*	65	110
_____	1021	90-degree Crossover (027), *32–42*	1	5
_____	1022	Tunnel, 18" long (0), *35–42*	15	30
_____	1023	Tunnel, 19" long, *34–42*	20	40
_____	1024	Switches, pair (027), *37–42*	5	15
_____	1025	Bumper (027), *40–42*	15	25
_____	1027	Transformer Station, *34*	50	115
_____	1028	Transformer, 40 watts, *39*	3	10
_____	1029	Transformer, 25 watts, *36*	5	20
_____	1030	Electric Locomotive 0-4-0 (0), *32*	75	135
_____	1030	Transformer, 40 watts, *35–38*	6	25
_____	1035	0-4-0 Locomotive (0), *32*	75	115
_____	1037	Transformer, 40 watts, *40–42*	7	25
_____	1038	Transformer, 30 watts, *40*	2	5
_____	1039	Transformer, 35 watts, *37–40*	7	20

		Good	Exc
1040	Transformer, 60 watts, *37–39*	10	30 ____
1041	Transformer, 60 watts, *39–42*	15	30 ____
1045	Watchman, *38–42*	30	65 ____
1050	Passenger Car Trailer (2⅞"), *05**	5000	7200 ____
1100	Summer Trolley Trailer (std), *10–13*		NRS ____
1100	Mickey Mouse Handcar, *35–37**		
	(A) Red base	405	640 ____
	(B) Apple green base, orange shoes	500	880 ____
	(C) Orange base	600	1225 ____
1103	Peter Rabbit Handcar (O), *35–37**	330	820 ____
1105	Santa Claus Handcar (O), *35–35**		
	(A) Red base	660	1050 ____
	(B) Green base	720	1200 ____
1107	Transformer Station, *33*	25	70 ____
1107	Donald Duck Handcar (O), *36–37**		
	(A) White dog house, red roof	475	1200 ____
	(B) White dog house, green roof	450	1100 ____
	(C) Orange dog house, green roof	640	1850 ____
1121	Switches, pair (027), *37–42*	15	35 ____
1506L	0-4-0 Locomotive (O), *33–34*	95	125 ____
1506M	0-4-0 Locomotive (O), *35*	250	430 ____
1508	0-4-0 Commodore Vanderbilt with 1509 Mickey Mouse stoker Tender, *35*	420	690 ____
1511	0-4-0 Locomotive (O), *36–37*	110	160 ____
1512	Gondola (O), *31–33, 36–37*	25	50 ____
1514	Boxcar (O), *31–37*	25	40 ____
1515	Tank Car (O), *33–37*	25	40 ____
1517	Caboose (O), *31–37*	25	40 ____
1518	Mickey Mouse Circus Dining Car (O), *35*	120	260 ____
1519	Mickey Mouse Band Car (O), *35*	120	260 ____
1520	Mickey Mouse Circus Car (O), *35*	120	260 ____
1536	Mickey Mouse Circus Set: 1508, 1509, 1518, 1519, 1520, *35*	770	1350 ____
1550	Switches, for windup trains, pair, *33–37*	2	5 ____
1555	90-degree Crossover, for windup trains, *33–37*	1	2 ____
1560	Station, *33–37*	15	35 ____
1569	Accessory Set, 8 pieces, *33–37*	35	70 ____
1588	0-4-0 Locomotive (O), *36–37*	150	250 ____
1630	Pullman Car (O), *38–42*		
	(A) Aluminum windows	35	70 ____
	(B) Light gray windows	45	80 ____
1631	Observation Car (O), *38–42*		
	(A) Aluminum windows	35	70 ____
	(B) Light gray windows	45	80 ____

			Good	Exc
____	**1651E**	Electric Locomotive 0-4-0 (O), *33*	130	240
____	**1661E**	2-4-0 Locomotive (O), *33*	75	160
____	**1662**	0-4-0 Locomotive (027), *40–42*	218	420
____	**1663**	0-4-0 Locomotive (027), *40–42*	200	385
	1664/E	2-4-2 Locomotive (027), *38–42*		
____		(A) Gunmetal	60	100
____		(B) Black	60	95
	1666/E	2-6-2 Locomotive (027), *38–42*		
____		(A) Gunmetal	115	170
____		(B) Black	95	145
	1668/E	2-6-2 Locomotive (027), *37–41*		
____		(A) Gunmetal	75	115
____		(B) Black	75	130
	1673	Coach (O), *36–37*		
____		(A) Aluminum windows	35	75
____		(B) Light gray windows	45	90
____	**1674**	Pullman Car (O), *36–37*	35	75
____	**1675**	Observation Car (O), *36–37*	30	70
	1677	Gondola (O), *33–35, 39–42*		
____		(A) Light blue, Ives	40	60
____		(B) Blue or red, Lionel	20	40
	1679	Boxcar (O), *33–42*		
____		(A) Cream, Ives	25	40
____		(B) Cream, Lionel	25	40
____		(C) Cream or yellow, Baby Ruth	20	40
	1680	Tank Car (O), *33–42*		
____		(A) Aluminum, Ives Tank Lines	60	95
____		(B) Aluminum, no Ives lettering	20	35
____		(C) Orange, Shell Oil	15	30
	1681	2-4-0 Locomotive (O), *34–35*		
____		(A) Black, red frame	55	120
____		(B) Red, red frame	110	145
	1681E	2-4-0 Locomotive (O), *34–35*		
____		(A) Black, red frame	65	130
____		(B) Red, red frame	130	165
	1682	Caboose (O), *33–42*		
____		(A) Vermilion, Ives	35	70
____		(B) Red or tuscan, Lionel	15	40
	1684	2-4-2 Locomotive (027), *41–42*		
____		(A) Black	45	70
____		(B) Gunmetal	45	70
	1685	Coach (O), *33–37 u*		
____		(A) Gray, maroon roof	240	495
____		(B) Red, maroon roof	170	335
____		(C) Blue, silver roof	170	315

		Good	Exc	
1686	Baggage Car (O), *33–37 u*			
	(A) Gray, maroon roof	240	495	____
	(B) Red, maroon roof	170	335	____
	(C) Blue, silver roof	170	315	____
1687	Observation Car (O), *33–37 u*			
	(A) Gray, maroon roof	170	315	____
	(B) Red, maroon roof	180	315	____
	(C) Blue, silver roof	170	315	____
1688/E	2-4-2 Locomotive (027), *36–46*	50	125	____
1689E	2-4-2 Locomotive (027), *36–37*			
	(A) Gunmetal	75	115	____
	(B) Black	60	100	____
1689T	Tender, black	15	30	____
1690	Pullman Car (O), *33–40*	35	60	____
1691	Observation Car (O), *33–40*	35	60	____
1692	Pullman Car (027), *39 u*	45	70	____
1693	Observation Car (027), *39 u*	45	70	____
1700E	Diesel, power unit only (027), *35–37*	45	70	____
1700E	Set: 1700, 1701 (2), 1702, *35–37 u*			
	(A) Aluminum and light red	140	250	____
	(B) Chrome and light red	140	250	____
	(C) Orange and gray	155	285	____
1701	Coach (027), *35–37*			
	(A) Chrome sides and roof	20	45	____
	(B) Silver sides and roof	30	55	____
	(C) Orange and gray	75	150	____
1702	Observation Car (027), *35–37*			
	(A) Chrome sides and roof	20	45	____
	(B) Silver sides and roof	30	55	____
	(C) Orange and gray	75	150	____
1703	Observation Car, hooked coupler, *35–37 u*	50	110	____
1717	Gondola (O), *33–40 u*	30	50	____
1717X	Gondola (O), *40 u*	25	50	____
1719	Boxcar (O), *33–40 u*	30	50	____
1719X	Boxcar (O), *41–42 u*	30	50	____
1722	Caboose (O), *33–42 u*	25	50	____
1722X	Caboose (O), *39–40 u*	25	40	____
1766	Pullman Car (std), *34–40**			
	(A) Terra-cotta, maroon roof, brass trim	300	650	____
	(B) Red, maroon roof, nickel trim	300	540	____
1767	Baggage Car (std), *34–40**			
	(A) Terra-cotta, maroon roof, brass trim	295	850	____
	(B) Red, maroon roof, nickel trim	295	700	____

		Good	Exc
1768	Observation Car (std), *34–40**		
____	(A) Terra-cotta, maroon roof, brass trim	300	650
____	(B) Red, maroon roof, nickel trim	300	540
____ **1811**	Pullman Car (O), *33–37*	35	70
____ **1812**	Observation Car (O), *33–37*	30	65
____ **1813**	Baggage Car (O), *33–37*	60	135
____ **1816/W**	Diesel (O), *35–37*	100	240
____ **1817**	Coach (O), *35–37*	25	50
____ **1818**	Observation Car (O), *35–37*	25	50
____ **1835E**	2-4-2 Locomotive (std), *34–39*	470	730
____ **1910**	Electric Locomotive 0-6-0, early (std), *10–11*	920	1550
____ **1910**	Electric Locomotive 0-6-0, late (std), *12*	550	1350
____ **1910**	Pullman Car (std), *09–10 u*	860	1800
____ **1911**	Electric Locomotive 0-4-0, early (std), *10–12*	860	1700
____ **1911**	Electric Locomotive 0-4-0, late (std), *13*	700	1100
1911	Electric Locomotive 0-4-4-0 Special (std), *11–12*	860	2500
1912	Electric Locomotive 0-4-4-0 (std), *10–12**		
____	(A) New York, New Haven & Hartford	1550	3200
____	(B) New York Central Lines	1300	2700
____ **1912**	Electric Locomotive 0-4-4-0 Special (std), *11**	2500	4500
____ **2200**	Summer Trolley Trailer (std), *10–13*	1100	2250
____ **2203B**	Tender	40	80
____ **2224W**	Tender	55	115
____ **2225W**	Tender	30	60
____ **2228B**	Tender	140	280
____ **2235W**	Tender	25	50
____ **2600**	Pullman Car (O), *38–42*	80	155
____ **2601**	Observation Car (O), *38–42*	60	115
____ **2602**	Baggage Car (O), *38–42*	90	185
2613	Pullman Car (O), *38–42**		
____	(A) Blue, 2-tone blue roof	100	300
____	(B) State green, 2-tone green roof	200	440
2614	Observation Car (O), *38–42**		
____	(A) Blue, 2-tone blue roof	100	300
____	(B) State green, 2-tone green roof	200	440
2615	Baggage Car (O), *38–42**		
____	(A) Blue, 2-tone blue roof	115	300
____	(B) State green, 2-tone green roof	200	420
____ **2620**	Floodlight Car (O), *38–42*	65	100
2623	Pullman Car (O), *41–42*		
____	(A) Irvington	175	335
____	(B) Manhattan	165	310
____ **2624**	Pullman Car (O), *41–42*	750	1700
____ **2630**	Pullman Car (O), *38–42*	30	70

		Good	Exc
2631	Observation Car (O), *38–42*	30	70 ___
2640	Pullman Car, illuminated (O), *38–42*		
	(A) Light blue, aluminum roof	30	70 ___
	(B) State green, dark green roof	30	70 ___
2641	Observation Car, illuminated (O), *38–42*		
	(A) Light blue, aluminum roof	30	70 ___
	(B) State green, dark green roof	30	70 ___
2642	Pullman Car (O), *41–42*	30	70 ___
2643	Observation Car (O), *41–42*	30	65 ___
2651	Flatcar (O), *38–42*	30	50 ___
2652	Gondola (O), *38–41*	25	65 ___
2653	Hopper Car (O), *38–42*		
	(A) Stephen Girard green	35	70 ___
	(B) Black	60	130 ___
2654	Tank Car (O), *38–42*		
	(A) Aluminum, Sunoco	35	60 ___
	(B) Orange, Shell	35	60 ___
	(C) Light gray, Sunoco	40	70 ___
2655	Boxcar (O), *38–42*		
	(A) Cream, maroon roof	35	65 ___
	(B) Cream, tuscan roof	40	70 ___
2656	Stock Car (O), *38–41*		
	(A) Light gray, red roof	45	75 ___
	(B) Burnt orange, tuscan roof	75	115 ___
2657	Caboose (O), *40–41*	30	45 ___
2657X	Caboose (O), *40–41*	25	40 ___
2659	Dump Car (O), *38–41*	40	70 ___
2660	Crane Car (O), *38–42*	85	165 ___
2672	Caboose (O27), *41–42*	20	50 ___
2677	Gondola (O27), *39–41*	25	40 ___
2679	Boxcar (O27), *38–42*	15	30 ___
2680	Tank Car (O27), *38–42*		
	(A) Aluminum, Sunoco	15	40 ___
	(B) Orange, Shell	15	40 ___
2682	Caboose (O27), *38–42*	15	30 ___
2682X	Caboose (O27), *38–42*	20	35 ___
2689T	Tender	15	35 ___
2689W	Tender	35	50 ___
2717	Gondola (O), *38–42 u*	20	40 ___
2719	Boxcar (O), *38–42 u*	30	50 ___
2722	Caboose (O), *38–42 u*	25	50 ___
2755	Tank Car (O), *41–42*	70	130 ___
2757	Caboose (O), *41–42*	25	45 ___
2757X	Caboose (O), *41–42*	25	40 ___
2758	Automobile Boxcar (O), *41–42*	35	60 ___

			Good	Exc
___	2810	Crane Car (O), *38–42*	145	210
___	2811	Flatcar (O), *38–42*	50	95
	2812	Gondola (O), *38–42*		
___		(A) Green	40	85
___		(B) Dark orange	45	95
___	2813	Stock Car (O), *38–42*	120	225
	2814	Boxcar (O), *38–42*		
___		(A) Cream, maroon roof	85	150
___		(B) Orange, brown roof, rubber-stamped lettering	200	700
	2814R	Refrigerator Car (O), *38–42*		
___		(A) White, light blue roof, nickel plates	140	260
___		(B) White, brown roof, no plates	375	660
	2815	Tank Car (O), *38–42*		
___		(A) Aluminum	85	165
___		(B) Orange	135	215
	2816	Hopper Car (O), *35–42*		
___		(A) Red	100	190
___		(B) Black	110	220
	2817	Caboose (O), *36–42*		
___		(A) Light red body and roof	78	140
___		(B) Flat red body, tuscan roof	115	180
	2820	Floodlight Car (O), *38–42*		
___		(A) Stamped nickel searchlights	110	205
___		(B) Gray die-cast searchlights	120	260
___	2954	Boxcar (O), *40–42**	145	350
	2955	Sunoco Tank Car (O), *40–42**		
___		(A) Shell decal	225	500
___		(B) Sunoco decal	340	690
___	2956	Hopper Car (O), *40–42**	160	400
___	2957	Caboose (O), *40–42**	70	260
___	3300	Summer Trolley Trailer (std), *10–13*	1400	2250
___	3651	Operating Lumber Car (O), *39–42*	25	55
___	3652	Operating Gondola (O), *39–42*	35	75
___	3659	Operating Dump Car (O), *39–42*	20	40
___	3811	Operating Lumber Car (O), *39–42*	35	90
___	3814	Operating Merchandise Car (O), *39–42*	90	195
___	3859	Operating Dump Car (O), *38–42*	45	90

Other Transformers and Motors

		Good	Exc	
A	Miniature Motor, *04*	50	95	
A	Transformer, 40, 60 watts, *21–37*	10	25	
B	New Departure Motor, *06–16*	75	135	
B	Transformer, 50, 75 watts, *16–38*	7	25	
C	New Departure Motor, *06–16*	100	180	
D	New Departure Motor, *06–14*	100	180	
E	New Departure Motor, *06–14*	100	180	
F	New Departure Motor, *06–14*	100	180	
G	Fan Motor, battery-operated, *06–14*	100	180	
K	Transformer, 150, 200 watts, *13–38*	20	75	
L	Transformer, 50, 75 watts, *13–16, 33–38*	10	25	
M	Peerless Motor, battery-operated, *15–20*	30	80	
N	Transformer, 50 watts, *41–42*	7	20	
Q	Transformer, 50 watts, *14–15*	10	20	
Q	Transformer, 75 watts, *38–42*	12	28	
R	Peerless Motor, battery-operated, reversing, *15–20*	30	75	
R	Transformer, 100 watts, *38–42*	20	45	
S	Transformer, 50 watts, *14–17*	13	28	
T	Transformer, 75, 100, 150 watts, *14–28*	8	30	
U	Transformer, Aladdin, *32–33*	5	15	
V	Transformer, 150 watts, *39–42*	40	75	
W	Transformer, 75 watts, *32–33*	10	35	
Y	Peerless Motor, battery-operated, 3-speed, *15–20*	40	80	
Z	Transformer, 250 watts, *39–42*	85	140	

Track, Lockons, and Contactors

	Good	Exc	
O Straight		1	
O Curve		1	
O72 Straight	1	2	
O72 Curve	1	2	
O27 Straight		1	
O27 Curve		1	
Standard Straight	1	3	
Standard Curve	1	2	
Standard Insulated Straight, *33–42*	2	4	
Standard Insulated Curve, *33–42*	1	2	
O Gauge Lockon		1	
Standard Gauge Lockon		1	
UTC Lockon		1	
145C Contactor	3	10	
153C Contactor	3	7	
Track Clips, dozen (O), *37*	5	10	

			Good	Exc
___	5C	Test Set	700	1200
___	5D	Test Set, *54*	1225	2500
___	5E	Electronic Set Tester, *46–49*	1000	3000
___	5F	Test Set	700	2180
___	011-11	Fiber Pins, dozen (O), *46–50*	1	3
___	011-43	Insulating Pins, dozen (O), *61*	1	2
___	020	90-degree Crossover (O), *45–61*	3	5
___	020X	45-degree Crossover (O), *46–59*	3	8
___	022	Remote Control Switches, pair (O), *45–69*	23	42
___	022-500	Adapter Set (O), *57–61*	1	7
___	022A	Remote Control Switches, pair (O), *47*	27	98
___	022C-1	Switch Controller	5	12
___	25	Bumper (O), *46–47*	5	15
	26	Bumper, *48–50*		
___		(A) Red, *49–50*	5	14
___		(B) Gray, *48*	16	60
___	027C-1	Track Clips, box of 12 (027), *47, 49*	4	17
___	027C-1	Track Clips, box of 50 (027)	21	64
	30	Water Tower, *47–50*		
___		(A) Single-walled	19	75
___		(B) Double-walled	20	90
___	31	Curved Track (Super O), *57–66*	1	4
___	31-7	Power Blade Connection, dozen (Super O), *57–60*		11
___	31-15	Ground Rail Pin, dozen (Super O), *57–66*	1	4
___	31-45	Power Blade Connection, dozen (Super O), *61–66*	2	11
___	32	Straight Track (Super O), *57–66*	2	5
___	32-10	Insulating Pin, dozen (Super O), *57–60*		12
___	32-20	Power Blade Insulator, dozen (Super O), *57–60*	1	5
___	32-25	Insulating Pin (Super O), *57–61*		1
___	32-30	Ground Pin (Super O), *57–61*		1
___	32-31	Power Pin (Super O), *57–61*		1
___	32-32	Insulating Pin (Super O), *57–61*		1
___	32-33	Ground Pin (Super O), *57–61*		1
___	32-34	Power Pin (Super O), *57–61*		1
___	32-35	Insulating Pin, dozen (Super O to 027), *57–61*		3
___	32-45	Power Blade Insulators, dozen (Super O), *61–66*	3	8
___	32-55	Insulating Pins, dozen (Super O), *61–66*	3	8
___	33	Half Curved Track (Super O), *57–66*	1	3
___	34	Half Straight Track (Super O), *57–66*	2	4
___	35	Boulevard Lamp, *45–49*	10	38

		Good	Exc	
36	Operating Car Remote Control Set (Super O), *57–66*	10	20	____
37	Uncoupling Track Set (Super O), *57–66*	8	18	____
38	Accessory Adapter Tracks, pair (Super O), *57–61*	6	15	____
38	Operating Water Tower, *46–47*	103	295	____
39	Operating Set (Super O), *57*	4	8	____
39-5	Operating Set (Super O), *57–58*	4	8	____
39-6	Operating Set (Super O), *57–58*	4	11	____
39-10	Operating Set (Super O), *58*	4	8	____
39-15	Operating Set with blade (Super O), *57–58*	4	8	____
39-20	Operating Set (Super O), *57–58*	4	8	____
39-25	Operating Set (Super O), *61–66*	8	25	____
39-35	Operating Set (Super O), *59*	8	25	____
40	Hookup Wire, *50–51, 53–63*			
	(A) Single reel, orange or gray, with tape	7	34	____
	(B) 8 sealed reels in dealer box	103	383	____
40-25	Conductor Wire with envelope, *56–59*	9	35	____
40-50	Cable Reel with envelope, *60–61*	10	71	____
41	Contactor (Super O)	1	2	____
41	U.S. Army Switcher, *55–57*			
	(A) Unpainted black body	50	103	____
	(B) Black-painted body	225	850	____
042/42	Manual Switches, pair (O), *46–59*	10	25	____
42	Picatinny Arsenal Switcher, *57*	80	281	____
43	Power Track (Super O), *59–66*	4	13	____
44	U.S. Army Mobile Launcher, *59–62*	60	168	____
44-80	Missiles, *59–60*	10	23	____
45	U.S. Marines Mobile Launcher, *60–62*	80	260	____
45	Automatic Gateman, *46–49*	15	43	____
45N	Automatic Gateman, *45*	18	48	____
48	Insulated Straight Track (Super O), *57–66*	4	10	____
49	Insulated Curved Track (Super O), *57–66*	4	10	____
50	Section Gang Car, *54–64*			
	(A) Gray bumpers, rotating blue man and fixed olive men, center horn, *54*	195	716	____
	(B) Blue bumpers, rotating olive man and fixed blue men, center horn	31	57	____
	(C) Blue bumpers, rotating olive man and fixed blue men, off-center horn	23	41	____
51	Navy Yard Switcher, *56–57*	69	137	____
52	Fire Car, *58–61*	64	178	____
53	Rio Grande Snowplow, *57–60*			
	(A) Backwards "a" in Rio Grande	68	205	____
	(B) Correctly printed "a"	150	518	____
54	Ballast Tamper, *58–61, 66, 68–69*	55	167	____
55	PRR Tie-Jector Car, *57–61*			
	(A) Ventilation slot behind motorman	52	153	____
	(B) No slot behind motorman	45	105	____

			Good	Exc
____	55-150	Ties, 24 pieces, *57–60*	13	30
____	56	Lamp Post, *46–49*	23	45
____	56	M&StL Mine Transport, *58*	135	363
____	57	AEC Switcher, *59–60*	140	504
____	58	GN Snowplow, *59–61*	145	373
____	58	Lamp Post, *46–50*	17	39
____	59	Minuteman Switcher, *62–63*	181	453
	60	Lionelville Rapid Transit Trolley, *55–58*		
____		(A) Metal motorman silhouettes	95	248
		(B) No motorman silhouettes	37	100
____	61	Ground Lockon (Super O), *57–66*	2	5
____	61-25	Super O Ground clips, dozen, with dealer envelope	5	17
____	62	Power Lockon (Super O), *57–66*	1	4
____	64	Highway Lamp Post, *45–49*	15	38
	65	Handcar, *62–66*		
____		(A) Light yellow	80	270
____		(B) Dark yellow	70	240
____	68	Executive Inspection Car, *58–61*	61	155
____	69	Maintenance Car, *60–62*	68	215
____	70	Yard Light, *49–50*	9	28
____	71	Lamp Post, *49–59*	8	12
____	75	Goose Neck Lamps, set of 2, *61–63*	10	20
	76	Boulevard Street Lamps, set of 3, *59–66, 68–69*	15	30
____	80	Controller, *60*	5	25
____	88	Controller, *46–60*	9	15
____	89	Flagpole, *56–58*	15	50
	90	Controller, *55–66*		
____		(A) Metal clip	6	10
____		(B) No metal clip	5	8
____	91	Circuit Breaker, *57–60*	10	23
____	92	Circuit Breaker, *59–66, 68–69*	6	13
____	93	Water Tower, *46–49*	17	44
____	96C	Controller, *45–54*	4	8
____	97	Coal Elevator, *46–50*	55	139
____	108	Trestle Set, 12 black piers,	9	23
____	109	Partial Trestle Set, *61*	5	17
____	110	Graduated Trestle Set, 22 or 24 piers, *55–69*	8	16
____	110-75	Graduated Trestle Set with 110-78 envelope	10	28
____	111	Elevated Trestle Set, 10 A piers, *56–69*	7	13
____	111-100	Elevated Trestle Piers, set of 2, *60–63*	13	35
	112	Remote Control Switches, pair (Super O), *57–66*	43	83
____	114	Newsstand with horn, *57–59*	34	80
____	115	Passenger Station, *46–49*	110	270
____	118	Newsstand with whistle, *57–58*	38	85
____	119	Landscaped Tunnel, *57–58*	200	400
____	120	90-degree Crossing (Super O), *57–66*	6	13

		Good	Exc
121	Landscaped Tunnel, *59–66*		NRS ____
122	Lamp Assortment, *48–52*	33	165 ____
123	Lamp Assortment, *55–59*	60	155 ____
123-60	Lamp Assortment, *60–63*	28	153 ____
125	Whistle Shack, *50–55*		
	(A) Gray base	13	40 ____
	(B) Green base	22	48 ____
128	Animated Newsstand, *57–60*	57	102 ____
130	60-degree Crossing (Super O), *57–66*	7	14 ____
131	Curved Tunnel, *59–66*		NRS ____
132	Passenger Station, *49–55*	35	68 ____
133	Passenger Station, *57, 61–62, 66*	20	48 ____
138	Water Tower, *53–57*	23	63 ____
140	Automatic Banjo Signal, *54–66*	13	27 ____
142	Manual Switches, pair (Super O), *57–66*	28	56 ____
145	Automatic Gateman, *50–66*		
	(A) Red roof	11	38 ____
	(B) Maroon roof	10	32 ____
145C	Contactor, *50–60*	3	8 ____
147	Whistle Controller, *61–66*	2	6 ____
148	Dwarf Trackside Signal, *57–60*	23	48 ____
148-100	Controller (SPDT switch), *57–60*	6	17 ____
150	Telegraph Pole Set, *47–50*	30	39 ____
151	Automatic Semaphore, *47–69*		
	(A) Green base, yellow blade, *47*	20	55 ____
	(B) Black base, yellow blade, *47*	10	25 ____
	(C) Black base, red blade, *47*	155	373 ____
	(D) Green base, yellow blade with raised lenses	18	74 ____
152	Automatic Crossing Gate, *45–49*	8	17 ____
153	Automatic Block Control Signal, *45–59*	13	23 ____
153C	Contactor	3	7 ____
154	Automatic Highway Signal, *45–69*	12	21 ____
154C	Contactor	4	8 ____
155	Blinking Light Signal with bell, *55–57*	20	48 ____
156	Station Platform, *46–49*	29	85 ____
156-5	Station Platform Fence with envelope	23	57 ____
157	Station Platform, *52–59*		
	(A) Maroon base	15	37 ____
	(B) Red base	25	75 ____
157-23	Station Platform Fence with envelope	14	48 ____
160	Unloading Bin, *52–57*		
	(A) Black plastic, long	2	8 ____
	(B) Black metal, short	31	71 ____
	(C) Multicolor Bakelite, short	6	23 ____
	(D) Black Bakelite, short	4	10 ____
161	Mail Pickup Set, *61–63*	23	67 ____
163	Single Target Block Signal, *61–69*	15	30 ____

			Good	Exc
___	**164**	Log Loader, *46–50*	64	160
___	**164-64**	Log Set, 5 pieces, *52–58*	26	68
___	**167**	Whistle Controller, *45–46*	3	10
___	**175**	Rocket Launcher, *58–60*	54	162
___	**175-50**	Extra Rocket, *59–60*	10	26
___	**182**	Magnetic Crane, *46–49*	129	250
___	**182-22**	Steel Scrap with bag, *46–49*	45	124
___	**192**	Operating Control Tower, *59–60*	107	242
	193	Industrial Water Tower, *53–55*		
___		(A) Red	43	78
___		(B) Black, *53*	83	168
	195	Floodlight Tower, *57–69*		
___		(A) Medium tan base, rubber-stamped lettering	25	70
___		(B) All other variations	23	55
___	**195-75**	Floodlight Extension, 8-bulb (with box), *58–60*	30	86
___	**196**	Smoke Pellets, *46–47*	28	100
	197	Rotating Radar Antenna, *57–59*		
___		(A) Orange platform	33	99
___		(B) Gray platform	27	70
___	**197-75**	Separate Sale Radar Head with box	48	172
___	**199**	Microwave Relay Tower, *58–59*	30	70
___	**202**	UP Alco Diesel A Unit, *57*	33	75
___	**204**	Santa Fe Alco Diesel AA Units, *57*	72	192
	205	Missouri Pacific Alco Diesel AA Units, *57–58*		
___		(A) Pilot without support	45	123
___		(B) Pilot with painted metal support	70	165
___	**206**	Artificial Coal, large bag, *46–68*	12	21
___	**207**	Artificial Coal, small bag, *46–48*	7	15
___	**208**	Santa Fe Alco Diesel AA Units, *58–59*	57	230
___	**209**	New Haven Alco Diesel AA Units, *58*	192	685
___	**209**	Wooden Barrels, set of 6, *46–50*	9	18
___	**210**	Texas Special Alco Diesel AA Units, *58*	50	130
___	**211**	Texas Special Alco Diesel AA Units, *62–66*	60	132
___	**212**	Santa Fe Alco Diesel AA Units, *64–66*	75	175
___	**212T**	Santa Fe Alco Diesel Dummy A Unit, *64–66*	25	60
___	**212**	USMC Alco Diesel A Unit, *58–59*	65	156
___	**212T**	USMC Diesel Dummy A Unit, *58 u*	315	975
___	**213**	M&StL Alco Diesel AA Units, *64*	75	205
___	**214**	Plate Girder Bridge, *53–69*	7	15
	215	Santa Fe Alco Diesel Units, *65 u*		
___		(A) AB Units	63	130
___		(B) AA Units	75	150
___	**216**	Burlington Alco Diesel A Unit, *58*	105	333
___	**216**	M&StL Alco Diesel AA Units (213T dummy A unit), *64 u*	63	190
___	**217**	B&M Alco Diesel AB Units, *59*	90	208
___	**217C**	B&M Alco Diesel B Unit, *59*	30	70

		Good	Exc	
218	Santa Fe Alco Diesel Units, *59–63*			
	(A) AA Units	70	155	____
	(B) AB Units	65	145	____
	(C) AA Units, solid nose decal	70	208	____
218C	Santa Fe Alco B Unit, *61–63*	40	96	____
219	Missouri Pacific Alco Diesel AA Units, *59 u*	75	153	____
220	Santa Fe Alco Diesel Units, *60–61*			
	(A) A Unit	35	102	____
	(B) AA Units	65	170	____
221	2-6-4 Locomotive, 221W Tender, *46–47*			
	(A) Gray body, black drivers	60	138	____
	(B) Black body, nickel-rimmed black drivers, *47*	70	170	____
	(C) Gray body, cast-aluminum drivers, *46*	110	240	____
221	Rio Grande Alco Diesel A Unit, *63–64*	28	60	____
221	Santa Fe Alco Diesel A Unit, *63–64 u*	176	600	____
221	U.S. Marine Corps Alco Diesel A Unit, *63–64 u*	180	505	____
221T	Tender			
	(A) Gray	18	40	____
	(B) Black	15	45	____
221W	Whistle Tender	28	60	____
222	Rio Grande Alco Diesel A Unit, *62*	25	60	____
223	Santa Fe Alco Diesel AB Units, *63*	64	182	____
224	2-6-2 Locomotive, 2466W or 2466WX Tender, *45–46*			
	(A) Blackened handrails, *45*	118	245	____
	(B) Silver handrails	75	153	____
224	U.S. Navy Alco Diesel AB Units, *60*	120	248	____
225	C&O Alco Diesel A Unit, *60*	40	75	____
226	B&M Alco Diesel AB Units, *60 u*	73	162	____
226C	B&M Alco Diesel B Unit, *60 u*	35	83	____
227	CN Alco Diesel A Unit, *60 u*	70	145	____
228	CN Alco Diesel A Unit, *61 u*	70	145	____
229	M&StL Alco Diesel Units, *61–62*			
	(A) A Unit, *61*	55	99	____
	(B) AB Units, *62*	80	185	____
229C	M&StL Alco Diesel B Unit, *61–62*	30	65	____
230	C&O Alco Diesel A Unit, *61*	48	98	____
231	Rock Island Alco Diesel A Unit, *61–63*			
	(A) With red stripe	50	103	____
	(B) Without red stripe	150	413	____
232	New Haven Alco Diesel A Unit, *62*	57	134	____
233	2-4-2 Scout Locomotive, 233W Tender, *61–62*	30	68	____
233W	Whistle Tender	20	43	____
234T	Lionel Lines Tender	8	23	____
234T	Pennsylvania Tender	13	50	____
234W	Lionel Whistle Tender	23	48	____

		Good	Exc
____ 234W	Pennsylvania Whistle Tender	25	100
235	2-4-2 Scout Locomotive, 1130T or 1060T Tender, *60 u*	75	224
____			
236	2-4-2 Scout Locomotive, *61–62*		
____	(A) 1050T slope-back Tender	15	43
____	(B) 1130T Tender	15	45
237	2-4-2 Scout Locomotive, *63–66*		
____	(A) 1060T Tender	25	65
____	(B) 234W Tender	31	75
238	2-4-2 Scout Locomotive, stripe on running board, 234W Tender, *63–64*	55	150
____ 239	2-4-2 Scout Locomotive, 234W Tender, *65–66*	40	88
____ 240	2-4-2 Scout Locomotive, 242T Tender, *64 u*	87	267
241	2-4-2 Scout Locomotive, *65 u*		
____	(A) Narrow stripe, 234W Tender	32	98
____	(B) Wide stripe, 1130T Tender	25	69
242	2-4-2 Scout Locomotive, 1060T or 1062T Tender, *62–66*	18	38
____			
____ 243	2-4-2 Scout Locomotive, 243W Tender, *60*	32	88
____ 243W	Whistle Tender	15	45
244	2-4-2 Scout Locomotive, 244T or 1130T Tender, *60–61*	18	44
____			
____ 244T	Tender	7	18
____ 245	2-4-2 Scout Locomotive, 1130T Tender, *59 u*	25	71
246	2-4-2 Scout Locomotive, 244T or 1130T Tender, *59–61*	13	27
____			
247	2-4-2 Scout Locomotive, 247T Tender, *59*		
____	(A) Closed pilot	15	70
____	(B) Open pilot	15	150
____ 247T	B&O Tender	15	30
____ 248	2-4-2 Scout Locomotive, 1130T Tender, *58*	25	75
____ 249	2-4-2 Scout Locomotive, 250T Tender, *58*	20	58
____ 250	2-4-2 Scout Locomotive, 250T Tender, *57*	20	58
____ 250T	Tender	10	24
251	2-4-2 Scout Locomotive, *66 u*		
____	(A) 1062T slope-back Tender	82	210
____	(B) 250T-type Tender	78	210
____ 252	Crossing Gate, *50–62*	9	21
____ 253	Block Control Signal, *56–59*	14	28
256	Illuminated Freight Station, *50–53*		
____	(A) Standard	23	45
____	(B) Light green roof	58	128
257	Freight Station with diesel horn, *56–57*		
____	(A) Maroon base	30	85
____	(B) Brown base	40	105
____	(C) Maroon or brown base, light green roof	68	145
260	Bumper, *51–69*		
____	(A) Die-cast	7	13
____	(B) Black plastic	15	38

POSTWAR 1945-1969

		Good	Exc	
262	Highway Crossing Gate, *62–69*	15	43	___
264	Operating Forklift Platform, *57–60*	85	232	___
282	Portal Gantry Crane, *54–57*	80	172	___
282R	Portal Gantry Crane, *56–57*	70	171	___
299	Code Transmitter Beacon Set, *61–63*	43	111	___
308	Railroad Sign Set, die-cast, *45–49*	23	35	___
309	Yard Sign Set, plastic, *50–59*	8	22	___
310	Billboard Set, *50–68*	10	20	___
313	Bascule Bridge, *46–49*	95	332	___
313-82	Fiber Pins, dozen, *46–60*	1	2	___
313-121	Fiber Pins, dozen, *61*	1	2	___
314	Scale Model Girder Bridge, *45–50*	10	32	___
315	Illuminated Trestle Bridge, *46–48*	36	84	___
316	Trestle Bridge, *49*	18	37	___
317	Trestle Bridge, *50–56*	17	31	___
321	Trestle Bridge, *58–64*	15	38	___
321-100	Trestle Bridge	23	72	___
332	Arch-Under Trestle Bridge, *59–66*	20	38	___
334	Operating Dispatching Board, *57–60*	80	200	___
342	Culvert Loader, *56–58*	38	162	___
345	Culvert Unloader, *57–59*	40	163	___
346	Culvert Unloader, manual, *65 u*	55	140	___
347	Cannon Firing Range Set, *64 u*	277	748	___
348	Culvert Unloader, manual, *66–69*	75	160	___
350	Engine Transfer Table, *57–60*	105	247	___
350-50	Transfer Table Extension, *57–60*	78	154	___
352	Ice Depot with 6352 Ice Car, *55–57*	55	137	___
353	Trackside Control Signal, *60–61*	11	33	___
356	Operating Freight Station, *52–57*			
	(A) Dark green roof, *52–57*	36	93	___
	(B) Light green roof, *57*	70	178	___
362	Barrel Loader, *52–57*			
	(A) Gold lettering	24	68	___
	(B) Red lettering	97	355	___
362-78	Wooden Barrels, 6 pieces, *52–57*			
	(A) Brown	7	18	___
	(B) Red	88	287	___
364	Conveyor Lumber Loader, *48–57*	25	73	___
364C	On/Off Switch, *48–64*	6	11	___
365	Dispatching Station, *58–59*	47	113	___
375	Turntable, *62–64*	67	173	___
390C	Switch, double-pole, double-throw, *60–64*	6	13	___
394	Rotary Beacon, *49–53*			
	(A) Steel tower, red platform	20	45	___
	(B) Steel tower, green platform	33	77	___
	(C) Aluminum tower, platform, and base	18	35	___
	(D) Aluminum tower, red steel base	33	63	___
	(E) Steel tower, red platform, stick-on nameplate	32	77	___

			Good	Exc
395	Floodlight Tower, *49–56*			
____	(A) Light green, silver, or unpainted aluminum		20	45
____	(B) Red		33	104
____	(C) Dark green		87	300
____	(D) Yellow		44	125
397	Operating Coal Loader, *48–57*			
____	(A) Yellow generator, *48*		120	312
____	(B) Blue generator, *49–57*		35	85
____ **400**	B&O Passenger Rail Diesel Car, *56–58*		75	168
____ **404**	B&O Baggage-Mail Rail Diesel Car, *57–58*		135	307
____ **410**	Billboard Blinker, *56–58*		18	43
____ **413**	Countdown Control Panel, *62*		17	58
____ **415**	Diesel Fueling Station, *55–57*		48	128
____ **419**	Heliport Control Tower, *62*		165	358
____ **443**	Missile Launching Platform with ammo dump, *60–62*		28	63
____ **445**	Switch Tower, lighted, *52–57*		23	53
____ **448**	Missile Firing Range Set, *61–63*		47	152
____ **450**	Operating Signal Bridge, *52–58*		22	48
____ **450L**	Signal Light Head, *52–58*		13	26
____ **452**	Overhead Gantry Signal, *61–63*		40	98
455	Operating Oil Derrick, *50–54*			
____	(A) Dark green tower, green top		50	119
____	(B) Dark green tower, red top		58	163
____	(C) Apple green tower, red top		88	377
456	Coal Ramp with 3456 Hopper, *50–55*			
____	(A) Light gray ramp		53	128
____	(B) Dark gray ramp		73	153
____ **456C**	Coal Ramp Controller		8	35
460	Piggyback Transportation Set, *55–57*			
____	(A) Metal stick-on signs on lift truck		49	113
____	(B) Rubber-stamped lettering on lift truck		70	142
____ **460P**	Piggyback Platform, *55–57*		20	65
____ **461**	Platform with truck and trailer, *66*		60	175
____ **462**	Derrick Platform Set, *61–62*		109	295
____ **464**	Lumber Mill, *56–60*		44	110
____ **465**	Sound Dispatching Station, *56–57*		37	84
____ **470**	Missile Launching Platform with target car, *59–62*		51	95
____ **479-1**	Truck for 6362 Truck Car with envelope, *55–56*		25	88
____ **480-25**	Conversion Magnetic Coupler, *50–60*		1	5
____ **480-32**	Conversion Magnetic Coupler, *61–69*		1	5
494	Rotary Beacon, *54–66*			
____	(A) Painted steel		23	43
____	(B) Unpainted aluminum		20	61
____ **497**	Coaling Station, *53–58*		55	124

		Good	Exc	
520	LL Boxcab Electric Locomotive, *56–57*			
	(A) Black pantograph	33	77	____
	(B) Copper-colored pantograph	40	98	____
600	MKT NW2 Switcher, *55*			
	(A) Black frame, black end rails	63	117	____
	(B) Gray frame, yellow or black end rails	80	201	____
601	Seaboard NW2 Switcher, *56*			
	(A) Red stripes with square ends	77	174	____
	(B) Red stripes with round ends	88	162	____
602	Seaboard NW2 Switcher, *57–58*	77	155	____
610	Erie NW2 Switcher, *55*			
	(A) Black frame	53	123	____
	(B) Black frame, two-axle Magnetraction	30	150	____
	(C) Yellow frame	124	402	____
	(D) Replacement body with nameplates	90	272	____
611	Jersey Central NW2 Switcher, *57–58*	60	152	____
613	UP NW2 Switcher, *58*	77	223	____
614	Alaska NW2 Switcher, *59–60*			
	(A) Plastic bell, no brake	100	190	____
	(B) No bell, yellow brake	113	234	____
	(C) "Built by Lionel" outlined in yellow near nose	178	332	____
616	Santa Fe NW2 Switcher, *61–62*			
	(A) Open E-unit slot and bell/horn slots	95	183	____
	(B) Plugged E-unit slot and open bell/horn slots	101	254	____
	(C) Plugged E-unit slot and bell/horn slots	108	278	____
617	Santa Fe NW2 Switcher, *63*	110	249	____
621	Jersey Central NW2 Switcher, *56–57*	70	147	____
622	Santa Fe NW2 Switcher, *49–50*			
	(A) Large GM decal on cab	138	279	____
	(B) Small GM decal on side	103	209	____
623	Santa Fe NW2 Switcher, *52–54*	75	137	____
624	C&O NW2 Switcher, *52–54*	75	175	____
625	LV GE 44-ton Switcher, *57–58*	42	104	____
626	B&O GE 44-ton Switcher, *56–57, 59*	108	305	____
627	LV GE 44-ton Switcher, *56–57*	33	75	____
628	NP GE 44-ton Switcher, *56–57*	46	103	____
629	Burlington GE 44-ton Switcher, *56*	146	330	____
633	Santa Fe NW2 Switcher, *62*	58	130	____
634	Santa Fe NW2 Switcher, *63, 65–66*			
	(A) Safety stripes	80	145	____
	(B) No safety stripes	48	110	____
635	UP NW2 Switcher, *65 u*	48	114	____
637	2-6-4 Locomotive, 2046 736W Tender, *59–63*			
	(A) 2046W Lionel Lines Tender	55	150	____
	(B) 736W Pennsylvania Tender	70	170	____

			Good	Exc
____	**638-2361**	Van Camp's Pork & Beans Boxcar, *62 u*	15	40
____	**645**	Union Pacific NW2 Switcher, *69*	48	138
____	**646**	4-6-4 Locomotive, 2046W Tender, *54–58*	90	232
____	**665**	4-6-4 Locomotive, 2046W, 6026W, or 736W Tender, *54–59, 66*	83	233
____	**671**	6-8-6 Steam Turbine Locomotive, smoke bulb, *46*	105	198
	671	6-8-6 Steam Turbine Locomotive, *47–49*		
____		(A) 671W Tender	75	190
____		(B) 2671W Tender, backup lights	117	408
____		(C) 2671W Tender, no backup lights	101	223
____	**671-75**	Smoke Lamp, 12 volt, *46*	10	18
____	**671R**	6-8-6 Steam Turbine Locomotive, 4424W or 4671 Tender, *46–49*	165	303
____	**671RR**	6-8-6 Steam Turbine Locomotive, 2046W-50 Tender, *52*	90	195
____	**671S**	Smoke Conversion Kit	20	130
____	**671W**	Whistle Tender, *46–48*	30	63
	675	2-6-2 Locomotive, 2466WX or 6466WX Tender, *47–49*		
____		(A) Aluminum smokestack, *47*	74	211
____		(B) Black smokestack, *48–49*	63	177
____	**675**	2-6-4 Locomotive, 2046W Tender, *52*	69	183
____	**681**	6-8-6 Steam Turbine Locomotive, 2046W-50 or 2671W Tender, *50–51, 53*	98	212
____	**682**	6-8-6 Steam Turbine Locomotive, 2046W-50 Tender, *54–55*	136	318
____	**685**	4-6-4 Hudson Locomotive, 6026W Tender, *53*	80	208
____	**703-10**	Smoke Lamp, 18 volt, *46*	12	22
	726	2-8-4 Berkshire, *46–49*		
____		(A) 2426W Tender, smoke lamp, *46*	230	535
____		(B) 2426W Tender, *47–49*	210	463
____	**726RR**	2-8-4 Berkshire Locomotive, 2046W Tender, *52*	117	258
____	**726S**	Smoke Conversion Kit	40	115
____	**736**	2-8-4 Berkshire Locomotive, 2671WX, 2046W, or 736W Tender, *50–51*	225	325
____	**736**	2-8-4 Berkshire Locomotive, 2671WX, 2046W, or 736W Tender, *53–66*	146	298
____	**736W**	PRR Whistle Tender	22	65
	746	N&W 4-8-4 Class J Northern, *57–60*		
____		(A) Tender with long stripe	493	983
____		(B) Tender with short stripe	300	770
____	**746W**	Tender, short stripe	30	115
____	**760**	Curved Track, 16 sections (O72), *54–57*	18	45
____	**773**	4-6-4 Hudson Locomotive, 2426W Tender, *50*	673	1487
	773	4-6-4 Hudson Locomotive, *64–66*		
____		(A) 773W NYC Tender	667	1103
____		(B) 736W PRR Tender	535	930
____	**773T**	NYC Tender	70	150

		Good	Exc
773W	NYC Whistle Tender	100	220 ____
902	Elevated Trestle Set, *60*	25	133 ____
909	Smoke Fluid, large or small bottle, *57–66, 68–69*		
	(A) ½ ounce bottle	7	20 ____
	(B) 2 ounce bottle	9	35 ____
B909	Smoke Capsules, pack of three, *57–66, 68–69*	8	28 ____
919	Artificial Grass, *46–64*	7	15 ____
920	Scenic Display Set, *57–58*	34	69 ____
920-2	Tunnel Portals, pair, *58–59*	13	25 ____
920-3	Green Grass, *57*	3	12 ____
920-4	Yellow Grass, *57*	7	18 ____
920-5	Artificial Rock, *57–58*	3	11 ____
920-6	Dry Glue, *57–58*	3	10 ____
920-8	Dyed Lichen, *57–58*	3	15 ____
925	Lubricant, 2 ounce tube, *46–69*	3	12 ____
925-1	Lubricant, 1 ounce tube, *50–69*	1	5 ____
926	Lubricant, ½ ounce tube, *55*	2	3 ____
926-5	Instruction Booklet, *46–48*	1	5 ____
927	Lubricating Kit, *50–59*	11	27 ____
928	Maintenance and Lubricating Kit, *60–63*	31	60 ____
943	Ammo Dump, *59–61*	16	38 ____
950	U.S. Railroad Map, *58–66*	20	48 ____
951	Farm Set, 13 pieces, *58*	50	125 ____
952	Figure Set, 30 pieces, *58*	34	57 ____
953	Figure Set, 32 pieces, *59–62*	40	84 ____
954	Swimming Pool and Playground Set, 30 pieces, *59*	40	106 ____
955	Highway Set, 22 pieces, *58*	30	65 ____
956	Stockyard Set, 18 pieces, *59*	40	85 ____
957	Farm Building and Animal Set, 35 pieces, *58*	60	120 ____
958	Vehicle Set, 24 pieces, *58*	45	83 ____
959	Barn Set, 23 pieces, *58*	39	78 ____
960	Barnyard Set, 29 pieces, *59–61*	56	141 ____
961	School Set, 36 pieces, *59*	45	108 ____
962	Turnpike Set, 24 pieces, *58*	60	183 ____
963	Frontier Set, 18 pieces, *59–60*	60	150 ____
964	Factory Site Set, 18 pieces, *59*	70	230 ____
965	Farm Set, 36 pieces, *59*	55	145 ____
966	Firehouse Set, 45 pieces, *58*	70	168 ____
967	Post Office Set, 25 pieces, *58*	50	111 ____
968	TV Transmitter Set, 28 pieces, *58*	55	120 ____
969	Construction Set, 23 pieces, *60*	63	114 ____
970	Ticket Booth, *58–60*	35	118 ____
971	Lichen with box, *60–64*	33	80 ____
972	Landscape Tree Assortment, *61–64*	25	83 ____
973	Complete Landscaping Set, *60–64*	45	129 ____
974	Scenery Set, *58*	70	223 ____
980	Ranch Set, 14 pieces, *60*	50	123 ____

			Good	Exc
____	**981**	Freight Yard Set, 10 pieces, *60*	50	145
____	**982**	Suburban Split Level Set, 18 pieces, *60*	42	185
____	**983**	Farm Set, 7 pieces, *60–61*	33	75
____	**984**	Railroad Set, 22 pieces, *61–62*	56	137
____	**985**	Freight Area Set, 32 pieces, *61*	35	165
____	**986**	Farm Set, 20 pieces, *62*	45	168
____	**987**	Town Set, 24 pieces, *62*	35	65
____	**988**	Railroad Structure Set, 16 pieces, *62*	40	93
	1001	2-4-2 Scout Locomotive, plastic body, 1001T Tender, *48*		
____		(A) Silver rubber-stamped cab number	25	75
____		(B) White heat-stamped cab number	15	38
____	**1001T**	Tender	6	16
	1002	Gondola, *48–52*		
____		(A) Black, white lettering	4	12
____		(B) Blue, white lettering	5	14
____		(C) Silver, black lettering	125	412
____		(D) Yellow, black lettering	120	388
____		(E) Red, white lettering	120	337
____	**X1004**	PRR Baby Ruth Boxcar, *48–52*	5	9
____	**1005**	Sunoco 1-D Tank Car, *48–50*	6	11
	1007	LL SP-type Caboose, *48–52*		
____		(A) Red body	3	9
____		(B) Red body, raised board on catwalk	10	35
____		(C) Tuscan body	192	950
____	**1008**	Uncoupling Unit (027), *57–62*	2	6
____	**1008-50**	Uncoupling Track Section (027), *57–62*	3	7
____	**1009**	Manumatic Track Section (027), *48–52*	5	10
____	**1010**	Transformer, 35 watts, *61–66*	6	11
____	**1011**	Transformer, 25 watts, *48–49*	4	8
____	**1012**	Transformer, 35 watts, *50–54*	5	9
____	**1013**	Curved Track (027), *45–69*		1
____	**1013-17**	Steel Pins, dozen (027), *46–60*		1
____	**1013-42**	Steel Pins, dozen (027), *61–68*		2
____	**1014**	Transformer, 40 watts, *55*	5	10
____	**1015**	Transformer, 45 watts, *56–60*	8	10
____	**1016**	Transformer, 35 watts, *59–60*	6	10
____	**1018**	Half Straight Track (027), *55–69*		1
____	**1018**	Straight Track (027), *45–69*		1
____	**1019**	Remote Control Track Set (027), *46–48*	3	7
____	**1020**	90-degree Crossing (027), *55–69*	2	4
____	**1021**	90-degree Crossing (027), *45–54*	2	4
____	**1022**	Manual Switches, pair (027), *53–69*	6	14
____	**1023**	45-degree Crossing (027), *56–69*	3	5
____	**1024**	Manual Switches, pair (027), *46–52*	6	14
____	**1025**	Illuminated Bumper (027), *46–47*	8	14
____	**1025**	Transformer, 45 watts, *61–69*	5	13
____	**1026**	Transformer, 25 watts, *61–64*	3	5

		Good	Exc	
1032	Transformer, 75 watts, *48*	12	23	___
1033	Transformer, 90 watts, *48–56*	18	33	___
1034	Transformer, 75 watts, *48–54*	9	23	___
1035	Transformer, 60 watts, *47*	8	16	___
1037	Transformer, 40 watts, *46–47*	4	9	___
1041	Transformer, 60 watts, *45–46*	11	21	___
1042	Transformer, 75 watts, *47–48*	13	23	___
1043	Transformer, 50 watts, *53–57*	5	10	___
1043-500	Transformer, 60 watts, ivory, *57–58*	81	136	___
1044	Transformer, 90 watts, *57–69*	25	55	___
1045	Operating Watchman, *46–50*	18	50	___
1045C	Contactor	4	11	___
1047	Operating Switchman, *59–61*	21	93	___
1050	0-4-0 Scout Locomotive, 1050T Tender, *59 u*	42	142	___
1050T	Tender	5	18	___
1053	Transformer, 60 watts, *56–60*	9	18	___
1055	Texas Special Alco Diesel A Unit, *59–60*	25	60	___
1060	2-4-2 Locomotive, 1050T or 1060T Tender, *60–62*	10	30	___
1060T	Lionel Lines Tender	9	18	___
1060T-50	Southern Pacific Tender	12	28	___
1061	0-4-0 or 2–4–2 Scout Locomotive, 1061T Tender, *64, 69*			
	(A) Slope-back Lionel Lines tender	14	32	___
	(B) Paper number labels	39	174	___
	(C) No number stamped on cab	30	80	___
1061T	Tender	4	15	___
1062	0-4-0 or 2-4-2 Scout Locomotive, *63–64*			
	(A) Streamlined Southern Pacific Tender	20	45	___
	(B) Other tenders	18	33	___
1063	Transformer, 75 watts, *60–64*	13	24	___
1065	Union Pacific Alco Diesel A Unit, *61*	28	65	___
1066	Union Pacific Alco Diesel A Unit, *64 u*	33	75	___
1073	Transformer, 60 watts, *61–66*	10	19	___
1101	Transformer, 25 watts, *48*	3	7	___
1101	2-4-2 Scout Locomotive, 1001T Tender, *48 u*			
	(A) Cab correctly marked "1101"	15	38	___
	(B) Cab marked "1001"	121	311	___
1110	2-4-2 Locomotive, 1001T Tender, *49, 51–52*	13	28	___
1120	2-4-2 Scout Locomotive, 1001T Tender, *50*	18	33	___
1121	Remote Control Switches, pair (027), *46–51*	11	28	___
1122	Remote Control Switches, pair (027), *52–53*	13	30	___
1122-34	Remote Control Switches, pair, *52–53*	14	27	___
1122-500	Gauge Adapter (027), *57–66*	4	10	___
1122E	Remote Control Switches, pair (027), *53–69*	11	32	___
1130	2-4-2 Locomotive, 6066T or 1130T Tender, *53–54*			
	(A) Plastic body	15	35	___
	(B) Die-cast body	33	118	___

			Good	Exc
1130T		Tender		
____		(A) Black-painted shell	33	92
____		(B) Black plastic shell	7	21
____	**1130T-500**	Tender, pink, from Girls Set	83	175
____	**1144**	Transformer, 75 watts, *61–66*	10	23
____	**1232**	Transformer, 75 watts, made for export, *48*	15	40
	1615	0-4-0 Locomotive, 1615T Tender, *55–57*		
____		(A) No grab irons	69	140
____		(B) Grab irons on locomotive and tender	135	250
____	**1615T**	Tender	14	26
____	**1625**	0-4-0 Locomotive, 1625T Tender, *58*	138	335
____	**1625T**	Tender	23	46
____	**1640-100**	Presidential Kit, *60*	48	141
____	**1654**	2-4-2 Locomotive, 1654W Tender, *46–47*	35	78
____	**1654T**	Tender	10	20
____	**1654W**	Whistling Tender	15	33
____	**1655**	2-4-2 Locomotive, 6654W Tender, *48–49*	38	74
	1656	0-4-0 Locomotive, 6403B Tender, *48–49*		
____		(A) Large silver cab number	120	245
____		(B) Small silver cab number	125	254
____	**1665**	0-4-0 Locomotive, 2403B Tender, *46*	190	362
	1666	2-6-2 Locomotive, 2466W or 2466WX Tender, *46–47*		
____		(A) Number plate and two-piece bell	53	125
____		(B) Rubber-stamped number and one-piece bell	68	150
____	**1666T**	Tender	10	25
	1862	4-4-0 Civil War General, 1862T Tender, *59–62*		
____		(A) Gray smokestack	89	169
____		(B) Black smokestack	90	190
____	**1862T**	Tender	24	39
____	**1865**	Western & Atlantic Coach, *59–62*	25	45
____	**1866**	Western & Atlantic Mail-Baggage Car, *59–62*	28	47
____	**1872**	4-4-0 Civil War General, 1872T Tender, *59–62*	105	255
____	**1872T**	Tender	28	48
____	**1875**	Western & Atlantic Coach, *59–62*	75	239
____	**1875W**	Western & Atlantic Coach, whistle, *59–62*	50	138
____	**1876**	Western & Atlantic Baggage Car, *59–62*	35	101
____	**1877**	Flatcar with fence and horses, *59–62*	43	90
____	**1882**	4-4-0 Civil War General, 1882T Tender, *60 u*	184	385
____	**1882T**	Tender, *60 u*	33	70
____	**1885**	Western & Atlantic Coach, *60 u*	105	263
____	**1887**	Flatcar with fences and horses, *60 u*	70	165
____	**2001**	Track Make-up Kit (O27), *63*	300	750
____	**2002**	Track Make-up Kit (O27), *63*	495	1300
____	**2003**	Track Make-up Kit (O27), *63*	600	1900
____	**2016**	2-6-4 Locomotive, 6026W Tender, *55–56*	45	88

		Good	Exc	
2018	2-6-4 Locomotive, *56–59, 61*			
	(A) 6026T Tender	33	63	____
	(B) 6026W Tender	50	98	____
	(C) 1130T Tender	35	65	____
2020	6-8-6 Steam Turbine Locomotive, 2020W or 2466WX Tender, smoke lamp, *46*	83	180	____
2020	6-8-6 Steam Turbine Locomotive, 2020W or 6020W Tender, *47–49*	67	163	____
2020W	Whistling Tender	33	58	____
2023	Union Pacific Alco Diesel AA Units, *50–51*			
	(A) Yellow body	98	217	____
	(B) Gray nose and side frames	1080	3088	____
	(C) Silver body	65	199	____
2024	C&O Alco Diesel A Unit, *69*	27	74	____
2025	2-6-2 Locomotive, 2466WX or 6466WX Tender, *47–49*			
	(A) Black smokestack, *48–49*	73	165	____
	(B) Aluminum smokestack, *47*	83	185	____
2025	2-6-4 Locomotive, 6466W Tender, *52*	81	162	____
2026	2-6-2 Locomotive, 6466WX Tender, *48–49*	55	90	____
2026	2-6-4 Locomotive, 6466W, 6466T, or 6066T Tender, *51–53*	38	85	____
2028	Pennsylvania GP7 Diesel, *55*			
	(A) Gold lettering	142	258	____
	(B) Yellow lettering	108	230	____
	(C) Tan frame	238	568	____
2029	2-6-4 Locomotive, *64–69*			
	(A) 234W Lionel Lines Tender	48	112	____
	(B) LL Tender with "Hagerstown" on bottom	58	128	____
	(C) 234W Pennsylvania Tender	88	195	____
2031	Rock Island Alco Diesel AA Units, *52–54*	67	224	____
2032	Erie Alco Diesel AA Units, *52–54*	87	178	____
2033	Union Pacific Alco Diesel AA Units, *52–54*	72	202	____
2034	2-4-2 Scout Locomotive, 6066T Tender, *52*	27	63	____
2035	2-6-4 Locomotive, 6466W Tender, *50–51*	57	150	____
2036	2-6-4 Locomotive, 6466W Tender, *50*	48	110	____
2037	2-6-4 Locomotive, *54–55, 57–63*			
	(A) 6026T or 1130T Tender	34	84	____
	(B) 6026W, 233W, or 234W whistle Tender	65	123	____
2037-500	2-6-4 Locomotive, pink, 1130T-500 Tender, *57–58*	257	815	____
2041	Rock Island Alco Diesel AA Units, *69*	52	145	____
2046	4-6-4 Locomotive, 2046W Tender, *50–51, 53*	81	175	____
2046T	Tender, for export	70	223	____
2046W	Whistle Tender	30	61	____
2046W-50	PRR Whistle Tender	31	66	____
2055	4-6-4 Locomotive, 2046W or 6026W Tender, *53–55*	74	158	____
2056	4-6-4 Locomotive, 2046W Tender, *52*	73	203	____

			Good	Exc
2065		4-6-4 Locomotive, 2046W or 6026W Tender, *54–56*	76	170
___	**2203B**	Tender	58	120
___	**2224W**	Whistle Tender	24	75
___	**2240**	Wabash F3 AB Units, *56*	183	463
___	**2242**	New Haven F3 AB Units, *58–59*	173	607
___	**2242C**	New Haven F3 B Unit, *58–59*	50	143
	2243	Santa Fe F3 AB Units, *55–57*		
___		(A) Gray body mold, raised molded cab door ladder	108	277
___		(B) Typical molded cab door ladder	90	226
___	**2243C**	Santa Fe F3 B Unit, *55–57*	60	143
	2245	Texas Special F3 AB Units, *54–55*		
___		(A) B Unit with portholes, *54*	184	416
___		(B) B Unit without portholes, *55*	233	744
	2257	SP-type caboose, *47*		
___		(A) Red body, no smokestack	5	15
___		(B) Tuscan body and smokestack	74	301
___		(C) Red body and smokestack	110	411
	2321	Lackawanna FM Train Master Diesel, *54–56*		
___		(A) Gray roof	161	298
___		(B) Maroon roof	152	437
	2322	Virginian FM Train Master Diesel, *65–66*		
___		(A) Unpainted blue body, yellow stripes	245	498
___		(B) Blue or black body, painted blue and yellow stripes	315	630
___	**2328**	Burlington GP7 Diesel, *55–56*	90	215
___	**2329**	Virginian GE E-33 or EL-C Electric Locomotive, *58–59*	160	492
___	**2330**	Pennsylvania GG1 Electric Locomotive, green, *50*	362	1042
	2331	Virginian FM Train Master Diesel, *55–58*		
___		(A) Black and yellow stripes, gray mold, *55*	323	673
___		(B) Yellow stripes, blue mold, *56–58*	235	548
___		(C) Blue and yellow stripes, gray mold	525	1038
	2332	Pennsylvania GG1 Electric Locomotive, *47–49*		
___		(A) Black	527	1228
___		(B) Dark green	167	440
	2333	NYC F3 Diesel AA Units, *48–49*		
___		(A) Rubber-stamped lettering	229	585
___		(B) Heat-stamped lettering	173	471
___	**2333**	Santa Fe F3 Diesel AA Units, *48–49*	190	395
___	**2337**	Wabash GP7 Diesel, *58*	97	237
	2338	Milwaukee Road GP7 Diesel, *55–56*		
___		(A) Orange band around shell	383	1051
___		(B) Interrupted orange band	73	183
___	**2339**	Wabash GP7 Diesel, *57*	126	262

		Good	Exc	
2340	Pennsylvania GG1 Electric Locomotive, *55*			
	(A) Tuscan	442	1143	____
	(B) Dark green	322	758	____
2341	Jersey Central FM Train Master Diesel, *56*			
	(A) High-gloss orange	980	2088	____
	(B) Dull orange	875	1690	____
2343	Santa Fe F3 Diesel AA Units, *50–52*	143	438	____
2343C	Santa Fe F3 B Unit, *50–55*			
	(A) Screen roof vents	89	250	____
	(B) Louver roof vents	73	183	____
2344	NYC F3 Diesel AA Units, *50–52*	163	472	____
2344C	NYC F3 B Unit, *50–55*	96	223	____
2345	Western Pacific F3 Diesel AA Units, *52*	447	968	____
2346	B&M GP9 Diesel, *65–66*	128	310	____
2347	C&O GP7 Diesel, *65 u*	1440	3925	____
2348	M&StL GP9 Diesel, *58–59*	146	253	____
2349	Northern Pacific GP9 Diesel, *59–60*	148	355	____
2350	New Haven EP-5 Electric Locomotive, *56–58*			
	(A) Painted nose trim, white N and orange H	232	573	____
	(B) Decaled nose trim, white N and orange H	127	285	____
	(C) Painted nose trim, orange N and black H	760	1525	____
	(D) Decaled nose trim, orange N and black H	323	815	____
	(E) Orange and white stripes go through doorjambs	345	1027	____
2351	Milwaukee Road EP-5 Electric Locomotive, *57–58*	147	421	____
2352	Pennsylvania EP-5 Electric Locomotive, *58–59*			
	(A) Tuscan body	159	414	____
	(B) Chocolate brown body	186	390	____
2353	Santa Fe F3 Diesel AA Units, *53–55*	167	416	____
2354	NYC F3 Diesel AA Units, *53–55*	215	443	____
2355	Western Pacific F3 Diesel AA Units, *53*	438	880	____
2356	Southern F3 Diesel AA Units, *54–56*	344	657	____
2356C	Southern F3 B Unit, *54–56*	134	249	____
2357	SP-type Caboose, *47–48*			
	(A) Red body and smokestack	137	514	____
	(B) Tuscan body and smokestack	15	35	____
	(C) Tile red, no smokestack, "6357" stamped on bottom	70	231	____
2358	Great Northern EP-5 Electric Locomotive, *59–60*	211	580	____
2359	Boston & Maine GP9 Diesel, *61–62*	100	260	____
2360	Pennsylvania GG1 Electric Locomotive, *56–58, 61–63*			
	(A) Tuscan, 5 gold stripes	570	1253	____
	(B) Dark green, 5 gold stripes	374	823	____
	(C) Tuscan, gold stripe, heat-stamped letters	378	745	____
	(D) Tuscan, gold stripe, decaled lettering	393	713	____

			Good	Exc
	2363	Illinois Central F3 Diesel AB Units, *55–56*		
____		(A) Black lettering	344	702
____		(B) Brown lettering	372	812
____	**2365**	C&O GP7 Diesel, *62–63*	101	254
____	**2367**	Wabash F3 Diesel AB Units, *55*	315	642
____	**2367C**	Wabash F3 Diesel B Unit, *55*	80	175
____	**2368**	B&O F3 Diesel AB Units, *56*	445	1266
____	**2373**	CP F3 Diesel AA Units, *57*	653	1438
	2378	Milwaukee Road F3 Diesel AB Units, *56*		
____		(A) Yellow roof line stripes	495	1258
____		(B) No roof line stripes	522	1075
	2378C	Milwaukee Road F3 Diesel B Unit, yellow roof line stripe, *56*		
____			270	532
____	**2379**	Rio Grande F3 Diesel AB Units, *57–58*	358	712
____	**2383**	Santa Fe F3 Diesel AA Units, *58–66*	179	419
____	**2400**	Maplewood Pullman Car, green, *48–49*	45	112
____	**2401**	Hillside Observation Car, green, *48–49*	37	100
____	**2402**	Chatham Pullman Car, green, *48–49*	43	109
____	**2404**	Santa Fe Vista Dome Car, *64–65*	33	75
____	**2405**	Santa Fe Pullman Car, *64–65*	33	75
____	**2406**	Santa Fe Observation Car, *64–65*	32	70
____	**2408**	Santa Fe Vista Dome Car, *66*	45	80
____	**2409**	Santa Fe Pullman Car, *66*	43	80
____	**2410**	Santa Fe Observation Car, *66*	35	75
	2411	Lionel Lines Flatcar, *46–48*		
____		(A) With pipes, *46*	32	80
____		(B) With logs, *47–48*	13	38
____	**2412**	Santa Fe Vista Dome Car, *59–63*	35	78
____	**2414**	Santa Fe Pullman Car, *59–63*	35	79
____	**2416**	Santa Fe Observation Car, *59–63*	28	70
____	**2419**	DL&W Work Caboose, *46–47*	20	48
	2420	DL&W Work Caboose with searchlight, *46–48*		
____		(A) Light or dark gray, heat-stamped lettering	52	99
____		(B) Light or dark gray, rubber-stamped lettering	62	139
	2421	Maplewood Pullman Car, *50–53*		
____		(A) Gray roof	30	70
____		(B) Silver roof	25	50
	2422	Chatham Pullman Car, *50–53*		
____		(A) Gray roof	32	70
____		(B) Silver roof	25	52
	2423	Hillside Observation Car, *50–53*		
____		(A) Gray roof	27	67
____		(B) Silver roof	22	47
____	**2426W**	Whistle Tender, *50*	128	242
____	**2429**	Livingston Pullman Car, *52–53*	50	98
____	**2430**	Pullman Car, blue, *46–47*	30	95
____	**2431**	Observation Car, blue, *46–47*	25	90

		Good	Exc	
2432	Clifton Vista Dome Car, *54–58*	34	80	___
2434	Newark Pullman Car, *54–58*	35	80	___
2435	Elizabeth Pullman Car, *54–58*	40	113	___
2436	Mooseheart Observation Car, *57–58*	30	75	___
2436	Summit Observation Car, *54–56*	28	59	___
2440	Pullman Car, green, *46–47*			
	(A) Silver lettering	40	73	___
	(B) White lettering	26	68	___
2441	Observation Car, green, *46–47*			
	(A) Silver lettering	40	73	___
	(B) White lettering	29	63	___
2442	Clifton Vista Dome Car, *56*	45	95	___
2442	Pullman Car, brown, *46–48*			
	(A) Silver lettering	43	78	___
	(B) White lettering	30	65	___
2443	Observation Car, brown, *46–48*			
	(A) Silver lettering	38	73	___
	(B) White lettering	30	65	___
2444	Newark Pullman Car, *56*	45	100	___
2445	Elizabeth Pullman Car, *56*	85	213	___
2446	Summit Observation Car, *56*	45	99	___
2452	Pennsylvania Gondola, *45–47*			
	(A) Whirly wheels, *45*	18	40	___
	(B) Regular wheels	9	20	___
	(C) Early flying shoe trucks, two holes in floor, *45*	33	117	___
2452X	Pennsylvania Gondola, *46–47*	8	18	___
X2454	Baby Ruth Boxcar, PRR logo, *46–47*	20	40	___
X2454	Pennsylvania Boxcar, *46*			
	(A) Brown door	70	189	___
	(B) Orange door	126	386	___
2456	Lehigh Valley Hopper, *48*			
	(A) Flat black, 2 lines of data, *48*	13	33	___
	(B) Flat black, 3 lines of data, *48*	93	230	___
2457	PRR N5-type Caboose "477618," tintype, *45–47*			
	(A) Red, white lettering	18	38	___
	(B) Brown, offset white lettering	173	590	___
	(C) Brown, centered white lettering	30	90	___
X2458	PRR Automobile Boxcar, *46–48*	28	53	___
2460	Bucyrus Erie Crane Car, 12-wheel, *46–50*			
	(A) Gray cab	78	245	___
	(B) Black cab	35	85	___
2461	Transformer Car, die-cast, *47–48*			
	(A) Red transformer	28	85	___
	(B) Black transformer	30	75	___
	(C) Red transformer, number rubber-stamped on bottom	42	157	___

			Good	Exc
	2465	Sunoco 2-D Tank Car, *46–48*		
____		(A) "Gas, Sunoco, and Oils" in diamond, centered	150	370
____		(B) "Sunoco" in diamond	7	18
____		(C) "Sunoco" extends beyond diamond	8	18
____	**2466T**	Tender	19	43
____	**2466WX**	Whistle Tender, *45–48*	25	65
____	**2472**	PRR N5-type Caboose, tintype, *46–47*	10	28
____	**2481**	Plainfield Pullman Car, yellow, *50*	89	253
____	**2482**	Westfield Pullman Car, yellow, *50*	92	251
____	**2483**	Livingston Observation Car, yellow, *50*	77	238
____	**2521**	President McKinley Observation Car, *62–66*	55	160
____	**2522**	President Harrison Vista Dome Car, *62–66*	67	170
____	**2523**	President Garfield Pullman Car, *62–66*	63	163
	2530	REA Baggage Car, *54–60*		
____		(A) Large doors	173	369
____		(B) Small doors	64	136
	2531	Silver Dawn Observation Car, *52–60*		
____		(A) Ribbed channels, round rivets	35	96
____		(B) Ribbed channels, hex rivets	44	99
____		(C) Ribbed channels, hex rivets, red center taillight	59	148
____		(D) Flat channels, glued nameplates	56	118
	2532	Silver Range Vista Dome Car, *52–60*		
____		(A) Ribbed channels, round rivets	41	97
____		(B) Flat channels, glued nameplates	38	148
	2533	Silver Cloud Pullman Car, *52–59*		
____		(A) Ribbed channels, round rivets	39	88
____		(B) Flat channels, glued nameplates	42	148
	2534	Silver Bluff Pullman Car, *52–59*		
____		(A) Ribbed channels, round rivets	46	108
____		(B) Flat channels, glued nameplates	33	160
____	**2541**	Alexander Hamilton Observation Car, *55–56**	58	160
____	**2542**	Betsy Ross Vista Dome Car, *55–56**	59	163
____	**2543**	William Penn Pullman Car, *55–56**	60	165
____	**2544**	Molly Pitcher Pullman Car, *55–56**	60	165
____	**2550**	B&O Baggage-Mail Rail Diesel Car, *57–58*	132	421
____	**2551**	Banff Park Observation Car, *57**	109	249
____	**2552**	Skyline 500 Vista Dome Car, *57**	124	258
____	**2553**	Blair Manor Pullman Car, *57**	171	392
____	**2554**	Craig Manor Pullman Car, *57**	167	392
____	**2555**	Sunoco 1-D Tank Car, *46–48*	21	59
____	**2559**	B&O Passenger Rail Diesel Car, *57–58*	110	278
	2560	Lionel Lines Crane Car, 8-wheel, *46–47*		
____		(A) Black boom	22	80
____		(B) Brown boom	25	84
____		(C) Green boom	31	95
____	**2561**	Vista Valley Observation Car, *59–61**	73	230

		Good	Exc	
2562	Regal Pass Vista Dome Car, *59–61**	80	262	____
2563	Indian Falls Pullman Car, *59–61**	90	272	____
2625	Irvington Pullman Car, *46–50**			
	(A) No silhouettes	55	150	____
	(B) Silhouettes	85	253	____
2625	Madison Pullman Car, *46–47**	65	167	____
2625	Manhattan Pullman Car, *46–47**	65	167	____
2627	Madison Pullman Car, *48–50**			
	(A) No silhouettes	58	160	____
	(B) Silhouettes	87	247	____
2628	Manhattan Pullman Car, *48–50**			
	(A) No silhouettes	58	147	____
	(B) Silhouettes	88	249	____
2671T	PRR Tender, for export	38	105	____
2671W	Whistle Tender	40	83	____
2671WX	Whistle Tender	44	82	____
2755	Sunoco 1-D Tank Car, *45*	27	73	____
X2758	PRR Automobile Boxcar, *45–46*	29	48	____
2855	Sunoco 1-D Tank Car, *46–47*			
	(A) Black	76	240	____
	(B) Black, decal without "Gas" and "Oils"	60	203	____
	(C) Gray	45	179	____
3309	Turbo Missile Launch Car, red body, *63–64*	16	49	____
3309-50	Turbo Missile Launch Car, olive body, *63–64*	166	639	____
3330	Flatcar with submarine kit, *60–62*	60	165	____
3330-100	Operating Submarine Kit with box, *60–61*	105	346	____
3349	Turbo Missile Launch Car, red body, *62–65*	16	45	____
3356	Operating Horse Car and Corral Set, *56–60, 64–66*	43	125	____
3356	Operating Horse Car only, *56–60, 64–66*			
	(A) Built date, bar-end trucks, *56–60*	30	73	____
	(B) No built date, AAR trucks, *64–66*	43	137	____
3356-100	Black Horses, 9 pieces, *56–59*	15	28	____
3356-150	Horse Car Corral, *57–60*	24	49	____
3357	Hydraulic Maintenance Car, *62–64*	20	65	____
3357-27	Trestle Components for Cop and Hobo Car, *62*	23	50	____
3359	Lionel Lines Twin-bin Coal Dump Car, *55–58*	18	42	____
3360	Operating Burro Crane, self-propelled, *56–57*	73	183	____
3361	Operating Log Dump Car, *55–58*	15	37	____
3362	Helium Tank Unloading Car, *61–63, 69*	20	45	____
3364	Operating Dump Car with 3 logs, *65–66, 68*	15	34	____
3366	Circus Car Corral Set, *59–62*	97	253	____
3366	Circus Car only, *59–62*	68	134	____
3366-100	White Horses, 9 pieces, *59–62*	32	57	____
3370	W&A Sheriff and Outlaw Car, *61–64*			
	(A) AAR trucks	18	48	____
	(B) Archbar trucks	25	63	____

			Good	Exc
	3376	Bronx Zoo Car, *60–66, 69*		
____		(A) Blue, white lettering	21	56
____		(B) Green, yellow lettering	35	58
____		(C) Blue, yellow lettering	98	296
____	**3386**	Bronx Zoo Car, *60*	25	60
____	**3409**	Helicopter Car, *61*	33	117
	3410	Helicopter Car, *61–63*		
____		(A) 2 operating couplers, gray Navy helicopter	33	85
____		(B) Single operating coupler, yellow helicopter, *63*	58	139
____	**3413**	Mercury Capsule Car, *62–64*	42	155
____	**3419**	Helicopter Car, *59–65*	35	80
____	**3424**	Wabash Operating Boxcar, *56–58*	25	60
____	**3424-75**	Low Bridge Signal, *56–57*	80	250
____	**3424-100**	Low Bridge Signal Set, *56–58*	20	45
____	**3428**	U.S. Mail Operating Boxcar, *59–60*	40	75
____	**3429**	USMC Helicopter Car, *60*	170	474
	3434	Poultry Dispatch Car, *59–60, 64–66*		
____		(A) Gray man	50	100
____		(B) Blue man	58	120
	3435	Traveling Aquarium Car, *59–62*		
____		(A) Gold lettering, tank designations, and circle around L	425	1017
____		(B) Gold lettering, tank designations, no circle around L	260	664
____		(C) Gold lettering, no tank designations, no circle around L	115	267
____		(D) Yellow lettering, no tank designations, no circle around L	50	132
____	**3444**	Erie Operating Gondola, *57–59*	28	60
	3451	Operating Log Dump Car, *46–48*		
____		(A) Heat-stamped lettering	15	38
____		(B) Rubber-stamped lettering	20	65
	3454	PRR Operating Merchandise Car, *46–47*		
____		(A) Red lettering	1120	4027
____		(B) Blue lettering	35	127
____	**3456**	N&W Operating Hopper, *50–55*	18	55
	3459	LL Operating Coal Dump Car, *46–48*		
____		(A) Aluminum bin	87	250
____		(B) Black bin	18	50
____		(C) Green bin	26	72
____	**3460**	Flatcar with trailers, *55–57*	32	65
	3461	LL Operating Log Car, *49–55*		
____		(A) Black car, heat-stamped lettering	20	36
____		(B) Black car, rubber-stamped lettering	132	357
____	**3461-25**	LL Operating Log Car, green	18	53

		Good	Exc
3462	Automatic Milk Car, *47–48*		
	(A) Flat white or cream, steel base mechanism	13	52 ____
	(B) Flat white or cream, brass base mechanism	25	65 ____
	(C) Glossy cream	64	238 ____
3462-70	Magnetic Milk Cans, *52–59*	8	17 ____
3462P	Milk Car Platform, *47–48*	7	16 ____
X3464	ATSF Operating Boxcar, *49–52*		
	(A) Orange body	9	21 ____
	(B) Tan body	400	1200 ____
X3464	NYC Operating Boxcar, *49–52*	10	23 ____
3469	LL Operating Coal Dump Car, *49–55*	15	45 ____
3470	Target Launching Car, dark blue, *62–64*	23	65 ____
3470-100	Target Launching Car, light blue, *63*	58	214 ____
3472	Automatic Milk Car, *49–53*	20	53 ____
3474	Western Pacific Operating Boxcar, *52–53*	25	60 ____
3482	Automatic Milk Car, *54–55*		
	(A) "RT3472" on right	31	86 ____
	(B) "RT3482" on right	21	62 ____
3484	Pennsylvania Operating Boxcar, *53*	22	55 ____
3484-25	ATSF Operating Boxcar, *54*		
	(A) White lettering	25	70 ____
	(B) Black lettering	320	1170 ____
3494-1	NYC Operating Boxcar, *55*	37	108 ____
3494-150	MP Operating Boxcar, *56*	52	139 ____
3494-275	State of Maine Operating Boxcar, *56–58*		
	(A) "3494275" on side	40	100 ____
	(B) No number on side	61	162 ____
3494-550	Monon Operating Boxcar, *57–58*	171	383 ____
3494-625	Soo Operating Boxcar, *57–58*	183	454 ____
3509	Satellite Launching Car, *61*		
	(A) Chrome satellite cover	30	70 ____
	(B) Gray satellite cover	75	246 ____
3510	Satellite Launching Car, *62*	43	107 ____
3512	Fireman and Ladder Car, *59–61*		
	(A) Black extension ladder	45	122 ____
	(B) Silver extension ladder	63	218 ____
3519	Satellite Launching Car, *61–64*	23	60 ____
3520	Searchlight Car, *52–53*		
	(A) Serif lettering	17	54 ____
	(B) Sans serif lettering	16	35 ____
3530	GM Generator Car, *56–58*		
	(A) Blue fuel tank	45	130 ____
	(B) Black fuel tank	43	115 ____
	(C) 3530 underscored	415	1767 ____
3530-50	Searchlight with pole and base, *56–56*	19	59 ____

			Good	Exc
___	**3535**	Security Car with searchlight, *60–61*	33	105
___	**3540**	Operating Radar Car, *59–60*	33	103
___	**3545**	Operating TV Monitor Car, *61–62*	49	161
	3559	Operating Coal Dump Car, *46–48*		
___		(A) Black coil housing	15	44
___		(B) Brown coil housing	40	126
	3562-1	ATSF Operating Barrel Car, *54*		
___		(A) Black, black unloading trough	61	201
___		(B) Black, yellow unloading trough	58	185
___		(C) Gray, red lettering	800	2970
	3562-25	ATSF Operating Barrel Car, gray, *54*		
___		(A) Red lettering, no bracket tab	160	477
___		(B) Blue lettering, no bracket tab	17	50
___		(C) Blue lettering, bracket tab	17	72
	3562-50	ATSF Operating Barrel Car, yellow, *55–56*		
___		(A) Painted	37	96
___		(B) Unpainted	28	60
___	**3562-75**	ATSF Operating Barrel Car, orange, *57–58*	36	83
	3619	Helicopter Reconnaissance Car, *62–64*		
___		(A) Light yellow	43	128
___		(B) Dark yellow	65	194
	3620	Searchlight Car, orange generator, *54–56*		
___		(A) Unpainted gray plastic searchlight	17	38
___		(B) Gray-painted gray plastic searchlight	28	45
___		(C) Unpainted orange plastic searchlight	48	125
___		(D) Gray-painted orange plastic searchlight	50	183
	3650	Extension Searchlight Car, *56–59*		
___		(A) Light gray	28	78
___		(B) Dark gray	45	148
___		(C) Olive gray	85	265
	3656	Armour Operating Cattle Car, some with an open coil, *49–55*		
___		(A) Black letters, Armour sticker	105	245
___		(B) White letters, Armour sticker	25	63
___		(C) Black letters, no Armour sticker	67	190
___		(D) White letters, no Armour sticker	25	56
___	**3656**	Stockyard with cattle, *49–55*	24	58
	3656-34	Cattle, black, 9 pieces, *49–58*		
___		(A) Rounded ridge on base, *49*	60	111
___		(B) Plain base	15	40
___	**3656-150**	Corral Platform, yellow tray	215	490
___	**3662**	Automatic Milk Car, *55–60, 64–66*	39	73
___	**3662-79**	Nonmagnetic Milk Cans, 7 pieces, white envelope	19	52
___	**3662-80**	Nonmagnetic Milk Cans, 7 pieces, manila envelope	17	48
	3665	Minuteman Operating Car, *61–64*		
___		(A) Medium blue roof	60	190
___		(B) Dark blue roof	38	94

		Good	Exc	
3666	Minuteman Boxcar with cannon, *64 u*	192	485	___
3672	Bosco Operating Milk Car, *59–60*			
	(A) Unpainted yellow body	85	180	___
	(B) Painted yellow body	140	267	___
3672-79	Bosco Can Set, 7 pieces, *59–60*	25	72	___
3820	USMC Operating Submarine Car, *60–62*	96	207	___
3830	Operating Submarine Car, *60–63*	38	87	___
3854	Automatic Merchandise Car, *46–47*	170	513	___
3927	Lionel Lines Track Cleaning Car, *56–60*	30	46	___
3927-38	Track Cleaning Fluid Bottle	9	17	___
3927-50	Track Wiping Cylinders, 25 pieces, *57–60*	13	30	___
3927-75	Track-Clean Detergent, can, *56–69*	5	14	___
4357	SP-type Caboose, electronic, die-cast stack, *48–49*			
	(A) Die-cast metal smokestack	60	200	___
	(B) Matching plastic smokestack	115	270	___
	(C) Matching plastic smokestack, raised board on catwalk	110	255	___
4452	PRR Gondola, electronic, *46–49*	48	122	___
4454	Baby Ruth PRR Boxcar, electronic, *46–49*	60	160	___
4457	PRR N5-type Caboose, tintype, electronic, *46–47*	43	150	___
4671W	Whistle Tender	80	178	___
5102	Railroad and Roadway Crossing	10	60	___
5159-50	Maintenance and Lube Kit, *66–69*	25	63	___
5160	Viewing Stand, *63*	40	125	___
5459	LL Coal Dump Car, electronic, *46–49*	49	134	___
6001T	Tender	8	17	___
6002	NYC Gondola, *50*	4	8	___
X6004	Baby Ruth PRR Boxcar, *50*	4	7	___
6007	Lionel Lines SP-type Caboose, *50*	3	7	___
6009	Remote Control Uncoupling Track, *53–54*	2	7	___
6012	Gondola, *51–56*	2	6	___
6014	Bosco PRR Boxcar, *58*			
	(A) White body	22	49	___
	(B) Red body	4	9	___
	(C) Orange body	4	7	___
6014	Chun King Boxcar, *57 u*	46	138	___
6014	Frisco Boxcar, *57, 63–69*			
	(A) White body	5	11	___
	(B) Red body	5	7	___
	(C) White body, coin slot	16	45	___
	(D) Orange body, *57*	18	50	___
	(E) Orange body, *69*	10	23	___
X6014	Baby Ruth PRR Boxcar, *51–56*			
	(A) White body	5	9	___
	(B) Red body	3	8	___
6014-100	Airex Boxcar, *60 u*	14	40	___
6014-150	Wix Boxcar, *59 u*	62	195	___

		Good	Exc
6015	Sunoco 1-D Tank Car, *54–55*		
	(A) Painted tank	70	303
	(B) Unpainted tank	4	12
6017	Lionel Lines SP-type Caboose, *51–62*		
	(A) Glossy tuscan-painted orange mold	23	80
	(B) Semigloss tuscan-painted, orange mold	13	34
	(C) Tile red-painted, blue mold	13	34
	(D) Common red, tuscan, and brown bodies	4	9
	(E) Bright red, black mold, *62*	63	213
6017	SP-type Caboose, maroon, "Lionel" only, *56*	10	35
6017-50	U.S. Marine Corps SP-type Caboose, *58*	23	70
6017-85	LL SP-type Caboose, gray, *58*	22	67
6017-100	B&M SP-type Caboose, *59, 62, 65–66*		
	(A) Purple-blue	118	408
	(B) Medium or light blue	15	42
6017-185	ATSF SP-type Caboose, *59–60*	12	33
6017-200	U.S. Navy SP-type Caboose, *60*	43	145
6017-225	ATSF SP-type Caboose, *61–62*	15	40
6017-235	ATSF SP-type Caboose, *62*	15	40
6019	Remote Control Track (027), *48–66*	2	10
6020W	Whistle Tender	34	67
6024	Nabisco Shredded Wheat Boxcar, *57*	10	30
6024	RCA Whirlpool Boxcar, *57 u*	20	60
6025	Gulf 1-D Tank Car, *56–58*		
	(A) Gray body, blue lettering	5	12
	(B) Orange body, blue lettering	6	16
	(C) Black body, red-orange Gulf emblem	5	15
6026T	Tender	11	28
6026W	Whistle Tender	22	59
6027	Alaska SP-type Caboose, *59*	23	65
6029	Remote Control Uncoupling Track, *55–63*	3	7
6032	Short Gondola, black (027), *52–54*	2	6
X6034	Baby Ruth PRR Boxcar, *53–54*		
	(A) Orange, blue lettering	5	10
	(B) Orange, black lettering	5	11
6035	Sunoco 1-D Tank Car, *52–53*	3	8
6037	Lionel Lines SP-type Caboose, *52–54*		
	(A) Tuscan	3	6
	(B) Red	5	11
6042	Short Gondola, *59–61, 62–64 u*	3	11
6044	Airex Boxcar, orange lettering, *59–60 u*		
	(A) Medium blue	8	20
	(B) Teal blue	23	65
	(C) Purple-blue	81	275
6044-1X	Nestles/McCall's Boxcar, *62–63 u*	350	1533
6045	Lionel Lines 2-D Tank Car, *59–64*		
	(A) Gray	10	20
	(B) Orange	15	33
	(C) Beige	10	30

		Good	Exc
6045	Cities Service 2-D Tank, *60 u*	15	35 ____
6047	Lionel Lines SP-type Caboose, *62*		
	(A) Unpainted, medium red	2	5 ____
	(B) Painted, brown	160	733 ____
	(C) Unpainted, coral pink	15	62 ____
6050	Lionel Savings Bank Boxcar, *61*		
	(A) Type I body, Blt by Lionel	19	48 ____
	(B) Type I body, Built by Lionel	43	160 ____
	(C) Type IIa body, Blt by Lionel	150	275 ____
6050-110	Swift Boxcar, *62–63*		
	(A) Red body	8	24 ____
	(B) Dark red body, 2 open holes in roof walk	45	127 ____
6050-175	Libby's Tomato Juice Boxcar, *63 u*		
	(A) Green stems on tomatoes	15	40 ____
	(B) Green stems missing	19	55 ____
	(C) No white lines between glass and tomatoes	25	82 ____
6057	LL SP-type Caboose, *59–62*		
	(A) Unpainted red plastic	3	7 ____
	(B) Red-painted	32	98 ____
	(C) Unpainted coral pink plastic	18	65 ____
6057-50	LL SP-type Caboose, orange, *62*	20	52 ____
6058	C&O SP-type Caboose, *61*		
	(A) Blue lettering	17	48 ____
	(B) Black lettering	28	83 ____
6059	M&StL SP-type Caboose, *61–69*		
	(A) Painted, red	13	38 ____
	(B) Unpainted, red	5	11 ____
	(C) Unpainted, maroon	6	13 ____
6062	NYC Gondola with 3 cable reels, *59–62*		
	(A) No metal undercarriage	10	28 ____
	(B) Metal undercarriage	19	66 ____
	(C) No metal undercarriage, no paint on bottom	45	80 ____
6062-50	NYC Gondola with 2 canisters, *69*	7	17 ____
6066T	Tender	8	18 ____
6067	SP-type Caboose, unmarked, *61–62*		
	(A) Red	3	8 ____
	(B) Yellow	6	14 ____
	(C) Brown	9	18 ____
6076	ATSF Hopper, *63 u*	8	28 ____
6076	Lehigh Valley Hopper, short, *63*		
	(A) Gray body	8	14 ____
	(B) Black body	7	13 ____
	(C) Red body	8	13 ____
	(D) Yellow body, painted	350	1294 ____
6076-100	Hopper, gray, unmarked, *63*	10	24 ____
6110	2-4-2 Locomotive, 6001T Tender, *50–51*	15	35 ____

			Good	Exc
	6111	Flatcar with logs, *55–57*		
____		(A) Yellow with black lettering	10	35
____		(B) Yellow with white lettering	106	507
	6112	Short Gondola with 4 canisters, *56–58*		
____		(A) Black body	6	18
____		(B) Blue body	6	18
____		(C) White body	14	40
	6112-5	Canister, *56–58*		
____		(A) Red or white	1	3
____		(B) Red with black letters	18	55
____	6112-25	Canister Set, 4 pieces, red or white, with box, *56–58*	28	63
____	6119	DL&W Work Caboose, red, *55–56*	12	24
____	6119-25	DL&W Work Caboose, orange, *56–59*	15	35
____	6119-50	DL&W Work Caboose, brown, *56*	23	53
	6119-75	DL&W Work Caboose, *57*		
____		(A) Heat-stamped letters on frame	15	35
____		(B) Closely spaced rubber-stamped letters on frame	55	219
____		(C) Widely spaced rubber-stamped letters on frame	47	186
	6119-100	DL&W Work Caboose, red cab, gray tool tray, *57–66, 69*		
____		(A) Black frame, white letters	10	25
____		(B) "Built By Lionel" builders plate, *66*	22	84
____		(C) Black frame, red-painted cab	53	199
____		(D) Santa Fe cab, gray tool box	10	35
____	6119-125	Rescue Caboose, olive, black frame, *64*	63	180
____	6120	Work Caboose, yellow, unmarked, *61–62*	8	14
	6121	Flatcar with pipes, *56–57*		
____		(A) Yellow, red, or gray	10	63
____		(B) Maroon	16	84
	6130	ATSF Work Caboose, *61, 65–69*		
____		(A) Red painted, no builders plate	14	35
____		(B) Red unpainted, builders plate	10	30
____		(C) Red painted, builders plate	64	251
____	6139	Remote Control Uncoupling Track (027), *63*	1	4
____	6142	Short Gondola, green, blue, or black, with 2 canisters, *63–66, 69*	6	14
____	6142-175	Short Gondola, olive drab, with 2 canisters	48	145
____	6149	Remote Control Uncoupling Track (027), *64–69*	1	4
	6151	Flatcar with patrol truck, *58*		
____		(A) Yellow frame	35	85
____		(B) Orange frame	25	73
____		(C) Cream frame	35	89
	6162	NYC Gondola with 3 white canisters, *59–68*		
____		(A) Blue body	9	25
____		(B) Red body	74	295

		Good	Exc
6162-60	Alaska Gondola with 3 red canisters, *59*	39	85 ____
6167	LL SP-type Caboose, red, *63–64*		
	(A) Unpainted	5	9 ____
	(B) Painted	30	127 ____
6167	SP-type Caboose, unmarked, no end rails, *63–64*		
	(A) Red body	3	9 ____
	(B) Brown body	7	22 ____
6167-50	SP-type Caboose, unmarked, yellow	5	19 ____
6167-85	Union Pacific SP-type Caboose, *69*	10	35 ____
6167-175	SP-type Caboose, unmarked, olive	109	380 ____
6175	Flatcar with rocket, *58–61*		
	(A) Black frame	28	67 ____
	(B) Red frame	25	67 ____
6176	Hopper, unmarked, *63–69*		
	(A) Dark yellow	10	34 ____
	(B) Gray	8	15 ____
	(C) Red	10	25 ____
	(D) Bright yellow	25	63 ____
6176	Lehigh Valley Hopper, *64–66, 69*		
	(A) Dark yellow	5	9 ____
	(B) Gray	6	11 ____
	(C) Black	3	8 ____
	(D) Red	13	29 ____
	(E) Bright yellow	25	55 ____
6176-100	Olive Drab Hopper, unmarked	35	111 ____
6219	C&O Work Caboose, *60*	20	45 ____
6220	Santa Fe NW2 Switcher, *49–50*		
	(A) Large GM decal on cab	120	268 ____
	(B) Small GM decal on side	85	205 ____
6250	Seaboard NW2 Switcher, *54–55*		
	(A) Seaboard decal	89	230 ____
	(B) Widely spaced rubber-stamped letters	99	245 ____
	(C) Closely spaced rubber-stamped letters	126	460 ____
6257	SP-type Caboose, *48–52*		
	(A) Dark red, matching plastic smokestack	165	434 ____
	(B) All other variations	5	14 ____
6257-25	SP-type Caboose, circled-L logo, *53–55*		
	(A) Red painted	7	16 ____
	(B) Unpainted red plastic	4	11 ____
6257-50	SP-type Caboose, *56*	4	11 ____
6257-100	Lionel Lines SP-type Caboose, smokestack, *63–64*	10	25 ____
6257X	SP-type Caboose, red, 2 couplers, with box, *48*	27	51 ____
6262	Flatcar with wheel load, *56–57*		
	(A) Black frame, *56–57*	28	60 ____
	(B) Red frame, *56*	346	786 ____

			Good	Exc
	6264	Flatcar with lumber for 264 Fork Lift Platform, *57–60*		
____		(A) Bar-end trucks	27	58
____		(B) Plastic trucks	33	70
____		(C) Separate-sale box and envelope	100	256
____	**6311**	Flatcar with 3 pipes, *55*	20	47
	6315	Gulf 1-D Chemical Tank Car, *56–59, 68–69*		
____		(A) Early, painted	30	78
____		(B) Late, unpainted	22	55
____		(C) Late, unpainted, built date	50	130
	6315	Lionel Lines 1-D Tank Car, *63–66*		
____		(A) Unpainted orange body	15	30
____		(B) Painted orange body	93	340
	6342	NYC Gondola with culvert channel and		
____		7 pipes, *56–58, 64–66*	18	42
____	**6343**	Barrel Ramp Car with 6 barrels, *61–62*	20	39
____	**6346**	Alcoa Quad Hopper, *56*	28	60
	6352-1	PFE Ice Car from 352 Ice Depot, *55–57*		
____		(A) 3 lines of data	63	117
____		(B) 4 lines of data	48	98
____		(C) Separate-sale box	875	3217
	6356	NYC Stock Car, 2-level, *54–55*		
____		(A) Heat-stamped lettering	18	40
____		(B) Rubber-stamped lettering	25	85
	6357	SP-type Caboose, SP logo, *48–53*		
____		(A) Tile red, tuscan, or maroon	10	31
____		(B) Tile red, extra board on catwalk	138	496
	6357	SP-type Caboose, no logo, *57–61*		
____		(A) Number to left	9	40
____		(B) Number to right	16	65
	6357-25	SP-type Caboose, circle L logo, *53–56*		
____		(A) Maroon or tuscan body, black metal smokestack	10	25
____		(B) Maroon body, maroon metal smokestack	103	388
____	**6357-50**	ATSF SP-type Caboose, lighted, *60*	297	947
	6361	Timber Transport Car, *60–61, 64–69*		
____		(A) White lettering	27	69
____		(B) No lettering	53	145
	6362	Truck Car with 3 trucks, *55–56*		
____		(A) Shiny orange	23	44
____		(B) Dull orange	33	91
____	**6376**	LL Circus Stock Car, *56–57*	27	62
____	**6401**	Flatcar, no load, gray, *60*	4	10
	6401-25	Gray flatcar with load, *64–67*		
____		(A) Jeep and cannon	115	263
____		(B) Tank	95	200
____		(C) Payton automobile	25	50
____		(D) Logs	11	21
____	**6402**	Flatcar with orange or gray reels, *62, 64–66*	10	25

		Good	Exc
6402	Flatcar with blue boat, *69*	28	60 ___
6402-150	Maroon Flatcar with white trailer	13	35 ___
6403B	Tender	35	80 ___
6404	Black Flatcar with auto, *60*		
	(A) Red auto	28	65 ___
	(B) Yellow auto	50	125 ___
	(C) Brown auto	75	234 ___
	(D) Green auto	90	243 ___
6405	Flatcar with piggyback van, *61*	17	48 ___
6406	Flatcar with auto, *61*		
	(A) Maroon frame, red auto	25	60 ___
	(B) Maroon frame, yellow auto	55	134 ___
	(C) Gray frame, dark brown auto	80	305 ___
	(D) Gray frame, green auto	90	219 ___
	(E) Gray frame, yellow auto	50	100 ___
6407	Flatcar with rocket, *63*	120	420 ___
6408	Flatcar with pipes, *63*	18	42 ___
6408	Flatcar with 2 orange cable reels, *67*	15	45 ___
6409-25	Flatcar with pipes, *63*	15	43 ___
6410-25	Flatcar with 2 automobiles, *63*		
	(A) Yellow autos	115	505 ___
	(B) Brown autos	150	630 ___
6411	Flatcar with logs, *48–50*	13	39 ___
6413	Mercury Capsule Carrying Car, *62–63*		
	(A) Medium blue frame	67	152 ___
	(B) Aquamarine frame	98	210 ___
	(C) Teal frame	90	258 ___
6414	Evans Auto Loader with 4 cars, *55–66*		
	(A) Premium cars (chrome bumpers, windows, rubber wheels): red, yellow, blue-green, and white	55	107 ___
	(B) Cheapie cars (no wheels): 2 red and 2 yellow	160	303 ___
	(C) Red cars with gray bumpers	70	160 ___
	(D) Yellow cars with gray bumpers	160	395 ___
	(E) Brown cars with gray bumpers	258	808 ___
	(F) Green cars with gray bumpers	457	932 ___
	(G) Metal trucks, number right of Lionel, premium cars	50	123 ___
6414-25	Set of 4 Automobiles, separate sale box, *55–58*	120	325 ___
6415	Sunoco 3-D Tank Car, *53–55, 64–66, 69*	13	32 ___
6416	Boat Transport Car, 4 boats, *61–63*	85	260 ___
6417	PRR N5c Porthole Caboose, *53–57*		
	(A) New York Zone	15	35 ___
	(B) Without New York Zone	151	251 ___
6417-25	Lionel Lines N5c Porthole Caboose, *54*	15	35 ___
6417-50	LV N5c Porthole Caboose, *54*		
	(A) Tuscan	398	1350 ___
	(B) Gray	60	130 ___

Good   Exc

		Good	Exc
6418	Machinery Car with 2 steel girders, *55–57*		
___	(A) Black girders, "Lionel" in raised letters	68	130
___	(B) Orange girders, "Lionel" in raised letters	58	105
___	(C) Pinkish orange girders, U.S. Steel	68	120
___	(D) Black girders, U.S. Steel	70	128
___ **6419**	DL&W Work Caboose, *48–50, 52–55*	15	36
___ **6419-25**	DL&W Work Caboose, one coupler, *54–55*	15	35
6419-50	DL&W Work Caboose, short smokestack, *56–57*		
___		15	39
___ **6419-75**	DL&W Work Caboose, one coupler, *56–57*	15	38
___ **6419-100**	N&W Work Caboose, *57–58*	45	109
6420	DL&W Work Caboose with searchlight, *48–50*		
___	(A) Heat-stamped serif lettering	38	75
___	(B) Rubber-stamped sans serif lettering	68	158
6424	Twin Auto Flatcar, *56–59*		
___	(A) Black frame, premium cars	21	58
___	(B) 6805 slots, no rail stops	53	123
___	(C) AAR trucks, number on right	29	74
6424-110	Twin Auto Flatcar, 6805 slots and rail stops, *58–59*		
___		85	184
___ **6425**	Gulf 3-D Tank Car, *56–58*	13	35
___ **6427**	Lionel Lines N5c Porthole Caboose, *54–60*	15	33
___ **6427-60**	Virginian N5c Porthole Caboose, *58*	180	406
6427-500	PRR N5c Porthole Caboose, sky blue, from Girls Set, *57–58**		
___		163	335
___ **6428**	U.S. Mail Boxcar, *60–61, 65–66*	20	47
___ **6429**	DL&W Work Caboose, AAR trucks, *63*	130	265
6430	Flatcar with 2 trailers, *56–58*		
___	(A) Gray Cooper-Jarrett trailers	25	60
___	(B) White Cooper-Jarrett trailers	27	74
___	(C) Green Fruehauf trailers	25	54
___	(D) Gray Cooper-Jarrett trailers with Fruehauf stickers	35	90
6431	Flatcar with 2 vans and Midgetoy tractor, *66*		
___	(A) White vans, *66*	65	225
___	(B) Yellow vans, *66*	85	350
___ **6434**	Poultry Dispatch Stock Car, *58–59*	32	70
6436-1	LV Open Quad Hopper, black, *55*		
___	(A) No spreader brace holes	45	143
___	(B) Spreader brace with holes	15	35
6436-25	LV Open Quad Hopper, maroon, *55–57*		
___	(A) No spreader brace holes	153	488
___	(B) Spreader brace with holes	20	45
6436-110	LV Quad Hopper, red, *63–68*		
___	(A) No built date	20	40
___	(B) Built date "New 3-55"	36	92

		Good	Exc
6436-500	LV Open Quad Hopper, lilac, from Girls Set, *57–58**		
	(A) No spreader brace holes	117	390 ____
	(B) Spreader brace with holes	75	302 ____
6437	PRR N5c Porthole Caboose, *61–68*	17	37 ____
6440	Flatcar with gray vans, *61–63*	35	80 ____
6440	Green Pullman Car, *48–49*	35	90 ____
6441	Green Observation Car, *48–49*	30	80 ____
6442	Brown Pullman Car, *49*	40	83 ____
6443	Brown Observation Car, *49*	37	73 ____
6445	Fort Knox Gold Reserve Boxcar with coin slot, *61–63*	45	99 ____
6446	N&W Covered Quad Hopper, black or gray, *54–55*	25	55 ____
6446-25	N&W Covered Quad Hopper, *55–57*		
	(A) Black, white lettering	26	65 ____
	(B) Gray, black lettering	32	73 ____
	(C) Gray, plastic trucks, spreader brace holes	64	189 ____
6446-60	LV Covered Quad Hopper, *63*	90	227 ____
6447	PRR N5c Porthole Caboose, *63*	104	305 ____
6448	Exploding Target Range Boxcar, *61–64*		
	(A) Red sides, white roof and ends	16	40 ____
	(B) White sides, red roof and ends	17	40 ____
6452	Pennsylvania Gondola, black, *48–49*		
	(A) Numbered "6462", *48*	15	48 ____
	(B) Numbered "6452", *49*	8	23 ____
X6454	Baby Ruth PRR Boxcar, *48*	90	269 ____
X6454	Santa Fe Boxcar, *48*	10	32 ____
X6454	NYC Boxcar, *48*		
	(A) Brown body	15	34 ____
	(B) Orange body	53	139 ____
	(C) Tan body	23	60 ____
X6454	Erie Boxcar, *49–52*	15	40 ____
X6454	PRR Boxcar, *49–52*	18	45 ____
X6454	SP Boxcar, *49–52*		
	(A) Break in herald circle between R and N, *49*	27	85 ____
	(B) Complete herald circle	17	44 ____
6456	Lehigh Valley Short Hopper, *48–55*		
	(A) Black	10	25 ____
	(B) Maroon	8	20 ____
6456-25	Lehigh Valley Short Hopper, gray, *54–55*	20	40 ____
6456-50	Lehigh Valley Short Hopper, enamel red, white lettering, *54*	261	587 ____
6456-75	Lehigh Valley Short Hopper, enamel red, yellow lettering, *54*	65	158 ____
6457	SP-type Caboose, *49–52*	14	25 ____
6460	Bucyrus Erie Crane Car, black cab, 8-wheel, *52–54*	20	45 ____
6460-25	Bucyrus Erie Crane Car, red cab, 8-wheel, *54*	38	95 ____

			Good	Exc
____	**6461**	Transformer Car, *49–50*	33	70
	6462	NYC Gondola, black or red, with 6 barrels, *49–54*		
____			8	20
	6462-25	NYC Gondola, green, with 6 barrels, *54–57*		
____		(A) N in second panel, 2 lines of data	11	35
____		(B) N in third panel, 3 lines of data	15	45
	6462-75	NYC Gondola, red-painted, with 6 barrels, *52–55*		
____			11	28
	6462-125	NYC Gondola, red plastic, with 6 barrels, *55–57*		
____			8	21
	6462-500	NYC Gondola, pink, from Girls Set, with 4 canisters, *57–58**		
____			55	175
____	**6463**	Rocket Fuel 2-D Tank Car, *62–63*	19	59
	6464-1	WP Boxcar, *53–54*		
____		(A) Blue lettering	28	55
____		(B) Red lettering	425	1220
____	**6464-25**	GN Boxcar, *53–54*	31	85
____	**6464-50**	M&StL Boxcar, *53–56*	23	75
	6464-75	RI Boxcar, green, *53–54, 69*		
____		(A) Built date, *53–54*	30	60
____		(B) No built date, *69*	40	85
	6464-100	Western Pacific Boxcar, *54–55*		
____		(A) Silver body, yellow feather	40	125
____		(B) Orange body, blue feather	197	733
____	**6464-125**	NYC Pacemaker Boxcar, *54–56*	43	83
____	**6464-150**	MP Boxcar, *54–55, 57*	45	108
	6464-175	Rock Island Boxcar, *54–55*		
____		(A) Blue lettering	40	108
____		(B) Black lettering	375	1033
____	**6464-200**	Pennsylvania Boxcar, *54–55, 69*	70	131
____	**6464-225**	SP Boxcar, *54–56*	45	117
____	**6464-250**	WP Boxcar, *66*	65	237
	6464-275	State of Maine Boxcar, *55, 57–59*		
____		(A) Striped doors	35	75
____		(B) Solid doors	55	127
	6464-300	Rutland Boxcar, *55–56*		
____		(A) Rubber-stamped lettering	45	85
____		(B) Split door with bottom painted green	230	420
____		(C) Rubber-stamped lettering with solid shield	1413	3888
____		(D) Heat-stamped lettering	75	160
____		(E) Painted yellow body	300	848
____	**6464-325**	B&O Sentinel Boxcar, *56*	182	424
____	**6464-350**	MKT Boxcar, *56*	95	297
	6464-375	Central of Georgia Boxcar, *56–57, 66*		
____		(A) Unpainted maroon body	40	80
____		(B) Painted red body	775	3264

	Good	Exc
6464-400 B&O Time-Saver Boxcar, *56–57, 69*		
(A) BLT 5-54	43	90 ____
(B) BLT 2-56	109	250 ____
(C) No built date	45	103 ____
6464-425 New Haven Boxcar, *56–58*	29	60 ____
6464-450 Great Northern Boxcar, *56–57, 66*	63	130 ____
6464-475 B&M Boxcar, *57–60, 65–66, 68*		
(A) Medium blue-painted or unpainted plastic	38	75 ____
(B) Dark purple-painted, gray or blue mold	74	283 ____
(C) Dark blue-painted, yellow mold	127	460 ____
6464-500 Timken Boxcar, white side band and charcoal lettering, *57–59, 69*		
(A) Unpainted yellow body	45	128 ____
(B) Painted yellow body, Type IV	48	135 ____
(C) Painted yellow body, Type II	140	433 ____
6464-510 NYC Pacemaker Boxcar, *57–58*	260	675 ____
6464-515 MKT Boxcar, *57–58*	260	672 ____
6464-525 M&StL Boxcar, *57–58, 64–66*		
(A) Red, white lettering	27	75 ____
(B) Maroon, white lettering	115	455 ____
6464-650 D&RGW Boxcar, *57–58, 66*		
(A) Yellow body, silver roof, black stripe	65	135 ____
(B) Yellow body, silver roof, no black stripe	95	229 ____
(C) Painted yellow body and yellow roof	500	2540 ____
6464-700 Santa Fe Boxcar, *61, 66*	40	145 ____
6464-725 New Haven Boxcar, *62–66, 68*		
(A) Orange body	23	50 ____
(B) Black body	63	237 ____
6464-825 Alaska Boxcar, *59–60*	89	315 ____
6464-900 NYC Boxcar, *60–66*	37	90 ____
6465 Gulf 2-D Tank Car, *58*		
(A) Black tank	15	53 ____
(B) Gray tank	11	35 ____
6465 Sunoco 2-D Tank Car, *48–56*		
(A) Silver tank, rubber-stamped "6465"	6	12 ____
(B) Silver tank, rubber-stamped "6455"	20	65 ____
(C) Silver tank, no number on frame	7	18 ____
(D) Glossy gray tank	10	40 ____
6465-85 LL 2-D Tank Car, black, *59*	20	53 ____
6465-110 Cities Service 2-D Tank, *60–62*	23	59 ____
6465-160 LL 2-D Tank Car, orange with black ends, *63–64*	10	27 ____
6466T Tender, *49–53*	13	30 ____
6466W Whistle Tender, *49–53*	18	45 ____
6466WX Whistle Tender, *49–53*	20	50 ____
6467 Miscellaneous Car, *56*	25	52 ____
6468 B&O Auto Boxcar, blue, *53–55*	15	42 ____
6468X B&O Auto Boxcar, tuscan, *53–55*	128	189 ____

			Good	Exc
	6468-25	NH Auto Boxcar, *56–58*		
____		(A) Black N over white H, black doors	25	75
____		(B) White N over black H, black doors	66	258
____		(C) Black N over white H, painted Tuscan doors	33	80
____	**6469**	Liquified Gas Tank Car, *63*	39	111
____	**6470**	Explosives Boxcar, *59–60*	12	36
____	**6472**	Refrigerator Car, *50–53*	11	25
____	**6473**	Horse Transport Car, *62–69*	13	25
____	**6475**	Libby's Crushed Pineapple Vat Car, *63 u*	35	90
____	**6475**	Pickles Vat Car, *60–62*	20	77
	6476	LV Short Hopper, *57–63*		
____		(A) Red body	6	19
____		(B) Gray body	8	20
____		(C) Black body	6	19
____	**6476-75**	LV Short Hopper, black, Type VI body, *63*	8	20
____	**6476-135**	LV Short Hopper, yellow, *64–66, 68*	6	19
____	**6476-160**	LV Short Hopper, black, *69*	6	17
____	**6476-185**	LV Short Hopper, yellow, *69*	6	19
____	**6477**	Miscellaneous Car with pipes, *57–58*	20	65
____	**6480**	Explosives Boxcar, red, *61*	17	43
____	**6482**	Refrigerator Car, *57*	14	40
	6500	Flatcar with Bonanza airplane, *62, 65*		
____		(A) Plane, red top and wings	342	662
____		(B) Plane, white top and wings	385	800
____	**6501**	Flatcar with jet boat, *62–63*	52	148
	6502	Flat Car with Girder, *62*		
____		(A) Black flatcar	19	70
____		(B) Red flatcar	35	109
____	**6502-50**	Flatcar, blue or teal, no lettering, with bridge girder, *62*	10	44
	6511	Flatcar with pipes, *53–56*		
____		(A) Die-cast truck plates, *53*	18	58
____		(B) Stamped metal truck plates	13	40
____	**6511-24**	Set of 6 pipes with box, *55–58*	40	150
____	**6512**	Cherry Picker Car, *62–63*	28	85
	6517	LL Bay Window Caboose, *55–59*		
____		(A) Built date underscored	25	75
____		(B) Built date not underscored	20	50
____		(C) Built date not underscored, lettering higher	20	53
____	**6517-75**	Erie Bay Window Caboose, *66*	147	460
____	**6518**	Transformer Car, *56–58*	23	64
	6519	Allis-Chalmers Flatcar, *58–61*		
____		(A) Dark or medium orange base	25	70
____		(B) Dull light orange base	42	130

		Good	Exc	
6520	Searchlight Car, *49–51*			
	(A) Tan generator	625	1388	____
	(B) Green generator	93	263	____
	(C) Maroon generator	17	47	____
	(D) Orange generator	15	41	____
	(E) Green generator, black searchlight housing	88	300	____
6530	Firefighting Instruction Car, *60–61*			
	(A) Red body, white lettering	25	83	____
	(B) Black body, white lettering	105	415	____
6536	M&StL Open Quad Hopper, *58–59, 63*			
	(A) AAR trucks, *59, 63*	27	69	____
	(B) Bar-end trucks, *58*	45	135	____
6544	Missile Firing Car, 4 missiles, *60–64*			
	(A) White-lettered console	45	159	____
	(B) Black-lettered console	100	333	____
6555	Sunoco 1-D Tank Car, *49–50*	15	65	____
6556	MKT Stock Car, *58*	118	315	____
6557	SP-type Smoking Caboose, *58–59*			
	(A) Tuscan, with non-reverse lettering	83	215	____
	(B) Brown, with reverse lettering	463	1125	____
6560	Bucyrus Erie Crane Car, smokestack, *55–58, 68–69*			
	(A) Black frame, red-orange cab	36	102	____
	(B) Black frame, gray cab	27	72	____
	(C) Black frame, red cab	19	40	____
	(D) Dark blue frame, red cab	30	95	____
	(E) Black frame, red cab, rubber-stamped "6560"	86	327	____
	(F) Black frame, black cab	53	150	____
6560-25	Bucyrus Erie Crane Car, 8-wheel, *56*	33	84	____
6561	Cable Car, 2 reels, *53–56*			
	(A) Orange reels	23	58	____
	(B) Gray reels	23	93	____
6562	NYC Gondola with 4 red canisters, *56–58*			
	(A) Gray body, *56*	15	45	____
	(B) Red body, *56, 58*	10	30	____
	(C) Black body, *57*	9	28	____
6572	REA Refrigerator Car, *58–59, 63*			
	(A) Passenger trucks	99	227	____
	(B) Bar-end trucks	35	101	____
	(C) AAR trucks, *63*	25	69	____
6630	Missile Launching Car, *61*	22	73	____
6636	Alaska Open Quad Hopper, *59–60*	36	91	____
6640	USMC Missile Launching Car, *60*	73	220	____
6646	Lionel Lines Stock Car, *57*	14	43	____
6650	IRBM Rocket Launcher, *59–63*			
	(A) "6650" stamped on left	18	50	____
	(B) "6650" stamped on right	76	233	____

			Good	Exc
___	**6650-80**	Missile, *60*	4	10
___	**6651**	USMC Cannon Car, *64 u*	73	212
___	**6654W**	Whistle Tender	18	40
	6656	Lionel Lines Stock Car, *49–55*		
___		(A) Brown Armour decal	22	66
___		(B) No decal	9	25
	6657	Rio Grande SP-type Caboose, *57–58*		
___		(A) With ladder slots	55	158
___		(B) Without ladder slots	135	409
___	**6660**	Boom Car, *58*	25	77
	6670	Derrick Car, *59–60*		
___		(A) "6670" stamped on left	22	75
___		(B) "6670" stamped on right	62	219
	6672	Santa Fe Refrigerator Car, *54–56*		
___		(A) Blue lettering, 2 lines of data	18	39
___		(B) Black lettering, 2 lines of data	22	63
___		(C) Blue lettering, 3 lines of data	91	303
___	**6736**	Detroit & Mackinac Open Quad Hopper, *60–62*	14	40
	6800	Flatcar with airplane, *57–60*		
___		(A) Plane, black top and wings	33	87
___		(B) Plane, yellow top and wings	40	112
___	**6800-60**	Airplane, *57–58*	46	243
___	**6801**	Flatcar with boat, white hull, brown deck, *57*	28	68
___	**6801-50**	Flatcar with boat, yellow hull, white deck, *58–60*	32	82
___	**6801-60**	Boat, *57–58*	20	110
___	**6801-75**	Flatcar with boat, blue hull, white deck, *58–60*	33	88
___	**6802**	Flatcar with 2 U.S. Steel girders, *58–59*	15	37
___	**6803**	Flatcar with USMC tank and sound truck, *58–59*	104	221
___	**6804**	Flatcar with USMC antiaircraft and sound trucks, *58–59*	107	208
___	**6805**	Atomic Energy Disposal Flatcar, *58–59*	40	170
___	**6806**	Flatcar with USMC radar and medical trucks, *58–59*	98	206
___	**6807**	Flatcar with amphibious vehicle, *58–59*	62	141
___	**6808**	Flatcar with USMC tank and searchlight truck, *58–59*	97	272
___	**6809**	Flatcar with USMC antiaircraft and medical trucks, *58–59*	97	209
___	**6810**	Flatcar with trailer, *58*	20	48
	6812	Track Maintenance Car, *59*		
___		(A) Dark yellow superstructure	17	64
___		(B) Black base, gray platform and crank handle	17	62
___		(C) Gray base, black platform and crank handle	17	63
___		(D) Cream superstructure	40	190
___		(E) Light yellow superstructure	20	70

		Good	Exc	
6814	Rescue Caboose, *59–61*	43	108	___
6816	Flatcar with Allis-Chalmers bulldozer, *59–60*			
	(A) Red car	170	440	___
	(B) Black car	575	1100	___
6816-100	Allis-Chalmers Bulldozer, *59–60*			
	(A) No box	70	233	___
	(B) Separate-sale box	234	707	___
6817	Flatcar with Allis-Chalmers motor scraper, *59–60*			
	(A) Red car	193	435	___
	(B) Black car	520	1178	___
6817-100	Allis-Chalmers Motor Scraper, *59–60*			
	(A) No box	118	258	___
	(B) Separate-sale box	233	650	___
6818	Flatcar with transformer, *58*	10	35	___
6819	Flatcar with helicopter, *59–60*	17	61	___
6820	Aerial Missile Transport Car with helicopter, *60–61*			
	(A) Light blue frame	85	225	___
	(B) Medium blue frame	68	190	___
6821	Flatcar with crates, *59–60*	15	38	___
6822	Searchlight Car, *61–69*			
	(A) Black base, gray light	15	38	___
	(B) Gray base, black light	23	47	___
6823	Flatcar with 2 IRBM missiles, *59–60*	25	65	___
6824	USMC Work Caboose, *60*	88	262	___
6824-50	Rescue Caboose, white, *64*	37	113	___
6825	Flatcar with arch trestle bridge, *59–62*	18	38	___
6826	Flatcar with Christmas trees, *59–60*	26	90	___
6827	Flatcar with Harnischfeger power shovel, *60–63*	70	225	___
6827-100	Harnischfeger Power Shovel, *60*			
	(A) No box	55	122	___
	(B) Separate-sale box	115	253	___
6828	Flatcar with Harnischfeger crane, *60–63, 66*			
	(A) Black flatcar, light yellow crane cab	79	235	___
	(B) Black flatcar, dark yellow crane cab	75	265	___
	(C) Red flatcar, dark yellow crane cab	323	1185	___
6828-100	Harnischfeger Construction Crane, *60*			
	(A) No box	35	105	___
	(B) Separate-sale box	90	258	___
6830	Flatcar with submarine, *60–61*	48	150	___
6844	Missile Carrying Car, 6 missiles, *59–60*			
	(A) Black frame	23	85	___
	(B) Red frame	345	1150	___

			Good	Exc
	Other Track, Transformers, and Assorted Items			
___ A	Transformer, 90 watts, *47–48*		13	35
___ CO-1	Track Clips, dozen, with envelope (O), *49*		5	12
___ CO-1	Track Clips, box of 50 (O), *49*		25	85
___ CO-1	Track Clips, box of 100 (O), *49*		33	113
___ CTC	Lockon (O and O27), *47–69*		1	2
___ CTC-14	Lockons, dozen, with envelope		13	38
___ ECU-1	Electronic Control Unit, *46*		30	80
___ KW	Transformer, 190 watts, *50–65*		33	74
___ LTC	Lockon (O and O27), *50–69*		2	8
___ LW	Transformer, 125 watts, *55–56*		36	65
___ OC	Curved Track (O), *45–61*		0	1
___ OC½	Half Section Curved Track (O), *45–66*		0	1
___ OCS	Curved Insulated Track (O), *46–50*		8	20
___ OS	Straight Track (O), *45–61*		0	2
___ OSS	Straight Insulated Track, *46–50*		5	18
___ OTC	Lockon Track (O and O27)		2	4
___ Q	Transformer, 75 watts, *46*		11	26
___ R	Transformer, 110 watts, *46–47*		13	32
___ RCS	Remote Control Track (O), *45–48*		4	10
___ RW	Transformer, 110 watts, *48–54*		11	28
___ RX	Transformer, 100 watts, *47–48*		13	33
___ S	Transformer, 80 watts, *47*		13	33
SP	Smoke Pellets, bottle, *48–69*			
___	(A) Tall, light amber bottle		13	48
___	(B) Tall, dark amber bottle		10	50
___	(C) Short, light amber bottle		16	56
___	(D) All other bottles		5	12
___	(E) Bottle on blister pack, *65*		20	58
___ SP-12	Dealer Display Box with 12 full smoke bottles		105	310
___ ST-300	Nut Driver Set with holder, service station item		485	1025
___ ST-301	Wheel Puller, service station item		50	160
___ ST-303	E Unit Spreader, service station item		31	85
___ ST-311	Wheel Puller, service station item		73	176
___ ST-320	Phillips Screwdriver, service station item		143	280
___ ST-321	Flathead Screwdriver, short, service station item		180	440
___ ST-322	Flathead Screwdriver, long, service station item		40	150
___ ST-325	Screwdriver Set, service station item		400	900
___ ST-342	Track Pliers, service station item		75	165
___ ST-343	O Gauge Track Pliers, service station item		400	858
___ ST-350	Rivet Press, service station item		424	698
___ ST-350-5	Rivet Press Tool Block with tools, service station item		300	525
___ ST-350-17	Sliding Shoe Anvil, service station item		7	18
___ ST-375	Wheel Cup Tool Set, service station item		400	900
___ ST-378	E Unit Vice, service station item		133	249
___ ST-384	Track Pliers, service station item		125	250

POSTWAR 1945-1969

		Good	Exc	
SW	Transformer, 130 watts, *61–66*	25	65	____
TW	Transformer, 175 watts, *53–60*	33	80	____
TOC	Curved Track (O), *62–66, 68–69*		1	____
TOC½	Half Section Straight Track (O), *62–66*		1	____
TOS	Straight Track (O), *62–69*		1	____
UCS	Remote Control Track (O), *45–69*	5	13	____
UTC	Lockon (O, 027, Standard), *45*	1	2	____
V	Transformer, 150 watts, *46–47*	45	85	____
VW	Transformer, 150 watts, *48–49*	37	83	____
Z	Transformer, 250 watts, *45–47*	63	115	____
ZW	Transformer, 250 watts, *48–49*	41	102	____
ZW	Transformer, 275 watts, *50–56*	63	152	____
ZW	Transformer, 275 watts, R type, *57–66*	87	172	____

Section 3
MODERN ERA 1970-2018

		Exc	Min
366	Menards C&NW 4-4-2 Locomotive with tender, *09*	45	75
_____**400**	Menards C&NW Chicago Combine Car, *09*	25	40
403	Menards C&NW Lake Superior Observation Car, *09*	25	40
_____**410**	Menards C&NW Lake Michigan Coach, *09*	40	65
_____**0512**	Toy Fair Reefer, *81 u*	60	70
_____**550C**	31" Diameter Curved Track (O), *70*	1	2
_____**550S**	Straight Track (O), *70*	1	2
_____**665E**	Johnny Cash Blue Train 4-6-4 Locomotive, *71 u*		NRS
_____**1050**	New Englander Set, *80–81*	155	205
_____**1052**	Chesapeake Flyer Set, *80*	140	150
_____**1053**	James Gang Set, *80–82*	155	195
_____**1070**	Royal Limited Set, *80*	285	350
_____**1071**	Mid Atlantic Limited Set, *80*	225	230
_____**1072**	Cross Country Express Set, *80–81*	240	385
_____**1081**	Wabash Cannonball Set, *70–72*	105	120
_____**1082**	Yard Boss Set, *70*	120	165
_____**1083**	Pacemaker Set, *70*	105	120
_____**1084**	Grand Trunk Western Freight Set, *70*	120	140
_____**1085**	Santa Fe Express Diesel Freight Set, *70*	175	190
_____**1091**	Sears Special Steam Freight Set, *70 u*	150	165
_____**1092**	Sears GTW Steam Freight Set, *70 u*	150	165
_____**1100**	Happy Huff n' Puff, *74–75 u*	55	70
_____**1150**	L.A.S.E.R. Train Set, *81–82*	155	195
_____**1151**	Union Pacific Thunder Freight Set, *81–82*	150	175
_____**1153**	JCPenney Thunderball Freight Set, *81 u*	165	180
_____**1154**	Reading Yard King Set, *81–82*	170	190
_____**1155**	Cannonball Freight Set, *82*	75	85
_____**1157**	Lionel Leisure Wabash Cannonball Set, *81 u*		250
_____**1158**	Maple Leaf Limited Set, *81*	405	435
_____**1159**	Toys "R" Us Midnight Flyer Set, *81 u*	130	140
_____**1160**	Great Lakes Limited Set, *81*	280	330
_____**T-1171**	CN Locomotive Set, *71 u*	240	275
_____**T-1172**	Yardmaster Set, *71 u*		200
_____**T-1173**	Grand Trunk Western Freight Set, *71–73 u*	175	195
_____**T-1174**	Canadian National, *71–73 u*	265	300
_____**1182**	Yardmaster Set, *71–72*	85	105
_____**1183**	Silver Star Set, *71–72*	65	80
_____**1184**	Allegheny Set, *71*	120	150
_____**1186**	Cross Country Express Set, *71–72*	210	260
_____**1187**	Illinois Central Set (SSS), *71*	400	485
_____**1190**	Sears Special #1 Set, *71 u*	85	100
_____**1195**	JCPenney Special Set, *71 u*	150	165
_____**1198**	Unnamed Set, *71 u*		175
_____**1199**	Ford-Autolite Allegheny Set, *71 u*	187	207
_____**1200**	Gravel Gus, *75 u*	75	100
_____**1250**	New York Central Set (SSS), *72*	315	380
_____**1252**	Heavy Iron Set, *82–83*	90	130
_____**1253**	Quicksilver Express Set, *82–83*	265	340
_____**1254**	Black Cave Flyer Set, *82*	75	105

		Exc	Mint	
1260	Continental Limited Set, *82*	290	385	___
1261	Sears Black Cave Flyer Set, *82 u*	165	195	___
1262	Toys "R" Us Heavy Iron Set, *82 u*	150	165	___
1263	JCPenney Overland Freight Set, *82 u*	150	165	___
1264	Nibco Express Set, *82 u*	190	195	___
1265	Tappan Special Set, *82 u*	130	155	___
T-1272	Yardmaster Set, *72–73 u*	150	165	___
T-1273	Silver Star Set, *72–73 u*	90	115	___
1280	Kickapoo Valley & Northern Set, *72*	60	75	___
1284	Allegheny Set, *72*	140	165	___
1285	Santa Fe Twin Diesel Set, *72*	95	140	___
1287	Pioneer Dockside Switcher Set, *72*	95	100	___
1290	Sears Steam Freight Set, *72 u*	150	165	___
1291	Sears Steam Freight Set, *72 u*	150	165	___
1300	Gravel Gus Junior, *75 u*	70	90	___
1350	Canadian Pacific Set (SSS), *73*	460	620	___
1351	Baltimore & Ohio Set, *83–84*	205	280	___
1352	Rocky Mountain Freight Set, *83–84*	75	95	___
1353	Southern Streak Set, *83–85*	75	95	___
1354	Northern Freight Flyer Set, *83–85*	230	280	___
1355	Commando Assault Train, *83–84*	175	248	___
1359	Display Case for Set 1355, *83 u*	75	95	___
1361	Gold Coast Limited Set, *83*	390	400	___
1362	Lionel Leisure BN Express Set, *83 u*	200	300	___
1380	U.S. Steel Industrial Switcher Set, *73–75*	60	75	___
1381	Cannonball Set, *73–75*	70	75	___
1382	Yardmaster Set, *73–74*	110	135	___
1383	Santa Fe Freight Set, *73–75*	100	125	___
1384	Southern Express Set, *73–76*	75	120	___
1385	Blue Streak Freight Set, *73–74*	100	120	___
1386	Rock Island Express Set, *73–74*	120	140	___
1387	Milwaukee Road Special Set, *73*	185	285	___
1388	Golden State Arrow Set, *73–75*	215	240	___
1390	Sears 7-unit Steam Freight Set, *73 u*	170	190	___
1392	Sears 8-unit Steam Freight Set, *73 u*	150	165	___
1393	Sears 6-unit Diesel Freight Set, *73 u*	150	165	___
1395	JCPenney Set, *73 u*	150	165	___
1400	Happy Huff n' Puff Junior, *75 u*	130	140	___
1402	Chessie System Set, *84–85*	125	150	___
1403	Redwood Valley Express Set, *84–85*	170	205	___
1450	D&RGW Set (SSS), *74*	335	415	___
1451	Erie-Lackawanna Limited Set, *84*	415	465	___
1460	Grand National Set, *74*	300	330	___
1461	Black Diamond Set, *74 u, 75*	100	120	___
1463	Coca-Cola Special Set, *74 u, 75*	216	265	___
1487	Broadway Limited Set, *74–75*	160	255	___
1489	Santa Fe Double Diesel Set, *74–76*	140	165	___
1492	Sears 7-unit Steam Freight Set, *74 u*	150	165	___
1493	Sears 7-unit Steam Freight Set, *74 u*	150	165	___
1499	JCPenney Great Express Set, *74 u*	150	165	___
1501	Midland Freight Set, *85–86*	75	95	___
1502	Yard Chief Set, *85–86*	205	230	___
1506	Sears Centennial Chessie System Set, *85 u*	165	195	___
1512	JCPenney Midland Freight Set, *85 u*	90	115	___

		Exc	Mint
___**1549**	Toys "R" Us Heavy Iron Set, *85–89 u*	180	215
___**1552**	Burlington Northern Limited Set, *85*	500	570
___**1560**	North American Express Set, *75*	275	365
___**1562**	Fast Freight Flyer Set, *85 u*	120	140
___**1577**	Liberty Special Set, *75 u*	224	232
___**1579**	Milwaukee Road Set (SSS), *75*	325	410
___**1581**	Thunderball Freight Set, *75–76*	90	100
___**1582**	Yard Chief Set, *75–76*	115	155
___**1584**	N&W "Spirit of America" Set, *75*	160	180
___**1585**	75th Anniversary Special Set, *75–77*	216	228
___**1586**	Chesapeake Flyer Set, *75–77*	160	190
___**1587**	Capitol Limited Set, *75*	270	300
___**1593**	Sears Set, *75 u*		100
___**1595**	Sears 6-unit Diesel Freight Set, *75 u*	150	165
___**1602**	Nickel Plate Special Set, *86–91*	120	125
___**1606**	Sears Centennial Nickel Plate Set, *86 u*	165	195
___**1608**	American Express General Set, *86 u*	205	320
___**1615**	Cannonball Express Set, *86–90*	65	75
___**1632**	Santa Fe Work Train (SSS), *86*	220	255
___**1652**	B&O Freight Set, *86*	140	185
___**1658**	Town House TV and Appliances Set, *86 u*	80	95
___**1660**	Yard Boss Set, *76*	100	115
___**1661**	Rock Island Line Set, *76–77*	80	100
___**1662**	Black River Freight Set, *76–78*	75	95
___**1663**	Amtrak Lake Shore Limited Set, *76–77*	215	265
___**1664**	Illinois Central Freight Set, *76–77*	265	355
___**1665**	NYC Empire State Express Set, *76*	310	435
___**1672**	Northern Pacific Set (SSS), *76*	215	280
___**1685**	True Value Freight Flyer Set, *86–87 u*	60	75
___**1686**	Kay Bee Toys Freight Flyer Set, *86 u*	150	165
___**1687**	Freight Flyer Set, *87–90*	39	47
___**1693**	Toys "R" Us Rock Island Line Set, *76 u*	110	130
___**1694**	Toys "R" Us Black River Freight Set, *76 u*	110	130
___**1696**	Sears Steam Freight Set, *76 u*	110	130
___**1698**	True Value Rock Island Line Set, *76 u*	125	145
___**1760**	Trains n' Truckin' Steel Hauler Set, *77–78*	105	110
___**1761**	Trains n' Truckin' Cargo King Set, *77–78*	95	165
___**1762**	Wabash Cannonball Set, *77*	135	190
___**1764**	Heartland Express Set, *77*	185	240
___**1765**	Rocky Mountain Special Set, *77*	210	315
___**1766**	B&O Budd Car Set (SSS), *77*	335	390
___**1776**	Seaboard U36B Diesel, *74–76*	74	120
___**1790**	Lionel Leisure Steel Hauler Set, *77 u*	150	200
___**1791**	Toys "R" Us Steel Hauler Set, *77 u*	130	175
___**1792**	True Value Rock Island Line Set, *77 u*	100	135
___**1793**	Toys "R" Us Black River Freight Set, *77 u*	120	155
___**1796**	JCPenney Cargo Master Set, *77 u*		200
___**1860**	"Workin' on the Railroad" Timberline Set, *78*	65	85
1862	"Workin' on the Railroad" Logging Empire Set, *78*		
___		85	110
___**1864**	Santa Fe Double Diesel Set, *78–79*	155	190
___**1865**	Chesapeake Flyer Set, *78–79*	155	180
___**1866**	Great Plains Express Set, *78–79*	195	285
___**1867**	Milwaukee Road Limited Set, *78*	230	275
___**1868**	M&StL Set (SSS), *78*	215	255

		Exc	Mint	
1892	JCPenney Logging Empire Set, *78 u*	95	125	___
1893	Toys "R" Us Logging Empire Set, *78 u*	175	225	___
1960	Midnight Flyer Set, *79–81*	55	75	___
1962	Wabash Cannonball Set, *79*	90	105	___
1963	Black River Freight Set, *79–81*	75	85	___
1965	Smokey Mountain Line Set, *79*	65	85	___
1970	Southern Pacific Limited Set, *79 u*	340	365	___
1971	Quaker City Limited Set, *79*	315	335	___
1990	Mystery Glow Midnight Flyer Set, *79 u*	75	90	___
1991	JCPenney Wabash Cannonball Deluxe Express Set, *79 u*	150	165	___
1993	Toys "R" Us Midnight Flyer Set, *79 u*	110	130	___
2110	Graduated Trestle Set, 22 pieces, *70–88*	9	13	___
2111	Elevated Trestle Set, 10 pieces, *70–88*	8	11	___
2113	Tunnel Portals, pair, *84–87*	11	16	___
2115	Dwarf Signal, *84–87*	9	13	___
2117	Block Target Signal, *84–87*	23	29	___
2122	Extension Bridge, rock piers, *76–87*	24	34	___
2125	Whistling Freight Shed, *71*	36	43	___
2126	Whistling Freight Shed, *76–87*	18	26	___
2127	Diesel Horn Shed, *76–87*	25	30	___
2128	Operating Switchman, *83–86*	26	29	___
2129	Illuminated Freight Station, *83–86*	30	33	___
2133	Lighted Freight Station, *72–78, 80–84*	34	38	___
2140	Automatic Banjo Signal, *70–84*	17	21	___
2145	Automatic Gateman, *72–84*	31	47	___
2151	Operating Semaphore, *78–82*	15	19	___
2152	Automatic Crossing Gate, *70–84*	21	25	___
2154	Automatic Highway Flasher, *70–87*	19	24	___
2156	Illuminated Station Platform, *70–71*	26	34	___
2162	Automatic Crossing Gate and Signal "262," *70–87, 94, 96–98, 05*	16	27	___
2163	Block Target Signal, *70–78*	14	19	___
2170	Street Lamps, set of 3, *70–87*	13	19	___
2171	Gooseneck Street Lamps, set of 2, *80–81, 83–84*	15	18	___
2175	"Sandy Andy" Gravel Loader Kit, *76–79*	34	55	___
2180	Road Signs, 16 pieces, *77–98*		6	___
2181	Telephone Pole Set "150," *77–98*		5	___
2195	Floodlight Tower, *70–71*	38	50	___
2199	Microwave Tower, *72–75*	30	39	___
2214	Girder Bridge, *70–71, 72 u, 73–87*	5	9	___
2256	Station Platform, *73–81*	12	18	___
2260	Illuminated Bumper, *70–71, 72 u, 73*	23	35	___
2280	Nonilluminated Bumpers, set of 3, *73–84*	2	4	___
2282	Die-cast Bumpers, pair, *83 u*	12	18	___
2283	Die-cast Illuminated Bumpers "260," *84–99*	10	16	___
2290	Illuminated Bumpers, pair, *75 u, 76–86*	7	11	___
2292	Station Platform, *85–87*	5	9	___
2300	Operating Oil Drum Loader, *83–87*	80	90	___
2301	Operating Sawmill, *80–84*	60	65	___
2302	Union Pacific Manual Gantry Crane, *80–82*	24	31	___
2303	Santa Fe Manual Gantry Crane, *80–81, 83 u*	17	21	___
2305	Getty Operating Oil Derrick, *81–84*	105	115	___
2306	Operating Ice Station with 6700 Ice Car, *82–83*	90	105	___

			Exc	Mint
____	2307	Lighted Billboard, *82–86*	12	13
____	2308	Animated Newsstand, *82–83*	105	120
____	2309	Mechanical Crossing Gate, *82–92*	4	7
____	2310	Mechanical Crossing Gate, *73–77*	2	4
____	2311	Mechanical Semaphore, *82–92*	4	7
____	2312	Mechanical Semaphore, *73–77*	2	4
____	2313	Floodlight Tower, *75–86*	22	27
____	2314	Searchlight Tower, *75–84*	22	27
____	2315	Operating Coaling Station, *83–84*	80	83
____	2316	N&W Operating Gantry Crane, *83–84*	90	125
____	2317	Operating Drawbridge, *75 u, 76–81*	100	130
____	2318	Operating Control Tower, *83–86*	40	50
____	2319	Illuminated Watchtower, *75–78, 80*	29	56
____	2320	Flagpole Kit, *83–87*	10	14
____	2321	Operating Sawmill, *84, 86–87*	115	133
____	2323	Operating Freight Station, *84–87*	43	47
____	2324	Operating Switch Tower, *84–87*	60	65
____	2390	Lionel Mirror, *82 u*	80	115
____	2494	Rotary Beacon, *72–74*	37	44
____	2709	Rico Station Kit, *81–98*		42
____	2710	Billboards, set of 5, *70–84*	4	10
____	2714	Tunnel, *75 u, 76–77*	36	43
____	2716	Short Extension Bridge, *88–98*	3	8
____	2717	Short Extension Bridge, *77–87*	2	4
____	2718	Barrel Platform Kit, *77–84*	3	5
____	2719	Watchman's Shanty Kit, *77–87*	3	5
____	2720	Lumber Shed Kit, *77–84, 87*	3	5
____	2721	Operating Log Mill Kit, *78*	2	4
____	2722	Barrel Loader Kit, *78*	2	4
____	2783	Freight Station Kit, *84*	6	10
____	2784	Freight Platform Kit, *81–90*	5	8
____	2785	Engine House Kit, *73–77*	31	39
____	2786	Freight Platform Kit, *73–77*	4	6
____	2787	Freight Station Kit, *73–77, 83*	7	10
____	2788	Coal Station Kit, *75 u, 76–77*	18	30
____	2789	Water Tower Kit, *75–77, 80*	19	24
____	2791	Cross Country Set, *70–71*	22	30
____	2792	Whistle Stop Set, *70–71*	24	34
____	2792	Layout Starter Pack, *80–84*	9	21
____	2793	Alamo Junction Set, *70–71*	22	30
____	2796	Grain Elevator Kit, *76 u, 77*	43	47
____	2797	Rico Station Kit, *76–77*	23	37
____	2900	Lockon, *70–98*		1
____	2901	Track Clips, dozen (027), *71–98*		6
____	2905	Lockon and Wire, *74–00*		3
____	2909	Smoke Fluid, *70–98*		8
____	2910	OTC Contactor, *84–86, 88*	4	7
____	2911	Smoke Pellets, *70–73*	18	35
____	2925	Lubricant, *70–71, 72 u, 73–75*		2
____	2927	Maintenance Kit, *70, 78–98*		11
____	2928	Oil, *71*		2
____	2951	Track Layout Book, *70–86*	1	2
____	2952	Train and Accessory Manual, *70–74*	1	2
____	2953	Train and Accessory Manual, *75–86*	1	2

		Exc	Mint
2960	Lionel 75th Anniversary Book, *75 u, 76*	14	26____
2980	Magnetic Conversion Coupler, *70–71*	1	2____
2985	The Lionel Train Book, *86–98*		11____
3100	Great Northern 4-8-4 (FARR 3), *81*	335	388____
4044	Transformer, 45-watt, *70–71*	2	7____
4045	Safety Transformer, *70–71*	2	3____
4050	Safety Transformer, *72–79*	2	3____
4060	Power Master Transformer, *80–93*		13____
4090	Power Master Transformer, *70–84*	47	65____
4125	Transformer, 25-watt, *72*	2	3____
4150	Trainmaster Transformer, *72–73, 75–77*	6	15____
4250	Trainmaster Transformer, *74*	5	10____
4651	Trainmaster Transformer, *78–79*	1	2____
4690	MW Transformer, *86–89*	60	80____
4851	AC Transformer, red or black, *85–91, 94–96*	5	10____
5012	27" Diameter Curved Track, card of 4 (027), *70–96*		17____
5013	27" Diameter Curved Track (027), *70–78*		1____
5014	Half Curved Track (027), *70–98*		1____
5016	36" Straight Track (027), *87–88*	1	2____
5017	Straight Track, card of 4 (027), *70–96*		4____
5018	Straight Track (027), *70–78*		1____
5019	Half Straight Track (027), *70–98*		1____
5020	90-degree Crossover (027), *70–98*		7____
5021	27" Manual Switch, left hand (027), *70–98*		15____
5022	27" Manual Switch, right hand (027), *70–98*		15____
5023	45-degree Crossover (027), *70–98*		6____
5024	35" Straight Track (027), *88–98, 05*		3____
5025	Manumatic Uncoupler, *71–72*	1	2____
5027	27" Manual Switches, pair (027), *74–84*	13	21____
5030	Track Expander Set (027), *71–84*	18	26____
5031	Ford-Autolite Layout Expander Set, *71 u*	50	65____
5033	27" Diameter Curved Track (027), *79–98*		1____
5038	Straight Track (027), *79–98*		1____
5041	Insulator Pins, dozen (027), *70–98*		1____
5042	Steel Pins, dozen (027), *70–98*		1____
5045	54" Diameter Curved Track Ballast (027), *87–88*	1	2____
5046	27" Diameter Curved Track Ballast (027), *87–88*	1	2____
5047	Straight Track Ballast (027), *87–88*	1	2____
5049	42" Diameter Curved Track (027), *88–98*	1	2____
5090	27" Manual Switches, 3 pair (027), *78–84*	55	70____
5113	54" Diameter Curved Track (027), *79–98*	1	2____
5121	27" Remote Switch, left hand (027), *70–98*	18	22____
5122	27" Remote Switch, right hand (027), *70–98*	20	22____
5125	27" Remote Switches, pair (027), *71–83*	20	30____
5132	31" Remote Switch, right hand (0), *80–94*	29	30____
5133	31" Remote Switch, left hand (0), *80–94*	22	30____
5149	Remote Uncoupling Section (027), *70–98*		15____
5165	72" Remote Switch, right hand (0), *87–98*	23	65____
5166	72" Remote Switch, left hand (0), *87–98*	23	75____
5167	42" Remote Switch, right hand (027), *88–98*	25	37____
5168	42" Remote Switch, left hand (027), *88–98*	25	37____
5193	27" Remote Switches, 3 pair (027), *78–83*	80	95____
5500	10" Straight Track (0), *71–98*		1____
5501	31" Diameter Curved Track (0), *71–98*		1____

Exc Mint

		Exc	Mint
____5502	Remote Uncoupling Section (0), *71–72*	7	9
____5504	Half Curved Track (0), *83–98*		1
____5505	Half Straight Track (0), *83–98*		1
____5520	90-degree Crossover (0), *71–72*	6	9
____5522	36" Straight, *87–88*		3
____5523	40" Straight Track (0), *88–98*		4
____5530	Remote Uncoupling Section (0), *81–98*	10	19
____5540	90-degree Crossover (0), *81–98*		10
____5543	Insulator Pins, dozen (0), *70–98*		1
____5545	45-degree Crossover (0), *83–98*		11
____5551	Steel Pins, dozen (0), *70–98*		1
____5554	54" Diameter Curved Track (0), *90–98*		2
____5560	72" Diameter Curved Track Ballast (0), *87–88*	1	2
____5561	31" Diameter Curved Track Ballast (0), *87–88*	1	2
____5562	Straight Track Ballast (0), *87–88*	1	2
____5572	72" Diameter Curved Track (0), *79–98*	2	3
____5600	Curved Track (Trutrack), *73–74*	1	2
____5601	Curved Track, card of 4 (Trutrack), *73–74*	6	10
____5602	Curved Track Ballast, card of 4 (Trutrack), *73–74*	5	9
____5605	Straight Track (Trutrack), *73–74*	1	2
____5606	Straight Track, card of 4 (Trutrack), *73–74*	5	9
____5607	Straight Track Ballast, card of 4 (Trutrack), *73–74*	5	9
____5620	Manual Switch, left hand (Trutrack), *73–74*	4	13
____5625	Remote Switch, left hand (Trutrack), *73–74*	9	17
____5630	Manual Switch, right hand (Trutrack), *73–74*	4	13
____5635	Remote Switch, right hand (Trutrack), *73–74*	9	17
____5640	Left Switch Ballast, card of 2 (Trutrack), *73–74*	5	9
____5650	Right Switch Ballast, card of 2 (Trutrack), *73–74*	5	9
____5655	Lockon (Trutrack), *73–74*	1	2
____5660	Terminal Track with lockon (Trutrack), *74*	1	3
____5700	Oppenheimer Reefer, *81*	30	38
____5701	Dairymen's League Reefer, *81*	21	23
____5702	National Dairy Despatch Reefer, *81*	16	21
____5703	North American Despatch Reefer, *81*	22	26
____5704	Budweiser Reefer, *81–82*	64	70
____5705	Ball Glass Jars Reefer, *81–82*	30	35
____5706	Lindsay Brothers Reefer, *81–82*	26	27
____5707	American Refrigerator Transit Reefer, *81–82*	17	20
____5708	Armour Reefer, *82–83*	16	21
____5709	REA Reefer, *82–83*	22	26
____5710	Canadian Pacific Reefer, *82–83*	22	25
____5711	Commercial Express Reefer, *82–83*	13	15
____5712	Lionel Lines Reefer, *82 u*	47	75
____5713	Cotton Belt Reefer, *83–84*	19	22
____5714	Michigan Central Reefer, *83–84*	17	24
____5715	Santa Fe Reefer, *83–84*	19	26
____5716	Vermont Central Reefer, *83–84*	20	23
____5717	Santa Fe Bunk Car, *83*	22	30
____5719	Canadian National Reefer, *84*	10	16
____5720	Great Northern Reefer, *84*	75	90
____5721	Soo Line Reefer, *84*	21	23
____5722	NKP Reefer, *84*	16	18
____5724	PRR Bunk Car, *84*	15	23
____5726	Southern Bunk Car, *84 u*	22	27

		Exc	Mint
5727	USMC Bunk Car, *84–85*	25	30____
5728	Canadian Pacific Bunk Car, *86*	18	23____
5730	Strasburg Reefer, *85–86*	20	27____
5731	L&N Reefer, *85–86*	19	24____
5732	Jersey Central Reefer, *85–86*		24____
5733	Lionel Lines Bunk Car, *86 u*	18	24____
5735	NYC Bunk Car, *85–86*	33	35____
5739	B&O Tool Car, *86*	32	37____
5745	Santa Fe Bunk Car (SSS), *86*	39	45____
5760	Santa Fe Tool Car (SSS), *86*	30	35____
5900	AC/DC Converter, *79–83*	3	10____
6076	LV Hopper (O27), *70 u*	17	21____
6100	Ontario Northland Covered Quad Hopper, *81–82*	30	34____
6101	BN Covered Quad Hopper, *81–82*	17	31____
6102	GN Covered Quad Hopper (FARR 3), *81*	26	28____
6103	Canadian National Covered Quad Hopper, *81*	35	38____
6104	Southern Quad Hopper with coal (FARR 4), *83*	50	60____
6105	Reading Operating Hopper, *82*	34	39____
6106	N&W Covered Quad Hopper, *82*	30	40____
6107	Shell Covered Quad Hopper, *82*	22	26____
6109	C&O Operating Hopper, *83*	29	41____
6110	MP Covered Quad Hopper, *83–84*	17	27____
6111	L&N Covered Quad Hopper, *83–84*	13	20____
6113	Illinois Central Hopper (O27), *83–85*	15	25____
6114	C&NW Covered Quad Hopper, *83*	54	80____
6115	Southern Hopper (O27), *83–86*	15	19____
6116	Soo Line Ore Car, *84*	21	27____
6117	Erie Operating Hopper, *84*	29	39____
6118	Erie Covered Quad Hopper, *84*	31	45____
6122	Penn Central Ore Car, *84*	20	25____
6123	PRR Covered Quad Hopper (FARR 5), *84–85*	55	105____
6124	D&H Covered Quad Hopper, *84*	19	32____
6126	Canadian National Ore Car, *86*	18	24____
6127	Northern Pacific Ore Car, *86*	20	24____
6131	Illinois Terminal Covered Quad Hopper, *85–86*	15	21____
6134	BN 2-bay ACF Hopper (std O), *86 u*	95	115____
6135	C&NW 2-bay ACF Hopper (std O), *86 u*	65	80____
6137	NKP Hopper (O27), *86–91*	13	17____
6138	B&O Quad Hopper with coal, *86*	21	28____
6142	Gondola, black, *70*	20	33____
6150	Santa Fe Hopper (O27), *85–86, 92 u*	10	15____
6177	Reading Hopper (O27), *86–90*	14	19____
6200	FEC Gondola with canisters, *81–82*	13	24____
6201	Union Pacific Animated Gondola, *82–83*	19	25____
6202	WM Gondola with coal, *82*	34	36____
6203	Black Cave Gondola (O27), *82*	2	4____
6205	CP Gondola with canisters, *83*	18	26____
6206	C&IM Gondola with canisters, *83–85*	18	26____
6207	Southern Gondola with canisters (O27), *83–85*	6	8____
6208	Chessie System Gondola with canisters, *83 u*	21	24____
6209	NYC Gondola with coal (std O), *84–85*	42	46____
6210	Erie-Lackawanna Gondola with canisters, *84*	21	30____
6211	C&O Gondola with canisters, *84–85*		10____
6214	Lionel Lines Gondola with canisters, *84 u*	38	45____

		Exc	Mint
____6230	Erie-Lackawanna Reefer (std O), *86 u*	95	120
____6231	Railgon Gondola with coal (std O), *86 u*	66	76
____6232	Illinois Central Boxcar (std O), *86 u*	65	80
____6233	CP Flatcar with stakes (std O), *86 u*	47	50
____6234	Burlington Northern Boxcar (std O), *85*	55	75
____6235	Burlington Northern Boxcar (std O), *85*	33	43
____6236	Burlington Northern Boxcar (std O), *85*	33	43
____6237	Burlington Northern Boxcar (std O), *85*	32	47
____6238	Burlington Northern Boxcar (std O), *85*	33	43
____6239	Burlington Northern Boxcar (std O), *86 u*	37	55
____6251	NYC Coal Dump Car, *85*	25	42
____6254	NKP Gondola with canisters, *86–91*	6	11
6258	Santa Fe Gondola with canisters (O27), *85–86, 92 u*		3
____X6260	NYC Gondola with canisters, *85–86*	13	15
____6272	Santa Fe Gondola with cable reels (SSS), *86*	20	25
____6300	Corn Products 3-D Tank Car, *81–82*	19	25
____6301	Gulf 1-D Tank Car, *81*	20	26
____6302	Quaker State 3-D Tank Car, *81*	42	46
____6304	GN 1-D Tank Car (FARR 3), *81*	44	55
____6305	British Columbia 1-D Tank Car, *81*	55	76
____6306	Southern 1-D Tank Car (FARR 4), *83*	45	50
____6307	PRR 1-D Tank Car (FARR 5), *84–85*	70	75
____6308	Alaska 1-D Tank Car (O27), *82–83*	27	35
____6310	Shell 2-D Tank Car (O27), *83–84*	19	24
____6312	C&O 2-D Tank Car (O27), *84–85*	18	26
____6313	Lionel Lines 1-D Tank Car, *84 u*	43	50
____6314	B&O 3-D Tank Car, *86*	31	38
____6317	Gulf 2-D Tank Car (O27), *84–85*	18	22
____6357	Frisco 1-D Tank Car, *83*	42	50
____6401	Virginian Bay Window Caboose, *81*	37	47
____6403	Amtrak Vista Dome Car (O27), *76–77*	24	31
____6404	Amtrak Passenger Coach (O27), *76–77*	24	31
____6405	Amtrak Passenger Coach (O27), *76–77*	24	31
____6406	Amtrak Observation Car (O27), *76–77*	22	29
____6410	Amtrak Passenger Coach (O27), *77*	28	48
____6411	Amtrak Passenger Coach (O27), *77*	24	35
____6412	Amtrak Vista Dome Car (O27), *77*	22	33
____6420	Reading Transfer Caboose, *81–82*	20	28
____6421	Joshua L. Cowen Bay Window Caboose, *82*	34	40
____6422	DM&IR Bay Window Caboose, *81*	32	38
____6425	Erie-Lackawanna Bay Window Caboose, *83–84*	35	43
____6426	Reading Transfer Caboose, *82–83*	14	24
____6427	BN Transfer Caboose, *83–84*	12	21
____6428	C&NW Transfer Caboose, *83–85*	22	25
____6430	Santa Fe SP-type Caboose, *83–89*	4	14
____6431	Southern Bay Window Caboose (FARR 4), *83*	42	55
____6432	Union Pacific SP-type Caboose, *81–82*	6	10
____6433	Canadian Pacific Bay Window Caboose, *81*	60	70
____6435	U.S. Marines Transfer Caboose, *83–84*	9	17
____6438	GN Bay Window Caboose (FARR 3), *81*	48	65
____6439	Reading Bay Window Caboose, *84–85*	22	30
____6441	Alaska Bay Window Caboose, *82–83*	45	50
____6446-25	N&W Covered Quad Hopper, *70 u*	203	290
____6449	Wendy's N5c Caboose, *81–82*	64	74

Exc Mint

		Exc	Mint
6464-500	Timken Boxcar, orange, *70 u*	208	290____
6464-500	Timken Boxcar, yellow, *70 u*	210	350____
6476-135	LV Hopper "25000" (O27), *70–71 u*	6	11____
6478	Black Cave SP-type Caboose, *82*	5	9____
6482	Nibco Express SP-type Caboose, *82 u*	26	34____
6485	Chessie System SP-type Caboose, *84–85*	6	10____
6486	Southern SP-type Caboose, *83–85*	5	7____
6490	NKP N5c Caboose, *84 u*		NRS____
6491	Erie-Lackawanna Transfer Caboose, *85–86*	9	17____
6493	L&C Bay Window Caboose, *86–87*	21	36____
6494	Santa Fe Bobber Caboose, *85–86*	7	9____
6496	Santa Fe Work Caboose (SSS), *86*	21	29____
6504	L.A.S.E.R. Flatcar with helicopter (O27), *81–82*	18	26____
6505	L.A.S.E.R. Radar Car, *81–82*	17	25____
6506	L.A.S.E.R. Security Car, *81–82*	18	26____
6507	L.A.S.E.R. Flatcar with cruise missile, *81–82*	21	30____
6508	Canadian Pacific Crane Car, *81*	50	70____
6509	Depressed Center Flatcar with girders, *81*	60	85____
6510	Union Pacific Crane Car, *82*	55	60____
6515	Union Pacific Flatcar (O27), *83–84, 86*	5	9____
6521	NYC Flatcar with stakes (std O), *84–85*	29	35____
6522	C&NW Searchlight Car, *83–85*	27	30____
6524	Erie Crane Car, *84*	55	60____
6526	Searchlight Car, *84–85*	23	25____
6529	NYC Searchlight Car, *85–86*	21	27____
6531	Express Mail Flatcar with trailers, *85–86*	23	32____
6560	Bucyrus Erie Crane Car, *71*	100	130____
6561	Flatcar with cruise missile (O27), *83–84*	13	26____
6562	Flatcar with fences (O27), *83–84*	13	21____
6564	U.S. Marines Flatcar with 2 tanks (O27), *83–84*	13	21____
6573	Redwood Valley Express Log Dump Car (O27), *84–85*	8	13____
6574	Redwood Valley Express Crane Car (O27), *84–85*	7	13____
6575	Redwood Valley Express Flatcar with fences (O27), *84–85*	7	13____
6576	Santa Fe Crane Car (O27), *85–86, 92 u*	7	10____
6579	NYC Crane Car, *85–86*	36	44____
6585	PRR Flatcar with fences (O27), *86–90*	5	9____
6587	W&ARR Flatcar with horses, *86 u*	18	26____
6593	Santa Fe Crane Car (SSS), *86*	41	48____
6700	PFE Ice Car, *82–83*		70____
6900	N&W Extended Vision Caboose, *82*	60	65____
6901	Ontario Northland Extended Vision Caboose, *82 u*	44	55____
6903	Santa Fe Extended Vision Caboose, *83*	80	95____
6904	Union Pacific Extended Vision Caboose, *83*	115	135____
6905	NKP Extended Vision Caboose, *83 u*	50	65____
6906	Erie-Lack. Extended Vision Caboose, *84*	75	90____
6907	NYC Wood-sided Caboose (std O), *86 u*	90	92____
6908	PRR N5c Caboose (FARR 5), *84–85*	43	47____
6910	NYC Extended Vision Caboose, *84 u*	55	60____
6912	Redwood Valley Express SP-type Caboose, *84–85*	9	16____
6913	Burlington Northern Extended Vision Caboose, *85*	70	90____
6916	NYC Work Caboose, *85–86*	16	22____
6917	Jersey Central Extended Vision Caboose, *86*	36	50____

Exc Mint

		Exc	Mint
____**6918**	B&O SP-type Caboose, *86*	10	15
____**6919**	Nickel Plate Road SP-type Caboose, *86–91*	5	9
____**6920**	B&A Wood-sided Caboose (std O), *86 u*	65	80
____**6921**	PRR SP-type Caboose, *86–90*	5	9
____**7200**	Quicksilver Passenger Coach (027), *82–83*	26	34
____**7201**	Quicksilver Passenger Coach (027), *82–83*	26	34
____**7202**	Quicksilver Observation Car (027), *82–83*	26	34
____**7203**	N&W Diner "491," *82 u*	130	180
____**7204**	Southern Pacific Diner, *82 u*	190	235
____**7207**	NYC Diner, *83 u*	70	140
____**7208**	PRR Diner, *83 u*	80	90
____**7210**	Union Pacific Diner, *84*	85	110
____**7211**	Southern Pacific Vista Dome Car, *83 u*	145	185
____**7215**	B&O Passenger Coach, *83–84*	43	50
____**7216**	B&O Passenger Coach, *83–84*	43	50
____**7217**	B&O Baggage Car, *83–84*	43	50
____**7220**	Illinois Central Baggage Car, *85, 87*	105	135
____**7221**	Illinois Central Combination Car, *85, 87*	85	105
____**7222**	Illinois Central Passenger Coach, *85, 87*	85	105
____**7223**	Illinois Central Passenger Coach, *85, 87*	85	105
____**7224**	Illinois Central Diner, *85, 87*	75	90
____**7225**	Illinois Central Observation Car, *85, 87*	95	115
____**7227**	Wabash Diner (FF 1), *86–87*	115	130
____**7228**	Wabash Baggage Car (FF 1), *86–87*	90	100
____**7229**	Wabash Combination Car (FF 1), *86–87*	90	100
____**7230**	Wabash Passenger Coach (FF 1), *86–87*	90	100
____**7231**	Wabash Passenger Coach (FF 1), *86–87*	90	100
____**7232**	Wabash Observation Car (FF 1), *86–87*	85	95
____**7241**	W&ARR Passenger Coach, *86 u*	43	50
____**7242**	W&ARR Baggage Car, *86 u*	43	50
____**7301**	Norfolk & Western Stock Car, *82*	34	45
____**7302**	Texas & Pacific Stock Car (027), *83–84*	11	14
____**7303**	Erie Stock Car, *84*	41	50
____**7304**	Southern Stock Car (FARR 4), *83 u*	41	45
____**7309**	Southern Stock Car (027), *85–86*	12	16
____**7312**	W&ARR Stock Car (027), *86 u*	25	30
____**7401**	Chessie System Stock Car (027), *84–85*	13	17
____**7404**	Jersey Central Boxcar, *86*	26	40
____**7500**	Lionel 75th Anniversary U36B Diesel, *75–77*	127	147
____**7501**	Lionel 75th Anniversary Boxcar, *75–77*	24	34
____**7502**	Lionel 75th Anniversary Reefer, *75–77*	27	36
____**7503**	Lionel 75th Anniversary Reefer, *75–77*	32	43
7504____	Lionel 75th Anniversary Covered Quad Hopper, *75–77*	28	40
____**7505**	Lionel 75th Anniversary Boxcar, *75–77*	29	41
____**7506**	Lionel 75th Anniversary Boxcar, *75–77*	16	21
____**7507**	Lionel 75th Anniversary Reefer, *75–77*	27	39
____**7508**	Lionel 75th Anniversary N5c Caboose, *75–77*	24	29
____**7509**	Kentucky Fried Chicken Reefer, *81–82*	69	79
____**7510**	Red Lobster Reefer, *81–82*	64	72
____**7511**	Pizza Hut Reefer, *81–82*	64	72
____**7512**	Arthur Treacher's Reefer, *82*	62	69
____**7513**	Bonanza Reefer, *82*	63	71
____**7514**	Taco Bell Reefer, *82*	66	85
____**7515**	Denver Mint Car, *81*	64	81

		Exc	Mint	
7517	Philadelphia Mint Car, *82*	38	39	____
7518	Carson City Mint Car, *83*	34	43	____
7519	Toy Fair Reefer, *82 u*	35	42	____
7520	Nibco Express Boxcar, *82 u*	265	440	____
7521	Toy Fair Reefer, *83 u*	50	65	____
7522	New Orleans Mint Car, *84 u*	33	38	____
7523	Toy Fair Reefer, *84 u*	44	49	____
7524	Toy Fair Reefer, *85 u*	55	60	____
7525	Toy Fair Boxcar, *86 u*	65	80	____
7530	Dahlonega Mint Car, *86 u*	37	48	____
7600	Frisco "Spirit of '76" N5c Caboose, *74–76*	33	39	____
7601	Delaware Boxcar, *74–76*	14	19	____
7602	Pennsylvania Boxcar, *74–76*	17	27	____
7603	New Jersey Boxcar, *74–76*	15	24	____
7604	Georgia Boxcar, *74 u, 75–76*	22	26	____
7605	Connecticut Boxcar, *74 u, 75–76*	17	32	____
7606	Massachusetts Boxcar, *74 u, 75–76*	25	29	____
7607	Maryland Boxcar, *74 u, 75–76*	17	34	____
7608	South Carolina Boxcar, *75 u, 76*	38	50	____
7609	New Hampshire Boxcar, *75 u, 76*	38	46	____
7610	Virginia Boxcar, *75 u, 76*	155	200	____
7611	New York Boxcar, *75 u, 76*	50	65	____
7612	North Carolina Boxcar, *75 u, 76*	35	60	____
7613	Rhode Island Boxcar, *75 u, 76*	36	50	____
7700	Uncle Sam Boxcar, *75 u*	44	51	____
7701	Camel Boxcar, *76–77*	60	70	____
7702	Prince Albert Boxcar, *76–77*	62	78	____
7703	Beechnut Boxcar, *76–77*	33	51	____
7704	Toy Fair Boxcar, *76 u*	110	120	____
7705	Canadian Toy Fair Boxcar, *76 u*	130	145	____
7706	Sir Walter Raleigh Boxcar, *77–78*	63	71	____
7707	White Owl Boxcar, *77–78*	63	71	____
7708	Winston Boxcar, *77–78*	62	76	____
7709	Salem Boxcar, *78*	62	71	____
7710	Mail Pouch Boxcar, *78*	62	72	____
7711	El Producto Boxcar, *78*	58	71	____
7712	Santa Fe Boxcar (FARR 1), *79*	25	44	____
7800	Pepsi Boxcar, *76 u, 77*	74	82	____
7801	A&W Boxcar, *76 u, 77*	48	62	____
7802	Canada Dry Boxcar, *76 u, 77*	44	57	____
7803	Trains n' Truckin' Boxcar, *77 u*	20	26	____
7806	Season's Greetings Boxcar, *76 u*	70	95	____
7807	Toy Fair Boxcar, *77 u*	70	95	____
7808	Northern Pacific Stock Car, *77*	37	44	____
7809	Vernors Boxcar, *77 u, 78*	50	65	____
7810	Orange Crush Boxcar, *77 u, 78*	40	55	____
7811	Dr Pepper Boxcar, *77 u, 78*	48	63	____
7813	"Season's Greetings" Boxcar, *77 u*	65	90	____
7814	"Season's Greetings" Boxcar, *78 u*	70	95	____
7815	Toy Fair Boxcar, *78 u*	65	85	____
7816	Toy Fair Boxcar, *79 u*	65	85	____
7817	Toy Fair Boxcar, *80 u*	95	105	____
7900	D&RGW Operating Cowboy Car (O27), *82–83*	22	26	____
7901	LL Cop and Hobo Car (O27), *82–83*	24	27	____

			Exc	Mint
___	7902	Santa Fe Boxcar (027), *82–85*	5	9
___	7903	Rock Island Boxcar (027), *83*	8	13
___	7904	San Diego Zoo Giraffe Car (027), *83–84*	44	55
___	7905	Black Cave Boxcar (027), *82*	6	9
___	7908	Tappan Boxcar (027), *82 u*	39	55
___	7909	L&N Boxcar (027), *83–84*	40	49
___	7910	Chessie System Boxcar (027), *84–85*	18	23
___	7912	Toys "R" Us Giraffe Car (027), *82–84 u*	70	80
___	7913	Turtleback Zoo Giraffe Car (027), *85–86*	50	60
___	7914	Toys "R" Us Giraffe Car (027), *85–89 u*	70	90
___	7920	Sears Centennial Boxcar (027), *85–86 u*	39	44
___	7925	Erie-Lackawanna Boxcar (027), *86–90*	10	18
___	7926	NKP Boxcar (027), *86–91*	8	10
___	7930	True Value Boxcar (027), *86–87 u*	34	50
	7931	Town House TV and Appliances Boxcar (027), *86 u*	31	39
___	7932	Kay Bee Toys Boxcar (027), *86–87 u*	40	49
___	8001	NKP 2-6-4 Locomotive, *80 u*	55	65
___	8002	Union Pacific 2-8-4 Locomotive (FARR 2), *80*	310	345
___	8003	Chessie System 2-8-4 Locomotive, *80*	360	540
___	8004	Rock Island 4-4-0 Locomotive, *80–82*	190	220
___	8005	Santa Fe 4-4-0 Locomotive, *80–82*	65	75
___	8006	ACL 4-6-4 Locomotive, *80 u*	245	340
___	8007	NYNH&H 2-6-4 Locomotive, *80–81*	65	75
___	8008	Chessie System 4-4-2 Locomotive, *80*	65	75
___	8010	Santa Fe NW2 Switcher, *70, 71 u*	48	79
___	8020	Santa Fe Alco Diesel A Unit, *70–72, 74–76*	65	85
___	8020	Santa Fe Alco Diesel A Unit, dummy, *70*	45	60
___	8021	Santa Fe Alco Diesel B Unit, *71–72, 74–76*	47	70
___	8022	Santa Fe Alco Diesel A Unit, *71 u*	80	105
___	8025	CN Alco Diesel A Unit, *71–73 u*	85	105
___	8025	CN Alco Diesel A Unit, dummy, *71–73 u*	45	65
___	8030	Illinois Central GP9 Diesel, *70–72*	103	140
___	8031	Canadian National GP7 Diesel, *71–73 u*	80	150
___	8031	Illinois Central GP9 Diesel Dummy Unit, *70*		NRS
___	8040	Canadian National 2-4-2 Locomotive, *71 u*	43	85
___	8040	NKP 2-4-2 Locomotive, *70–72*	26	34
___	8041	NYC 2-4-2 Locomotive, *70*	55	65
___	8041	PRR 2-4-2 Locomotive, *71 u*	55	65
___	8042	GTW 2-4-2 Locomotive, *70, 71–73 u*	26	34
___	8043	NKP 2-4-2 Locomotive, *70 u*	45	65
___	8050	D&H U36C Diesel, *80*	105	220
___	8051	D&H U36C Diesel Dummy Unit, *80*	95	115
___	8054/55	Burlington F3 Diesel AA Set, *80*	360	385
___	8056	C&NW FM Train Master Diesel, *80*	175	225
___	8057	Burlington NW2 Switcher, *80*	100	115
___	8059	Pennsylvania F3 Diesel B Unit, *80 u*	190	290
___	8060	Pennsylvania F3 Diesel B Unit, *80 u*	335	420
___	8061	Chessie System U36C Diesel, *80*	110	140
___	8062	Burlington F3 Diesel B Unit, *80 u*	205	255
___	8063	Seaboard SD9 Diesel, *80*	80	100
___	8064	Florida East Coast GP9 Diesel, *80*	150	200
___	8065	Florida East Coast GP9 Diesel Dummy Unit, *80*	95	120
___	8066	TP&W GP20 Diesel, *80–81, 83 u*	65	80
___	8071	Virginian SD18 Diesel, *80 u*	135	155

Exc Mint

		Exc	Mint	
8072	Virginian SD18 Diesel Dummy Unit, *80 u*	75	110	___
8100	Norfolk & Western 4-8-4 "611," *81*	360	402	___
8101	Chicago & Alton 4-6-4 Locomotive "659," *81*	275	445	___
8102	Union Pacific 4-4-2 Locomotive, *81–82*	49	65	___
8104	Union Pacific 4-4-0 Locomotive "3," *81 u*	180	235	___
8111	DT&I NW2 Switcher, *71–74*	55	65	___
8140	Southern 2-4-0 Locomotive, *71 u*	22	30	___
8141	PRR 2-4-2 Locomotive, *71–72*	41	43	___
8142	C&O 4-4-2 Locomotive, *71–72*		55	___
8150	PRR GG1 Electric Locomotive "4935," *81*	330	395	___
8151	Burlington SD28 Diesel, *81*	120	145	___
8152	Canadian Pacific SD24 Diesel, *81*	170	180	___
8153	Reading NW2 Switcher, *81–82*	100	155	___
8154	Alaska NW2 Switcher, *81–82*	120	160	___
8155	Monon U36B Diesel, *81–82*	110	135	___
8156	Monon U36B Diesel Dummy Unit, *81–82*		65	___
8157	Santa Fe FM Train Master, *81*	280	325	___
8158	DM&IR GP35 Diesel, *81–82*	90	150	___
8159	DM&IR GP35 Diesel Dummy Unit, *81–82*	55	75	___
8160	Burger King GP20 Diesel, *81–82*	106	128	___
8161	L.A.S.E.R. Switcher, *81–82*	23	55	___
8162	Ontario Northland SD18 Diesel, *81 u*	150	210	___
8163	Ontario Northland SD18 Diesel Dummy Unit, *81 u*	95	140	___
8164	Pennsylvania F3 Diesel B Unit, *81 u*	340	370	___
8182	Nibco Express NW2 Switcher, *82 u*	90	130	___
8190	Diesel Horn Kit, *81 u*		30	___
8200	Kickapoo Dockside 0-4-0T, *72*	28	39	___
8203	PRR 2-4-2 Locomotive, *72, 74 u, 75*	26	34	___
8204	C&O 4-4-2 Locomotive, *72*	55	60	___
8206	NYC 4-6-4 Locomotive, *72–75*	140	155	___
8209	Pioneer Dockside 0-4-0T with tender, *72*	45	65	___
8209	Pioneer Dockside 0-4-0T, no tender, *73–76*	42	55	___
8210	Joshua L. Cowen 4-6-4 Locomotive, *82*	245	350	___
8212	Black Cave 0-4-0 Locomotive, *82*	30	49	___
8213	D&RGW 2-4-2 Locomotive, *82–83, 84–91 u*	65	70	___
8214	Pennsylvania 2-4-2 Locomotive, *82–83*	55	65	___
8215	Nickel Plate Road 2-8-4 Locomotive "779," *82 u*	245	285	___
8250	Santa Fe GP9 Diesel, *72, 74–75*	120	145	___
8251-50	Horn/Whistle Controller, *72–74*	1	2	___
8252	D&H Alco Diesel A Unit, *72*	85	125	___
8253	D&H Alco Diesel B Unit, *72*	50	70	___
8254	Illinois Central GP9 Diesel Dummy Unit, *72*	60	65	___
8255	Santa Fe GP9 Diesel Dummy Unit, *72*	60	65	___
8258	Canadian National GP7 Diesel Dummy Unit, *72–73 u*	65	85	___
8260/62	Southern Pacific F3 Diesel AA Set, *82*	490	520	___
8261	Southern Pacific F3 Diesel B Unit, *82 u*	435	445	___
8263	Santa Fe GP7 Diesel, *82*	65	80	___
8264	CP Vulcan Switcher Snowplow, *82*	80	100	___
8265	Santa Fe SD40 Diesel, *82*	205	225	___
8266	Norfolk & Western SD24 Diesel, *82*	150	225	___
8268	Quicksilver Alco Diesel A Unit, *82–83*	85	105	___
8269	Quicksilver Alco Diesel A Unit, dummy, *82–83*	55	65	___
8272	Pennsylvania EP-5 Electric Locomotive, *82 u*	205	265	___

		Exc	Mint
____8300	Santa Fe 2-4-0 Locomotive, *73–74*	22	25
____8302	Southern 2-4-0 Locomotive, *73–76*	29	30
____8303	Jersey Central 2-4-2 Locomotive, *73–74*	55	59
____8304	B&O 4-4-2 Locomotive, *75*	75	105
____8304	C&O 4-4-2 Locomotive, *75–77*	75	105
____8304	Pennsylvania 4-4-2 Locomotive, *74–75*	75	105
____8304	Rock Island 4-4-2 Locomotive, *73–75*	85	105
____8305	Milwaukee Road 4-4-2 Locomotive, *73*	95	120
____8307	Southern Pacific 4-8-4 Locomotive "4449," *83*	490	560
____8308	Jersey Central 2-4-2 Locomotive, *73–74 u*	36	43
____8309	Southern 2-8-2 Locomotive "4501" (FARR 4), *83*	385	495
____8310	Jersey Central 2-4-0 Locomotive, *74–75 u*	26	50
____8310	Nickel Plate Road 2-4-0 Locomotive, *73 u*	26	50
____8310	Santa Fe 2-4-0 Locomotive, *74–75 u*	26	34
____8311	Southern 0-4-0 Locomotive, *73 u*	26	34
____8313	Santa Fe 0-4-0 Locomotive, *83–84*	13	17
____8314	Southern 2-4-0 Locomotive, *83–85*	17	21
____8315	B&O 4-4-0 Locomotive, *83–84*	85	120
____8341	ACL SP-type Caboose, *86 u, 87–90*	6	8
____8350	U.S. Steel Switcher, *73–75*	18	26
____8351	Santa Fe Alco Diesel A Unit, *73–75*	60	65
____8352	Santa Fe GP20 Diesel, *73–75*	65	105
____8353	Grand Trunk Western GP7 Diesel, *73–75*	90	120
____8354	Erie NW2 Switcher, *73, 75*	80	105
____8355	Santa Fe GP20 Diesel Dummy Unit, *73–74*	65	90
8356 ____	Grand Trunk Western GP7 Diesel Dummy Unit, *73–75*	65	75
____8357	PRR GP9 Diesel, *73–75*	100	120
____8358	PRR GP9 Diesel Dummy Unit, *73–75*	55	100
____8359	Chessie System GP7 Diesel "GM50," *73*	95	120
____8360	Long Island GP20 Diesel, *73–74*	70	105
____8361	Western Pacific Alco Diesel A Unit, *73–75*	50	70
____8362	Western Pacific Alco Diesel B Unit, *73–75*	45	65
____8363	B&O F3 Diesel A Unit, *73–75*	280	310
____8364	B&O F3 Diesel A Unit, dummy, *73–75*	120	160
____8365/66	CP F3 Diesel AA Set (SSS), *73*	355	405
____8367	Long Island GP20 Diesel Dummy Unit, *73–75*	80	100
____8368	Alaska Vulcan Switcher, *83*	120	129
____8369	Erie-Lackawanna GP20 Diesel, *83–85*	125	140
____8370/72	NYC F3 Diesel AA Set, *83*	330	435
____8371	NYC F3 Diesel B Unit, *83*	105	150
____8374	Burlington Northern NW2 Switcher, *83–85*	105	110
____8375	C&NW GP7 Diesel, *83–85*	135	165
____8376	Union Pacific SD40 Diesel, *83*	175	200
____8377	U.S. Marines Switcher, *83–84*	55	65
____8378	Wabash FM Train Master Diesel "550," *83 u*	500	690
____8379	PRR Fire Car, *83 u*	80	100
____8380	Lionel Lines SD28 Diesel, *83 u*	235	315
____8402	Reading 4-4-2 Locomotive, *84–85*	47	55
____8403	Chessie System 4-4-2 Locomotive, *84–85*	55	65
____8404	PRR 6-8-6 "6200" (FARR 5), *84–85*	360	460
____8406	NYC 4-6-4 Locomotive "783," *84*	445	571
8410 ____	Redwood Valley Express 4-4-0 Locomotive, *84–85*	34	50
____8452	Erie Alco Diesel A Unit, *74–75*	75	95

		Exc	Mint	
8453	Erie Alco Diesel B Unit, *74–75*	55	75	___
8454	D&RGW GP7 Diesel, *74–75*	80	110	___
8455	D&RGW GP7 Diesel Dummy Unit, *74–75*	50	85	___
8458	Erie-Lackawanna SD40 Diesel, *84*	160	190	___
8459	D&RGW Vulcan Rotary Snowplow, *84*	125	146	___
8460	MKT NW2 Switcher, *74–75*	45	65	___
8463	Chessie System GP20 Diesel, *74 u*	130	190	___
8464/65	D&RGW F3 Diesel AA Set (SSS), *74*	220	325	___
8466	Amtrak F3 Diesel A Unit, *74–76*	225	250	___
8467	Amtrak F3 Diesel A Unit, dummy, *74–76*	80	90	___
8468	B&O F3 Diesel B Unit, *74–75*	95	100	___
8469	CP F3 Diesel B Unit (SSS), *74*	85	110	___
8470	Chessie System U36B Diesel, *74*	80	110	___
8471	Pennsylvania NW2 Switcher, *74–76*	170	195	___
8473	Coca-Cola NW2 Switcher, *74 u, 75*	109	128	___
8474	D&RGW F3 Diesel B Unit (SSS), *74*	95	110	___
8475	Amtrak F3 Diesel B Unit, *74*	85	105	___
8477	NYC GP9 Diesel, *84 u*	150	205	___
8480/82	Union Pacific F3 Diesel AA Set, *84*	280	365	___
8481	Union Pacific F3 Diesel B Unit, *84*	150	155	___
8485	USMC NW2 Switcher, *84–85*	105	135	___
8500	Pennsylvania 2-4-0 Locomotive, *75–76*	17	21	___
8502	Santa Fe 2-4-0 Locomotive, *75*	17	21	___
8506	PRR 0-4-0 Locomotive, *75–77*	75	90	___
8507	Santa Fe 2-4-0 Locomotive, *75 u*	25	30	___
8512	Santa Fe 0-4-0T Locomotive, *85–86*	22	30	___
8516	NYC 0-4-0 Locomotive, *85–86*	115	140	___
8550	Jersey Central GP9 Diesel, *75–76*	120	155	___
8551	Pennsylvania EP-5 Electric Locomotive, *75–76*	115	120	___
8552/53/54	SP Alco Diesel ABA Set, *75–76*	200	245	___
8555/57	Milwaukee Road F3 Diesel AA Set (SSS), *75*	240	315	___
8556	Chessie System NW2 Switcher, *75–76*	160	200	___
8558	Milwaukee Road EP-5 Electric Locomotive, *76–77*	160	195	___
8559	N&W GP9 Diesel "1776," *75*	115	145	___
8560	Chessie System U36B Diesel Dummy Unit, *75*	85	130	___
8561	Jersey Central GP9 Diesel Dummy Unit, *75–76*	70	95	___
8562	Missouri Pacific GP20 Diesel, *75–76*	130	145	___
8563	Rock Island Alco Diesel A Unit, *75–76 u*	65	90	___
8564	Union Pacific U36B Diesel, *75*	110	155	___
8565	Missouri Pacific GP20 Diesel Dummy Unit, *75–76*	55	70	___
8566	Southern F3 Diesel A Unit, *75–77*	220	370	___
8567	Southern F3 Diesel A Unit, dummy, *75–77*	105	135	___
8568	Preamble Express F3 Diesel A Unit, *75 u*	90	115	___
8569	Soo Line NW2 Switcher, *75–77*	60	65	___
8570	Liberty Special Alco Diesel A Unit, *75 u*	75	90	___
8571	Frisco U36B Diesel, *75–76*	75	95	___
8572	Frisco U36B Diesel Dummy Unit, *75–76*	20	55	___
8573	Union Pacific U36B Diesel Dummy Unit, *75 u*	145	190	___
8575	Milwaukee Road F3 Diesel B Unit (SSS), *75*	105	160	___
8576	Penn Central GP7 Diesel, *75 u, 76–77*	90	120	___
8578	NYC Ballast Tamper, *85, 87*	85	90	___
8580/82	Illinois Central F3 Diesel AA Set, *85, 87*	420	485	___
8581	Illinois Central F3 Diesel B Unit, *85, 87*	130	155	___
8585	Burlington Northern SD40 Diesel, *85*	355	385	___

		Exc	Mint
___8587	Wabash GP9 Diesel "484," *85 u*	250	280
___8600	NYC 4-6-4 Locomotive, *76*	175	195
___8601	Rock Island 0-4-0 Locomotive, *76–77*	17	21
___8602	D&RGW 2-4-0 Locomotive, *76–78*	22	26
___8603	C&O 4-6-4 Locomotive, *76–77*	135	190
___8604	Jersey Central 2-4-2 Locomotive, *76 u*	39	44
___8606	B&A 4-6-4 Locomotive "784," *86 u*	720	760
___8610	Wabash 4-6-2 "672" (FF 1), *86–87*	435	610
___8615	L&N 2-8-4 Locomotive "1970," *86 u*	540	630
___8616	Santa Fe 4-4-2 Locomotive, *86*	60	65
___8617	Nickel Plate Road 4-4-2 Locomotive, *86–91*	60	65
___8625	Pennsylvania 2-4-0 Locomotive, *86–90*	21	34
___8630	W&ARR 4-4-0 Locomotive "3," *86 u*	125	150
___8635	Santa Fe 0-4-0 (SSS), *86*	80	100
___8650	Burlington Northern U36B Diesel, *76–77*	120	170
8651	Burlington Northern U36B Diesel Dummy Unit, *76–77*	70	90
___8652	Santa Fe F3 Diesel A Unit, *76–77*	260	510
___8653	Santa Fe F3 Diesel A Unit, dummy, *76–77*	135	160
___8654	Boston & Maine GP9 Diesel, *76–77*	155	195
___8655	Boston & Maine GP9 Diesel Dummy Unit, *76–77*	90	110
___8656	Canadian National Alco Diesel A Unit, *76*	150	195
___8657	Canadian National Alco Diesel B Unit, *76*	60	75
___8658	CN Alco Diesel A Unit, dummy, *76*	85	170
___8659	Virginian Electric Locomotive, *76–77*	125	137
___8660	CP Rail NW2 Switcher, *76–77*	100	135
___8661	Southern F3 Diesel B Unit, *76*	165	170
___8662	B&O GP7 Diesel, *86*	120	130
___8664	Amtrak Alco Diesel A Unit, *76–77*	85	120
___8665	BAR Jeremiah O'Brien GP9 Diesel "1776," *76 u*	100	170
___8666	Northern Pacific GP9 Diesel (SSS), *76*	125	175
___8667	Amtrak Alco Diesel B Unit, *76–77*	60	80
8668	Northern Pacific GP9 Diesel Dummy Unit (SSS), *76*	100	130
___8669	Illinois Central Gulf U36B Diesel, *76–77*	125	165
___8670	Chessie System Switcher, *76*	30	55
___8679	Northern Pacific GP20 Diesel, *86*	90	105
___8687	Jersey Central FM Train Master Diesel, *86*	198	276
___8690	Lionel Lines Trolley, *86*	105	115
___8701	W&ARR 4-4-0 Locomotive "3," *77–79*	157	210
___8702	Southern 4-6-4 Locomotive, *77–78*	280	398
___8703	Wabash 2-4-2 Locomotive, *77*	22	30
___8750	Rock Island GP7 Diesel, *77–78*	110	125
___8751	Rock Island GP7 Diesel Dummy Unit, *77–78*	50	70
___8753	Pennsylvania GG1 Electric Locomotive, *77 u*	290	315
___8754	New Haven Electric Locomotive, *77–78*	100	115
___8755	Santa Fe U36B Diesel, *77–78*	130	150
___8756	Santa Fe U36B Diesel Dummy Unit, *77–78*	75	95
___8757	Conrail GP9 Diesel, *76 u, 77–78*	110	140
___8758	Southern GP7 Diesel Dummy Unit, *77 u, 78*	75	95
___8759	Erie-Lackawanna GP9 Diesel, *77–79*	115	175
8760	Erie-Lackawanna GP9 Diesel Dummy Unit, *77–79*	95	115
___8761	GTW NW2 Switcher, *77–78*	95	130
___8762	Great Northern EP-5 Electric Locomotive, *77–78*	130	140

		Exc	Mint	
8763	Norfolk & Western GP9 Diesel, *76 u, 77–78*	110	120	____
8764	B&O Budd RDC Passenger (SSS), *77*	110	135	____
8765	B&O Budd RDC Baggage Dummy Unit (SSS), *77*	80	100	____
8766	B&O Budd RDC Baggage (SSS), *77*		310	____
8767	B&O Budd RDC Passenger Dummy Unit (SSS), *77*	85	105	____
8768	B&O Budd RDC Passenger Dummy Unit (SSS), *77*	85	105	____
8769	Republic Steel Switcher, *77–78*	22	39	____
8770	NW2 Switcher, *77–78*		65	____
8771	Great Northern U36B Diesel, *77*	110	140	____
8772	GM&O GP20 Diesel, *77*	85	95	____
8773	Mickey Mouse U36B Diesel, *77–78*	493	645	____
8774	Southern GP7 Diesel, *77 u, 78*	110	135	____
8775	Lehigh Valley GP9 Diesel, *77 u, 78*	85	105	____
8776	C&NW GP20 Diesel, *77 u, 78*	87	129	____
8777	Santa Fe F3 Diesel B Unit (SSS), *77*	160	175	____
8778	Lehigh Valley GP9 Diesel Dummy Unit, *77 u, 78*	90	110	____
8779	C&NW GP20 Diesel Dummy Unit, *77 u, 78*	73	109	____
8800	Lionel Lines 4-4-2 Locomotive, *78–81*	75	105	____
8801	Blue Comet 4-6-4 Locomotive, *78–80*	380	500	____
8803	Santa Fe 0-4-0 Locomotive, *78*	14	24	____
8850	Penn Central GG1 Electric Locomotive, *78 u, 79*	250	305	____
8851/52	New Haven F3 Diesel AA Set, *78 u, 79*	320	430	____
8854	CP Rail GP9 Diesel, *78–79*	100	120	____
8855	Milwaukee Road SD18 Diesel, *78*		115	____
8857	Northern Pacific U36B Diesel, *78–80*	140	180	____
8858	Northern Pacific U36B Diesel Dummy Unit, *78–80*	55	85	____
8859	Conrail Electric Locomotive, *78–82*	105	150	____
8860	Rock Island NW2 Switcher, *78–79*	85	100	____
8861	Santa Fe Alco Diesel A Unit, *78–79*	65	85	____
8862	Santa Fe Alco Diesel B Unit, *78–79*	36	43	____
8864	New Haven F3 Diesel B Unit, *78*	85	105	____
8866	M&StL GP9 Diesel (SSS), *78*	85	120	____
8867	M&StL GP9 Diesel Dummy Unit (SSS), *78*	65	95	____
8868	Amtrak Budd RDC Baggage, *78, 80*	195	235	____
8869	Amtrak Budd RDC Passenger Dummy Unit, *78, 80*	75	95	____
8870	Amtrak Budd RDC Passenger Dummy Unit, *78, 80*	85	115	____
8871	Amtrak Budd RDC Baggage Dummy Unit, *78, 80*	85	105	____
8872	Santa Fe SD18 Diesel, *78 u*	125	155	____
8873	Santa Fe SD18 Diesel Dummy Unit, *78 u*	60	85	____
8900	Santa Fe 4-6-4 Locomotive (FARR 1), *79*	270	310	____
8902	ACL 2-4-0 Locomotive, *79–82, 86 u, 87–90*	13	17	____
8903	D&RGW 2-4-2 Locomotive, *79–81*	17	21	____
8904	Wabash 2-4-2 Locomotive, *79, 81 u*	30	34	____
8905	Smokey Mountain Dockside 0-4-0T Locomotive, *79*	9	17	____
8950	Virginian FM Train Master Diesel, *79*	230	285	____
8951	Southern Pacific FM Train Master Diesel, *79*	237	335	____
8952/53	PRR F3 Diesel AA Set, *79*	350	500	____
8955	Southern U36B Diesel, *79*	120	195	____
8956	Southern U36B Diesel Dummy Unit, *79*	80	125	____
8957	Burlington Northern GP20 Diesel, *79*	120	150	____
8958	Burlington Northern GP20 Diesel Dummy Unit, *79*	85	90	____

		Exc	Mint
___8960	Southern Pacific U36C Diesel, *79 u*	130	180
___8961	Southern Pacific U36C Diesel Dummy Unit, *79 u*	70	80
___8962	Reading U36B Diesel, *79*	115	130
___8970/71	PRR F3 Diesel AA Set, *79 u, 80*	330	425
___9001	Conrail Boxcar (027), *86–87 u, 88–90*	5	10
___9010	GN Hopper (027), *70–71*	6	8
___9011	GN Hopper (027), *70 u, 75–76, 78–83*	8	10
___9012	TA&G Hopper (027), *71–72*	7	8
___9013	Canadian National Hopper (027), *72–76*	5	8
___9015	Reading Hopper (027), *73–75*	17	21
9016	Chessie System Hopper (027), *75–79, 87–88, 89 u*	4	6
___9017	Wabash Gondola with canisters (027), *78–82*	3	5
___9018	DT&I Hopper (027), *78–79, 81–82*	6	7
___9019	Flatcar (027), *78*	2	3
___9020	Union Pacific Flatcar (027), *70–78*	3	5
___9021	Santa Fe Work Caboose, *70–71, 73–75*	9	13
___9022	Santa Fe Bulkhead Flatcar (027), *70–72, 75–79*	7	13
___9023	MKT Bulkhead Flatcar (027), *73–74*	7	10
___9024	C&O Flatcar (027), *73–75*	3	6
___9025	DT&I Work Caboose, *71–74, 77–78*	8	10
___9026	Republic Steel Flatcar (027), *75–82*	5	7
___9027	Soo Line Work Caboose, *75–76*	7	9
___9030	Kickapoo Gondola (027), *72, 79*	5	9
9031	NKP Gondola with canisters (027), *73–75, 82–83, 84–91 u*	4	8
___9032	SP Gondola with canisters (027), *75–78*		3
9033	PC Gondola with canisters (027), *76–78, 82, 86 u, 87–90, 92 u*		3
___9034	Lionel Leisure Hopper (027), *77 u*	30	34
___9035	Conrail Boxcar (027), *78–82*	5	12
___9036	Mobilgas 1-D Tank Car (027), *78–82*	7	19
___9037	Conrail Boxcar (027), *78 u, 80*	7	10
___9038	Chessie System Hopper (027), *78 u, 80*	15	19
___9039	Mobilgas 1-D Tank Car (027), *78 u, 80*	10	15
___9040	General Mills Wheaties Boxcar (027), *70–72*	9	13
___9041	Hershey's Boxcar (027), *70–71, 73–76*	16	25
___9042	Ford-Autolite Boxcar (027), *71 u, 72 74–76*	13	21
___9043	Erie-Lackawanna Boxcar (027), *73–75*	13	20
___9044	D&RGW Boxcar (027), *75–76*	5	8
___9045	Toys "R" Us Boxcar (027), *75 u*	35	42
___9046	True Value Boxcar (027), *76 u*	26	34
___9047	Toys "R" Us Boxcar (027), *76 u*	40	43
___9048	Toys "R" Us Boxcar (027), *76 u*	33	41
___9049	Toys "R" Us Boxcar (027), *78 u*		NRS
___9050	Sunoco 1-D Tank Car (027), *70–71*	17	23
___9051	Firestone 1-D Tank Car (027), *74–75, 78*	15	19
___9052	Toys "R" Us Boxcar (027), *77 u*	26	34
___9053	True Value Boxcar (027), *77 u*	28	40
___9054	JCPenney Boxcar (027), *77 u*	14	19
___9055	Republic Steel Gondola with canisters, *78 u*	9	10
___9057	CP Rail SP-type Caboose, *78–79*	10	15
___9058	Lionel Lines SP-type Caboose, *78–79, 83*	5	7
___9059	Lionel Lines SP-type Caboose, *79 u, 81 u*	7	9
___9060	Nickel Plate Road SP-type Caboose, *70–72*	5	7

		Exc	Mint
9061	Santa Fe SP-type Caboose, *70–76*	5	8____
9062	Penn Central SP-type Caboose, *70–72, 74–76*	7	9____
9063	GTW SP-type Caboose, *70, 71–73 u*	15	19____
9064	C&O SP-type Caboose, *71–72, 75–77*	7	10____
9065	Canadian National SP-type Caboose, *71–73 u*	19	24____
9066	Southern SP-type Caboose, *73–76*	7	9____
9067	Kickapoo Valley Bobber Caboose, *72*	6	9____
9068	Reading Bobber Caboose, *73–76*	5	7____
9069	Jersey Central SP-type Caboose, *73–74, 75–76 u*	5	8____
9070	Rock Island SP-type Caboose, *73–74*	13	17____
9071	Santa Fe Bobber Caboose, *74 u, 77–78*	7	9____
9073	Coca-Cola SP-type Caboose, *74 u, 75*	30	35____
9075	Rock Island SP-type Caboose, *75–76 u*	13	17____
9076	"We The People" SP-type Caboose, *75 u*	19	28____
9077	D&RGW SP-type Caboose, *76–83, 84–91 u*	7	8____
9078	Rock Island Bobber Caboose, *76–77*	5	7____
9079	GTW Hopper (O27), *77*	28	32____
9080	Wabash SP-type Caboose, *77*	9	10____
9085	Santa Fe Work Caboose, *79–82*	4	5____
9090	General Mills Mini-Max Car, *71*	27	32____
9106	Miller Vat Car, *84–85*	33	52____
9107	Dr Pepper Vat Car, *86–87*	30	36____
9110	B&O Quad Hopper, *71*	25	30____
9111	N&W Quad Hopper, *72–75*	15	20____
9112	D&RGW Covered Quad Hopper, *73–75*	20	23____
9113	Norfolk & Western Quad Hopper (SSS), *73*	27	32____
9114	Morton Salt Covered Quad Hopper, *74–76*	18	27____
9115	Planter's Covered Quad Hopper, *74–76*	21	33____
9116	Domino Sugar Covered Quad Hopper, *74–76*	22	29____
9117	Alaska Covered Quad Hopper (SSS), *74–76*	29	33____
9119	Detroit & Mackinac Covered Hopper, *75 u*		20____
9120	Northern Pacific Flatcar with trailers, *70–71*	33	38____
9121	L&N Flatcar with bulldozer and scraper, *71–79*	47	54____
9122	Northern Pacific Flatcar with trailers, *72–75*	19	32____
9123	C&O Auto Carrier, 3-tier, *72 u, 73–74*	18	27____
9124	P&LE Flatcar with logs, *73–74*	18	25____
9125	Norfolk & Western Auto Carrier, 2-tier, *73–77*	23	28____
9126	C&O Auto Carrier, 3-tier, *73–75*	23	34____
9128	Heinz Vat Car, *74–76*	25	34____
9129	N&W Auto Carrier, 3-tier, *75–76*	17	19____
9130	B&O Quad Hopper, *70*	23	24____
9131	D&RGW Gondola with canisters, *73–77*	5	8____
9132	Libby's Vat Car (SSS), *75–77*	16	23____
9133	BN Flatcar with trailers, *76–77, 80*	20	28____
9134	Virginian Covered Quad Hopper, *76–77*		32____
9135	N&W Covered Quad Hopper, *70 u, 71, 75*	17	26____
9136	Republic Steel Gondola with canisters, *72–76, 79*	9	11____
9138	Sunoco 3-D Tank Car (SSS), *78*	33	37____
9139	PC Auto Carrier, 3-tier, *76–77*	21	29____
9140	Burlington Gondola with canisters, *70, 73–82, 87–89*	7	9____
9141	BN Gondola with canisters, *70–72*	8	10____
9143	CN Gondola with canisters, *71–73 u*	30	34____

		Exc	Mint
___9144	D&RGW Gondola with canisters (SSS), *74–76*	9	13
___9145	ICG Auto Carrier, 3-tier, *77–80*	21	29
___9146	Mogen David Vat Car, *77–81*	21	26
___9147	Texaco 1-D Tank Car, *77–78*	46	63
___9148	Du Pont 3-D Tank Car, *77–81*	25	28
___9149	CP Rail Flatcar with trailers, *77–78*	22	35
___9150	Gulf 1-D Tank Car, *70 u, 71*	22	28
___9151	Shell 1-D Tank Car, *72*	27	31
___9152	Shell 1-D Tank Car, *73–76*	25	34
___9153	Chevron 1-D Tank Car, *74–76*	28	35
___9154	Borden 1-D Tank Car, *75–76*	33	47
___9156	Mobilgas 1-D Tank Car, *76–77*	30	40
___9157	C&O Crane Car, *76–78, 81–82*	35	44
___9158	PC Flatcar with shovel, *76–77, 80*	40	55
___9159	Sunoco 1-D Tank Car, *76*	35	50
___9160	Illinois Central N5c Caboose, *70–72*	17	23
___9161	CN N5c Caboose, *72–74*	14	25
___9162	PRR N5c Caboose, *72–76*	25	30
___9163	Santa Fe N5c Caboose, *73–76*	17	24
___9165	Canadian Pacific N5c Caboose (SSS), *73*	21	30
___9166	D&RGW SP-type Caboose (SSS), *74–75*	20	25
___9167	Chessie System N5c Caboose, *74–76*	24	31
___9168	Union Pacific N5c Caboose, *75–77*	17	19
___9169	Milwaukee Road SP-type Caboose (SSS), *75*	16	19
___9170	N&W N5c Caboose "1776," *75*	27	30
___9171	MP SP-type Caboose, *75 u, 76–77*	19	20
___9172	Penn Central SP-type Caboose, *75 u, 76–77*	23	31
___9173	Jersey Central SP-type Caboose, *75 u, 76–77*	22	33
___9174	NYC (P&E) Bay Window Caboose, *76*	65	70
___9175	Virginian N5c Caboose, *76–77*	24	26
___9176	BAR N5c Caboose, *76 u*	17	30
___9177	Northern Pacific Bay Window Caboose (SSS), *76*	25	35
___9178	ICG SP-type Caboose, *76–77*	19	24
___9179	Chessie System Bobber Caboose, *76*	7	11
___9180	Rock Island N5c Caboose, *77–78*	12	23
___9181	B&M N5c Caboose, *76 u, 77*	39	49
___9182	N&W N5c Caboose, *76 u, 77–80*	20	26
___9183	Mickey Mouse N5c Caboose, *77–78*	32	50
___9184	Erie Bay Window Caboose, *77–78*	24	30
___9185	GTW N5c Caboose, *77*	21	28
___9186	Conrail N5c Caboose, *76 u, 77–78*	27	29
___9187	Gulf, Mobile & Ohio SP-type Caboose, *77*	10	16
___9188	GN Bay Window Caboose, *77*	22	27
___9189	Gulf 1-D Tank Car, *77*	40	60
___9193	Budweiser Vat Car, *83–84*	92	121
___9200	Illinois Central Boxcar, *70–71*	19	25
___9201	Penn Central Boxcar, *70*	17	25
___9202	Santa Fe Boxcar, *70*	20	24
___9203	Union Pacific Boxcar, *70*		21
___9204	Northern Pacific Boxcar, *70*		21
___9205	Norfolk & Western Boxcar, *70*	22	25
___9206	Great Northern Boxcar, *70–71*		20
___9207	Soo Line Boxcar, *71*	11	18
___9208	CP Rail Boxcar, *71*	21	23

		Exc	Mint
9209	Burlington Northern Boxcar, *71–72*	16	21____
9210	B&O DD Boxcar, *71*	16	20____
9211	Penn Central Boxcar, *71*	17	28____
9213	M&StL Covered Quad Hopper (SSS), *78*	20	29____
9214	Northern Pacific Boxcar, *71–72*	16	21____
9215	Norfolk & Western Boxcar, *71*	19	24____
9216	Great Northern Auto Carrier, 3-tier, *78*	25	39____
9217	Soo Line Operating Boxcar, *82–84*	29	36____
9218	Monon Operating Boxcar, *81*	25	30____
9219	Missouri Pacific Operating Boxcar, *83*	27	33____
9220	Borden Operating Milk Car, *83–86*	95	113____
9221	Poultry Dispatch Operating Chicken Car, *83–85*	45	50____
9222	L&N Flatcar with trailers, *83–84*	38	60____
9223	Reading Operating Boxcar, *84*	33	40____
9224	Churchill Downs Operating Horse Car, *84–86*	85	110____
9225	Conrail Operating Barrel Car, *84*	42	55____
9226	Delaware & Hudson Flatcar with trailers, *84–85*	31	34____
9228	Canadian Pacific Operating Boxcar, *86*	24	37____
9229	Express Mail Operating Boxcar, *85–86*	21	27____
9230	Monon Boxcar (SSS), *71, 72 u*	17	24____
9231	Reading Bay Window Caboose, *79*	24	32____
9232	Allis-Chalmers Condenser Car, *80–81, 83 u*	42	50____
9233	Depressed Center Flatcar with transformer, *80*	55	65____
9234	Radioactive Waste Car, *80*	53	78____
9235	Union Pacific Derrick Car, *83–84*	16	22____
9236	C&NW Derrick Car, *83–85*	22	30____
9238	Northern Pacific Log Dump Car, *84*	16	24____
9239	Lionel Lines N5c Caboose, *83 u*	50	60____
9240	NYC Hopper (O27), *87 u*	20	29____
9240	NYC Operating Hopper, *86*	32	39____
9241	PRR Log Dump Car, *85–86*	21	27____
9250	WaterPoxy 3-D Tank Car, *70–71*	23	34____
9260	Reynolds Aluminum Covered Quad Hopper, *75–77*	19	22____
9261	Sun-Maid Raisins Covered Quad Hopper, *75 u, 76*	22	29____
9262	Ralston Purina Covered Quad Hopper, *75 u, 76*	36	58____
9263	PRR Covered Quad Hopper, *75 u, 76–77*	23	30____
9264	Illinois Central Covered Quad Hopper, *75 u, 76–77*	28	39____
9265	Chessie System Covered Quad Hopper, *75 u, 76–77*	21	27____
9266	Southern "Big John" Covered Quad Hopper, *76*	46	65____
9267	Alcoa Covered Quad Hopper (SSS), *76*	20	25____
9268	Northern Pacific Bay Window Caboose, *77 u*	33	40____
9269	Milwaukee Road Bay Window Caboose, *78*	34	47____
9270	Northern Pacific N5c Caboose, *78*	14	27____
9271	M&StL Bay Window Caboose (SSS), *78–79*	18	30____
9272	New Haven Bay Window Caboose, *78–80*	20	34____
9273	Southern Bay Window Caboose, *78 u*	36	45____
9274	Santa Fe Bay Window Caboose, *78 u*	40	47____
9276	Peabody Quad Hopper, *78*	19	28____
9277	Cities Service 1-D Tank Car, *78*	41	45____
9278	Life Savers 1-D Tank Car, *78–79*	112	152____
9279	Magnolia 3-D Tank Car, *78, 79 u*	13	19____

		Exc	Mint
____**9280**	Santa Fe Operating Stock Car (O27), *77–81*	20	24
____**9281**	Santa Fe Auto Carrier, 3-tier, *78–80*	21	27
____**9282**	GN Flatcar with trailers, *78–79, 81–82*	22	28
____**9283**	Union Pacific Gondola with canisters, *77*	15	21
____**9284**	Santa Fe Gondola with canisters, *77*	16	27
____**9285**	ICG Flatcar with trailers, *77*	47	48
____**9286**	B&LE Covered Quad Hopper, *77*	14	26
____**9287**	Southern N5c Caboose, *77 u, 78*	18	30
____**9288**	Lehigh Valley N5c Caboose, *77 u, 78, 80*	25	31
____**9289**	C&NW N5c Caboose, *77 u, 78, 80*	25	36
____**9290**	Union Pacific Operating Barrel Car, *83*	65	75
____**9300**	PC Log Dump Car, *70–75, 77*	18	24
____**9301**	U.S. Mail Operating Boxcar, *73–84*	32	42
____**9302**	L&N Searchlight Car, *72 u, 73–78*	21	24
____**9303**	Union Pacific Log Dump Car, *74–78, 80*	17	22
____**9304**	C&O Coal Dump Car, *74–78*	11	23
____**9305**	Santa Fe Operating Cowboy Car (O27), *80–82*	16	23
____**9306**	Santa Fe Flatcar with horses, *80–82*	18	26
____**9307**	Erie Animated Gondola, *80–84*	55	70
____**9308**	Aquarium Car, *81–84*	125	129
____**9309**	TP&W Bay Window Caboose, *80–81, 83 u*	19	25
____**9310**	Santa Fe Log Dump Car, *78 u, 79–83*	13	24
____**9311**	Union Pacific Coal Dump Car, *78 u, 79–82*	13	24
____**9312**	Conrail Searchlight Car, *78 u, 79–83*	18	27
____**9313**	Gulf 3-D Tank Car, *79 u*	43	50
____**9315**	Southern Pacific Gondola with canisters, *79 u*	16	23
____**9316**	Southern Pacific Bay Window Caboose, *79 u*	47	50
____**9317**	Santa Fe Bay Window Caboose, *79*	21	36
____**9320**	Fort Knox Mint Car, *79 u*	110	135
____**9321**	Santa Fe 1-D Tank Car (FARR 1), *79*	25	31
____**9322**	Santa Fe Covered Quad Hopper (FARR 1), *79*	30	38
____**9323**	Santa Fe Bay Window Caboose (FARR 1), *79*	39	49
____**9324**	Tootsie Roll 1-D Tank Car, *79–81*	67	96
____**9325**	Norfolk & Western Flatcar with fences, *79–81 u*	6	10
9326	Burlington Northern Bay Window Caboose, *79–80*	34	44
____**9327**	Bakelite 3-D Tank Car, *80*	19	29
____**9328**	Chessie System Bay Window Caboose, *80*	33	42
____**9329**	Chessie System Crane Car, *80*	40	47
____**9330**	Kickapoo Dump Car, *72, 79*	3	7
____**9331**	Union 76 1-D Tank Car, *79*	39	44
____**9332**	Reading Crane Car, *79*	37	50
____**9333**	Southern Pacific Flatcar with trailers, *79–80*	33	47
____**9334**	Humble 1-D Tank Car, *79*	21	26
____**9335**	B&O Log Dump Car, *86*	16	22
____**9336**	CP Rail Gondola with canisters, *79*	20	29
____**9338**	Pennsylvania Power & Light Quad Hopper, *79*	60	75
____**9339**	GN Boxcar (O27), *79–83, 85 u, 86*	7	10
9340	Illinois Central Gondola with canisters (O27), *79–81, 82 u, 83*	5	9
____**9341**	ACL SP-type Caboose, *79–82, 86 u 87–90*	6	8
____**9344**	Citgo 3-D Tank Car, *80*	23	38
____**9345**	Reading Searchlight Car, *84–85*	20	25
____**9346**	Wabash SP-type Caboose, *79*	6	10
____**9348**	Santa Fe Crane Car (FARR 1), *79 u*	60	70

		Exc	Mint
9349	San Francisco Mint Car, *80*	55	70____
9351	PRR Auto Carrier, 3-tier, *80*	23	40____
9352	Trailer Train Flatcar with C&NW trailers, *80*	29	55____
9353	Crystal Line 3-D Tank Car, *80*	18	26____
9354	Pennzoil 1-D Tank Car, *80, 81 u*	60	85____
9355	Delaware & Hudson Bay Window Caboose, *80*	37	45____
9357	Smokey Mountain Bobber Caboose, *79*	8	10____
9359	National Basketball Association Boxcar (O27), *79–80 u*	19	24____
9360	National Hockey League Boxcar (O27), *79–80 u*	21	26____
9361	C&NW Bay Window Caboose, *80*	47	50____
9362	Major League Baseball Boxcar (O27), *79–80 u*	17	21____
9363	N&W Log Dump Car "9325" (O27), *79*	4	7____
9364	N&W Crane Car "9325" (O27), *79*	7	9____
9365	Toys "R" Us Boxcar (O27), *79 u*	30	37____
9366	UP Covered Quad Hopper (FARR 2), *80*	19	23____
9367	Union Pacific 1-D Tank Car (FARR 2), *80*	21	30____
9368	Union Pacific Bay Window Caboose (FARR 2), *80*	30	36____
9369	Sinclair 1-D Tank Car, *80*	60	85____
9370	Seaboard Gondola with canisters, *80*	19	21____
9371	Atlantic Sugar Covered Quad Hopper, *80*	19	22____
9372	Seaboard Bay Window Caboose, *80*	30	41____
9373	Getty 1-D Tank Car, *80–81, 83 u*	31	42____
9374	Reading Covered Quad Hopper, *80–81, 83 u*	39	40____
9376	Soo Line Boxcar (O27), *81 u*	40	50____
9378	Derrick Car, *80–82*	18	22____
9379	Santa Fe Gondola with canisters, *80–81, 83 u*	22	30____
9380	NYNH&H SP-type Caboose, *80–81*	7	10____
9381	Chessie System SP-type Caboose, *80*	7	9____
9382	Florida East Coast Bay Window Caboose, *80*	34	48____
9383	UP Flatcar with trailers (FARR 2), *80 u*	27	34____
9384	Great Northern Operating Hopper, *81*	50	55____
9385	Alaska Gondola with canisters, *81*	27	34____
9386	Pure Oil 1-D Tank Car, *81*	38	50____
9387	Burlington Bay Window Caboose, *81*	46	52____
9388	Toys "R" Us Boxcar (O27), *81 u*	38	45____
9389	Radioactive Waste Car, *81–82*	63	78____
9398	PRR Coal Dump Car, *83–84*	28	38____
9399	C&NW Coal Dump Car, *83–85*	17	22____
9400	Conrail Boxcar, *78*	14	20____
9401	Great Northern Boxcar, *78*	18	23____
9402	Susquehanna Boxcar, *78*	30	33____
9403	Seaboard Coast Line Boxcar, *78*	12	17____
9404	NKP Boxcar, *78*	19	21____
9405	Chattahoochee Boxcar, *78*	14	19____
9406	D&RGW Boxcar, *78–79*	17	21____
9407	Union Pacific Stock Car, *78*	18	25____
9408	Lionel Lines Circus Stock Car (SSS), *78*	31	40____
9411	Lackawanna Phoebe Snow Boxcar, *78*	35	43____
9412	RF&P Boxcar, *79*	21	27____
9413	Napierville Junction Boxcar, *79*	18	24____
9414	Cotton Belt Boxcar, *79*	19	23____
9415	Providence & Worcester Boxcar, *79*	17	25____
9416	MD&W Boxcar, *79, 81*	13	19____
9417	CP Rail Boxcar, *79*	45	50____

		Exc	Mint
____**9418**	FARR Boxcar, *79 u*	50	60
____**9419**	Union Pacific Boxcar (FARR 2), *80*	10	17
____**9420**	B&O Sentinel Boxcar, *80*	21	26
____**9421**	Maine Central Boxcar, *80*	10	17
____**9422**	EJ&E Boxcar, *80*	12	20
____**9423**	NYNH&H Boxcar, *80*	14	22
____**9424**	TP&W Boxcar, *80*	17	21
____**9425**	British Columbia DD Boxcar, *80*	27	35
____**9426**	Chesapeake & Ohio Boxcar, *80*	19	30
____**9427**	Bay Line Boxcar, *80–81*	12	17
____**9428**	TP&W Boxcar, *80–81, 83 u*		23
____**9429**	"The Early Years" Boxcar, *80*	20	27
____**9430**	"The Standard Gauge Years" Boxcar, *80*	22	25
____**9431**	"The Prewar Years" Boxcar, *80*	20	25
____**9432**	"The Postwar Years" Boxcar, *80*	50	55
____**9433**	"The Golden Years" Boxcar, *80*	33	43
____**9434**	Joshua Lionel Cowen "The Man" Boxcar, *80 u*	29	37
____**9436**	Burlington Boxcar, *81*	25	30
____**9437**	Northern Pacific Stock Car, *81*	22	36
____**9438**	Ontario Northland Boxcar, *81*	25	31
____**9439**	Ashley Drew & Northern Boxcar, *81*	11	19
____**9440**	Reading Boxcar, *81*	50	65
____**9441**	Pennsylvania Boxcar, *81*	32	42
____**9442**	Canadian Pacific Boxcar, *81*	13	21
____**9443**	Florida East Coast Boxcar, *81*	19	24
____**9444**	Louisiana Midland Boxcar, *81*	14	18
____**9445**	Vermont Northern Boxcar, *81*	14	17
____**9446**	Sabine River & Northern Boxcar, *81*	15	21
____**9447**	Pullman Standard Boxcar, *81*	16	21
____**9448**	Santa Fe Stock Car, *81–82*	34	40
____**9449**	Great Northern Boxcar (FARR 3), *81*	27	31
____**9450**	Great Northern Stock Car (FARR 3), *81 u*	50	60
____**9451**	Southern Boxcar (FARR 4), *83*	26	32
____**9452**	Western Pacific Boxcar, *82–83*	12	16
____**9453**	MPA Boxcar, *82–83*	14	19
____**9454**	New Hope & Ivyland Boxcar, *82–83*	21	27
____**9455**	Milwaukee Road Boxcar, *82–83*	15	19
____**9456**	PRR DD Boxcar (FARR 5), *84–85*	24	30
____**9461**	Norfolk & Southern Boxcar, *82*	25	43
____**9462**	Southern Pacific Boxcar, *83–84*	18	23
____**9463**	Texas & Pacific Boxcar, *83–84*	15	19
____**9464**	NC&StL Boxcar, *83–84*	16	22
____**9465**	Santa Fe Boxcar, *83–84*	12	19
____**9466**	Wanamaker Boxcar, *82 u*	60	70
____**9467**	Tennessee World's Fair Boxcar, *82 u*	26	31
____**9468**	Union Pacific DD Boxcar, *83*	31	34
____**9469**	NYC Pacemaker Boxcar (std O), *84–85*	37	53
____**9470**	Chicago Beltline Boxcar, *84*	15	20
____**9471**	Atlantic Coast Line Boxcar, *84*	13	20
____**9472**	Detroit & Mackinac Boxcar, *84*	22	26
____**9473**	Lehigh Valley Boxcar, *84*	24	28
____**9474**	Erie-Lackawanna Boxcar, *84*	31	35
____**9475**	D&H "I Love NY" Boxcar, *84 u*	28	37
____**9476**	PRR Boxcar (FARR 5), *84–85*	27	36

		Exc	Mint
9480	MN&S Boxcar, *85–86*	15	18____
9481	Seaboard System Boxcar, *85–86*	15	18____
9482	Norfolk & Southern Boxcar, *85–86*	13	17____
9483	Manufacturers Railway Boxcar, *85–86*	14	19____
9484	Lionel 85th Anniversary Boxcar, *85*	22	26____
9486	GTW "I Love Michigan" Boxcar, *86*	23	34____
9490	Christmas Boxcar for Lionel Employees, *85 u*		1800____
9491	Christmas Boxcar, *86 u*	26	37____
9492	Lionel Lines Boxcar, *86*	23	29____
9500	Milwaukee Road Passenger Coach, *73*	28	75____
9501	Milwaukee Road Passenger Coach, *73 u, 74–76*	33	37____
9502	Milwaukee Road Observation Car, *73*	30	48____
9503	Milwaukee Road Passenger Coach, *73*	33	48____
9504	Milwaukee Road Passenger Coach, *73 u, 74–76*	33	37____
9505	Milwaukee Road Passenger Coach, *73 u, 74–76*	35	38____
9506	Milwaukee Road Combination Car, *74 u, 75–76*	32	37____
9507	PRR Passenger Coach, *74–75*	34	55____
9508	PRR Passenger Coach, *74–75*	32	50____
9509	PRR Observation Car, *74–75*	41	60____
9510	PRR Combination Car, *74 u, 75–76*	30	47____
9511	Milwaukee Road Passenger Coach, *74 u*	33	48____
9513	PRR Passenger Coach, *75–76*	25	44____
9514	PRR Passenger Coach, *75–76*	23	36____
9515	PRR Passenger Coach, *75–76*	22	34____
9516	B&O Passenger Coach, *76*	27	42____
9517	B&O Passenger Coach, *75*	45	65____
9518	B&O Observation Car, *75*	45	65____
9519	B&O Combination Car, *75*	55	85____
9521	PRR Baggage Car, *75 u, 76*	65	95____
9522	Milwaukee Road Baggage Car, *75 u, 76*	65	80____
9523	B&O Baggage Car, *75 u, 76*	60	70____
9524	B&O Passenger Coach, *76*	27	37____
9525	B&O Passenger Coach, *76*	30	43____
9527	Milwaukee Road Campaign Observation Car, *76 u*	38	60____
9528	PRR Campaign Observation Car, *76 u*	48	75____
9529	B&O Campaign Observation Car, *76 u*	35	59____
9530	Southern Baggage Car, *77–78*	45	65____
9531	Southern Combination Car, *77–78*	29	37____
9532	Southern Passenger Coach, *77–78*	33	47____
9533	Southern Passenger Coach, *77–78*	27	38____
9534	Southern Observation Car, *77–78*	31	47____
9536	Blue Comet Baggage Car, *78–80*	39	55____
9537	Blue Comet Combination Car, *78–80*	35	50____
9538	Blue Comet Passenger Coach, *78–80*	35	47____
9539	Blue Comet Passenger Coach, *78–80*	35	48____
9540	Blue Comet Observation Car, *78–80*	27	40____
9541	Santa Fe Baggage Car, *80–82*	21	30____
9545	Union Pacific Baggage Car, *84*	135	200____
9546	Union Pacific Combination Car, *84*	85	105____
9547	Union Pacific Observation Car, *84*	85	105____
9548	UP Placid Bay Passenger Coach, *84*	90	110____
9549	UP Ocean Sunset Passenger Coach, *84*	85	105____
9551	W&ARR Baggage Car, *77 u, 78–80*	36	48____
9552	W&ARR Passenger Coach, *77 u, 78–80*	46	60____

		Exc	Mint
____9553	W&ARR Flatcar with horses, *77 u, 78–80*	32	50
____9554	Chicago & Alton Baggage Car, *81*	55	85
____9555	Chicago & Alton Combination Car, *81*	50	75
____9556	Chicago & Alton Wilson Passenger Coach, *81*	50	75
9557	Chicago & Alton Webster Groves Passenger Coach, *81*	45	65
____9558	Chicago & Alton Observation Car, *81*	50	75
____9559	Rock Island Baggage Car, *81–82*	42	65
____9560	Rock Island Passenger Coach, *81–82*	43	65
____9561	Rock Island Passenger Coach, *81–82*	42	65
____9562	N&W Baggage Car "577," *81*	80	110
____9563	N&W Combination Car "578," *81*	80	105
____9564	N&W Passenger Coach "579," *81*	90	100
____9565	N&W Passenger Coach "580," *81*	85	100
____9566	N&W Observation Car "581," *81*	90	95
____9567	N&W Vista Dome Car "582," *81 u*	160	255
____9569	PRR Combination Car, *81 u*	115	160
____9570	PRR Baggage Car, *79*	85	115
____9571	PRR Passenger Coach, *79*	125	145
____9572	PRR Passenger Coach, *79*	110	125
____9573	PRR Vista Dome Car, *79*	95	120
____9574	PRR Observation Car, *79*	75	100
____9575	PRR Passenger Coach, *79–80 u*	100	135
____9576	Burlington Baggage Car, *80*	145	175
____9577	Burlington Passenger Coach, *80*	95	105
____9578	Burlington Passenger Coach, *80*	105	110
____9579	Burlington Vista Dome Car, *80*	95	110
____9580	Burlington Observation Car, *80*	95	110
____9581	Chessie System Baggage Car, *80*	55	62
____9582	Chessie System Combination Car, *80*	47	55
____9583	Chessie System Passenger Coach, *80*	40	47
____9584	Chessie System Passenger Coach, *80*	31	37
____9585	Chessie System Observation Car, *80*	55	65
____9586	Chessie System Diner, *86 u*	85	90
____9588	Burlington Vista Dome Car, *80 u*	110	120
____9589	Southern Pacific Baggage Car, *82–83*	110	135
____9590	Southern Pacific Combination Car, *82–83*	90	105
9591	Southern Pacific Pullman Passenger Coach, *82–83*	85	105
9592	Southern Pacific Pullman Passenger Coach, *82–83*	85	105
____9593	Southern Pacific Observation Car, *82–83*	100	130
____9594	NYC Baggage Car, *83–84*	105	130
____9595	NYC Combination Car, *83–84*	75	85
____9596	NYC Wayne County Passenger Coach, *83–84*	80	95
____9597	NYC Hudson River Passenger Coach, *83–84*	70	85
____9598	NYC Observation Car, *83–84*	75	85
____9599	Chicago & Alton Diner, *86 u*	80	90
____9600	Chessie System Hi-Cube Boxcar, *75 u, 76–77*	19	25
____9601	ICG Hi-Cube Boxcar, *75 u, 76–77*	20	21
____9602	Santa Fe Hi-Cube Boxcar, *75 u, 76–77*	17	20
____9603	Penn Central Hi-Cube Boxcar, *76–77*	12	18
____9604	Norfolk & Western Hi-Cube Boxcar, *76–77*	23	26
____9605	NH Hi-Cube Boxcar, *76–77*	17	21
____9606	Union Pacific Hi-Cube Boxcar, *76 u, 77*	10	17

		Exc	Mint
9607	Southern Pacific Hi-Cube Boxcar, *76 u, 77*	12	15____
9608	Burlington Northern Hi-Cube Boxcar, *76 u, 77*	21	23____
9610	Frisco Hi-Cube Boxcar, *77*	25	34____
9620	NHL Wales Boxcar, *80*	27	35____
9621	NHL Campbell Boxcar, *80*	27	34____
9622	NBA Western Boxcar, *80*	24	30____
9623	NBA Eastern Boxcar, *80*	26	34____
9624	National League Baseball Boxcar, *80*	27	34____
9625	American League Baseball Boxcar, *80*	27	35____
9626	Santa Fe Hi-Cube Boxcar, *82–84*	10	14____
9627	Union Pacific Hi-Cube Boxcar, *82–83*	15	21____
9628	Burlington Northern Hi-Cube Boxcar, *82–84*	14	19____
9629	Chessie System Hi-Cube Boxcar, *83–84*	24	36____
9660	Mickey Mouse Hi-Cube Boxcar, *77–78*	34	46____
9661	Goofy Hi-Cube Boxcar, *77–78*	53	61____
9662	Donald Duck Hi-Cube Boxcar, *77–78*	38	49____
9663	Dumbo Hi-Cube Boxcar, *77 u, 78*	43	58____
9664	Cinderella Hi-Cube Boxcar, *77 u, 78*	56	86____
9665	Peter Pan Hi-Cube Boxcar, *77 u, 78*	49	77____
9666	Pinocchio Hi-Cube Boxcar, *78*	113	161____
9667	Snow White Hi-Cube Boxcar, *78*	354	466____
9668	Pluto Hi-Cube Boxcar, *78*	149	193____
9669	Bambi Hi-Cube Boxcar, *78 u*	67	105____
9670	Alice In Wonderland Hi-Cube Boxcar, *78 u*	61	91____
9671	Fantasia Hi-Cube Boxcar, *78 u*	56	91____
9672	Mickey Mouse 50th Anniversary Hi-Cube Boxcar, *78 u*	368	468____
9700	Southern Boxcar, *72–73*	22	30____
9701	B&O DD Boxcar, *72*	14	19____
9702	Soo Line Boxcar, *72–73*	15	21____
9703	CP Rail Boxcar, *72*	34	44____
9704	Norfolk & Western Boxcar, *72*	10	17____
9705	D&RGW Boxcar, *72*	13	20____
9706	C&O Boxcar, *72*	17	19____
9707	MKT Stock Car, *72–75*	14	22____
9708	U.S. Mail Boxcar, *72–75*	18	23____
9708	U.S. Mail Toy Fair Boxcar, *73 u*	85	95____
9709	BAR State of Maine Boxcar (SSS), *72–74*	29	32____
9710	Rutland Boxcar (SSS), *72–74*	24	28____
9711	Southern Boxcar, *74–75*	19	25____
9712	B&O DD Boxcar, *73–74*	31	34____
9713	CP Rail Boxcar, *73–74*	24	30____
9713	CP Rail "Season's Greetings" Boxcar, *74 u*	95	120____
9714	D&RGW Boxcar, *73–74*	16	20____
9715	C&O Boxcar, *73–74*	17	22____
9716	Penn Central Boxcar, *73–74*	15	20____
9717	Union Pacific Boxcar, *73–74*	21	25____
9718	Canadian National Boxcar, *73–74*	23	31____
9719	New Haven DD Boxcar, *73 u*	23	32____
9723	Western Pacific Boxcar (SSS), *73–74*	27	29____
9723	Western Pacific Toy Fair Boxcar, *74 u*	20	60____
9724	Missouri Pacific Boxcar (SSS), *73–74*	21	24____
9725	MKT Stock Car (SSS), *73–75*	15	18____
9726	Erie-Lackawanna Boxcar (SSS), *78*	25	30____
9729	CP Rail Boxcar, *78*		34____

Exc Mint

		Exc	Mint
____9730	CP Rail Boxcar, *74–75*	23	27
____9731	Milwaukee Road Boxcar, *74–75*	16	21
____9732	Southern Pacific Boxcar, *79 u*	24	31
____9734	Bangor & Aroostook Boxcar, *79*	30	38
____9735	Grand Trunk Western Boxcar, *74–75*	15	21
____9737	Vermont Central Boxcar, *74–76*	27	34
____9738	Illinois Terminal Boxcar, *82*	33	45
____9739	D&RGW Boxcar (SSS), *74–76*	17	25
____9740	Chessie System Boxcar, *74–75*	15	19
____9742	M&StL Boxcar, *73 u*	12	19
____9742	M&StL "Season's Greetings" Boxcar, *73 u*	85	105
____9743	Sprite Boxcar, *74 u, 75*	19	27
____9744	Tab Boxcar, *74 u, 75*	17	24
____9745	Fanta Boxcar, *74 u, 75*	19	29
____9747	Chessie System DD Boxcar, *75–76*	24	28
____9748	CP Rail Boxcar, *75–76*	16	20
____9749	Penn Central Boxcar, *75–76*	16	21
____9750	DT&I Boxcar, *75–76*	13	20
____9751	Frisco Boxcar, *75–76*	21	23
____9752	L&N Boxcar, *75–76*	20	23
____9753	Maine Central Boxcar, *75–76*	16	22
____9754	NYC Pacemaker Boxcar (SSS), *75–77*	20	30
____9755	Union Pacific Boxcar, *75–76*	20	24
____9757	Central of Georgia Boxcar, *74 u*	16	17
____9758	Alaska Boxcar (SSS), *75–77*	24	31
____9759	Paul Revere Boxcar, *75 u*	36	43
____9760	Liberty Bell Boxcar, *75 u*	30	40
____9761	George Washington Boxcar, *75 u*	36	43
____9762	Toy Fair Boxcar, *75 u*	125	170
____9763	D&RGW Stock Car, *76–77*	15	20
____9764	GTW DD Boxcar, *76–77*	40	55
____9767	Railbox Boxcar, *76–77*	15	20
____9768	B&M Boxcar, *76–77*	18	27
____9769	B&LE Boxcar, *76–77*	15	21
____9770	Northern Pacific Boxcar, *76–77*	14	18
____9771	Norfolk & Western Boxcar, *76–77*	16	24
____9772	Great Northern Boxcar, *76*	60	85
____9773	NYC Stock Car, *76*	32	39
____9775	M&StL Boxcar (SSS), *76*	19	23
____9776	SP Overnight Boxcar (SSS), *76*	32	34
____9777	Virginian Boxcar, *76–77*	22	25
____9778	"Season's Greetings" Boxcar, *75 u*	165	185
____9780	Johnny Cash Boxcar, *76 u*	50	61
____9781	Delaware & Hudson Boxcar, *77–78*	19	23
____9782	Rock Island Boxcar, *77–78*	14	17
____9783	B&O Time-Saver Boxcar, *77–78*	18	27
____9784	Santa Fe Boxcar, *77–78*	13	17
____9785	Conrail Boxcar, *77–78*	20	23
____9786	C&NW Boxcar, *77–79*	18	27
____9787	Jersey Central Boxcar, *77–79*	12	19
____9788	Lehigh Valley Boxcar, *77–79*	17	21
____9789	Pickens Boxcar, *77*	25	33
____9801	B&O Sentinel Boxcar (std O), *73–75*	18	26
____9802	Miller High Life Reefer (std O), *73–75*	32	36

		Exc	Mint
9803	Johnson Wax Boxcar (std O), *73–75*	27	33____
9805	Grand Trunk Western Reefer (std O), *73–75*	20	31____
9806	Rock Island Boxcar (std O), *74–75*	38	46____
9807	Stroh's Beer Reefer (std O), *74–76*	67	79____
9808	Union Pacific Boxcar (std O), *75–76*	36	50____
9809	Clark Reefer (std O), *75–76*	33	41____
9811	Pacific Fruit Express Reefer (FARR 2), *80*	26	33____
9812	Arm & Hammer Reefer, *80*	24	30____
9813	Ruffles Reefer, *80*	18	26____
9814	Perrier Reefer, *80*	21	30____
9815	NYC "Early Bird" Reefer (std O), *84–85*	34	40____
9816	Brach's Candy Reefer, *80*	21	26____
9817	Bazooka Bubble Gum Reefer, *80*	24	31____
9818	Western Maryland Reefer, *80*	18	23____
9819	Western Fruit Express Reefer (FARR 3), *81*	22	29____
9820	Wabash Gondola with coal (std O), *73–74*	24	38____
9821	SP Gondola with coal (std O), *73–75*	28	32____
9822	GTW Gondola with coal (std O), *74–75*	24	29____
9823	Santa Fe Flatcar with crates (std O), *75–76*	34	44____
9824	NYC Gondola with coal (std O), *75–76*	41	56____
9825	Schaefer Reefer (std O), *76–77*	45	60____
9826	P&LE Boxcar (std O), *76–77*	34	39____
9827	Cutty Sark Reefer, *84*	34	44____
9828	J&B Reefer, *84*	31	44____
9829	Dewar's White Label Reefer, *84*	39	46____
9830	Johnnie Walker Red Label Reefer, *84*	29	47____
9831	Pepsi Cola Reefer, *82*	79	90____
9832	Cheerios Reefer, *82*	159	185____
9833	Vlasic Pickles Reefer, *82*	23	29____
9834	Southern Comfort Reefer, *83–84*	34	47____
9835	Jim Beam Reefer, *83–84*	43	60____
9836	Old Grand-Dad Reefer, *83–84*	38	50____
9837	Wild Turkey Reefer, *83–84*	64	96____
9840	Fleischmann's Gin Reefer, *85*	38	43____
9841	Calvert Gin Reefer, *85*	38	45____
9842	Seagram's Gin Reefer, *85*	40	45____
9843	Tanqueray Gin Reefer, *85*	41	44____
9844	Sambuca Reefer, *86*	37	49____
9845	Baileys Irish Cream Reefer, *86*	60	89____
9846	Seagram's Vodka Reefer, *86*	39	46____
9847	Wolfschmidt Vodka Reefer, *86*	36	41____
9849	Lionel Lines Reefer, *83 u*	20	32____
9850	Budweiser Reefer, *72 u, 73–75*	54	65____
9851	Schlitz Reefer, *72 u, 73–75*	29	35____
9852	Miller Reefer, *72 u, 73–77*	32	38____
9853	Cracker Jack Reefer, *72 u, 73–75*		
	(A) Caramel-colored body	29	34____
	(B) White body, black logo border	23	28____
9854	Baby Ruth Reefer, *72 u, 73–76*	22	26____
9855	Swift Reefer, *72 u, 73–77*	23	28____
9856	Old Milwaukee Reefer, *75–76*	33	40____
9858	Butterfinger Reefer, *73 u, 74–76*	22	28____
9859	Pabst Reefer, *73 u, 74–75*	40	47____
9860	Gold Medal Reefer, *73 u, 74–76*	12	21____

			Exc	Mint
____	9861	Tropicana Reefer, 75–77	23	35
____	9862	Hamm's Reefer, 75–76	35	42
____	9863	REA Reefer (SSS), 74–76	24	28
____	9866	Coors Reefer, 76–77	41	56
____	9867	Hershey's Reefer, 76–77	73	85
____	9869	Santa Fe Reefer (SSS), 76	32	37
____	9870	Old Dutch Cleanser Reefer, 77–78, 80	15	21
____	9871	Carling Black Label Reefer, 77–78, 80	33	45
____	9872	Pacific Fruit Express Reefer, 77–79	24	28
____	9873	Ralston Purina Reefer, 78	25	38
____	9874	Miller Lite Beer Reefer, 78–79	52	59
____	9875	A&P Reefer, 78–79	23	31
____	9876	Vermont Central Reefer, 78	26	31
____	9877	Gerber Reefer, 79–80	68	78
____	9878	Good and Plenty Reefer, 79	24	31
____	9879	Hills Bros. Reefer, 79–80	23	29
____	9880	Santa Fe Reefer (FARR 1), 79	27	31
____	9881	Rath Packing Reefer, 79 u	23	31
____	9882	NYC "Early Bird" Reefer, 79	25	29
____	9883	Nabisco Oreo Reefer, 79	86	91
____	9884	Fritos Reefer, 81–82	26	34
____	9885	Lipton Tea Reefer, 81–82	30	38
____	9886	Mounds Reefer, 81–82	24	30
____	9887	Fruit Growers Express Reefer (FARR 4), 83	29	38
____	9888	Green Bay & Western Reefer, 83	42	49
____	11000	Holiday Express Freight Set, 08		280
____	11004	NASCAR Diesel Freight Set, 06–07		300
____	11005	Dale Earnhardt Jr. Diesel Freight Set, 06–07		240
____	11006	Kasey Kahne Expansion Pack, 06–07		130
____	11006	Lionel Lion Set, 03 u		230
____	11007	Dale Earnhardt Sr. Expansion Pack, 06–07		130
____	11008	Dale Earnhardt Jr. Expansion Pack, 06–07		130
____	11009	Tony Stewart Expansion Pack, 06–07		130
____	11010	Jimmie Johnson Expansion Pack, 06–07		130
____	11011	Jeff Gordon Expansion Pack, 06–07		130
	11020	Harry Potter Hogwarts Express Steam Passenger		
____		Set, 08–13		330
____	11025	Jimmie Johnson 2006 Champion Boxcar, 07		45
____	11038	Snow-covered Straight Track 4-pack, 08		14
____	11041	Holiday Calliope Car, 08		45
____	11067	Lionel Bear, 08		25
____	11077	Harry Potter Figures, 08		27
____	11096	Engineer Hat, 08		18
____	11098	Holiday Toy Soldier Car, 08		50
____	11100	PRR 2-8-2 Mikado Locomotive "9631," CC, 07		370
____	11101	LL 2-8-4 Berkshire Locomotive "737," CC, 06		350
	11103	Southern PS-4 4-6-2 Pacific Locomotive "1403,"		
____		CC, 06		1000
____	11104	UP Big Boy Locomotive "4014," CC, 06		1800
	11105	NYC L-2A 4-8-2 Mohawk Locomotive "2770,"		
____		CC, 06		1100
	11107	LionMaster SP Cab Forward Locomotive "4276,"		
____		RailSounds, 06–07		850
	11108	C&O F-19 4-6-2 Pacific Locomotive "494," CC,		
____		06–07		1160
____	11109	C&O 0-8-0 Locomotive "79," TrainSounds, 06		420

		Exc	Mint
11110	NYC 0-8-0 Locomotive "7805," TrainSounds, *06*		420____
11116	UP 4-8-4 FEF-3 Locomotive "844," gray, CC, *08–09*		1160____
11117	Santa Fe E6 4-4-2 Atlantic Locomotive "1484," CC, *07–09*		600____
11119	Southern 0-8-0 Locomotive "6535," TrainSounds, *07*		420____
11122	UP Big Boy Locomotive "4024," CC, *06*		1700____
11123	UP Big Boy Locomotive "4023," CC, *06*		1700____
11126	UP Big Boy Locomotive "4012," CC, *06*		1700____
11127	SP GS-4 4-8-4 Northern Locomotive "4436," CC, *07–09*		1200____
11128	C&O F-19 4-6-2 Pacific Locomotive "490," CC, *07*		1160____
11131	UP 4-8-4 FEF-3 Locomotive "844," black, CC, *08–09*		1160____
11132	Reading 2-8-0 Consolidation Locomotive "1914," RailSounds, *08*		450____
11133	NYC 2-8-0 Consolidation Locomotive "1149," RailSounds, *08*		450____
11134	WM 2-8-0 Consolidation Locomotive "729," RailSounds, *08*		450____
11135	B&O 2-8-0 Consolidation Locomotive "2784," RailSounds, *08*		450____
11136	WP 2-8-2 Mikado Locomotive "322," CC, *08*		800____
11137	UP 2-8-2 Mikado Locomotive "1925," CC, *08*		800____
11138	ATSF 2-8-2 Mikado Locomotive "3156," CC, *08*		800____
11139	MILW 2-8-2 Mikado Locomotive "462," CC, *08*		800____
11140	Cass Scenic Shay Locomotive "7," CC, *07*		800____
11141	Birch Valley Lumber Shay Locomotive "5," CC, *07*		800____
11142	Hogwarts Express Add-on 2-pack, *09–10*		120____
11143	SP AC-4 Cab Forward Locomotive "4100," CC, *08*		1670____
11146	Pere Marquette 2-8-4 Berkshire Locomotive "1225," CC, *08*		1290____
11147	PRR 4-8-2 Mib Locomotive "6750," CC, *08*		1290____
11148	NYC Dreyfuss J-3a 4-6-4 Hudson Locomotive "5448," CC, *08*		1130____
11149	LionMaster UP Big Boy 4-8-8-4 Locomotive "4006," CC, *08*		860____
11150	NYC F-12e 4-6-0 10-wheel Locomotive "827," CC, *08*		700____
11151	Polar Express Tender, RailSounds, *08–10*		440____
11152	D&RGW LionMaster 4-6-6-4 Challenger Locomotive "3805," CC, *09*		900____
11153	Stourbridge Lion Steam Locomotive, *09–10*		430____
11154	PRR CC2s 0-8-8-0 Mallet Locomotive "8183," CC, *09–10*		2000____
11155	ATSF 2-10-10-2 Mallet Locomotive "3000," CC, *09–10*		2500____
11156	C&O 4-6-0 Ten-Wheeler Locomotive, CC, *10*		740____
11157	WM Shay Locomotive "6," CC, *10*		800____
11162	Lone Ranger Add-on 3-pack, *10*		165____
11164	Dewitt Clinton Passenger Set, *10*		630____
11165	Dewitt Clinton Add-on Coach, *10*		70____
11166	CSX Merger Freight 2-pack #1, *10–11*		130____

		Exc	Mint
___11167	CSX Merger Freight 2-pack #2, *10–11*		105
___11168	CSX Merger Freight 2-pack #3, *10–11*		130
___11169	Strasburg Freight Add-on 2-pack, *10*		100
___11170	Three Rivers Fast Freight Set, *10–12*		400
___11172	Santa Fe 4-4-2 Steam Freight Set, *13*		200
___11173	Texan Freight Add-on 2-pack, *10–11*		130
___11174	Maple Leaf Freight Add-on 2-pack, *10–11*		110
___11175	Operation Eagle Justice Add-on 2-pack, *10–11*		125
11180	Motor City Express Diesel Freight Train Set, CC, *12–13*		1150
___11181	CN GP9 Diesel Piggyback Train Set, CC, *12*		850
___11182	Dixie Special FT Diesel Freight Set, *11*		700
___11183	Lincoln Funeral Train, *13*		1140
___11194	Texas Special Diesel Passenger Set, CC, *13–14*		1110
___11195	PRR Diesel Passenger Set, CC, *13–14*		1110
___11199	UP NW2 Diesel Switcher Work Train Set, CC, *12*		600
11200	UP LionMaster Challenger Locomotive "3985," CC, *10*		900
11201	WM LionMaster Challenger Locomotive "1204," CC, *10*		900
___11202	CP 4-6-0 Ten-Wheeler Locomotive "914," CC, *10*		740
11203	Pere Marquette Berkshire Locomotive "1225," CC, *09*		980
___11204	Pere Marquette Tender, RailSounds, *09*		440
11207	PRR LionMaster T1 Duplex Locomotive "5511," CC, *10*		800
11208	UP LionMaster Big Boy Locomotive "4011," CC, *10*		900
___11209	Vision NYC Hudson Locomotive "5344," CC, *10*		1600
___11210	UP Challenger Locomotive "3967," CC, *10*		1825
11211	UP 4-6-6-4 Challenger Locomotive "3976," CC, *10*		1825
___11212	NKP Berkshire Locomotive "765," CC, *10*		1400
___11215	LV 4-6-0 Camelback Locomotive "1598," CC, *10*		550
11216	Jersey Central 4-6-0 Camelback Locomotive, CC, *10*		550
___11217	PRR 4-6-0 Camelback Locomotive "822," CC, *10*		550
___11218	Vision NYC Hudson Locomotive "5331," CC, *10*		1600
___11219	Clinchfield Challenger Locomotive "672," CC, *10*		1825
___11220	UP Challenger Locomotive "3989," CC, *10*		1825
___11221	UP Challenger Locomotive "3983," CC, *10*		1825
___11224	PRR Atlantic Locomotive "460," CC, *10–11*		700
___11225	B&O Atlantic Locomotive "1440," CC		700
___11226	UP Water Tender, black, CC, *11*		300
___11227	UP Water Tender, gray, CC, *11*		300
___11228	Clinchfield Water Tender, CC, *11*		300
___11229	MILW 4-8-4 Northern Locomotive "261," CC, *11*		995
___11230	MILW 4-8-4 Northern Locomotive "267," CC, *11*		995
___11232	Reading Atlantic Locomotive "351," CC, *11*		700
11233	Pennsylvania Power & Light 2-Truck Shay Locomotive, CC, *11*		900
11234	Pennsylvania Power & Light 2-Truck Shay Locomotive, *11*		750
11235	West Side Lumber 2-Truck Shay Steam Locomotive, CC, *11*		900

		Exc	Mint
11236	West Side Lumber 2-Truck Shay Steam Locomotive, *11*		750____
11237	Sugar Pine Lumber Shay Locomotive "4," CC, *11*		900____
11238	Sugar Pine Lumber Shay Locomotive "5," *11*		750____
11239	Merrill & Ring Lumber 2-Truck Shay Steam Locomotive, CC, *11*		900____
11240	Merrill & Ring Lumber 2-Truck Shay Steam Locomotive, *11*		750____
11247	Erie USRA 0-8-0 Steam Switcher "121," CC, *11–12*		700____
11248	Erie USRA 0-8-0 Steam Switcher "127," *11–12*		550____
11249	L&N USRA 0-8-0 Steam Switcher "2119," CC, *11–12*		700____
11250	L&N USRA 0-8-0 Steam Switcher "2121," *11–12*		550____
11251	Pere Marquette USRA 0-8-0 Steam Switcher "1300," CC, *11–12*		700____
11252	Pere Marquette USRA 0-8-0 Steam Switcher "1307," *11–12*		550____
11253	NH 0-8-0 Steam Switcher "3603," CC, *11–13*		700____
11254	NH 0-8-0 Steam Switcher "3606," *11–13*		550____
11255	C&O 2-8-2 Mikado Steam Locomotive "1062," CC, *12*		900____
11256	NH 2-8-2 Mikado Steam Locomotive "3021," CC, *12*		900____
11257	PRR 2-8-2 Mikado Steam Locomotive "8631," CC, *12*		900____
11258	Southern 2-8-2 Mikado Steam Locomotive "4501," CC, *12*		900____
11259	UP 2-8-2 Mikado Steam Locomotive "2840," CC, *12*		900____
11260	Rio Grande 2-8-2 Mikado Steam Locomotive "1207," CC, *12*		900____
11261	DM&I 2-8-2 Mikado Steam Locomotive "1305," CC, *12*		900____
11262	Erie 2-8-2 Mikado Steam Locomotive "3007," CC, *12*		900____
11264	PRR K4 4-6-2 Pacific Steam Locomotive "1361," CC, *11*		900____
11265	PRR K4 4-6-2 Pacific Steam Locomotive "1330," CC, *11*		900____
11266	PRR K4 4-6-2 Pacific Steam Locomotive "1361," *11*		750____
11268	Strasburg 2-6-0 Mogul Steam Locomotive "89," *11*		550____
11269	RI 2-6-0 Mogul Steam Locomotive "750," *11–13*		550____
11270	GN 2-6-0 Mogul Steam Locomotive "453," *11*		550____
11271	C&O 2-6-0 Mogul Steam Locomotive "49," *11–12*		550____
11272	ATSF 2-6-0 Mogul Steam Locomotive "573," *11*		550____
11273	Central Pacific 2-6-0 Mogul Steam Locomotive "1470," *11–13*		550____
11274	MKT USRA 0-8-0 Steam Switcher "46," CC, *11–12*		700____
11275	MKT 0-8-0 Steam Switcher "51," CC, *11*		550____
11276	Lionelville & Western 0-8-0 Steam Switcher "1," CC, *11–13*		700____
11277	Lionelville & Western 0-8-0 Steam Switcher "2," *11–13*		550____

		Exc	Mint
11278	WP 2-8-2 Mikado Steam Locomotive "322," CC, *11*		900
____11279	WP 2-8-2 Mikado Steam Locomotive "327," *11*		750
11280	B&O 2-8-2 Mikado Steam Locomotive "4507," CC, *11*		900
____11281	B&O 2-8-2 Mikado Steam Locomotive "451," *11*		750
11282	GN 2-8-2 Mikado Steam Locomotive "3125," CC, *11*		900
11284	MP 2-8-2 Mikado Steam Locomotive "1310," CC, *11*		900
11286	RI 2-8-2 Mikado Steam Locomotive "2302," CC, *11*		900
____11287	RI 2-8-2 Mikado Steam Locomotive "2305," *11*		750
11288	T&P 2-8-2 Mikado Steam Locomotive "552," CC, *11*		900
____11289	T&P 2-8-2 Mikado Steam Locomotive "557," *11*		750
11290	Bethlehem Steel 2-6-0 Mogul Steam Locomotive "28," *11*		550
11291	Weyerhaeuser 2-6-0 Mogul Locomotive "288," *11–13*		550
11295	Elk River Lumber 2-Truck Shay Locomotive "1," CC, *11*		900
11296	Elk River Lumber 2-Truck Shay Locomotive "2," *11*		750
11297	P. Bunyan Lumber 2-Truck Shay Locomotive "18," CC, *11*		900
11298	P. Bunyan Lumber 2-Truck Shay Locomotive "23," *11*		750
11299	C&O 2-6-6-2 Mallet Steam Locomotive "875," CC, *12*		1300
11300	PRR 2-10-4 Texas Steam Locomotive "6479," CC, *11*		1300
11301	PRR 2-10-4 Texas Steam Locomotive "6498," CC, *11*		1300
11303	C&O 2-10-4 Texas Steam Locomotive "3011," CC, *11*		1300
11304	C&O 2-10-4 Texas Steam Locomotive "3025," CC, *11*		1300
11306	NKP 2-10-4 Texas Steam Locomotive "801," CC, *11*		1300
11308	Erie 2-10-4 Texas Steam Locomotive "3405," CC, *11*		1300
11310	Pere Marquette 2-10-4 Texas Locomotive "1241," CC, *11*		1300
11312	MILW S3 4-8-4 Northern Steam Locomotive "265," CC, *11*		995
11315	Pennsylvania-Reading Seashore Atlantic Locomotive, *11*		550
____11316	PRR 4-4-2 Atlantic Steam Locomotive "272," *11*		550
11317	Southern 4-4-2 Atlantic Steam Locomotive "1910," *11*		550
____11318	CN 4-4-2 Atlantic Steam Locomotive "1630," *11*		550
____11319	PRR K4 4-6-2 Pacific Locomotive "5409," *13*		900
____11320	PRR K4 4-6-2 Pacific Locomotive, "5436," *13*		750
11321	C&O 2-6-6-2 Mallet Steam Locomotive "1525," CC, *12*		1300
11322	NKP 2-6-6-2 Mallet Steam Locomotive "943," CC, *12*		1300

Exc Mint

		Exc	Mint
11323	W&LE 2-6-6-2 Mallet Steam Locomotive "8002," CC, *12*	1300	___
11327	PRR Prewar K4 4-6-2 Pacific Locomotive "3667," CC, *11*	900	___
11328	PRR Prewar K4 4-6-2 Pacific Locomotive "3672," CC, *11*	900	___
11329	PRR Prewar K4 4-6-2 Pacific Locomotive "3678," *11*	750	___
11330	Polar K4 4-6-2 Pacific Locomotive, CC, *11–14*	900	___
11331	Polar K4 4-6-2 Pacific Locomotive, *11*	750	___
11332	ATSF 4-8-4 Northern Steam Locomotive "3751," CC, *12*	1300	___
11333	ATSF 4-8-4 Northern Steam Locomotive "3759," CC, *12*	1300	___
11334	Southern Crescent Limited 4-6-2 Pacific Locomotive, CC, *12*	1100	___
11335	Blue Comet 4-6-2 Pacific Steam Locomotive "832," CC, *12*	1100	___
11337	B&O 2-8-8-4 Steam Locomotive "7621," CC, *12*	1300	___
11338	Alton Limited 4-6-2 Pacific Steam Locomotive "657," CC, *12*	1100	___
11339	N&W 2-6-6-2 Mallet Steam Locomotive "1409," CC, *12*	1300	___
11340	B&O 2-8-8-4 Steam Locomotive "659," CC, *12*	1300	___
11341	Pilot 4-12-2 Locomotive, CC, *13*	1300	___
11342	UP 4-12-2 Steam Locomotive "9004," CC, *12–13*	1300	___
11343	UP 4-12-2 Steam Locomotive, black, "9000," CC, *12–13*	1300	___
11344	UP 4-12-2 Steam Locomotive, greyhound, "9000," CC, *12*	1300	___
11363	Cass Scenic RR 2-Truck Shay Steam Locomotive "3," CC, *12*	900	___
11364	Meadow River 2-Truck Shay Steam Locomotive "1," CC, *12–13*	900	___
11365	Weyerhaeuser 2-Truck Shay Steam Locomotive "3," CC, *12–13*	900	___
11366	Pickering Lumber 2-Truck Shay Locomotive "3," CC, *12–13*	900	___
11367	CP 2-Truck Shay Steam Locomotive "111," CC, *12–13*	900	___
11368	WM 2-Truck Shay Steam Locomotive "2," CC, *12*	900	___
11369	Bethlehem Steel 2-Truck Shay Steam Locomotive "5," CC, *12–13*	900	___
11374	DM&I 2-8-8-4 Steam Locomotive "223," CC, *12*	1300	___
11375	WP 2-8-8-4 Steam Locomotive "258," CC, *12*	1300	___
11376	NP 2-8-8-4 Steam Locomotive "5000," CC, *12*	1300	___
11377	GN 2-8-8-4 Steam Locomotive "2060," CC, *12*	1300	___
11379	PRR 0-4-0 Shifter Steam Locomotive "112," *12*	450	___
11380	PRR 0-4-0 Shifter Steam Locomotive "94," *12*	450	___
11381	North Pole Central 0-4-0 Switcher (std O), *12*	450	___
11382	Transylvania 0-4-0 Shifter Steam Locomotive "13," *12*	450	___
11383	Bethlehem Steel 0-4-0 Shifter Steam Locomotive "134," *12*	450	___
11384	ATSF 0-4-0 Shifter Steam Locomotive "2301," *13*	450	___
11385	UP 0-4-0 Shifter Steam Locomotive "206," *13*	450	___

		Exc	Mint
11386	B&M 2-8-4 Berkshire Steam Locomotive "4018," CC, *12–13*		1250
11387	ATSF 2-8-4 Berkshire Steam Locomotive "4199," CC, *12–13*		1250
11388	SP 2-8-4 Berkshire Steam Locomotive "3505," CC, *12–13*		1250
11389	B&A 2-8-4 Berkshire Steam Locomotive "1404," CC, *12–13*		1250
11390	Lima Demonstrator 2-8-4 Berkshire Locomotive "1," CC, *12–13*		1250
11391	IC 2-8-4 Berkshire Steam Locomotive "7020," CC, *12–13*		1250
11392	Michigan Central 2-8-4 Berkshire Locomotive "1420," CC, *12–13*		1250
11399	UP H7 Class 2-8-8-2 Steam Locomotive "3595," CC, *13–14*		1350
11400	C&O H7 Class 2-8-8-2 Steam Locomotive "1578," CC, *13–14*		1350
11401	Pilot H7 Class 2-8-8-2 Locomotive, CC, *14–15*		1350
11402	Virginian USRA Y3 2-8-8-2 Locomotive, CC, *13–14*		1350
11403	Pilot USRA 2-8-8-2 Locomotive, CC, *13–15*		1350
11404	ATSF USRA Y3 2-8-8-2 Locomotive, CC, *13–14*		1350
11405	N&W USRA Y3 2-8-8-2 Locomotive, CC, *13–14*		1350
11410	Pilot 4-8-2 Mohawk Locomotive, CC, *13–15*		1300
11411	NYC 4-8-2 Mohawk Locomotive "2854," CC, *12–13*		1300
11412	NYC 4-8-2 Mohawk Locomotive "2867," CC, *12–13*		1300
11413	Pilot 4-8-4 J-Class Locomotive, CC, *13–15*		1300
11414	N&W 4-8-4 Steam Locomotive "612," CC, *12–13*		1300
11415	Pilot S2 6-8-6 Turbine Locomotive, CC, *14–15*		1300
11416	PRR S2 6-8-6 Steam Turbine Locomotive "6200," CC, *12–14*		1300
11417	PRR S2 6-8-6 Steam Turbine Locomotive "6200," CC, *12–13*		1300
11418	Pilot GS-6 Locomotive, CC, *13–14*		1300
11419	SP 4-8-4 GS-2 Locomotive, black, CC, *12–13*		1300
11420	SP 4-8-4 GS-2 Locomotive, Daylight, CC, *12*		1300
11421	SP 4-8-4 GS-6 Locomotive, black, CC, *12*		1300
11422	WP 4-8-4 GS-64 Locomotive "482," CC, *12*		1300
11423	CNJ Blue Comet Locomotive "833," CC, *12–13*		1100
11425	Alaska 0-4-0 Locomotive, RailSounds, *12–13*		1100
11426	Rio Grande 0-4-0 Locomotive, RailSounds, *12–13*		450
11427	SP 0-4-0 Locomotive "14," RailSounds, *12–13*		450
11428	MILW 0-4-0 Locomotive, RailSounds, *12–13*		450
11429	Southern 0-4-0 Locomotive, RailSounds, *12–13*		450
11430	GN 0-4-0 Locomotive "1066," RailSounds, *12–13*		450
11431	N&W 4-8-4 Locomotive "611," CC, *12*		1300
11432	LL S2 6-8-6 Steam Turbine Locomotive, CC, *13–14*		1300
11433	PRR S2 6-8-6 Steam Turbine Locomotive CC, *13–14*		1300
11434	UP Big Boy Locomotive "4006," CC, *14*		2700
11435	UP Big Boy Locomotive "4018," CC, *14*		2700

		Exc	Mint
11436	UP Big Boy Locomotive "4005," CC, *14*		2700____
11437	UP Big Boy Locomotive "4014," CC, *14*		2700____
11438	UP Big Boy Locomotive "4017," CC, *14*		2700____
11446	UP USRA Y3 2-8-8-2 Locomotive "3671," CC, *13–14*		1350____
11447	PRR USRA Y3 2-8-8-2 Locomotive "376," CC, *13–14*		1350____
11448	UP Big Boy Locomotive "4012," CC, *14*		2700____
11449	UP Big Boy Locomotive "4004," CC, *14*		2700____
11450	Polar Express Berkshire Scale Locomotive, gold, CC, *14*		1500____
11451	Polar Express Berkshire Scale Locomotive, black, CC, *14*		1500____
11452	C&O 2-8-4 Berkshire Locomotive "2687," CC, *14*		1500____
11453	Erie 2-8-4 Berkshire Locomotive "3321," CC, *14*		1500____
11454	NKP 2-8-4 Berkshire Locomotive "765," CC, *14*		1500____
11455	Pere Marquette 2-8-4 Berkshire Locomotive "1225," CC, *14*		1500____
11456	Pere Marquette 2-8-4 Berkshire Locomotive "1227," CC, *14*		1500____
11462	SP AC-12 Cab-Forward Locomotive "4291," CC, *14*		1700____
11463	SP AC-12 Cab-Forward Locomotive "4286," CC, *14*		1700____
11464	SP AC-12 Cab-Forward Locomotive "4294," CC, *14*		1700____
11465	SP AC-12 Cab-Forward Locomotive "4275," CC, *14*		1700____
11469	Pilot AC-12 Cab-Forward Locomotive, CC, *14–15*		1700____
11528	Frosty the Snowman Figure Pack, *14, 16*		30____
11650	Alderney Dairy General American Milk Car 2-pack (std O), *07*		130____
11651	Freeport General American Milk Car 2-pack (std O), *07*		130____
11652	BNSF Mechanical Reefer 2-pack (std O), *07–09*		140____
11653	SPFE Mechanical Reefer 2-pack (std O), *07*		140____
11654	UPFE Mechanical Reefer 2-pack (std O), *07*		140____
11655	GN WFE Mechanical Reefer 2-pack (std O), *07*		140____
11657	PFE Wood-sided Reefer 3-pack (std O), *06*		190____
11658	John Bull Add-on Coach, *08*		80____
11700	Conrail Limited Set, *87*	320	370____
11701	Rail Blazer Set, *87–88*		60____
11702	Black Diamond Set, *87*	195	265____
11703	Iron Horse Freight Set, *88–91*	100	105____
11704	Southern Freight Runner Set (SSS), *87*	210	285____
11705	Chessie System Unit Train, *88*	360	450____
11706	Dry Gulch Line Set (SSS), *88*	190	260____
11707	Silver Spike Set, *88–89*	175	245____
11708	Midnight Shift Set, *88 u, 89*	60	75____
11710	CP Rail Freight Set, *89*	375	447____
11711	Santa Fe F3 Diesel ABA Set, *91*	480	590____
11712	Great Lakes Express Set (SSS), *90*	260	280____
11713	Santa Fe Dash 8-40B Set, *90*	395	480____
11714	Badlands Express Set, *90–91*	49	60____
11715	Lionel 90th Anniversary Set, *90*	345	370____
11716	Lionelville Circus Special Set, *90–91*	155	190____

		Exc	Mint
____11717	CSX Freight Set, *90*	230	240
____11718	Norfolk Southern Dash 8-40C Unit Train, *92*	445	481
____11719	Coastal Freight Set (SSS), *91*	165	215
____11720	Santa Fe Special Set, *91*	49	60
____11721	Mickey's World Tour Train Set, *91, 92 u*	118	158
____11722	Girls Train Set, *91*	549	823
____11723	Amtrak Maintenance Train, *91, 92 u*	210	245
____11724	GN F3 Diesel ABA Set, *92*	730	840
____11726	Erie-Lackawanna Freight Set, *91 u*	225	275
____11727	Coastal Limited Set, *92*	90	110
____11728	High Plains Runner Set, *92*	120	130
____11733	Feather River Set (SSS), *92*	285	330
____11734	Erie Alco Diesel ABA Set (FF 7), *93*	250	305
____11735	NYC Flyer Freight Set "1735WS," *93–99*	125	160
____11736	Union Pacific Express Set, *93–95*	110	130
____11738	Soo Line Set (SSS), *93*	250	280
____11739	Super Chief Set, *93–94*	135	155
____11740	Conrail Consolidated Set, *93*	200	240
____11741	Northwest Express Set, *93*	130	155
____11742	Coastal Limited Set, *93 u*	90	115
____11743	Chesapeake & Ohio Freight Set, *94*	240	280
____11744	NYC Passenger/Freight Set (SSS), *94*	295	335
____11745	U.S. Navy Set, *94–95*	253	295
____11746	Seaboard Freight Set, *94, 95 u*	90	115
____11747	Lionel Lines Steam Set, *95*	310	340
____11748	Amtrak Alco Diesel Passenger Set, *95–96*	130	185
____11749	Western Maryland Set (SSS), *95*	275	300
____11750	McDonald's Nickel Plate Special Set, *87 u*	143	153
____11751	Sears PRR Passenger Set, *87 u*	120	155
____11752	JCPenney Timber Master Set, *87 u*	75	115
____11753	Kay Bee Toys Rail Blazer Set, *87 u*	80	100
____11754	Key America Set, *87 u*	150	165
____11755	Timber Master Set, *87 u*	150	165
____11756	Hawthorne Freight Flyer Set, *87–88 u*	65	85
____11757	Chrysler Mopar Express Set, *88 u*	320	380
____11758	Desert King Set (SSS), *89*	195	250
____11759	JCPenney Silver Spike Set, *88 u*	175	250
____11761	JCPenney Iron Horse Freight Set, *88 u*	120	125
____11762	True Value Cannonball Express Set, *89 u*	95	145
____11763	United Model Freight Hauler Set, *88 u*	135	145
____11764	Sears Iron Horse Freight Set, *88 u*	155	190
____11765	Spiegel Silver Spike Set, *88 u*	175	250
____11767	Shoprite Freight Flyer Set, *88 u*	80	125
____11769	JCPenney Midnight Shift Set, *89 u*	100	175
____11770	Sears Circus Set, *89 u*	185	220
____11771	K-Mart Microracers Set, *89 u*	80	110
____11772	Macy's Freight Flyer Set, *89 u*	170	220
____11773	Sears NYC Passenger Set, *89 u*	175	200
____11774	Ace Hardware Cannonball Express Set, *89 u*	145	175
____11775	Anheuser-Busch Set, *89–92 u*	250	347
____11776	Pace Iron Horse Freight Set, *89 u*	115	135
____11777	Sears Lionelville Circus Set, *90 u*	175	190
____11778	Sears Badlands Express Set, *90 u*	49	60
____11779	Sears CSX Freight Set, *90 u*	190	230

		Exc	Mint
11780	Sears NP Passenger Set, *90 u*	155	190____
11781	True Value Cannonball Express Set, *90 u*	75	115____
11783	Toys "R" Us Heavy Iron Set, *90–91 u*	135	160____
11784	Pace Iron Horse Freight Set, *90 u*	115	135____
11785	Costco Union Pacific Express Set, *90 u*	200	230____
11789	Sears Illinois Central Passenger Set, *91 u*	170	200____
11793	Santa Fe Set, *91 u*	49	60____
11794	Mickey's World Tour Set, *91 u*	80	100____
11796	Union Pacific Express Set, *91 u*	150	160____
11797	Sears Coastal Limited Set, *92 u*	80	100____
11800	Toys "R" Us Heavy Iron Thunder Limited Set, *92–93 u*	235	295____
11803	Nickel Plate Special Set, *92 u*	135	145____
11804	K-Mart Coastal Limited Set, *92 u*	80	100____
11809	Village Trolley Set, *95–97*	55	85____
11810	Budweiser Modern Era Set, *93–94 u*	208	218____
11811	United Auto Workers Set, *93 u*	189	447____
11812	Coastal Limited Special Set, *93 u*	95	115____
11813	Crayola Activity Train Set, *94 u, 95*	115	139____
11814	Ford Limited Edition Set, *94 u*	214	259____
11818	Chrysler Mopar Set, *94 u*	231	268____
11819	Georgia Power Set, *95 u*	519	546____
11820	Red Wing Shoes NYC Flyer Set, *95 u*	258	313____
11821	Sears Zenith Set, *95 u*		780____
11822	Chevrolet Set, *96 u*	279	324____
11825	Bloomingdale's Set, *96 u*		322____
11826	Sears Freight Set, *95–96 u*		769____
11827	Zenith Employees Set, *96 u*		808____
11828	NJ Transit Passenger Set, *96 u*		180____
11833	NJ Transit GP38 Diesel Passenger Set, *97*	275	300____
11837	Union Pacific GP9 Diesel Set, *97*		520____
11838	ATSF Warhorse Hudson Freight Set, *97*		810____
11839	SP&S 4-6-2 Steam Freight Set, *97*		280____
11841	Bloomingdale's Set, *97 u*		301____
11843	Boston & Maine GP9 Diesel ABA Set, *98*		510____
11844	Union Pacific Die-cast Ore Cars 4-pack, *98*		225____
11846	Kal Kan Pet Care Train Set, *97 u*		803____
11849	Lionel Centennial Series Reefer 4-pack, *98*		115____
11850	Rice A Roni Trolley Set, *02 u*		265____
11851	PFE Reefer 6-pack (std 0), *02*	225	255____
11852	Clinchfield PS-2 2-bay Hopper, *04*		70____
11853	B&M PS-2 2-bay Hopper 2-pack, *05*		128____
11854	N&W PS-2 Covered Hopper 2-pack, *04*		70____
11855	GN Offset Hopper with coal, 2-pack, *05*		120____
11856	Green Bay & Western Offset Hopper 2-pack, *05*		120____
11857	Baltimore & Ohio Offset Hopper 2-pack, *05*		120____
11858	PRR PS-4 Flatcar with trailers, 2-pack (std 0), *05*		160____
11859	GN PS-4 Flatcar with trailers (std 0), *05*		160____
11860	SP PS-4 Flatcar with trailers (std 0), *05*		160____
11861	C&O PS-4 Flatcar with trailers (std 0), *05*		160____
11863	Southern Pacific GP9 Diesel "2383," *98*		225____
11864	New York Central GP9 Diesel "2383," *98*		275____
11865	Alaska GP7 Diesel "1802," *98–99*		90____
11866	Govt. of Canada Cylindrical Hopper 2-pack (std 0), *05*		120____

		Exc	Mint
___11867	CN Cylindrical Hopper 2-pack (std O), *05*		120
___11868	BN Husky Stack Car 2-pack (std O), *05*		160
___11869	SP Husky Stack Car 2-pack (std O), *05*		160
___11870	CSX Husky Stack Car 2-pack (std O), *05*		220
___11871	TTX Trailer Train Stack Car 2-pack (std O), *05*		160
11872 ___	PFE Orange Steel-sided Reefer 3-pack (std O), *05*		130
___11873	C&O Offset Hopper 3-pack (std O), *05*		130
11874 ___	PFE Orange Steel-sided Reefer 3-pack (std O), *05*		130
___11875	NP Steel-sided Reefer 3-pack (std O), *05*		130
___11876	PFE Silver Steel-sided Reefer 3-pack (std O), *05*		130
___11877	C&NW Steel-sided Reefer 3-pack (std O), *05*		130
11878	Santa Fe PS-2 2-bay Covered Hopper 3-pack (std O), *06*		125
11879 ___	MKT PS-2 2-bay Covered Hopper 3-pack (std O), *06*		125
11880 ___	Boraxo PS-2 2-bay Covered Hopper 3-pack (std O), *06*		125
11881 ___	PRR PS-2 2-bay Covered Hopper 3-pack (std O), *06*		125
___11882	RI Offset Hopper with gravel, 3-pack (std O), *06*		125
___11883	CNJ Offset Hopper 3-pack (std O), *06*		145
___11884	Maine Central Offset Hopper 3-pack (std O), *06*		145
___11891	Pennsylvania 3-bay Hopper 3-pack (std O), *06*		155
___11892	Conrail ACF 3-bay Hopper 3-pack (std O), *06*		155
___11893	N&W 3-bay Hopper 3-pack (std O), *06*		155
___11894	UP 3-bay Hopper 3-pack (std O), *06*		155
___11895	GN Steel-sided Reefer 3-pack (std O), *06*		145
___11896	Santa Fe Steel-sided Reefer 3-pack (std O), *06*		145
11897 ___	Pepper Packing Steel-sided Reefer 3-pack (std O), *06*		145
___11900	SF Steam Freight Set, *96–01*		130
___11903	ACL F3 Diesel ABA Set, *96*		716
___11905	U.S. Coast Guard Set, *96*	160	180
___11906	Factory Selection Special Set, *95 u*		85
___11909	N&W J 4-8-4 Warhorse Set, *96*	560	720
___11910	Lionel Lines Set (O27), *96*	140	160
___11912	"57" Switcher Service Exclusive, *96*		310
___11913	SP GP9 Diesel Freight Set, *97*		440
___11914	NYC GP9 Diesel Freight Set, *97*		370
11918 ___	Conrail SD20 Service Exclusive "X1144" (SSS), *97*		255
___11919	Docksider Set, *97*		70
___11920	Port of Lionel City Dive Team Set, *97*		185
___11921	Lionel Lines Freight Set, *97*		130
___11929	ATSF Warbonnet Passenger Set, *97–99*		132
___11930	ATSF Warbonnet Passenger Car 2-pack, *97–99*		80
___11931	Chessie Flyer Freight Set "1931S," *97–99*		165
___11933	Dodge Motorsports Freight Set, *96 u*		308
___11934	Virginian Electric Locomotive Freight Set, *97–99*		260
___11935	NYC Flyer Freight Set, *97*		155
___11936	Little League Baseball Steam Set, *97*	229	295
___11939	SP&S 4-6-2 Steam Freight Set, *97*		220
___11940	Southern Pacific SD40 Warhorse Coal Set, *98*		600
___11944	Lionel Lines 4-4-2 Steam Freight Set, *98*		175

MODERN ERA 1970-2018

		Exc	Mint
11956	UP GP9 Diesel Set, *97*	325	375 ____
11957	Mobil Oil Steam Special Set, *97*		429 ____
11971	D&H 4-4-2 Steam Freight Set, *98*	125	155 ____
11972	Alaska GP7 Diesel Set, *98–99*	180	215 ____
11974	Station Accessory Set, *98*		22 ____
11975	Freight Accessory Pack, *98*		23 ____
11977	NP Freight Cars 4-pack, *98*		170 ____
11979	N&W 4-4-2 Steam Freight Set, *98*		75 ____
11981	1998 Holiday Trolley Set, *98*		75 ____
11982	New Jersey Transit Ore Car Set, *98*		250 ____
11983	Farmrail Agricultural Set, *99*		475 ____
11984	Corvette GP7 Diesel Set, *99*		451 ____
11988	NYC Firecar "18444" and Instruction Car "19853," *99*		210 ____
12000	NY Yankees Berkshire Passenger Set, *13*		380 ____
12004	Philadelphia Phillies Berkshire Passenger Set, *13*		380 ____
12008	Boston Red Sox Berkshire Passenger Set, *13*		380 ____
12012	Chicago Cubs Berkshire Passenger Set, *13*		380 ____
12013	NY Mets and Yankees Subway Series Set, *13*		400 ____
12014	10" Straight Track (FasTrack), *03–17*		6 ____
12015	O36 Curved Track (FasTrack), *03–17*		6 ____
12016	10" Terminal Track (FasTrack), *03–14, 16*		6 ____
12017	O36 Manual Switch, left hand (FasTrack), *03–17*		50 ____
12018	O36 Manual Switch, right hand (FasTrack), *03–17*		50 ____
12019	90-degree Crossover (FasTrack), *03–17*		26 ____
12020	5" Uncoupling Track (FasTrack), *03–17*		42 ____
12022	O36 Half Curved Track (FasTrack), *03–14, 16*		5 ____
12023	O36 Quarter Curved Track (FasTrack), *03–14, 16*		5 ____
12024	5" Straight Track (FasTrack), *03–17*		5 ____
12025	4" Straight Track (FasTrack), *03–14, 16*		5 ____
12026	1" Straight Track (FasTrack), *03–14, 16*		5 ____
12027	10" Insulated Track (FasTrack), *03–14, 16*		5 ____
12028	Inner Passing Loop Track Pack (FasTrack), *03–16*		115 ____
12029	Accessory Activator Pack (FasTrack), *03–17*		21 ____
12030	Figure 8 Track Pack (FasTrack), *03–16*		75 ____
12031	Outer Passing Loop Track Pack (FasTrack), *03–16*		145 ____
12032	10" Straight Track 4-pack (FasTrack), *03–17*		22 ____
12033	O36 Curved Track, card of 4 (FasTrack), *03–17*		22 ____
12035	FasTrack Lighted Bumper 2-pack, *05–17*		33 ____
12036	Grade Crossing 2-pack (FasTrack), *05–16*		14 ____
12037	Graduated Trestle Set (FasTrack), *05–16*		85 ____
12038	Elevated Trestle Set (FasTrack), *05–16*		45 ____
12039	Railer (FasTrack), *04–16*		9 ____
12040	O Gauge Transition Piece (FasTrack), *04–14, 16*		9 ____
12041	O72 Curved Track (FasTrack), *04–14, 16*		7 ____
12042	30" Straight Track (FasTrack), *04–14, 16*		15 ____
12043	O48 Curved Track (FasTrack), *04–14, 16*		5 ____
12044	Siding Track Add-on Track Pack (FasTrack), *04–16*		120 ____
12045	O36 Remote Switch, left hand (FasTrack), *04–17*		95 ____
12046	O36 Remote Switch, right hand (FasTrack), *04–17*		95 ____
12047	O72 Wye Remote Switch (FasTrack), *04–14*		97 ____

		Exc	Mint
12048	072 Remote Switch, left hand (FasTrack), *04–14*		104
12049	072 Remote Switch, right hand (FasTrack), *04–14*		104
12050	22½-degree Crossover (FasTrack), *04–14, 16*		46
12051	45-degree Crossover (FasTrack), *04–14, 16*		24
12052	Grade Crossing with flashers (FasTrack), *05–16*		100
12053	Accessory Power Wire (FasTrack), *04–17*		6
12054	Operating Track with half straight (FasTrack), *05–17*		45
12055	072 Half Curved Track (FasTrack), *04–14, 16*		6
12056	060 Curved Track (FasTrack), *05–14, 16*		7
12057	060 Remote Switch, left hand, *05–14*		104
12058	060 Remote Switch, right hand (FasTrack), *05–14*		104
12059	Earthen Bumper (FasTrack), *04–16*		9
12060	Block Section (FasTrack), *05–14, 16*		9
12061	084 Curved Track (FasTrack), *05–14, 16*		7
12062	Grade Crossing with gates and flashers (FasTrack), *06–14*		160
12065	048 Remote Switch, left hand (FasTrack), *07–14*		104
12066	048 Remote Switch, right hand (FasTrack), *07–14*		104
12073	1⅜" Track Section (FasTrack), *07–14, 16*		5
12074	1⅜" Track Section, no roadbed (FasTrack), *07–14, 16*		5
12080	42" Path Remote Switch, right hand, *07–12*		80
12081	42" Path Remote Switch, left hand, *07–12*		80
12700	Erie Magnetic Gantry Crane, *87*	125	150
12701	Operating Fueling Station, *87*	60	74
12702	Control Tower, *87*	60	75
12703	Icing Station, *88–89*	60	65
12704	Dwarf Signal, *88–93*	9	11
12705	Lumber Shed Kit, *88–99*		9
12706	Barrel Loader Building Kit, *87–99*		10
12707	Billboards, set of 3, *87–99*		5
12708	Street Lamps, set of 3, *88–93*	6	9
12709	Banjo Signal, *87–91, 95–00*		29
12710	Engine House Kit, *87–91*	21	25
12711	Water Tower Kit, *87–99*		13
12712	Automatic Ore Loader, *87–88*	17	21
12713	Automatic Gateman, *87–88, 94–00*	30	40
12714	Crossing Gate, *87–91, 93–17*		50
12715	Illuminated Bumpers, set of 2, *87–15*		13
12716	Searchlight Tower, *87–89, 91–92*	15	22
12717	Nonilluminated Bumpers, set of 3, *87–17*		7
12718	Barrel Shed Kit, *87–99*		10
12719	Animated Refreshment Stand, *88–89*	65	70
12720	Rotary Beacon, *88–89*	40	45
12721	Illuminated Extension Bridge, rock piers, *89*	26	38
12722	Roadside Diner, smoke, *88–89*	27	38
12723	Microwave Tower, *88–91, 94–95*	14	19
12724	Double Signal Bridge, *88–90*	39	50
12725	Lionel Tractor and Trailer, *88–89*	10	18
12726	Grain Elevator Kit, *88–91, 94–99*		36
12727	Operating Semaphore, *89–99*		26

		Exc	Mint
12728	Illuminated Freight Station, *89*	29	38
12729	Mail Pickup Set, *88–91, 95*	12	16
12730	Lionel Girder Bridge, *88–03, 08-17*		21
12731	Station Platform, *88–00*		8
12732	Coal Bag, *88–17*		7
12733	Watchman Shanty Kit, *88–99*		5
12734	Passenger/Freight Station, *89–99*		18
12735	Diesel Horn Shed, *88–91*	19	24
12736	Coaling Station Kit, *88–91*	21	31
12737	Whistling Freight Shed, *88–99*		28
12739	Lionel Gas Company Tractor and Tanker, *89*	20	25
12740	Genuine Wood Logs, set of 3, *88–92, 94–95, 97–99*		5
12741	Union Pacific Intermodal Crane, *89*	165	185
12742	Gooseneck Lamps, set of 2, *89–00*		21
12743	Track Clips, dozen (O), *89–16*		12
12744	Rock Piers, set of 2, *89–92, 94–05, 08, 11–15*		15
12745	Barrel Pack, set of 6, *89–17*		8
12746	Operating/Uncoupling Track (O27), *89–16*		10
12748	Illuminated Passenger Platform, *89–99*		18
12749	Rotary Radar Antenna, *89–92, 95*	28	38
12750	Crane Kit, *89–91*	8	10
12751	Shovel Kit, *89–91*	8	10
12752	History of Lionel Trains Video, *89–92, 94*	19	21
12753	Ore Load, set of 2, *89–91, 95*	1	2
12754	Graduated Trestle Set, 22 pieces, *89–15*		27
12755	Elevated Trestle Set, 10 pieces, *89–15*		27
12756	The Making of the Scale Hudson Video, *91–94*	20	22
12759	Floodlight Tower, *90–00*		25
12760	Automatic Highway Flasher, *90–91*	23	27
12761	Animated Billboard, *90–91, 93, 95*	12	23
12763	Single Signal Bridge, *90–91, 93*	31	35
12767	Steam Clean and Wheel Grind Shop, *92–93, 95*	240	290
12768	Burning Switch Tower, *90, 93*	85	90
12770	Arch-Under Bridge, *90–03, 08-17*		30
12771	Mom's Roadside Diner, smoke, *90–91*	34	50
12772	Truss Bridge, flasher and piers, *90–16*		70
12773	Freight Platform Kit, *90–98*		32
12774	Lumber Loader Kit, *90–99*		19
12777	Chevron Tractor and Tanker, *90–91*	9	15
12778	Conrail Tractor and Trailer, *90*	9	16
12779	Lionelville Grain Company Tractor and Trailer, *90*	11	19
12780	RS-1 50-watt Transformer, *90–93*	95	130
12781	N&W Intermodal Crane, *90–91*	145	160
12782	Lift Bridge, *91–92*	428	518
12783	Monon Tractor and Trailer, *91*	11	19
12784	Intermodal Containers, set of 3, *91*	12	17
12785	Lionel Gravel Company Tractor and Trailer, *91*	9	15
12786	Lionel Steel Company Tractor and Trailer, *91*	10	16
12791	Animated Passenger Station, *91*	45	60
12794	Lionel Tractor, *91*	7	13
12795	Cable Reels, pair, *91–98*	3	5
12798	Forklift Loader Station, *92–95*	33	44
12800	Scale Hudson Replacement Pilot Truck, *91 u*	13	17

		Exc	Mint
12802	Chat & Chew Roadside Diner, smoke and lights, *92–95*	41	50
____**12804**	Highway Lights, set of 4, *92–99, 02–04, 13–17*	9	27
____**12805**	Intermodal Containers, set of 3, *92*	10	14
____**12806**	Lionel Lumber Company Tractor and Trailer, *92*	10	15
____**12807**	Little Caesars Tractor and Trailer, *92*	9	14
____**12808**	Mobil Tractor and Tanker, *92*	8	13
____**12809**	Animated Billboard, *92–93*	12	22
____**12810**	American Flyer Tractor and Trailer, *94*	12	18
____**12811**	Alka Seltzer Tractor and Trailer, *92*	11	19
____**12812**	Illuminated Freight Station, *93–00*		27
____**12818**	Animated Freight Station, *92, 94–95*	50	60
____**12819**	Inland Steel Tractor and Trailer, *92*	9	16
____**12821**	Lionel Catalog Video, *92*	13	17
____**12826**	Intermodal Containers, set of 3, *93*	10	16
____**12831**	Rotary Beacon, *93–95*	22	32
____**12832**	Block Target Signal, *93–98*		25
____**12833**	RoadRailer Tractor and Trailer, *93*	9	15
____**12834**	Pennsylvania Magnetic Gantry Crane, *93*	130	170
____**12835**	Operating Fueling Station, *93*	55	60
____**12836**	Santa Fe Quantum Tractor and Trailer, *93*	8	14
____**12837**	Humble Oil Tractor and Tanker, *93*	9	16
____**12838**	Crate Load, set of 2, *93–97*		3
____**12839**	Grade Crossings, set of 2, *93–16*		7
____**12840**	Insulated Straight Track (O), *93–16*		8
____**12841**	Insulated Straight Track (027), *93–16*		5
____**12842**	Dunkin' Donuts Tractor and Trailer, *92 u*	13	25
____**12843**	Die-cast Sprung Trucks, pair, *93–99*		10
____**12844**	Coil Covers, pair (O), *93–98*		3
____**12847**	Animated Ice Depot, *94–99*		65
____**12848**	Lionel Oil Company Derrick, *94*	55	75
____**12849**	Lionel Controller with wall pack, *94, 95 u*		NRS
____**12852**	Die-cast Intermodal Trailer Frame, *94–01*		6
____**12853**	Coil Covers, pair (std O), *94–98*		7
____**12854**	U.S. Navy Tractor and Tanker, *94–95*		33
____**12855**	Intermodal Containers, set of 3, *94–95*	9	13
____**12860**	Lionel Visitor's Center Tractor and Trailer, *94 u*	10	14
____**12861**	Lionel Leasing Company Tractor, *94*	8	13
____**12862**	Oil Drum Loader, *94–95*	75	85
____**12864**	Little Caesars Tractor and Trailer, *94*	8	14
____**12865**	Wisk Tractor and Trailer, *94*	12	55
12866	TMCC 135-watt PowerHouse Power Supply, *94 u, 95–03*		46
12867	TMCC 135 PowerMaster Power Distribution Center, *94 u, 95–04*		49
____**12868**	TMCC CAB-1 Remote Controller, *94 u, 95–09*		115
____**12869**	Marathon Oil Tractor and Tanker, *94*	15	22
____**12873**	Operating Sawmill, *95–97*		70
____**12874**	Classic Street Lamps, set of 3, *94–00*		13
____**12877**	Operating Fueling Station, *95*	75	85
____**12878**	Control Tower, *95*	49	60
____**12881**	Chrysler Mopar Tractor and Trailer, *94 u*	41	52
____**12882**	Lighted Billboard, *95*	9	14
____**12883**	Dwarf Signal, *95–17*		27
____**12884**	Truck Loading Dock Kit, *95–98*		16

		Exc	Mint
12885	40-watt Control System, *94 u, 95–05*		35____
12886	Floodlight Tower, *95–98*		31____
12888	Railroad Crossing Flasher, *95–17*		56____
12889	Operating Windmill, *95–98*		34____
12890	Big Red Control Button, *94 u, 95–00*		43____
12891	Lionel Refrigerator Lines Tractor and Trailer, *95*	12	16____
12892	Automatic Flagman, *92–98*		25____
12893	TMCC PowerMaster Power Adapter Cable, *94 u, 95–13, 17*		20____
12894	Signal Bridge, *95–01*		22____
12895	Double-track Signal Bridge, *95–00*		44____
12896	Tunnel Portals, pair, *95–17*		20____
12897	Engine House Kit, *96–98*		29____
12898	Flagpole, *95–97*		9____
12899	Searchlight Tower, *95–98*	10	25____
12900	Crane Kit, *95–98*		8____
12901	Shovel Kit, *95–98*		7____
12902	Marathon Oil Derrick, *94 u, 95*	109	161____
12903	Diesel Horn Shed, *95–98*		29____
12904	Coaling Station Kit, *95–98*		19____
12905	Factory Kit, *95–98*		20____
12906	Maintenance Shed Kit, *95–98*		20____
12907	Intermodal Containers, set of 3, *95*	9	14____
12911	TMCC Command Base, *95–09*		80____
12912	Oil Pumping Station, *95–98*	38	65____
12914	SC-1 Switch and Accessory Controller, *95–98*		35____
12915	Log Loader, *96*		115____
12916	Water Tower, *96–97*		56____
12917	Animated Switch Tower, *96–98*		29____
12922	NYC Operating Gantry Crane, coil covers, *96*	75	90____
12923	Red Wing Shoes Tractor and Trailer, *95 u*	34	38____
12925	42" Diameter Curved Track Section (O), *96–16*		4____
12926	Globe Street Lamps, set of 3, *96–03, 08–09, 16–17*		25____
12927	Yard Light, set of 3, *96–17*		27____
12929	Rail-truck Loading Dock, *96*		44____
12930	Lionelville Oil Company Derrick, *95 u, 96*	55	75____
12931	Electrical Substation, *96*		22____
12932	Laimbeer Packaging Tractor and Trailer Set, *96*		14____
12933	GM Parts Tractor and Trailer, *95*		NRS____
12935	Zenith Tractor and Trailer, *96*		24____
12936	SP Intermodal Crane, *97*		195____
12937	NS Intermodal Crane, *97*		200____
12938	PowerStation Controller and PowerHouse 135-watt Power Supply, *97–00*		150____
12943	Illuminated Station Platform, *97–00*		24____
12944	Sunoco Oil Derrick, *97*		85____
12945	Sunoco Pumping Oil Station, *97*		80____
12948	Bascule Bridge, *97*	75	315____
12949	Billboards, set of 3, *97–00*		7____
12951	Airplane Hangar Kit, *97–98*		29____
12952	Big L Diner Kit, *97*		24____
12953	Linex Gas Tall Oil Tank, *97*		9____
12954	Linex Gas Wide Oil Tank, *97*		10____

		Exc	Mint
12955	Road Runner and Wile E. Coyote Ambush Shack, *97*		93
12958	Industrial Water Tower, *97–98*		50
12960	Rotary Radar Antenna, *97*		26
12961	Newsstand with diesel horn, *97*		30
12962	LL Passenger Service Train Whistle, *97–99*		30
12964	Donald Duck Radar Antenna, *97*		69
12965	Goofy Rotary Beacon, *97*		52
12966	Rotary Aircraft Beacon, *97–00*		35
12968	Girder Bridge Building Kit, *97*		22
12969	TMCC Command Set, *97–09*		148
12974	Blinking Light Billboard, *97–00*		15
12975	Steiner Victorian Building Kit, *97–98*		33
12976	Dobson Victorian Building Kit, *97–98*		24
12977	Kindler Victorian Building Kit, *97–98*		35
12982	Culvert Loader, conventional, *98–00*		190
12983	Culvert Unloader, conventional, *99*		185
12987	Intermodal Containers, set of 3, *98*		15
12989	Lionel Tractor and Trailer, *98*		16
12991	Linex Gas Tractor-Tanker, *98*		16
14000	Operating Forklift Platform, *00*		160
14001	Operating Belt Lumber Loader, *00*		95
14002	ZW Amp/Volt Meter, *00–04*		80
14003	80-watt Transformer/Controller, *00–03*		70
14004	Operating Coal Loader, *00*		135
14005	Operating Coal Ramp, *00*		130
14018	ElectroCoupler Kit for Command Upgradeable GP9s, *00*		20
14062	31" Path Remote Switch, left hand, *01–14*		55
14063	31" Path Remote Switch, right hand, *01–14*		75
14065	Nuclear Reactor, *00*		233
14071	Yard Light 3-pack, *00–17*		35
14072	Haunted House, *01*		181
14073	History of Lionel, The First 90 Years Video, *00*		15
14075	A Century of Lionel, 1900-1969 Video, *00*		15
14076	A Century of Lionel, 1970-2000 Video, *00*		15
14077	ZW Amp/Volt Meter, *00–03*		70
14078	Die-cast Sprung Trucks, *00–05, 07–17*		24
14079	Operating North Pole Pylon, *01*		70
14080	Hobo Hotel, *01*	30	65
14081	Shell Oil Derrick, *01*		100
14082	Pedestrian Walkover, speed sensor, *01–03*		50
14083	Pedestrian Walkover, *01–03, 08, 12–16*		55
14084	Lionel Heliport, *01*		85
14085	Newsstand, *01*		75
14086	Water Tower, *00*		105
14087	Lighthouse, *01*		95
14090	Banjo Signal, *01–17*		60
14091	Automatic Gateman, *01–03, 07–09*		38
14092	Floodlight Tower, *01–05, 08–16*		48
14093	Single Signal Bridge, *01–04, 08*		22
14094	Double Signal Bridge, *01–04, 08*		30
14095	Illuminated Station Platform, *01–04*		20
14096	Station Platform, *01–04*		10
14097	Rotary Aircraft Beacon, *01–04, 07–10*		40

		Exc	Mint
14098	Auto Crossing Gate, *01–17*	100	
14099	Block Target Signal, *01–04, 07–08*	22	
14100	Blinking Light Billboard, *01–03*	23	
14101	Red Baron Pylon, *01*	85	
14102	Rocket Launcher, *01*	250	
14104	Burning Switch Tower, *00*	70	
14105	Aquarium, *01*	175	
14106	Operating Freight Station, *00*	70	
14107	Coaling Station, *01–03*	95	
14109	Carousel, *01*	230	
14110	Operating Ferris Wheel, *01–02, 04*	170	
14111	1531R Controller, *00–17*	46	
14112	Lighted Lockon, *01–10, 13–16*	6	
14113	Engine Transfer Table, *01*	210	
14114	Engine Transfer Table Extension, *01*	75	
14116	PRR Die-cast Girder Bridge, *01*	20	
14117	NYC Die-cast Girder Bridge, *01*	20	
14119	Gooseneck Lamps, set of 2, *01–04, 07*	22	
14121	Classic Billboards, set of 3, *01–03*	10	
14124	ZW Controller with 2 transformers, *01*	300	
14125	Christmas Tree with 400E Train, *00*	65	
14126	Exploding Ammo Dump	55	
14133	Madison Hobby Shop, *01*	290	
14134	Triple Action Magnetic Crane, *01*	230	
14135	NS Black Die-cast Girder Bridge, *02*	15	
14137	Die-cast Girder Bridge, *01–07*	25	
14138	Snap-On Tool Animated Billboard, *01 u*	NRS	
14142	Industrial Smokestack, *02–04*	50	
14143	Industrial Tank, *02–04*	40	
14145	Operating Lumberjacks, *02–03*	65	
14147	Die-cast Old Style Clock Tower, *02–04, 08–17*	47	
14148	Operating Billboard Signmen, *02–03*	60	
14149	Scale-sized Banjo Signal, *02–05*	40	
14151	Mainline Dwarf Signal, *02–08*	43	
14152	Passenger Station, *02–04*	37	
14153	Lion Oil Derrick, *02–03*	50	
14154	Water Tower, *01–02*	65	
14155	Floodlight Tower, *02–03*	55	
14156	Lion Oil Diesel Fueling Station, *02–03*	70	
14157	Coal Loader, *01–03*	120	
14158	Icing Station, *01–02*	75	
14159	Animated Billboard, *02–04*	20	
14160	Frank's Hotdog Stand, *03–04*	55	
14161	Smoking Hobo Shack, *02*	60	
14162	Missile Launching Platform, *02–03*	48	
14163	Industrial Power Station, *02–03*	550	
14164	Lionelville Bandstand, *02*	140	
14166	Train Orders Building, *04–05*	49	
14167	Operating Lift Bridge, *02*	380	
14168	Operating Harry's Barber Shop, *02–04*	100	
14170	Amusement Park Swing Ride, *03–04*	150	
14171	Pirate Ship Ride, *02–04*	130	
14172	NYC Railroad Tugboat, *02*	180	
14173	Drawbridge, *02–04*	70	

		Exc	Mint
____14175	Santa Fe Die-cast Girder Bridge, *01–03*		17
____14176	Norfolk Southern Die-cast Girder Bridge, *02–03*		18
____14178	TMCC Direct Lockon, *02–03*		25
____14179	TMCC Track Power Controller, *02–13*		230
____14180	B&O Railroad Tugboat, *02–03*		155
____14181	TMCC Action Recorder Controller, *02–13*		115
____14182	TMCC Accessory Switch Controller, *02–13*		115
____14183	TMCC Accessory Motor Controller, *02–13*		115
____14184	TMCC Block Power Controller, *02–12*		90
____14185	TMCC Operating Track Controller, *02–13*		100
____14186	TMCC Accessory Voltage Controller, *02–13*		160
____14187	TMCC How-to Video, *02–04*		11
____14189	TMCC Track Power Controller, *02–13*		175
____14190	The Lionel Train Book, *04–14*		30
____14191	TMCC Command Base Cable, 6 feet, *02–13*		14
____14192	TMCC 3-wire Command Base Cable, *02–13*		15
____14193	TMCC Controller to Controller Cable, 1 foot, *02–13*		6
____14194	TMCC TPC Cable Set, *02–13*		16
____14195	TMCC Command Base Cable, 20 feet, *02–07*		12
14196	TMCC Controller to Controller Cable, 6 feel, *02–13*		9
14197	TMCC Controller to Controller Cable, 20 feet, *02–07*		9
____14198	CW-80 80-watt Transformer, *03–17*	65	150
____14199	Playground Swings, *03–04, 08–09*		50
____14201	Burning Switch Tower, *05*		70
____14202	Water Tower, *05*		140
____14203	Amusement Park Swing Ride, *06–07*		230
____14209	U.S. Steel Gantry Crane, *05*		180
____14210	Pony Ride, *06–07*		70
____14211	Road Crew, *07–08*		90
____14214	Lionelville Mini Golf, *06*		80
____14215	Tug-of-War, *06–08*		60
____14217	Helicopter Pylon, *06–09*		140
____14218	Downtown People Pack, *06–17*		27
____14219	Ice Rink, *06–08*		80
____14220	Lionelville Water Tower, *06–08*		21
____14221	Witches Cauldron, *06–08*		70
____14222	Die-cast Girder Bridge, *06–09*		30
____14225	Sunoco Industrial Tank, *06–09*		70
____14227	Yard Tower, *06–08*		45
____14229	Crossing Shanty, *06–09*		20
____14230	Milk Bottle Toss Midway Game, *06*		20
____14231	Cotton Candy Midway Booth, *06*		20
____14236	Operating Freight Station, *06–07*		105
____14237	Rocket Launcher, *06–07*		320
____14240	Ice Block Pack, *06–17*		6
____14241	Work Crew People Pack, *06–17*		27
____14242	Hard Rock Cafe, *06*		50
____14243	U.S. Army Water Tower, *06–08*		95
____14244	Ammo Loader, *06–07*		105
14251	Die-cast Sprung Trucks, rotating bearing caps, *07–17*		25
____14255	Sand Tower, *06–17*		35

		Exc	Mint
14257	Passenger Station, *06–13*		60
14258	North Pole Passenger Station, *06–10*		53
14259	Christmas People Pack, *06–12*		23
14260	Christmas Tractor and Trailer, *06–08*		25
14261	Christmas Tree Lot, *06*		70
14262	Elevated Tank, *07*		70
14265	Sawmill with sound, *08*		130
14267	Sir Topham Hatt Gateman, *07–12*		80
14273	Polar Express Add-on Figures, *06–07, 12–14, 16–7*		30
14289	Operating Santa Gateman, *08*		80
14290	UPS Store, *06*		30
14291	Operating Milk Loading Depot, K-Line, *08*		100
14294	993 Legacy Expansion Set, *07–16*		290
14295	990 Legacy Command Set, *07–16*		400
14297	Halloween Witch Pylon, *07–08*		140
14500	KCS F3 Diesel AA Set, Railsounds, CC, *01*	380	660
14512	F3 Diesel ABA Demonstrator "291," CC, *01*	360	425
14517	Santa Fe F3 Diesel B Unit "2343C," powered, *01*		280
14518	CP F3 Diesel B Unit "2373C," RailSounds, CC, *01*		345
14520	Texas Special F3 Diesel B Unit, RailSounds, *01*		360
14521	Rock Island E6 Diesel AA Set, *01*		530
14524	Atlantic Coast Line E6 Diesel AA Set, *01*		630
14536	Santa Fe F3 Diesel AA Set, RailSounds, CC, *03–04*		800
14539	Santa Fe F3 Diesel B Unit, *03*		300
14540	D&RGW F3 Diesel B Unit, RailSounds, CC, *01*		315
14541	C&O F3 Diesel B Unit, RailSounds, CC, *01*		300
14542	KCS F3 Diesel B Unit "2388C," RailSounds, CC, *01*		375
14543	SP F3 Diesel B Unit, RailSounds, CC, *01*		282
14544	Southern E6 AA Diesel Set, CC, *02*		560
14547	Burlington E5 AA Diesel Set, CC, *02*		570
14552	NYC F3 Diesel AA Set, RailSounds, CC, *03–04*		740
14555	NYC F3 Diesel B Unit, *03*		200
14557	WP F3 Diesel B Unit, nonpowered, *03–04*		190
14558	B&O F3 Diesel B Unit, nonpowered, *03–04*		155
14559	D&RGW F3 Diesel AA Set, *01*		620
14560	NP F3 Diesel A Unit "2390B," freight, *02*		175
14561	NP F3 Diesel A Unit "2390B," passenger, *02*		190
14562	Milwaukee Road F3 Diesel A Unit "75C," *02*		190
14563	Erie-Lackawanna F3 Diesel A Unit "7094," *02*		175
14564	CP F3 Diesel B Unit "237C," CC, *02*		350
14565	B&O F3 Diesel AA Set, *03–04*		650
14568	WP F3 Diesel AA Set, *03–04*		780
14571	Santa Fe PA Diesel AA Set, CC, *03*		660
14574	D&H PA Diesel AA Set, CC, *03*		580
14584	Wabash F3 Diesel A Unit, nonpowered, *03*		180
14586	D&H PB Unit, *03*		125
14587	Santa Fe PB Unit, *03*		125
14588	Santa Fe F3 Diesel ABA Set, CC, *04–05*		980
14592	PRR F3 Diesel ABA Set, CC, *04–05*		750
14596	NH Alco PA Diesel AA Set, *04–05*		700
14599	NH Alco PB Diesel B Unit "0767-B," *04–05*		150
15000	D&RGW Waffle-sided Boxcar, *95*	12	18

			Exc	Mint
____	**15001**	Seaboard Waffle-sided Boxcar, *95*	14	19
____	**15002**	Chesapeake & Ohio Waffle-sided Boxcar, *96*	16	20
____	**15003**	Green Bay & Western Waffle-sided Boxcar, *96*	16	20
____	**15004**	Bloomingdale's Boxcar, *97 u*		40
____	**15005**	"I Love NY" Boxcar, *97 u*		65
____	**15008**	CP Rail Boxcar		30
____	**15013**	L&N Waffle-sided Boxcar "102402," *00*		29
____	**15014**	Seaboard Waffle-sided Boxcar "125925," *00*		25
____	**15015**	C&NW Waffle-sided Boxcar "161013," *03*		18
____	**15016**	IC Waffle-sided Boxcar "12981," *04*		20
____	**15017**	CSX Waffle-sided Boxcar, *05*		27
____	**15018**	D&H Waffle-sided Boxcar "24052," *06*		30
____	**15020**	NH Waffle-sided Boxcar, *07*		30
____	**15021**	MKT Waffle-sided Boxcar, *08*		35
____	**15024**	UP Waffle Boxcar "960860," *09–11*		40
____	**15028**	Southern Waffle-sided Boxcar "539889," *10*		40
____	**15029**	Western & Atlantic Wood-sided Reefer, *10*		53
____	**15033**	MTK Stock Car, *10*		65
____	**15038**	CSX Hi-Cube Boxcar, *11–12*		40
____	**15039**	NS Waffle-sided Boxcar, *11–12*		40
____	**15041**	BNSF Hi-Cube Boxcar, *10*		50
____	**15042**	CSX Waffle-sided Boxcar, *11*		40
____	**15051**	Lionel Lines Boxcar, *11–12*		40
____	**15052**	Amtrak Hi-Cube Boxcar, *11–12*		40
____	**15053**	REA Waffle-sided Boxcar, *11–12*		40
____	**15054**	C&NW Wood-sided Reefer, *11–12*		40
____	**15060**	K-Line Boxcar, *06*		40
____	**15063**	U.S.A.F. Minuteman Boxcar, *11*		55
____	**15069**	Coke Wood-sided Reefer #1, *09–16*		65
____	**15071**	Coca-Cola Christmas Boxcar, *12*		70
____	**15072**	Halloween Boxcar, *09–11*		55
____	**15074**	Mr. Goodbar Wood-sided Reefer, *09–11*		55
____	**15075**	Boy Scouts of America Eagle Scout Boxcar, *11–14*		60
____	**15077**	ATSF Stock Car, *11*		55
____	**15078**	Pabst Wood-sided Reefeer, *11*		60
____	**15079**	Schlitz Wood-sided Reefer, *11*		58
____	**15080**	C&O 40' Boxcar, *11*		55
____	**15083**	CP Rail Waffle-sided Boxcar, *13*		43
____	**15084**	GN Hi-Cube Boxcar, *13–14*		43
____	**15086**	Alaska Wood-Sided Reefer, *12*		40
____	**15091**	Angela Trotta Thomas "High Hopes" Hi-Cube Boxcar, *12*		55
____	**15094**	Sleepy Hollow Halloween Reefer, *14–15*		60
____	**15095**	1953 Lionel Catalog Art Reefer, *13*		55
____	**15096**	Hershey's Kisses Christmas Boxcar, *12*		65
____	**15097**	Peanuts Christmas Boxcar, *12–13*		70
____	**15098**	Lone Ranger Boxcar, *12–14*		60
____	**15100**	Amtrak Passenger Coach, *95–97*		35
____	**15101**	Reading Baggage Car (027), *96*		34
____	**15102**	Reading Combination Car (027), *96*		23
____	**15103**	Reading Passenger Coach (027), *96*		23
____	**15104**	Reading Vista Dome Car (027), *96*		26
____	**15105**	Reading Full Vista Dome Car (027), *96*		26
____	**15106**	Reading Observation Car (027), *96*		23

		Exc	Mint
15107	Amtrak Vista Dome Car, *96*		38____
15108	Northern Pacific Vista Dome Car, *96*		34____
15109	ATSF Combine Car "2407," *97*		35____
15110	ATSF Vista Dome Car 2404," *97*		35____
15111	ATSF Observation Car "2406," *97*		35____
15112	ATSF Albuquerque Coach "2405," *97*		34____
15113	ATSF Culebra Vista Dome Car "2404," *97*		34____
15114	NJ Transit Coach "5610," *96 u*		45____
15115	NJ Transit Coach "5611," *96 u*		45____
15116	NJ Transit Coach "5612," *96 u*		45____
15117	Annie Passenger Coach, *97*		26____
15118	Clarabel Passenger Coach, *97*		26____
15122	NJ Transit Passenger Coach "5613," *97 u*		45____
15123	NJ Transit Passenger Coach "5614," *97 u*		45____
15124	NJ Transit Passenger Coach "5615," *97 u*		45____
15125	Amtrak Observation Car, *97 u*		50____
15126	Stars & Stripes Abraham Lincoln General Coach, *99*		60____
15127	Stars & Stripes Ulysses S. Grant General Coach, *99*		60____
15128	Pride of Richmond Robert E. Lee General Coach, *99*		60____
15129	Pride of Richmond Jefferson Davis General Coach, *99*		60____
15136	Custom Series Short Observation Car, blue, *99*		40____
15137	Custom Series Short Observation Car, red, *99*		34____
15138	Pratt's Hollow Baggage Car, *98*		100____
15139	Pratt's Hollow Vista Dome Car, *98*		100____
15140	Pratt's Hollow Coach, *98*		100____
15141	Pratt's Hollow Observation, *98*		100____
15142	U.S. Army Baby Heavyweight Coach, *00*		50____
15143	U.S. Army Baby Heavyweight Coach, *00*		50____
15153	Pullman Baby Madison Set 4-pack, *01*		190____
15163	T&P Baby Heavyweight Coach, *01*		30____
15166	Union Pacific Whistling Baggage Car, *04*		41____
15169	C&O Streamliner Car 4-pack, *03*		140____
15170	L&N Streamliner Car 4-pack, *03*		140____
15180	NYC Streamliner Car 4-pack, *04*		340____
15185	UP Streamliner Car 4-pack, *04*		340____
15300	NYC Superliner Aluminum Passenger Car 4-pack, *02*		360____
15301	NYC Manhattan Superliner Passenger Coach, *02*		90____
15302	NYC Queens Superliner Passenger Coach, *02*		90____
15304	NYC Staten Island Superliner Passenger Coach, *02*		90____
15305	NYC Brooklyn Superliner Passenger Coach, *02*		90____
15311	CB&Q California Zephyr Aluminum Passenger Car 4-pack, *03*		350____
15312	Santa Fe Super Chief Aluminum Passenger Car 4-pack, *03*		275____
15313	D&H Aluminum Passenger Car 4-pack, *03*		415____
15314	Amtrak Superliner 2-pack, *03*		220____
15315	Santa Fe Superliner 2-pack, *03*		200____
15316	NYC Superliner 2-pack, *03*		195____
15317	Southern Aluminum Passenger Car 4-pack, *03*		350____
15318	Lionel Lines Aluminum Passenger Car 2-pack, *03*		125____

			Exc	Mint
___	15319	Santa Fe Superliner Aluminum Passenger Car 2-pack, *03*		145
___	15326	NYC 20th Century Limited Aluminum Passenger Car 6-pack, *02*		485
___	15333	N&W Powhatan Arrow Aluminum Passenger Car 6-pack, *02*		435
___	15340	PRR South Wind Aluminum Passenger Car 6-pack, *02*		435
___	15379	Lionel Lines Silver Valley Aluminum Combination Car, *03*		100
___	15380	Lionel Lines Silver Spoon Aluminum Diner, *03*		100
___	15381	Santa Fe Aluminum Baggage Car "2571," *03*		100
___	15382	Santa Fe Regal Dome Aluminum Vista Dome Car, *03*		100
___	15383	NYC 20th Century Limited Diner, StationSounds, *03*		195
___	15384	N&W Powhatan Arrow Diner, StationSounds, *03*		190
___	15385	Pennsylvania South Wind Diner, StationSounds, *03*		190
___	15394	Amtrak Streamliner Car 4-pack, *03–04*		450
___	15395	Alaska Streamliner Car 4-pack, *03–04*		355
___	15396	Amtrak Superliner Diner, StationSounds, *03*		220
___	15397	Santa Fe Superliner Diner, StationSounds, *03*		200
___	15398	NYC Superliner Diner, StationSounds, *03*		200
___	15405	50th Anniversary Hillside Heavyweight Diner, StationSounds, *02*		195
___	15406	Blue Comet Giacobini Heavyweight Diner, StationSounds, *02*		300
___	15504	Alton Limited Diner, StationSounds, *03*		230
___	15507	Phantom III Passenger Car 4-pack (15508 Baggage, 15509 Vista Dome, 15510 Coach, 15511 Observation), *02*		245
___	15512	Phantom II Passenger Car 4-pack, *02*		250
___	15517	Southern Crescent Limited Heavyweight Passenger Car 2-pack, *03–04*		205
___	15520	Southern Crescent Limited Heavyweight Diner, StationSounds, *03–04*		220
___	15521	NYC 20th Century Limited Heavyweight Passenger Car 4-pack, *04*		345
___	15526	Santa Fe Chief Heavyweight Passenger Car 4-pack, *04*		370
___	15538	NYC 20th Century Limited Heavyweight Passenger Car 2-pack, *04*		200
___	15541	NYC 20th Century Limited Heavyweight Diner, StationSounds, *04*		200
___	15542	Santa Fe Chief Heavyweight Passenger Car 2-pack, *04*		195
___	15545	Santa Fe Chief Heavyweight Diner, StationSounds, *04*		200
___	15546	Napa Valley Wine Train Heavyweight 2-pack, *05*		250
___	15549	Napa Valley Wine Train Diner, StationSounds, *05*		280
___	15554	Pennsylvania Heavyweight Car 3-pack (std O), *05*		375
___	15558	Pennsylvania Heavyweight Add-on Coach (std O), *05*		140
___	15559	PRR Reading Seashore Heavyweight Car 3-pack (std O), *05*		370

		Exc	Mint
15563	PRR Reading Seashore Heavyweight Add-on Coach, *05*		130____
15564	LIRR Heavyweight Car 3-pack (std O), *05*		370____
15568	LIRR Heavyweight Add-on Coach (std O), *05*		130____
15570	LIRR Heavyweight Car 3-pack (std O), *06*		230____
15574	LIRR Heavyweight Car Add-on (std O), *06*		140____
15575	C&O Heavyweight Diner, StationSounds (std O), *06–07*		295____
15576	C&O Heavyweight Passenger Car 2-pack (std O), *06–07*		265____
15577	NYC Heavyweight 3-pack (std O), *05–06*		370____
15581	NYC Heavyweight Add-on Coach (std O), *05–06*		130____
15584	Amtrak Acela Passenger Car 3-pack (std O), *06*		580____
15588	Southern Heavyweight Passenger Car 4-pack, *06*		495____
15593	Southern Heavyweight Passenger Car 2-pack, *06*		265____
15596	Southern Heavyweight Diner, StationSounds, *06*		295____
15597	C&O Heavyweight Passenger Car 4-pack (std O), *06–07*		495____
15906	RailSounds Trigger Button, *90–95*		12____
16000	PRR Vista Dome Car (027), *87–88*	37	55____
16001	PRR Passenger Coach (027), *87–88*	33	41____
16002	PRR Passenger Coach (027), *87–88*	24	29____
16003	PRR Observation Car (027), *87–88*	24	29____
16009	PRR Combination Car (027), *88*	36	38____
16010	Virginia & Truckee Passenger Coach (SSS), *88*	36	47____
16010	Railbox Modern Boxcar 6-pack, LionScale, *16*		360____
16011	Virginia & Truckee Passenger Coach (SSS), *88*	36	47____
16012	Virginia & Truckee Baggage Car (SSS), *88*	36	47____
16013	Amtrak Combination Car (027), *88–89*	21	34____
16014	Amtrak Vista Dome Car (027), *88–89*	21	34____
16015	Amtrak Observation Car (027), *88–89*	21	34____
16016	NYC Baggage Car (027), *89*	36	55____
16017	NYC Combination Car (027), *89*	21	29____
16018	NYC Passenger Coach (027), *89*	21	29____
16019	NYC Vista Dome Car (027), *89*	21	29____
16020	NYC Passenger Coach (027), *89*	23	33____
16020	BNSF Modern Boxcar 6-pack, LionScale, *16*		360____
16021	NYC Observation Car (027), *89*	20	28____
16022	Pennsylvania Baggage Car (027), *89*	27	38____
16023	Amtrak Passenger Coach (027), *89*	21	30____
16024	Northern Pacific Diner (027), *92*	39	44____
16027	LL Combination Car (027, SSS), *90*	39	48____
16028	LL Passenger Coach (SSS, 027), *90*	35	42____
16029	LL Passenger Coach (SSS, 027), *90*	35	42____
16030	LL Observation Car (SSS, 027), *90*	35	42____
16030	CSX Modern Boxcar 6-pack, LionScale, *16*		360____
16031	Pennsylvania Diner (027), *90*	35	39____
16033	Amtrak Baggage Car (027), *90*	28	38____
16034	NP Baggage Car (027), *90–91*	30	45____
16035	NP Combination Car (027), *90–91*	18	26____
16036	NP Passenger Coach (027), *90–91*	21	30____
16037	NP Vista Dome Car (027), *90–91*	18	26____
16038	NP Passenger Coach (027), *90–91*	17	25____
16039	NP Observation Car (027), *90–91*	21	30____
16040	Southern Pacific Baggage Car, *90–91*	22	30____

Exc | Mint

		Exc	Mint
____16040	NS Modern Boxcar 6-pack, LionScale, *16*		360
____16041	NYC Diner (027), *91*	37	47
____16042	Illinois Central Baggage Car (027), *91*	24	34
____16043	Illinois Central Combination Car (027), *91*	22	30
____16044	Illinois Central Passenger Coach (027), *91*	24	34
____16045	Illinois Central Vista Dome Car (027), *91*	22	30
____16046	Illinois Central Passenger Coach (027), *91*	24	34
____16047	Illinois Central Observation Car (027), *91*	24	34
____16048	Amtrak Diner (027), *91–92*	33	40
____16049	Illinois Central Diner (027), *92*	27	38
____16050	C&NW Baggage Car "6620," *93*	44	55
16050	AT&SF 3-bay Offset Hopper 6-pack, LionScale, *16*		330
____16051	C&NW Combination Car "6630," *93*	40	50
____16052	C&NW Passenger Coach "6616," *93*	34	42
____16053	C&NW Passenger Coach "6602," *93*	37	46
____16054	C&NW Observation Car "6603," *93*	38	47
____16055	Santa Fe Passenger Coach (027), *93–94*	29	38
____16056	Santa Fe Vista Dome Car (027), *93–94*	25	32
____16057	Santa Fe Passenger Coach (027), *93–94*	30	40
____16058	Santa Fe Combination Car (027), *93–94*	27	35
____16059	Santa Fe Vista Dome Car (027), *93–94*	26	34
____16060	Santa Fe Observation Car (027), *93–94*	25	31
____16060	B&O 3-bay Offset Hopper 6-pack, LionScale, *16*		330
____16061	N&W Baggage Car "6061," *94*	60	85
____16062	N&W Combination Car "6062," *94*	38	50
____16063	N&W Passenger Coach "6063," *94*	43	55
____16064	N&W Passenger Coach "6064," *94*	43	55
____16065	N&W Observation Car "6065," *94*	36	48
____16066	NYC Combination Car "6066" (SSS), *94*	55	70
____16067	NYC Passenger Coach "6067" (SSS), *94*	38	47
____16068	UP Baggage Car "6068" (027), *94*	50	65
____16069	UP Combination Car "6069" (027), *94*	36	43
____16070	UP Passenger Coach "6070" (027), *94*	36	43
____16070	B&M 3-bay Offset Hopper 6-pack, LionScale, *16*		330
____16071	UP Diner "6071" (027), *94*	36	46
____16072	UP Vista Dome Car "6072" (027), *94*	36	43
____16073	UP Passenger Coach "6073" (027), *94*	36	42
____16074	UP Observation Car "6074" (027), *94*	36	43
____16075	Missouri Pacific Baggage Car "6620," *95*	44	55
____16076	Missouri Pacific Combination Car "6630," *95*	34	41
____16077	Missouri Pacific Passenger Coach "6616," *95*	34	41
____16078	Missouri Pacific Passenger Coach "7805," *95*	34	39
____16079	Missouri Pacific Observation Car "6609," *95*	34	41
____16080	New Haven Baggage Car "6080" (027), *95*	35	44
16080	C&O 3-bay Offset Hopper 6-pack #1, LionScale, *16*		330
____16081	New Haven Combination Car "6081" (027), *95*	28	37
____16082	New Haven Passenger Coach "6082" (027), *95*	28	37
____16083	New Haven Vista Dome Car "6083" (027), *95*	30	39
16084	New Haven Full Vista Dome Car "6084" (027), *95*	33	39
____16086	New Haven Observation Car "6086" (027), *95*	31	40
____16087	NYC Baggage Car "6087" (SSS), *95*	48	65
____16088	NYC Passenger Coach "6088" (SSS), *95*	36	43

		Exc	Mint
16089	NYC Diner "6089" (SSS), *95*	36	43____
16090	NYC Observation Car "6090" (SSS), *95*	38	46____
16090	C&O 3-bay Offset Hopper 6-pack #2, LionScale, *16*		330____
16091	NYC Passenger Cars, set of 4 (SSS), *95*	140	165____
16092	Santa Fe Full Vista Dome Car (027), *95*	30	38____
16093	Illinois Central Full Vista Dome Car (027), *95*	29	38____
16094	Pennsylvania Full Vista Dome Car (027), *95*	30	39____
16095	Amtrak Combination Car (027), *95*	19	23____
16096	Amtrak Vista Dome Car (027), *95*	19	23____
16097	Amtrak Observation Car (027), *95*	19	23____
16098	Amtrak Passenger Coach, *95–97*	20	33____
16099	Amtrak Vista Dome Car, *95–97*	20	33____
16100	Alaska RR 3-bay 9-panel Hopper 6-pack, LionScale, *16*		330____
16102	Southern 3-D Tank Car (SSS), *87*	23	30____
16103	Lehigh Valley 2-D Tank Car (027), *88*	19	25____
16104	Santa Fe 2-D Tank Car (027), *89*	19	23____
16105	D&RGW 3-D Tank Car (SSS), *89*	48	65____
16106	Mopar Express 3-D Tank Car, *88 u*	100	151____
16107	Sunoco 2-D Tank Car (027), *90*	16	20____
16108	Racing Fuel 1-D Tank Car "6108" (027), *89 u, 92 u*	9	13____
16109	B&O 1-D Tank Car (SSS), *91*	29	34____
16110	Circus Animals Operating Stock Car "1989" (027), *89 u*	24	34____
16110	Chessie 3-bay 9-panel Hopper 6-pack, LionScale, *16*		330____
16111	Alaska 1-D Tank Car (027), *90–91*	22	27____
16112	Dow Chemical 3-D Tank Car, *90*	20	26____
16113	Diamond Shamrock 2-D Tank Car (027), *91*	20	25____
16114	Hooker Chemicals 1-D Tank Car (027), *91*	13	17____
16115	MKT 3-D Tank Car, *92*	13	16____
16116	U.S. Army 1-D Tank Car, *91 u*	36	42____
16119	MKT 2-D Tank Car (027), *92, 93 u*	14	19____
16120	Southern 3-bay 9-panel Hopper 6-pack, LionScale, *16*		330____
16121	C&NW Stock Car (SSS), *92*	33	43____
16123	Union Pacific 3-D Tank Car, *93–95*	16	22____
16124	Penn Salt 3-D Tank Car, *93*	21	26____
16125	Virginian Stock Car, *93*	19	24____
16126	Jefferson Lake 3-D Tank Car, *93*	22	26____
16127	Mobil 1-D Tank Car, *93*	28	33____
16128	Alaska 1-D Tank Car, *94*	24	29____
16129	Alaska 1-D Tank Car (027), *93 u, 94*	21	28____
16130	SP Stock Car (027), *93 u, 94*	10	13____
16130	WM 3-bay 9-panel Hopper 6-pack, LionScale, *16*		330____
16131	T&P Reefer, *94*	19	24____
16132	Deep Rock 3-D Tank Car, *94*	25	30____
16133	Santa Fe Reefer, *94*	22	28____
16134	Reading Reefer, *94*	17	21____
16135	C&O Stock Car, *94*	23	27____
16136	B&O 1-D Tank Car, *94*	28	32____
16137	Ford 1-D Tank Car "12," *94 u*	34	39____
16138	Goodyear 1-D Tank Car, *95*	28	34____

		Exc	Mint
____16140	Domino Sugar 1-D Tank Car, *95*	24	29
16140	Klemme Coop PS-2CD Covered Hopper 6-pack, LionScale, *16*		360
____16141	Erie Stock Car, *95*	22	30
____16142	Santa Fe 1-D Tank Car, *95*	26	30
____16143	Reading Reefer, *95*	18	23
____16144	San Angelo 3-D Tank Car, *95*	22	25
____16146	Dairy Despatch Reefer, *95*	15	20
____16147	Clearly Canadian 1-D Tank Car (O27), *94 u*	25	40
____16149	Zep Chemical 1-D Tank Car (O27), *95 u*	63	78
____16150	Sunoco 1-D Tank Car "6315," *97*	35	38
16150	D&RGW PS-2CD Covered Hopper 6-pack, LionScale, *16*		360
____16152	Sunoco 3-D Tank Car "6415," *97*		26
____16153	AEC Reactor Fluid 1-D Tank Car "6515-1," *97*		90
____16154	AEC Reactor Fluid 1-D Tank Car "6515-2," *97*		101
____16155	AEC Reactor Fluid 1-D Tank Car "6515-3," *97*		103
16157	Gatorade Little League Baseball 1-D Tank Car "6315," *97 u*		58
____16160	AEC Tank Car "6515" with reactor fluid, *98*		77
16160	MILW PS-2CD Covered Hopper 6-pack, LionScale, *16*		360
____16162	Hooker 1-D Tank Car "6315-1," *97*		50
____16163	Hooker 1-D Tank Car "6315-2," *97*		50
____16164	Hooker 1-D Tank Car "6315-3," *97*		50
____16165	Mobilfuel 3-D Tank Car "6415," *97 u*		50
16170	RFMX PS-2CD Covered Hopper 6-pack, LionScale, *16*		360
16170	RFMX PS-2CD Covered Hopper 6-pack, LionScale, *16*		360
____16171	Alaska 1-D Tank Car "6171," *98–99*		33
____16173	Harold the Helicopter Flatcar, *98*	45	60
____16175	NJ Transit Port Morris Ore Car "9125," *98*		45
____16176	NJ Transit Raritan Yard Ore Car "9126," *98 u*		45
____16177	NJ Transit Gladstone Yard Ore Car "9127," *98 u*		45
____16178	NJ Transit Bay Head Yard Ore Car "9128," *98 u*		45
____16179	NJ Transit Dover Yard Ore Car "9129," *98 u*		45
____16180	Tabasco 1-D Tank Car, *98*	63	79
____16181	Biohazard Tank Car with Lights, *98*		84
____16182	Gatorade 1-D Tank Car "6315," *98 u*		64
____16187	Linex 3-D Tank Car "6425," *99*		30
____16188	Kodak 1-D Tank Car "6515," *99*	74	91
____16199	UP 1-D Tank Car "6035," *99–00*		25
____16200	Rock Island Boxcar (O27), *87–88*	7	10
____16201	Wabash Boxcar (O27), *88–91*	7	10
____16203	Key America Boxcar (O27), *87 u*	45	65
____16204	Hawthorne Boxcar (O27), *87 u*	50	85
____16205	Mopar Express Boxcar "1987" (O27), *87–88 u*	50	60
____16206	D&RGW Boxcar (SSS), *89*	37	42
____16207	True Value Boxcar (O27), *88 u*	32	115
____16208	PRR Auto Carrier, 3-tier, *89*	24	37
____16209	Disney Magic Boxcar (O27), *88 u*	90	110
____16211	Hawthorne Boxcar (O27), *88 u*	45	65
____16213	Shoprite Boxcar (O27), *88 u*	55	80
____16214	D&RGW Auto Carrier, *90*	24	32

		Exc	Mint
16215	Conrail Auto Carrier, *90*	27	38____
16217	Burlington Northern Auto Carrier, *92*	24	36____
16219	True Value Boxcar (O27), *89 u*	55	75____
16220	Ace Hardware Boxcar (O27), *89 u*	55	80____
16221	Macy's Boxcar (O27), *89 u*	55	80____
16222	Great Northern Boxcar (O27), *90–91*	8	15____
16223	Budweiser Reefer, *89–92 u*	61	84____
16224	True Value "Lawn Chief" Boxcar (O27), *90 u*	45	60____
16225	Budweiser Vat Car, *90–91 u*	123	161____
16226	Union Pacific Boxcar "6226" (O27), *90–91 u*	15	19____
16227	Santa Fe Boxcar (O27), *91*	13	17____
16228	Union Pacific Auto Carrier, *92*	26	33____
16229	Erie-Lackawanna Auto Carrier, *91 u*	45	55____
16232	Chessie System Boxcar, *92, 93 u, 94, 95 u*	25	30____
16233	MKT DD Boxcar, *92*	20	29____
16234	ACY Boxcar (SSS), *92*	34	41____
16235	Railway Express Agency Reefer, *92*	19	23____
16236	NYC Pacemaker Boxcar, *92 u*	18	24____
16237	Railway Express Agency Boxcar, *92 u*	21	23____
16238	NYNH&H Boxcar, *93–95*		3____
16239	Union Pacific Boxcar, *93–95*	15	20____
16241	Toys "R" Us Boxcar, *92–93 u*	35	45____
16242	Grand Trunk Western Auto Carrier, *93*	35	40____
16243	Conrail Boxcar, *93*	26	34____
16244	Duluth, South Shore & Atlantic Boxcar, *93*	20	24____
16245	Contadina Boxcar, *93*	16	20____
16247	ACL Boxcar, *94*	15	19____
16248	Budweiser Boxcar, *93–94 u*	46	63____
16249	United Auto Workers Boxcar, *93 u*		55____
16250	Santa Fe Boxcar (O27), *93 u, 94*	8	10____
16251	Columbus & Greenville Boxcar, *94*	8	15____
16252	U.S. Navy Boxcar "6106888," *94–95*		30____
16253	Santa Fe Auto Carrier, *94*	32	38____
16255	Wabash DD Boxcar, *95*	20	26____
16256	Ford DD Boxcar, *94 u*	30	34____
16257	Crayola Boxcar, *94 u, 95*	17	23____
16258	Lehigh Valley Boxcar, *95*	17	22____
16259	Chrysler Mopar Boxcar, *97 u*	33	43____
16260	Chrysler Mopar Auto Carrier, *96 u*	54	64____
16261	Union Pacific DD Boxcar, *95*	26	29____
16263	ATSF Boxcar, *96–99*		25____
16264	Red Wing Shoes Boxcar, *95*	24	28____
16265	Georgia Power "Atlanta '96" Boxcar, *95 u*	194	234____
16266	Crayola Boxcar, *95*	17	23____
16267	Sears Zenith Boxcar, *95–96 u*		55____
16268	GM/AC Delco Boxcar, *95 u*		51____
16269	Lionel Lines Boxcar, *96*		10____
16272	Christmas Boxcar, *97*		36____
16273	Lionel Employee Christmas Boxcar, *97*		55____
16274	Marvin the Martian Boxcar, *97*		55____
16279	Dodge Motorsports Boxcar, *96 u*	139	180____
16284	Galveston Wharves Boxcar, *98*		28____
16285	Savannah State Docks Boxcar, *98*		26____
16291	Christmas Boxcar, *98*		34____

			Exc	Mint
____	**16292**	Lionel Employee Christmas Boxcar, *98*	309	369
____	**16293**	JCPenney Boxcar, *97*		100
____	**16294**	Pedigree Boxcar, *97*	143	163
____	**16295**	Kal Kan Boxcar, *97*	143	164
____	**16296**	Whiskas Boxcar, *97*	135	160
____	**16297**	Sheba Boxcar, *97*	134	157
____	**16298**	Mobil Boxcar, *97*		50
____	**16300**	Rock Island Flatcar with fences (O27), *87–88*	8	10
____	**16301**	Lionel Barrel Ramp Car, *87*	14	19
____	**16303**	PRR Flatcar with trailers, *87*	26	33
____	**16304**	RI Gondola with cable reels (O27), *87–88*	5	9
____	**16305**	Lehigh Valley Ore Car, *87*	80	130
____	**16306**	Santa Fe Barrel Ramp Car, *88*	12	16
____	**16307**	NKP Flatcar with trailers, *88*	30	40
____	**16308**	Burlington Northern Flatcar with trailer, *88–89*	20	25
____	**16309**	Wabash Gondola with canisters, *88–91*	9	13
____	**16310**	Mopar Express Gondola with canisters, *87–88 u*	35	39
____	**16311**	Mopar Express Flatcar with trailers, *87–88 u*	116	160
____	**16313**	PRR Gondola with cable reels (O27), *88 u, 89*	5	10
____	**16314**	Wabash Flatcar with trailers, *89*	26	30
____	**16315**	PRR Flatcar with fences (O27), *88 u, 89*	7	9
____	**16317**	PRR Barrel Ramp Car, *89*	18	22
____	**16318**	LL Depressed Center Flatcar with cable reels, *89*	22	26
____	**16320**	Great Northern Barrel Ramp Car, *90*	13	19
____	**16321/22**	Sealand TTUX Flatcar Set with trailers, *90*	65	73
____	**16323**	Lionel Lines Flatcar with trailers, *90*	21	25
____	**16324**	PRR Depressed Center Flatcar with cable reels, *90*	16	20
____	**16325**	Microracers Exhibition Ramp Car, *89 u*	21	28
____	**16326**	Santa Fe Depressed Center Flatcar with cable reels, *91*	16	21
____	**16327**	"The Big Top" Circus Gondola with canisters, *89 u*	19	24
____	**16328**	NKP Gondola with cable reels, *90–91*	17	23
____	**16329**	SP Flatcar with horses (O27), *90–91*	19	24
____	**16330**	MKT Flatcar with trailers, *91*	25	30
____	**16332**	LL Depressed Center Flatcar with transformer, *91*	28	33
____	**16333**	Frisco Bulkhead Flatcar with lumber, *91*	17	22
____	**16334**	C&NW Flatcar Set ("16337, 16338") with trailers, *91*	55	60
____	**16335**	NYC Pacemaker Flatcar with trailer (SSS), *91*	46	65
____	**16336**	UP Gondola "6336" with canisters, *90–91 u*	17	21
____	**16339**	Mickey's World Tour Gondola with canisters (O27), *91, 92 u*	17	21
____	**16341**	NYC Depressed Center Flatcar with transformer, *92*	29	32
____	**16342**	CSX Gondola with coil covers, *92*	18	23
____	**16343**	Burlington Gondola with coil covers, *92*	20	23
____	**16345/46**	SP TTUX Flatcar Set with trailers, *92*	55	65
____	**16347**	Ontario Northland Bulkhead Flatcar with pulp load, *92*	22	26
____	**16348**	Erie Liquefied Petroleum Car, *92*	23	25
____	**16349**	Allis Chalmers Condenser Car, *92*	28	35
____	**16350**	CP Rail Bulkhead Flatcar with lumber, *91 u*	20	29
____	**16351**	Flatcar with U.S. Navy submarine, *92*	27	33

		Exc	Mint
16352	U.S. Military Flatcar with cruise missile, *92*	33	43____
16353	B&M Gondola with coil covers, *91 u*	33	39____
16355	Burlington Gondola, *92, 93 u, 94–95*	11	17____
16356	MKT Depressed Center Flatcar with cable reels, *92*	17	21____
16357	L&N Flatcar with trailer, *92*	24	31____
16358	L&N Gondola with coil covers, *92*	17	21____
16359	Pacific Coast Gondola with coil covers (SSS), *92*	33	38____
16360	N&W Maxi-Stack Flatcar Set ("16361, 16362") with containers, *93*	44	55____
16363	Southern TTUX Flatcar Set ("16364, 16365") with trailers, *93*	38	49____
16367	Clinchfield Gondola with coil covers, *93*	18	21____
16368	MKT Liquid Oxygen Car, *93*	21	22____
16369	Amtrak Flatcar with wheel load, *92 u*	19	28____
16370	Amtrak Flatcar with rail load, *92 u*	19	28____
16371	BN I-Beam Flatcar with load, *92 u*	24	29____
16372	Southern I-Beam Flatcar with load, *92 u*	24	34____
16373	Erie-Lackawanna Flatcar with stakes, *93*	19	23____
16374	D&RGW Flatcar with trailer, *93*	25	28____
16375	NYC Bulkhead Flatcar, *93–95*	21	25____
16376	UP Flatcar with trailer, *93–95*	31	37____
16378	Toys "R" Us Flatcar with trailer, *92–93 u*	60	95____
16379	NP Bulkhead Flatcar with pulp load, *93*	16	23____
16380	UP I-Beam Flatcar with load, *93*	20	26____
16381	CSX I-Beam Flatcar with load, *93*	20	25____
16382	Kansas City Southern Bulkhead Flatcar, *93*	14	18____
16383	Conrail Flatcar with trailer, *93*	50	58____
16384	Soo Line Gondola with cable reels, *93*	14	19____
16385	Soo Line Ore Car, *93*	65	75____
16386	SP Flatcar with lumber, *94*	15	19____
16387	KCS Gondola with coil covers, *94*	13	16____
16388	LV Gondola with canisters, *94*	16	20____
16389	PRR Flatcar with wheel load, *94*	27	32____
16390	Flatcar with water tank, *94*	24	27____
16391	Lionel Lines Gondola, *93 u*		15____
16392	Wabash Gondola with canisters (O27), *93 u, 94*	7	9____
16393	Wisconsin Central Bulkhead Flatcar, *94*	13	19____
16394	Vermont Central Bulkhead Flatcar, *94*	20	30____
16395	CP Flatcar with rail load, *94*	18	23____
16396	Alaska Bulkhead Flatcar, *94*	17	22____
16397	Milwaukee Road I-Beam Flatcar with load, *94*	30	34____
16398	C&O Flatcar with trailer, *94*	80	85____
16399	Western Pacific I-Beam Flatcar with load, *94*	31	35____
16400	PRR Hopper (O27), *88 u, 89*	15	18____
16402	Southern Quad Hopper with coal (SSS), *87*	30	42____
16406	CSX Quad Hopper with coal, *90*	29	34____
16407	B&M Covered Quad Hopper (SSS), *91*	28	37____
16408	UP Hopper "6408" (O27), *90–91 u*	17	21____
16410	MKT Hopper (O27), *92, 93 u*	19	24____
16411	L&N Quad Hopper with coal, *92*	28	32____
16412	C&NW Covered Quad Hopper, *94*	16	21____
16413	Clinchfield Quad Hopper with coal, *94*	16	22____
16414	CCC&StL Hopper (O27), *94*	18	25____
16416	D&RGW Covered Quad Hopper, *95*	16	20____

		Exc	Mint
____**16417**	Wabash Quad Hopper with coal, *95*	19	21
____**16418**	C&NW Hopper with coal (O27), *95*	15	21
____**16419**	Tennessee Central Hopper, *96*		17
____**16420**	WM Quad Hopper with coal (SSS), *95*	30	34
____**16421**	WM Quad Hopper with coal (SSS), *95*	30	33
____**16422**	WM Quad Hopper with coal (SSS), *95*		33
____**16423**	WM Quad Hopper with coal (SSS), *95*		30
____**16424**	WM Covered Quad Hopper (SSS), *95*	34	39
____**16425**	WM Covered Quad Hopper (SSS), *95*	25	29
____**16426**	WM Covered Quad Hopper (SSS), *95*	24	27
____**16427**	WM Covered Quad Hopper (SSS), *95*	27	30
____**16429**	WM Quad Hopper with coal, set of 2		70
16430	Georgia Power Quad Hopper "82947" with coal, *95 u*		109
____**16431**	Lionel Corporation 2-bay Hopper "6456-1," *96*		30
____**16432**	Lionel Corporation 2-bay Hopper "6456-2," *96*		64
____**16433**	Lionel Corporation 2-bay Hopper "6456-3," *96*		18
____**16434**	LV 2-bay Hopper "6456," "TLDX," *97*		25
____**16435**	Virginian 2-bay Hopper "6456-1," *97*		30
____**16436**	N&W 2-bay Hopper "6456-2," *97*		33
____**16437**	C&O 2-bay Hopper "6456-3," *97*		33
____**16438**	Frisco 4-bay Covered Hopper "87538," *98*		34
____**16439**	Southern 4-bay Covered Hopper "77836," *98*		34
____**16440**	Alaska 2-bay Hopper "7100," *98–99*		35
____**16441**	New York Central 4-bay Hopper, *99*		26
____**16442**	Bethlehem Gondola "6462" (SSS), *99*		40
____**16443**	GN 2-bay Hopper "172364," *99–00*		20
____**16444**	CNJ 2-bay Hopper "643," *00*		20
____**16445**	Frisco 2-bay Hopper "93108," *00*		20
____**16446**	Burlington 2-bay Hopper, *00*		20
____**16447**	PRR Tuscan 2-bay Hopper, *00 u*		30
____**16448**	PRR Gray 2-bay Hopper, *00 u*		30
____**16449**	PRR Black 2-bay Hopper, *00 u*		30
____**16450**	PRR Green 2-bay Hopper, *00 u*		30
____**16451**	Lionel Mines 2-bay Hopper, *00 u*		50
____**16453**	SP 2-bay Hopper "460604," *01*		15
____**16454**	Bethlehem Steel Hopper "41025," *01*		37
____**16455**	Pioneer Seed 2-bay Hopper, *00 u*		50
____**16456**	B&O 2-bay Hopper, *01*		20
____**16459**	LV 2-bay Hopper "51102," *01*		23
____**16460**	Reading 2-bay Hopper "79636," *02*		25
____**16463**	Rio Grande Icebreaker Tunnel Car "18936," *02*		32
____**16464**	NYC Icebreaker Tunnel Car "X3200," *02*		32
____**16465**	WP 2-bay Hopper "100340," *03*		19
____**16466**	Pennsylvania Icebreaker Tunnel Car, *03*		33
____**16467**	"Naughty and Nice" Hopper 2-pack, *02*		60
____**16469**	B&O Hopper "435351," *02*		22
____**16470**	"Naughty and Nice" Ore Car 2-pack, *03*		43
____**16473**	Rock Island Ore Car "99122," *03*		18
____**16474**	Alaska Ore Car "16474," *04*		21
____**16475**	Santa Fe Hopper "16475," *04*		18
____**16480**	Lionelville Snow Transport Quad Hopper, *04*		45
____**16482**	Norfolk Southern Hopper, traditional, *05*		27
____**16487**	Alaska 2-bay Hopper, *05*		35
____**16489**	BNSF Ore Car, traditional, *05*		15

		Exc	Mint
16490	Sodor Mining Hopper, *05, 13*		35____
16491	CNJ Hopper "60714," *06*		30____
16492	C&NW Ore Car "114023," *06*		30____
16493	Christmas Ice Breaker Car, *06*		55____
16500	Rock Island Bobber Caboose, *87–88*	9	13____
16501	Lehigh Valley SP-type Caboose, *87*	19	24____
16503	NYC Transfer Caboose, *87*	16	22____
16504	Southern N5c Caboose (SSS), *87*	17	30____
16505	Wabash SP-type Caboose, *88–91*	10	15____
16506	Santa Fe Bay Window Caboose, *88*	18	28____
16507	Mopar Express SP-type Caboose, *87–88 u*	42	54____
16508	Lionel Lines SP-type Caboose "6508," *89 u*	13	17____
16509	D&RGW SP-type Caboose (SSS), *89*	19	24____
16510	New Haven Bay Window Caboose, *89*	25	30____
16511	PRR Bobber Caboose, *88 u, 89*	9	13____
16513	Union Pacific SP-type Caboose, *89*	14	21____
16515	Lionel Lines SP-type Caboose, RailScope, *89*	20	23____
16516	Lehigh Valley SP-type Caboose, *90*	15	26____
16517	Atlantic Coast Line Bay Window Caboose, *90*	22	26____
16518	Chessie System Bay Window Caboose, *90*	41	50____
16519	Rock Island Transfer Caboose, *90*	13	17____
16520	"Welcome to the Show" Circus SP-type Caboose, *89 u*	13	21____
16521	PRR SP-type Caboose, *90–91*	8	11____
16522	"Chills & Thrills" Circus N5c Caboose, *90–91*	10	15____
16523	Alaska SP-type Caboose, *91*	24	31____
16524	Anheuser-Busch SP-type Caboose, *89–92 u*	34	45____
16525	D&H Bay Window Caboose (SSS), *91*	30	39____
16526	Kansas City Southern SP-type Caboose, *91*	17	21____
16528	UP SP-type Caboose "6528," *90–91 u*	17	21____
16529	Santa Fe SP-type Caboose "16829," *91*	9	13____
16530	Mickey's World Tour SP-type Caboose "16830," *91, 92 u*	13	17____
16531	Texas & Pacific SP-type Caboose, *92*	18	23____
16533	C&NW Bay Window Caboose, *92*	22	30____
16534	Delaware & Hudson SP-type Caboose, *92*	14	19____
16535	Erie-Lackawanna Bay Window Caboose, *91 u*	42	50____
16536	Chessie System SP-type Caboose, *92, 93 u, 94, 95 u*		23____
16537	MKT SP-type Caboose, *92, 93 u*	17	21____
16538	L&N Bay Window Caboose "1041," *92 u*	29	33____
16539	WP Steelside Caboose "539," smoke, SSS (std O), *92*	50	55____
16541	Montana Rail Link Extended Vision Caboose "10131" with smoke, *93*	55	65____
16543	NYC SP-type Caboose, *93–95*		20____
16544	Union Pacific SP-type Caboose, *93–95*	22	26____
16546	Clinchfield SP-type Caboose, *93*	22	26____
16547	"Happy Holidays" SP-type Caboose, *93–95*	46	55____
16548	Conrail SP-type Caboose, *93*	15	20____
16549	Soo Line Work Caboose, *93*	18	26____
16550	U.S. Navy Searchlight Caboose, *94–95*	16	21____
16551	Budweiser SP-type Caboose, *93–94 u*	30	33____
16552	Frisco Searchlight Caboose, *94*	23	26____
16553	United Auto Workers SP-type Caboose, *93 u*		40____

		Exc	Mint
____16554	GT Extended Vision Caboose "79052," smoke, *94*	40	47
____16555	C&O SP-type Caboose, *94*	22	26
____16557	Ford SP-type Caboose, *94 u*	19	24
____16558	Crayola SP-type Caboose, *94 u, 95*	17	21
____16559	Seaboard Center Cupola Caboose "5658," *95*	23	24
____16560	Chrysler Mopar Caboose, *94 u*	24	26
____16561	UP Center Cupola Caboose "25766," *95*	27	31
____16562	Reading Center Cupola Caboose, *95*	25	29
____16563	Lionel Lines SP-type Caboose, *95*	22	26
16564	Western Maryland Center Cupola Caboose (SSS), *95*	30	34
____16565	Milwaukee Road Bay Window Caboose, *95*	50	60
____16566	U.S. Army SP-type Caboose "907," *95*		28
____16568	ATSF SP-type Caboose, *96–99*		23
____16571	Georgia Power SP-type Caboose "52789," *95 u*		68
____16575	Sears Zenith SP-type Caboose, *95*		38
____16577	U.S. Coast Guard Work Caboose, *96*		26
____16578	Lionel Lines SP-type Caboose, *95 u*		20
____16579	GM/AC Delco, SP-type Caboose, *95*		35
____16580	SP-type Caboose, *96–99*		11
____16581	UP Illuminated Caboose, *96*		30
____16586	SP Illuminated Caboose "6357," *97*		42
____16590	Dodge Motorsports SP-type Caboose "6950," *96*		54
16591	Little League Baseball SP-type Caboose "6397," *97*		40
____16593	Lionel Belt Line Caboose "6257," *98*		32
____16594	Caboose "6357," *98*		29
____16600	Illinois Central Coal Dump Car, *88*	14	23
____16601	Canadian National Searchlight Car, *88*	19	24
____16602	Erie-Lackawanna Coal Dump Car, *87*	16	26
____16603	Detroit Zoo Giraffe Car (O27), *87*	40	49
____16604	NYC Log Dump Car, *87*	15	27
____16605	Bronx Zoo Giraffe Car (O27), *88*	39	44
____16606	Southern Searchlight Car, *87*	13	21
____16607	Southern Coal Dump Car "16707" (SSS), *87*	18	26
____16608	Lehigh Valley Searchlight Car, *87*	22	30
____16609	Lehigh Valley Derrick Car, *87*	22	30
____16610	Track Maintenance Car, *87–88*	15	25
____16611	Santa Fe Log Dump Car, *88*	15	23
____16612	Soo Line Log Dump Car, *89*	14	24
____16613	MKT Coal Dump Car, *89*	17	26
____16614	Reading Cop and Hobo Car (O27), *89*	24	25
____16615	Lionel Lines Extension Searchlight Car, *89*	20	28
____16616	D&RGW Searchlight Car (SSS), *89*	22	30
____16617	C&NW Boxcar with ETD, *89*	23	34
____16618	Santa Fe Track Maintenance Car, *89*	11	19
____16619	Wabash Coal Dump Car, *90*	14	25
____16620	C&O Track Maintenance Car, *90–91*	16	19
____16621	Alaska Log Dump Car, *90*	24	31
____16622	CSX Boxcar with ETD, *90–91*	20	28
____16623	MKT DD Boxcar with ETD, *91*	16	23
____16624	NH Cop and Hobo Car (O27), *90–91*	23	31
____16625	NYC Extension Searchlight Car, *90*	22	30
____16626	CSX Searchlight Car, *90*	18	26
____16627	CSX Log Dump Car, *90*	19	23

		Exc	Mint
16628	Cop and Hobo Circus Gondola, *90–91*	36	43____
16629	Operating Circus Elephant Car (O27), *90–91*	38	50____
16630	SP Operating Cowboy Car (O27), *90–91*	22	26____
16631	RI Boxcar, steam RailSounds, *90*	110	130____
16632	BN Boxcar, diesel RailSounds, *90*	90	100____
16634	WM Coal Dump Car, *91*	26	32____
16636	D&RGW Log Dump Car, *91*	19	25____
16637	WP Extension Searchlight Car, *91*	27	30____
16638	Operating Circus Animal Car (O27), *91*	50	55____
16639	B&O Boxcar, steam RailSounds, *91*	100	120____
16640	Rutland Boxcar, diesel RailSounds, *91*	100	120____
16641	Toys "R" Us Giraffe Car (O27), *90–91 u*	45	65____
16642	Mickey's World Tour Goofy Car (O27), *91, 92 u*	33	41____
16644	Amtrak Crane Car, *91, 92 u*	36	42____
16645	Amtrak Searchlight Caboose, *91*	27	30____
16649	Railway Express Agency Boxcar, steam RailSounds, *92*	110	140____
16650	NYC Pacemaker Boxcar, diesel RailSounds, *92*	100	135____
16651	Operating Circus Clown Car (O27), *92*	24	30____
16652	Radar Car, *92*	25	29____
16653	Western Pacific Crane Car (SSS), *92*	44	60____
16655	Steam Tender "1993," RailSounds, *93*	115	140____
16656	Burlington Log Dump Car, *92 u*	18	25____
16657	Lehigh Valley Coal Dump Car, *92 u*	22	29____
16658	Erie-Lackawanna Crane Car, *93*	47	65____
16659	Union Pacific Searchlight Car, *93–95*	15	18____
16660	Fire Car with ladders, *93–94*	28	33____
16661	Flatcar with boat, *93*	20	22____
16662	Bugs Bunny and Yosemite Sam Outlaw Car (O27), *93–94*	28	30____
16663	Missouri Pacific Searchlight Car, *93*	16	19____
16664	L&N Coal Dump Car, *93*	22	25____
16665	Maine Central Log Dump Car, *93*	23	27____
16666	Toxic Waste Car, *93–94*	25	32____
16667	Conrail Searchlight Car, *93*	27	30____
16668	Ontario Northland Log Dump Car, *93*	20	24____
16669	Soo Line Searchlight Car, *93*	17	21____
16670	TV Car, *93–94*	12	22____
16673	Lionel Lines Tender, whistle, *94–97*	33	42____
16674	Pinkerton Animated Gondola, *94*	28	32____
16675	Great Northern Log Dump Car, *94*	21	25____
16676	Burlington Coal Dump Car, *94*	23	28____
16677	NATO Flatcar with Royal Navy submarine, *94*	34	44____
16678	Rock Island Searchlight Car, *94*	12	23____
16679	U.S. Mail Operating Boxcar, *94*	45	50____
16680	Cherry Picker Car, *94*	25	28____
16681	Aquarium Car, *95*	35	44____
16682	Lionelville Farms Operating Stock Car (O27), *94*	23	27____
16683	Los Angeles Zoo Elephant Car (O27), *94*	22	26____
16684	U.S. Navy Crane Car, *94–95*	35	40____
16685	Erie Extension Searchlight Car, *95*	30	34____
16686	Mickey Mouse Animated Boxcar, *95*	28	35____
16687	U.S. Mail Operating Boxcar, *94*	29	37____
16688	Fire Car with ladders, *94*	35	43____
16689	Toxic Waste Car, *94*	29	32____

		Exc	Mint
16690	Bugs Bunny and Yosemite Sam Outlaw Car (O27), *94*	30	34
16701	Southern Tool Car (SSS), *87*	43	55
16702	Amtrak Bunk Car, *91, 92 u*	25	27
16703	NYC Tool Car, *92*	24	31
16704	TV Car, *94*	27	29
16705	Chesapeake & Ohio Cop and Hobo Car, *95*	28	34
16706	Animal Transport Service Giraffe Car, *95*	27	30
16708	C&NW Track Maintenance Car, *95*	24	31
16709	New York Central Derrick Car, *95*	22	28
16710	U.S. Army Operating Missile Car, *95*	40	42
16711	Pennsylvania Searchlight Car, *95*	27	31
16712	Pinkerton Animated Gondola, *95*	34	39
16715	ATSF Log Dump Car, *96–99*		24
16717	Jersey Central Crane Car, *96*		41
16718	USMC Missile Launching Flatcar, *96*	26	31
16719	Exploding Boxcar, *96*		38
16720	Lionel Lines Searchlight Car "3650," *96–97*		50
16724	Mickey and Friends Submarine Car, *96*		39
16725	Rhino Transport Car, *97*		31
16726	U.S. Army Fire Ladder Car, *96*		43
16734	U.S. Coast Guard Searchlight Car, *96*		30
16735	U.S. Coast Guard Flatcar with radar, *96*	28	35
16736	U.S. Coast Guard Derrick Car, *96*		34
16737	Road Runner and Wile E. Coyote Gondola "3444," *96*		60
16738	Pepe LePew Boxcar "3370," *96*		40
16739	Foghorn Leghorn Poultry Car "6434," *96*		44
16740	Lionel Corporation Mail Car "3428," *96*		37
16741	Union Pacific Illuminated Bunk Car, *97*		25
16742	Trout Ranch Aquarium Car "3435," *96*		32
16744	Port of Lionel City Searchlight Car, *97*		30
16745	Port of Lionel City Flatcar with radar, *97*		30
16746	Port of Lionel City Derrick Car, *97*		30
16747	Breyer Animated Horse Car "6473," *97*		34
16748	U.S. Forest Service Log-Dump Car "3361," *97*		30
16749	Midget Mines Ore-Dump Car "3479," *97*		36
16750	Lionel City Aquarium Car "3436," *97*		32
16751	AIREX Sports Channel TV Car "3545," *97*		25
16752	Marvin the Martian Missile Launching Flatcar "6655," *97*	130	140
16754	Porky Pig and Instant Martians Flatcar "6805," *97*	130	179
16755	Daffy Duck Animated Balloon Car "3470," *97*	131	168
16760	Pluto and Cats Animated Gondola "3444," *97*		55
16765	Bureau of Land Management Log Car "3351," *98*		30
16766	Bureau of Land Management Ore Car "3479," *98*		31
16767	New York Central Ice Docks Ice Car "6352," *98*		47
16776	Holiday Boxcar, RailSounds, *98*		68
16777	Animated Cola Car and Platform, *98*		100
16782	Bethlehem Ore Dump Car "3479," *99*		95
16783	Westside Lumber Log Dump Car "3351," *99*		32
16784	Pratt's Hollow Seed Dump Car "3479," *99*		36
16785	"Happy Holidays" Music Reefer "5700," *99*		100
16789	Easter Operating Boxcar, *99*		39

		Exc	Mint
16790	UP Stock Car "3356," Crowsounds, *99*		90___
16791	New York City Lights Boxcar, *99*		44___
16792	Constellation Boxcar "9600," *99*		37___
16793	Animated Glow-in-the-Dark Alien Boxcar, *99*		44___
16794	Wicked Witch Halloween Boxcar, *99*		46___
16795	Elf Chasing Rudolph Gondola "6462," *99*		55___
16796	Snowman Loading Ice Car "6352," *99*		55___
16805	Budweiser Malt Nutrine Reefer "3285," *91–92 u*	76	102___
16806	Toys "R" Us Boxcar, *92 u*	21	26___
16807	H.J. Heinz Reefer "301," *93*	23	27___
16808	Toys "R" Us Boxcar, *93 u*	28	30___
16817	Ambassador 1-D Tank Car, *00 u*		170___
16818	Engineer Award Tank Car, *00 u*		710___
16819	JLC Award Tank Car, *00 u*		760___
16820	Ambassador Boxcar, *00 u*	309	505___
16822	CSX Water Tower, *08*		23___
16824	O36 Command Control Switch, left hand (FasTrack), *09–14*		110___
16825	O36 Command Control Switch, right hand (FasTrack), *09–14*		110___
16826	O72 Command Control Switch, left hand (FasTrack), *09–14*		120___
16827	O72 Command Control Switch, right hand (FasTrack), *09–14*		120___
16828	O60 Command Control Switch, left hand (FasTrack), *09–14*		120___
16829	O60 Command Control Switch, right hand (FasTrack), *09–14*		120___
16830	O48 Command Control Switch, left hand (FasTrack), *09–14*		120___
16831	O48 Command Control Switch, right hand (FasTrack), *09–14*		120___
16832	O72 Command Control Wye Switch (FasTrack), *09–14*		115___
16834	O48 Half-Curved Track (FasTrack), *09–14, 16*		5___
16835	O48 Quarter-Curved Track (FasTrack), *09–14, 16*		5___
16836	Christmas Girder Bridge, *09*		21___
16837	Christmas Operating Billboard, *09*		45___
16841	Halloween Gateman, *09*		80___
16842	Big Moe Crane, *10*		70___
16843	City and Western Diorama, *10–11*		15___
16845	Bookstore, *09–10*		60___
16846	Burning Hobo Depot, *09*		90___
16847	Legacy Hotel, *10–11*		70___
16848	Creature Comforts Pet Store, sound, *09–10*		80___
16849	Rotary Dumper with coal conveyor, CC, *10*		600___
16850	Operating Wind Turbine, 3-pack, *09–11*		225___
16851	Sunoco Cylindrical Oil Tank, gray, *10–11*		100___
16852	Sunoco Cylindrical Oil Tank, yellow, *10–11*		90___
16853	Polar Express Diorama, *09–11, 13*		18___
16854	MTA LIRR Blinking Billboard, *09*		30___
16855	MTA LIRR Illuminated Station Platform, *09*		37___
16856	MTA LIRR Passenger Station, *09*		60___
16857	Thomas & Friends Diorama, *10–16*		18___
16859	Grand Central Terminal, *09*		1500___
16861	50,000-gallon Water Tank, *09–11*		150___

		Exc	Mint
___16863	Santa's Christmas Wish Station, *09–11*		125
___16868	Straight O Gauge Tunnel, *09–17*		55
___16871	Winter Wonderland Diorama, *09–11*		15
___16872	Illuminated Christmas Station Platform, *09*		35
___16873	Bathtub Gondola Coal Load 3-pack, *10–17*		20
___16874	Coaling Station, *10–11*		80
___16880	Freight Platform, *10–12*		30
___16881	Barrel Shed, *10–11*		30
___16882	12" Covered Bridge, *10–17*		60
___16883	Neil's Guitar Shop, *10–11*		60
___16889	Coal Tipple Pack, *11–17*		15
___16891	Tank Car Accident, *10–11*		130
___16896	Flagpole with lights, *10–16*		28
___16897	75th Anniversary Gateman, *10*		75
___16903	CP Bulkhead Flatcar with pulp load (SSS), *94*	22	25
___16904	NYC Pacemaker Flatcar Set with trailers, *94*	55	60
___16907	Flatcar with farm tractors, *94*	27	33
16908	U.S. Navy Flatcar "04039" with submarine, *94–95*	39	46
16909	U.S. Navy Gondola "16556" with canisters, *94–95*	16	22
___16910	Missouri Pacific Flatcar with trailer, *94*	22	27
___16911	B&M Flatcar with trailer, *94*	28	34
___16912	CN Maxi-Stack Flatcar Set with containers, *94*	70	75
___16915	Lionel Lines Gondola (O27), *93–94 u*	7	10
___16916	Ford Flatcar with trailer, *94 u*	38	45
___16917	Crayola Gondola with crayons, *94 u, 95*	8	9
___16919	Chrysler Mopar Gondola with coil covers, *94–96*	33	36
___16922	Chesapeake & Ohio Flatcar with trailer, *95*	25	31
16923	Intermodal Service Flatcar with wheel chocks, *95*	15	22
___16924	Lionel Corporation Flatcar "6424" with trailer, *96*		24
___16925	New York Central Flatcar with trailer, *95*	65	85
___16926	Frisco Flatcar with trailers, *95*	24	31
___16927	New York Central Flatcar with gondola, *95*	17	22
___16928	Soo Line Flatcar with dump bin (O27), *95*	12	15
___16929	BC Rail Gondola with cable reels, *95*	21	25
___16930	Santa Fe Flatcar with wheel load, *95*	20	25
___16932	Erie Flatcar with rail load, *95*	17	22
___16933	Lionel Lines Flatcar with autos, *95*	23	25
___16934	Pennsylvania Flatcar with Ertl road grader, *95*	28	39
16935	UP Depressed Center Flatcar with Ertl bulldozer, *95*	22	35
16936	Sealand Maxi-Stack Flatcar Set with containers, *95*	70	85
___16939	U.S. Navy Flatcar "04040" with boat, *95*	25	30
___16940	ATSF Flatcar with trailer, *96–99*		40
___16941	ATSF Flatcar with autos, *96–99*		25
___16943	Jersey Central Gondola, *96*		18
16944	Georgia Power Depressed Center Flatcar "31438" with transformer, *95 u*		50
16945	Georgia Power Depressed Center Flatcar "31950" with cable reels, *95 u*		53
___16946	C&O F9 Well Car "3840," *96*		31
___16951	Southern I-Beam Flatcar "9823" with load, *97*		25

		Exc	Mint
16952	U.S. Navy Flatcar with Ertl helicopter, *96*		25____
16953	NYC Flatcar with Red Wing Shoes trailer, *95 u*	39	45____
16954	NYC Flatcar "6424" with Ertl scraper, *96*		30____
16955	ATSF Flatcar with Ertl Challenger, *96*		30____
16956	Zenith Flatcar with trailer, *95 u*		136____
16957	Depressed Center Flatcar "6461" with Ertl Case tractor, *96*		29____
16958	Flatcar with Ertl New Holland loader, *96*		26____
16960	U.S. Coast Guard Flatcar with boat, *96*		40____
16961	GM/AC Delco Flatcar with trailer, *95*		73____
16963	Lionel Corporation Flatcar "6411," *96–97*		34____
16964	Lionel Corporation Gondola "6462," *97*		22____
16965	Scout Flatcar "6424" with stakes, *96–97*		20____
16967	Depressed Center Flatcar "6461" with transformer, *96*		21____
16968	Depressed Center Flatcar "6461" with Ertl Helicopter, *96*		35____
16969	Flatcar "6411" with Beechcraft Bonanza, *96*		33____
16970	LA County Flatcar "6424" with motorized powerboat, *96*		20____
16971	Port of Lionel City Flatcar with boat, *97*		35____
16972	P&LE Gondola "6462," *97*		22____
16975	Well Car Doublestack Set, *97*		75____
16978	MILW Flatcar "6424" with P&H shovel, *97*		43____
16980	Speedy Gonzales Missile Flatcar "6823," *97*		46____
16982	BC Rail Bulkhead Flatcar "9823" with lumber, *97*		28____
16983	PRR F9 Well Car "6983" with cable reels, *97*		39____
16986	Sears Zenith Bulkhead Flatcar, *96 u*		45____
16987	Musco Lighting Bulkhead Flatcar, *97 u*		35____
16997	Lionel Lines Recovery Crane Car, *99*		50____
17002	Conrail 2-bay ACF Hopper (std O), *87*	42	47____
17003	Du Pont 2-bay ACF Hopper (std O), *90*	39	45____
17004	MKT 2-bay ACF Hopper (std O), *91*	23	27____
17005	Cargill 2-bay ACF Hopper (std O), *92*	29	37____
17006	Soo Line 2-bay ACF Hopper (std O, SSS), *93*	31	36____
17007	GN 2-bay ACF Hopper "173872" (std O), *94*	26	31____
17008	D&RGW 2-bay ACF Hopper "10009" (std O), *95*		31____
17009	New York Central 2-bay ACF Hopper, *96*		35____
17010	Govt. of Canada ACF 2-bay Covered Hopper "7000," *98*		32____
17010	NP PS-1 Boxcar 6-pack, LionScale, *17*		360____
17011	NP ACF 2-bay Covered Hopper "75052," *98*		44____
17012	Govt. of Canada ACF 2-bay Covered Hopper "7001," *98*		30____
17013	NYC Graffiti 2-bay Covered Hopper "7000," *99*		55____
17014	Graffiti 2-bay Covered Hopper "7000" (std O), *99*		45____
17015	Corning 2-bay Hopper "90409" (std O), *01*		40____
17016	C&NW 2-bay Hopper "96644" (std O), *01*		46____
17017	Chessie System 2-bay Hopper "605527" (std O), *02*		32____
17018	Nickel Plate Road Offset Hopper "33074," *02*		43____
17019	Santa Fe Offset Hopper "78299," *02*		43____
17020	Frisco Offset Hopper "92092," *02*		43____
17020	UP PS-1 Boxcar 6-pack, LionScale, *17*		360____
17021	NYC Offset Hopper "867999," *02*		43____

		Exc	Mint
17022	Burlington 2-bay ACF Hopper "183925" (std O), 03		30
17023	BNSF 2-bay Hopper "409038" (std O), 04		30
17024	Reading Offset Hopper "81089" (std O), 03–04		43
17025	C&O Offset Hopper "300027" (std O), 03–04		43
17026	D&H Offset Hopper "7215" (std O), 03–04		41
17027	IC Offset Hopper "92142" (std O), 03–04		49
17028	GE PS-2 2-bay Covered Hopper "326" (std O), 03–04		35
17029	CNJ PS-2 2-bay Covered Hopper "803" (std O), 03–04		35
17030	MILW PS-2 2-bay Covered Hopper "99708" (std O), 03–04		35
17030	Reading PS-1 Boxcar 6-pack, LionScale, 17		360
17031	SP PS-2 2-bay Covered Hopper "401306" (std O), 03–04		38
17038	Clinchfield PS-2 Covered Hopper, 05		70
17039	Boston & Maine PS-2 2-bay Covered Hopper, 05		55
17040	Norfolk & Western PS-2 2-bay Covered Hopper, 05		55
17040	NYC PS-1 Boxcar 6-pack, LionScale, 17		360
17041	Great Northern Offset Hopper, 05		60
17042	Green Bay & Western Offset Hopper, 05		60
17043	Baltimore & Ohio Offset Hopper, 05		60
17050	NYC 14-panel Hopper 6-pack, LionScale, 17		330
17060	D&RGW 14-panel Hopper 6-pack, LionScale, 17		330
17063	Santa Fe PS-2 2-bay Covered Hopper "82297" (std O), 06		55
17064	MKT PS-2 2-bay Covered Hopper "1311" (std O), 06		55
17065	Boraxo PS-2 2-bay Covered Hopper "31062" (std O), 06		55
17066	PRR PS-2 2-bay Covered Hopper "256177" (std O), 06		55
17067	Rock Island Offset Hopper "89500" with gravel (std O), 06		65
17068	CNJ Offset Hopper "61261" (std O), 06		65
17069	Maine Central Offset Hopper "3785" (std O), 06		65
17070	P&LE Offset Hopper "4990" (std O), 06		65
17070	Conrail 14-panel Hopper 6-pack, LionScale, 17		330
17080	EL 14-panel Hopper 6-pack, LionScale, 17		330
17083	C&O Offset Hopper "47386" (std O), 05		40
17100	Chessie System 3-bay ACF Hopper	49	85
17101	Chessie System 3-bay ACF Hopper (std O), 88	37	45
17102	Chessie System 3-bay ACF Hopper (std O), 88	35	41
17103	Chessie System 3-bay ACF Hopper (std O), 88	31	34
17104	Chessie System 3-bay ACF Hopper (std O), 88	38	46
17105	Chessie System 3-bay ACF Hopper (std O), 88	39	46
17107	Sinclair 3-bay ACF Hopper (std O), 89	40	48
17108	Santa Fe 3-bay ACF Hopper (std O), 90	42	48
17109	N&W 3-bay ACF Hopper (std O), 91	24	31
17110	UP Hopper with coal (std O), 91	24	30
17111	Reading Hopper with coal (std O), 91	23	28
17112	Erie-Lack. 3-bay ACF Hopper (std O), 92	24	34
17113	LV Hopper with coal (std O), 92–93	25	32
17114	Peabody Hopper with coal (std O), 92–93	26	30

		Exc	Mint
17118	Archer Daniels Midland 3-bay ACF Hopper "60029" (std O), *93*	28	35____
17120	CSX Hopper "295110" with coal (std O), *94*	28	30____
17121	ICG Hopper "72867" with coal (std O), *94*	26	33____
17122	RI 3-bay ACF Hopper "800200" (std O), *94*	32	39____
17123	Cargill Covered Grain Hopper "844304" (std O), *95*	25	34____
17124	Archer Daniels Midland 3-bay ACF Hopper "50224" (std O), *95*	24	30____
17127	Delaware & Hudson 3-bay Hopper, *96*		34____
17128	Chesapeake & Ohio 3-bay Hopper, *96*		30____
17129	WM 3-bay Hopper "9300" with coal (std O), *97*		34____
17130	ACFX ACF 4-bay Covered Hopper 6-pack, LionScale, *17*		360____
17132	PRR 3-bay ACF Hopper "260815," *98*		40____
17133	BNSF ACF 3-bay Covered Hopper "403698," *98*		38____
17134	BNSF 3-bay Covered Hopper "403698" (std O), *01*		38____
17135	BNSF ACF 3-bay Covered Hopper with ETD, *98*		39____
17137	Cargill 3-bay Covered Hopper "1219" (std O), *99*		45____
17138	Farmers Elevator 3-bay Covered Hopper (std O), *99*		45____
17139	"Grain Train" 3-bay Hopper "BLMR 1025," *99–00*		39____
17140	Virginian 3-bay Hopper 6-pack, "5260-5265," *99*		230____
17140	GN ACF 4-bay Covered Hopper 6-pack, LionScale, *17*		360____
17147	C&O 3-bay Hopper 6-pack, "156330-156335," *99*		230____
17150	AT&SF ACF 4-bay Covered Hopper 6-pack, LionScale, *17*		360____
17154	Alberta Cylindrical Hopper "628373" (std O), *01*		40____
17155	Shell Cylindrical Hopper "3527" (std O), *01*		40____
17156	ACF Pressureaide 3-bay Hopper "59267" (std O), *01*		27____
17157	Wonder Bread "56670" 3-bay Hopper (std O), *01*		40____
17158	Conrail Coal Hopper "487739" (std O), *01*		42____
17159	N&W Coal Hopper "1776" (std O), *01*		45____
17160	C&NW (UP) B145ACF 4-bay Covered Hopper 6-pack, LionScale, *17*		360____
17163	C&O 3-bay Hopper (std O), *01*		30____
17170	General Mills 3-bay Covered Hopper (std O), *00 u*		60____
17170	PFE 57' Mechanical Reefer, *17*		390____
17171	Lionel Lion Cylindrical Hopper (std O), *01*		45____
17172	CP Rail Cylindrical Hopper "385206" (std O), *02*		37____
17173	Govt. of Canada Cylindrical Hopper "111031" (std O), *02*		33____
17174	GN 3-bay Hopper "171250" (std O), *02*		29____
17175	IC PS-2CD 4427 Covered Hopper "57031" (std O), *02*		40____
17176	Cargill PS-2CD 4427 Covered Hopper "2514" (std O), *02*		46____
17177	PS-2CD 4427 Covered Hopper "2500" (std O), *02*		40____
17178	Santa Fe PS-2CD 4427 Covered Hopper "304774" (std O), *02*		40____
17179	Indianapolis Power & Light Coal Hopper "10074" (std O), *02*		40____

		Exc	Mint
___17180	Rock Island Coal Hopper "700665" (std O), *02*		40
17180	SPFE 57' Mechanical Reefer 6-pack, LionScale, *17*		390
17181	NYC 4-bay ACF Centerflow Hopper "892138" (std O), *03*		45
17182	Sigco Hybrids 4-bay ACF Centerflow Hopper "1100" (std O), *03*		46
___17183	C&O Hopper "156341" (std O), *01*		30
___17184	Virginian Hopper "5271" (std O), *01*		30
___17185	LLCX Bathtub Gondola "877900" (std O), *01*		36
17186	Cannonaide 4-bay ACF Centerflow Hopper "96169" (std O), *03*		40
17187	Rio Grande 4-bay ACF Centerflow Hopper "15521" (std O), *03*		40
17188	Govt. of Canada 3-bay Cylindrical Hopper (std O), *03*		48
17189	Saskatchewan Grain 3-bay Cylindrical Hopper (std O), *03*		48
___17190	Soo/CP 3-bay ACF Hopper "119303" (std O), *03*		37
17190	UPFE 57' Mechanical Reefer 6-pack, LionScale, *17*		390
17191	BN PS-2CD 4427 Hopper "450669" (std O), *03–04*		45
17192	Lehigh Valley PS-2CD 4427 Hopper "51118" (std O), *03–04*		40
17193	Chessie System/WM PS-2CD 4427 Hopper "4673" (std O), *03–04*		30
17194	MKT PS-2CD 4427 Hopper "1122" (std O), *03–04*		40
___17195	L&N 3-bay Hopper "240850" (std O), *04*		40
___17196	Firestone 4-bay Hopper "53240" (std O), *04*		40
17197	Diamond Chemicals 4-bay Hopper "53286" (std O), *04*		40
___17198	Hercules 4-bay Hopper "50503" (std O), *04*		40
___17199	Conrail 4-bay Hopper "888367" (std O), *04*		46
___17200	Canadian Pacific Boxcar (std O), *89*	26	32
17200	BNFE 57' Mechanical Reefer 6-pack, LionScale, *17*		390
___17201	Conrail Boxcar (std O), *87*	33	38
___17202	Santa Fe Boxcar (std O), diesel RailSounds, *90*	80	85
___17203	Cotton Belt DD Boxcar (std O), *91*	33	38
___17204	Missouri Pacific DD Boxcar (std O), *91*	27	30
___17207	C&IM DD Boxcar (std O), *92*	36	42
___17208	Union Pacific DD Boxcar (std O), *92*	35	40
___17209	B&O DD Boxcar "296000" (std O), *93*	37	43
17210	Chicago & Illinois Midland Boxcar "16021" (std O), *92 u*	30	39
17211	Chicago & Illinois Midland Boxcar "16022" (std O), *92 u*	30	39
17212	Chicago & Illinois Midland Boxcar "16023" (std O), *92 u*	24	31
___17213	Susquehanna Boxcar "501" (std O), *93*	28	31
___17214	Railbox Boxcar (std O), diesel RailSounds, *93*	75	85
17216	PRR DD Boxcar "60155" (std O), *94*	34	38
17217	New Haven State of Maine Boxcar "45003" (std O), *95*	28	35
___17218	BAR State of Maine Boxcar "2184" (std O), *95*	23	36

		Exc	Mint
17219	Tazmanian Devil 40th Birthday Boxcar (std O), *95*	40	50____
17220	Pennsylvania Boxcar (std O), *96*		23____
17221	NYC Boxcar (std O), *96*		34____
17222	Western Pacific Boxcar (std O), *96*	28	34____
17223	Milwaukee Road DD Boxcar (std O), *96*		34____
17224	Central of Georgia Boxcar "9464-197" (std O), *97*	15	29____
17225	Penn Central Boxcar "9464-297" (std O), *97*	13	26____
17226	Milwaukee Road Boxcar "9464-397" (std O), *97*		23____
17227	UP DD Boxcar "9200" (std O), *97*		35____
17231	Wisconsin Central DD Boxcar "9200" with auto frames, *98*		40____
17232	SP/UP Merger DD Boxcar "9200," *98*		33____
17233	Western Pacific Boxcar "9464-198," *98*		27____
17234	Port Huron & Detroit Boxcar "9464-298," *98*		33____
17235	Boston & Maine Boxcar "9464-398," *98*		41____
17239	ATSF "Texas Chief" Boxcar "9464-1," *97*		50____
17240	ATSF "Super Chief" Boxcar "9464-2," *97*		50____
17241	ATSF" El Capitan" Boxcar "9464-3," *97*		50____
17242	ATSF "Grand Canyon" Boxcar "9464-4," *97*		60____
17243	NP Boxcar "8722," *98*		48____
17244	Santa Fe "Chief" Boxcar, *98*		37____
17245	C&O Boxcar with Chessie kitten, *98*		44____
17246	NYC Pacemaker Rolling Stock 4-pack, *98*		200____
17247	NYC 9464 Boxcar "174940," *98*		135____
17248	NYC 9464 Boxcar "174945," *98*		115____
17249	NYC 9464 Boxcar "174949," *98*		60____
17250	UP Boxcar "507406" (std O), *99*		45____
17251	BNSF Boxcar "103277," *99*		41____
17252	NS Boxcar "564824" (std O), *99*		41____
17253	CSX Boxcar "141756" (std O), *99*		35____
17254	UP Boxcar "551967" (std O), *99*		42____
17255	Chevy DD Boxcar "9200" (std O), *99*		38____
17257	Atlantic Coast Line Boxcar "28809" (std O), *99*		36____
17258	D&H 9464 Boxcar "29055" std O, *99*		41____
17259	MKT 9464 Boxcar "1422" (std O), *99*		34____
17260	CP Rail 9464 Boxcar "286138" (std O), silver, *00*		45____
17261	CP Rail 9464 Boxcar "85154," green, *00*		44____
17262	CP Rail 9464 Boxcar "56776," red (std O), *00*		48____
17263	NYC Boxcar "45725" (std O), *00*		46____
17264	C&O Boxcar "6054" (std O), *00*		44____
17265	U.S. Army Boxcar (std O), *00*		35____
17266	Monon Boxcar "911" (std O), *00*		45____
17268	C&O 9464 Boxcar "12700" (std O), *01*		44____
17269	Western Maryland 9464 Boxcar "29140" (std O), *01*		44____
17270	B&O Time-Saver 9464 Boxcar "467439" (std O), *01*		42____
17271	"The Rock" Boxcar "300324" (std O), *01*		37____
17272	Railbox Boxcar "15150" (std O), *01*		27____
17273	DT&I DD Boxcar "26852" (std O), *01*		44____
17274	Soo Line DD Boxcar "177587" (std O), *01*		42____
17275	NYC PS-1 Boxcar "175008" (std O), *02*		43____
17276	Cotton Belt PS-1 Boxcar "75000" (std O), *02*		44____
17277	Rio Grande PS-1 Boxcar "69676" (std O), *02*		40____

			Exc	Mint
____	17278	WP PS-1 Boxcar "1953" (std O), *02*		44
____	17279	Ontario Northland Boxcar "7428" (std O), *02*		40
	17280	Santa Fe Boxcar "600194" with auto frames (std O), *02*		45
____	17281	PRR DD Boxcar "83158" (std O), *04*		42
____	17282	UP DD Boxcar "160300" (std O), *04*		42
____	17283	GM&O DD Boxcar "9077" (std O), *04*		41
____	17284	Erie DD Boxcar "66000" (std O), *04*		41
____	17285	CSX Big Blue Boxcar "151296" (std O), *03*		36
____	17287	BAR Boxcar "5976" (std O), *03*		35
____	17288	NYC PS-1 Boxcar "175012" (std O), *03–04*		38
____	17289	GN PS-1 Boxcar "18485" (std O), *03*		40
____	17290	Seaboard PS-1 Boxcar "24452" (std O), *03–04*		42
____	17291	RI PS-1 Boxcar "21110" (std O), *03–04*		42
____	17292	B&M PS-1 Boxcar "76182" (std O), *04*		34
____	17293	IC PS-1 Boxcar "400666" (std O), *04*		40
____	17294	TP&W PS-1 Boxcar "5036" (std O), *04*		36
____	17295	Santa Fe PS-1 Boxcar "276749" (std O), *04*		40
____	17297	UP PS-1 Boxcar, *03*		100
____	17300	Canadian Pacific Reefer (std O), *89*	28	33
____	17301	Conrail Reefer (std O), *87*	35	42
____	17302	Santa Fe Reefer with ETD (std O), *90*	35	41
____	17303	C&O Reefer "7890" (std O), *93*	23	30
____	17304	Wabash Reefer "26269" (std O), *94*	29	37
____	17305	Pacific Fruit Express Reefer "459400" (std O), *94*	27	40
____	17306	Pacific Fruit Express Reefer "459401" (std O), *94*	19	27
____	17307	Tropicana Reefer "300" (std O), *95*	44	65
____	17308	Tropicana Reefer "301" (std O), *95*	22	35
____	17309	Tropicana Reefer "302" (std O), *95*	21	29
____	17310	Tropicana Reefer "303" (std O), *95*	20	27
____	17311	REA Reefer (std O), *96*	28	30
____	17314	PFE Reefer "9800-198," *98*		42
____	17315	PFE Reefer "9800-298," *98*		39
____	17316	NP Reefer "98583," *98*		50
____	17317	PRR Reefer FGE "91904," *98*		36
____	17318	UP Reefer "170650," *99*		47
____	17319	PFE Reefer 6-pack (std O), *01*		300
	17331	Hood's General American Milk Car "802" (std O), *02*		100
	17332	Pfaudler General American Milk Car "501" (std O), *02*		70
	17334	REA General American Milk Car "1741" (std O), *02*		100
	17335	New Haven General American Milk Car "102" (std O), *02*		75
____	17336	PFE Steel-sided Reefer "17760" (std O), *03*		45
____	17337	CN Steel-sided Reefer "209712" (std O), *03*		38
	17338	Merchants Dispatch Transit Steel-sided Reefer "12322" (std O), *03*		39
	17339	Burlington Steel-sided Reefer "74825" (std O), *03*		45
	17340	White Bros. General American Milk Car "891" (std O), *03*		44
	17341	Dairymen's League General American Milk Car "779" (std O), *03*		43
____	17342	Miller Beer Steel-sided Reefer (std O), *03 u*		58

		Exc	Mint
17343	Miller Beer Steel-sided Reefer (std O), *03 u*		64___
17349	NYC General American Milk Car "6581" (std O), *03 u*		42___
17350	Hood's General American Milk Car "503" (std O), *03 u*		45___
17351	Santa Fe Steel-sided Reefer "3526" (std O), *04*		43___
17352	PFE Steel-sided Reefer "20043" (std O), *04*		41___
17353	Needham Packing Steel-sided Reefer "60507" (std O), *04*		44___
17354	Swift Steel-sided Reefer "15392" (std O), *04*		42___
17355	Hood's Steel-sided Reefer "550" (std O), *04*		40___
17356	Nestle Nesquik Steel-sided Reefer (std O), *04*		44___
17357	Borden's Steel-sided Reefer "522" (std O), *04*		47___
17358	Fairfield Farms Steel-sided Reefer (std O), *04*		44___
17360	Hood's General American Milk Car "810" (std O), *03*		46___
17361	Hood's General American Milk Car "811" (std O), *03*		43___
17362	Pfaudler General American Milk Car "502" (std O), *03*		47___
17363	Pfaudler General American Milk Car "503" (std O), *03*		40___
17364	REA General American Milk Car "1742" (std O), *03*		38___
17365	REA General American Milk Car "1743" (std O), *03*		44___
17366	NH General American Milk Car "103" (std O), *03*		43___
17367	NH General American Milk Car "104" (std O), *03*		47___
17368	White Brothers General American Milk Car "892" (std O), *03*		43___
17369	White Brothers General American Milk Car "893" (std O), *03*		47___
17370	Dairymen's League General American Milk Car "780" (std O), *03*		47___
17371	Dairymen's League Milk Car "781" (std O), *03*		47___
17372	NYC General American Milk Car "6582" (std O), *03*		47___
17373	NYC General American Milk Car "6583" (std O), *03*		40___
17374	Hood's General American Milk Car "504" (std O), *03*		43___
17375	Hood's General American Milk Car "505" (std O), *03*		47___
17377	Railway Express Operating Milk Car "302" (std O), *05*		172___
17378	Supplee General American Milk Car (std O), *05*		63___
17379	NP Steel-sided Reefer "91353" (std O), *05*		60___
17380	PFE Silver Steel-sided Reefer "45698" (std O), *05*		60___
17381	North Western Steel-sided Reefer "751" (std O), *05*		40___
17397	PFE Steel-sided Reefer "47767" (std O), *05*		45___
17398	A&P General American Milk Car "737" (std O), *06*		65___
17399	Bowman Dairy General American Milk Car "117" (std O), *06*		65___
17400	CP Rail Gondola with coal (std O), *89*	30	34___
17401	Conrail Gondola with coal (std O), *87*	24	26___

		Exc	Mint
___17402	Santa Fe Gondola with coal (std O), *90*	19	25
17403 ___	Chessie System Gondola "371629" with coil covers (std O), *93*	18	25
17404 ___	ICG Gondola "245998" with coil covers (std O), *93*	26	32
17405 ___	Reading Gondola "24876" with coil covers (std O), *94*	27	31
17406 ___	PRR Gondola "385405" with coil covers (std O), *95*	37	42
___17407	NKP Gondola with scrap load, *96*		24
17408 ___	Cotton Belt Gondola "9820" with scrap load (std O), *97*		32
___17410	UP Gondola "903004" with scrap load (std O), *99*		30
___17412	Gondola, blue, online store, *98*		20
___17413	Service Center Gondola with parts load (SSS), *00*		24
17414 ___	Nickel Plate PS-5 Gondola "44801" (std O), *01–02*		40
___17415	Frisco PS-5 Gondola "61878" (std O), *01–02*		35
17416 ___	D&H Gondola "14011" with scrap load (std O), *01*		33
___17417	BN Rotary Bathtub Gondola 3-pack, *01*		140
___17421	CSX Rotary Bathtub Gondola 3-pack, *01*		135
17425 ___	Western Maryland PS-5 Gondola "354903" (std O), *01–02*		36
17426 ___	Maine Central PS-5 Gondola "1116" (std O), *01–02*		40
17427 ___	CSX Rotary Bathtub Gondola Add-on Unit (std O), *02*		47
17428 ___	BN Rotary Bathtub Gondola Add-on Unit (std O), *02*		42
17429 ___	Conrail Rotary Bathtub Gondola 3-pack (std O), *02–03*		115
17433 ___	BNSF Rotary Bathtub Gondola 3-pack (std O), *02–03*		145
___17439	UP PS-5 Gondola "229606" (std O), *03*		35
___17440	Algoma Central PS-5 Gondola "801" (std O), *03*		32
17441 ___	Conrail Rotary Bathtub Gondola "507673" (std O), *03*		39
17442 ___	BNSF Rotary Bathtub Gondola "668330" (std O), *03*		46
___17443	NS Rotary Bathtub Gondola 3-pack (std O), *03*		90
___17447	UP Rotary Bathtub Gondola 3-pack (std O), *03*		100
___17457	GN PS-5 Gondola "72839" (std O), *03*		35
___17458	Reading PS-5 Gondola "33267" (std O), *03*		35
___17459	CP Rail PS-5 Gondola "338966" (std O), *04*		35
___17460	NYC PS-5 Gondola "749592" (std O), *04*		40
___17461	Pennsylvania PS-5 Gondola "374256" (std O), *04*		36
___17462	Santa Fe PS-5 Gondola "167340" (std O), *04*		35
___17463	NS Bathtub Gondola "10303" (std O), *04*		40
___17464	UP Bathtub Gondola "28100" (std O), *04*		35
___17465	CP Rail Bathtub Gondola 3-pack (std O), *04*		105
___17470	CP Rail Bathtub Gondola, *05*		50
___17471	Burlington PS-5 Gondola with covers (std O), *05*		44
___17472	New Haven PS-5 Gondola with covers (std O), *05*		53
___17473	NYC PS-5 Gondola "502351" (std O), *06–07*		65

		Exc	Mint
17474	D&H PS-5 Gondola "13816" (std 0), *06–07*		65___
17475	Koppers PS-5 Gondola "213" (std 0), *06–07*		65___
17477	L&N PS-5 Gondola "170012" (std 0), *06–07*		46___
17478	N&W PS-5 Gondola "275005" with containers (std 0), *08*		70___
17479	LV PS-5 Gondola "33455" with containers (std 0), *08*		70___
17480	RI PS-5 Gondola with coke containers (std 0), *08–09*		70___
17488	UP Bathtub Gondola 3-pack (std 0), *09*		190___
17500	CP Flatcar with logs (std 0), *89*	17	29___
17501	Conrail Flatcar with stakes (std 0), *87*	37	45___
17502	Santa Fe Flatcar with trailer (std 0), *90*	70	75___
17503	NS Flatcar with trailer (std 0), *92*	55	65___
17504	NS Flatcar with trailer (std 0), *92*	55	65___
17505	NS Flatcar with trailer (std 0), *92*	50	55___
17506	NS Flatcar with trailer (std 0), *92*	46	55___
17507	NS Flatcar with trailer (std 0), *92*	50	55___
17510	NP Flatcar "61200" with logs (std 0), *94*	31	36___
17511	WM Flatcar with logs, set of 3 (std 0), *95*		145___
17512	WM Flatcar with logs (std 0), *95*	35	41___
17513	WM Flatcar with logs (std 0), *95*	43	50___
17514	WM Flatcar with logs (std 0), *95*	39	45___
17515	Norfolk Southern Flatcar with tractors (std 0), *95*	24	42___
17516	T&P Flatcar "9823" with 2 Beechcraft Bonanzas (std 0), *97*		50___
17517	WP Flatcar "9823" with Ertl Caterpillar frontloader (std 0), *97*		39___
17518	PRR Flatcar "9823" with 2 Corgi Mack trucks (std 0), *97*	29	50___
17522	Flatcar with Plymouth Prowler, *98*		41___
17527	Flatcar with 2 Dodge Vipers, *98*		38___
17529	ATSF Flatcar "90010" with Ford milk truck, *99*		55___
17533	MTTX Ford Flatcar with auto frames, *99*		38___
17534	Diamond T Flatcar with Mack trucks "9823," *99*		55___
17536	Route 66 Flatcar "9823-3" with 2 luxury coupes, *99*		37___
17537	Route 66 Flatcar "9823-4" with 2 touring coupes, *99*		32___
17538	NYC Flatcar with Ford tow truck, *99*		43___
17539	Flatcar "9823" with 2 Corvettes (std 0), *99*		70___
17540	Flatcar "9823" with 2 Corvettes (std 0), *99*		70___
17546	LL Recovery Flatcar "6424" with rail load, *99*		50___
17547	Lionel Lines Recovery Flatcar "6429" with machinery, *99*		50___
17548	Route 66 Flatcar "9823-6" with 2 luxury coupes, *99*		42___
17549	Route 66 Flatcar "9823-5" with station wagon and trailer, *99*		42___
17550	BN Center Beam Flatcar "6216" with lumber (std 0), *99*		39___
17551	NYC Flatcar with NYC pickups "499," *99*		49___
17553	Trailer Train Flatcar "98102" with combine (std 0), *99*		125___

		Exc	Mint
17554	GN Flatcar "61042" with logs, *00*		32
17555	Ford Mustang Flatcar with 2 cars (std O), *01*		NRS
17556	Ford Mustang Flatcar with 2 cars (std O), *01*		NRS
17557	Route 66 Flatcar "9823-7" with black sedans, *99–00*		39
17558	Route 66 Flatcar "9823-8" with brown sedans, *99*		39
17559	Route 66 Flatcar "9823-9" with 2 wagons (std O), *01*		40
17560	Route 66 Flatcar "9823-10" with 2 sedans (std O), *01*		40
17563	Santa Fe Flatcar "90011" with pickup trucks (std O), *01*		49
17564	West Side Lumber Shay Log Car 3-pack #2 (std O), *01*		95
17568	PRR Flatcar "470333" with pickup trucks (std O), *02*		50
17571	UP Flatcar "909231" with pickup trucks (std O), *03*		50
17572	Pioneer Seed Flatcar with pedal cars, *02 u*		190
17573	WM PS-4 Flatcar "2631" (std O), *03*		35
17574	Santa Fe PS-4 Flatcar "90081" (std O), *03*		35
17575	NYC PS-4 Flatcar "506098" (std O), *03*		40
17576	Ontario Northland PS-4 Flatcar "2020" (std O), *03*		35
17577	B&O PS-4 Flatcar "8651" (std O), *04*		35
17578	B&M PS-4 Flatcar "34007" (std O), *04*		35
17579	Milwaukee Road PS-4 Flatcar "64073" (std O), *04*		35
17580	UP PS-4 Flatcar "54603" (std O), *04*		35
17581	GN Flatcar "X4168" with pickup trucks (std O), *04*		42
17582	PRR PS-4 Flatcar "469617" with trailers (std O), *05*		110
17583	GN PS-4 Flatcar with trailers, *05*		80
17584	SP PS-4 Flatcar with trailers, *05*		80
17585	C&O PS-4 Flatcar "81000" with trailers (std O), *05*		80
17586	BN Husky Stack Car "63322" (std O), *05*		80
17587	SP Husky Stack Car "513915" (std O), *05*		80
17588	CSX Husky Stack Car "620350" (std O), *05*		80
17589	TTX Trailer Train Husky Stack Car "456249" (std O), *05*		65
17600	NYC Wood-sided Caboose (std O), *87 u*	35	45
17601	Southern Wood-sided Caboose (std O), *88*	35	44
17602	Conrail Wood-sided Caboose (std O), *87*	65	75
17603	RI Wood-sided Caboose (std O), *88*	19	34
17604	Lackawanna Wood-sided Caboose (std O), *88*	42	53
17605	Reading Wood-sided Caboose (std O), *89*	34	37
17606	NYC Steel-sided Caboose, smoke (std O), *90*	49	65
17607	Reading Steel-sided Caboose, smoke (std O), *90*	55	65
17608	C&O Steel-sided Caboose, smoke (std O), *91*	46	55
17610	Wabash Steel-sided Caboose, smoke (std O), *91*	39	55
17611	NYC Wood-sided Caboose "6003" (std O), *90 u*	40	55
17612	NKP Steel-sided Caboose, smoke (FF 6), *92*	60	65
17613	Southern Steel-sided Caboose "7613," smoke (std O), *92*	60	65

		Exc	Mint
17615	NP Wood-sided Caboose, smoke (std O), *92*	65	70____
17617	D&RGW Steel-sided Caboose (std O), *95*	50	55____
17618	Frisco Wood-sided Caboose (std O), *95*	65	75____
17620	NP Wood-sided Caboose "1746," *98*		70____
17623	Farmrail Extended Vision Caboose, *99*		74____
17624	Conrail Extended Vision Caboose "6900," *99*		43____
17625	Burlington Northern Steel-sided Caboose "7606," *99*		65____
17626	Service Center Extended Vision Caboose (SSS), *00*		29____
17627	C&O Extended Vision Caboose, *01*		65____
17628	BNSF Extended Vision Caboose, *01*		65____
17629	Santa Fe Extended Vision Caboose, *01*		80____
17630	UP Extended Vision Caboose, *01*		85____
17631	Virginian Bay Window Caboose, *01*		85____
17632	CSX Bay Window Caboose, *01*		75____
17633	NYC Bay Window Caboose, *01*		90____
17634	Delaware & Hudson Bay Window Caboose, *01*		75____
17635	100th Anniversary Die-cast Gold Caboose, *00*		345____
17636	NYC Die-cast Caboose "18096," *00–01*		100____
17637	NYC "Quicker via Peoria" Die-cast Caboose, *00*		135____
17638	RI Extended Vision Caboose "17011" (std O), *02*		55____
17639	Chessie Extended Vision Caboose "3322" (std O), *02*		55____
17640	CP Extended Vision Caboose "434604" (std O), *02*		57____
17641	Soo Line Extended Vision Caboose "2" (std O), *02*		55____
17642	Conrail Bay Window Caboose "21023" (std O), *02*		65____
17643	NKP Bay Window Caboose "480" (std O), *02*		60____
17644	Erie Bay Window Caboose "C307," (std O), *02*		55____
17645	N&W Bay Window Caboose "C-6," (std O), *02*		55____
17646	UP Bay Window Caboose "24555," (std O), *02*		65____
17647	B&O Caboose "C-2820" (std O), *03–04*		65____
17648	Chessie System Caboose "C-2800" (std O), *03–04*		75____
17649	Lionel Lines Caboose "7649" (std O), *03–04*		65____
17650	Rio Grande Extended Vision Caboose "01500" (std O), *03*		65____
17651	BN Extended Vision Caboose "10531" (std O), *03–05*		80____
17652	NYC Bay Window Caboose "20200" (std O), *03*		75____
17653	SP Bay Window Caboose "1337" (std O), *03*		65____
17654	Alaska Extended Vision Caboose "989" (std O), *03*		75____
17655	WP Bay Window Caboose "448" (std O), *03–04*		75____
17657	Norman Rockwell Holiday Caboose, *03*		30____
17658	Burlington Extended Vision Caboose "13611" (std O), *04*		70____
17659	CN Extended Vision Caboose "79646" (std O), *04*		70____
17660	Seaboard Extended Vision Caboose "5700" (std O), *04*		65____
17661	C&NW Bay Window Caboose "10871" (std O), *04*		65____
17662	PC Bay Window Caboose "21001" (std O), *04*		65____

		Exc	Mint
____	**17663** Southern Bay Window Caboose "X546" (std 0), 04		65
____	**17664** B&O Caboose "C-2824" (std 0), 03–04		65
____	**17665** Chessie System Caboose "C-2802" (std 0), 03–04		75
____	**17669** NYC Bay Window Caboose, smoke, 05		85
____	**17670** CP Rail Bay Window Caboose, smoke, 05		85
____	**17671** BN Extended Vision Caboose, 05		85
____	**17672** GN Extended Vision Caboose "X-106" (std 0), 05		85
____	**17673** Santa Fe Extended Vision Caboose, 05		85
____	**17674** Reading Extended Vision Caboose "94119" (std 0), 05		75
____	**17675** Rio Grande Extended Vision Caboose "01507" (std 0), 06		90
____	**17676** NYC Bay Window Caboose "20300," 07		60
____	**17677** Erie-Lack. Bay Window Caboose "C359" (std 0), 06		90
____	**17678** B&O I-12 Caboose "C2421" (std 0), 06		90
____	**17679** Long Island Bay Window Caboose "C-62" (std 0), 06		90
____	**17682** Reading Northeastern Caboose "92841" (std 0), 06–07		85
____	**17683** Chessie System Northeastern Caboose "1893" (std 0), 07		85
____	**17684** Conrail Northeastern Caboose "18873" (std 0), 07		85
____	**17685** Jersey Central Northeastern Caboose "91533" (std 0), 07		85
____	**17690** UP CA-4 Caboose "3826" (std 0), 06		90
____	**17691** UP CA-4 Caboose "25103" (std 0), 06		90
____	**17692** LL CA-4 B22 Caboose "7629" (std 0), 06		90
____	**17693** Chessie Extended Vision Caboose "3285" (std 0), 06		90
____	**17694** NS Extended Vision Caboose "555582" (std 0), 06		90
____	**17695** Alaska I-12 Caboose "1001" (std 0), 06		90
____	**17696** CP Bay Window Caboose "437266" (std 0), 06		90
____	**17697** CN Extended Vision Caboose "78128" (std 0), 06		90
____	**17699** UP Ca-4 Caboose "25193" (std 0), 07		90
____	**17700** UP ACF 40-ton Stock Car "47456" (std 0), 01–02		85
____	**17701** Rio Grande ACF 40-ton Stock Car "39269" (std 0), 01–02		60
____	**17702** CP ACF 40-ton Stock Car "277083" (std 0), 01–02		75
____	**17703** NYC ACF 40-ton Stock Car "23334" (std 0), 01–02		85
____	**17703** Crayola 2-bay Hopper, LionScale, 17		70
____	**17704** B&O ACF 40-ton Stock Car "110234" (std 0), 02		40
____	**17705** CB&Q ACF 40-ton Stock Car "52886" (std 0), 02		40
____	**17707** PRR ARF 40-ton Stock Car "128994" (std 0), 03		35
____	**17708** CP Rail ACF 40-ton Stock Car "277313" (std 0), 03		38
____	**17709** UP Stock Car "48154" (std 0), 04		45
____	**17710** Great Northern Stock Car "56385" (std 0), 04		40
____	**17711** C&O ACF 40-ton Stock Car "95237" (std 0), 06		60
____	**17712** N&W ACF 40-ton Stock Car "33000" (std 0), 06		60
____	**17713** MKT ACF 40-ton Stock Car "47150" (std 0), 06		60

		Exc	Mint
17714	CN 40-ton Stock Car "172755" (std O), *06*	60	
17715	MP 40-ton Stock Car "52428" (std O), *06*	60	
17716	CGW 40-ton Stock Car "838," *08*	60	
17717	UP 40-ton Stock Car "48217," *08*	60	
17718	NS Heritage 3-bay Hopper 2-pack (std O), *12*	160	
17719	C&BQ ACF Stock Car "52925" (std O), *09*	70	
17720	UP ACF Stock Car (std O), *10*	70	
17721	Postwar Scale Stock Car 2-pack, *10–11*	140	
17724	CN Scale Steel-sided Reefer "210552," (std O), *11*	80	
17725	NP Scale Steel-sided Reefer "98528," (std O), *11*	80	
17726	IC Scale Steel-sided Reefer "16644," (std O), *11*	80	
17727	Mopac/Wabash Scale Steel-sided Reefer "30790," (std O), *11*	80	
17729	C&O Scale PS-1 Boxcar "2992" (std O), *12*	70	
17730	Seaboard Scale Round-roof Boxcar "19293" (std O), *11*	70	
17731	Pere Marquette Scale Boxcar "81805" (std O), *12*	70	
17732	L&N Scale PS-1 Boxcar "4798" (std O), *12*	70	
17733	PRR Scale Round-roof Boxcar "78948" (std O), *11*	70	
17734	PRR Scale Round-roof Boxcar "76644" (std O), *11*	70	
17735	PRR Round-roof DD Boxcar "77851" (std O), *12*	70	
17736	PRR Round-roof DD Boxcar "60156" (std O), *12*	70	
17737	N&W Scale Round-roof Boxcar "46494" (std O), *11*	70	
17738	NP Round-roof DD Boxcar "39300" (std O), *12*	70	
17739	DT&I Round-roof DD Boxcar "12250" (std O), *12*	70	
17740	Alaska Scale Round-roof Boxcar "27781" (std O), *11*	70	
17741	Santa Fe Scale Slogan Reefer 5-car Set (std O), *12*	320	
17747	Santa Fe Scale Boxcar "39009" (std O), *12*	70	
17748	Grave's Mortuary Supply Scale PS-1 Boxcar (std O), *12-13*	70	
17749	Erie Scale PS-1 Boxcar "90300" (std O), *12*	70	
17750	NYC Round-roof DD Boxcar "77147" (std O), *12*	70	
17751	NKP Scale PS-1 Boxcar "6605" (std O), *12*	70	
17752	Polar Round-roof Boxcar "1202" (std O), *12–13, 16–17*	70	
17753	LV Scale PS-1 Boxcar "65124" (std O), *12*	70	
17754	EL DD Boxcar "65000" (std O), *12*	75	
17755	D&H DD Boxcar "25025" (std O), *12*	75	
17756	CP Rail DD Boxcar "42630" (std O), *12*	75	
17757	Milwaukee Road DD Boxcar "13441" (std O), *12*	75	
17758	ATSF Map and Slogan Reefer 3-pack, *12*	190	
17762	BN 57' Mechanical Reefer "9618" (std O), *12*	85	
17763	NYC 57' Mechanical Reefer "6762" (std O), *12*	85	
17764	ATSF 57' Mechanical Reefer "56244" (std O), *12*	85	
17765	Virginian Round-roof DD Boxcar "3131" (std O), *13–14*	80	
17766	NH Round-roof Boxcar "39303" (std O), *13*	70	
17767	SP Round-roof DD Boxcar "166052" (std O), *13–14*	80	

		Exc	Mint
17768	Grave's Mortuary Supply Round-roof Boxcar (std O), *13*		70
____**17769**	D&RGW PS-1 Boxcar "60046" (std O), *13*		70
____**17770**	MILW PS-1 Boxcar "8777" (std O), *13*		70
____**17771**	CNJ PS-1 Boxcar "23522" (std O), *13–14*		80
____**17772**	Central of Georgia PS-1 Boxcar (std O), *13*		70
____**17773**	D&M Round-roof Boxcar "3148" (std O), *13–14*		80
____**17774**	D&M PS-1 Boxcar "2833" (std O), *13*		70
____**17775**	NS Heritage 3-bay Hopper 3-pack (std O), *13–15*		240
____**17779**	NS Heritage 3-bay Hopper 3-pack (std O), *13–15*		240
____**17783**	NS Heritage 3-bay Hopper 3-pack (std O), *13–15*		240
____**17787**	NS Heritage 3-bay Hopper 3-pack (std O), *13*		240
____**17791**	NS Heritage 3-bay Hopper 3-pack (std O), *13*		240
____**17795**	NS Heritage 3-bay Hopper 3-pack (std O), *13*		240
____**17800**	Ontario Northland Ore Car "6126," *00*		30
____**17801**	CN Ore Car "345165," *00*		37
____**17802**	CP Ore Car "377249," *00*		28
____**17803**	DMIR Ore Car "31456," *00*		30
____**17804**	UP Ore Car "8023," *01*		29
____**17805**	CP Rail Ore Car "377238," *01*		29
____**17806**	UP Ore Car "27250," *03*		30
____**17807**	BN Ore Car "95887," *02*		28
____**17900**	Santa Fe Unibody Tank Car (std O), *90*	37	46
____**17901**	Chevron Unibody Tank Car (std O), *90*	26	32
____**17902**	NJ Zinc Unibody Tank Car (std O), *91*	26	34
____**17903**	Conoco Unibody Tank Car (std O), *91*	24	29
____**17904**	Texaco Unibody Tank Car (std O), *92*	34	43
17905	Archer Daniels Midland Unibody Tank Car (std O), *92*	24	33
____**17906**	SCM Unibody Tank Car "78286" (std O), *93*	47	55
____**17908**	Marathon Oil Unibody Tank Car (std O), *95*	51	56
____**17909**	Hooker Chemicals Unibody Tank Car (std O), *96*		55
____**17910**	Sunoco Unibody Tank Car "7900," *97*		37
____**17913**	J.M. Huber Tank Car, *98*		29
____**17914**	Englehard Tank Car, *98*		36
____**17915**	Gulf Unibody Tank Car "8438," *00*		43
____**17916**	Burlington Unibody Tank Car "130000," *00*	24	38
____**17918**	Southern Unibody Tank Car, *01*		32
____**17919**	Koppers Unibody Tank Car, *01*		39
17924	Safety Kleen Unibody Tank Car "77603" (std O), *02*		40
17925	Beefmaster Unibody Tank Car "120021" (std O), *02*		38
____**17926**	Cargill Unibody 1-D Tank Car "5836" (std O), *03*		40
17927	Union Starch Unibody 1-D Tank Car "59137" (std O), *03*		35
____**17928**	Merck 1-D Tank Car "25421" (std O), *03*		35
17929	Wyandotte Chemicals 1-D Tank Car "1325" (std O), *03*		34
____**17930**	CSX Unibody Tank Car "993369" (std O), *04*		35
____**17931**	UP Unibody Tank Car "6" (std O), *04*		35
17932	CIBRO TankTrain Intermediate Car "26263" (std O), *04*		35
17933	GATX TankTrain Intermediate Car 3-pack (std O), *04*		100

		Exc	Mint
17946	Candy Cane Unibody Tank Car, *04*		60____
17948	Philadelphia Quartz 1-D Tank Car "806" (std O), *06*		55____
17949	Skelly Oil 1-D Tank Car "2293" (std O), *06*		55____
17950	ADM Unibody Tank Car "19020" (std O), *06*		60____
17951	Cerestar Unibody Tank Car "190177" (std O), *06*		60____
17959	Dow 1-D Tank Car "310101" (std O), *07*		55____
17960	Amaizo 1-D Tank Car "15440" (std O), *07*		55____
17962	Domino Sugar 1-D Tank Car "3008" (std O), *07*		60____
17966	Procor 1-D Tank Car "82607" (std O), *07*		60____
17972	Union Starch 1-D Tank Car "724" (std O), *08*		60____
17973	UP 1-D Tank Car "907838" (std O), *08*		60____
17975	Cargill Foods Unibody Tank Car 3-pack (std O), *08–09*		195____
17976	Huber Unibody Tank Car 3-pack (std O), *08–09*		195____
17983	GATX TankTrain Intermediate Car 3-pack, *08*		195____
18000	PRR 0-6-0 Locomotive "8977," *89, 91*	258	405____
18001	Rock Island 4-8-4 Locomotive "5100," *87*	305	315____
18002	NYC 4-6-4 Locomotive "785," *87 u*	510	576____
18003	DL&W 4-8-4 Locomotive "1501," *88*	235	294____
18004	Reading 4-6-2 Locomotive "8004," *89*	185	205____
18005	NYC 4-6-4 Locomotive "5340," display case, *90*	705	799____
18006	Reading 4-8-4 Locomotive "2100," *89 u*	490	528____
18007	Southern Pacific 4-8-4 Locomotive "4410," *91*	374	392____
18008	Disneyland 35th Anniversary 4-4-0 Locomotive, display case, *90*	256	305____
18009	NYC 4-8-2 Locomotive "3000," *90 u, 91*	370	561____
18010	PRR 6-8-6 Steam Turbine Locomotive "6200," *91–92*	900	1041____
18011	Chessie System 4-8-4 Locomotive "2101," *91*	440	536____
18012	NYC 4-6-4 Locomotive "5340," *90*	710	900____
18013	Disneyland 35th Anniversary 4-4-0 Locomotive, *90*	245	282____
18014	Lionel Lines 2-6-4 Locomotive "8014," *91*	145	190____
18016	Northern Pacific 4-8-4 Locomotive "2626," *92*	385	440____
18018	Southern 2-8-2 Locomotive "4501," *92*	640	650____
18022	Pere Marquette 2-8-4 Locomotive "1201," *93*	550	650____
18023	Western Maryland Shay Locomotive "6," *92*	1050	1350____
18024	Sears T&P 4-8-2 Locomotive "907," display case, *92 u*	750	790____
18025	T&P 4-8-2 Locomotive "907," *92 u*		640____
18026	NYC 4-6-4 Dreyfuss Hudson Locomotive, 2-rail, *92 u*		2350____
18027	NYC 4-6-4 Dreyfuss Hudson Locomotive, 3-rail, *93 u*		1450____
18028	Smithsonian PRR 4-6-2 Locomotive "3768," 2-rail, *93 u*		2150____
18029	NYC 4-6-4 Dreyfuss Hudson Locomotive, 3-rail, *93 u*	1900	2150____
18030	Frisco 2-8-2 Locomotive "4100," *93 u*	530	625____
18031	2-10-0 Bundesbahn BR-50 Locomotive, 2-rail, *93 u*		NRS____
18034	Santa Fe 2-8-2 Locomotive "3158," *94*	540	620____
18035	2-10-0 Reichsbahn BR-50 Locomotive, 2-rail, *93 u*		NRS____
18036	2-10-0 French BR-50 Locomotive, 2-rail, *93 u*		NRS____

		Exc	Mint
__**18040**__	N&W 4-8-4 Locomotive "612," *95*	640	710
__**18042**__	Boston & Albany 4-6-4 Locomotive "618," *95*		250
__**18043**__	Chesapeake & Ohio 4-6-4 Locomotive "490," *95*	680	750
__**18044**__	Southern 4-6-2 Locomotive "1390," *96*		255
__**18045**__	Commodore Vanderbilt Locomotive "777," *96*		678
__**18046**__	Wabash 4-6-4 Locomotive "700," *96*	190	375
__**18049**__	N&W Warhorse 4-8-4 Locomotive "600," *96*		490
__**18050**__	JCPenney 4-6-2 Locomotive "2055," *96*	235	245
__**18052**__	Pennsylvania Torpedo Locomotive "238E," *97*		455
__**18054**__	NYC 0-4-0 Switcher "1665," black, *97*		145
18056	NYC J1-e Hudson Locomotive "763E," Vanderbilt tender, *97*		603
18062	ATSF 4-6-4 Hudson Locomotive "3447," *97*		680
18063	NYC 4-6-4 Commodore Vanderbilt Locomotive, *99*		952
18064	NYC 4-8-2 Mohawk L-3A Locomotive "3005," tender, *98*	275	450
18067	NYC Weathered Commodore Vanderbilt Scale Hudson Locomotive, *97*		840
__**18071**__	SP Daylight Locomotive "4449," *98*		680
__**18072**__	Lionel Lines Torpedo Locomotive, tender, *98*		360
__**18079**__	NYC 2-8-2 Mikado Locomotive "1967," *99*		710
__**18080**__	D&RGW 2-8-2 Mikado Locomotive "1210," *99*		720
__**18082**__	NYC 4-6-4 Hudson Locomotive "5404," *99*		230
__**18083**__	C&O 4-6-4 Hudson Locomotive "305," *99*		205
__**18084**__	Santa Fe 4-6-4 Hudson Locomotive "305," *99*		225
__**18085**__	NH 4-6-2 Pacific Locomotive "1334," *99*		275
__**18086**__	NYC 4-6-2 Pacific Locomotive "4929," *99*		235
__**18087**__	Santa Fe 4-6-2 Pacific Locomotive "3448," *99*		265
__**18088**__	SP 4-6-2 Pacific Locomotive "1407," *99*		350
__**18089**__	CNJ 4-6-0 Camelback Locomotive "771," *99*		405
__**18091**__	PRR 4-6-0 Camelback Locomotive "821," *99*		405
__**18092**__	SP 4-6-0 Camelback Locomotive "2283," *99*		395
__**18093**__	C&NW 4-6-0 Camelback Locomotive "3006," *99*		285
__**18094**__	B&O 4-4-2 E6 Atlantic Locomotive, CC, *99–00*		345
__**18095**__	PRR 4-4-2 E6 Atlantic Locomotive, CC, *99–00*	275	455
__**18096**__	ATSF 4-4-2 E6 Atlantic Locomotive, CC, *99–00*		370
__**18097**__	CNJ 4-6-0 Camelback Locomotive "770," *99*		330
__**18098**__	PRR 4-6-0 Camelback Locomotive "820," *99*		355
__**18099**__	SP 4-6-0 Camelback Locomotive "2282," *99*		360
__**18100**__	Santa Fe F3 Diesel A Unit "8100" (see 11711)		NRS
__**18101**__	Santa Fe F3 Diesel B Unit "8101" (see 11711)		NRS
18102	Santa Fe F3 Diesel A Unit "8102," dummy (see 11711)		NRS
__**18103**__	Santa Fe F3 Diesel B Unit "8103," dummy, *91 u*	180	190
__**18104**__	GN F3 Diesel A Unit "366A," dummy (see 11724)		500
__**18105**__	GN F3 Diesel B Unit "370B," dummy (see 11724)		NRS
__**18106**__	GN F3 Diesel A Unit "351C," dummy (see 11724)		NRS
__**18107**__	D&RGW Alco PA1 Diesel ABA Set, *92*	640	740
__**18108**__	Great Northern F3 Diesel B Unit "371B," *93*	85	105
__**18109**__	Erie Alco Diesel A Unit "725A" (see 11734)		NRS
__**18110**__	Erie Alco Diesel B Unit "725B" (see 11734)		160
18111	Erie Alco Diesel A Unit "736A," dummy (see 11734)		NRS

		Exc	Mint	
18115	Santa Fe F3 Diesel B Unit, *93*	90	115	___
18116	Erie-Lackawanna Alco PA1 Diesel AA Set, *93*	450	490	___
18117/18	Santa Fe F3 Diesel AA Set "200," *93*	330	410	___
18119/20	UP Alco Diesel AA Set, *94*	200	235	___
18121	Santa Fe F3 Diesel B Unit "200A," *94*	75	95	___
18122	Santa Fe F3 Diesel B Unit "200B," *95*	140	150	___
18123	ACL F3 Diesel A Unit "342" (see 11903)		NRS	___
18124	ACL F3 Diesel B Unit "342B" (see 11903)		NRS	___
18125	ACL F3 Diesel A Unit "343," dummy (see 11903)		NRS	___
18128	Santa Fe F3 Diesel A Unit "2343," *96*		435	___
18129	Santa Fe F3 Diesel B Unit "2343C," *96*		245	___
18130	Santa Fe F3 Diesel AB Set, *96*		580	___
18131	NP F3 Diesel AB Set, "2390A, 2390C," *97*	295	360	___
18132	NP F3 Diesel A Unit, powered		300	___
18133	NP F3 Diesel B Unit, dummy		150	___
18134	Santa Fe F3 Diesel A Unit "2343," dummy, *97*		195	___
18136	Santa Fe F3 Diesel B Unit "2343C," *97*	135	240	___
18138	Milwaukee Road F3 Diesel A Unit "75A," *98*		400	___
18139	Milwaukee Road F3 Diesel B Unit "2378B," *98*		250	___
18140	Milwaukee Road F3 Diesel AB Set, *98*	390	600	___
18145	NP F3 Diesel A Unit "2390A," *97*	300	360	___
18146	NP F3 Diesel B Unit "2390C," *97*		170	___
18147	NP F3 Diesel AB Set, *97*	450	580	___
18149	UP Veranda Gas Turbine Locomotive "61," *98*	860	900	___
18154	Deluxe Santa Fe FT Diesel AA Set, *98–00*		375	___
18155	Deluxe Santa Fe FT Diesel A Unit, powered (see 18154)		NRS	___
18156	Deluxe Santa Fe FT Diesel A Unit, dummy (see 18154)		NRS	___
18157	Santa Fe FT Diesel AA Set, *98–00*		240	___
18158	Santa Fe FT Diesel A Unit, powered (see 18157)		NRS	___
18159	Santa Fe FT Diesel A Unit, dummy (see 18157)		NRS	___
18160	NYC Deluxe FT Diesel AA Set, "1602, 1603," *98–00*		500	___
18163	NYC FT Diesel AA Set, "1600, 2400," *98–00*		300	___
18166	B&O FT Diesel AA Set, CC, *99–00*		340	___
18169	B&O FT Diesel AA Set, traditional, *99–00*		240	___
18189	Army of Potomac Operating Stock Car, *99*		45	___
18190	McNeil's Rangers Operating Stock Car "2," *99*		45	___
18191	WP F3 Diesel AA Set, *98*	153	570	___
18192	WP F3 Diesel A Unit, powered, *98*		485	___
18193	WP F3 Diesel A Unit, dummy, *98*		495	___
18197	WP F3 Diesel B Unit "2355C," *99*	88	255	___
18198	WP F3 Diesel B Unit "2345C" CC, *99*		360	___
18200	Conrail SD40 Diesel "8200," *87*	180	200	___
18201	Chessie System SD40 Diesel "8201," *88*	245	340	___
18202	Erie-Lack. SD40 Diesel Unit "8459," dummy, *89 u*	90	140	___
18203	CP Rail SD40 Diesel "8203," *89*	195	250	___
18204	Chessie SD40 Diesel Unit "8204," dummy, *90 u*	135	190	___
18205	Union Pacific Dash 8-40C Diesel "9100," *89*	275	335	___
18206	Santa Fe Dash 8-40B Diesel "8206," *90*	195	235	___
18207	Norfolk Southern Dash 8-40C Diesel "8689," *92*	230	270	___

		Exc	Mint
____18208	BN SD40 Diesel Dummy Unit "8586," *91 u*	115	165
____18209	CP Rail SD40 Diesel Dummy Unit "8209," *92 u*	135	165
____18210	Illinois Central SD40 "6006," *93*	220	250
____18211	Susquehanna Dash 8-40B Diesel "4002," *93*	145	165
18212	Santa Fe Dash 8-40B Diesel Dummy Unit "8212," *93*	155	180
____18213	Norfolk Southern Dash 8-40C Diesel "8688," *94*	225	240
____18214	CSX Dash 8-40C Diesel "7500," *94*	235	255
____18215	CSX Dash 8-40C Diesel "7643," *94*	240	260
____18216	Conrail SD-60M Diesel "5500," *94*	355	380
____18217	Illinois Central SD40 Diesel "6007," *94*	170	175
____18218	Susquehanna Dash 8-40B Diesel "4004," *94*	205	225
____18219	C&NW Dash 8-40C Diesel "8501," *95*	325	330
____18220	C&NW Dash 8-40C Diesel "8502," *95*	215	315
____18221	D&RGW SD50 Diesel "5512," *95*	455	520
____18222	D&RGW SD50 Diesel "5517," *95*	280	325
____18223	Milwaukee Road SD40 Diesel "154," *95*	375	380
____18224	Milwaukee Road SD40 Diesel "155," *95*	240	265
____18226	GE Dash 9 Diesel, *97*		295
____18228	SP Dash 9 Diesel "8228," gray with red nose, *97*		340
____18229	SP SD40 Diesel "7333," *98*	300	425
____18231	BNSF Dash 9 Diesel "739," *98*		435
____18232	Soo Line SD60 Diesel "5500," *97*		350
____18233	BNSF Dash 9 Diesel "745," *98*		330
____18234	BNSF Dash 9 Diesel "740," CC, *98–99*		405
____18235	BNSF Dash 9 Diesel 2-pack, "739, 740," *98*		710
____18238	Conrail SD70 Diesel "4145," *99–00*		300
____18240	Conrail Dash 8-40B Diesel "5065" CC, *98*		260
____18241	BN SD70 Diesel "9413," *99–00*		345
____18245	PRR Alco PA1 Diesel AA Set, *99*		495
____18248	PRR Alco PB-1 Diesel "5750B," *99*		215
____18249	Erie Alco PB-1 Diesel "850B," *00*		250
____18250	BNSF SD70 Diesel "9870," *99–00*		365
____18251	CSX SD60 Diesel "8701," *99–00*		300
____18252	Amtrak Dash 9 Diesel, CC, *99*		285
____18253	BNSF Dash 9 Diesel, CC, *99*		305
____18254	ATSF Dash 9 Diesel, CC, *99*		340
____18255	NS Dash 9 Diesel, CC, *99*		315
____18256	Amtrak Dash 9 Diesel, traditional, *99*		200
____18257	BNSF Dash 9 Diesel, traditional, *99*		190
____18258	ATSF Dash 9 Diesel, traditional, *99*		205
____18259	NS Dash 9 Diesel, traditional, *99*		215
____18260	Conrail SD70 Diesel "4144," *99–00*		280
____18261	BN SD60 Diesel "9412," *99–00*		255
____18262	BNSF SD70 Diesel "9869," *99–00*		250
____18263	CSX SD60 Diesel "8700," *99–00*		255
____18264	Southern Pacific SD70M Diesel "8238," *99–00*		245
____18265	Southern Pacific SD70M Diesel "9803," *99–00*		340
18266	Norfolk Southern SD60 Diesel "6552," CC, *01–02*		400
____18268	Lionel Centennial SD90MAC Diesel, CC, *00*		415
____18269	UP SD90MAC Diesel "8006," CC, *00*		405
____18271	CP SD90MAC Diesel "9129," CC, *00*		440
____18273	UP SD40 Diesel "8071," *99–00*		330
____18274	Burlington U30C Diesel "891," CC, *01*		370

		Exc	Mint
18276	Seaboard U30C Diesel "7274," CC, *01*		325
18278	UP U30C Diesel "2938," CC, *01*		330
18280	Maersk SD70 Diesel, CC, *00*		345
18281	BNSF Dash 9-44CW Diesel "788," CC, *00*		340
18282	BNSF Dash 9-44CW Diesel "789," traditional, *00*		225
18283	CSX Dash 9-44CW Diesel "9019," CC, *00*		340
18284	CSX Dash 9-44CW Diesel "9020," traditional, *00*		300
18285	UP Dash 9-44C Diesel "9659," CC, *01*		325
18286	UP Dash 9-44CW Diesel "9717," CC, *01*		355
18287	CN Dash 9-44C Diesel "2529," CC, *01*		460
18288	Odyssey System SD70 Diesel, CC, *00 u*		400
18290	Amtrak Dash 8-32BWH Diesel "509," CC, *01*		325
18291	BNSF Dash 8-32BWH Diesel "580," CC, *02*		340
18292	Chessie GE U30C Diesel "3312," CC, *02*		340
18293	Santa Fe U30C Diesel, CC, *03*		395
18294	Alaska SD70MAC Diesel "4005," CC, *01–02*		435
18295	Conrail SD80MAC Diesel "7200," CC, *02–03*		365
18296	CSX SD80MAC Diesel "801," CC, *02–03*		405
18297	NYC SD80MAC Diesel "9914," CC, *02–03*		405
18298	UP "Desert Victory" SD40-2 Diesel "3593," CC, *02–03*		380
18299	CP Rail SD40-2 Diesel "5420," CC, *02–03*		375
18300	PRR GG1 Electric Locomotive "8300," *87*	285	335
18301	Southern FM Train Master Diesel "8301," *88*	150	204
18302	GN EP-5 Electric Locomotive "8302" (FF 3), *88*	190	250
18303	Amtrak GG1 Electric Locomotive "8303," *89*	275	338
18304	Lackawanna MU Commuter Car Set, *91*	380	435
18305	Lackawanna MU Commuter Car Dummy Set, *92*	230	255
18306	PRR MU Commuter Car Set, *92*	260	330
18307	PRR FM Train Master Diesel "8699," *94*	170	202
18308	PRR GG1 Electric Locomotive "4866," *92*	193	278
18309	Reading FM Train Master Diesel "863," *93*	173	212
18310	PRR MU Commuter Car Dummy Set, *93*	265	345
18311	Disney EP-5 Electric Locomotive "8311," *94*	296	397
18313	Pennsylvania GG1 Electric Locomotive "4907," *96*	75	297
18314	PRR GG1 Electric Locomotive "2332," 5 gold stripes, *97*	300	507
18315	Virginian E33 Electric Locomotive "2329," *97*		240
18319	New Haven EP-5 Electric Locomotive, *99*	200	365
18321	CNJ Train Master Diesel "2341," *99*		405
18322	Lackawanna Train Master Diesel "2321," *99*		465
18326	PRR Congressional GG1 Electric Locomotive, *00*		600
18327	Virginian FM Train Master Diesel "2331," *99–00*		410
18328	NH MU Commuter Car Set, CC, *00*		385
18331	Reading MU Commuter Car Set, CC, *00*		460
18334	NH MU Commuter Car Dummy Set, CC, *01*		180
18337	Reading MU Commuter Car Dummy Set, CC, *01*		200
18343	PRR GG1 Electric Locomotive "2332," CC, *01*		610
18344	LIRR MU Commuter Car Set, powered, CC, *01*		470
18347	IC MU Commuter Car Set, powered, CC, *01*		470
18351	NYC S1 Electric Locomotive, *03*		400
18352	JCPenney SP MU Commuter Car, display case, *02*		140

		Exc	Mint
18353	Pennsylvania E33 Electric Locomotive "4403," CC, *02*		280
18354	PRR GG1 Electric Locomotive "4918," tuscan, CC, *04*		790
18355	PRR GG1 Electric Locomotive "4876," green, CC, *04*		900
18356	Penn Central GG1 Electric Locomotive "4901," CC, *04*		1050
18364	PRR BB1 Electric Locomotive "3900," CC, *05–07*		530
18367	LIRR BB3 Electric Locomotive "328 A," CC, *05*		530
18371	PRR GG1 Electric Locomotive "4912," tuscan, 5 stripes, CC, *05–07*		780
18372	PRR GG1 Electric Locomotive "4925," green, 1 stripe, CC, *05–07*		780
18373	NYC S2 Electric Locomotive "125," CC, *05–07*		410
18374	PRR GG1 Electric Locomotive "4866," silver, CC, *06–08*		900
18375	Lackawanna FM Train Master Diesel "850," CC, *06*		400
18376	Lackawanna FM Train Master Diesel "851," nonpowered (std O), *06*		130
18378	New York City R27 Subway Car 2-pack, *07*		360
18384	MILW EP-2 Electric Locomotive, CC, *07–08*		950
18385	NYC H-16-44 Diesel "7001," *07–09*		202
18386	NYC H-16-44 Diesel "7002," nonpowered (std O), *07–09*		123
18389	MILW EP-2 Electric Locomotive "E-1," CC, *07–08*		950
18399	NH EF-4 Rectifier Locomotive "306," CC, *09*		360
18400	Santa Fe Vulcan Rotary Snowplow "8400," *87*	135	170
18401	Workmen Handcar, *87–88*	30	37
18402	Lionel Lines Burro Crane, *88*	65	80
18403	Santa Claus Handcar, *88*	26	29
18404	San Francisco Trolley "8404," *88*	55	85
18405	Santa Fe Burro Crane, *89*	70	83
18406	Track Maintenance Car, *89, 91*	34	49
18407	Snoopy and Woodstock Handcar, *90–91*	89	103
18408	Santa Claus Handcar, *89*	26	35
18410	PRR Burro Crane, *90*	100	115
18411	Canadian Pacific Fire Car, *90*	70	98
18413	Charlie Brown and Lucy Handcar, *91*	40	68
18416	Bugs Bunny and Daffy Duck Handcar, *92–93*	117	165
18417	Section Gang Car, *93*	65	80
18419	Lionelville Electric Trolley "8419," *94*	75	90
18421	Sylvester and Tweety Handcar, *94*	44	50
18422	Santa and Snowman Handcar, *94*	32	37
18423	On-track Step Van, *95*	23	28
18424	On-track Pickup Truck, *95*	20	25
18425	Goofy and Pluto Handcar, *95*	40	55
18426	Santa and Snowman Handcar, *95*	25	30
18427	Tie-Jector Car "55," *97*		60
18429	Workmen Handcar, *96*	28	34
18430	Crew Car, *96*		28
18431	Trolley Car, *96–97*		46
18433	Mickey and Minnie Handcar, *96–97*	43	82
18434	Porky and Petunia Handcar, *96*		35
18436	Dodge Ram Track Inspection Vehicle, *97*		39

		Exc	Mint
18438	PRR High-rail Inspection Vehicle, *98*		50____
18439	Union Pacific High-rail Inspection Vehicle, *98*		42____
18440	NJ Transit High-rail Inspection Vehicle, *98*		50____
18444	Lionelville Fire Car (SSS), *98*		150____
18445	NYC Fire Car, *98*		90____
18446	Postwar "58" GN Rotary Snowplow, *99*		181____
18447	Executive Inspection Vehicle, *99*		125____
18452	Boston Trolley "3321," *99–00*		65____
18454	Executive Inspection Vehicle, blue, *00*		105____
18455	NYC Tie-Jector Car "X-2," *00–01*		74____
18456	Postwar "59" Minuteman Motorized Unit, *01–02*		290____
18457	Postwar "65" Handcar, *00–01*		45____
18458	Postwar "53" D&RGW Snowplow, *00*		160____
18459	Christmas Handcar, *01*		35____
18461	Track Cleaning Car, *02–03*		90____
18463	Hot Rod Inspection Vehicle, *01–02*		100____
18464	Postwar "54" Track Ballast Tamper, *02–03*		170____
18465	Postwar "50" Gang Car, *03*		78____
18466	UP Rotary Snow Plow, *01–02*		150____
18467	Train Robbery Handcar, *02*		45____
18468	CN Railroad Speeder, *03–04*		49____
18469	Chessie System Railroad Speeder, *03–04*		49____
18470	Postwar "52" Fire Car, *02*		105____
18471	UP GP20 Diesel "1977," *03*		105____
18473	Lehigh Valley GP38 Diesel "310," *03*		160____
18474	Postwar "41" U.S. Army Switcher, *03–04*		145____
18475	Toy Story Handcar, *03*		55____
18476	Mickey and Minnie Mouse Handcar, *03–04*		55____
18480	Hobo Motorized Handcar, *03–04*		35____
18481	Christmas Yuletide Trolley, *03*		50____
18482	New Haven Rail Bonder "16," *04*		35____
18483	C&O Ballast Tamper "48," *04*		55____
18484	NS Dodge Inspection Vehicle, *04–05*		55____
18485	NYC Gang Car, *04–05*		100____
18486	Donald and Daisy Duck Handcar, *04–05*		63____
18487	Postwar "56" M&StL Mine Transport Car, *04–05*		230____
18489	Great Northern Rail Bonder "HR-73," *04*		35____
18490	UP Ballast Tamper, *04–05*		150____
18491	MOW Ballast Tamper "325," *04*		44____
18492	MOW Rail Bonder "58," *04*		35____
18493	Santa's Speeder, *05*		60____
18497	N&W Speeder "541005," traditional, *05*		65____
18498	New York Central Rotary Snowplow, *05*		210____
18500	Milwaukee Road GP9 Diesel "8500" (FF 2), *87*	175	230____
18501	WM NW2 Switcher "8501" (FF 4), *89*	185	215____
18502	LL 90th Anniversary GP9 Diesel "1900," *90*	148	173____
18503	Southern Pacific NW2 Switcher "8503," *90*	250	280____
18504	Frisco GP7 Diesel "504" (FF 5), *91*	155	240____
18505	NKP GP7 Diesel Set "400, 401" (FF 6)	295	365____
18506	CN Budd RDC Set, "D202, D203"	210	261____
18507	CN Budd RDC Baggage Car "D202," powered, *92*	50	75____
18508	CN Budd RDC Passenger Dummy Unit "D203," *92*	125	150____
18510	CN Budd RDC Passenger Dummy Unit "D200"	50	75____
18511	CN Budd RDC Passenger Dummy Unit "D250"	50	75____

Exc Mint

		Exc	Mint
18512	CN Budd RDC Dummy Set, "D200, D250," 93	125	195
18513	NYC GP7 Diesel "7420," 94	90	125
18514	Missouri Pacific GP7 Diesel "4124," 95	245	310
18515	Lionel Steel Vulcan Diesel "57" (SSS), 96		190
18516	Phantom III Locomotive, CC, 02		345
18550	JCPenney MILW GP9 Diesel "8500," display case, 87 u	180	245
18551	JCPenney Susquehanna RS3 Diesel "8809," display case, 89 u	180	195
18552	JCPenney DM&IR SD18 Diesel "8813," display case, 90 u	170	195
18553	Sears UP GP9 Diesel "150," display case, 91 u	100	150
18554	JCPenney GM&O RS3 "721," display case, 92–93 u	160	180
18555	Sears C&IM SD9 Diesel "52," 92 u	165	190
18556	Sears Chicago & Illinois Midland Freight Car Set, 92 u	110	120
18557	Chessie System 4-8-4 Locomotive "2101," display case, export, 92 u		NRS
18558	JCPenney MKT GP9 Diesel "91," display case, 94 u	160	180
18562	SP GP9 Diesel "2380," 96		195
18563	NYC GP9 Diesel "2380," 96		230
18564	CP GP9 Diesel "2380," 97		265
18565	Milwaukee Road GP9 Diesel "2338," 97		220
18566	CR SD20 Diesel "8495" (SSS), 97		150
18567	PRR GP9 Diesel "2028," 97		225
18569	CB&Q GP9 Diesel "2380," 98		190
18573	Santa Fe GP9 Diesel "2380," 98		155
18574	Milwaukee Road GP20 Diesel "975," 98		250
18575	Custom Series I GP9 Diesel "2398," 98		350
18576	SP GP9 Diesel B Unit "2385," nonpowered, 98		135
18577	NYC GP9 Diesel B Unit "2385," nonpowered, 98		145
18579	MILW GP9 Diesel "2384," nonpowered, 99		135
18580	Pennsylvania GP9 Diesel B Unit "2027," 98		165
18582	Seaboard NW2 Switcher, 98	250	455
18583	AEC Switcher "57," 98		217
18585	Centennial SD40 Diesel, 99		447
18587	NKP Alco C420 Switcher "577," CC, 99–01	215	255
18588	D&H Alco C420 Switcher "412," CC, 99–01	250	275
18589	LV Alco C420 Switcher "409," CC, 99–01	255	300
18590	NKP Alco C420 Switcher "578," traditional, 99–01		170
18591	D&H Alco C420 Switcher "411," traditional, 99–01		215
18592	LV Alco C420 Switcher "410," traditional, 99–01		175
18596	D&H Alco RS-11 Switcher "5001," CC, 99–01		370
18598	NYC Alco RS-11 Switcher "8010," CC, 99–01		380
18599	C&O GP38 Diesel "3855," 99–00		145
18600	ACL 4-4-2 Locomotive "8600," 87 u	65	75
18601	Great Northern 4-4-2 Locomotive "8601," 88	80	95
18602	PRR 4-4-2 Locomotive "8602," 87	75	85
18604	Wabash 4-4-2 Locomotive "8604," 88–91	65	75
18605	Mopar Express 4-4-2 Locomotive "1987," 87–88 u	75	120
18606	NYC 2-6-4 Locomotive "8606," 89	170	190

		Exc	Mint
18607	Union Pacific 2-6-4 Locomotive "8607," *89*	130	155____
18608	D&RGW 2-6-4 Locomotive "8608" (SSS), *89*	90	105____
18609	Northern Pacific 2-6-4 Locomotive "8609," *90*	170	195____
18610	Rock Island 0-4-0 Locomotive "8610," *90*	105	115____
18611	Lionel Lines 2-6-4 Locomotive (SSS), *90*	125	140____
18612	C&NW 4-4-2 Locomotive "8612," *89*	75	100____
18613	NYC 4-4-2 Locomotive "8613," *89 u*	75	95____
18614	Circus Train 4-4-2 Locomotive "1989," *89 u*	95	125____
18615	GTW 4-4-2 Locomotive "8615," *90*	70	85____
18616	Northern Pacific 4-4-2 Locomotive "8616," *90 u*	85	110____
18617	Adolphus III 4-4-2 Locomotive, *89–92 u*	100	125____
18620	Illinois Central 2-6-2 Locomotive "8620," *91*	165	190____
18622	Union Pacific 4-4-2 Locomotive "8622," *90–91 u*	65	80____
18623	Texas & Pacific 4-4-2 Locomotive "8623," *92*	80	110____
18625	Illinois Central 4-4-2 Locomotive "8625," *91 u*	70	95____
18626	Delaware & Hudson 2-6-2 Locomotive "8626," *92*	105	115____
18627	C&O 4-4-2 Locomotive "8627" or "8633," *92, 93 u, 94, 95 u*	75	95____
18628	MKT 4-4-2 Locomotive "8628," *92, 93 u*	70	85____
18630	C&NW 4-6-2 Locomotive "2903," *93*	325	370____
18632	C&O Columbia 4-4-2 Locomotive "8632," *97–99*	75	95____
18632	NYC 4-4-2 Locomotive "8632," *93–95*	75	95____
18633	C&O 4-4-2 Locomotive "8633," *94–95*	65	85____
18633	UP 4-4-2 Locomotive "8633," *93–95*	65	85____
18635	Santa Fe 2-6-4 Locomotive "8625," *93*	135	155____
18636	B&O 4-6-2 Locomotive "5300," *94*	295	315____
18637	United Auto Workers 4-4-2 Locomotive "8633," *93 u*		90____
18638	Norfolk & Western 2-6-4 Locomotive "638," *94*	170	220____
18639	Reading 4-6-2 Locomotive "639," *95*	145	170____
18640	Union Pacific 4-6-2 Locomotive "8640," *95*	110	130____
18641	Ford 4-4-2 Locomotive "8641," *94 u*	65	85____
18642	Lionel Lines 4-6-2 Locomotive, *95*	110	130____
18644	ATSF 4-4-2 Columbia Locomotive "8644," *96–99*	75	90____
18648	Sears Zenith 4-4-2 Locomotive "8632," *96 u*		132____
18649	Chevrolet 4-4-2 Locomotive "USA-1," *96 u*		112____
18650	LL 4-4-2 Columbia Locomotive "X-1110," *96–99*	95	120____
18653	B&A 4-6-2 Pacific Locomotive "2044," *97*		140____
18654	SP 4-6-2 Pacific Locomotive "2044," *97*		140____
18656	Bloomingdale's 4-4-2 Columbia Locomotive "8632," *96*		108____
18657	Sears Zenith 4-4-2 Columbia Locomotive "8632," *96*		115____
18658	LL Little League 4-4-2 Columbia Locomotive "X-1110," *97*		90____
18660	CN 4-6-2 Locomotive "2044," tender, *98*		175____
18661	N&W 4-6-2 Locomotive "2044," tender, *98*		160____
18662	Pennsylvania 0-4-0 Switcher, *98*	165	230____
18666	SP&S 4-6-2 Pacific Locomotive "2044," *97*		200____
18668	Bloomingdale's 4-4-2 Columbia Locomotive "8632," *97*		130____
18669	JCPenney IC 4-6-2 Pacific Locomotive "2099," *98*		205____
18670	D&H Columbia 4-4-2 Locomotive "1400," *98*		80____
18671	N&W Columbia 4-4-2 Locomotive "1201," *98*		70____

		Exc	Mint
18678	Quaker Oats Columbia 4-4-2 Locomotive "8632," *98*		162
18679	JCPenney T&P 4-6-2 Locomotive "2000," traditional, *99, 00 u*		250
18681	PRR 4-4-2 Locomotive "460," *99*		75
18682	Santa Fe 4-4-2 Columbia Locomotive "524," traditional, *00–01*		70
18696	ACL 4-6-4 Locomotive "1800," *01*		120
18697	Santa Fe 4-6-4 Locomotive "3465," *01*		100
18699	Alaska 4-4-2 Locomotive "64," *01*		105
18700	Rock Island 0-4-0T Locomotive "8700," *87–88*	36	43
18702	V&TRR 4-4-0 Locomotive "8702" (SSS), *88*	160	195
18704	Lionel Lines 2-4-0 Locomotive, *89 u*	36	43
18705	Neptune 0-4-0T Locomotive "8705," *90–91*	35	42
18706	Santa Fe 2-4-0 Locomotive "8706," *91*	36	43
18707	Mickey's World Tour 2-4-0 Locomotive "8707," *91, 92 u*	58	68
18709	Lionel Employee Learning Center 0-4-0T Locomotive, *92 u*		140
18710	SP 2-4-0 Locomotive "2000," *93*	30	38
18711	Southern 2-4-0 Locomotive "2000," *93*	30	38
18712	Jersey Central 2-4-0 Locomotive "2000," *93*	30	38
18713	Chessie System 2-4-0 Locomotive "1993," *94–95*	30	38
18716	Lionelville Circus 4-4-0 Locomotive, *90–91*	90	110
18718	LL 0-4-0 Dockside Switcher "8200," *97–98*		40
18719	Thomas the Tank Engine "1," *97*		158
18720	Union 4-4-0 General Locomotive "1865," *99*		175
18721	Confederate 4-4-0 General Locomotive "1861," *99*		175
18722	Percy the Tank Engine "6," *99*		170
18723	Union Pacific 4-4-0 General Locomotive, *05*		100
18730	Transylvania RR 4-4-0 Locomotive "13," traditional, *05*		105
18732	North Pole Central 4-4-0 Locomotive "25," *06*		110
18733	Percy the Tank Engine "6," *05–12*		120
18734	James the Tank Engine "5," *06–12*		120
18741	Thomas the Tank Engine, *08–13*		120
18745	Hallow's Eve 4-6-0 Steam Locomotive, *11–12*		190
18753	Route of the Reindeer RS3 Diesel, *11*		190
18754	Polar Express 2-8-4 Berkshire Steam Locomotive, *11, 13*		300
18755	C&O Berkshire Steam Locomotive "2751," TrainSounds, *11*		290
18771	Percy, remote system, *13–16*		140
18774	James, remote system, *13–16*		140
18775	Diesel, remote system, *13–16*		140
18799	Bethlehem Steel Switcher "44," *99*		100
18800	Lehigh Valley GP9 Diesel "8800," *87*	80	95
18801	Santa Fe U36B Diesel "8801," *87*	100	120
18802	Southern GP9 Diesel "8802" (SSS), *87*	100	115
18803	Santa Fe RS3 Diesel "8803," *88*	90	105
18804	Soo Line RS3 Diesel "8804," *88*	95	115
18805	Union Pacific RS3 Diesel "8805," *89*	100	125
18806	New Haven SD18 Diesel "8806," *89*	100	115
18807	Lehigh Valley RS3 Diesel "8807," *90*	90	120

		Exc	Mint
18808	ACL SD18 Diesel "8808," *90*	85	105____
18809	Susquehanna RS3 Diesel "8809," *89 u*		130____
18810	CSX SD18 Diesel "8810," *90*	95	130____
18811	Alaska SD9 Diesel "8811," *91*	95	135____
18812	Kansas City Southern GP38 Diesel "4000," *91*	120	140____
18813	DM&IR SD18 Diesel "8813," *90 u*	90	145____
18814	D&H RS3 Diesel "8814" (SSS), *91*	90	120____
18815	Amtrak RS3 Diesel "1815," *91, 92 u*	100	130____
18816	C&NW GP38-2 Diesel "4600," *92*	105	130____
18817	UP GP9 Diesel "150" (see 18553), *91 u*		135____
18819	L&N GP38-2 Diesel "4136," *92*	115	145____
18820	WP GP9 Diesel "8820" (SSS), *92*	120	140____
18821	Clinchfield GP38-2 Diesel "6005," *93*	125	150____
18822	Gulf, Mobile & Ohio RS3 Diesel "721," *92–93 u*		NRS____
18823	Chicago & Illinois Midland SD9 Diesel "52," *92 u*		235____
18824	Montana Rail Link SD9 Diesel "600," *93*	185	230____
18825	Soo Line GP38-2 Diesel "4000" (SSS), *93*	120	145____
18826	Conrail GP7 Diesel "5808," *93*	100	120____
18827	"Happy Holidays" RS3 Diesel "8827," *93*	165	220____
18830	Budweiser GP9 Diesel "1947," *93–94 u*	118	158____
18831	SP GP20 Diesel "4060," *94*	105	120____
18832	PRR RSD-4 Diesel "8446," *95*	110	135____
18833	Milwaukee Road RS3 Diesel "2487," *94*	100	110____
18834	C&O SD28 Diesel "8834," *94*	110	140____
18835	NYC RS3 Diesel "8223" (SSS), *94*	135	195____
18836	CN (Grand Trunk) GP38-2 Diesel "5800," *94*	135	160____
18837	"Happy Holidays" RS3 Diesel "8837," *94–95*	150	190____
18838	Seaboard RSC-3 Diesel "1538," *95*	110	140____
18840	U.S. Army GP7 Diesel "1821," *95*	85	124____
18841	Western Maryland GP20 Diesel "27" (SSS), *95*	120	150____
18842	JCPenney B&LE SD38 Diesel "868," *95 u*		265____
18843	Great Northern RS3 Diesel "197," *96*		145____
18845	D&RGW RS3 Diesel "5204," *97*		100____
18846	Lionel Centennial Series GP9 Diesel, *98*		415____
18847	Santa Fe H-12-44 Switcher "602," *99*		385____
18848	PRR H-12-44 Switcher "9087," *99*		420____
18853	JCPenney Santa Fe GP9 Diesel "2370," *97 u*		150____
18854	UP GP9 Diesel Dummy Set, "2380, 2387," *97*		450____
18856	NJ Transit GP38-2 Diesel "4303," *99*		315____
18857	Union Pacific GP9 Diesel "2397," *97*		240____
18858	Lionel Centennial GP20 Diesel, *98*		450____
18859	Phantom II, *99*		360____
18860	Pratt's Hollow Collection I: Phantom, *98*		400____
18864	Southern Pacific GP9 Diesel B Unit, *98*		140____
18865	New York Central GP9 Diesel B Unit, *98*		170____
18866	Milwaukee Road GP7 Diesel "2383," *98*		205____
18868	NJ Transit GP38-2 Diesel "4300," *98 u*		140____
18870	Pennsylvania GP9 Diesel "2029," *98*		180____
18872	Wabash GP7 Diesel Set, "453, 454, 455," *99*		560____
18876	C&NW H-12-44 Switcher "1053," *99*	125	319____
18877	Union Pacific GP9 Diesel "2399," nonpowered, *99*		175____
18878	Alaska GP7 Diesel "1803," *99*		115____
18879	B&O GP9 Diesel "5616," *99*		260____
18881	Custom GP9 Diesel "5616," *99*		350____

		Exc	Mint
___ **18892**	Burlington GP9 Diesel "2328," *99*		205
___ **18897**	Christmas GP7 Diesel "1999," *99*		200
___ **18900**	PRR Switcher "8900," *88 u, 89*	26	34
___ **18901/02**	PRR Alco Diesel AA Set, *88*	110	130
___ **18903/04**	Amtrak Alco Diesel AA Set, *88–89*	90	130
___ **18903**	Amtrak "Mopar Express," *99*		500
___ **18905**	PRR 44-ton Switcher "9312," *92*	80	116
___ **18906**	Erie-Lackawanna RS3 Diesel "8906," *91 u*	70	90
___ **18907**	Rock Island 44-ton Switcher "371," *93*	95	110
___ **18908/09**	NYC Alco Diesel AA Set, *93*	105	115
___ **18910**	CSX Switcher "8910," *93*	40	46
___ **18911**	UP Switcher "8911," *93*	33	37
___ **18912**	Amtrak Switcher "8912," *93*	37	43
___ **18913**	Santa Fe Alco Diesel A Unit "8913," *93–94*	55	65
___ **18915**	WM Alco Diesel A Unit "8915," *93*	65	80
___ **18916**	WM Alco Diesel A Unit "8916," dummy, *93*	38	42
___ **18917**	Soo Line NW2 Switcher, *93*	65	75
___ **18918**	B&M NW2 Switcher "8918," *93*	75	90
___ **18919**	Santa Fe Alco Diesel A Unit "8919," dummy, *93–94*	36	55
___ **18920**	Frisco NW2 Switcher "254," *94*	70	75
___ **18921**	C&NW NW2 Switcher "1017," *94*	60	80
___ **18922**	New Haven Alco Diesel A Unit "8922," *94*	75	105
___ **18923**	New Haven Alco Diesel A Unit "8923," dummy, *94*	50	55
___ **18924**	IC Switcher "8924," *94–95*	37	44
___ **18925**	D&RGW Switcher "8925," *94–95*	32	37
___ **18926**	Reading Switcher "8926," *94–95*	31	39
___ **18927**	U.S. Navy NW2 Switcher "65-00637," *94–95*	65	85
___ **18928**	C&NW NW2 Switcher Calf Unit, *95*	50	55
___ **18929**	B&M NW2 Switcher Calf Unit, *95*	44	49
___ **18930**	Crayola Switcher, *94 u, 95*	27	30
___ **18931**	Chrysler Mopar NW2 Switcher "1818," *94 u*	76	88
___ **18932**	Jersey Central NW2 Switcher "8932," *96*		65
___ **18933**	Jersey Central NW2 Switcher Calf Unit "8933," *96*		55
___ **18934/35**	Reading Alco Diesel AA Set, *95*	75	95
___ **18936**	Amtrak Alco Diesel A Unit "8936," *95*		65
___ **18937**	Amtrak FA2 Alco Diesel, nonpowered, *95–97*		50
___ **18938**	U.S. Navy NW2 Switcher Calf Unit, *95*	55	65
___ **18939**	Union Pacific NW2 Switcher Set, *96*		145
___ **18943**	Georgia Power NW2 Switcher "1960," *95 u*		170
___ **18946**	U.S. Coast Guard NW2 Switcher "8946," *96*		80
___ **18947**	Port of Lionel City Alco FA2 Diesel "2030," *97*		70
___ **18948**	Port of Lionel City Alco FB2 Diesel "2030B," *97*		45
___ **18952**	ATSF Alco PA1 Diesel "2000," *97*		345
___ **18953**	NYC Alco PA1 Diesel "2000," *97*		260
___ **18954**	ATSF Alco FA2 Diesel "212," powered, *97–99*		80
___ **18955**	NJ Transit NW2 Switcher "500," *96 u*		110
___ **18956**	Dodge Motorsports NW2 Switcher "8956," *96 u*		172
___ **18959**	New York Central NW2 Switcher "622," *97*		475
___ **18961**	Erie Alco PA1 Diesel "850," *98*		315
___ **18965**	Santa Fe Alco PB1 Diesel, *98*		255
___ **18966**	New York Central Alco BP1 Diesel "2008," *98*		250
___ **18971**	Alco Diesel A Unit, nonpowered, *98*		60

		Exc	Mint
18973	RI Alco FA2 Diesel "2031," powered, *98–99*		NRS____
18974	RI Alco FA2 Diesel Dummy Unit, *98–99*		NRS____
18975	Southern 44-ton Switcher "1955," *99*		190____
18978	C&O NW2 Switcher "624," *99–00*		410____
18981	Pennsylvania Railroad Speeder "16," *04*		45____
18982	Santa Fe Railroad Speeder "122," *04–05*		65____
18988	MP15 Diesel, K-Line, *06*		140____
18989	Bethlehem Steel Plymouth Switcher, traditional, K-Line, *06*		100____
18992	SP S2 Diesel Switcher "1440," CC, *08*		410____
18993	C&NW S2 Diesel Switcher "1031," CC, *08*		410____
18994	Lionel Lines FA Diesel, traditional, *08–09*		90____
19000	Blue Comet Diner, *87 u*	60	75____
19001	Southern Diner, *87 u*	55	65____
19002	Pennsylvania Diner, *88 u*	29	41____
19003	Milwaukee Road Diner, *88 u*	29	44____
19010	B&O Diner, *89 u*	36	55____
19011	Lionel Lines Baggage Car, *93*	184	299____
19015	Lionel Lines Passenger Coach, *91*	125	180____
19016	Lionel Lines Passenger Coach, *91*	100	135____
19017	Lionel Lines Passenger Coach, *91*	85	110____
19018	Lionel Lines Observation Car, *91*	95	120____
19019	SP Baggage Car "9019," *93*	120	153____
19023	SP Passenger Coach "9023," *92*	125	160____
19024	SP Passenger Coach "9024," *92*	85	100____
19025	SP Passenger Coach "9025," *92*	100	115____
19026	SP Observation Car "9026," *92*	85	100____
19038	Adolphus Busch Observation Car, *92–93 u*		85____
19039	Pere Marquette Baggage Car, *93*		75____
19040	Pere Marquette Passenger Coach "1115," *93*		75____
19041	Pere Marquette Passenger Coach "1116," *93*		75____
19042	Pere Marquette Observation Car "36," *93*		75____
19047	Baltimore & Ohio Combination Car "9047," *96*		55____
19048	Baltimore & Ohio Passenger Coach "9048," *96*		50____
19049	Baltimore & Ohio Diner "9049," *96*		42____
19050	Baltimore & Ohio Observation Car "9050," *96*		42____
19056	NYC Heavyweight Baggage Car, *96*		105____
19057	NYC Willow Run Heavyweight Coach, *96*		95____
19058	NYC Willow Trail Heavyweight Coach, *96*		90____
19059	NYC Seneca Valley Heavyweight Observation Car, *96*		100____
19060	Pullman Heavyweight Set, *96*		473____
19061	Wabash Passenger Set, *97*		235____
19062	Wabash City of Columbia Coach "2361," *97*		90____
19063	Wabash City of Danville Coach "2362," *97*		75____
19064	Wabash REA Baggage Car "2360," *97*		47____
19065	Wabash Windy City Observation Car "2363," *97*		90____
19066	Commodore Vanderbilt Pullman Heavyweight 2-pack, *97*		190____
19067	Commodore Vanderbilt Willow River Pullman "2543," *97*		115____
19068	Commodore Vanderbilt Willow Valley Pullman "2544," *97*		100____
19069	Pullman Baby Madison Set "9500-02," *97*		155____
19070	Baby Madison Combination Car "9501," *97*		40____

		Exc	Mint
19071	Laurel Gap Baby Madison Coach "9500," 97		34
19072	Laurel Summit Baby Madison Coach "9500," 97		40
19073	Catskill Valley Baby Madison Observation Car "9502," 97		34
19074	Legends of Lionel Madison Set, 97		385
19075	Mazzone Lionel Legends Coach "2621," 97		105
19076	Caruso Lionel Legends Coach "2624," 97		90
19077	Raphael Lionel Legends Coach "2652," 97		90
19078	Cowen Lionel Legends Observation Car "2600," 97		95
19079	NYC Heavyweight Passenger Car Set, 97		275
19080	NYC Heavyweight REA Baggage Car "2564," 97		100
19081	NYC Park Place Heavyweight Coach "2565," 97		100
19082	NYC Star Beam Heavyweight Coach "2566," 97		100
19083	NYC Hudson Valley Heavyweight Observation Car "2567," 97		100
19087	C&O Heavyweight Passenger Car 4-pack, "2571-74," 97		290
19088	C&O Heavyweight Baggage Car "2571," 97		100
19089	C&O Heavyweight Sleeper Car "2572," 97		100
19090	C&O Heavyweight Diner "2573," 97		110
19091	C&O Heavyweight Observation Car "2574," 97		100
19093	Commodore Vanderbilt Heavyweight Sleeper Car 2-pack, 98		170
19094	Commodore Vanderbilt Niagara Falls Sleeper, 98		75
19095	Commodore Vanderbilt Highland Falls Sleeper, 98		75
19096	Legends of Lionel Madison Car 2-pack, 98		130
19097	Bonnano Lionel Legends Coach "2653," 98		80
19098	Pagano Lionel Legends Coach "2654," 98		105
19099	PRR Liberty Gap Baggage Car "2623," 99		80
19100	Amtrak Baggage Car "9100," 89	125	165
19101	Amtrak Combination Car "9101," 89	75	85
19102	Amtrak Passenger Coach "9102," 89	75	85
19103	Amtrak Vista Dome Car "9103," 89	70	90
19104	Amtrak Diner "9104," 89	65	80
19105	Amtrak Full Vista Dome Car "9105," 89 u	70	80
19106	Amtrak Observation Car "9106," 89	75	90
19107	SP Full Vista Dome Car, 90 u	70	88
19108	N&W Full Vista Dome Car "576," 91 u	75	85
19109	Santa Fe Baggage Car "3400," 91	225	300
19110	Santa Fe Combination Car "3500," 91	80	110
19111	Santa Fe Diner "601," 91	100	135
19112	Santa Fe Passenger Coach, 91	125	175
19113	Santa Fe Vista Dome Car, 91	100	135
19116	Great Northern Baggage Car "1200," 92	135	165
19117	Great Northern Combination Car "1240," 92	65	80
19118	Great Northern Passenger Coach "1212," 92	75	95
19119	Great Northern Vista Dome Car "1322," 92	75	95
19120	Great Northern Observation Car "1192," 92	75	95
19121	Union Pacific Vista Dome Car "9121," 92 u	90	100
19122	D&RGW California Zephyr Baggage Car, 93	170	210
19123	D&RGW California Zephyr Silver Bronco Vista Dome Car, 93	95	115

		Exc	Mint
19124	D&RGW California Zephyr Silver Colt Vista Dome Car, *93*	95	115____
19125	D&RGW California Zephyr Silver Mustang Vista Dome Car, *93*	100	125____
19126	D&RGW California Zephyr Silver Pony Vista Dome Car, *93*	95	115____
19127	D&RGW California Zephyr Vista Dome Car, *93*	85	100____
19128	Santa Fe Full Vista Dome Car "507," *92 u*	175	185____
19129	IC Full Vista Dome Car "9129," *93*	75	85____
19130	Lackawanna Passenger Cars, set of 4, *94*	280	350____
19131	Lackawanna Baggage Car "2000" (see 19130)		150____
19132	Lackawanna Diner "469" (see 19130)		100____
19133	Lackawanna Passenger Coach "260" (see 19130)		100____
19134	Lackawanna Observation Car "789" (see 19130)		85____
19135	Lackawanna Combination Car "425," *94*	85	100____
19136	Lackawanna Passenger Coach "211," *94*	65	75____
19137	New York Central Roomette Car, *95*	90	105____
19138	Santa Fe Roomette Car, *95*	75	95____
19139	N&W Baggage Car "577," *95*	150	200____
19140	N&W Combination Car "494," *95*	60	80____
19141	N&W Diner "495," *95*	105	135____
19142	N&W Passenger Coach "538," *95*	75	95____
19143	N&W Passenger Coach "537," *95*	75	95____
19144	N&W Observation Car "582," *95*	80	95____
19145	C&O Combination Car "1403," *96*		65____
19146	C&O Passenger Coach "1623," *96*		60____
19147	C&O Passenger Coach "1803," *96*		55____
19148	C&O Chessie Club Coach "1903," *96*		55____
19149	C&O Coach/Diner "1950," *96*		50____
19150	C&O Observation Car "2504," *96*		55____
19151	Norfolk & Western Duplex Roomette car, *96*		108____
19152	Union Pacific Duplex Roomette Car, *96*		75____
19153	C&O Passenger Cars, set of 4, *96*		340____
19154	Atlantic Coast Line Passenger Car Set, *96*		340____
19155	ACL Combination Car "101," *96*		90____
19156	ACL Talladega Diner, *96*		90____
19157	ACL Moultrie Coach, *96*		95____
19158	ACL Observation Car "256," *96*		90____
19159	N&W Passenger Cars, set of 4, *95 u*	300	385____
19160	LL REA Baggage Car, *96*		90____
19161	LL Silver Mesa Coach, *96*		80____
19162	LL Silver Sky Vista Dome Car, *96*		75____
19163	LL Silver Rail Observation Car, *96*		75____
19164	Chesapeake & Ohio Passenger Cars, *96*		160____
19165	ATSF Super Chief Set, *96*		305____
19166	NP Vista Dome Car Set, *97*		305____
19167	NP Pullman Coach "2571," *97*		105____
19168	NP Pullman Coach "2571," *97*		105____
19169	NP Pullman Coach "2570," *97*		95____
19170	NP Pullman Coach "2571," *97*		100____
19171	NYC Streamliner Car 4-pack, *97*		285____
19172	NYC Aluminum Passenger/Baggage Car "2570," *97*		95____

			Exc	Mint
	19173	NYC Manhattan Island Aluminum Passenger Diner, 97		100
	19174	NYC Queensboro Bridge Aluminum Passenger Coach, 97		100
	19175	NYC Windgate Brook Aluminum Observation Car, 97		90
	19176	ATSF Indian Arrow Diner "2572," 97		90
	19177	ATSF Grass Valley Coach "2573," 97		90
	19178	ATSF Citrus Valley Coach "2574," 97		90
	19179	ATSF Vista Heights Coach "2575," 97		90
	19180	ATSF Surfliner Passenger Car 4-pack, 97		250
	19181	GN Empire Builder Prairie View Full Vista Dome Car, 98		75
	19182	GN Empire Builder River View Full Vista Dome Car, 98		75
	19183	GN Empire Builder Vista Dome Car 2-pack, 98		125
	19184	Milwaukee Road Passenger Car 4-pack, 99		390
	19185	MILW Red River Valley Aluminum Passenger Coach "194," 99		125
	19186	MILW Aluminum Coach/Diner "170," 99		110
	19187	MILW Cedar Rapids Aluminum Observation Car "186," 99		120
	19188	MILW Aluminum REA Passenger/Baggage Car "1336," 99		95
	19194	KCS Aluminum Passenger Car 4-pack, 00		380
	19200	Tidewater Southern Boxcar, 87	14	21
	19201	Lancaster & Chester Boxcar, 87	23	37
	19202	PRR Boxcar, 87	22	30
	19203	D&TS Boxcar, 87	11	18
	19204	Milwaukee Road Boxcar (FF 2), 87	29	41
	19205	Great Northern DD Boxcar (FF 3), 88	20	24
	19206	Seaboard System Boxcar, 88	18	23
	19207	CP Rail DD Boxcar, 88	17	22
	19208	Southern DD Boxcar, 88	11	13
	19209	Florida East Coast Boxcar, 88	15	19
	19210	Soo Line Boxcar, 89	19	23
	19211	Vermont Railway Boxcar, 89	18	21
	19212	PRR Boxcar, 89	21	25
	19213	SP&S DD Boxcar, 89	16	19
	19214	Western Maryland Boxcar (FF 4), 89	23	27
	19215	Union Pacific DD Boxcar, 90	17	21
	19216	Santa Fe Boxcar, 90	17	22
	19217	Burlington Boxcar, 90	16	21
	19218	New Haven Boxcar, 90	16	20
	19219	Lionel Lines 1900-1906 Boxcar, diesel RailSounds, 90	120	145
	19220	Lionel Lines 1926-1934 Boxcar, 90	27	30
	19221	Lionel Lines 1935-1937 Boxcar, 90	27	30
	19222	Lionel Lines 1948-1950 Boxcar, 90	27	30
	19223	Lionel Lines 1979-1989 Boxcar, 90	18	25
	19228	Cotton Belt Boxcar, 91	16	22
	19229	Frisco Boxcar, diesel RailSounds (FF 5), 91	75	90
	19230	Frisco DD Boxcar (FF 5), 91	21	26
	19231	TA&G DD Boxcar, 91	13	16
	19232	Rock Island DD Boxcar, 91	17	20
	19233	Southern Pacific Boxcar, 91	15	19

		Exc	Mint
19234	NYC Boxcar, *91*	60	65____
19235	MKT Boxcar, *91*	55	65____
19236	NKP DD Boxcar (FF 6), *92*	22	30____
19237	C&IM Boxcar, *92*	17	24____
19238	Kansas City Southern Boxcar, *92*	18	23____
19239	Toronto, Hamilton & Buffalo DD Boxcar, *92*	15	20____
19240	Great Northern DD Boxcar, *92*	15	20____
19241	Mickey Mouse 60th Anniversary Hi-Cube Boxcar, *91 u*	130	175____
19242	Donald Duck 50th Anniversary Hi-Cube Boxcar, *91 u*	130	140____
19243	Clinchfield Boxcar "9790," *91 u*	35	41____
19244	L&N Boxcar "9791," *92*	35	38____
19245	Mickey's World Tour Hi-Cube Boxcar, *92 u*	35	40____
19246	Disney World 20th Anniversary Hi-Cube Boxcar, *92 u*	33	40____
19247	Postwar "6464" Series Boxcar Set I, 3 cars, *93*	445	610____
19248	Western Pacific Boxcar "6464," *93*	75	95____
19249	Great Northern Boxcar "6464," *93*	75	95____
19250	M&StL Boxcar "6464," *93*	80	105____
19251	Montana Rail Link DD Boxcar "10001," *93*	21	27____
19254	Erie Boxcar (FF 7), *93*	21	25____
19255	Erie DD Boxcar (FF 7), *93*	22	26____
19256	Goofy Hi-Cube Boxcar, *93*	23	26____
19257	Postwar "6464" Series Boxcar Set II, 3 cars, *94*	80	97____
19258	Rock Island Boxcar "6464," *94*	25	34____
19259	Western Pacific Boxcar "6464100," *94*	33	46____
19260	Western Pacific Boxcar "6464100," *94*	35	49____
19261	Perils of Mickey Hi-Cube Boxcar #1, *93*	20	30____
19262	Perils of Mickey Hi-Cube Boxcar #2, *93*	20	28____
19263	NYC DD Boxcar (SSS), *94*	36	42____
19264	Perils of Mickey Hi-Cube Boxcar #3, *94*	28	31____
19265	Mickey Mouse 65th Anniversary Hi-Cube Boxcar, *94*	22	44____
19266	Postwar "6464" Series Boxcar Set III, 3 cars, *95*	75	90____
19267	NYC Pacemaker Boxcar "6464125," *95*	37	42____
19268	Missouri Pacific Boxcar "6464150," *95*	25	29____
19269	Rock Island Boxcar "6464," *95*	25	26____
19270	Donald Duck 60th Anniversary Hi-Cube Boxcar, *95*	30	34____
19271	Minnie Mouse Hi-Cube Boxcar, *95*	21	43____
19272	Postwar "6464" Series Boxcar Set IV, 3 cars, *96*	70	85____
19273	BAR State of Maine Boxcar "6464275," *96*		35____
19274	SP Overnight Boxcar "6464225," *96*		28____
19275	Pennsylvania Boxcar "6464," *96*		44____
19276	Postwar "6464" Series Boxcar Set V, 3 cars, *96*	65	85____
19277	Rutland Boxcar "6464-300," *96*		26____
19278	B&O Boxcar "6464-325," *96*		30____
19279	Central of Georgia Boxcar "6464-375," *96*		29____
19280	Mickey's Wheat Hi-Cube Boxcar, *96*		32____
19281	Mickey's Carrots Hi-Cube Boxcar, *96*		40____
19282	Santa Fe "Super Chief" Boxcar "6464-196," *96*		24____
19283	Erie Boxcar "6464-296," *96*		22____
19284	Northern Pacific Boxcar "6464-396," *96*		29____
19285	B&A State of Maine Boxcar "6464-275," *96*		27____

		Exc	Mint
____**19286**	Tweety and Sylvester Boxcar, *96*		46
____**19287**	NYC/PC Merger Boxcar "6464-125X" (SSS), *97*	50	75
____**19288**	PRR/CR Merger Boxcar "6464-200X" (SSS), *97*	43	56
____**19289**	Monon "Hoosier Line" Boxcar "6464," *97*		27
____**19290**	Seaboard "Silver Meteor" Boxcar "6464," *97*		24
____**19291**	GN Boxcar "6464-397," *97*		26
____**19292**	Postwar "6464" Series Boxcar Set VI, 3 cars, *97*		90
____**19293**	MKT Boxcar "6464-350," *97*	28	32
____**19294**	B&O Boxcar "6464-400," *97*	27	34
____**19295**	NH Boxcar "6464-425," *97*	25	34
____**19300**	PRR Ore Car, *87*	15	23
____**19301**	Milwaukee Road Ore Car, *87*	20	25
19302	Milwaukee Road Quad Hopper with coal (FF 2), *87*	24	35
____**19303**	Lionel Lines Quad Hopper with coal, *87 u*	20	31
____**19304**	GN Covered Quad Hopper (FF 3), *88*	18	25
____**19305**	Chessie System Ore Car, *88*	18	23
____**19307**	B&LE Ore Car with load, *89*	19	25
____**19308**	GN Ore Car with load, *89*	18	23
____**19309**	Seaboard Covered Quad Hopper, *89*	16	19
____**19310**	L&C Quad Hopper with coal, *89*	16	30
____**19311**	SP Covered Quad Hopper, *90*	13	19
____**19312**	Reading Quad Hopper with coal, *90*	21	36
____**19313**	B&O Ore Car with load, *90–91*	20	25
____**19315**	Amtrak Ore Car with load, *91*	22	30
____**19316**	Wabash Covered Quad Hopper, *91*	18	23
____**19317**	Lehigh Valley Quad Hopper with coal, *91*	47	55
____**19318**	NKP Quad Hopper with coal (FF 6), *92*	30	34
____**19319**	Union Pacific Covered Quad Hopper, *92*	19	23
____**19320**	PRR Ore Car with load, *92*	21	30
____**19321**	B&LE Ore Car with load, *92*	21	30
____**19322**	C&NW Ore Car with load, *93*	27	34
____**19323**	Detroit & Mackinac Ore Car with load, *93*	20	29
____**19324**	Erie Quad Hopper with coal (FF 7), *93*	25	33
____**19325**	N&W 4-bay Hopper "6446-1" with coal, *97*		65
____**19326**	N&W 4-bay Hopper "6446-2" with coal, *96*		60
____**19327**	N&W 4-bay Hopper "6446-3" with coal, *96*		60
____**19328**	N&W 4-bay Hopper "6446-4" with coal, *96*		60
____**19329**	N&W 4-bay Hopper "6436" with coal, *97*		55
____**19330**	Cotton Belt 4-bay Hopper "64661" with coal, *98*		45
____**19331**	Cotton Belt 4-bay Hopper "64662" with coal, *98*		45
____**19332**	Cotton Belt 4-bay Hopper "64663" with coal, *98*		45
____**19333**	Cotton Belt 4-bay Hopper "64664" with coal, *98*		45
____**19338**	Cotton Belt 4-bay Hopper 2-pack, *99*		120
____**19339**	Cotton Belt 4-bay Hopper "64469," *99*		NRS
____**19340**	Cotton Belt 4-bay Hopper "64470," *99*		NRS
____**19341**	LV 2-bay Hopper "6456," *99*		30
19344	D&RGW 3-bay Cylindrical Hopper "15990," *99–00*		42
____**19345**	CN 3-bay Cylindrical Hopper "370708," *99–00*		95
____**19346**	PRR 4-bay Hopper with coal "744433," *01*		40
____**19347**	LV 2-bay Hopper "643657," *01*		40
19348	Duluth, Missabe & Iron Range Ore Car "28000," *03*		25
____**19349**	U.S. Steel Ore Car "19349," *03*		29

		Exc	Mint
19350	Postwar "6636" Alaska Quad Hopper, *03*		34____
19357	N&W Hopper "6446-25," Archive Collection, *07*		50____
19361	Twizzlers Quad Hopper, *10*		55____
19362	Coursers Christmas Hopper with gifts, *10*		60____
19364	Milk Duds Covered Hopper, *11*		55____
19365	Coca-Cola Quad Hopper, *10*		60____
19366	Santa's Little Hopper, *10–11*		55____
19367	ATSF Quad Hopper, *11*		60____
19368	Southern Offset Hopper "106723," (std O), *11*		70____
19369	Alaska Quad Hopper "20756," *12*		60____
19371	Burlington Northern I-Beam Car, *04*		60____
19374	NS Bathtub Gondola 2-pack (std O), *15*		140____
19377	DETX Bathtub Gondola 2-pack (std O), *15*		140____
19380	CSX Bathtub Gondola 2-pack (std O), *15*		140____
19383	UP PS-4 Flatcar "57125" (std O), *13*		70____
19384	ATSF PS-4 Flatcar "90088" (std O), *13*		70____
19385	CNJ PS-4 Flatcar "339" (std O), *13*		70____
19386	BN PS-4 Flatcar "613200" (std O), *13*		70____
19388	BN 89' Auto Carrier (std O), *13–14*		110____
19389	SP 89' Auto Carrier (std O), *13–14*		110____
19390	CP 89' Auto Carrier (std O), *13–14, 16*		110____
19391	Soo Line 89' Auto Carrier (std O), *13–14, 16*		110____
19393	BNSF Auto Carrier 2-pack (std O), *12*		220____
19394	UP Auto Carrier 2-pack (std O), *12*		220____
19395	Grand Trunk Auto Carrier 2-pack (std O), *12*		220____
19396	CSX Auto Carrier 2-pack (std O), *12*		220____
19397	CN Auto Carrier 2-pack (std O), *12*		220____
19398	Conrail Auto Carrier 2-pack (std O), *12*		220____
19400	Milwaukee Road Gondola with cable reels (FF 2), *87*	23	31____
19401	GN Gondola with coal (FF 3), *88*	14	16____
19402	GN Crane Car (FF 3), *88*	47	65____
19403	WM Gondola with coal (FF 4), *89*	20	25____
19404	Trailer Train Flatcar with WM trailers (FF 4), *89*	29	33____
19405	Southern Crane Car, *91*	42	65____
19406	West Point Mint Car, *91 u*	38	50____
19408	Frisco Gondola with coil covers (FF 5), *91*	26	31____
19409	Southern Flatcar with stakes, *91*	18	22____
19410	NYC Gondola with canisters, *91*	47	55____
19411	NKP Flatcar with Sears trailer (FF 6), *92*	50	59____
19412	Frisco Crane Car, *92*	49	65____
19413	Frisco Flatcar with stakes, *92*	16	21____
19414	Union Pacific Flatcar with stakes (SSS), *92*	19	26____
19415	Erie Flatcar with trailer "7200" (FF 7), *93*	28	39____
19416	ICG TTUX Flatcar Set with trailers (SSS), *93*	70	75____
19419	Charlotte Mint Car, *93*	25	32____
19420	Lionel Lines Vat Car, *94*	18	22____
19421	Hirsch Brothers Vat Car, *95*	16	21____
19423	Circle L Racing Flatcar "6424" with stock cars, *96*		27____
19424	Edison Electric Depressed Center Flatcar "6461" with transformer, *97*		31____
19427	Evans Auto Loader "6414," *99*		55____
19428	Evans Boat Loader "6414," *99*		70____
19429	Culvert Gondola "6342," *98–99*		48____

		Exc	Mint
19430	ATSF Flatcar "6411" with Beechcraft Bonanza, *98*		47
19438	Christmas Gondola (std O), *98*		42
19439	Flatcar with safes, *98*		35
19440	Flatcar with FedEx trailer, *98*		34
19441	Lobster Vat Car, *98*		35
19442	Water Supply Flatcar with tank (SSS), *98*		31
19444	Flatcar with VW Bug, *98*		38
19445	Borden Milk Tank Car "520," *99*		38
19446	Pittsburgh Paint Vat Car, *99*		43
19447	Mama's Baked Beans Vat Car, *99*		35
19448	Easter Gondola "6462" with candy, *99*		27
19449	Liquified Gas Tank Car "6469," *99*		31
19450	Barrel Ramp Car "6343," *99*		31
19451	Wheel Car "6262," *99*		32
19454	PRR Flatcar "6424" with gondola, *99*		25
19455	Lionel Lines Flatcar "6430" with Cooper-Jarrett trailers, *99*		60
19457	Lionel Lines Extension Searchlight Car, *99*		40
19459	Valentine Gondola "6462" with candy, *99*		50
19471	Mobil Flatcar with 2 trailers, *00 u*		96
19472	Mobil Bulkhead Flatcar with tank, *00 u*		68
19474	L&N Flatcar "6424" with trailer frames, *99*		26
19476	Zoo Gondola "6462" with animals, *99–00*		43
19477	Monday Night Football Flatcar with trailer, *01*		30
19478	Culvert Gondola "6342," *99*		45
19479	Borden Milk Car "521," *00*		38
19480	Valentine's Vat Car "6475," *99–00*		30
19481	Easter Vat Car, *99–00*		38
19482	NYC Flat with trailer "6424," *00*		50
19483	VW Beetle Flatcar, *00*		48
19484	Flatcar "6264" with timber, *00*		34
19485	PRR Culvert Gondola "347004," *01*		41
19486	NYC Lumber Flatcar, *00*		34
19487	Flatcar "6800" with airplane, *00*		41
19489	Evans Auto Loader "500085," *00*		50
19490	Postwar "6475" Libby's Vat Car, *01–02*		36
19491	Christmas Vat Car, *01*		30
19492	WM Skeleton Log Car 3-pack, *01*		95
19496	Westside Lumber Skeleton Log Car 3-pack, *01*		112
19500	Milwaukee Road Reefer (FF 2), *87*	30	39
19502	C&NW Reefer, *87*	30	33
19503	Bangor & Aroostook Reefer, *87*	22	25
19504	Northern Pacific Reefer, *87*	16	22
19505	Great Northern Reefer (FF 3), *88*	29	35
19506	Thomas Newcomen Reefer, *88*	18	23
19507	Thomas Edison Reefer, *88*	21	27
19508	Leonardo da Vinci Reefer, *89*	19	27
19509	Alexander Graham Bell Reefer, *89*	17	20
19510	PRR Stock Car (FARR 5), *89 u*	18	26
19511	WM Reefer (FF 4), *89*	22	28
19512	Wright Brothers Reefer, *90*	17	21
19513	Ben Franklin Reefer, *90*	17	20
19515	Milwaukee Road Stock Car (FF 2), *90 u*	33	41
19516	George Washington Reefer, *89 u, 91*	14	19

Exc Mint

Number	Description	Exc	Mint
19517	Civil War Reefer, *89 u, 91*	14	19____
19518	Man on the Moon Reefer, *89 u, 91*	13	17____
19519	Frisco Stock Car (FF 5), *91*	26	31____
19520	CSX Reefer, *91*	18	23____
19522	Guglielmo Marconi Reefer, *91*	19	23____
19523	Dr. Robert Goddard Reefer, *91*	19	23____
19524	Delaware & Hudson Reefer (SSS), *91*	29	32____
19525	Speedy Alka Seltzer Reefer, *91 u*	31	32____
19526	Jolly Green Giant Reefer, *91 u*	21	33____
19527	Nickel Plate Road Reefer (FF 6), *92*	20	29____
19528	Joshua L. Cowen Reefer, *92*	23	28____
19529	A.C. Gilbert Reefer, *92*	18	23____
19530	Rock Island Stock Car, *92 u*	34	38____
19531	Rice Krispies Reefer, *92 u*	23	33____
19532	Hormel Reefer "901," *92 u*	18	24____
19535	Erie Reefer (FF 7), *93*	23	26____
19536	Soo Line REA Reefer (SSS), *93*	25	30____
19538	Hormel Reefer "102," *94*	22	25____
19539	Heinz Reefer, *94*	38	47____
19540	Broken Arrow Ranch Stock Car "3356," *97*		28____
19552	Rutland Reefer "395" (std O), *00*		32____
19553	ATSF Stock Car "23003," *00*		37____
19554	Postwar Celebration Milk Car "36621," *00*		125____
19555	Swift Reefer "5839," red, *01*		33____
19556	Swift Reefer "1020," silver, *01*		31____
19557	Circus Stock Car "6376," *00*		32____
19558	Postwar "6556" MKT Stock Car, *02*		27____
19559	MKT Stock Car, girls set add-on, *02*		95____
19560	NP 2-door Stock Car "6356," Archive Collection, *02*		33____
19561	Norman Rockwell Holiday Reefer, *03*		25____
19562	Norman Rockwell Holiday Reefer, *03*		25____
19563	Norman Rockwell Holiday Reefer, *03*		25____
19564	Postwar "6672" Santa Fe Reefer, *03*		35____
19565	Burlington Reefer "6672," Archive Collection, *03*		35____
19567	Postwar "6572" Railway Express Agency Reefer, *05*		45____
19568	GN Reefer, Archive Collection, *05*		45____
19569	Pillsbury Reefer, traditional, *05*		53____
19570	Nestle Nesquik Reefer, traditional, *05*		53____
19572	NYC Reefer "6672," Archive Collection, *06*		45____
19573	Postwar "6356" NYC Stock Car, *06–07*		50____
19574	GN Stock Car, *08*		50____
19575	REA Reefer "6721," *08–09*		50____
19576	Alaska Reefer, *08*		50____
19577	Krey's Reefer, *10–11*		60____
19578	Granny Smith Apples Wood-sided Reefer, *10–11*		53____
19585	NS Transparent Instruction Car, *10–11*		75____
19586	Alaska Husky Transport Car, *10–11*		75____
19587	Hershey's Chocolate Wood-sided Reefer, *10*		75____
19588	Santa's Wish Transparent Gift Car, *10*		75____
19589	Blood Transfusion Bunk Car, *10–11*		60____
19590	Wood-sided Reefer 2-pack, *10*		110____
19593	Hershey's Kisses Wood-sided Reefer, *11–15*		60____
19594	York Peppermint Patty Wood-sided Reefer, *10–11*		55____

		Exc	Mint
____19599	Old Glory Reefers, set of 3, *89 u, 91*	37	43
____19600	Milwaukee Road 1-D Tank Car (FF 2), *87*	33	40
____19601	North American 1-D Tank Car (FF 4), *89*	17	29
____19602	Johnson 1-D Tank Car (FF 5), *91*	24	30
____19603	GATX 1-D Tank Car (FF 6), *92*	32	41
____19604	Goodyear 1-D Tank Car (SSS), *93*	33	36
____19605	Hudson's Bay 1-D Tank Car (SSS), *94*	25	29
____19607	Sunoco 1-D Tank Car "6315," *96*		23
19608	Sunoco Aviation Services 1-D Tank Car "6315"		
____	(SSS), *97*		38
____19611	Gulf Oil 1-D Tank Car "6315," *98*		33
____19612	Gulf Oil 3-D Tank Car "6425," *98*		30
____19614	BASF 1-D Tank Car "UTLX 78252," *99–00*		25
____19615	Vulcan Chemicals 1-D Tank Car, *99–00*		25
____19621	Centennial 1-D Tank Car "6015-1," *99*		55
____19622	Centennial 1-D Tank Car "6015-2," *99*		62
____19623	Centennial 1-D Tank Car "6015-3," *99*		62
____19624	Centennial 1-D Tank Car "6015-4," *99*		58
____19625	Ethyl Tank Car " 6236," *01*		31
____19626	Diamond Chemical Tank Car "19419," *01*		29
____19627	Shell 1-D Tank Car "1227," *01*		37
____19628	Lion Oil 1-D Tank Car "2256," *01*		35
____19634	General American 1-D Tank Car, *01*		30
____19635	U.S. Army 1-D Tank Car "10936," *01*		31
____19636	Hooker Chemicals 1-D Tank Car "6180," *01*		36
19637	GATX TankTrain Intermediate Car "44589"		
____	(std O), *02*		55
19638	CN TankTrain Intermediate Car "75571" (std O),		
____	*02*		65
19639	GATX TankTrain Intermediate Car 3-pack		
____	(std O), *02*		140
____19644	Union Texas 1-D Tank Car "9922," *02*		33
____19645	Penn Salt 1-D Tank Car "4730," *02*		33
19646	CN TankTrain Intermediate Car "75571" (std O),		
____	*03*		45
19647	GATX TankTrain Intermediate Car "44589"		
____	(std O), *03*		45
____19649	Scrooge McDuck Mint Car, *05*		192
____19651	Santa Fe Tool Car, *87*	30	35
____19652	Jersey Central Bunk Car, *88*	25	33
____19653	Jersey Central Tool Car, *88*	26	28
____19654	Amtrak Bunk Car, *89*	22	25
____19655	Amtrak Tool Car, *90–91*	23	30
____19656	Milwaukee Road Bunk Car, smoke, *90*	40	50
____19657	Wabash Bunk Car, smoke, *91–92*	36	42
____19658	Norfolk & Western Tool Car, *91*	24	29
____19660	Mint Car, *98*		40
____19663	Pratt's Hollow Bunk Car "5717," *99*		40
____19664	Ambassador Award Bunk Car, bronze, *99 u*		410
____19665	Ambassador Engineer Bunk Car, silver, *99 u*		590
____19666	Ambassador Cowen Bunk Car, gold, *99 u*		435
____19667	Wellspring Gold Bullion Car, *99*		56
____19669	King Tut Museum Car "9660," *99*		70
____19670	NY Federal Reserve Bullion Car "6445," *00*		44

Exc Mint

		Exc	Mint
19671	Lionel Model Shop Display Car "6445-01," 99–00		50____
19672	Lionel Mines Mint Car, 00 u		250____
19673	Wellspring Capital Management Mint Car, 99 u		215____
19674	Lionel Lines Platinum Car, 00		43____
19675	Lionel Model Shop Display "6445-2," 01		42____
19676	Philadelphia Mint Car, 01		40____
19677	Fort Knox Mint Car "6445," 00		50____
19678	U.S. Army Bunk Car, 02		45____
19679	St. Louis Federal Reserve Mint Car, 02		38____
19681	Area 51 Alien Suspension Car, 02		47____
19682	Alaska Klondike Mining Mint Car, 02		40____
19683	Pony Express Mint Car, 02		50____
19686	Chicago Federal Reserve Mint Car "6445," 03–04		45____
19687	UP Bunk Car "3887," smoke, 03		40____
19688	Postwar "6445" Fort Knox Mint Car, 02–03		39____
19689	CIBRO TankTrain Intermediate Car 3-pack (std O), 03		100____
19694	Pony Express Mint Car, 03		50____
19696	U.S. Savings Bond Mint Car, 00		150____
19697	U.S. Bureau of Engraving and Printing Mint Car "19697," 04		40____
19698	San Francisco Federal Reserve Mint Car, 04		40____
19700	Chessie System Extended Vision Caboose, 88	43	50____
19701	Milwaukee Road N5c Caboose (FF 2), 88	50	65____
19702	PRR N5c Caboose, 87	44	55____
19703	GN Extended Vision Caboose (FF 3), 88	42	49____
19704	WM Extended Vision Caboose, smoke (FF 4), 89	42	49____
19705	CP Rail Extended Vision Caboose, smoke, 89	43	47____
19706	UP Extended Vision Caboose "9706," smoke, 89	40	56____
19707	SP Work Caboose with searchlight, smoke, 90	55	60____
19708	Lionel Lines Bay Window Caboose, 90	43	46____
19709	PRR Work Caboose, smoke, 89, 91	49	70____
19710	Frisco Extended Vision Caboose, smoke (FF 5), 91	43	47____
19711	NS Extended Vision Caboose, smoke, 92	47	65____
19712	PRR N5c Caboose, 91	44	47____
19714	NYC Work Caboose with searchlight, smoke, 92	100	130____
19715	DM&IR Extended Vision Caboose "C-217," 92 u	50	60____
19716	IC Extended Vision Caboose "9405," smoke, 93	105	135____
19717	Susquehanna Bay Window Caboose "0121," 93	44	55____
19718	C&IM Extended Vision Caboose "74," 92 u	38	45____
19719	Erie Bay Window Caboose "C-300" (FF 7), 93	47	55____
19720	Soo Line Extended Vision Caboose (SSS), 93	32	41____
19721	GM&O Extended Vision Caboose "2956," 93 u	47	50____
19723	Disney Extended Vision Caboose, 94	36	45____
19724	JCPenney MKT Extended Vision Caboose "125," 94 u	38	43____
19726	NYC Bay Window Caboose (SSS), 95	50	60____
19727	Pennsylvania N5c Caboose "477938," 96		30____
19728	N&W Bay Window Caboose, 96		70____
19732	ATSF Bay Window Caboose "6517," 96		43____
19733	New York Central Caboose "6357," 96		30____
19734	Southern Pacific Caboose "6357," 96		26____

		Exc	Mint
____19736	PRR N5c Caboose "6417," *97*		27
____19737	Lackawanna Searchlight Caboose "2420," *97*		75
____19738	Conrail N5c Caboose "6417" (SSS), *97*		55
____19739	NYC Wood-sided Caboose "6907," *97*		60
____19740	Virginian N5c Caboose "6427," *97 u*		65
____19741	Pennsylvania N5c Caboose "6417," *98*		50
19742	Erie Bay Window Caboose "C301," Caboose		
____	Talk, *98*		95
____19748	SP&S Bay Window Caboose "6517," *97 u*		50
____19749	SP Bay Window Caboose "6517," *98*		100
____19750	Holiday Music Bay Window Caboose, *98*		160
____19751	PRR N5c Caboose "492418," *98*		30
____19752	NP Bay Window Caboose "407," *98*		50
____19753	UP Extended Vision Caboose "25641," *98*		55
____19754	NYC Caboose "20112," *98*		55
____19755	Centennial Porthole Caboose, *99*		68
____19756	Lionel Lines Bay Window Caboose, *99*		50
____19758	DL&W Work Caboose "6419," *99*		55
____19759	Corvette N5c Caboose, *99*		60
____19772	Lionel Visitor's Center Vat Car, *99 u*		40
____19773	Lionel Kids Club Barrel Ramp Car "6343," *96 u*		48
19778	Case Cutlery Wood-sided Caboose "1889"		
____	(std O), *99 u*		NRS
____19779	SP Bay Window Caboose "1908," *99*		65
____19780	LV Porthole Caboose "641751," *99–00*		43
19781	Vapor Records Holiday Porthole Caboose "6417,"		
____	*99–00*		62
____19782	NYC Bay Window Caboose "21719," *00*		65
____19783	Ford Mustang Extended Vision Caboose, *01*		50
____19785	SP Bay Window Caboose "6517," *00*		55
____19786	PRR Extended Vision Caboose, *00 u*		40
____19787	PRR Extended Vision Caboose "477927," *01*		40
____19790	Postwar "6417" Lehigh Valley Caboose, *02*		41
____19792	Postwar "C301" Erie Bay Window Caboose, *03*		45
____19796	C&O Bay Window Caboose, *03*		50
____19800	Circle L Ranch Operating Cattle Car, *88*	75	95
____19801	Poultry Dispatch Chicken Car, *87*	20	27
____19802	Carnation Milk Car, *87*	87	102
____19803	Reading Ice Car, *87*	38	44
____19804	Wabash Operating Hopper, *87*	25	34
____19805	Santa Fe Operating Boxcar, *87*	28	36
____19806	PRR Operating Hopper, *88*	28	32
____19807	PRR Extended Vision Caboose, smoke, *88*	39	47
____19808	NYC Ice Car, *88*	38	49
____19809	Erie-Lackawanna Operating Boxcar, *88*	27	35
____19810	Bosco Milk Car, *88*	80	89
____19811	Monon Brakeman Car, *90*	50	55
____19813	Northern Pacific Ice Car, *89 u*	41	46
____19815	Delaware & Hudson Brakeman Car, *92*	49	60
19816	Madison Hardware Operating Boxcar "190991,"		
____	*91 u*	80	102
____19817	Virginian Ice Car, *94*	31	35
____19818	Dairymen's League Milk Car "788," *94*	65	80
____19819	Poultry Dispatch Car (SSS), *94*	36	43
____19820	Die-cast Tender, RailSounds II, *95–96*		175

		Exc	Mint
19821	UP Operating Boxcar, *95*	31	36____
19822	Pork Dispatch Car, *95*	29	39____
19823	Burlington Ice Car, *94 u, 95*	39	49____
19824	U.S. Army Target Launcher, *96*		30____
19825	Generator Car, *96*		48____
19827	NYC Operating Boxcar, *97*		37____
19828	C&NW Animated Stock Car "3356" and Stockyard, *96–97*		100____
19830	U.S. Mail Operating Boxcar "3428," *97*		39____
19831	GM Generator Car "3530," power pole and wire, *97*		46____
19832	Cola Ice Car "6352," *97*		47____
19833	Tender "2426RS," RailSounds II, *97*		240____
19834	LL 6-wheel Crane Car "2460," *97*		60____
19835	FedEx Animated Boxcar "3464X," *97*		38____
19837	Bucyrus 6-wheel Crane Car "2460," *99*		49____
19845	Aquarium Car "3435," CC, *98*		151____
19846	Animated Giraffe Car "3376C," *98*		105____
19850	Stock Car "33760," RailSounds, *00*		130____
19853	Firefighting Instruction Generator Car (SSS), *98*		60____
19854	Lionelville Fire Car (SSS), *98*		55____
19855	Christmas Aquarium Car, *98*		60____
19856	Mermaid Transport, *98*		65____
19857	NYC Firefighting Instruction Car "19853," *98–99*		175____
19858	Lionelville Operating Searchlight Car "19854," *99*		65____
19859	REA Boxcar "6267," steam RailSounds, *99*		170____
19860	Conrail Boxcar "169671," diesel RailSounds, *99*		140____
19864	Animated Ostrich Boxcar, *99*		37____
19867	Operating Poultry Dispatch Car "3434," *99*		48____
19868	Shark Aquarium Car "3435," *99*		190____
19869	Alien Aquarium Car "3435," *99*		49____
19877	ATSF Operating Barrel Car, *99*		55____
19878	Operating Helium Tank Flatcar "3362," *99*		40____
19880	Lionel Lines Extension Searchlight Car, *00*		50____
19882	Sanderson Farms Poultry Car "3434," *99*		41____
19883	LL Bucyrus Erie Crane Car "64608," *99*		45____
19884	Atlantis Travel Aquarium Car, *00 u*		95____
19885	N&W Operating Hopper Car, *00*		31____
19886	Seaboard Boxcar "16126," steam RailSounds, *00*		140____
19887	SP Boxcar "651663," diesel RailSounds, *00*		140____
19888	Christmas Music Boxcar, *01*		65____
19889	PRR Bay Window Caboose "477719," Crewtalk, *00*		140____
19890	Santa Fe Bay Window Caboose "999211," Crewtalk, *00*		100____
19894	Hood's Operating Milk Car with platform, *03–04*		95____
19894	Pony Express Mint Car, *03*		50____
19895	3356 Santa Fe Horse Car with corral, *04*		120____
19896	USMC Missile Launch Sound Car "45," *03–04*		165____
19897	NYC Crane Car, TMCC, *04*		255____
19898	Nestle Nesquik Operating Milk Car with platform, *04*		95____
19899	Pennsylvania Crane Car "19899" CC, *03–05*		260____
19900	Toy Fair Boxcar, *87 u*	65	80____
19901	"I Love Virginia" Boxcar, *87*	25	35____

		Exc	Mint
____19902	Toy Fair Boxcar, *88 u*	55	80
____19903	Christmas Boxcar, *87 u*	22	34
____19904	Christmas Boxcar, *88 u*	32	43
____19905	"I Love California" Boxcar, *88*	20	24
____19906	"I Love Pennsylvania" Boxcar, *89*	26	32
____19907	Toy Fair Boxcar, *89 u*	38	55
____19908	Christmas Boxcar, *89 u*	30	39
____19909	"I Love New Jersey" Boxcar, *90*	19	25
____19910	Christmas Boxcar, *90 u*	35	38
____19911	Toy Fair Boxcar, *90 u*	75	95
____19912	"I Love Ohio" Boxcar, *91*	21	28
____19913	Christmas Boxcar, *91*	34	52
____19913	Lionel Employee Christmas Boxcar, *91 u*	150	200
____19914	Toy Fair Boxcar, *91 u*	38	50
____19915	"I Love Texas" Boxcar, *92*	35	60
____19916	Lionel Employee Christmas Boxcar, *92 u*	190	220
____19917	Toy Fair Boxcar, *92 u*	45	53
____19918	Christmas Boxcar, *92 u*	49	70
____19919	"I Love Minnesota" Boxcar, *93*	40	60
____19920	Lionel Visitor's Center Boxcar, *92 u*	16	28
____19921	Lionel Employee Christmas Boxcar, *93 u*	140	185
____19922	Christmas Boxcar, *93*	33	41
____19923	Toy Fair Boxcar, *93 u*	65	95
____19925	Lionel Employee Learning Center Boxcar, *93 u*	55	63
____19926	"I Love Nevada" Boxcar, *94*	21	26
____19927	Lionel Visitor's Center Boxcar, *93 u*	26	33
____19928	Lionel Employee Christmas Boxcar, *94 u*	205	230
____19929	Christmas Boxcar, *94*	30	40
____19931	Toy Fair Boxcar, *94 u*	49	65
____19932	Lionel Visitor's Center Boxcar, *94 u*	26	33
____19933	"I Love Illinois" Boxcar, *95*	21	27
____19934	Lionel Visitor's Center Boxcar, *95 u*	18	22
____19937	Toy Fair Boxcar, *95 u*	55	75
____19938	Christmas Boxcar, *95*	26	34
____19939	Lionel Employee Christmas Boxcar, *95 u*	100	128
____19941	"I Love Colorado" Boxcar, *95*	23	30
____19942	"I Love Florida" Boxcar, *96*	19	27
____19943	"I Love Arizona" Boxcar, *96*	20	25
____19944	Lionel Visitor's Center Tank Car, *96 u*		35
____19945	Holiday Boxcar, *96*		29
____19946	Lionel Employee Christmas Boxcar, *96 u*		195
____19947	Lionel Toy Fair Boxcar, *96 u*		200
____19948	Visitor's Center Flatcar with trailer, *96 u*		34
____19949	"I Love NY" Boxcar, *97*		50
____19950	"I Love Montana" Boxcar, *97*		30
____19951	"I Love Massachusetts" Boxcar, *98*		26
____19952	"I Love Indiana" Boxcar, *98*		31
19955 ____	Lionel Visitor's Center Gondola with coil covers, *98 u*		20
____19956	Toy Fair Boxcar "777," *98 u*		65
____19957	Ambassador Caboose, *97 u*		484
____19958	Ambassador Caboose, silver (std O), *98 u*		553
____19959	Ambassador Caboose, gold (std O), *98 u*		744
____19964	U.S. JCI Senate Boxcar, *92 u*	55	63
____19968	"I Love Maine" Boxcar, *99*		40

		Exc	Mint
19969	"I Love Vermont" Boxcar, *99*		40____
19970	"I Love New Hampshire" Boxcar, *99*		34____
19971	"I Love Rhode Island" Boxcar, *99*		34____
19976	Lionel Employee Holiday Boxcar, *99 u*		150____
19977	Toy Fair Boxcar, *99 u*		50____
19981	Lionel Centennial Boxcar, *99*		36____
19982	Lionel Centennial Boxcar, *99*		36____
19983	Lionel Centennial Boxcar, *99*		36____
19984	Lionel Centennial Boxcar, *99*		36____
19985	"I Love Georgia" Boxcar, *99–00*		45____
19986	"I Love North Carolina" Boxcar, *99–00*		40____
19987	"I Love South Carolina" Boxcar, *99–00*		40____
19988	"I Love Tennessee" Boxcar, *99–00*		55____
19989	Toy Fair Boxcar, *00 u*		55____
19996	Toy Fair Boxcar, *01 u*		50____
19997	Lionel Employee Boxcar, *01 u*		125____
19998	Christmas Boxcar, *01*		33____
19999	Lionel Visitor's Center 4-bay Hopper, *02 u*		153____
20000	PRR Senator Coach 4-pack (std O), *13, 15*		640____
20005	SP Sunset Limited Coach 4-pack (std O), *13, 15*		640____
20010	UP City of Los Angeles Coach 4-pack (std O), *13, 15*		640____
20015	B&O Capitol Limited Coach 4-pack (std O), *13*		640____
20020	FEC City of Miami Coach 4-pack (std O), *13*		640____
20025	KCS Southern Belle Coach 4-pack (std O), *13*		640____
20030	MILW Olympian Coach 4-pack (std O), *13, 15*		640____
21029	World of Little Choo Choo Set, *94u, 95*	36	43____
21141	North Dakota State Quarter Gondola Bank, *07*		60____
21142	South Dakota State Quarter Hopper Bank, *07*		60____
21163	SuperStreets FasTrack Grade Crossing, *08–10*		20____
21164	SuperStreets 10" Transition to FasTrack, *08–10*		9____
21165	SuperStreets Transition to FasTrack, 2 pieces, *08–10*		17____
21168	City Traction Trolley Add-on, *08*		75____
21169	City Traction Speeder Add-on, *08*		75____
21170	NYC 15" Heavyweight Passenger Car 4-pack, *07*		250____
21175	NYC 15" Heavyweight Passenger Car 2-pack, *07*		125____
21198	ATSF Alco Diesel AA Set, horn, *08*		200____
21199	ATSF Midnight Chief Streamliner Car 4-pack, *08*		200____
21204	ATSF Midnight Chief Streamliner Car 2-pack, *08*		100____
21207	SP Diesel Work Train, *07*		175____
21212	NH Diesel Freight Set, *07*		250____
21217	Southern Diesel Executive Inspection Train, *07*		175____
21229	Ringling Bros. S2 Diesel Switcher, horn, *07*		80____
21230	Ringling Bros. Porter Locomotive, *07*		105____
21231	Ringling Bros. Streamliner Car 4-pack, *07*		210____
21234	Ringling Bros. Streamliner Car 2-pack, *07*		105____
21237	Ringling Bros. Flatcar with 3 wagons, *07*		50____
21238	Ringling Bros. Flatcar with 3 wagons, *07*		50____
21239	Ringling Bros. Flatcar with crates, *07*		45____
21240	Ringling Bros. Flatcar with front end loader and poles, *07*		45____
21252	Boy Flying Kite, *08*		60____
21253	Operating Bunk Car Yard Office, *07*		80____

		Exc	Mint
21261	SuperStreets 2.5" Straight-to-Curve Connector, 4 pieces, *08–10*		9
21265	Operating Voltmeter Car, *07*		75
21266	SuperStreets Intersection, 4 pieces, *08–10*		40
21267	PRR Boxcab Electric Locomotive, horn, *07*		77
21271	WP Operating Coal Dump Car with vehicle, *07*		33
21276	Congressional Diner, smoke, *07*		110
21277	Operating Flagman's Shanty, *08*		70
21279	Roach Wranglers Pest Control Van, *08*		30
21281	SuperStreets D21 Curve, *08–10*		3
21282	SuperStreets 2.5" Curve-to-Curve Connector, 4 pieces, *08–10*		9
21283	SuperStreets Tubular Track Grade Crossing, *08–10*		18
21284	SuperStreets 10" Tubular Transition, *08–10*		8
21285	SuperStreets 10" Tubular Transition, 2 pieces, *08–10*		14
21286	SuperStreets Intersection, *08–10*		10
21287	SuperStreets Y Roadway, *08–10*		12
21288	SuperStreets O Gauge Conversion Pins, *08–10*		2
21289	SuperStreets Connector Pins, *08–10*		2
21290	SuperStreets Hookup Wires, 2 pieces, *08–10*		3
21291	Dogbone Expander pack, *08–10*		25
21296	City Traction Classic Truck, *07*		30
21298	NYC 4-6-4 Hudson Locomotive "5279," CC, *07*		500
21316	PE RS3 Diesel "2815," CC, *07*		350
21324	Acrobats and Clowns Figures, 10 pieces, *08–10*		12
21325	Ringmaster Circus Figures, 5, with accessories, *08–10*		12
21326	PRR 15" Interurban Car 2-pack, *07*		200
21354	Fresh Never Frozen Fish Transport Car, *07*		80
21355	Dump Bin, *08–10*		20
21358	Special Addition Boxcar, Girl, *08–10*		25
21359	Special Addition Boxcar, Boy, *08–10*		25
21368	Passenger Coach Figures, 9 pieces, *08–10*		11
21369	Walking Figures, 8 pieces, *08–10*		11
21370	Sitting Figures, 6, with benches, *08–10*		11
21371	Standing Figures, 8 pieces, *08–10*		11
21372	Railroad Station Figures, 6, with accessories, *08–10*		11
21373	School Figures, 7, with accessories, *08–10*		11
21374	Service Station Figures, 5, with accessories, *08–10*		11
21375	Police Figures, 10, with dog, *08*		20
21376	Seated Passenger Figures, 40 pieces, *08*		27
21377	Mounted Police, 3, with horses, *08–10*		11
21378	Factory, *08–10*		18
21379	Police Station, *08–10*		16
21380	Colonial House, *08–10*		16
21381	Suburban Station, *08–10*		16
21382	School, *08–10*		17
21383	Suburban Ranch House, *08–10*		15
21384	Service Station with gas pumps, *08–10*		17
21385	Barn and Chicken Coop, *08–10*		20
21386	Firehouse, *08–10*		17

		Exc	Mint
21387	Church, *08–10*		15____
21388	Country L-shaped Ranch House, *08–10*		16____
21389	Supermarket, *08–10*		12____
21390	Diner, *08–10*		15____
21394	Rotating Beacon, *08–09*		31____
21396	Single Tunnel Portals, pair, *08–10*		15____
21397	SuperSnap 31" Remote Switch, left hand, *08–09*		55____
21398	SuperSnap 31" Remote Switch, right hand, *08–09*		55____
21399	SuperSnap 72" Remote Switch, left hand, *08–09*		70____
21400	SuperSnap 72" Remote Switch, right hand, *08–09*		70____
21412	NYC Plymouth Switcher Freight Set, *07*		155____
21430	SuperStreets D16 Curve, *08–10*		2____
21431	SuperStreets 10" Straight Track, *08–10*		2____
21432	SuperStreets D16 Curved Track, 8 pieces, *08–10*		18____
21433	SuperStreets 5" Straight Track, 4 pieces, *08–10*		14____
21434	SuperStreets 10" Straight Track, 8 pieces, *08–10*		19____
21435	World War II Seated Soldiers, 9, with benches, *08–09*		20____
21436	Rings and Things Circus Accessories, *08–09*		10____
21438	Remote Controller, *07–10*		35____
21442	City Figures, 7, with scooter, *08–10*		11____
21443	Factory Figures, 6, with accessories, *08–10*		11____
21444	Church Figures, 5, with accessories, *08–10*		11____
21445	Firefighting Figures, 11, with accessories, *08–10*		20____
21449	Operating Loading Platform with flatcar, *07–08*		80____
21450	Unloading Station with dump bins, *07*		100____
21451	Girder Bridge with stone piers, *07*		40____
21452	Graduated Trestle Set, 26 pieces, *07*		50____
21453	Elevated Trestle Set, 10 pieces, *07*		40____
21454	Double Tunnel Portals, 2 pieces, *08–10*		20____
21456	UPS Step Van, *07*		30____
21466	Ringling Bros. 15" Aluminum Advertising Car, *07*		110____
21469	Ringling Bros. Flatcar, white, with container, *07*		45____
21470	Ringling Bros. Flatcar, blue, with container, *07*		45____
21471	Ringling Bros. Flatcar with 2 trailers, *08–10*		60____
21472	Ringling Bros. Flatcar with 2 trailers, *08–10*		60____
21476	Strasburg Plymouth Diesel Switcher, *07*		100____
21494	WM RS3 Diesel "189," CC, *07*		350____
21529	Montana State Quarter Boxcar Bank, *08*		45____
21542	Washington State Quarter Tank Car Bank, *08*		45____
21543	Boyd Bros. Ford Classic Truck, *08*		33____
21549	Ringling Bros. Crew Bus, *08*		33____
21552	S.W.A.T. Team Step Van, *08*		30____
21560	Reading Flatcar with rail load, *07*		25____
21567	School Bus SuperStreets Set, *08*		110____
21568	Dirty Dogz Van SuperStreets Set, *08*		100____
21569	Angelo's Pizza Delivery Van, *08*		30____
21570	Flying Colors Painting Van, *08*		30____
21571	SuperStreets 10" Insulated Roadway, 2 pieces, *08–10*		8____
21572	SuperStreets 5" Straight School, 2 pieces, *08–10*		8____
21573	SuperStreets 5" Straight Stop Ahead, 2 pieces, *08–10*		8____

		Exc	Mint
____21574	SuperStreets 5" Straight Crosswalk, 2 pieces, *08–10*		8
____21575	SuperStreets 10" Crossing, 2 pieces, *08–10*		10
____21576	SuperStreets Skid Mark Roadway Pack, *08–10*		13
____21577	Snack-On Step Van, *08*		30
____21582	Keystone Coal Porter Locomotive, *08*		100
____21583	Keystone Coal Freight Car 4-pack, *08*		100
21590	ATSF "Midnight Chief" 2-bay Hopper "162277," *08*		25
21591	ATSF "Midnight Chief" Flatcar "94468" with trailer, *08*		43
____21592	ATSF "Midnight Chief" Caboose, *08*		25
____21593	ATSF "Midnight Chief" Boxcar "621593," *08*		35
21594	NYC Empire State Express 15" Aluminum Car 4-pack, *08–09*		420
____21599	SP flatcar with wheel load, *07*		35
____21600	B&M RS3 Diesel "1538," CC, *08–09*		350
____21607	Jack Frost Hopper "327" with sugar load, *08*		25
____21609	Elephants and Giraffes, 2 pair, *08–10*		13
____21610	Lions and Tigers, 2 pair, *08–10*		13
____21611	Horses, 4 pieces, *08*		13
____21621	ATSF Operating Boxcar "22658," *08–09*		90
____21623	Rutland Operating Milk Car with platform, *08–10*		150
____21626	Rath Wood-sided Reefer "622," *09*		45
____21627	Greenlee Packing Wood-sided Reefer "3862," *10*		45
____21628	CNJ Reefer "1438," *08–09*		35
____21629	C&O Reefer "7783," *08–09*		35
____21630	UP Stock Car "42005," *09*		45
____21631	Reading Boxcar "107984," *08–09*		35
____21632	GN Boxcar "34285," *08–09*		35
21633	RI "Route of the Rockets" Boxcar "21110," *09–10*		40
____21634	Tidewater Flying A 1-D Tank Car "1367," *09*		40
21635	Southern Depressed Center Flatcar, 2 transformers, *09*		43
____21636	NS Flatcar with bulkheads and stakes, *08–09*		35
____21637	Ontario Northland Ribbed Hopper with coal, *09*		40
____21639	Pan Am Boxcar "32126," *08–09*		55
____21640	UP Modern Steel-sided Reefer "499030," *08–09*		55
____21641	Ringling Bros. Merchandise Flatcar, *08*		50
____21643	PRR Die-cast Gondola with covers, *09*		73
____21644	PRR 16-wheel Flatcar with transformer, *08–09*		80
____21646	DT&I Work Crane and Boom Car, *09*		85
21649	City Traction Trolley with Ringling Bros. banner, *08–09*		80
____21651	Moo-Town Creamery Step Van, *08–09*		38
____21656	Quikrete Step Van, *08–09*		42
____21658	Ringling Bros. Vintage Truck, *08–09*		42
____21659	DT&I Flatcar "90059" with Ford trailer, *08–09*		60
____21662	Moo-Town Creamery Vending Machine, *08–09*		13
21663	Moo-Town Creamery Bunk Car Ice Cream Shop, *08–09*		115
____21664	RI Operating Coal Dump Car with vehicle, *08–09*		40
____21665	Alaska Operating Log Dump Car with vehicle, *09*		40
21667	Red River Lumber Boxcab Diesel with horn, *08–09*		100

		Exc	Mint
21668	CP Operating Hopper "9628," *08–09*		45____
21675	Mountain View Creamery Loading Depot, *08–10*		130____
21676	Beaver Creek Logging Die-cast Porter Locomotive, *08–09*		120____
21677	Ford Factory, *09*		22____
21679	Assured Comfort HVAC Van, *08–09*		38____
21680	Division of Prisons Bus SuperStreets Set, *08–09*		150____
21688	Ringling Bros. Heavyweight Coach 2-pack, *08–11*		240____
21691	Ringling Bros. Flatcar with 2 trailers, *08–10*		60____
21692	C&NW MP15 Diesel with Ringling Bros. banner, *08–09*		140____
21693	Southern MP15 Diesel Pair, powered and dummy, *10*		200____
21696	Ford Flatcar with 2 trucks, *08–09*		53____
21698	Lionel Van SuperStreets Set, *08–10*		130____
21701	Star Spangled GG1 Electric Locomotive "4837," *08–10*		260____
21702	Milwaukee Road Girder Bridge, *08–09*		15____
21703	ATSF Black Mesa Aluminum Business Car, *09–10*		160____
21704	C&O Double Searchlight Car with vehicle, *08–09*		50____
21706	Chatham Police Van, *08–09*		38____
21707	NYC Aluminum Business Car, *09*		160____
21708	CN Operating Log Dump Car, *10*		120____
21709	PRR Girder Bridge, *08–09*		15____
21715	Ringling Bros. Stock Car, *08–09*		60____
21717	Pullman-Standard 1-D Tank Car, *08–09*		35____
21719	NYC Bay Window Caboose, *99*		70____
21720	Ringling Bros. Billboard Set #2, *08–09*		10____
21721	Warning Sign Pack, 12 pieces, *08–10*		25____
21730	Regulatory Sign Pack, 12 pieces, *08–10*		25____
21738	Railroad Crossing Sign Pack, 6 pieces, *08–10*		21____
21750	NKP Rolling Stock 4-pack, *98*		160____
21751	PRR Rolling Stock 4-pack, *98*		145____
21752	Conrail Unit Trailer Train, *98*		285____
21753	Service Station Fire Rescue Train, *98*	500	585____
21754	BNSF 3-bay Covered Hopper 2-pack (std O), *98*		65____
21755	4-bay Covered Hoppers 2-pack, *98*		65____
21756	6464-style Overstamped Boxcars 2-pack, *98*		65____
21757	UP Freight Car Set, *98*		188____
21758	Bethlehem Steel "44" (SSS), *99*		375____
21759	Canadian Pacific F3 Diesel Passenger Set, *99*		930____
21761	B&M Boxcar Set, 4-pack, *99*		180____
21763	New Haven Freight Set, *99*		265____
21766	ACL Passenger Car 2-pack, *99*		385____
21769	Centennial 1-D Tank Car Set, 4-pack, *99*		225____
21770	NYC Reefer Set, 4-pack, *99*		225____
21771	D&RGW Stock Car Set, 4-pack, *99*		230____
21774	Custom Series Consist I, 3-pack, *99*		150____
21775	Train Wreck Recovery Set, *99*		190____
21778	ATSF Train Master Diesel Freight Set, *99*		NRS____
21779	Seaboard Freight Car Set, *99*		280____
21780	NYC Aluminum Passenger Car 2-pack, *99*		160____
21781	Case Cutlery Freight Set, *99 u*		1000____
21782	PRR Congressional Set, *00*		930____

		Exc Mint
____21783	Monday Night Football 2-pack, *01–02*	50
____21784	QVC PRR Coal Freight Steam Set, *00 u*	356
____21785	QVC Gold Mine Freight Steam Set, *00 u*	386
____21786	Santa Fe F3 Diesel ABBA Passenger Set, *00*	1500
____21787	Blue Comet Steam Passenger Set, *01–02*	1050
____21788	Postwar Missile Launch Freight Set, *02–03*	350
____21789	Norfolk Southern Piggyback Set, CC (SSS), *01*	370
____21790	CN TankTrain Dash 9 Diesel Freight Set, *02*	630
21791	Freedom Train Diesel Passenger Set, RailSounds, *03*	540
____21792	C&O Coal Hopper 6-pack #2 (std O), *01*	145
____21793	Virginian Coal Hopper 6-pack #2 (std O), *01*	160
____21794	Pioneer Seed GP7 Diesel Freight Set, *01 u*	900
____21795	Case Farmall Freight Set, *01 u*	990
____21796	NJ Medical Steam Freight Set, *01 u*	483
____21797	SP Daylight Passenger Set, *01*	670
____21852	MILW PS-2CD Hopper 3-pack (std O), *06*	155
____21853	BNSF PS-2CD Hopper 3-pack (std O), *06*	155
____21854	N&W PS-2CD Hopper 3-pack (std O), *06*	155
____21855	A&P Milk Car 3-pack, *06*	150
____21856	Bowman Dairy Milk Car 3-pack (std O), *06*	150
____21857	Western Dairy Milk Car 3-pack (std O), *06*	150
____21858	NP PS-4 Flatcar with trailers, 2-pack (std O), *06*	170
21859	C&NW PS-4 Flatcar with trailers, 2-pack (std O), *06*	170
____21860	UP PS-4 Flatcar with trailers, 2-pack (std O), *06*	170
____21861	PRR PS-4 Flatcar with trailers (std O), *06*	170
____21863	ADM Unibody Tank Car 3-pack (std O), *06*	135
____21864	Cerestar Unibody Tank Car 3-pack (std O), *06*	135
____21865	Coe Rail Husky Stack Car 2-pack (std O), *06*	170
____21866	Santa Fe Husky Stack Car 2-pack (std O), *06*	170
____21872	C&O Offset Hopper 3-pack (std O), *05*	130
____21873	P&LE Offset Hopper 3-pack (std O), *06*	145
____21874	TTX Trailer Train 2-pack (std O), *06*	170
____21875	CSX Husky Stack Car 2-pack (std O), *06*	170
____21876	Disney Villain Hi-Cube Boxcar 3-pack, *05–06*	135
____21877	Domino Sugar 1-D Tank Car 3-pack (std O), *07*	135
____21878	Procor 1-D Tank Car 3-pack (std O), *07*	135
____21879	C&EI Offset Hopper 3-pack (std O), *07*	145
____21880	Erie Offset Hopper 3-pack (std O), *07*	145
____21881	Frisco Offset Hopper 3-pack (std O), *07–08*	200
____21882	Chessie System Offset Hopper 3-pack (std O), *07*	145
____21883	C&O 3-bay Hopper 2-pack (std O), *07–08*	140
21884	Pennsylvania Power & Light 3-bay Hopper 2-pack (std O), *07*	140
____21885	Santa Fe 3-bay Hopper 2-pack (std O), *07*	140
____21886	C&NW 3-bay Hopper 2-pack (std O), *07–08*	140
____21888	IMC Canada Cylindrical Hopper 2-pack, *06*	130
____21893	Greenbrier Husky Stack Car 2-pack (std O), *07*	170
____21894	CSX Husky Stack Car 2-pack (std O), *07*	170
____21895	BN Husky Stack Car 2-pack (std O), *07*	170
21896	Arizona & California Husky Stack Car 2-pack (std O), *07*	170
21897	REA PS-4 Flatcar with trailers, 2-pack (std O), *07–08*	170

		Exc	Mint
21898	NYC PS-4 Flatcar with trailers, 2-pack (std O), *07–08*		170___
21899	Lackawanna PS-4 Flatcar with trailers, 2-pack (std O), *07*		170___
21900	Civil War Union Train Set, *99*		375___
21901	Civil War Confederate Train Set, *99*		375___
21902	Construction Zone Set, *99 u*		87___
21902	MILW PS-4 Flatcar with trailers, 2-pack (std O), *07–08*		170___
21904	Safari Adventure Set, *99 u*		90___
21904	UP PS-2 Covered Hopper 2-pack (std O), *07*		120___
21905	NYC Flyer Set, *99 u*		100___
21909	AGFA Film Steam Freight Set, *98 u*		1400___
21914	Lionel Lines Freight Set, *99*		120___
21916	Lionel Village Trolley, *99*		75___
21917	N&W Freight Set, *99*		70___
21918	Thomas Circus Play Set, *00*		100___
21918	PC PS-2 Covered Hopper 2-pack (std O), *07*		120___
21921	Imco PS-2 Covered Hopper 2-pack (std O), *07–08*		120___
21924	Holiday Trolley Set, *99*		65___
21925	Thomas the Tank Engine Island of Sodor Train Set, *99–00*		150___
21930	NYC PS-2 Covered Hopper 2-pack (std O), *07*		120___
21932	JCPenney NYC Freight Flyer Steam Set, *00 u*		170___
21934	Custom Series Consist II, 3-pack, *99*		140___
21936	Looney Tunes Train Set, *00 u*		380___
21937	NYC Steel-sided Reefer 2-pack (std O), *07*		130___
21939	Dubuque Steel-sided Reefer 2-pack (std O), *07–08*		130___
21940	ADM Steel-sided Reefer 2-pack (std O), *07*		130___
21941	National Car Steel-sided Reefer 2-pack (std O), *07*		130___
21944	"Celebrate a Lionel Christmas" Steam Set, *00–01*		165___
21945	Christmas Trolley Set, *00*		100___
21948	NYC Freight Flyer Set, air whistle, *00*		240___
21950	Maersk SD70 Diesel Maxi-Stack Set, *00*	560	700___
21951	World War II Troop Train, *00*		410___
21952	Lionel Lines Service Station Special Set, *00*		294___
21953	Ford Mustang GP7 Diesel Set, CC, *01*		345___
21955	D&RGW F3 Diesel AA Passenger Set, CC, *01*		740___
21956	New York Central Freight Set, *99–00*		355___
21969	Lionel Village Trolley Set, *00*		85___
21970	SP RS3 Diesel Freight Set, horn, *00–01*		110___
21971	Pennsylvania Flyer Steam Set, *00*		150___
21972	Frisco GP7 Diesel Freight Set, horn, *00*		150___
21973	ATSF Passenger Set, RailSounds, *00–01*		375___
21974	ATSF Passenger Set, SignalSounds, *00–01*		240___
21975	Burlington Steam Freight Set, SignalSounds, *00*		275___
21976	Centennial Steam Freight Starter Set, *00*		625___
21977	NYC Train Master Steam Freight Set, *99–00*		620___
21978	ATSF Train Master Diesel Freight Set, *99–00*		500___
21981	JCPenney NYC Flyer Set, *00 u*		150___
21988	NYC Freight Set, RailSounds, *00*		325___
21989	Burlington Steam Freight Set, RailSounds, *00*		300___

			Exc	Mint
___	21990	NYC Flyer Freight Set, RailSounds, *00*		175
___	21999	Whirlpool Steam Freight Set, *00 u*		710
___	22103	PRR A5 Scale Switcher "411," CC, *08–09*		330
	22104	PRR Freight Car 3-pack, *08*		135
	22105	NYC Empire State Express 4-6-4 Hudson Locomotive "5429," CC, *08–09*		420
___	22113	NYC Empire State Express 15" Aluminum Car 2-pack, *08–10*		210
___	22116	Ringling Bros. Diesel Freight Set, *08–10*		245
___	22121	Ringling Bros. Freight Set, *08–10*		390
___	22126	Ringling Bros. Expansion Pack, *08–10*		135
___	22131	NH Streamliner Car 3-pack, *07*		150
___	22135	CB&Q S2 Diesel Switcher "9305," horn, *07*		80
___	22136	Erie S2 Diesel Switcher "522," horn, *07*		80
___	22137	Alaska MP15 Diesel "1552," horn, *07*		100
___	22138	Astoria Heat & Power Porter Locomotive "4," *07*		100
___	22139	LIRR Speeder, *08*		50
___	22140	CNJ Boxcab Diesel "1000," horn, *08*		90
___	22141	Lackawanna 15" Interurban Car 2-pack, *07*		200
___	22142	FEC Operating Dump Car, *07*		70
___	22143	B&A Operating Log Dump Car, *08–09*		70
___	22144	Alaska Operating Coal Dump Car with vehicle, *08*		33
___	22145	WM Operating Log Dump Car with vehicle, *08*		33
___	22146	PFE Operating Boxcar, *08*		80
___	22147	B&O Operating Hopper with coal, *08*		35
___	22148	GN Operating Hopper with coal, *08*		35
	22149	Dairymen's League Operating Milk Car, green, with platform, *08*		140
___	22150	D&RGW Bunk Car, smoke, *08*		65
___	22151	Alaska Searchlight Car with vehicle, *08*		45
___	22152	NKP 2-bay Outside-braced Hopper "31299," *08*		50
___	22153	L&N 2-bay Offset Hopper "78660," *08*		50
___	22154	D&H 2-bay Rib Side Hopper "5737," *07*		50
___	22155	Erie-Lack. 2-bay Aluminum Hopper "21353," *08*		60
	22156	ACF Demonstrator 2-bay Aluminum Hopper "44586," *07*		60
___	22157	GN Aluminum Tank Car "74787," *08*		60
	22158	MILW Bulkhead Flatcar "967116" with wood, *08–09*		43
___	22159	BNSF Flatcar "585011" with trailer, *08*		43
___	22160	UP Flatcar "58059" with container, *08*		43
___	22161	Conrail Flatcar "705910" with NS container, *08*		43
___	22162	Foppiano Wine 3-D Tank Car "1112," *08*		45
___	22163	PRR Weed Control Car "6321226," *07*		45
___	22166	PRR Reefer "19492," *08*		25
___	22167	Seaboard Reefer "16622," *08*		25
___	22168	N&W Boxcar "645772," *08*		25
___	22169	ATSF Reefer "11744," *07*		25
___	22170	P&LE Reefer "22300," *07*		25
___	22171	B&O DD Boxcar "495289," *08*		25
___	22172	CB&Q Stock Car "52731," *08*		25
___	22174	Erie-Lack. Transfer Caboose, *07*		25
___	22176	PRR Caboose "478884," *07*		25
___	22177	L&N Caboose "100," *07*		25

		Exc	Mint
22179	NYC Depressed Center Flatcar "66256" with 2 girders, *08*		25____
22180	IC Depressed Center Flatcar with 2 transformers, *07*		25____
22182	RI Gondola "180043" with coils, *08*		25____
22184	B&O Covered Hopper "604321," *08*		25____
22185	UP Covered Hopper "53186," *08*		25____
22186	P&LE (NYC) Gondola "17243," *08–09*		35____
22187	PRR 2-D Tank Car "6351815," *07*		25____
22188	Deep Rock 3-D Tank Car "2152," *08*		25____
22189	NP Java Diner, smoke, *08*		110____
22190	C&O Operating Billboard, *08*		65____
22191	Operating Passenger Station, *08–09*		105____
22192	Hot Box Operating BBQ Shack, *07*		80____
22193	Cold Drinks Vending Machine, *08*		12____
22194	Water Tower with light, *08–09*		20____
22199	City Traction Trolley Barn, *08–09*		65____
22202	Loading Ramp, *08–10*		20____
22203	Dairymen's League Operating Milk Car, white, with platform, *07*		140____
22204	Snacks Vending Machine, *08*		12____
22205	Soup and Sandwich Vending Machine, *08*		12____
22206	PRR Crew Bus, *08*		30____
22222	Ringling Bros. Speeder Chase Set, *08–10*		92____
22225	Ringling Bros. Jomar Heavyweight Private Car, *08–11*		120____
22226	Ringling Bros. 18" Caledonia Heavyweight Private Car, *08*		100____
22227	Ringling Bros. 18" Advertising Car, *08*		100____
22228	Ringling Bros. Flatcar with 3 wagons, *08*		50____
22231	Ringling Bros. Flatcar with 3 wagons, *08*		50____
22235	Ringling Bros. Flatcar with pole wagon and truck, *08*		75____
22238	Ringling Bros. Work Caboose with calliope wagon, *08*		40____
22240	Ringling Bros. Flatcar/Stock Car with wagon, *08*		50____
22243	Ringling Bros. Human Cannonball Car, *08*		45____
22244	Ringling Bros. Operating Searchlight Car with 3 spotlights, *08*		60____
22247	Ringling Bros. Stock Car "54," *08*		50____
22248	Ringling Bros. Stock Car "47," *08*		50____
22249	Ringling Bros. Dining Dept. Billboard Reefer, *08*		80____
22250	Ringling Bros. Dining Dept. Wood-sided Reefer, *08–09*		90____
22251	Ringling Bros. Dormitory Bunk Car "22," *08*		75____
22252	Ringling Bros. Operating Billboard, *08–09*		75____
22253	Ringling Bros. Vintage Billboard Set #1, *08*		9____
22255	Ringling Bros. Aluminum Coach "40010," *08–10*		165____
22257	Ringling Bros. Aluminum Shop Car "63002," *08–10*		165____
22258	Ringling Bros. 18" Aluminum Large Animal Car, *08–10*		165____
22259	Ringling Bros. Flatcar with trailer, *08*		53____
22260	Ringling Bros. Tractor Trailer, *08*		30____
22261	Idaho State Quarter Hopper Bank, *08*		65____
22262	Wyoming State Quarter Tank Car Bank, *08*		50____

		Exc	Mint
___22263	Utah State Quarter Boxcar Bank, *08*		45
___22264	SuperStreets Figure-8 Expander Pack, *08–10*		35
___22267	Mulligan Spring Water Step Van, *08*		30
___22270	Quikrete Classic Truck with 2 pallets, *08*		33
___22271	MILW EP-5 Electric Locomotive "E20," CC, *08–09*		460
22272	MILW Olympian Hiawatha 18" Aluminum Car 4-pack, *08*		480
22277	MILW Olympian Hiawatha 18" Aluminum Car 2-pack, *08*		250
___22280	Erie-Lack. RS3 Diesel "933," CC, *08–09*		350
___22281	Southern Train Master Diesel "6300," CC, *08–09*		420
___22282	Southern Bay Window Caboose "X270," *08–09*		70
22283	UP S2 Diesel Switcher "1103" and Caboose "25384," *08*		130
22286	GN Boxcab Electric Locomotive "5008-A," horn, *08*		90
___22287	North Shore Line 15" Interurban Car 2-pack, *08*		230
22288	Commuter Train Station, 6 road name stickers, *09*		25
22289	Ringling Bros. 18" Aluminum Passenger Car 2-pack, *08*		270
___22290	Erie Boxcar "86448" with graffiti, *08*		46
___22291	C&NW Stock Car "14303," *08*		46
___22292	Land o' Lakes Butter Billboard Reefer, *08*		75
___22293	PRR 4-bay Hopper "253776," *08*		65
22294	Montana Rail Link 3-bay Aluminum Hopper "50049," *08*		70
22295	Canada Wheat 4-bay Aluminum Hopper "606418," *08*		73
___22296	Eaglebrook Aluminum Tank Car "19039," *08*		70
___22297	Petri Wine 3-D Tank Car "904," *08–09*		45
22298	Cotton Belt Offset Cupola Wood-sided Caboose "2230," *08*		80
___22299	MILW Bay Window Caboose "980502," *08–09*		70
___22300	Detroit, Toledo & Ironton Coil Car "1352," *08*		60
___22301	NYC Flatcar "506090" with freight kit, *08*		35
___22302	C&O Flatcar "80951" with freight kit, *08*		35
___22303	Extruded Aluminum I-Beam, 3 pieces, *08–09*		6
___22304	Rails, 12 pieces, *08–09*		6
___22305	Small Transformer Load, pair, *08–09*		15
___22306	Large Transformer Load, *08*		19
___22307	Forklifts, 3, with pallets, *08–09*		27
___22308	Loaders with crates, pair, *08–09*		13
___22309	Loaders with logs, pair, *08–09*		13
___22310	KBL Logistics Container 2-pack, *08*		40
22312	Commemorative Quarter Extended Vision Caboose, *09*		80
___22313	ATSF Boxcar "137460," *08*		25
___22314	Coastal King Seafood Wood-sided Reefer, *08*		25
22315	Wisconsin & Southern "God Bless America" Boxcar, *09*		43
22316	NP Depressed Center Flatcar "66130" with water tank, *08*		25
22317	U.S. Air Force Hopper "55175" with ballast load, *08*		25

		Exc	Mint
22318	DM&IR Ore Car "29991," *08*	25	___
22319	Celanese Chemicals 1-D Tank Car "12730," *08*	25	___
22320	Baldwin Locomotives Works 1-D Tank Car "6809," *08*	25	___
22321	B&O Operating Boxcar, *08*	45	___
22322	PRR Operating Ballast Dump Car, *08*	75	___
22323	FEMA Voltmeter Car, *08*	75	___
22324	C&NW Cop and Robber Chase Gondola, *08–09*	55	___
22325	White Milk Cans, 10 pieces, *08–10*	8	___
22326	Twin Searchlight Tower, *08–10*	33	___
22327	Tommy's Bunk Car Grill, *08–09*	100	___
22328	Santa Fe Operating Freight Transfer Platform, *08–09*	130	___
22329	Dual Track Signal Bridge, *08–10*	45	___
22330	Stella's Heavyweight Diner, smoke, *08–09*	140	___
22331	Coffee Vending Machine, *08*	12	___
22332	Spring Water Vending Machine, *08*	12	___
22333	Candy Vending Machine, *08*	12	___
22334	Ford Plymouth Diesel Switcher and Ore Car 6-pack, *08*	200	___
22335	NS Operating Paint Shop with boxcar, *08–09*	140	___
22344	KBL Logistics ISO Tank, *08*	19	___
22346	Tableau Circus Wagons, *08*	13	___
22349	Forklift with 6 pallets, *08–09*	23	___
22350	Twin Lamp Posts, 3 pieces, *08–09*	22	___
22352	Lamp Posts, 4 pieces, *08–09*	20	___
22354	Portable Spotlights, 3 pieces, *08–09*	15	___
22356	High Tension Poles, 4 pieces, *08–09*	8	___
22358	Rail Yard Signs, 12 pieces, *08–09*	10	___
22360	Telephone Poles, 6 pieces, *08–09*	7	___
22362	Girder Bridge, *08–09*	8	___
22363	Stone Bridge Piers, pair, *08–10*	27	___
22365	Heavyweight Passenger Coach 6-wheel Scale Trucks, pair, *08–09*	25	___
22366	Aluminum Passenger Coach 4-wheel Scale Trucks, pair, *08–09*	25	___
22367	Timkin Scale Sprung Trucks, pair, *08–09*	19	___
22368	Bettendorf Scale Sprung Trucks, pair, *08–09*	19	___
22369	Scale Couplers, pair, *08–09*	6	___
22379	SuperStreets Barricade, 2 pieces, *08–10*	11	___
22387	Kiosk with 3 vending machines, *08–09*	40	___
22391	Ford MP15 Diesel "10021," horn, *08*	115	___
22392	Ford Farming Boxcar "1681," *08*	30	___
22393	Ford Stampings DD Boxcar "101," *08*	35	___
22394	Ford 2-bay Covered Hopper "1667," *08*	30	___
22395	Ford Speeder "14," *08*	65	___
22396	Ford Water Tower, *08*	25	___
22397	Ford Rotating Sign Tower, *08*	55	___
22398	Boyd Bros. and Ford Barn and Chicken Coop, *08*	25	___
22399	Ford ISO Tank, *08–09*	21	___
22402	PRR Streamlined K4 4-6-2 Pacific Locomotive, tender, *09–10*	500	___
22408	Ringling Bros. Tractor Trailer #1, *08–09*	35	___
22411	Tableau Wagon Set #2, *08–10*	18	___
22412	PRR Operating Flagman's Shanty, *08–09*	90	___

			Exc	Mint
	22414	Linde Union Carbide Boxcar with aluminum tank, *08–09*		70
	22415	Ringling Bros. Flatcar with circus wagon, *08*		50
	22417	Ringling Bros. Flatcar with container, *09*		55
	22420	PRR Broadway Limited Aluminum Passenger Car 2-pack, *09–10*		300
	22423	GN Aluminum Passenger Car 2-pack, *09–10*		360
	22426	Ford Gondola "13447" with coils, *08–09*		43
	22427	Ford Operating Billboard, *08–09*		75
	22428	Ford Tin Sign Replica 4-pack, *08–09*		17
	22433	PRR Broadway Limited Aluminum Passenger Car 4-pack, *09–10*		600
	22438	Mail Crane, *08–10*		30
	22439	Milwaukee Road Aluminum Passenger Car 2-pack, *09–11*		360
	22447	Wabash Die-cast 2-bay Ribbed Hopper "37751," *08–09*		60
	22449	UP Crew Bus, *08–09*		38
	22450	Seaboard Die-cast Hopper with gravel, *10*		80
	22454	Oklahoma State Quarter Die-cast Hopper Bank, *08–09*		75
	22455	New Mexico State Quarter Die-cast Gondola Bank, *08–09*		74
	22456	Arizona State Quarter Tank Car Bank, *08–09*		55
	22457	Alaska State Quarter Boxcar Bank, *09*		55
	22458	Hawaii State Quarter Die-cast Hopper Bank, *09*		75
	22459	Southern Aluminum Passenger Car 2-pack #1, *09*		300
	22460	Southern Aluminum Passenger Car 2-pack #2, *09*		300
	22461	Scale Skeleton Log Car 4-pack, *08–09*		160
	22467	Railroad Water Tower, *08–09*		23
	22468	Fast Eddie's Used Car Lot with 2 die-cast vehicles, *08–09*		50
	22469	Cola Illuminated Vending Machine, *08–09*		13
	22470	SuperStreets Guard Rails, *08–10*		20
	22472	Ringling Bros. Tin Sign Replica 4-pack, *08–09*		17
	22477	Lionel Tin Sign Replica 4-pack, *08–09*		15
	22482	Vintage Tin Sign Replica 4-pack, *08–09*		15
	22487	Scooter Gang with scooters, *09–10*		13
	22492	Airport Revolving Searchlight, *10*		40
	22493	Ringling Bros. Lighted Clown Wood-sided Reefer, *09*		75
	22494	Ford Flatcar with 2 Thunderbird convertibles, *09*		53
	22496	Vita O Flavored Water Vending Machine, *09*		13
	22497	Top Pop Soda Illuminated Vending Machine, *09*		13
	22498	Ringling Bros. Flatcar with 3 circus wagons, *09–10*		55
	22500	Defense Dept. Flatcar with 2 jeeps and soldier, *09*		50
	22501	C&NW Railroad Van, CC, *09–10*		100
	22502	Ringling Bros. Flatcar with 3 circus wagons, *09–10*		55
	22504	Ford Water Tower with vintage Ford logo, *09–10*		25
	22505	Sparkling Springs Beverage Truck, *09*		45
	22506	SuperStreets Fishtail Roadway, *09*		25

		Exc	Mint
22507	Ringling Bros. Flatcar with boxcar and ticket wagon, *09*	60	___
22509	Pallet Pack with banded loads, *09*	20	___
22510	Lionel Step Van, CC, *09–10*	100	___
22511	BNSF Flatcar with helicopter, *09*	50	___
22513	Ringling Bros. Heavyweight Advertising Car, *09*	120	___
22514	NYC Girder Bridge, *09–10*	15	___
22515	Milwaukee Road/REA Scale Boxcar "6436," *09*	55	___
22516	BNSF MP15 Diesel "3704" with horn, *09*	120	___
22517	Quick Lane Ford Motorcraft Auto Parts Van, *09–10*	42	___
22518	Lionel Tank Container Leasing ISO Tank, *09–10*	23	___
22519	Roma Wine Wood-sided Billboard Reefer, *09–10*	70	___
22520	WWII Soldiers in Action, 10 pieces, *09–10*	20	___
22521	1959 Ford Billboard Set, *09*	10	___
22523	American Flyer Vintage Truck, *09*	38	___
22524	Ford Coil Car "749772," *09*	73	___
22525	Vermont Railway Operating Boxcar "177," *09*	50	___
22526	Crabby Matt's Smoking Heavyweight Diner, *09*	150	___
22527	Toledo, Peoria & Western Boxcar "5067," *09–10*	55	___
22528	GN Stock Car "55973," *09–10*	55	___
22529	U.S. Army 1-D Tank Car "11278," *09*	35	___
22530	Milwaukee Road Aluminum Coach "627," *09–11*	180	___
22531	Southern Girder Bridge, *09*	15	___
22532	Montana Rail Link 1-D Tank Car "100017," *09*	35	___
22533	GN Aluminum Coach "1377," *09–10*	180	___
22534	SuperStreets D16 Curve Guard Rails, *09–10*	20	___
22536	SuperStreets D21 Curve Guard Rails, *09–10*	22	___
22538	Ford Modern Aluminum Tank Car "30166," *09*	90	___
22539	BNSF Flatcar "922267" with Ford trailer, *09–10*	60	___
22542	PRR Flatcar "480227" with freight kit, *09*	40	___
22543	Biodiesel 2-D Tank Car "1544," *09*	40	___
22544	Ringling Bros. Wood-sided Gondola with equipment, *09*	63	___
22548	Kiosk #2 with 3 illuminated vending machines, *09*	40	___
22553	Convenience Mart, *09–10*	25	___
22554	Auto Parts Store, *09–10*	20	___
22555	Ringling Bros. Tractor with Gold Tour container, *09–10*	55	___
22558	PRR Flatcar "469301" with milk containers, *09*	50	___
22559	UP Gondola "229794" with freight kit, *09–10*	80	___
22560	CB&Q Wood-sided Gondola "85150" with spools, *09–10*	60	___
22561	Gondola Scrap Load, *09*	9	___
22562	Operation Lifesaver Boxcar with flashing LEDs, *09*	65	___
22563	Ringling Bros. Handcar and Trailer Set, *10–11*	70	___
22566	SuperStreets 2.5" Straight Roadway, 4 pieces, *10*	12	___
22568	Generators, 2 pieces, *09*	9	___
22570	Large transformer, *09*	22	___
22571	Cage Wagon Set, *09–10*	18	___
22573	Display Base, *09*	20	___
22574	Ringling Bros. Flatcar "39" with trailer, *09*	60	___
22577	Biodiesel Storage Tank with 2 figures, *09–10*	40	___

		Exc	Mint
___22578	Ringling Bros. Heavyweight Coach "70," *09*		120
___22579	Circus Horses, 4 pieces, *09–10*		15
___22580	Bollards and Chains, *09–10*		20
___22582	Pipe Stack Load, *09*		30
___22583	KBL Operating Wind Turbine, *09–10*		75
___22584	KBL Die-cast 16-wheel Flatcar "34807," *09*		85
22587	Old Reading Flatcar Foot Bridge with stone piers, *09–10*		50
___22590	Roadside Fender Bender, *09–10*		75
22592	SuperStreets D16 Turn Roadways, left and right, *10*		35
22595	SuperStreets D21 Turn Roadways, left and right, *10*		39
___22598	SuperStreets Adjustable Straight Kit, *09–10*		20
___22600	Wire Spool Load, 6 pieces, *09*		20
___22610	Napa Valley Wine Train Alco FA Diesel AA Set, *10*		230
22613	Napa Valley Wine Train 15" Passenger Car 4-pack, *10*		450
___22618	Signal Oil Co. 1-D Tank Car, *10*		40
___22619	PRR Paoli MU Commuter Train 2-pack, *10*		290
___22622	RR Paoli Motorized Combine, *10*		200
___22623	PRR Commuter Train Station, *10*		35
22624	NH Die-cast Plymouth Switcher with snowplow, *10*		160
22625	Ringling Bros. 18" Aluminum Generator Car, *10–11*		180
22627	Ringling Bros. Lighted Clown Wood-sided Reefer, *10–11*		90
22628	Ringling Bros. 18" Aluminum Advertising Car, *10–11*		180
___22629	Ringling Bros. Stock Car, *10–11*		60
___22630	Ringling Bros. Tractor and Trailer, *10–11*		35
___22633	Ringling Bros. 18" Aluminum Coach, *10–11*		180
22634	Ringling Bros. 18" Heavyweight Advertising Car, *10–11*		146
22635	Ringling Bros. Operating Dual Searchlight Car, *10–11*		60
___22637	Quikrete Step Van, *10*		48
___22638	PRR Crew Bus, *10*		45
___22639	B&O Boxcab Diesel "195," *10*		100
___22640	Central of Georgia Boxcar "5823," *10*		45
___22641	New Haven Boxcar "36438," *10*		45
22642	Ringling Bros. Operating Large Animal Feed Car, *10–11*		150
___22643	Ford MP15 Diesel "10022," *10–11*		135
___22644	Ford Motorcraft 48' Aluminum Tank Car, *10–11*		95
22645	Ringling Bros. Operating Tent Pole Dump Car, *10–11*		130
___22646	Ford Speeder, *10–11*		75
___22647	Rock Island Gondola "180044," *10*		35
___22648	PRR Gondola "353381," *10*		35
22651	Central Vermont Operating Milk Car with platform, *10*		175
___22653	Starlite Diner with parking lot, *10*		200
22654	Ringling Bros. Flatcar with 3 circus wagons, *10–11*		60

		Exc	Mint
22656	Ringling Bros. Flatcar with 3 circus wagons, *10–11*		60____
22658	Operating Flagman's Shanty, *10*		100____
22659	Union 76 1-D Tank Car "6322," *10*		40____
22660	Moose Pond Creamery Operating Loading Depot, *10*		140____
22661	WM 2-Bay Covered Hopper "5051," *10*		35____
22662	PRR Reefer "19494," *10*		45____
22663	New Haven Illuminated Caboose, *10*		40____
22667	Acme Scrap Platform Crane, *10*		60____
22670	ATSF Operating Boxcar, *10*		140____
22671	Smoking Southern Bay Window Caboose, *10*		90____
22672	Ringling Bros. 18" Sarasota Observation Car, *10–11*		146____
22673	Ford Water Tower with light, *10*		27____
22674	MILW 21" Aluminum Passenger Car 2-pack, *10–11*		400____
22679	Ringling Bros. Operating Billboard, *10–11*		100____
22902	Quonset Hut, *98–99*		22____
22907	Die-cast Girder Bridge, *98–01*		10____
22910	Gilbert Tractor Trailer, *98*		20____
22914	PowerHouse Lockon, *98–01*		24____
22915	Municipal Building, *98–99*		28____
22916	190-watt Power Accessory System, *98*		425____
22918	Locomotive Backshop, *98*	300	460____
22919	ElectroCouplers Kit for GP9 Diesel, *98–00*		20____
22922	Intermodal Crane, *98*		195____
22931	Die-cast Cantilever Signal Bridge, *98–06*		35____
22934	Walkout Cantilever Signal, *98–03*		42____
22936	Coaling Tower, 3 pieces, *98*		85____
22940	Mast Signal, *98–00*		37____
22942	Accessories Box, *98–01*		20____
22944	Automatic Operating Semaphore, *98–03, 08*		35____
22945	Block Target Signal, *98–00*		39____
22946	Automatic Crossing Gate and Signal, *98–99*		45____
22947	Auto Crossing Gate, *98–00*		36____
22948	Gooseneck Street Lamps, set of 2, *98–00*		30____
22949	Highway Lights, set of 4, *98–99*		20____
22950	Classic Street Lamps, set of 3, *98–02*		20____
22951	Dwarf Signal, *98–00*		24____
22952	Classic Billboards, set of 3, *98–00*		15____
22953	Linex Gasoline Tall Oil Tank, *98–99*		6____
22954	Linex Gasoline Wide Oil Tank, *98–99*		6____
22955	ElectroCouplers Kit for J Class and B&A tenders, *98–00*		20____
22956	ElectroCouplers Kit for NW2 Switcher, *98*		20____
22957	ElectroCouplers Kit for F3 Diesel, *98–01*		20____
22958	ElectroCouplers Kit for Dash 9 Diesel, *98–01*		20____
22959	ElectroCoupler Conversion Kit for Atlantic Locomotive, *98–01*		13____
22960	Trainmaster Command Basic Upgrade Kit, *98–01*		34____
22961	Standard GP9 Diesel B Unit Upgrade Kit, *98–01*		30____
22962	Deluxe GP9 Diesel B Unit Upgrade Kit, black trucks, *98–01*		44____
22963	RailSounds Upgrade Kit, steam RailSounds, *98–01*		55____

		Exc	Mint
22964	RailSounds Upgrade Kit, diesel RailSounds, *98–01*		55
22965	Culvert Loader, CC, *98–01*		255
22966	Figure-8 Add-on Track Pack (027), *98–16*		17
22967	Double Loop Add-on Track Pack (027), *98–16*		62
22968	Double Loop Track Pack (027), *98–03*		65
22969	Deluxe Complete Track Pack (0), *98–16*		120
22972	Bascule Bridge, *98–99*		337
22973	Lionel Corporation Tractor and Trailer, *98*		15
22975	Culvert Unloader, CC, *99–00*		225
22979	GP9 Diesel B-Unit Deluxe Upgrade Kit, silver trucks, *98–01*		34
22980	TMCC SC-2 Switch Controller, *99–16*		130
22982	Postwar ZW Controller and Transformer Set, *98*		265
22983	180-watt PowerHouse Power Supply, *99–16*		100
22990	Flatcar with Route 66 autos, 4-pack, *99*		37
22991	Christmas Tree and Blue Comet Train, *99–00*		60
22993	Route 66 Sinclair Dino Cafe, *99–00*		210
22997	Oil Drum Loader, *99–00*		100
22998	Triple Action Magnetic Crane, *99*		220
22999	Sound Dispatching Station, *99–00*		90
23000	NYC Dreyfuss Hudson Operating Base, 2-rail, *92 u*		190
23001	NYC Dreyfuss Hudson Operating Base, 3-rail, *93 u*		190
23002	NYC Hudson Operating Base, *92 u, 93–94*		190
23003	PRR B-6 Switcher Operating Base, *92 u, 93–94*		190
23004	NP 4-8-4 Operating Base, *92 u, 93–94*		190
23005	Reading T-1 Operating Base, *92 u, 93–94*		190
23006	Chessie System T-1 Operating Base, *92 u, 93–94*		190
23007	SP Daylight Operating Base, *92 u, 93–94*		190
23008	NYC L-3 Mohawk Operating Base, *92 u, 93–94*		190
23009	PRR S2 Turbine Locomotive Operating Base, *92 u, 93–94*		190
23010	31" Remote Switch, left hand (0), *95–99*	30	37
23011	31" Remote Switch, right hand (0), *95–99*	20	30
23012	F3 Diesel ABA Operating Base, *92 u, 93–94*		190
24018	PRR Boxcar, *05*		25
24101	Mainline Color Position Signal, *04–08*		25
24102	Industrial Water Tower, *03*		55
24103	Double Floodlight Tower, *03, 05–09*		42
24104	Hobo Tower, *03–05*		70
24105	Track Gang, *03–06*		70
24106	Exploding Ammunition Dump, *02*		25
24107	Missile Firing Range Set, *02*		60
24108	World War II Pylon, *03*		80
24109	Santa Fe Railroad Tugboat, *03*		125
24110	Pennsylvania Railroad Tugboat, *03*		118
24111	Swing Bridge, *03*		215
24112	Oil Field with bubble tubes, *03*		44
24113	Lionelville Ford Auto Dealership, *03*		225
24114	AMC/ARC Gantry Crane, CC, *03*		195
24115	AMC/ARC Log Loader, CC, *03, 06–07*		140
24117	Illuminated Covered Bridge, *02–16*		60

		Exc	Mint
24119	Big Bay Lighthouse, *04–05*		170____
24122	Lionelville People Pack, *03, 08–09, 15–17*		27____
24123	Passenger Station People Pack, *03, 08–09, 15–17*		27____
24124	Carnival People Pack, *03, 08–11, 13–16*	5	27____
24130	TMCC 135/180 PowerMaster, *04–12*		79____
24131	Dumbo Pylon, *03*		70____
24134	Bethlehem Steel Gantry Crane, *02*		200____
24135	Lionel Lighthouse, *02–03*		100____
24137	Mr. Spiff and Puddles, *03, 08*		34____
24138	Playtime Playground, *03, 08*		50____
24139	Duck Shooting Gallery, *03*		110____
24140	Charles Bowdish Homestead, *03*		60____
24147	Lionel Sawmill, *03*		90____
24148	Coal Tipple Coal Pack, *602, 08–10, 13–17*		15____
24149	NYC Hobo Hotel, *02*		42____
24151	Hobo Campfire, *03*		25____
24152	Conveyor Lumber Loader, *03*		65____
24153	Railroad Control Tower, *03, 08–10*		40____
24154	Maiden Rescue, *03*		35____
24155	Blinking Light Billboard, *04–10*		21____
24156	Lionelville Street Lamps, set of 4, *04–05, 07–17*		30____
24159	Illuminated Station Platform, *04–08*		32____
24160	Rub-a-Dub-Dub, *04*		42____
24161	Test O' Strength, *04–06*		70____
24164	Summer Vacation, *04–05*		80____
24168	Tire Swing, *04–05*		70____
24170	Rover's Revenge, *04–05*		70____
24171	Campbell's Soup Water Tower, *04*		45____
24172	Balancing Man, *04–05*		70____
24173	Derrick Platform, *03–05*		60____
24174	Icing Station, *04–06*		100____
24176	Irene's Diner, *06–07*		65____
24177	Hot Air Balloon Ride, *04, 06*		95____
24179	Scrambler Amusement Ride, *04–07*		165____
24180	Choo Choo Barn Lionelville Zoo, *04–05*		105____
24182	Lionelville Firehouse, *04*		100____
24183	Lionelville Gas Station, *04, 06–09*		115____
24187	Classic Billboard Set: 3 stands and 5 inserts, *04–08*		10____
24190	Station Platform, *05–09*		17____
24191	Park People Pack, *04–17*		27____
24192	Park Benches People Pack, *04–09*		23____
24193	Railroad Yard People Pack, *04–08, 14–17*		27____
24194	Civil Servants People Pack, *04–17*		27____
24196	Farm People Pack, *04–09*		23____
24197	City Accessory Pack, *04–17*		27____
24200	Lionel FasTrack Book, *07–10, 13–15*		35____
24201	UPS Centennial Operating Billboard Signmen, *07*		100____
24203	Polar Express Original Figures, 4 pieces, *08–14, 16*		30____
24204	Christmas Tractor Trailer with trees, *08*		25____
24205	Classic Billboard Set, *08–10*		20____
24206	MOW Gantry Crane, *08*		280____
24212	Lionel Art Blinking Billboard, *08–09*		23____

			Exc Mint
____	24213	Universal Lockon, *12–16*	4
____	24214	Postwar "395" Floodlight Tower, *08*	75
____	24215	MTA Metro-North Passenger Station, *07*	53
____	24218	Sunoco Elevated Tank, *08–09*	75
____	24219	PRR Plastic Girder Bridge, *08*	18
____	24220	ATSF Girder Bridge, *08–09*	18
____	24221	UP Die-cast Girder Bridge, *08*	30
____	24222	UPS Die-cast Girder Bridge, *08*	30
____	24223	Santa's Sleigh Pylon, *08*	150
____	24224	Postwar "38" Water Tower, *08–09*	150
____	24226	Christmas Toy Store, *08*	52
____	24227	Halloween Animated Billboard, *08–09*	54
____	24228	Christmas Operating Billboard, *08*	38
____	24229	Pennsylvania Water Tower, *08–09*	23
____	24230	Maiden Rescue, *08*	60
____	24232	Burning Switch Tower, *08*	80
____	24233	Exploding Ammunition Dump, *08*	36
____	24234	Missile Firing Range, *08*	43
____	24235	UPS Water Tower, *08*	80
____	24236	Wimpy's All-Star Burger Stand, *08*	97
____	24238	Sunoco Oil Derrick, *08*	90
____	24240	MTA Metro-North Blinking Billboard, *07*	21
____	24242	Postwar "352" Icing Station, *08*	100
____	24243	Rosie's Roadside Diner, *08*	85
____	24244	Commuter People, *08, 13–17*	27
____	24245	MTA Metro-North Illuminated Station Platform, *07*	32
____	24248	Manual Crossing Gate, *08–17*	20
____	24250	Mainline Gooseneck Lamps, pair, *08–09*	32
____	24251	Polar Express Caribou, *08–14, 16–17*	27
____	24252	Polar Express Wolves and Rabbits, *08–14, 16–17*	27
____	24264	Halloween People, *08–12*	23
____	24265	Trick or Treat People, *08–13*	23
____	24270	Operating Forklift Platform, *08–09*	280
____	24272	Train Orders Building, *08*	80
____	24273	Christmas Water Tower, *08–10*	23
____	24274	Christmas Girder Bridge, *08*	18
____	24279	PowerMaster Bridge, *08–13*	55
____	24283	NYC Girder Bridge, *09–10*	21
____	24284	Halloween Girder Bridge, *09–11*	21
____	24285	CP Rail Girder Bridge, *08–09*	30
____	24286	Polar Express Girder Bridge, *09–14*	21
____	24287	ATSF Blinking Light Water Tower, *09*	30
____	24288	NYC Blinking Light Water Tower, *09*	30
____	24293	Legacy Module Garage, *08–09*	50
____	24294	AEC Nuclear Reactor, *09–10*	328
____	24295	Cowen's Corner Hobby Shop, *09*	420
____	24296	Engine House, *09–12, 14*	70
____	24299	Main Street Ice Cream Parlor, *08*	37
____	24500	D&RGW Alco PA Diesel AA Set, *04*	530
____	24503	D&RGW Alco PB Diesel, *04*	150
____	24504	Santa Fe E6 Diesel AA Set, CC, *03*	530
____	24507	Milwaukee Road E6 Diesel AA Set, CC, *03*	530
____	24511	Burlington FT Diesel AA Set, RailSounds, *03*	225
____	24516	Santa Fe F3 Diesel B Unit, *03*	235

Exc Mint

No.	Description	Exc	Mint
24517	NYC F3 Diesel B Unit "2404," powered, CC, *03*		250____
24518	WP F3 Diesel B Unit, *03*		275____
24519	B&O F3 Diesel B Unit, *03*		270____
24520	Alaska F3 Diesel AA Set, *03*		650____
24521	Alaska F3 Diesel B Unit, nonpowered, *03*		200____
24522	Alaska F3 Diesel B Unit "1519," powered, CC, *03*		300____
24528	Postwar "2379T" Rio Grande F3 Diesel A Unit, nonpowered, *04*		175____
24529	Santa Fe F3 Diesel AA Set, CC, *04*		690____
24532	Santa Fe F3 Diesel B Unit "18A," nonpowered, *04*		150____
24533	Santa Fe F3 Diesel B Unit "18B," *04*		200____
24534	Erie-Lack. F3 Diesel ABA Set, CC, *05*		900____
24538	Erie-Lack. F3 Diesel B Unit "8042," powered, CC, *05*		225____
24544	NYC FA2 Diesel AA Set, CC, *05*		600____
24547	NYC FB2 Diesel B Unit "3330" (std O), *05*		150____
24548	CN FPA-4 Diesel AA Set, CC, *05*		600____
24551	CN FPB-4 Diesel B Unit "6865" (std O), *05*		150____
24552	UP F3 Diesel ABA Set, CC, *05*		680____
24556	UP F3 Diesel B Unit "900C," powered, CC, *05*		285____
24562	Santa Fe F3 Diesel B Unit, powered, *04–05*		300____
24563	PRR F3 Diesel B Unit, powered, *04–05*		195____
24570	Santa Fe FT Diesel B Unit, nonpowered, *05*		85____
24573	Postwar "2383C" Santa Fe F3 Diesel B Unit, nonpowered, *05*		180____
24574	UP E7 Diesel AA Set, CC, *06*		700____
24577	UP E7 Diesel B Unit "990," nonpowered (std O), *06*		150____
24578	UP E7 Diesel B Unit "988," powered, *06*		300____
24579	NYC E7 Diesel AA Set, CC, *06*		700____
24582	NYC E7 Diesel B Unit "4105," nonpowered (std O), *06*		150____
24583	NYC E7 Diesel B Unit "4104," powered, *06*		300____
24584	Pennsylvania F7 Diesel ABA Set, CC, *06*		900____
24588	Pennsylvania F7 Diesel B Unit "9643B," powered, *06–07*		300____
24589	Santa Fe F7 Diesel ABA Set, CC, *06–07*		900____
24593	Santa Fe F7 Diesel B Unit "332B," powered, *06–07*		300____
24594	PRR F7 Diesel Breakdown B Unit, RailSounds, *06–07*		160____
24595	Santa Fe F7 Diesel Breakdown B Unit, RailSounds, *06–07*		270____
24596	UP E7 Diesel Breakdown B Unit, RailSounds, *06*		270____
24597	NYC E7 Diesel Breakdown B Unit, RailSounds, *06*		270____
24928	Franklin Mutual Bank, *08*		60____
25003	WP Boxcar, orange with silver feather, *05*		30____
25008	Holiday Boxcar, *06*		50____
25009	Santa Fe Hi-Cube Boxcar "14064," *06*		30____
25010	NP Boxcar "48189," *06*		30____
25011	Angela Trotta Thomas "Santa's Break" Boxcar, *06*		50____
25014	PRR Boxcar, silver, *10*		30____
25016	ATSF Boxcar, *10*		35____
25022	NYC Boxcar, *06*		35____
25025	Reading Boxcar "106502," *07–08*		35____

		Exc	Mint
___25026	RI Hi-Cube Boxcar, *07–08*		35
___25030	Billboard Boxcar with catalog art, *06*		20
___25033	Holiday Boxcar, *07*		50
25034	Angela Trotta Thomas "Santa's Workshop" Boxcar, *07*		50
___25035	Disney Holiday Boxcar, *06*		50
___25041	UPS Centennial Boxcar #1, *06*		60
___25042	UPS Centennial Boxcar #2, *07*		60
___25043	Macy's Parade Boxcar, *06*		40
___25050	British Columbia Hi-Cube Boxcar "8008," *08*		35
___25051	Seaboard Boxcar, *08*		35
___25052	Disney Holiday Boxcar, *07*		75
___25053	NYC DD Boxcar "75500," *08*		55
25054	Angela Trotta Thomas "Christmas Memories" Boxcar, *08*		55
___25057	PRR Boxcar "19751," *08*		20
___25058	Santa Fe Boxcar, *10*		30
___25059	Democrat 2008 Election Boxcar, *08*		50
___25060	Republican 2008 Election Boxcar, *08*		50
___25061	Holiday Boxcar, *08*		55
___25063	Conrail Boxcar "25063," *09*		40
___25064	CP Rail Hi-Cube Boxcar, *09–10*		40
___25065	Disney Holiday Boxcar, *08*		40
___25066	Holiday Boxcar, *09*		65
25067	Angela Trotta Thomas "General Delivery" Boxcar, *09*		65
___25068	D&H Boxcar, *08 u*		60
___25077	Milwaukee Road Boxcar "8484," *09–10*		40
___25087	Wabash Boxcar "6439," *10–11*		40
___25093	Seaboard Boxcar, *10*		30
___25095	Texas Special Boxcar, *10*		100
___25096	CN Boxcar, *10*		45
25103	Chessie "Steam Special" Madison Car 2-pack, *05*		100
___25106	Pennsylvania Madison Car 4-pack, *05*		210
___25111	Pennsylvania Madison Car 2-pack, *05*		120
___25114	Lionel Lines Passenger Car 3-pack, *05*		120
___25118	Lionel Lines Passenger Car 2-pack, *05*		80
___25121	Southern Streamliner Car 4-pack, *05*		210
___25126	Southern Streamliner Car 2-pack, *05–06*		120
___25134	Polar Express Add-on Diner, *05–14, 16–17*		70
25135	Polar Express Add-on Baggage Car, *05–14, 16–17*		70
___25148	B&O Madison Car 4-pack, *06–07*		220
___25153	B&O Madison Car 2-pack, *06–07*		125
25156	California Zephyr Streamliner Car 4-pack (std O), *06–07*		220
___25161	California Zephyr Streamliner Car 2-pack, *06–07*		125
___25164	UP Madison Car 4-pack, *06–07*		220
___25169	UP Madison Car 2-pack, *06–07*		125
___25176	B&O Baggage Car, TrainSounds, *06–07*		160
___25177	UP Baggage Car, TrainSounds, *06–07*		160
25178	California Zephyr Streamliner Baggage Car, TrainSounds, *06–07*		160
25186	Polar Express Hot Chocolate Car Add-on, *06–14, 16–17*		70

MODERN ERA 1970-2018

Exc Mint

		Exc	Mint
25187	GN Streamliner Car 4-pack, *07*		220____
25188	GN Streamliner Car 2-pack, *07*		125____
25189	GN Streamliner Baggage Car, TrainSounds, *07*		160____
25196	North Pole Central Vista Dome Car, *07–08*		45____
25197	North Pole Central Baggage Car, *07–10*		45____
25198	PRR Vista Dome Car "4058," *07–09*		45____
25199	PRR Baggage Car "9359," *07–09*		45____
25404	FEC Champion Aluminum Passenger Car 2-pack, *04–05*		290____
25407	FEC Champion Aluminum Diner, StationSounds, *04–05*		290____
25408	Santa Fe El Capitan Aluminum Passenger Car 2-pack, *05*		290____
25411	Santa Fe El Capitan Aluminum Diner, StationSounds, *05*		290____
25412	B&O Columbian Aluminum Passenger Car 2-pack, *05*		275____
25415	B&O Columbian Aluminum Diner, StationSounds, *05*		290____
25416	SP Daylight Aluminum Passenger Car 2-pack, *04–05*		290____
25419	SP Daylight Aluminum Diner, StationSounds, *04–05*		290____
25420	PRR Trail Blazer Aluminum Passenger Car 2-pack, *04–05*		290____
25423	PRR Trail Blazer Aluminum Diner, StationSounds, *04–05*		290____
25433	UP City of Denver Aluminum Passenger Car 4-pack (std O), *05*		1000____
25438	Union Pacific Aluminum Passenger Car 2-pack, *05*		250____
25441	UP City of Denver 18" Aluminum Diner, StationSounds, *05*		290____
25446	Santa Fe Super Chief Streamliner Car 2-pack, *05*		150____
25450	PRR Congressional Aluminum Passenger Car 4-pack (std O), *06–07*		580____
25455	PRR Congressional Aluminum Passenger Car 2-pack (std O), *06–07*		300____
25458	PRR Congressional Diner, StationSounds (std O), *06–07*		300____
25473	NYC Commodore Vanderbilt Aluminum Passenger Car 2-pack (std O), *06*		300____
25476	NYC Commodore Vanderbilt Diner, StationSounds (std O), *06*		300____
25496	Texas Special 21" Streamliner Diner, StationSounds (std O), *07*		300____
25503	Santa Fe Heavyweight Passenger Car 4-pack (std O), *07–09*		495____
25504	Santa Fe Heavyweight Passenger Car 2-pack (std O), *07–09*		265____
25505	Santa Fe Heavyweight Diner, StationSounds (std O), *07–09*		295____
25506	SP Heavyweight Passenger Car 4-pack (std O), *07*		495____
25507	SP Heavyweight Passenger Car 2-pack (std O), *07–08*		265____
25508	SP Heavyweight Diner, StationSounds (std O), *07–08*		295____

25512	Texas Special Streamliner Car 2-pack (std 0), *07*	300
25514	Best Friend of Charleston Coach, *08*	125
25515	MILW Heavyweight Passenger Car 4-pack (std 0), *07*	495
25516	MILW Heavyweight Passenger Car 2-pack (std 0), *07*	265
25517	MILW Heavyweight Diner, StationSounds (std 0), *07–08*	295
25518	PRR Heavyweight Passenger Car 4-pack (std 0), *07*	495
25519	PRR Heavyweight Passenger Car 2-pack (std 0), *07*	265
25520	PRR Heavyweight Diner, StationSounds (std 0), *07–08*	295
25521	B&O Heavyweight Passenger Car 4-pack (std 0), *07*	495
25522	B&O Heavyweight Passenger Car 2-pack (std 0), *07*	265
25523	B&O Heavyweight Diner, StationSounds (std 0), *07–08*	295
25559	Phantom IV Passenger Car 4-pack, *08*	380
25574	UP Streamlined Diner, StationSounds (std 0), *08*	325
25575	Polar Express Heavyweight Car 2-pack, *09*	400
25576	Polar Express Scale Observation Car, *14, 16*	210
25578	Polar Express Heavyweight Add-on Coach, *09*	200
25582	New York City Transit R30 Subway 2-pack, *10*	400
25586	Polar Express Heavyweight Baggage Car, *10, 12–14*	210
25587	Polar Express Abandoned Toy Car, *10, 13*	200
25595	New York City Transit R16 Subway 2-pack, *10*	400
25598	Polar Express Heavyweight Combination Car, *12–14*	210
25600	Postwar Scale CP 18" Aluminum Passenger Car 4-pack, *11*	640
25605	Postwar Scale CP 18" Aluminum Passenger Car 2-pack, *11*	320
25608	ATSF Super Chief 18" Aluminum Passenger Cars 4-pack, *11*	640
25613	ATSF Super Chief 18" Aluminum Passenger Cars 2-pack, *11*	320
25616	UP 18" Passenger Car 2-pack (std 0), *11*	320
25619	PRR "Lindbergh Special" Passenger Car 2-pack, *11*	280
25622	Milwaukee Road 18" Passenger Car 4-pack, *11*	640
25623	Milwaukee Road 18" Passenger Car 2-pack, *11*	320
25630	Polar Express Scale Heavyweight Diner, *12–14, 16*	210
25631	Lionel Funeral Set Add-on 2-pack (std 0), *13*	300
25635	PRR Red Arrow Heavyweight Coach 3-pack (std 0), *13*	430
25639	PRR Red Arrow Heavyweight Diner (std 0), *13*	150
25646	ATSF Scout Heavyweight Coach 4-pack (std 0), *12–14*	550
25651	ATSF Scout Heavyweight Coach 2-pack (std 0), *12–14*	280
25654	Southern Crescent Limited Heavyweight Passenger Car 2-pack, *12*	550

		Exc	Mint
25655	Blue Comet Heavyweight Passenger Car 2-pack, *12–13*		550____
25656	Alton Limited Heavyweight Passenger Car 2-pack, *12–14*		550____
25665	Amtrak Acela Passenger Car 2-pack, *12*		500____
25713	NYC 20th Century Limited Heavyweight Passenger Car 4-pack (std O), *12–14*		550____
25714	NYC 20th Century Limited Van Twiller Combo Car (std O), *12*		140____
25715	NYC 20th Century Limited Schuyler Mansion Sleeper Car (std O), *12*		140____
25716	NYC 20th Century Limited Macomb House Sleeper Car (std O), *12*		140____
25717	NYC 20th Century Limited Catskill Valley Observation Car (std O), *12*		140____
25718	NYC 20th Century Limited Heavyweight Passenger Car 2-pack, *12–14*		280____
25719	NYC 20th Century Limited Baggage Car "4857" (std O), *12*		140____
25720	NYC 20th Century Limited Poplar Highlands Sleeper Car (std O), *12*		140____
25721	NYC 20th Century Limited Heavyweight Diner "655" (std O), *12*		280____
25722	D&RGW California Zephyr 18" Aluminum Passenger Car 4-pack, *12*		640____
25727	WP California Zephyr 18" Aluminum Passenger Car 2-pack, *12*		320____
25731	CB&Q California Zephyr 18" Aluminum Passenger Car 2-pack, *12*		320____
25757	Texas Special Passenger Car 2-pack, *13–14*		400____
25760	PRR Passenger Car 2-pack, *13–14*		400____
25773	SAL Round-roof Boxcar "19297" (std O), *14*		80____
25790	NYC 20th Century Limited Heavyweight Diner (std O), *12*		140____
25795	Polar Express 10th Anniversary Scale Coach, *14*		215____
25796	Polar Express 10th Anniversary Scale Observation Car, *14, 16*		215____
25930	John Adams Boxcar, *13, 15–16*		70____
25931	Andrew Johnson Boxcar, *13, 15–16*		70____
25932	Calvin Coolidge Boxcar, *13, 15–16*		70____
25933	Harry S. Truman Boxcar, *13, 15–16*		70____
25934	Santa Fe Reefer 3-pack, *14–17*		145____
25938	PRR Freight Expansion 3-pack, *13*		155____
25942	Western Freight Expansion 3-pack, *13–16*		155____
25946	SP Hi-Cube Boxcar "128132," *13, 15*		50____
25947	North Pole Express Jack Frost Reefer, *13*		43____
25958	Gingerbread Dough Vat Car, *13–14*		60____
25959	Gingerbread 3-D Tank Car, *13*		55____
25960	Christmas Tree Transparent Boxcar, *13–14*		75____
25961	Thanksgiving on Parade Boxcar, *13*		60____
25962	Thanksgiving Poultry Car, *13*		70____
25963	A Christmas Story 30th Anniversary Boxcar, *13–14*		65____
25964	Silver Bell Casting Co. Ore Car, *13*		55____
25965	Polar Express 10th Anniversary Boxcar, *13*		65____
25973	Seaboard Round-roof Boxcar "19297" (std O), *14*		80____
25977	A Christmas Story Leg Lamp Mint Car, *13*		80____

Exc Mint

		Exc Mint
_____ 26000	C&O Flatcar with pipes, *01*	20
_____ 26001	BP Flatcar "6424" with trailers, *01 u*	150
_____ 26002	Monopoly Flatcar with airplane, *00 u*	NRS
_____ 26003	Lackawanna Flatcar with NH trailer, *01*	60
_____ 26004	Conrail Flatcar "71693" with trailer, *01*	50
_____ 26005	Nickel Plate Flatcar with trailer, *01*	55
_____ 26006	Southern Flatcar "50126" with trailer, *01*	50
_____ 26007	NW Flatcar "203029" with trailer, *01*	50
_____ 26008	Farmall Flatcar, *01 u*	NRS
_____ 26011	B&M Bulkhead Flatcar, *01 u*	NRS
_____ 26013	CN Flatcar with Zamboni ice resurfacing machine, *01*	48
_____ 26014	JCPenney Flatcar, *01 u*	145
_____ 26016	Soo Line Flatcar with trucks, *01 u*	NRS
_____ 26017	Soo Line Flatcar with trailer, *01 u*	NRS
_____ 26018	Soo Line Flatcar with trailer, *01 u*	NRS
_____ 26019	Alaska Gondola "13801," *02*	30
_____ 26020	Postwar "3830" Flatcar with submarine, *02*	46
_____ 26021	CN Flatcar with trailer, *02*	44
_____ 26022	PFE Flatcar with trailer, *02*	32
_____ 26023	Postwar "6816" Flatcar with bulldozer, *02*	65
_____ 26024	Postwar "6817" Flatcar with scraper, *02*	65
_____ 26025	Postwar "6407" Flatcar with rocket, *02*	42
_____ 26026	Postwar "6413" Flatcar with Mercury capsules, *02*	95
_____ 26027	Flatcar "6425" with U.S. Army boat, *02*	30
_____ 26028	Conrail Well Car "768121," *02*	40
_____ 26030	NYC Flatcar "601172" with stakes and bulkheads, *02*	22
_____ 26033	NYC Gondola "6462," *01*	30
_____ 26035	LL Flatcar with traffic helicopter, *01*	50
_____ 26039	Lions Flatcar with 2 Zamboni ice resurfacing machines, *02*	39
_____ 26042	B&O Gondola "601272" with canisters, *03*	19
_____ 26043	Seaboard Flatcar "48109" with trailer, *03*	30
_____ 26044	NYC Flatcar "506089" with trailers, *03*	35
_____ 26045	Postwar "2411" Flatcar with pipes, *03*	40
_____ 26046	Postwar "6561" Flatcar with cable reels, *03*	30
_____ 26047	Postwar "2461" Flatcar with transformer, *03*	25
_____ 26048	Postwar "6801" Flatcar with boat, *02*	29
_____ 26049	Speedboat Willie Flatcar with boat, *03*	29
_____ 26053	PRR Gondola with canisters, *04 05*	20
_____ 26056	Southern Bulkhead Flatcar "50125," *02*	19
_____ 26057	SP Flatcar "599365" with tractors, *02*	37
_____ 26058	SP Flatcar "599366" with trailer frames, *02*	35
_____ 26061	Lionelville Tree Transport Gondola, *03*	40
_____ 26062	NYC Gondola "26062" with cable reels, *03*	19
_____ 26063	Pennsylvania Bulkhead Flatcar "26063," *03*	19
_____ 26064	Rock Island Flatcar "90088" with trailer, *04*	34
_____ 26065	REA Flatcar with trailers "TLCX2," *04*	35
_____ 26066	Great Northern Bulkhead Flatcar "26066," *04*	20
_____ 26067	Southern Gondola "60141" with cable reels, *04*	20
_____ 26070	Nestle Nesquik Flatcar "26070" with trailer, *03*	70
_____ 26077	LL Flatcar "6424" with autos, girls set add-on, *03*	44

		Exc	Mint
26078	LL Flatcar "6801" with boat, boys set add-on, *03*		40___
26080	NJ Medical School Flatcar with handcar, *03*		80___
26082	Frisco Auto Carrier, 2-tier, *04*		20___
26085	New York Auto Carrier, 2-tier, *05*		27___
26086	Alaska Flatcar with bulkheads, *05*		25___
26087	Rock Island Gondola with canisters, traditional, *05*		27___
26091	Elvis Flatcar with tractor and trailer, traditional, *05*		60___
26099	PRR Auto Carrier "500423," 3-tier, *07*		30___
26100	PRR 1-D Tank Car, *00*		27___
26101	Lenoil 1-D Tank Car "6015," *00*		34___
26102	AEC Glow-in-Dark 1-D Tank Car, *00*		55___
26103	GATX Tank Train 1-D Tank Car "44588," *00*		34___
26107	BP Petroleum 3-D Tank Car, *00 u*		99___
26108	Lionel Visitor's Center Reefer "206482," *00 u*		38___
26109	NYC (P&LE) 1-D Tank Car, *00*		42___
26110	SP 3-D Tank Car "6415," *00–01*		15___
26111	Frisco Tank Car, *00*		29___
26112	Gulf Oil Tank Car, *00*		40___
26113	U.S. Army 1-D Tank Car, *00*		35___
26114	Service Station 1-D Tank Car (SSS), *00*		32___
26115	Lionel Centennial Tank Car, *00 u*		90___
26116	Pepe LePew 1-D Tank Car, *00 u*		85___
26118	NYC Tank Car "101900," *01*		23___
26119	Protex 3-D Tank Car "1054," *00*		29___
26120	KCS Tank Car "1229," *00*		32___
26122	Pioneer Seed Tank Car, *00 u*		NRS___
26123	Santa Fe Stock Car "23002," *01*		35___
26124	C&O 1-D Tank Car "X1019," *01*		30___
26125	Winter Wonderland Clear Tank Car with confetti, *00*		50___
26126	Cheerios Boxcar, *98*		65___
26127	Wellspring Capital Management Tank Car with confetti, *00 u*		214___
26131	Santa Fe 1-D Tank Car "335268," *02*		22___
26132	UP 1-D Tank Car "69015, *02*		40___
26133	Tootsie Roll 1-D Tank Car "26133," *02*		37___
26135	Whirlpool Tank Car, *01*		NRS___
26136	Southern 1-D Tank Car "8790011," *03*		20___
26137	Jack Frost 1-D Tank Car "106," *03*		32___
26138	Nestle Nesquik 1-D Tank Car "26138," *03*		40___
26139	Lionel Lines Stock Car "26139" with horses, *03*		39___
26141	Whirlpool 1-D Tank Car, *03 u*		94___
26144	Chessie System 1-D Tank Car "2233," *02*		22___
26145	Do It Best 1-D Tank Car, *03 u*		80___
26146	Do It Best 1-D Tank Car, *03 u*		95___
26147	Diamond Chemicals 1-D Tank Car "6315," Archive Collection, *02*		33___
26149	Egg Nog 1-D Tank Car, *03*		43___
26150	Alaska 3-D Tank Car "26150," *03*		23___
26151	NP Wood-sided Reefer "26151," *03*		19___
26152	Morton Salt 1-D Tank Car "26152," *04*		40___
26153	Pillsbury 1-D Tank Car "26153," *04*		40___
26154	NYC 3-D Tank Car "26154," *04*		25___

____	26155	Pennsylvania 1-D Tank Car "26155," 04	20
____	26156	North Western Wood-sided Reefer "15356," 04	20
____	26157	Ballyhoo Brothers Circus Stock Car "26157," 04	35
____	26158	Campbell's Soup 1-D Tank Car, 04	35
____	26164	LL 1-D Tank Car "6315," girls set add-on, 03	43
____	26167	New Haven 1-D Tank Car, traditional, 05	27
____	26168	Conrail 3-D Tank Car, traditional, 05	27
____	26169	Santa Fe Wood-sided Reefer, traditional, 05	27
____	26171	Alaska 1-D Tank Car, 05	30
____	26176	Tidmouth Milk 1-D Tank Car, 05	35
____	26179	GN 3-D Tank Car, 06	30
____	26180	DM&IR 1-D Tank Car "S15," 06	30
____	26181	NYC Wood-sided Reefer, 06	30
____	26193	UP 1-D Tank Car, 07	15
____	26196	Candy Cane 1-D Tank Car, 06	60
____	26197	D&H 1-D Tank Car "55," 07–08	35
____	26198	D&RGW 3-D Tank Car, 07	30
____	26199	WP PFE Wood-sided Reefer "55327," 07	30
____	26200	NKP Boxcar "18211," 98	35
____	26201	Operation Lifesaver Boxcar, 98	29
____	26203	D&H Boxcar "1829," 98	25
____	26204	Alaska Boxcar "10806," 98–99	35
____	26205	Rocky & Bullwinkle Boxcar, 99	36
____	26206	Curious George Boxcar, 99	40
____	26208	Vapor Records Boxcar #2, 98	55
____	26214	Celebrate the Century Stamp Boxcar, 98 u	97
____	26215	AEC Glow-in-the-Dark Boxcar, 98	95
____	26216	Cheerios Boxcar, 98 u	80
____	26218	Quaker Oats Boxcar, 98 u	450
____	26219	Ace Hardware Boxcar, 98 u	NRS
____	26220	Smuckers Boxcar, 98 u	89
____	26222	Penn Central Boxcar "125962," 99	31
____	26223	FEC Boxcar "5027," 99	31
____	26224	D&H Boxcar, 99	24
____	26228	Vapor Records Holiday Boxcar, 99 u	125
____	26230	AEC Glow-in-the-Dark Boxcar #2, 99	55
____	26232	Martin Guitar Lumber Boxcar "9823," 99	50
____	26234	NYC Boxcar, 99	29
____	26235	Valentine Boxcar, 99	40
____	26236	Aircraft Boxcar, 99	28
____	26237	Boy Scout Boxcar, 99	85
____	26238	Detroit Historical Museum Boxcar, 99	29
____	26239	M.A.D.D. Boxcar, 99	19
____	26240	RailBox Boxcar, 99–00	24
____	26241	Norfolk & Western Boxcar, 99–00	17
____	26242	D.A.R.E. Boxcar, 99	30
____	26243	Christmas Boxcar, 99	35
____	26244	Woody Woodpecker Boxcar, 99	43
____	26247	Lionel Lines Boxcar, 99	38
____	26253	Acme Explosives Boxcar, 99 u	NRS
____	26254	Keebler Boxcar, 99 u	NRS
____	26255	NYC Boxcar "200495," 99 u	30
____	26256	Salvation Army Charity Boxcar, 99	29
____	26257	Wheaties Boxcar, 99	79

Exc Mint

		Exc	Mint
26264	Lionel Station Boxcar, *99*	44	
26265	NYC Pacemaker Boxcar, *00*	30	
26271	AEC Glow-in-the-Dark Boxcar, *99*	62	
26272	Christmas Boxcar, *00*	42	
26275	Boy Scout Boxcar, *00*	55	
26276	C&O Boxcar "23296," *99–00*	23	
26277	UP Boxcar "491050," *00*	20	
26278	Cap'n Crunch Christmas Boxcar, *99*	670	
26280	Tinsel Town Express Boxcar, music, *00*	50	
26284	Toy Fair Preview Boxcar, *99 u*	725	
26285	NYC Pacemaker Boxcar, *00*	40	
26288	AEC Glow-in-Dark Boxcar, *99*	50	
26290	SP Boxcar, *00*	20	
26291	Pennsylvania Boxcar "47158," *00*	20	
26292	Frisco Boxcar "22015," *00*	20	
26293	Burlington Boxcar, *00*	30	
26294	Centennial Express Boxcar, *00*	NRS	
26295	Trainmaster Boxcar, *99 u*	55	
26296	Service Station Boxcar Set (SSS), *00*	105	
26298	Taz Bobbing Boxcar, *00*	70	
26300	UPS Flatcar with trailers, *04*	50	
26301	UPS Flatcar with airplane, traditional, *05*	53	
26302	Troublesome Truck #1, *05*	35	
26303	Troublesome Truck #2, *05*	35	
26305	SP Auto Carrier, 2-tier, *06*	30	
26306	D&RGW Gondola "56135" with canisters, *06*	30	
26307	Chessie System Bulkhead Flatcar, *06*	30	
26308	Hard Rock Cafe Flatcar with billboards, *06*	55	
26309	Alaska Depressed Center Flatcar with cable reels, *06*	50	
26310	CGW Flatcar "3707" with trailer, *06*	55	
26311	Santa Fe Flatcar with pickups, *06*	60	
26317	AEC Gondola with toxic waste containers	30	
26318	AEC Gondola with toxic waste containers	30	
26330	Gondola with trees and presents, *06*	60	
26331	Lionel Lines Bulkhead Flatcar, *07*	30	
26332	CP Rail Gondola "337061" with canisters, *07*	30	
26335	Domino Sugar Flatcar with trailer, *07–08*	60	
26357	CSX Flatcar "600514" with pipes, *07–08*	50	
26366	REA Flatcar with trailers, *07*	60	
26367	Santa's Egg Nog Flatcar with container, *07*	60	
26368	Gondola with trees and presents, *07*	60	
26378	Conrail Auto Carrier "786414," 2-tier, *08*	35	
26379	PRR Gondola with cable reels, *08–09*	35	
26380	NYC Bulkhead Flatcar, *08*	35	
26389	ATSF Flatcar "108477" with 2 pickups, *08*	60	
26390	ATSF Flatcar with bulkheads, *09–10*	40	
26391	NYC Gondola "263910" with containers, *09*	40	
26392	BNSF Auto Carrier, *09*	40	
26400	C&NW Hopper, *07–08*	35	
26401	NP Ore Car "78540," *08*	35	
26410	Chessie System Hopper "47806," *08*	35	
26411	Lionel Lines Ore Car "2026," *08–09*	35	
26412	Chessie System 4-bay Hopper "60573," *08*	35	
26418	B&M Hopper, *09*	40	

Exc Mint

		Exc	Mint
26421	PRR Ore Car, *11*		40
26422	White Pass Ice Breaker Car, *09*		50
26423	Soo Line Ore Car, *10*		40
26424	LV Hopper, *11*		30
26425	UP Hopper, *11*		40
26429	PRR Hopper, *11*		40
26435	B&M Ice Breaker Hopper, *11*		50
26437	CSX Hopper, *11*		40
26439	Central of Georgia Hopper, *11–12*		40
26443	M&StL Ore Car "6700," *11*		40
26445	Polar Hopper with presents, *11–14*		60
26446	Thomas & Friends Troublesome Trucks Christmas 2-pack, *11–15*		70
26448	U.S. Army Gondola with reels, *11*		40
26449	CN Hi-Cube Boxcar "799346," *13*		55
26451	DM&IR Ore Car "28003," *13*		43
26452	PRR Hopper "153935," *13*		43
26457	PRR Ore Car, *12*		40
26473	Lackawanna NS Heritage 2-bay Hopper, *13*		55
26474	NYC NS Heritage Quad Hopper, *13*		55
26477	Monopoly Electric Company Hopper, *13*		65
26481	Boy Scouts of America Christmas Gondola, *13*		65
26488	Hershey's Ice Breakers Hopper, *13*		63
26489	Hershey's Chistmas Bells Boxcar, *13*		65
26491	Pennsylvania Power & Light Gondola with canisters, *13*		43
26492	Area 51 3-D Tank Car, *13*		43
26493	Monopoly Water Works 3-D Tank Car, *13*		65
26494	PRR Truss Rod Gondola with vats, *13*		60
26495	C&NW Poultry Car, *13*		60
26496	Lionelville Aquarium Co. Fish Food Vat Car, *13–16*		65
26497	Bethlehem Steel Depressed Flatcar with reels, *13*		43
26499	CN Hi-Cube Boxcar "799346," *14*		55
26502	UP Bay Window Caboose "6517," *97*		47
26503	ATSF High-Cupola Caboose "7606R," *97*		85
26504	Mobil Oil Square Window Caboose "6257," *97 u*		37
26505	Rescue Unit Caboose, *98*		50
26506	N&W Square Window Caboose "562748," *98*		15
26507	D&H Square Window Caboose "35707," *98*		20
26508	Alaska Square Window Caboose "1081," *98*		28
26511	Quaker Oats Square Window Caboose, *98 u*		48
26513	NYC Emergency Caboose "26505," *99*		47
26515	Lionel Lines Bobber Caboose, *99*		10
26516	Safari Bobber Caboose, *99 u*		10
26519	Christmas Work Caboose "6496," *99*		41
26520	Bethlehem Steel Work Caboose "6130" (SSS), *99*		55
26523	Keebler Cheezit Square Window Caboose, *99 u*		NRS
26524	NYC Square Window Caboose "295," *99 u*		20
26526	Santa Fe Square Window Caboose "999471," *01*		30
26527	Christmas Work Caboose with presents, *02*		27
26528	PRR Square Window Caboose "6257," *99*		21
26530	LL Square Window Caboose "6257," *99*		22
26532	NYC Square Window Caboose "296," *00*		20

		Exc	Mint
26533	SP Square Window Caboose, *00*	20	
26534	PRR Square Window Caboose "6257," *00*	20	
26535	Frisco Square Window Caboose "1700," *00*	20	
26536	Centennial Express Square Window Caboose, *00*	NRS	
26537	Lionel Mines Square Window Caboose, *00 u*	45	
26539	Whirlpool Square Window Caboose, *00 u*	NRS	
26542	ACL Square Window Caboose "069," *01*	31	
26543	GN Square Window Caboose "X66," *00–01*	28	
26544	Alaska Square Window Caboose "1084," *01*	25	
26545	Snap-On Square Window Caboose, *00 u*	NRS	
26548	Pioneer Seed Square Window Caboose, *00 u*	NRS	
26549	PRR Square Window Caboose "4977947," *01*	20	
26550	NYC Square Window Caboose "19293," *01*	20	
26551	Chessie System Center Cupola Caboose, *01*	25	
26552	Santa Fe Square Window Caboose "999472," *01*	25	
26553	C&O Center Cupola Caboose "A918," *01*	30	
26554	Monopoly Short Line Square Window Caboose, *00 u*	NRS	
26556	NH Center Cupola Caboose, *01*	35	
26557	Farmall Square Window Caboose, *01 u*	NRS	
26559	N&W Center Cupola Caboose "518408," *01*	20	
26560	B&M Square Window Caboose, *01 u*	20	
26564	Soo Line Center Cupola Caboose, *01 u*	20	
26565	Lionel Employee Square Window Caboose, *01 u*	150	
26566	WP Square Window Caboose "731," *02*	25	
26568	NKP Square Window Caboose "1155," *02*	25	
26569	Southern Square Window Caboose "252," *02*	25	
26570	B&O Square Window Caboose "295," *02*	25	
26572	Lionel 20th Century Square Window Caboose, *00 u*	25	
26580	Wabash Square Window Caboose "2805," *03*	22	
26581	C&O Square Window Caboose "C-1831," *03*	20	
26582	L&N Square Window Caboose "318," *03*	20	
26583	PRR Square Window Caboose "477814," *03*	25	
26594	Ontario Northland Work Caboose "26594," *03*	25	
26595	UP Caboose "26595," *03*	18	
26596	NYC Caboose "17716," *04*	25	
26597	Great Northern Caboose "X295," *04*	25	
26598	UP Caboose "26598," *04*	25	
26599	DM&IR Work Caboose "26599," *04*	25	
26600	American Fire and Rescue Water Tank Car, *09–11*	55	
26603	LV Depressed Flatcar with reels, *09*	40	
26604	Halloween Spooky Grave Gondola, *09*	58	
26609	NYC Gondola with Pacemaker canisters	40	
26612	Christmas Gifts Gondola, *09*	60	
26614	Tupelo Dairy Farms Milk Car, *10–11*	60	
26616	UP Bulkhead Flatcar with pipes, *10*	40	
26617	B&O Depressed Center Flatcar with generator, *10*	40	
26629	PRR Flatcar with generators	35	
26638	Pennsylvania Power & Light Flatcar with reels, *11*	40	
26639	Cities Service 3-Tier Auto Carrier, *11–12*	40	
26640	CN Maple Syrup Barrel Ramp Car, *11–12*	40	

		Exc	Mint
26641	Coca-Cola Flatcar with trailer, *11*		70
26642	CN Jet Snowblower, *11–12*		65
26643	D&RGW Jet Snowblower, *11–13*		65
26644	BNSF Flatcar with generator, *11*		40
26645	BNSF Flatcar with trailer, *11*		40
26646	Pennsylvania Power & Light Flatcar with transformer, *11–12*		40
26647	IC Bulkhead Flatcar with pipes, *11*		40
26649	Erie-Lack. Gondola with canisters, *11*		40
26650	M&StL Flatcar with pipes, *11*		40
26651	ATSF Scout Heavyweight Passenger Car 2-pack (std O), *12*		280
26652	NYC Gondola with canisters, *11*		40
26653	PC Flatcar with generator, *11*		35
26654	Boy Scouts Flatcar with Pinewood Derby Kit, *11–13*		75
26660	Coca-Cola Vat Car, *11–16*		70
26661	Reindeer Feed Barrel Ramp Car, *09*		60
26665	Hershey's Special Dark Flatcar with trailer, *11*		60
26666	Boy Scouts Flatcar with trailer, *11*		70
26667	Flatcar with Santa's sleigh, *12*		70
26668	Strasburg Flatcar with wheels, *11*		55
26669	U.S. Navy Flatcar with Shark submarine, *12–13*		60
26673	B&M Flatcar with Milk Tank, *12*		60
26675	Monopoly Auto Loader, *12*		80
26676	Heinz Baked Beans Vat Car, *12*		60
26677	LIRR Gondola with canisters, *12*		40
26679	ATSF Gondola with reels, *12–13*		55
26683	Christmas Track Maintenance Car, *12–13*		67
26685	Flatcar with Santa's plane, *12*		55
26686	Hershey's Cocoa Vat Car, *12–13*		63
26687	Lone Ranger Gondola with gunpowder vats, *12–14*		65
26693	Hershey's Krackel Piggyback Flatcar with trailer, *12–13*		70
26694	Carnegie Science Center Flatcar with submarine, *13*		65
26696	NJ Transit Gondola with wood ties, *12*		75
26699	PRR Flatcar with wheel load," *12–14*		55
26706	Lighted Christmas Boxcar, *00*		47
26707	Lionel Steel Operating Welding Flatcar "1108," *00*		90
26709	Flatcar "6511" with psychedelic submarine, *99*		32
26710	Southern Stock Car, Carsounds, *99*		95
26712	Churchill Downs Horse Car "6473," *99–00*		38
26713	Shay Log Car 3-pack, *99*		105
26714	Westside Lumber Flatcar with logs (std O), *99*		45
26715	Westside Lumber Flatcar with logs (std O), *99*		45
26716	Westside Lumber Flatcar with logs (std O), *99*		45
26717	Orion Star Boxcar 9600, *00*		30
26718	Christmas Boxcar, RailSounds, *00*		160
26719	Bobbing Ghost Halloween Boxcar, *00*		46
26721	Lionel Lines Coal Dump Car "3379," *00*		31
26722	Lionel Lines Log Dump Car "3351," *00*		31
26723	Lion Chasing Trainer Gondola "3444," *00*		49

		Exc	Mint
26724	Veterans Day Boxcar, *00*		70____
26725	NYC Jumping Hobo Boxcar "88160," *00*		38____
26726	T. Rex Bobbing Boxcar, *00*		41____
26727	San Francisco City Lights Boxcar, *00*		50____
26736	Lionel Birthday Boxcar, *02 u*		40____
26737	Operating Santa Gondola "6462," *00 u*		65____
26738	Lionel Mines Gondola, *00 u*		NRS____
26739	Santa and Snowman Boxcar, *00*		46____
26740	Reindeer Car, *00*		43____
26741	Operating Santa Boxcar, *00*		50____
26743	Christmas Reindeer Car, *01*		55____
26745	Traveling Aquarium Car "506," *01*		70____
26746	Bobbing Vampire Boxcar, *01*		46____
26747	Halloween Bats Aquarium Car, *01*		75____
26748	T&P Operating Hopper Car "9699," *01*		38____
26749	Alaska Log Dump Car, *01*		29____
26751	Chessie Coal Dump Car, *01*		27____
26752	Christmas Aquarium Car, *01*		55____
26753	Christmas Operating Dump Car, *01*		43____
26757	Operating Barrel Car "35621," *00*		55____
26758	AEC Nuclear Gondola "719766," *01*		90____
26759	Postwar "3459" Coal Dump Car, *02*		60____
26760	Postwar "3461" Log Dump Car, *02*		60____
26761	AEC Security Caboose 3535, *01*		63____
26762	Postwar "3665" Minuteman Car, *01*		55____
26763	Postwar "6448" Exploding Boxcar, *01*		40____
26764	Bethlehem Steel Operating Welding Car, *01*		75____
26765	Postwar "3370" Sheriff and Outlaw Car, *01–02*	40	49____
26766	Priority Mail Operating Boxcar, *01–02*		32____
26768	Postwar "6520" Searchlight Car, *02*		49____
26769	Santa Fe Crane Car "199793," CC, *03*		255____
26770	Wabash Brakeman Car "3424," *01*		70____
26773	Chessie Searchlight Car, *01*		20____
26774	Santa Fe Log Dump Car, *01*		25____
26775	U.S. Army Searchlight Car, *00*		50____
26776	U.S. Army Operating Boxcar "26413," *00*		55____
26777	U.S. Flag Boxcar, *01 u*		250____
26779	Burlington Operating Hopper "189312," *02*		40____
26780	Postwar "3376" Bronx Zoo Giraffe Car, *02*	35	36____
26781	Postwar "3540" Operating Radar Car, *02*		35____
26782	Lenny the Lion Bobbing Head Car, *02*		38____
26784	Stingray Express Aquarium Car, *02*		35____
26785	Flatcar with powerboat, *02*		31____
26786	Lionelville Operating Parade Car, *02*		40____
26787	Erie Jumping Hobo Boxcar, *01–02*		43____
26788	Christmas Music Boxcar, *02*		46____
26789	Kiss Kringle Chase Gondola, *02*		35____
26790	Lighted Christmas Boxcar, *02*		34____
26791	UP Animated Gondola, *02*	40	50____
26792	REA Operating Boxcar "6299," *03*		39____
26793	Alaska Extension Searchlight Car, *01*		44____
26794	Postwar "6352" PFE Ice Car, *01–02*		85____
26795	NYC Stock Car "3121," Cattle Sounds, *02*		50____
26796	Lionel Farms Poultry Dispatch Car, *01*		55____

		Exc	Mint
26797	GN Log Dump Car "60011," 02		48
26798	Bethlehem Steel Coal Dump Car "26798," 02		70
26801	Jumping Bart Simpson Boxcar, 04		44
26802	Simpsons Animated Gondola, 04		46
26803	Santa Fe Derrick Car "26803," 04		25
26804	NYC Coal Dump Car "26804," 04		22
26805	Pennsylvania Log Dump Car "26805," 04		24
26806	Pillsbury Operating Boxcar "3428," Archive Collection, 04		40
26807	Blue Chip Line Motorized Animated Gondola, 04		40
26808	Egg Nog Barrel Car, 04		55
26809	Santa's Extension Searchlight Car, 04		42
26810	NYC Operating Searchlight Car, 05		33
26811	Pennsylvania Coal Dump Car, 05		33
26812	Santa Fe Log Dump Car, 05		33
26813	Lionel Lines Derrick Car, 05		33
26814	NYC Walking Brakeman Car "174226," 05		40
26815	PRR "Workin' on the Railroad" Boxcar "24255," 05		42
26816	REA Boxcar, steam TrainSounds, 05		105
26817	Alaska Boxcar, diesel TrainSounds, 05		145
26818	Christmas Music Boxcar, 05		63
26819	Holiday Animated Gondola, 05		55
26820	Penguin Transport Aquarium Car, 05		60
26821	NP Moe & Joe Lumber Flatcar, 05		75
26826	Alaska Searchlight Car, 05		40
26827	UPS Operating Boxcar "9237," Archive Collection, 05		63
26828	Tornado Chaser Radar Tracking Car, 05		63
26829	UPS Holiday Operating Boxcar, 05		59
26832	Lionel Lines Tender, TrainSounds, 07–08		105
26833	Wellspring Radar Car, 04		70
26834	PFE Ice Car "20042" (std O), 05–06		63
26835	MOW Track Cleaning Car, 05		140
26836	Halloween Boxcar, SpookySounds, 05		105
26841	PRR Log Dump Car, 05		27
26842	NYC Coal Dump Car, 05		27
26845	Southern Derrick Car, 06		35
26846	GN Coal Dump Car, 06		38
26847	C&O Coal Dump Car, 06–07		80
26848	Lionel Lines Moe & Joe Flatcar, 06		80
26849	SP Log Dump Car, 06–07		80
26850	D&RGW Searchlight Car, 06		75
26851	WM Log Dump Car, 06		35
26852	Postwar "3562-25" Santa Fe Barrel Car, 06		75
26853	SeaWorld Aquarium Car, 06		75
26854	UP Walking Brakeman Car, 06–07		75
26855	Halloween Animated Gondola, 06		65
26856	Christmas Chase Gondola, 06		65
26857	Alien Radar Tracking Car, 06		65
26858	Christmas Music Boxcar, 06		65
26859	Christmas Parade Boxcar, 06		75
26860	B&O Boxcar "466035," steam TrainSounds (std O), 06–07		75

		Exc	Mint
26861	Santa Fe Boxcar, diesel TrainSounds (std O), *06–07*	110	____
26862	Hard Rock Cafe Boxcar, *06*	35	____
26863	Railway Express Operating Milk Car with platform, *06*	140	____
26864	Domino Sugar Operating Boxcar, *06–07*	40	____
26865	CP Animated Caboose, *06–07*	80	____
26867	Boxcar, AlienSounds, *06–07*	110	____
26868	U.S. Steel Operating Welding Car, *06*	75	____
26869	REA Jumping Hobo Boxcar, *06–07*	70	____
26870	Christmas Dump Car with presents, *06*	80	____
26871	PRR Tender, steam TrainSounds (std O), *06*	105	____
26872	U.S. Army Security Car, *06*	75	____
26876	Missile Firing Trail Car, *06*	75	____
26877	U.S. Army Missile Launch Car, *06–07*	190	____
26888	Weyerhaeuser Timber Co. Log Car	40	____
26889	Weyerhaeuser Timber Co. Log Car	40	____
26891	PRR Coal Dump Car, *05*	30	____
26897	Great Western Flatcar with handcar, *07*	65	____
26898	NYC Log Dump Car, *05*	25	____
26905	Bethlehem Steel Gondola "6462" with canisters, *98*	29	____
26906	SP Flatcar "9823" with Corgi `57 Chevy, *98*	40	____
26908	TTUX Flatcar "6300" with Apple trailers, *98*	70	____
26913	East St. Louis Gondola "9820," *98*	29	____
26920	Union Pacific Die-cast Ore Car "64861," *97*	70	____
26921	Union Pacific Die-cast Ore Car "64862," *97*	55	____
26922	Union Pacific Die-cast Ore Car "64863," *97*	65	____
26923	Union Pacific Die-cast Ore Car "64864," *97*	55	____
26924	Union Pacific Die-cast Ore Car "64865," *97*	55	____
26925	Union Pacific Die-cast Ore Car "64866," *97*	60	____
26926	Union Pacific Die-cast Ore Car, *98*	55	____
26927	Union Pacific Die-cast Ore Car, *98*	55	____
26928	Union Pacific Die-cast Ore Car, *98*	55	____
26929	Union Pacific Die-cast Ore Car, *98*	40	____
26936	Die-cast Tank Car 4-pack, *98*	335	____
26937	Die-cast Hopper 4-pack, *98*	325	____
26938	NYC Reefer, *99*	80	____
26940	Rio Grande Stock Car "37710," *99*	80	____
26946	D&H Semi-Scale Hopper "9642"	85	____
26947	Gulf Die-cast Tank Car, *98*	120	____
26948	P&LE Die-cast Hopper, *98*	65	____
26949	NP Flatcar with trailer "6424-2017," *98*	47	____
26950	NP Flatcar with trailer "6424-2016," *98*	47	____
26951	TTX Flatcar "475185" with PRR trailer, *98*	55	____
26952	J.B. Hunt Flatcar with trailer, *98*	40	____
26953	J.B. Hunt Flatcar with trailer, *98*	40	____
26954	J.B. Hunt Flatcar with trailer, *98*	40	____
26955	J.B. Hunt Flatcar with trailer, *98*	40	____
26956	C&O Gondola (O27), *98–99*	15	____
26957	Delaware & Hudson Flatcar with stakes, *98*	20	____
26971	Lionel Steel 16-wheel Depressed Center Flatcar, *98*	135	____
26972	Pony Express Animated Gondola, *98*	36	____
26973	Getty Die-cast Tank Car 3-pack, *98*	270	____

		Exc Mint
____26974	Getty Die-cast 1-D Tank Car "4003," *98*	80
____26975	Getty Die-cast 1-D Tank Car "4004," *98*	90
____26976	Getty Die-cast 1-D Tank Car "4005," *98*	80
____26977	Sinclair Die-cast Tank Car 3-pack, *98*	275
____26978	Sinclair Tank Car UTLX "64026," *98*	105
____26979	Sinclair Tank Car UTLX "64027," *98*	85
____26980	Sinclair Tank UTLX "64028," *98*	90
____26981	Gulf Die-cast Tank Car 2-pack, *99*	165
____26985	B&O Die-cast Hopper 2-pack, *99*	160
26987	Chessie System (B&O) Die-cast 4-bay Hopper "235154," *99*	
____		90
____26991	Lionelville Ladder Fire Car, *99*	47
____26992	NYC Reefer, *99*	75
____26993	NYC Reefer, *99*	85
____26994	NYC Reefer, *99*	135
____26995	Rio Grande Stock Car "37714," *99*	80
____26996	Rio Grande Stock Car "37715," *99*	80
____26997	Rio Grande Stock Car "37716," *99*	80
____27000	C&EI Offset Hopper "97393" (std O), *07*	65
____27001	Erie Offset Hopper "28001" (std O), *07*	65
____27002	Frisco Offset Hopper "92399" (std O), *07*	65
27003	Chessie System Offset Hopper "234355" (std O), *07*	
____		65
____27016	UP PS-2 Covered Hopper "1312" (std O), *07–08*	60
27019	Imco PS-2 Covered Hopper "41001" (std O), *07–08*	
____		60
____27022	PC PS-2 Covered Hopper "74217" (std O), *07*	60
____27025	NYC PS-2 Covered Hopper "883180" (std O), *07*	60
____27029	ATSF Offset Hopper 3-pack (std O), *08–09*	200
____27030	Monon Offset Hopper 3-pack (std O), *08–09*	200
____27031	MoPac Offset Hopper 3-pack (std O), *08–09*	200
____27032	NYC Offset Hopper 3-pack (std O), *08–09*	200
27033	Chessie System PS-2 Hopper 3-pack (std O), *08–09*	
____		180
27034	Nickel Plate Road PS-2 Hopper 3-pack (std O), *08–09*	
____		180
27053	CB&Q ACF 2-bay Covered Hopper "183925" (std O), *08–09*	
____		55
27059	Bakelite Plastics PS-2 Hopper "61445" (std O), *10–11*	
____		70
____27061	Clinchfield Freight Car 2-pack (std O), *10*	150
27064	PRR Flatcar with PRR piggyback trailers (std O), *12*	
____		98
____27065	SP Flatcar with SP piggyback trailers (std O), *12*	98
____27066	IC Flatcar with IC piggyback trailers (std O), *12*	98
27067	C&O Flatcar with REA piggyback trailers (std O), *12*	
____		98
27068	ATSF Flatcar with Santa Fe piggyback trailers (std O), *12*	
____		98
____27069	Conrail PS-2 Hopper "878330" (std O), *12–13*	70
____27070	N&W Scale Offset Hopper "279850" (std O), *12*	70
____27071	CSX 4-Bay Covered Hopper "256300" (std O), *12*	90
____27072	C&NW Scale PS-1 Boxcar "7" (std O), *12–13*	70
____27073	PRR Scale Offset Hopper 3-pack (std O), *12*	200
____27077	L&N Scale Offset Hopper "88494" (std O), *12–13*	70

		Exc	Mint
27078	Frisco Scale 3-Bay Open Hopper "88299" (std O), *12–14*	75	____
27079	NYC Boxcar, *09*	30	____
27080	Lionel Vision Boxcar, *14–15*	60	____
27081	BN PS-2 Hopper "424796" (std O), *12–13*	70	____
27082	Grand Trunk 4-Bay Covered Hopper "38111" (std O), *12*	90	____
27083	RI PS-2 Hopper "500751" (std O), *12–13*	70	____
27084	Seaboard 8000-gallon 1-D Tank Car "27084" (std O), *12*	70	____
27085	Wabash PS-2 Hopper "30425" (std O), *12–13*	70	____
27086	Grand Trunk 60' Boxcar "383575" (std O), *12, 14*	85	____
27087	CN 60' Boxcar "799424" (std O), *12, 14*	85	____
27088	MKT PS-5 Gondola "12447" (std O), *12–13*	65	____
27089	LIRR PS-5 Gondola "6053" (std O), *12*	65	____
27090	NP 8000-gallon 1-D Tank Car "27090" (std O), *12*	70	____
27091	WM Scale 3-Bay Open Hopper "85125" (std O), *12*	80	____
27092	CSX Heritage 60' Boxcar "176740" (std O), *12*	85	____
27093	Boy Scouts PS-2 Hopper "2013" (std O), *13*	70	____
27094	BNSF PS-2 Hopper 2-pack (std O), *13–14*	130	____
27095	KCS PS-2 Hopper 2-pack (std O), *13*	130	____
27096	C&NW PS-2 Hopper 2-pack (std O), *13*	130	____
27099	North Pole Central PS-1 Boxcar "125025" (std O), *13*	70	____
27100	C&NW PS-2CD 4427 Hopper "450669" (std O), *04*	40	____
27101	Morton Salt PS-2CD 4427 Hopper "504" (std O), *04*	43	____
27102	Pillsbury PS-2CD 4427 Hopper "3980" (std O), *04*	42	____
27103	Soo Line PS-2CD 4427 Hopper "70207" (std O), *04*	49	____
27104	Wabash Cylindrical Hopper "33007" (std O), *03*	43	____
27105	PC Cylindrical Hopper "884312" (std O), *03*	42	____
27113	Govt. of Canada Cylindrical Hopper, *04–05*	60	____
27114	Canadian National Cylindrical Hopper, *04–05*	60	____
27115	D&H 3-bay ACF Hopper "3454" (std O), *05–06*	65	____
27116	NYC 3-bay ACF Hopper "886270" (std O), *05–06*	65	____
27117	DM&IR 3-bay ACF Hopper "5017" (std O), *05*	65	____
27118	WP 3-bay ACF Hopper "11774" (std O), *05–06*	65	____
27129	N&W 3-bay ACF Hopper "10717" (std O), *06*	70	____
27130	PRR 3-bay ACF Hopper "180658" (std O), *06*	70	____
27131	Conrail 3-bay ACF Hopper "473877" (std O), *06*	70	____
27132	UP 3-bay ACF Hopper "18137" (std O), *06*	70	____
27133	MILW PS-2CD Hopper "98606" (std O), *06*	70	____
27134	BNSF PS-2CD Hopper "414367" (std O), *06*	70	____
27135	N&W PS-2CD Hopper "71573" (std O), *06*	70	____
27142	CP Rail 3-bay Hopper, *06*	48	____
27146	CP Soo 3-bay Hopper, *06*	48	____
27165	C&O 3-bay Hopper "86912" (std O), *07*	70	____
27166	Pennsylvania Power & Light 3-bay Hopper "347" (std O), *07*	70	____
27167	Santa Fe 3-bay Hopper "178558" (std O), *07–08*	70	____
27168	C&NW 3-bay Hopper "135000" (std O), *07*	70	____

		Exc	Mint
27169	CN Cylindrical Hopper "370708" (std O), *06*		65
27172	IMC Canada Cylindrical Hopper "45726" (std O), *06*		65
27177	Union Starch Cylindrical Hopper 3-pack (std O), *08*		210
27186	PRR Cylindrical Hopper 3-pack (std O), *08*		210
27187	TH&B Cylindrical Hopper 3-pack (std O), *08*		210
27188	KCS 3-bay Covered Hopper 3-pack, *08*		225
27189	BNSF 3-bay Aluminum Covered Hopper 3-pack, *08*		225
27190	C&NW PS-2CD Covered Hopper 3-pack (std O), *08*		225
27191	RI PS-2CD Covered Hopper 3-pack, *08*		225
27192	NP PS-2CD Covered Hopper 3-pack (std O), *08*		225
27203	NYC DD Boxcar "75509" (std O), *05*		63
27204	Grand Trunk Western DD Boxcar "596377" (std O), *05*		63
27205	D&RGW DD Boxcar "63798" (std O), *05*		40
27206	UP PS 60' Boxcar "960342" (std O), *08*		75
27207	IC PS 60' Boxcar "44295" (std O), *08*		75
27208	ATSF PS 60' Boxcar "37287" (std O), *08*		75
27209	D&RGW PS 60' Boxcar "63835" (std O), *08*		75
27210	PRR PS-1 Boxcar "47009" (std O), *05*		60
27211	MKT PS-1 Boxcar "948" (std O), *05*		60
27212	Rutland PS-1 Boxcar "358" (std O), *05*		60
27213	N&W DD Boxcar, *05*		35
27214	Chessie System PS-1 Boxcar "23770" (std O), *06*		60
27215	Rock Island PS-1 Boxcar "57607" (std O), *06*		60
27216	Erie-Lack. PS-1 Boxcar "84433" (std O), *06*		60
27217	Frisco PS-1 Boxcar "17826" (std O), *06*		19
27218	Santa Fe DD Boxcar "9870" (std O), *06–07*		70
27219	GN DD Boxcar "35449" (std O), *06–07*		70
27220	L&N DD Boxcar "41237" (std O), *06–07*		70
27221	CB&Q DD Boxcar "48500" (std O), *06–07*		70
27224	CGW PS-1 Boxcar "5180" (std O), *06*		60
27225	WP PS-1 Boxcar "19528" (std O), *06*		60
27226	NH PS-1 Boxcar "32196" (std O), *06*		60
27227	UP PS-1 Boxcar "100306" (std O), *06*		60
27228	UP DD Boxcar "454400" (std O), *07*		70
27229	Nickel Plate Road DD Boxcar "87100" (std O), *08*		70
27230	LV DD Boxcar "8505" (std O), *08*		70
27231	GN USRA Double-sheathed Boxcar (std O), *07*		65
27232	UP USRA Double-sheathed Boxcar (std O), *07*		65
27233	Cotton Belt USRA Double-sheathed Boxcar (std O), *07*		65
27234	C&NW USRA Double-sheathed Boxcar (std O), *07*		65
27235	Railbox Boxcar "10011" (std O), *07*		55
27239	SP DD Boxcar "232852" with auto rack (std O), *08*		75
27240	Pere Marquette DD Boxcar with auto rack (std O), *08*		75
27241	C&O PS-1 Boxcar "18719," *08*		60
27242	LV PS-1 Boxcar "62080," *08*		60
27243	SP PS-1 Boxcar "128131," *08*		60
27244	GN PS-1 Boxcar "39404," *08*		60
27246	SP Double-sheathed Boxcar "133" (std O), *08*		70

Exc Mint

		Exc	Mint
27247	MP Double-sheathed Boxcar "45111" (std O), *08*		70____
27249	GN Express Boxcar "2500" (std O), *08*		65____
27250	CN Express Boxcar "11061" (std O), *08–09*		65____
27251	WP Express Boxcar "220116," *08–09*		65____
27254	Western Pacific UP Heritage Boxcar (std O), *09–11, 13*		85____
27259	PRR ACF Stock Car "128988" (std O), *10*		70____
27260	ATSF Tool Car "190021" (std O), *09–10*		80____
27261	D&RGW Double-sheathed Boxcar "3282," *09*		80____
27263	Polar Railroad PS-1 Boxcar, *09*		70____
27264	C&O Double-sheathed Boxcar "3502," *10*		80____
27265	Virginian PS-1 Boxcar "63300" (std O), *10*		70____
27266	PRR Express Boxcar "504141" (std O), *10*		70____
27267	SP UP Heritage 60' Boxcar "6991" (std O), *10*		85____
27270	B&O PS-1 Boxcar 2-pack (std O), *10–11*		140____
27273	Ann Arbor PS-1 Boxcar "1314" (std O), *11*		70____
27274	Polar Railroad Double-sheathed Boxcar "1201," *10*		70____
27275	SP Overnight PS-1 Boxcar "97938" (std O), *10*		70____
27276	NKP Double-sheathed Boxcar "10580" (std O), *10–11*		70____
27277	WP Scale PS-1 Boxcar "1925" (std O), *11*		70____
27278	Cryo-Trans Trans-Mechanical Reefer (std O), *10*		95____
27282	UP DD Boxcar "163100" (std O), *10*		70____
27283	Postwar Scale Boxcar 2-pack, *10*		140____
27286	Postwar Scale 6464 Boxcar 2-pack #2, *11–13*		140____
27287	LV Boxcar and Caboose Set (std O), *10–11*		160____
27289	Jersey Central Boxcar and Caboose Set (std O), *10–11*		160____
27291	PRR Double-sheathed Boxcar "539335" (std O), *10–11*		70____
27294	ATSF 57' Mechanical Reefer "3006" (std O), *10*		85____
27296	Cryo-Trans 57' Mechanical Reefer (std O), *11*		85____
27299	WM Steel-sided Reefer (std O), *11*		80____
27300	Western Dairy General American Milk Car (std O), *06*		65____
27305	GN Steel-sided Reefer "70290" (std O), *06*		65____
27306	Santa Fe Steel-sided Reefer "3494" (std O), *06*		42____
27307	Pepper Packing Steel-sided Reefer "2330" (std O), *06*		65____
27327	BNSF Mechanical Reefer "798870" (std O), *07*		70____
27328	SP Fruit Express Reefer "456465" (std O), *07–09*		70____
27329	UP Fruit Express Reefer "55962" (std O), *07*		70____
27330	Great Northern WFE Reefer "8873" (std O), *07–08*		70____
27331	Alderney Dairy General American Milk Car (std O), *07*		65____
27332	Freeport General American Milk Car (std O), *07*		65____
27345	Milwaukee Road 40' Steel-sided Reefer "5317" (std O), *12*		80____
27349	ADM Steel-sided Reefer "7019" (std O), *07*		65____
27350	National Car Steel-sided Reefer "2430" (std O), *07*		48____
27355	NYC Steel-sided Reefer "2570" (std O), *07–08*		65____
27358	Dubuque Steel-sided Reefer "63648" (std O), *07*		65____
27361	PFE Wood-sided Reefer "97680" (std O), *06*		65____

		Exc Mint
27364	Erie URTX Steel-sided Reefer (std O), *11*	80
27365	Sheffield Farms Milk Car 2-pack (std O), *08*	140
27368	CNJ 40' Steel-sided Reefer "1443" (std O), *12*	80
27369	Borden's Milk Car 2-pack (std O), *08*	140
27372	PFE Steel-sided Reefer 3-pack (std O), *08*	210
27373	MILW Reefer 3-pack (std O), *08–09*	225
27374	Alaska Reefer 3-pack (std O), *08–09*	225
27375	NP Reefer 3-pack (std O), *08–09*	225
27394	Detroit, Toledo & Ironton Steel-sided Reefer (std O), *09–10*	80
27395	Amtrak ExpressTrak Baggage Car, *10*	75
27396	C&NW UP Heritage Mechanical Reefer (std O), *10*	85
27409	ATSF Water Tank Car "100844" (std O), *09–10*	70
27410	30,000-gallon Ethanol Tank Car 3-pack, sound, *09*	270
27411	30,000-gallon Ethanol Tank Car 3-pack, *09*	210
27412	GATX TankTrain Car "53782" (std O), *10*	70
27418	PRR NS Heritage Unibody Tank Car (std O), *10*	70
27419	Pennsylvania Power & Light 3-bay Open Hopper, *08*	80
27421	MoPac UP Heritage Cylindrical Hopper (std O), *09–11*	80
27422	N&W 3-bay Open Hopper "1776" (std O), *09*	80
27424	Penn Central PS-2 Hopper "440774" (std O), *10–11*	80
27425	Saskatchewan Cylindrical Hopper "397015" (std O), *09*	80
27426	Stourbridge Lion Anthracite Coal Car 2-pack, *09–10*	130
27429	MKT UP Heritage PS2-CD Hopper (std O), *09*	80
27431	CSX B&O Quad Hopper, *11*	50
27432	UP 3-bay Open Hopper "78123" (std O), *10*	80
27433	Conrail NS Heritage Cylindrical Hopper (std O), *10–11*	80
27434	D&RGW UP Heritage PS2-CD Hopper (std O), *10*	80
27435	Polar Railroad Tank Car, *09*	70
27436	Alberta Cylindrical Hopper "396363" (std O), *10*	80
27438	Virginian NS Heritage 3-bay Open Hopper (std O), *10*	80
27439	NS Heritage Unibody Tank Car "14098" (std O), *10*	70
27440	BN Cylindrical Hopper "458456" (std O), *10*	80
27441	D&M PS-2 Hopper "6133" (std O), *11*	70
27445	N&W NS Heritage PS-2CD Hopper (std O), *10*	80
27446	Southern NS Heritage Cylindrical Hopper (std O), *10*	80
27448	PRR NS Heritage 3-Bay Open Hopper (std O), *11*	80
27449	UP Boy Scouts 100th Anniversary Cylindrical Hopper (std O), *11*	80
27450	NW NS Heritage 3-Bay Open Hopper (std O), *11*	80
27451	Conrail NS Heritage Unibody 1-D Tank Car (std O), *11*	70
27452	PRR NS Heritage PS-1 Boxcar "45540" (std O), *11*	70
27453	NS Heritage PS-1 Boxcar "67850" (std O), *11*	70
27454	CP Cylindrical Hopper (std O), *11*	80

Exc Mint

		Exc	Mint
27455	Amtrak 57' Mechanical Reefer (std O), *11*	85	
27456	Soo Line PS2 Covered Hopper "70702" (std O), *11*	70	
27457	NS 3-Bay Open Hopper "148028" (std O), *11*	80	
27458	UP Mechanical Reefer "457244" (std O), *11*	85	
27459	WP DD Boxcar "19404" (std O), *11*	70	
27460	M&StL Double-sheathed Boxcar "26002" (std O), *11*	70	
27461	UP ACF 4-Bay Covered Hopper "91341" (std O), *11*	85	
27462	Chessie ACF 4-Bay Covered Hopper "601878" (std O), *11*	85	
27463	PRR ACF 3-Bay Covered Hopper "259900" (std O), *11–12*	80	
27464	BNSF ACF 3-Bay Covered Hopper "453403" (std O), *11*	80	
27465	CSX 89' Auto Rack Car "604540" (std O), *12–13*	150	
27466	UP 89' Auto Rack Car (std O), *12–13*	150	
27467	ATSF 89' Auto Rack Car (std O), *12–13*	150	
27468	Grand Truck 89' Auto Rack Car (std O), *12–13*	150	
27469	Frisco Cylindrical Hopper "81021" (std O), *11*	80	
27470	MKT Scale 1-D Tank Car (std O), *11*	70	
27471	DT&I 3-Bay Hopper "2070" (std O), *11*	80	
27472	CP Scale 1-D Tank Car "9943" (std O), *11*	70	
27473	Conrail 89' Auto Rack Car "456249" (std O), *12*	150	
27474	SP Cylindrical Hopper "491020" (std O), *11*	80	
27475	Lionelville & Western Scale 1-D Tank Car "2747" (std O), *11*	80	
27476	U.S. Army Scale 1-D Tank Car (std O), *11*	70	
27477	D&RGW 3-Bay Hopper "14901" (std O), *11*	80	
27478	NYC 3-Bay Hopper "922158" (std O), *11*	80	
27479	BN Scale 3-Bay Open Hopper "516400" (std O), *12*	80	
27480	NKP Scale Offset Hopper "33060" (std O), *12*	70	
27481	W&LE Scale Offset Hopper "62240" (std O), *12*	70	
27482	CP Scale Offset Hopper "354000" (std O), *12*	70	
27483	SP Unibody 1-D Tank Car "67200" (std O), *12*	70	
27484	D&H Unibody 1-D Tank Car "59" (std O), *12*	70	
27485	KCS Unibody 1-D Tank Car "996" (std O), *12*	70	
27488	Clinchfield CSX Heritage 3-Bay Open Hopper (std O), *12*	80	
27489	Chessie System CSX Heritage 3-Bay Open Hopper (std O), *12*	80	
27490	ATSF 3-Bay Covered Hopper "314000" (std O), *12–13*	85	
27491	GN 3-Bay Covered Hopper "171400" (std O), *12*	85	
27492	CN 89' Auto Rack Car "710833" (std O), *12*	150	
27493	CN PS-4 Flatcar with piggyback trailers (std O), *12*	98	
27494	CN PS-4 Flatcar with piggyback trailers (std O), *12*	98	
27495	CN PS-4 Flatcar with piggyback trailers (std O), *12*	98	
27496	Polar PS-2 Covered Hopper "1245" (std O), *12, 14*	70	
27497	UP Offset Hopper "74556" (std O), *12*	80	

		Exc	Mint
27498	DM&I 8000-gallon 1-D Tank Car "S19" (std O), *12*		70
____**27499**	Monon Scale PS-1 Boxcar "916" (std O), *12*		70
____**27510**	WP PS-4 Flatcar "2001" (std O), *05–06*		53
____**27511**	P&LE PS-4 Flatcar "1154" (std O), *05–06*		35
____**27512**	Reading PS-4 Flatcar "9314" (std O), *05*		53
____**27513**	UP 40' Flatcar "51219" (std O), *06*		55
____**27514**	CP 40' Flatcar "307401" (std O), *06*		55
____**27515**	Pennsylvania 40' Flatcar "473567" (std O), *06*		55
____**27516**	N&W 40' Flatcar "32900" (std O), *06*		55
____**27517**	NP PS-4 Flatcar "62829" with trailers (std O), *06*		85
27518	C&NW PS-4 Flatcar "44503" with trailers (std O), *06*		85
____**27519**	UP PS-4 Flatcar "53007" with trailers (std O), *06*		85
____**27520**	Coe Rail Husky Stack Car "5540" (std O), *06*		85
____**27521**	Santa Fe Husky Stack Car "254220" (std O), *06*		85
____**27535**	UP PS-4 Flatcar "53008" with trailers (std O), *07*		65
____**27536**	UP PS-4 Flatcar "53009" with trailers (std O), *08*		65
____**27537**	UP Flatcar with wood load, *06*		39
____**27541**	NYC 40' Flatcar "496299" with load (std O), *07*		63
____**27542**	NH 40' Flatcar "17808" with load (std O), *07–08*		70
27543	ATSF 40' Flatcar "191549" with load (std O), *07–08*		70
____**27544**	GT 40' Flatcar "64301" with load (std O), *07–08*		70
27545	REA PS-4 Flatcar "81003" with trailers (std O), *07–08*		85
____**27546**	Greenbrier Husky Stack Car "1993" (std O), *07*		85
____**27552**	Arizona & California Husky Stack Car (std O), *07*		85
27562	NYC PS-4 Flatcar "506075" with trailers (std O), *07–08*		85
27563	Lackawanna PS-4 Flatcar "16540" with trailers (std O), *07*		85
27564	Milwaukee Road PS-4 Flatcar with trailers "64074" (std O), *07–08*		85
____**27583**	UP 40' Flatcar "59292" with load (std O), *08*		70
____**27584**	Reading Flatcar with covered load (std O), *08–09*		70
27585	B&M 40' Flatcar "33773" with stakes (std O), *08–09*		65
____**27586**	Cass Scenic Skeleton Log Car 3-pack, *07*		170
____**27587**	Birch Valley Lumber Skeleton Log Car 3-pack, *07*		170
____**27594**	Wabash PS-4 Flatcar with stakes (std O), *08–09*		65
____**27600**	RI Bay Window Caboose "17070" (std O), *07*		90
27601	MILW Extended Vision Caboose "992300" (std O), *07*		90
27603	MP UP Heritage Ca-4 Caboose "2891" (std O), *08*		95
27604	UP Caboose "3881" (std O), *08*		90
27605	Pere Marquette Northeastern Caboose "A986" (std O), *08*		90
____**27606**	LL Northeastern Caboose "4679" (std O), *08*		90
____**27607**	Monongahela NS Heritage Caboose (std O), *12*		95
____**27608**	WM Caboose "1863" (std O), *08*		85
____**27609**	B&O Caboose "C-2445" (std O), *07*		90
____**27612**	WP Bay Window Caboose "446" (std O), *08*		90
____**27615**	NYC Bay Window Caboose "20383" (std O), *07*		90
____**27617**	D&H Bay Window Caboose "35725" (std O), *08*		90

		Exc	Mint
27618	MKT UP Heritage Ca-4 Caboose "8891" (std O), *08*		95____
27619	WP UP Heritage Ca-4 Caboose "3891" (std O), *08*		95____
27623	N&W Northeastern Caboose "500837" (std O), *09*		90____
27624	D&RGW UP Heritage CA-4 Caboose (std O), *09*		95____
27625	C&NW UP Heritage CA-4 Caboose (std O), *09*		95____
27626	SP UP Heritage CA-4 Caboose (std O), *09*		95____
27628	Wabash Northeastern Caboose "02222" (std O), *09–10*		90____
27629	C&O Northeastern Caboose (std O), *10*		90____
27630	Virginian NS Heritage CA-4 Caboose (std O), *10*		95____
27631	NS Heritage CA-4 Caboose (std O), *10*		95____
27633	UP CA-3 Caboose (std O), *10*		95____
27634	ATSF Extended Vision Caboose (std O), *10*		85____
27635	B&O I-12 Caboose (std O), *10*		85____
27636	NKP Northeastern Caboose (std O), *10–11*		85____
27638	Southern NS Heritage CA-4 Caboose (std O), *10–11*		95____
27639	N&W NS Heritage CA-4 Caboose (std O), *10*		95____
27640	Clinchfield Northeastern CA-3 Caboose, *10–11*		90____
27642	Virginian Scale Caboose with smoke, *10–13*		90____
27645	UP Boy Scouts 100th Anniversary Ca-3 Caboose (std O), *11*		95____
27648	PRR NS Heritage Ca-3 Caboose (std O), *11*		95____
27649	Baldwin Locomotive Works I-12 Caboose "6000" (std O), *12–13*		85____
27650	CSX Heritage Scale Bay Window Caboose "2510" (std O), *12*		90____
27651	B&O CSX Heritage I-12 Caboose (std O), *11*		90____
27652	CSX Heritage Chessie System Scale Caboose (std O), *12*		90____
27653	Family Lines CSX Heritage Ca-4 Caboose (std O), *11*		90____
27654	CSX/Clinchfield Scale Bay-Window Caboose (std O), *12*		90____
27655	WM CSX Heritage Extended Vision Caboose (std O), *11*		90____
27658	Pennsylvania Power & Light Work Caboose (std O), *11*		80____
27659	Bethlehem Steel Work Caboose (std O), *11*		80____
27660	UP George Bush Extended Vision Caboose (std O), *11*		90____
27661	KCS Extended Vision Caboose (std O), *11*		90____
27662	GTW Northeastern Caboose (std O), *11*		90____
27663	IC Extended Vision Caboose (std O), *11*		90____
27664	Lionel & Western Northeastern Caboose (std O), *11–12*		90____
27665	BN Bicentennial Extended Vision Caboose (std O), *11*		90____
27666	NH Scale Northeastern Caboose "C-666" (std O), *12*		90____
27667	UP Scale Ca-4 Caboose "3857" (std O), *12–13*		95____
27668	UP Scale Ca-3 Caboose "3779" (std O), *12–13*		95____
27669	PC Scale Northeastern Caboose "18420" with smoke (std O), *12–13*		90____

		Exc	Mint
27670	CP Scale Northeastern Caboose "400501" (std O), *12–13*		90
27671	West Side Lumber Scale Work Caboose "8" (std O), *12*		80
27672	Weyerhaeuser Timber Scale Work Caboose "12" (std O), *12–13*		80
27673	NYC Scale Northeastern Caboose "20090" (std O), *12*		90
27674	Elk River Lumber Work Caboose "6" (std O), *12, 14*		80
27676	CN Wood-Sided Caboose (std O), *12*		90
27677	UP Work Caboose "907306" (std O), *12*		80
27678	ATSF Wood-Sided Caboose "1790" (std O), *12*		85
27679	NP Wood-Sided Caboose "1282" (std O), *12*		85
27680	GN Wood-Sided Caboose "X499" (std O), *12*		85
27681	Southern NS Heritage Caboose (std O), *12*		95
27682	Conrail NS Heritage Caboose (std O), *12*		95
27683	Erie NS Heritage Caboose (std O), *12, 14–15*		95
27684	Illinois Terminal NS Heritage Caboose (std O), *12, 14–15*		95
27685	Central of Georgia NS Heritage Caboose (std O), *12*		95
27686	LV NS Heritage Caboose (std O), *12*		95
27687	Reading NS Heritage Caboose (std O), *13–15*		95
27688	NYC NS Heritage Caboose (std O), *13*		95
27689	Wabash NS Heritage Caboose (std O), *13–15*		95
27690	Virginian NS Heritage Caboose (std O), *13*		95
27691	PRR NS Heritage Caboose (std O), *12*		95
27692	N&W NS Heritage Caboose (std O), *12*		95
27693	CNJ NS Heritage Caboose (std O), *13–14*		95
27694	NS Heritage Caboose (std O), *12*		95
27695	DL&W NS Heritage Caboose (std O), *13–15*		95
27696	Savannah & Atlanta NS Heritage Caboose (std O), *13–15*		95
27697	Nickel Plate Road NS Heritage Caboose (std O), *12*		95
27698	Interstate NS Heritage Caboose (std O), *12*		95
27699	PC NS Heritage Caboose (std O), *13*		95
27702	Maersk Husky Stack Car 2-pack (std O), *09*		225
27705	ATSF Wedge Plow Flatcar "191369" (std O), *09*		90
27706	ATSF Idler Flatcar "191852" with load (std O), *09*		75
27707	UP Husky Stack Car 2-pack (std O), *09–10*		225
27710	No. 6464 Variation Boxcar 2-pack #2, *09*		110
27767	Santa Fe Passenger 4-pack, *11–12*		240
27771	Postwar "6572" REA Reefer, *11–13*		60
27772	Santa Fe Baggage Car and Diner 2-pack, *11–12*		120
27775	Postwar "2414" Santa Fe Blue-stripe Coach, *11–13*		60
27776	No. 6464 Variation Boxcar 2-pack #3, *11*		105
27779	Postwar Archive UP Caboose "8561," *11–12*		48
27791	Archive 6464-50 M&StL Boxcar, *12*		55
27792	Archive Pastel Freight Car 3-pack, *12*		170
27800	B&M Gondola with coke containers, *09–11*		80
27816	D&RGW Flatcar "22177" with pipes, *09–10*		80
27820	Wabash PS-4 Flatcar with piggyback trailers (std O), *09–10*		98

27824	MILW 40' Flatcar with metal pipes (std O), *10*	80____
27825	West Side Lumber Skeleton Log Car, *11*	70____
27826	CP Skeleton Log Car 2-pack (std O), *10*	133____
27827	UP Bathtub Gondola "28081" (std O), *10*	65____
27828	CN Bathtub Gondola "193140" (std O), *10*	65____
27829	WM Skeleton Log Car 2-pack, *10*	133____
27834	Pere Marquette PS-5 Gondola "18400," *11*	70____
27835	P. Bunyan Lumber Skeleton Log Car, *11–12*	70____
27836	Elk River Lumber Skeleton Log Car "11203" (std O), *11*	70____
27837	B&M PS-4 Flatcar with bulkheads (std O), *10–11*	80____
27838	PRR PS-4 Flatcar with bulkheads (std O), *10*	80____
27840	Polar Railroad PS-4 Flatcar with trailers, *10*	98____
27841	CSX Bathtub Gondola 2-pack (std O), *11*	130____
27842	UP Scale Flatcar with bulkheads "15775" (std O), *11*	70____
27843	WP Scale PS-5 Gondola "6774" (std O), *11*	70____
27844	BNSF Bathtub Gondola 3-pack (std O), *10*	200____
27848	Virginian NS Heritage 60' Boxcar (std O), *11*	85____
27849	Southern NS Heritage 60' Boxcar (std O), *11*	85____
27850	CSX 60' Boxcar "196911" (std O), *11*	85____
27851	BNSF Bathtub Gondola 2-pack, *11*	130____
27854	B&O Double-sheathed Boxcar "196500" (std O), *11*	70____
27855	NYC 60' DD Boxcar "53423" (std O), *11*	85____
27856	KCS PS-1 Boxcar "18741" (std O), *11*	70____
27857	PRR DD Boxcar "81919" (std O), *11, 14*	75____
27858	MP DD Boxcar "90103" (std O), *11*	70____
27860	Sugar Creek Lumber Skeleton Log Car "1749" (std O), *11*	70____
27863	Merrill & Ring Lumber Skeleton Log Car, *11–12*	70____
27868	NS Bathtub Gondola 2-pack (std O), *11*	130____
27871	NS 60' Boxcar "499646" (std O), *11*	85____
27872	Polar Hot Cocoa Milk Car, *11, 13*	70____
27873	Polar Reindeer Stock Car, *11, 13*	70____
27874	Grove's Mortuary Double-sheathed Boxcar (std O), *11*	70____
27875	NYC DD Boxcar "45395" (std O), *11*	70____
27876	State of Maine PS-1 Boxcar "5141" (std O), *11*	70____
27877	NH DD Boxcar "40510" (std O), *11*	70____
27882	Southern ACF 40-ton Stock Car "45655" (std O), *11*	70____
27883	T&P ACF 40-ton Stock Car "24042" (std O), *11*	70____
27884	RI ACF 40-ton Stock Car "77601" (std O), *11*	70____
27885	ATSF ACF 40-ton Stock Car "60390" (std O), *11*	70____
27886	GN PS-1 Boxcar "11310" (std O), *11*	70____
27887	D&RGW PS-5 Gondola "56316" with covers (std O), *11*	65____
27888	LIRR 40' Flatcar with wheels (std O), *11*	70____
27889	Erie 40' Flatcar "6361" with wheels (std O), *11*	70____
27890	L&N 40' Flatcar "22269" with wheels (std O), *11*	70____
27891	NKP Heritage PS-4 Flatcar with trailers (std O), *11*	98____
27892	Conrail PS-5 Gondola "612690" with covers (std O), *11*	65____
27893	GTW PS-1 Boxcar "516650" (std O), *11*	70____

		Exc	Mint
____ 27894	C&O PS-5 Gondola "362600" with covers (std O), *11*		65
____ 27895	ATSF PS-4 Bulkhead Flatcar "90085" (std O), *11*		80
____ 27896	CP 40' Flatcar with pipe load (std O), *11*		80
____ 27899	UP Scale PS-1 Boxcar "196889" (std O), *12*		70
____ 27903	Sager Place Observation Car, *09*		65
____ 27912	Postwar "2445" Elizabeth Coach, *08*		60
27917	Postwar "2550" Baggage-Mail Rail Diesel Car, nonpowered, *13–14*		70
27928	UP Boy Scouts 100th Anniversary PS-1 Boxcar (std O), *11*		70
27929	Postwar Nos. 2484/2485 UP Passenger Car 2-pack, *12–13*		120
____ 27935	Postwar "6820" Aerial Missile Transport Car, *13*		60
____ 27941	Postwar "3854" Merchandise Car, *12*		75
27946	Postwar "6050-25" Christmas Savings Boxcar, *13–14*		55
____ 27947	Postwar "6473-25" Reindeer Transport Car, *13*		60
27948	Postwar "6464-25" Great Northern Christmas Boxcar, *13*		60
27949	Postwar "3854-25" PRR Christmas Merchandise Car, *13–14*		75
____ 27953	Reading PS-2 Hopper 2-pack (std O), *13–14*		140
____ 27962	L&N PS-2 Hopper 2-pack (std O), *13–14*		140
____ 27965	P&WV Offset Hopper 3-pack (std O), *13–15*		210
____ 27969	N&W Offset Hopper 3-pack (std O), *13–15*		210
____ 27973	C&O Offset Hopper 3-pack (std O), *13–15*		210
____ 27977	GN Offset Hopper 3-pack (std O), *13–15*		210
____ 27981	PRR USRA Double-sheathed Boxcar (std O), *13*		70
____ 27982	SP USRA Double-sheathed Boxcar (std O), *13–14*		80
____ 27983	UP USRA Double-sheathed Boxcar (std O), *13–14*		70
27984	Procor 30,000-gallon 1-D Tank Car 3-pack (std O), *13*		240
27988	UTLX 30,000-gallon 1-D Tank Car 3-pack (std O), *13*		240
27992	ADM 30,000-gallon 1-D Tank Car 3-pack (std O), *13*		240
27996	ACFX 30,000-gallon 1-D Tank Car 3-pack (std O), *13*		240
____ 28000	C&NW 4-6-4 Hudson Locomotive "3005," *99*		205
28004	B&O 4-4-2 E6 Atlantic Locomotive, traditional, *99–00*		410
28005	PRR 4-4-2 E6 Atlantic Locomotive, traditional, *99–00*		345
28006	ATSF 4-4-2 E6 Atlantic Locomotive, traditional, *99–00*		285
____ 28007	NYC 4-6-4 Hudson Locomotive "5406," *99*		380
____ 28008	C&O 4-6-4 Hudson Locomotive "306," *99*		345
____ 28009	Santa Fe 4-6-4 Hudson Locomotive "3463," *99*		330
____ 28011	C&O 2-6-6-6 Allegheny Locomotive "1601," *99*		1800
28012	4-6-4 Commodore Vanderbilt Locomotive, red, *00 u*		1700
____ 28013	NH 4-6-2 Pacific Locomotive "1335," *99*		325
____ 28014	NYC 4-6-2 Pacific Locomotive "4930," *99*		305
28015	Santa Fe Pacific 4-6-2 Pacific Locomotive "3449," *99*		340
____ 28016	Southern 4-6-2 Pacific Locomotive "1407," *99*		345

		Exc	Mint
28017	Case Cutlery 4-6-2 Pacific Locomotive, *99 u*	313	___
28018	Reading 4-6-0 Camelback Locomotive "571," CC, *01*	495	___
28020	Lionel Lines 4-6-2 Pacific Locomotive "3344," *99*	250	___
28022	West Side Lumber Shay Locomotive "800," *99*	810	___
28023	PRR K4 4-6-2 Pacific Locomotive "3755," CC, *99*	375	___
28024	4-6-4 Commodore Vanderbilt Locomotive, blue, *00 u*	1663	___
28025	PRR K4 4-6-2 Pacific Locomotive, traditional, *99*	330	___
28026	LL 4-6-2 Pacific Locomotive, CC, *99*	325	___
28027	NYC 4-6-4 Hudson Locomotive "5413," *00*	590	___
28028	Virginian 2-6-6-6 Allegheny Locomotive "1601," *99*	1318	___
28029	UP 4-8-8-4 Big Boy Locomotive "4006," *99–00*	1500	___
28030	NYC 4-6-4 Hudson Locomotive "5450," gray, CC, *00*	315	___
28032	B&O 4-6-2 Pacific Locomotive, CC, *00*	315	___
28033	B&O 4-6-2 Pacific Locomotive, traditional, *00*	195	___
28034	UP 4-6-2 Pacific Locomotive, CC, *00*	310	___
28035	UP 4-6-2 Pacific Locomotive, traditional, *00*	210	___
28036	SP 2-8-0 Consolidation Locomotive "2685," CC, *00–01*	270	___
28037	SP 2-8-0 Consolidation Locomotive "2686," traditional, *00–01*	295	___
28038	UP 2-8-0 Consolidation Locomotive "324," CC, *00–01*	315	___
28039	UP 2-8-0 Consolidation Locomotive "326," traditional, *00–01*	240	___
28051	B&O 2-8-8-4 EM-1 Articulated Locomotive "7617," *00*	970	___
28052	N&W 2-6-6-4 Class A Locomotive "1218," *00*	870	___
28055	GN 4-6-4 Hudson Locomotive "1725," traditional, *00–01*	170	___
28057	Southern 4-8-2 Mountain Locomotive "1491," CC, *00*	690	___
28058	NH 4-8-2 Mountain Locomotive "3310," CC, *00*	670	___
28059	WP 4-8-2 Mountain Locomotive "179," CC, *00*	630	___
28062	LL Gold-plated 700E J-1E 4-6-4 Hudson Locomotive, display case, *00*	1050	___
28063	PRR T-1 4-4-4-4 Duplex Locomotive "5511," CC, *00*	910	___
28064	UP Challenger Coal Tender "3985," CC, *00 u*	1350	1800 ___
28065	NYC Hudson 4-6-4 Locomotive "5412," RailSounds, *00*	290	___
28066	B&O President Polk 4-6-2 Locomotive, CC, *01*	750	___
28067	Erie 4-6-2 Locomotive "2934," CC, *01*	570	___
28068	D&RGW 4-6-4 Hudson Locomotive, traditional, *01 u*	300	___
28070	SP Daylight 4-4-2 Atlantic Locomotive "3000," CC, *01*	425	___
28071	NP 4-4-2 Atlantic Locomotive "604," CC, *01*	415	___
28072	NYC 4-6-4 Hudson J3a Locomotive "5444," CC, *01*	790	___
28074	NP 2-8-4 Berkshire Locomotive "759," CC, *01*	640	___
28075	C&O 2-6-6-2 Locomotive "1521," CC, *01*	930	___
28076	NKP 2-6-6-2 Locomotive "921," CC, *01*	960	___

		Exc	Mint
28077	UP 4-6-6-4 Challenger Locomotive "3983," CC, *01*		680
28078	PRR 2-10-4 J1a Locomotive "6496," CC, *01*		880
28079	C&O 2-10-4 Class T Locomotive "3004," CC, *01*		882
28080	NYC 0-8-0 Locomotive "7745," CC, *01–02*		540
28081	C&O 0-8-0 Locomotive "75," CC, *01–02*		520
28084	NYC Dreyfuss Hudson 4-6-4 Locomotive "5452," CC, *01–02*		790
28085	N&W 2-8-8-2 Y6b Class Locomotive "2200," CC, *03*		1207
28086	PRR H9 Consolidation Locomotive "1111," CC, *01*		480
28087	UP Auxiliary Tender, yellow, CC, *01*		210
28088	N&W Auxiliary Water Tender, CC, *01–02*		200
28089	PRR 4-4-4-4 T-1 Duplex Locomotive "5511," 2-rail, *00*		1150
28090	UP Challenger Oil Tender "3977," 2-rail, *00 u*		1800
28098	NYC 4-6-0 10-wheel Locomotive "1916," CC, *01–02*		520
28099	UP Challenger Oil Tender "3977," CC, *00 u*		1700
28200	D&H U30C Diesel "702," CC (SSS), *02*		375
28201	UP SD90MAC Diesel "8049," *03*		345
28202	Conrail SD80MAC Diesel "7203," *03*		325
28203	CSX SD80MAC Diesel "803," *03*		325
28204	NS SD80MAC Diesel "7201," *03*		345
28205	Chessie System SD9 Diesel "1833," CC, *03*		230
28207	Erie-Lackawanna U33C Diesel "3304," CC, *02*		355
28208	BN U33C Diesel "5734," CC, *02*		355
28211	CP SD90MAC Diesel "9107," *03*		300
28213	Amtrak GE Dash 8 Diesel "516," CC, *02*		300
28214	BNSF GE Dash 8 Diesel "582," CC, *02*		325
28215	B&O GP30 Diesel "6939," CC, *02*		315
28216	Reading GP30 Diesel "5518," CC, *02*		315
28217	Rio Grande GP30 Diesel "3013," CC, *02*		315
28218	Lehigh Valley Alco C420 Switcher "407," CC, *04*		325
28219	Seaboard Alco C420 Switcher "136," CC, *04*		300
28222	Santa Fe Dash 9 Diesel "605" CC, *05*		250
28223	BNSF SD70MAC Diesel "9433," CC, *05*		250
28224	Jersey Central SD40-2 Diesel "3067," CC, *04*		350
28225	SPSF SD40T-2 Diesel "8521," CC, *04–05*		430
28226	NS SD80MAC Diesel "7204," CC, *04–05*		430
28227	UP SD70MAC Diesel "4979," CC, *04*		375
28228	C&NW Dash 9-44CW Diesel "8669," CC, *03*		350
28229	SP Dash 9-44CW Diesel "8132," CC, *03*		350
28230	Amtrak Dash 8 Diesel "505," CC, *04*		295
28235	Great Northern U33C Diesel "2543," CC, *05*		455
28237	Reading U30C Diesel "6301," CC, *05*		455
28239	Union Pacific SD70 Diesel, TMCC, *04*		360
28241	C&NW U30C Diesel "935," CC, *06*		455
28242	SP U33C Diesel "8773," CC, *06*		475
28243	LIRR Alco C420 Hi-nose Switcher "206," CC, *06*		420
28244	N&W Alco C420 Hi-nose Switcher "417," CC, *06–07*		420
28245	Chessie System SD40T-2 Diesel "7617," RailSounds, *06*		265

		Exc	Mint
28246	Chessie System SD40T-2 Diesel "7618," nonpowered (std O), 06		160___
28247	Rio Grande SD40T-2 Diesel "5348," RailSounds, 06		265___
28248	Rio Grande SD40T-2 Diesel "5349," nonpowered (std O), 06		160___
28250	N&W Alco C420 Hi-nose Switcher "416," nonpowered (std O), 06–07		160___
28251	LIRR Alco C420 Hi-nose Switcher "206," nonpowered (std O), 06		160___
28252	SP U33C Diesel "8774," nonpowered (std O), 06		160___
28253	C&NW U30C Diesel "936," nonpowered (std O), 06		160___
28255	UP SD40T-2 Diesel "4551," traditional, CC, 07–08		265___
28256	UP SD40T-2 Diesel "4596," nonpowered (std O), 07		170___
28257	NS SD40-2 Diesel "3340," CC, 06		430___
28258	NS SD40-2 Diesel "3341," nonpowered (std O), 06		170___
28259	CN SD40-2 Diesel "5383," CC, 06		430___
28260	CN SD40-2 Diesel "5384," nonpowered (std O), 06		170___
28261	UP (MP) SD70ACe Diesel "1982," CC, 07		450___
28262	UP (WP) SD70ACe Diesel "1983," CC, 07		450___
28263	UP (MKT) SD70ACe Diesel "1988," CC, 07		450___
28264	UP "Building America" SD70ACe Diesel "8348," CC, 07		450___
28265	MILW U30C Diesel "5657," CC, 07		455___
28266	MILW U30C Diesel "5657," nonpowered (std O), 07–08		170___
28267	Conrail U30C Diesel "6837," CC, 07		455___
28268	Conrail U30C Diesel "6838," nonpowered (std O), 07–08		170___
28269	ATSF Dash 8-40BW Diesel "562," CC, 08		500___
28270	ATSF Dash 8-40CW Diesel "563," nonpowered, 08		220___
28272	"I Love USA" SD60 Diesel "1776," traditional, 06		250___
28279	UP SD70ACe Diesel "1989," CC, 07		450___
28280	UP (C&NW) SD70ACe Diesel "1995," CC, 07		450___
28281	UP (SP) SD70ACe Diesel "1996," CC, 07		450___
28283	UP "Building America" SD70AC3 Diesel, nonpowered (std O), 07		170___
28284	Ferromex SD70ACe Diesel "4011," CC, 08		495___
28287	KCS SD70ACe Diesel "4050," CC, 08		495___
28292	Chessie System U30C Diesel "3312," CC, 02		300___
28293	Santa Fe U28CG Diesel "354," CC, 02		375___
28295	Conrail LionMaster SD80MAC Diesel, nonpowered, 08		200___
28296	UP AC6000 Diesel "7526," CC, 08		660___
28297	SP GP9 Diesel "446," CC, 10		390___
28298	CSX AC6000 Diesel "608," CC, 08		660___
28299	CSX AC6000 Diesel "609," nonpowered, 08		220___
28300	NS Dash 9 Diesel "9607," nonpowered, 08		220___
28302	BNSF SD70ACe Diesel "9380," CC, 08		495___
28305	CSX AC6000 Diesel "610," nonpowered, RailSounds, 08		430___

		Exc Mint
	28306	GE ES44AC Evolution Hybrid Diesel "2010," CC, 09–10
		1000
_____	28307	Wabash Train Master Diesel "550," CC, 09–10	495
_____	28311	UP DD35A Diesel, CC, 11	600
_____	28312	BN SD60 Diesel "8301," CC, 09	800
_____	28314	UP 3GS21B Genset Switcher "2701," CC, 10	675
	28316	PRR NS Heritage SD70ACe Diesel "1854," CC, 10
_____		500
	28318	Conrail NS Heritage SD70ACe Diesel "1209," CC, 10
_____		500
_____	28320	CP Evolution Hybrid Diesel, 10	875
_____	28323	NS Genset Switcher, CC, 11	800
_____	28327	UP AC6000 Diesel "7050," CC, 10	700
_____	28328	UPAC6000 Diesel "7055," nonpowered, CC, 10	350
_____	28330	UP SD70ACe Diesel "8444," CC, 10	500
_____	28331	CSX AC6000 Diesel "618," CC, 10	700
_____	28333	Virginian NS Heritage SD70ACe Diesel, CC, 10	500
_____	28334	NS Heritage SD70ACe Diesel "1982," CC, 10	500
_____	28338	PRR NS Heritage SD70ACe Diesel, CC, 11	500
_____	28339	ATSF AC6000 Diesel "9876," CC, 10	550
_____	28340	WP GP7 Diesel "705," CC, 10	450
_____	28343	Amtrak Dash 9 Diesel "519," CC, 10	500
_____	28344	Southern NS Heritage SD70ACe Diesel, CC, 10	500
_____	28345	N&W NS Heritage SD70ACe Diesel "247," CC, 10	500
	28347	UP Boy Scouts 100th Anniversary ES44AC Diesel, CC, 11
_____		875
_____	28350	BNSF ES44AC Diesel, CC, 11	850
_____	28351	KCS ES44AC Diesel "4655," CC, 11	850
_____	28353	Erie GP7 Diesel, CC, 11	450
_____	28354	CSX Genset Switcher "1303," CC, 11	800
_____	28355	BNSF Genset Switcher "1249," CC, 11	800
_____	28356	CSX SD60 Diesel, CC, 11	500
_____	28357	CSX SD60 Diesel, CC, 11	500
_____	28358	Soo Line SD60 Diesel, CC, 11	500
_____	28359	Soo Line SD60 Diesel, CC, 11	500
_____	28360	WP GP7 Diesel "707," CC, 11	450
_____	28361	WM GP7 Diesel "21," CC, 11	450
_____	28362	WM GP7 Diesel "23," CC, 11	450
_____	28363	BN SD60 Diesel "8302," CC, 11	500
_____	28364	BNSF Dash-9 Diesel "4081," CC, 11	500
_____	28365	BNSF Dash-9 Diesel "5121," CC, 11	500
_____	28366	CN Dash-9 Diesel "2643," CC, 11	500
_____	28367	CN Dash-9 Diesel "2692," CC, 11	500
_____	28368	Amtrak Dash-9 Diesel, CC, 11	500
_____	28369	NYC DD35A Diesel "9950," CC, 11	600
_____	28370	UP DD35 Diesel "84," CC, 12	600
_____	28371	UP DD35A Diesel "72," CC, 11	600
_____	28372	NYC DD35A Diesel "9955," CC, 11	600
_____	28373	C&NW UP Heritage SD70ACe Diesel, CC, 11	500
_____	28374	SP UP Heritage SD70ACe Diesel, CC, 11	500
_____	28375	Katy UP Heritage SD70ACe Diesel, CC, 11	500
_____	28376	MoPac UP Heritage SD70ACe Diesel, CC, 11	500
_____	28377	Rio Grande UP Heritage SD70ACe Diesel, CC, 11	500
_____	28378	WP UP Heritage SD70ACe Diesel, CC, 11	500
_____	28380	NYC DD35A Diesel, nonpowered, 11	440

		Exc Mint
28381	ATSF GP30 Diesel, CC, *11*	500____
28382	U.S. Army Genset Switcher, CC, *11*	800____
28383	Conrail Genset Switcher, CC, *11*	800____
28384	CN Genset Switcher "7990," CC, *11–12*	800____
28385	ATSF GP30 Diesel "1214," CC, *11*	500____
28386	ATSF GP30 Diesel "2710," *11*	380____
28387	ATSF GP30 Diesel "2715," nonpowered, *11*	240____
28388	ICG GP30 Diesel "2268," CC, *11*	500____
28389	ICG GP30 Diesel "2271," CC, *11*	500____
28390	UP DD35 Diesel "79," nonpowered, *12*	440____
28394	ICG GP30 Diesel "2277," *11*	380____
28395	ICG GP30 Diesel "2279," nonpowered, *11*	240____
28396	UP ES44AC Diesel "7454," CC, *11*	850____
28397	UP ES44AC Diesel "7459," CC, *11*	850____
28398	BNSF ES44AC Diesel "6436," CC, *11*	850____
28399	KCS ES44AC Diesel "4682," CC, *11*	850____
28400	Amtrak Rail Bonder, *05*	65____
28403	Pennsylvania Ballast Tamper, traditional, *05–06*	105____
28404	Maintenance Car, *05*	105____
28405	Picatinny Arsenal Switcher, CC, *05*	290____
28406	CSX Rail Bonder "92794," traditional, *05*	65____
28407	UP Speeder, *05*	65____
28408	CNJ Speeder "MW840," traditional, *06*	70____
28409	Conrail Rail Bonder "X409," traditional, *06*	70____
28411	U.S. Army Missile Launcher Locomotive, *06–07*	300____
28412	Santa's Speeder, *06*	70____
28413	Milwaukee Road Snowplow "X903," traditional, *06*	210____
28414	Lionel Lines Burro Crane, traditional, *06*	160____
28415	Third Avenue Trolley "1651," traditional, *06*	70____
28416	Hobo Handcar, traditional, *06*	70____
28417	Christmas Rotary Snowplow, *06*	180____
28418	Christmas Trolley, *06*	70____
28419	Lionel Lines Speeder, *07–08*	70____
28420	D&RGW Handcar, *07–08*	70____
28421	Fort Collins Trolley, *07*	73____
28422	PRR Burro Crane, *07–08*	160____
28423	Alaska Rotary Snowplow, *06–07*	220____
28424	Postwar "51" Navy Switcher, *07*	210____
28425	Polar Express Elf Handcar, *06–17*	100____
28427	Christmas Snowplow, *08–10*	210____
28428	Halloween Handcar, *07*	70____
28430	Wellspring Capital Management Trolley, *06*	85____
28432	Bethlehem Steel Switcher, traditional, *07*	210____
28434	Christmas Trolley, *07*	70____
28438	Portland Birney Trolley, *08–09*	65____
28440	PRR Inspection Vehicle, *08–09*	170____
28441	Transylvania Trolley, *08*	75____
28442	Postwar "50" Gang Car, *08*	120____
28444	NH Handcar, *08–09*	75____
28445	AEC Burro Crane Car	100____
28446	Silver Bell Trolley, *09*	90____
28447	4850TM Factory Trackmobile, CC, *10*	300____
28448	CSX 4850TM Trackmobile, CC, *10*	300____
28449	UP 4850TM Trackmobile, CC, *10*	300____

			Exc Mint
____	28450	CP Rail Trackmobile, CC, *11*	300
____	28451	Christmas Track Cleaning Car, *10–13*	150
____	28452	MOW Early Era Inspection Vehicle, *10*	130
____	28453	PRR Early Era Inspection Vehicle, *10*	130
____	28454	CP Early Era Inspection Vehicle, *10*	130
____	28455	NYC Trackmobile, CC, *11–13*	300
____	28456	Coca-Cola Trolley, *10*	90
____	28457	B&M Rotary Snowplow "8457," *11*	250
____	28466	U.S. Army Trackmobile, CC, *11*	300
____	28467	PRR Trackmobile, CC, *11*	300
____	28468	Amtrak Trackmobile, CC, *11*	300
____	28469	BNSF Trackmobile, CC, *11*	300
____	28470	NYC Early Era Inspection Vehicle, *11*	130
____	28471	ATSF Early Era Inspection Vehicle, CC, *11*	130
____	28472	Southern Early Era Inspection Vehicle, *11*	130
____	28473	GN Early Era Inspection Vehicle, CC, *11*	130
____	28474	North Pole Central Elf Handcar, *11*	80
____	28475	UP Early Era Inspection Vehicle, *11*	130
____	28476	IC Early Era Inspection Vehicle, *11*	130
____	28478	Frisco Early Era Inspection Vehicle, CC, *11*	130
____	28479	Christmas Early Era Inspection Vehicle, *11*	130
____	28480	Grand Trunk Early Era Inspection Vehicle, CC, *11*	130
____	28500	Mopac GP20 Diesel "2274," *99–00*	205
____	28501	ATSF GP9 Diesel "2924," traditional, *99*	200
____	28502	ATSF GP9 Diesel "2925," CC, *99–00*	255
____	28503	ACL GP7 Diesel, CC, *00*	245
____	28504	ACL GP7 Diesel, traditional, *00*	170
____	28505	Monon Alco C420 Switcher "505," CC, *00–01*	230
____	28506	Monon Alco C420 Switcher "506," traditional, *00–01*	170
____	28507	NH Alco C420 Switcher "2556," CC, *00–01*	275
____	28508	NH Alco C420 Switcher "2557," traditional, *00–01*	290
____	28509	FEC GP7 Diesel Set, *99*	560
____	28514	B&O GP9 Diesel "6590," *00*	85
____	28515	Lionel Service Station Alco C420 Switcher, CC, *00*	205
____	28516	Lehigh & Hudson River Alco C420 Diesel, *00*	160
____	28517	C&NW GP7 Diesel "1518," CC, *00–01*	275
____	28518	PRR EP-5 Electric Locomotive "2352," CC, *00*	410
____	28519	NP GP9 Diesel "2349," CC, *01*	290
____	28521	SP Alco RS-11 Switcher "5725," CC, *01–02*	280
____	28522	MP Alco RS-11 Switcher "4611," CC, *01–02*	305
____	28523	Soo SD40-2 Diesel "6622," CC, *01*	375
____	28524	Chessie SD40-2 Diesel "7616," CC, *01*	355
____	28527	AEC GP9 Diesel "2001," CC, *01*	378
____	28529	Norfolk Southern GP9 Diesel, CC, *02*	200
____	28530	NP Alco S4 Diesel "722," CC, *02*	285
____	28531	Santa Fe Alco S2 Switcher "2337," CC, *02*	285
____	28532	LV Alco S2 Switcher "150," CC, *02*	280
____	28533	Seaboard Air Line Alco S4 Diesel "1489," CC, *02*	290
____	28536	Rock Island GP7 Diesel "1274," CC, *02–03*	230
____	28538	WP Alco S2 Switcher "553," CC, *03*	340
____	28539	B&O Alco S2 Switcher "9045," CC, *03*	320
____	28540	UP SD40T-2 Diesel "4455," CC, *03*	390

Exc Mint

		Exc	Mint
28541	SP SD40T-2 Diesel "8239," CC, 03	400	___
28542	Rio Grande SD40T-2 Diesel "5350," CC, 03	400	___
28543	Ontario Northland RS3 Diesel "1308," 03	80	___
28544	Pennsylvania Alco RS-11 Switcher "8618," CC, 04	350	___
28545	NP Alco RS-11 Switcher "900," CC, 03	325	___
28548	Chessie System S4 Diesel "9009," CC, 05	400	___
28553	PRR Alco RS-11 Switcher "8620," traditional, 07–08	285	___
28554	Pennsylvania Alco RS-11 Switcher "8618," nonpowered, CC, 07	170	___
28554	PRR RS-11 Diesel "8621," nonpowered, 08	170	___
28555	Alaska GP38-2 Diesel "2001," CC, 06	400	___
28556	Alaska GP38-2 Diesel "2002," nonpowered (std O), 06	160	___
28557	CP GP30 Diesel "5000," CC, 06–07	400	___
28558	CP GP30 Diesel "5001," nonpowered (std O), 06–07	150	___
28559	Chessie System GP30 Diesel "3044," CC, 06–07	400	___
28560	Chessie System GP30 Diesel "3045," nonpowered (std O), 06–07	150	___
28561	NYC GP7 Diesel "5628," CC, 07–08	340	___
28562	NYC GP7 Diesel "5629," nonpowered (std O), 07	170	___
28563	GN GP7 Diesel "626," CC, 07	400	___
28564	GN GP7 Diesel "627," nonpowered (std O), 07	170	___
28565	RI GP7 Diesel "1265," CC, 07	400	___
28566	RI GP7 Diesel "1266," nonpowered (std O), 07	170	___
28567	UP GP7 Diesel "105," CC, 07	400	___
28568	UP GP7 Diesel "106," nonpowered (std O), 07	170	___
28570	D&RGW GP7 Diesel "5101," CC, 08	440	___
28573	PRR GP7 Diesel "8512," CC, 08	440	___
28578	D&H GP38-2 Diesel "7307," CC, 08	440	___
28587	PRR GP7 Diesel "8510," CC, 10	450	___
28592	N&W GP7 Diesel "2446," CC, 09	500	___
28594	White Pass & Yukon NW2 Diesel Switcher, traditional, 09–10	300	___
28595	ATSF SD40 Diesel "5004," CC, 09	380	___
28596	Erie GP7 Diesel "1210," CC, 11	450	___
28598	ATSF GP7 Diesel "2791," CC, 10	450	___
28599	Erie GP9 Diesel "1261," CC, 10	390	___
28612	WP 4-4-2 Atlantic Locomotive, traditional, 02	80	___
28613	Reading 0-6-0 Dockside Switcher "1251," traditional, 04	100	___
28615	B&O 4-6-4 Hudson Locomotive, traditional, 02	225	___
28616	Nickel Plate 2-8-4 Berkshire Locomotive, traditional, 02	190	___
28617	Southern 2-8-4 Berkshire Locomotive, traditional, 02	235	___
28624	Santa Fe 0-6-0 Dockside Switcher "2174," traditional, 04	175	___
28625	Wabash 4-4-2 Atlantic Locomotive "8625," traditional, 03	85	___
28626	PRR 4-6-4 Hudson Locomotive "626," traditional, 03	175	___
28627	C&O 2-8-4 Berkshire Locomotive "2755," traditional, 03	200	___

		Exc	Mint
28628	L&N 2-8-4 Berkshire Locomotive "1970," traditional, *03*	150	200
____28633	JCPenney B&O 2-8-4 Berkshire Locomotive, *07*		135
28636	D&RGW 4-4-2 Atlantic Locomotive "8636," traditional, *04*		95
28637	UP 4-6-4 Hudson Locomotive "673," traditional, *04*		160
28638	GN 2-8-4 Berkshire Locomotive "3414," traditional, *04*		200
28639	NYC 2-8-4 Berkshire Locomotive "9401," traditional, *04*		200
28646	North Pole Central 2-8-4 Berkshire "1900," traditional, *04*		230
28649	Polar Express 2-8-4 Berkshire Locomotive, *03–10*		120
28650	NYC 0-6-0 Dockside Switcher "X-8688," traditional, *05*		80
28651	Bethlehem Steel 0-6-0 Dockside Switcher "72," traditional, *05*		80
____28652	LL 4-4-2 Locomotive "8652," traditional, *05*		105
28655	Erie 2-8-4 Berkshire Locomotive "3338," traditional, *05*		240
28656	PRR 2-8-4 Berkshire Locomotive "56," traditional, *05*		240
28660	North Pole Central 0-6-0 Dockside Switcher "25," traditional, *05*		105
28661	Santa Fe 0-4-0 Locomotive "2300" traditional, *05*		160
____28662	C&O 0-4-0 Locomotive "39," traditional, *05*		160
28674	C&O 0-6-0 Dockside Switcher "67," traditional, *06–07*		110
28675	SP 0-6-0 Dockside Switcher "675," traditional, *06–07*		110
28676	U.S. Steel 0-6-0 Dockside Switcher "76," traditional, *06–07*		110
28677	WM 4-4-2 Atlantic Locomotive "103," traditional, *06*		110
28678	Rio Grande 0-4-0 Locomotive "55," traditional, *06–07*		170
28679	U.S. Army Transportation Corps 0-4-0 Locomotive "40," traditional, *06*		170
28680	Reading 0-4-0 Locomotive "1152," traditional, *06*		170
28681	Virginian 2-8-4 Berkshire Locomotive "509," traditional, *06*		260
28683	B&O 2-8-2 Mikado Locomotive "1520," TrainSounds, *06–07*		260
28684	UP 2-8-2 Mikado Locomotive "2498," TrainSounds, *06–07*		260
____28693	B&O 4-4-2 Locomotive "28," traditional, *05*		105
28694	NYC 4-4-2 Atlantic Locomotive "8637," traditional, *06*		100
28695	Halloween 0-6-0 Dockside Switcher "X-131," traditional, *06–07*		85
28699	Holiday 2-8-2 Mikado Locomotive "25," red, RailSounds, *08*		260
____28700	CB&Q 0-8-0 Locomotive "543," RailSounds, *05*		650
____28701	NP 0-8-0 Locomotive "1178," RailSounds, *05*		650

Exc Mint

		Exc	Mint
28702	Boston & Albany 0-8-0 Locomotive "53," RailSounds, *05*		650____
28704	PRR 4-4-2 Atlantic Locomotive "68," CC, *05*		550____
28706	PRR Reading Seashore 4-4-2 Atlantic Locomotive "6064," CC, *05*		550____
28742	B&O 4-6-0 Camelback Locomotive "1630," CC, *03*		335____
28743	B&O 4-6-0 Camelback Locomotive "1632," traditional, *03*		300____
28744	D&H 4-6-0 Camelback Locomotive "548," CC, *03*		325____
28745	D&H 4-6-0 Camelback Locomotive "555," traditional, *03*		300____
28746	Erie 4-6-0 Camelback Locomotive "860," CC, *03*		375____
28747	Erie 4-6-0 Camelback Locomotive "878," traditional, *03*		300____
28748	Jersey Central 4-6-0 Camelback Locomotive "772," CC, *03*		300____
28749	Jersey Central 4-6-0 Camelback Locomotive "773," traditional, *03*		300____
28750	Lackawanna 4-6-0 Camelback Locomotive "690," CC, *03*		375____
28751	Lackawanna 4-6-0 Camelback Locomotive "1031," traditional, *03*		300____
28752	LIRR 4-6-0 Camelback Locomotive "126," CC, *03*		300____
28753	LIRR 4-6-0 Camelback Locomotive "127," traditional, *03*		300____
28754	NYO&W 4-6-0 Camelback Locomotive "249," CC, *03*		300____
28755	NYO&W 4-6-0 Camelback "253" Locomotive, traditional, *03*		300____
28756	PRR Reading Seashore 4-6-0 Camelback Locomotive "6000," CC, *03*		325____
28757	PRR Reading Seashore 4-6-0 Camelback Locomotive "6001," traditional, *03*		300____
28758	Susquehanna 4-6-0 Camelback Locomotive "30," CC, *03*		305____
28759	Susquehanna 4-6-0 Camelback Locomotive "36," traditional, *03*		300____
28800	N&W GP7 Diesel "507," *99–00*		80____
28801	Lionel Lines 44-ton Switcher, *99*		135____
28806	Jersey Central FM H16-44 Diesel "1516," CC, *01*		335____
28811	Santa Fe FM H16-44 Diesel "3003," CC, *01*		290____
28813	Milwaukee Road FM H16-44 Diesel "406," CC, *01*		280____
28815	B&O GP30 Diesel "6935," CC, *02*		295____
28817	Reading GP30 Diesel "5513," CC, *02*		310____
28819	Rio Grande GP30 Diesel "3013," CC, *02*		310____
28821	GT GP7 Diesel "4438," *01*		100____
28822	Southern RS3 Diesel "2127," *01*		70____
28823	Virginian Electric Locomotive "234," *01*		122____
28826	Pioneer Seed GP7 Diesel "2001," traditional, *00 u*		NRS____
28827	Chessie GP38 Diesel, traditional, *01*		100____
28830	Soo Line GP9 Diesel, traditional, *01 u*		NRS____
28831	Conrail U36B Diesel "2971," traditional, *02*		100____
28832	Santa Fe RS3 Diesel "2099," traditional, *02*		70____

			Exc	Mint
___	28836	NYC FM H-16-44 Diesel "7000," CC, *02*		330
___	28837	NH FM H-16-44 Diesel "591," CC, *02*		325
___	28838	UP FM H-16-44 Diesel "1340," CC, *02*		325
___	28839	Alaska GP 30 Diesel "2000," CC, *04*		315
___	28840	Burlington GP30 Diesel "945," CC, *03*		325
___	28841	Seaboard GP30 Diesel "1315," CC, *03*		220
___	28842	C&O GP9 Diesel, horn, *04*		160
___	28843	Southern GP38 Diesel, horn, *04*		140
___	28845	Amtrak RS3 Diesel "106," *03*		70
	28846	Western Pacific U36B Diesel "3067," traditional, *04*		100
___	28847	DM & IR GP38 Diesel "203," traditional, *04*		170
___	28848	JCPenney Santa Fe GP38 Diesel, *04*		125
___	28849	Western Maryland GP7 Diesel, horn, *04*		185
___	28850	NYC GP30 Diesel "6115" CC, *04*		360
___	28851	Pennsylvania RS3 Diesel, *04*		75
___	28852	CSX U36B Diesel "1976," traditional, *05*		140
___	28853	Santa Fe GP38 Diesel "2371," traditional, *05*		210
___	28857	Alaska GP9 Diesel, *05*		125
	28859	Pennsylvania GP30 Diesel "2206," nonpowered, *06*		160
___	28860	UP GP30 Diesel "844," CC, *06*		360
___	28861	UP GP30 Diesel "845," nonpowered (std O), *06*		150
___	28862	CSX GP30 Diesel "4249," CC, *06*		400
	28863	CSX GP30 Diesel "4250," nonpowered (std O), *06*		150
___	28864	UP RS3 Diesel "1195," traditional, *06*		85
___	28865	GN GP9 Diesel "688," traditional, *06*		210
___	28866	NYC GP20 Diesel "6110," traditional, *06*		140
___	28868	ATSF GP38 Diesel		140
___	28873	NYC RS3 Diesel "8226," traditional, *06*		85
___	28874	UP GP9 Diesel "178," traditional, *06–07*		210
___	28875	Santa Fe GP20 "1107," traditional, *06*		140
___	28876	GN FT Diesel "418," traditional, *07–08*		245
___	28879	UPS Centennial GP38 Diesel, traditional, *06*		210
___	28881	Conrail GP20 Diesel "2107," traditional, *07*		140
___	28882	Alaska RS3 Diesel "1079," traditional, *07*		85
___	28883	Diesel, *07–13*		120
___	28884	PRR GP38 Diesel "2389," traditional, *08–09*		210
___	28886	RI RS3 Diesel "492," traditional, *08*		95
___	28887	Southern RS3 Diesel "2028," traditional, *08*		95
___	28890	CN GP9 Diesel "4573," traditional, *08*		210
___	28897	Seaboard U36B Diesel "1762," traditional, *08*		140
___	28900	Iron 'Arry and Iron Bert 2-pack, *08–09*		240
___	28905	ATSF FT Diesel "160," nonpowered, *09–10*		120
___	29000	PRR Caleb Strong Madison Coach "2622," *99*		80
___	29001	PRR Villa Royal Madison Coach "2621," *99*		80
___	29002	PRR Philadelphia Madison Coach "2624," *99*	30	80
___	29003	PRR Madison Car 4-pack, *98*		220
___	29004	NYC Heavyweight Passenger Car 2-pack, *99*		170
___	29007	NYC Pullman Passenger Car 2-pack, *98 u*		95
___	29008	NYC Heavyweight Diner "383," *98*		95
	29009	NYC Van Twiller Heavyweight Combination Car, *98*		95
___	29010	C&O Heavyweight Passenger Car 2-pack, *99*		150

		Exc	Mint
29039	Lionel Lines Recovery Combination Car "9501," 99		NRS___
29041	Alaska Streamliner Car 4-pack, 99–00		230___
29042	Alaska Streamliner Baggage Car "6310," 99–00		50___
29043	Alaska Streamliner Coach "5408," 99–00		65___
29044	Alaska Streamliner Vista Dome Car "7014," 99–00		65___
29046	B&O Streamliner Car 4-pack, 99–00		165___
29047	B&O Streamliner Baggage Car, 99–00		35___
29048	B&O Streamliner Coach, 99–00		50___
29049	B&O Streamliner Vista Dome Car, 99–00		50___
29050	B&O Streamliner Observation Car, 99–00		40___
29051	ATSF Streamliner Car 4-pack, 99–00		200___
29052	ATSF Streamliner Baggage Car, 99–00		40___
29053	ATSF Streamliner Coach, 99–00		60___
29054	ATSF Streamliner Vista Dome Car, 99–00		60___
29055	ATSF Streamliner Observation Car, 99–00		40___
29056	NYC Streamliner Car 4-pack, 99–00		180___
29057	NYC Streamliner Baggage Car, 99–00		40___
29058	NYC Streamliner Coach, 99–00		50___
29059	NYC Streamliner Vista Dome Car, 99–00		50___
29060	NYC Streamliner Observation Car, 99–00		45___
29061	PRR Madison Passenger Car 4-pack, 99–00		190___
29062	PRR Indian Point Madison Baggage Car, 99–00		50___
29063	PRR Christopher Columbus Madison Coach, 99–00		50___
29064	PRR Andrew Jackson Madison Coach, 99–00		50___
29065	PRR Broussard Madison Observation Car, 99–00		50___
29066	CNJ Madison Passenger Car 4-pack, 99–00		210___
29067	CNJ Madison Baggage Car "420," 99–00		50___
29068	CNJ Beachcomber Madison Coach, 99–00		50___
29069	CNJ Echo Lake Madison Coach, 99–00		50___
29070	CNJ Madison Observation Car "1178," 99–00		50___
29071	NYC Baby Madison Car 4-pack, 00		155___
29072	NYC Baby Madison Baggage Car "1001," 00		50___
29073	NYC Baby Madison Coach "1005," 00		50___
29074	NYC Baby Madison Coach "1006," 00		50___
29075	NYC Detroit Baby Madison Observation Car "1019," 00		40___
29076	Southern Baby Madison Car 4-pack, 00		155___
29077	Southern Delaware Madison Baggage Car "702," 00		30___
29078	Southern North Carolina Madison Coach "800," 00		50___
29079	Southern Maryland Madison Coach "801," 00		50___
29080	Southern Madison Observation Car "1100," 00		40___
29081	ATSF Baby Madison Car 4-pack, 00		160___
29082	ATSF Baby Madison Baggage Car "1765," 00		30___
29083	ATSF Baby Madison Coach "3040," 00		50___
29084	ATSF Baby Madison Coach "1535," 00		50___
29085	ATSF Baby Madison Observation Car "10," 00		45___
29086	Madison Car 3-pack, 99		280___
29090	Lionel Liontech Madison Car "2656," 99		75___
29091	Lawrence Cowen Lionel Legends Madison Coach "2657," 99–00		75___

		Exc	Mint
29105	PRR Trail Blazer Aluminum Passenger Car 4-pack, *04–05*		550
29108	Searchlight Car, *00*		30
29110	B&O Columbian Aluminum Passenger Car 4-pack, *04*		425
29115	SP Daylight Aluminum Passenger Car 4-pack, *04–05*		550
29122	Erie-Lack. F3 Diesel AB Passenger Set, *99*		840
29123	Erie-Lack. Aluminum Coach/Baggage Car "203," *99*		100
29124	Erie-Lack. Aluminum Coach/Diner "770," *99*		100
29125	Erie-Lack. Eleanor Lord Aluminum Coach, *99*		100
29126	Erie-Lack. Tavern Lounge Aluminum Observation Car "789," *99*		125
29127	ACL Aluminum Baggage Car "152," *99*		NRS
29128	ACL North Hampton Aluminum Coach, *99*		NRS
29129	Texas Special Passenger Car 4-pack, *99*		700
29130	Texas Special Edward Burleson Aluminum Coach "1200," *99*		115
29131	Texas Special David G. Burnett Aluminum Coach "1201," *99*		115
29132	Texas Special J. Pinckney Henderson Aluminum Coach "1202," *99*		115
29133	Texas Special Stephen F. Austin Aluminum Observation Car "1203," *99*		100
29135	California Zephyr Silver Poplar Aluminum Vista Dome Car, *99*		150
29136	California Zephyr Silver Palm Aluminum Vista Dome Car, *99*		150
29137	California Zephyr Silver Tavern Aluminum Vista Dome Car, *99*		150
29138	California Zephyr Silver Planet Aluminum Vista Dome Car, *99*		150
29139	Kughn Lionel Legends Madison Car "2655," *99*		113
29140	NYC Castleton Bridge Aluminum Sleeper Car, *99*		120
29141	NYC Martin Van Buren Aluminum Combination Car, *99*		120
29142	CP Skyline Aluminum Vista Dome Car "596," *99*		125
29143	CP Banff Park Aluminum Observation Car, *99*		125
29144	Santa Fe El Capitan Aluminum Passenger Car 4-pack, *04*		400
29149	CB&Q California Zephyr Aluminum Passenger Car 2-pack, *03*		300
29152	Santa Fe Super Chief Aluminum Passenger Car 2-pack, *03*		190
29155	D&H Aluminum Passenger Car 2-pack, *03*		190
29158	Southern Aluminum Passenger Car 2-pack, *03*		205
29165	Amtrak Superliner Passenger Car 2-pack, Phase IV, *04*		195
29168	Amtrak Superliner Diner, StationSounds, Phase IV, *04*		200
29169	Alaska Superliner Passenger Car 2-pack, *04*		200
29172	Alaska Superliner Diner, StationSounds, *04*		200
29182	N&W Powhatan Arrow Aluminum Passenger Car 4-pack (std O), *05*		550
29187	N&W Powhatan Arrow Aluminum Passenger Car 2-pack (std O), *05*		290

		Exc	Mint
29190	N&W Powhatan Arrow Aluminum Diner, StationSounds, *05*		290____
29191	MILW Hiawatha Passenger Car 4-pack, *06*		370____
29196	MILW Hiawatha Passenger Car 2-pack, *06*		190____
29199	MILW Hiawatha Diner, StationSounds, *06*		190____
29202	Santa Fe Map Boxcar "6464," *97 u*		53____
29203	Maine Central Boxcar "6464-597," *97 u*		35____
29205	Mickey Mouse Hi-Cube Boxcar "9555," *97*		70____
29206	Vapor Records Boxcar #1, *97*		90____
29209	Postwar "6464" Boxcar Series VII, 3 cars, *98*		87____
29210	GN Boxcar "6464-450," *98*		33____
29211	B&M Boxcar "6464-475," *98*		27____
29212	Timken Boxcar "6464-500," *98*		28____
29213	ATSF Grand Canyon Route 6464 Boxcar "6464-198," *98*		26____
29214	Southern 6464 Boxcar "6464-298," *98*		27____
29215	Canadian Pacific 6464 Boxcar "6464-398," *98*		26____
29217	1997 Toy Fair Airex Boxcar, *97*		78____
29218	Vapor Records Boxcar "6464-496," *97 u*		85____
29220	Lionel Centennial Series Hi-Cube Boxcar Set, 4 cars, *97*		225____
29221	Centennial Series Hi-Cube Boxcar "9697-1," *97*		62____
29222	Centennial Series Hi-Cube Boxcar "9697-2," *97*		70____
29223	Centennial Series Hi-Cube Boxcar "9697-3," *97*		63____
29224	Centennial Series Hi-Cube Boxcar "9697-4," *97*		60____
29225	H.O.R.D.E. Music Festival Boxcar, *97*		70____
29229	Vapor Records Holiday Car, *98*		160____
29231	Halloween Animated Boxcar, *98*		42____
29233	Conrail PC Overstamped Boxcar "6464-598," *98*		38____
29234	Conrail Erie Overstamped Boxcar "6464-698," *98*		32____
29235	NYC Boxcar "6464-510," *99*		47____
29236	MKT Boxcar "6464-515," *99*		40____
29237	M&StL Boxcar "6464-525," *99*		25____
29247	Mainline Classic Street Lamps, 3 pieces, *08–16*		40____
29250	Phoebe Snow Boxcar "6464-199," *99*		41____
29251	BN Boxcar "6464-299," *99*		31____
29252	CP Boxcar "6464-399," *99*		33____
29253	B&M Boxcar "76032," *99*		50____
29254	B&M Boxcar "76033," *99*		50____
29255	B&M Boxcar "76034," *99*		50____
29256	B&M Boxcar "76035," *99*		50____
29257	Southern Boxcar "9464-199," *99*		38____
29258	Reading Boxcar "9464-299," *99*		36____
29259	NP Bicentennial Boxcar "9464-399," *99*		34____
29265	Maine Central Boxcar "8661," *99*		36____
29266	Frisco Boxcar "8722," *99*		36____
29267	No. 6464 Boxcar 3-pack, Series VIII, *99*		85____
29268	Rio Grande Boxcar "63067," *99*		40____
29271	Lionel Cola Tractor and Trailer, *98*		12____
29279	Conrail Jersey Central Overstamped Boxcar "6464-28X," *99*		40____
29280	Conrail LV Overstamped Boxcar "6464-31X," *99*		41____
29281	Conrail Overstamped Boxcar 2-pack, *99*		70____
29282	Postwar "6464" Boxcar 3-pack, *99*		130____

		Exc	Mint
____29283	NYC Boxcar, *99*		55
____29284	GN Boxcar, *99*		40
____29285	Seaboard Boxcar, *99*		36
____29286	Overstamped Boxcar 2-pack, *99*		65
____29287	NH PC Overstamped Boxcar "6464-29X," *99*		34
____29288	Conrail Reading Overstamped Boxcar "6464-32X," *99*		38
____29289	Postwar "6464" Series IX, 3 cars, *99–00*		70
____29290	D&RGW Boxcar "6464-650," *00*		41
____29291	ATSF Boxcar "6464-700," *00*		38
____29292	NH Boxcar "6464-725," *00*		39
____29293	NH Boxcar "6464-425," *99*		95
____29294	Hellgate Bridge Boxcar "1900-2000," *99 u*		38
____29295	PRR "Don't Stand Me Still" Boxcar "24018," *99–00*		65
____29296	PRR "Merchandise" Boxcar "29296," *99–00*		65
____29297	PRR "No Damage" Boxcar "47158," *99–00*		65
____29298	Lionel Boxcar "6464-2000," *00*		46
____29300	50th Anniversary Clear Shell Aquarium Car, *10*		85
____29301	Postwar "3662" Transparent Milk Car with platform, *11, 13*		155
____29302	Christmas Music Reefer, *10*		75
____29303	North Pole Central Crane Car, *10–11*		65
____29305	UP Chisholm Trail Stock Car, Cattle Sounds, *11, 13*		200
____29306	PRR Hi-Cube Lighted Garland Boxcar, *10–11*		70
____29309	GN Pullman-Standard Diesel Freight Set, CC, *13*		830
____29310	Marine Science Deep Sea Exhibition Aquarium Car, *11*		75
____29311	Strasburg Derrick Car, *11*		45
____29312	Santa's Operating Boxcar, *11–12*		75
____29314	SP DD Boxcar "214051" (std O), *13–14*		75
____29317	CN DD Boxcar "214051" (std O), *13–14*		75
____29320	CNJ DD Boxcar "214051" (std O), *13–14*		75
____29321	Ice Skating Aquarium Car, *12*		80
____29322	Koi Aquarium Car, *13–14*		80
____29323	UP DD Boxcar "500019" (std O), *13–14*		75
____29324	Walking Zombie Brakeman Car, *12*		80
____29326	NP "Pig Palace" Operating Stock Car "84144," *12*		200
____29327	Bethlehem Steel Operating Hopper "2025," *12*		60
____29328	Beatles "Nothing is Real" Aquarium Car, *12–13*		85
____29329	Peanuts Halloween Aquarium Car, *12–13*		85
____29333	ATSF 89' Auto Carrier 2-pack (std O), *13–14, 16*		220
____29338	BN 89' Auto Carrier 2-pack (std O), *13–14*		220
____29344	C&NW DD Boxcar "57766" (std O), *13*		75
____29345	ATSF 89' Auto Carrier (std O), *13–14*		110
____29346	Soo Line 89' Auto Carrier 2-pack (std O), *13–16*		220
____29349	SP 89' Auto Carrier 2-pack (std O), *13–16*		220
____29364	NYC Water Level Steam Freight Set, CC, *12–13*		1600
____29365	N&W Pocahontas Steam Passenger Set, CC, *12*		1950
____29366	SP TankSet Diesel Set, CC, *12*		850
____29372	BNSF 89' Auto Carrier "300267" (std O), *13*		110
____29373	CN 89' Auto Carrier "710771" (std O), *13, 16*		110
____29376	Conrail 89' Auto Carrier "964444" (std O), *13*		110

		Exc	Mint
29377	CP 89' Auto Carrier 2-pack (std O), *13–14, 16*	220	___
29380	CSX 89' Auto Carrier "604544" (std O), *13*	110	___
29381	GTW 89' Auto Carrier "50450" (std O), *14–15*	110	___
29382	UP 89' Auto Carrier "604545" (std O), *13*	110	___
29384	DL&W USRA Double-sheathed Boxcar "44153" (std O), *13*	70	___
29385	ATSF USRA Double-sheathed Boxcar "39012" (std O), *13*	70	___
29386	PRR PS-4 Flatcar with stakes "469614" (std O), *13*	70	___
29387	GN PS-4 Flatcar with stakes "629387" (std O), *13*	70	___
29400	Bethlehem Steel Slag Car 3-pack (std O), *03*	185	___
29404	Bethlehem Steel Hot Metal Car 3-pack (std O), *03*	210	___
29408	PRR Coil Car, *01*	40	___
29411	Sherwin-Williams Vat Car, *02*	35	___
29412	Tabasco Brand Vat Car, *02*	36	___
29413	Airex Boat Loader Car "29413," *02*	42	___
29414	PRR Evans Auto Loader "480123," *01*	56	___
29415	WM Skeleton Log Car 3-pack #2 (std O), *02*	90	___
29419	West Side Lumber Skeleton Log Car 3-pack #2 (std O), *02*	90	___
29423	Wellspring Capital Management Happy Holidays Vat Car, *03 u*	255	___
29424	Meadow River Lumber Skeleton Log Car 3-pack (std O), *03*	90	___
29429	Campbell's Soup Vat Car "29429," *03*	38	___
29430	Meadow River Lumber Skeleton Log Car 3-pack #2 (std O), *03*	90	___
29434	Weyerhauser Skeleton Log Car 3-pack, *05*	100	___
29438	Trailer Train Flatcar with 2 UP trailers, *03*	60	___
29439	Postwar "6414" Evans Auto Loader, *02*	43	___
29441	UP Flatcar "53471" with grader, *02*	43	___
29442	CSX Flatcar "600513" with backhoe, *02*	43	___
29453	Elk River Lumber Skeleton Log Car 3-pack #2 (std O), *03*	90	___
29457	NS Flatcar "157590" with Caterpillar loader, *03*	42	___
29458	BNSF Flatcar "922268" with Caterpillar truck, *03*	44	___
29459	Water Barrel Car "1878," Archive Collection, *03*	40	___
29460	LL Flatcar "3460" with trailers, Archive Collection, *03*	39	___
29461	Postwar "6500" Flatcar with red-and-white airplane, *03*	32	___
29462	Postwar "6500" Flatcar with white-and-red airplane, *03*	31	___
29463	Postwar "6414" Evans Auto Loader, *03*	30	___
29464	U.S. Army Vat Car "29464," *04*	35	___
29465	U.S. Steel Slag Car 3-pack (std O), *04–05*	160	___
29469	U.S. Steel Hot Metal Car 3-pack (std O), *04–05*	190	___
29473	Youngstown Sheet & Tube Slag Car 3-pack (std O), *03*	150	___
29477	Youngstown Sheet & Tube Hot Metal Car 3-pack (std O), *03*	170	___
29481	Cass Scenic Railroad Skeleton Log Car 3-pack (std O), *03*	80	___
29487	Boat-loader with 4 boats, *04*	65	___

		Exc	Mint
29488	Cass Scenic Railroad Skeleton Log Car 3-pack #2 (std O), 04		90
29492	Pickering Lumber Skeleton Log Car 3-pack #1 (std O), 04		100
29496	Pickering Lumber Skeleton Log Car 3-pack #2 (std O), 04		90
29602	Celanese Chemicals 1-D Tank Car, 05		45
29603	Comet 1-D Tank Car, traditional, 05		53
29604	Meadow Brook Molasses 1-D Tank Car, traditional, 05		53
29606	Elvis Presley Gold Record Transport Car, 04		120
29607	Las Vegas Mint Car, traditional, 05		58
29609	Alien Suspension Car, 06		60
29610	Dixie Honey 1-D Tank Car, 06		60
29611	Sunoco 1-D Tank Car, 06		60
29612	Las Vegas Poker Chip Car, 06		40
29613	Postwar "6463" Rocket Fuel 2-D Tank Car, 06		75
29617	Cities Service Tank Car, 06–07		48
29618	Hooker Chemicals 3-D Tank Car, 07		60
29619	Grave's Formaldehyde 1-D Tank Car, 07		60
29622	Fort Knox Mint Car, lilac, Archive Collection, 07		60
29624	Monopoly Mint Car with money, 08		65
29626	"Case Closed" Mint Car with shredded documents, 08		109
29628	Poinsettia Mint Car, 09		70
29629	AEC Glow-in-the-Dark Tank Car, 09–10		60
29633	Christmas Ornament Lighted Mint Car, 10		70
29634	Federal Reserve Bailout Mint Car, 10		70
29635	Monopoly "Go To Jail" Mint Car, 10		70
29636	Vampire Transport Mint Car, 10–11		70
29637	Candy Cane 2-D Tank Car, 10–11		55
29640	Coca-Cola Tank Car, 10		62
29642	Jolly Rancher 1-D Tank Car, 11		55
29643	Hershey's Syrup 1-D Tank Car, 11		58
29644	ATSF 1-D Tank Car, 11		55
29645	Atlantic City Casino Mint Car, 11		70
29646	Alaska Oil 2-D Tank Car, 11		50
29647	Gingerbread Man Mint Car, 11		70
29649	Lionel SP Smoke Pellets Mint Car, 12–13		70
29650	Cleveland Federal Reserve Mint Car, 11		70
29651	Richmond Federal Reserve Mint Car, 12		70
29654	Boston Federal Reserve Mint Car, 13		70
29655	PRR 16-wheel Flatcar with girders "469846," 12		75
29656	ATSF 16-wheel Flatcar with transformer "90096," 12		75
29671	Smoke Pellet Mint Car #2, 13–15		70
29694	Hershey's Mint Car, 14		85
29695	Trailer Set Maxi-Stack Pair "48," 13		120
29697	Santa's Flatcar with submarine, 13		70
29698	Tree Topper Star Transport Car, 13–14		80
29699	Silver and Gold Christmas Mint Car, 13–14		70
29703	PRR Porthole Caboose, 01		45
29708	C&O Bay Window Caboose "8315," 04		45
29709	Pennsylvania N5c Caboose "477938," 04		40
29711	Santa Fe Bay Window Caboose, 05		60

		Exc	Mint
29712	Postwar "2420" Searchlight Caboose, *04*	50	___
29718	N&W Work Caboose, *06*	48	___
29719	Santa Fe Caboose "6427," Archive Collection, *06*	48	___
29726	Virginian Caboose "6427," Archive Collection, *06–07*	50	___
29727	"I Love U.S.A." Bay Window Caboose "1985," *06*	60	___
29729	Bethlehem Steel Searchlight Caboose, *06*	90	___
29732	PRR Caboose "477871," *08*	45	___
29733	White Pass & Yukon Extended Vision Caboose, *09–10*	90	___
29734	PRR NS Heritage CA-4 Caboose (std O), *10*	95	___
29735	Conrail NS Heritage CA-4 Caboose (std O), *10*	95	___
29737	ATSF Bay Window Caboose, traditional, *10–11*	70	___
29739	B&M Transfer Caboose, *11*	50	___
29765	TankSet Add-on 3-pack (std O), *12*	240	___
29771	CN TankSet 2-pack (std O), *12*	160	___
29774	GATX TankSet 2-pack (std O), *12*	160	___
29777	Cibro TankSet 2-pack (std O), *12*	160	___
29786	Bethlehem Steel PS-2 3-bay Hopper (std O), *13*	80	___
29787	PRR PS-2 3-bay Hopper (std O), *13*	80	___
29791	Wizard of Oz Anniversary Boxcar, *13–15*	70	___
29792	Angela Trotta Thomas "Toyland Express" Boxcar, *13*	65	___
29793	Where the Wild Things Are Boxcar, *13–15*	70	___
29800	MOW Crane Car, TMCC, *04*	250	___
29804	UP Crane Car "JPX 250," CC, *05*	320	___
29805	Conrail Crane Car "50202," CC, *05*	320	___
29806	Weyerhaeuser Log Dump Car, *05*	75	___
29807	DM&IR Coal Dump Car, *05*	75	___
29808	Candy Cane Dump Car, *05*	55	___
29809	Dump Car with presents, *05*	60	___
29810	Operating Egg Nog Car with platform, *05*	140	___
29811	Merchant's Despatch Transit Hot Box Reefer "12425," *05*	85	___
29812	Santa Fe Hot Box Reefer "20699," *05*	90	___
29813	Santa Fe Boom Car "19144," Crane Sounds, *05*	210	___
29814	Pennsylvania Boom Car "491063," Crane Sounds, *05*	210	___
29815	NYC Boom Car "X923," Crane Sounds, *05*	210	___
29816	MOW Boom Car "X-816," Crane Sounds, *05*	210	___
29817	UP Boom Car "909438," Crane Sounds, *05*	210	___
29818	Conrail Boom Car, Crane Sounds, *05*	210	___
29821	Postwar "2460" Lionel Lines Crane Car, gray cab, *05*	43	___
29822	Postwar "773W" NYC Tender, whistle, *05*	48	___
29823	Postwar "3484" Pennsylvania Operating Boxcar, *05*	38	___
29827	Postwar "3419" Helicopter Launching Car, *06*	49	___
29828	Postwar "3666" Minuteman Car with cannon, *06*	85	___
29829	Postwar "6905" Radioactive Waste Car, *06*	85	___
29830	PFE Hot Box Reefer "5890" (std O), *06*	105	___
29831	Swift Hot Box Reefer "15342" (std O), *06*	150	___
29832	Chessie System Crane Car "940504," CC, *06*	320	___
29833	Chessie System Boom Car "940561," CC, *06*	210	___
29834	LL Bay Window Caboose "834," TrainSounds (std O), *06–07*	110	___

		Exc	Mint
29835	SP Bay Window Caboose "4667," TrainSounds (std O), _06–07_		160
29839	Cherry Picker Car, _06_		63
29849	Lionel Lines Crane Car, silver cab, _06_		60
29850	N&W J Class Tender, air whistle, _06–07_		70
29853	Postwar "6651" Big John Cannon Car, _08_		75
29854	Satellite Launching Car, _07_		70
29855	Lionel Lines Operating Milk Car with platform, _07_		140
29856	Monon Operating Boxcar, _06–07_		65
29857	Lionel Lines Boom Car, _06–07_		55
29858	CP Rail Crane Car "414475," CC, _07_		320
29859	CP Rail Boom Car "412567," CC, _07_		210
29865	Southern Operating Barrel Car, _07–08_		75
29866	Pirates Aquarium Car, _07_		75
29867	NYC Jet Snow Blower "X27207," _07_		120
29868	Alaska Jet Snow Blower, _07_		120
29869	Bethlehem Steel Crane Car, _06_		60
29870	MOW Jet Snow Blower "MWX-16," _07_		120
29874	Peanuts Halloween Aquarium Car, _12_		85
29877	Southern Crane Car "D76," CC, _08_		350
29882	Witches Operating Brew Car, _08_		150
29884	CNJ Twin Dump Car, _08_		85
29885	BN Crane Car "S-104," CC, _10_		340
29886	BN Boom Car "S-1040," CC, _10_		220
29888	Postwar "3494-625" Soo Lines Operating Boxcar, _08_		70
29893	PRR Operating Stock Car "129893," RailSounds, _09_		150
29894	Christmas Chase Gondola, _09_		65
29895	Christmas Operating Snow Globe Car, _10_		75
29897	CSX Chessie System Research Car "3440," _11_		65
29900	"I Love Wisconsin" Boxcar, _01_		35
29901	"I Love Kentucky" Boxcar, _01_		30
29902	"I Love Iowa" Boxcar, _01_		31
29903	"I Love Missouri" Boxcar, _01_		31
29904	2002 Toy Fair Boxcar, _02_		22
29906	"I Love Connecticut" Boxcar, _02_		33
29907	"I Love West Virginia" Boxcar, _02_		33
29908	"I Love Delaware" Boxcar, _02_		33
29909	"I Love Maryland" Boxcar, _02_		65
29910	Toy Fair Centennial Boxcar, _03_		40
29912	"I Love Alabama" Boxcar, _03_		30
29913	"I Love Mississippi" Boxcar, _03_		35
29914	"I Love Louisiana" Boxcar, _03_		35
29915	"I Love Arkansas" Boxcar, _03_		30
29918	2003 Toy Fair Boxcar, _03_		48
29919	2004 Toy Fair Boxcar, _04_		37
29920	"I Love North Dakota" Boxcar, _03_		35
29921	"I Love South Dakota" Boxcar, _03_		40
29922	"I Love Nebraska" Boxcar, _03_		30
29923	"I Love Kansas" Boxcar, _03_		30
29925	Toy Fair Polar Express Boxcar, _05_		250
29927	"I Love Washington" Boxcar, _05_		45
29928	"I Love Oregon" Boxcar, _05_		40
29929	"I Love Idaho" Boxcar, _05_		45

Exc Mint

		Exc	Mint
29930	"I Love Utah" Boxcar, 05	45	___
29932	"I Love Oklahoma" Boxcar, 06	45	___
29933	"I Love New Mexico" Boxcar, 06	45	___
29934	"I Love Hawaii" Boxcar, 06	45	___
29935	"I Love Alaska" Boxcar, 06	45	___
29936	"I Love Wyoming" Boxcar, 06	45	___
29937	2006 Toy Fair Boxcar, 06	38	___
29942	Santa Fe Railroad Art Boxcar, 06	50	___
29943	Texas Special Railroad Art Boxcar, 06	50	___
29944	1957 Lionel Art Boxcar, 06	50	___
29945	1947 Lionel Art Boxcar, 06	50	___
29949	Weyerhaeuser Timber Skeleton Log Car 3-pack #2 (std O), 03	90	___
29950	1948 Lionel Art Boxcar, 08	50	___
29951	1954 Lionel Art Boxcar, 08	50	___
29952	GN Art Boxcar, 08	50	___
29953	SP Art Boxcar, 08	50	___
29954	Dealer Christmas Boxcar, 07	75	___
29955	Dealer Boxcar, 08	75	___
29958	Dealer Boxcar, 09	50	___
29959	1952 Lionel Art Boxcar, 09	58	___
29960	Rock Island Art Boxcar, 09–10	58	___
29961	Meet the Beatles Boxcar 2-pack, 10–14	130	___
29965	Lionel Art Boxcar 2-pack, 10–11	116	___
29968	Beatles "A Hard Day's Night" Boxcar, 11–14	65	___
29969	Beatles "Something New" Boxcar, 11–14	65	___
29973	NYC Pacemaker Boxcar "175005," 11	60	___
29974	SP Boxcar "128133," 11	60	___
29975	Holiday Boxcar, 11	60	___
29976	Holiday Boxcar, 12–13	65	___
29978	Railroad Museum of Pennsylvania Boxcar, 12	65	___
29979	Angela Trotta Thomas "Christmas Morning" Boxcar, 12–13	60	___
29980	Elvis Presley 35th Anniversary Boxcar, 12	70	___
29982	CV Milk Car "575" (std O), 16	80	___
29985	B&M Milk Car "1903" (std O), 16	80	___
29989	PFE Steel-sided Refrigerator Car 3-pack (std O), 14–15	240	___
29994	U.S. Army Boxcar, 13–15	70	___
29995	U.S. Navy Boxcar, 13–15	70	___
29996	U.S. Marines Boxcar, 13–15	70	___
29997	U.S. Air Force Boxcar, 13–15	70	___
29998	U.S. National Guard Boxcar, 13–16	70	___
29999	U.S. Coast Guard Boxcar, 13–16	70	___
30000	PRR Keystone Super Freight Steam Train, TMCC, 05	450	___
30001	Santa Fe El Capitan Passenger Set, TrainSounds, 05–10	370	___
30002	Neil Young's Greendale Diesel Freight Set, 04	420	___
30003	Pennsylvania Flyer Operating Freight Expansion Pack, 05	99	___
30004	Pennsylvania Flyer Passenger Expansion Pack, 05–08	120	___
30005	Disney Passenger Train, 05	190	___
30007	NYC Flyer Operating Freight Expansion Pack, 05	99	___

		Exc	Mint
____30008	NYC Flyer Passenger Expansion Pack, *05–08*		120
____30011	Holiday Expansion Pack, *05*		100
30012	Thomas the Tank Engine Expansion Pack, *05–13, 16*		150
____30016	NYC Flyer Steam Freight Set, *06–08*		290
____30018	Pennsylvania Flyer Steam Freight Set, *06–07*		200
____30020	North Pole Central Christmas Steam Train, *06–07*		220
____30021	Cascade Range Steam Logging Train, *06–08*		190
____30022	Southwest Diesel Freight Set, TrainSounds, *06*		295
____30024	UP Fast Freight Steam Set, TrainSounds, *06–07*		340
30025	Chesapeake Super Freight Steam Set, TMCC, *06–07*		475
____30026	CP Diesel Freight Set, TMCC, *06*		540
30034	Great Western Train Set with Lincoln Logs, *07–09*		230
____30035	Sodor Freight Expansion Pack, *06–09*		120
____30036	Great Western Expansion Pack, *07–08*		120
30037	Pennsylvania Flyer Operating Freight Expansion Pack, *06–08*		120
30038	NYC Flyer Operating Freight Expansion Pack, *06–08*		120
30039	North Pole Central Passenger Expansion Pack, *06–11*		110
30040	North Pole Central Freight Expansion Pack, *06–11*		110
____30041	Southwest Diesel Freight Expansion Pack, *06*		110
____30042	Cascade Range Expansion Pack, *06*		110
____30044	NYC Empire Builder Steam Freight Set, TMCC, *06*		2800
____30045	Alaska Steam Work Train, *07–09*		270
____30046	Alaska Work Train Expansion Pack, *07–08*		110
30047	Northwest Special Diesel Freight Set, TrainSounds, *07–08*		295
30048	Northwest Special Freight Expansion Pack, *07–08*		110
____30049	D&RGW Fast Freight Set, TrainSounds, *08–09*		320
____30050	Pennsylvania Super Freight Set, CC, *08*		450
____30051	UP Diesel Freight Set, TMCC, *07*		500
____30056	Halloween Steam Freight Set, *07–10*		225
____30061	UPS Centennial Stream Freight Set, *07–08*		230
____30064	Pennsylvania Speeder Set, traditional, K-Line, *06*		75
____30065	Best Friend of Charleston Locomotive, *07*		425
30066/67	C&O Empire Builder Steam Freight Set, CC, *07–09*		2700
____30068	North Pole Central Christmas Freight Set, *08*		220
____30069	Thomas & Friends Passenger Train, *08–12*		170
____30070	Lionel Lines 4-4-2 Steam Freight Set, *07*		300
____30076	Disney Christmas Train, *07*		400
____30081	UP Merger Special GP38 Freight Set, *08*		300
____30082	UP Heritage Freight Car 3-pack, *08*		100
30084	British Great Western Shakespeare Express Passenger Train, *08*		300
____30085	MTA Metro-North M-7 Commuter Car Set, *07–08*		280
____30087	Alien Spaceship Recovery Freight Set, *08–09*		230
____30088	John Bull Passenger Train, *08*		430
____30089	Pennsylvania Flyer Freight Set, *08–10*		200
____30091	ATSF Steam Freight Set, *08–09*		270

		Exc	Mint
30094	Chicago & North Western Passenger Set, *08*		150____
30096	Pennsylvania Keystone Special Steam Freight Set, *09*		260____
30103	NYC 0-8-0 Steam Freight Set, *09–10*		300____
30108	American Fire and Rescue GP20 Freight Set, *09–10*		400____
30109	Nutcracker Route Christmas Train Set, *10–11*		270____
30111	Pullman Passenger Expansion Pack, *09–16*		155____
30112	Eastern Freight Expansion Pack, *09–17*		155____
30114	MTA LIRR M-7 Commuter Set, *09*		320____
30116	Lone Ranger Wild West Freight Set, *09–13*		400____
30118	A Christmas Story Steam Freight Set, *09–12*		330____
30120	Menards C&NW Steam Passenger Set, *09*		250____
30121	ATSF Baby Madison Car 3-pack, *10–11*		190____
30122	Wizard of Oz Steam Freight Set, *10–12*		310____
30123	Boy Scouts of America Steam Freight Set, *10*		310____
30124	Thunder Valley Quarry Steam Freight Set, *10–11*		300____
30125	Rio Grande Ski Train, TrainSounds, *10–11*		340____
30126	Pennsylvania Flyer Steam Freight Set, *10*		230____
30127	Scout Steam Freight Set, *10–12*		200____
30128	Western Freight Expansion Pack, *10–12*		138____
30131	Chessie System Merger Diesel Freight Set, *10*		300____
30133	Strasburg Steam Passenger Set, *10–13*		330____
30135	Scout Freight Expansion Pack, *11–15*		115____
30136	Thunder Valley Quarry Freight Car Add-on 2-pack, *10–11*		110____
30138	Chessie System Merger Freight Car Add-on 2-pack, *10–11*		120____
30139	Santa Fe Flyer Steam Freight Set, *10*		270____
30141	Sodor Tank and Wagon Expansion Pack, *10–16*		150____
30142	Texas Special Freight Set, TrainSounds, *10–11*		700____
30144	Operation Eagle Justice Diesel Freight Set, *10–11*		500____
30145	Maple Leaf Diesel Freight Set, *10–11*		550____
30146	Menards Soo Line Freight Set, *10*		275____
30147	MTA Long Island M-7 Commuter Set, *11*		320____
30153	CSX Diesel Freight Set, *11*		330____
30154	BNSF Diesel Freight Set, *11*		340____
30155	M&StL Diesel Freight Set, *11–12*		230____
30156	NYC Flyer Freight Set, TrainSounds, *11*		300____
30157	M&StL Flatcar and Erie-Lack. Gondola 2-pack, *11–15*		110____
30158	Norfolk Southern GP38 Diesel Freight Train Set, *11*		320____
30159	Wabash Blue Bird Passenger Set, *11–12*		360____
30161	Boy Scouts Steam Freight Set, *11–13*		320____
30162	Thomas & Friends Christmas Set, *13–15*		200____
30164	Santa's Flyer Steam Freight Set, *11–13*		250____
30165	Candy Cane Transit Commuter 2-pack, *11–13*		180____
30166	Coca-Cola 125th Anniversary Steam Set, *11–12*		350____
30167	SP Merger Steam Freight Train Set, *12*		400____
30168	Rio Grande General Set, TrainSounds, *11–12*		300____
30169	NJ Transit Train Set, *11*		350____
30170	Sodor Freight 3-pack, *11–13*		100____
30171	GG1 Electric Freight Train Set, *11–13*		550____

		Exc	Mint
_____30173	Santa Fe Flyer Freight Set, *11–12*		270
_____30174	Pennsylvania Flyer Freight Set, *11–13*		290
30178	ATSF Super Chief Diesel Passenger Train Set, *12–13*		400
_____30179	RI Rocket Diesel Freight Train Set, *12–13*		400
_____30180	Horseshoe Curve Steam Freight Train Set, *12–13*		440
_____30181	CP Diesel Passenger Set, RailSounds, *13, 15*		450
_____30183	Scout Remote Steam Freight Set, *13, 15*		220
_____30184	Polar Express Steam Freight Set, *13*		420
_____30185	NJ Transit Diesel MOW Train Set, *12–13*		350
30186	KCS Southern Belle Diesel Freight Train Set, *12–13*		350
30187	Titanic Centennial Diesel Freight Train Set, *12–13*		450
_____30188	UP Flyer Steam Freight Train Set, *12–13*		330
_____30189	LIRR Diesel Passenger Train Set, *12–13*		330
_____30190	Thomas & Friends Set, LionChief, *12–16*		200
_____30191	Sodor Work Set 3-pack, *12–15*		100
_____30193	Peanuts Christmas Steam Freight Set, *12–15*		370
_____30194	North Pole Express Steam Freight Set, *12–13*		290
30195	Grand Central Express Diesel Passenger Train Set, *12–14*		440
_____30196	Hershey's Steam Freight Train Set, *12–13*		312
_____30200	NYC Flyer Steam Freight Train Set, *12–13*		350
30205	Silver Bells Christmas Steam Freight Set, *513–14*		240
_____30206	Area 51 RS3 Diesel Freight Set, *13*		250
_____30207	Santa Fe RS3 Diesel Freight Set, *13*		200
_____30210	CP Rail Grain SetDiesel Freight Set, *13*		390
_____30211	BNSF Maxi Stack Diesel Freight Set, *13*		440
_____30213	Northeast NS Heritage Diesel Freight Set, *13*		410
_____30214	Peanuts Halloween Steam Freight Set, *13, 15–16*		320
_____30217	SP Black Widow Diesel Freight Set, *13, 15*		460
_____30218	Polar Express Steam Passenger Set, *13–16*		400
_____30219	Gingerbread Junction Steam Freight Set, *13–14*		290
30220	Polar Express 10th Anniversary Passenger Set, *13–14, 16*		500
_____30221	Diesel Remote Control Set, *13–16*		200
_____30222	Percy Remote Control Set, *13–15*		200
_____30223	James Remote Control Set, *13–15*		200
_____30224	Pennsylvania Limited Steam Passenger Set, *13*		340
_____30225	Medal of Honor Train, *13*		430
_____30226	NS Diesel Freight Set, RailSounds, *13*		410
_____30228	Chattanooga Express Steam Passenger Set, *13*		250
30233	Pennsylvania Flyer Remote Steam Freight Set, *13–17*		280
_____31569	Western & Atlantic Passenger Car 2-pack, *08*		100
_____31700	Postwar Girls Freight Set, *01*		570
_____31701	Postwar Boys Freight Set, *02*		345
_____31704	Alton Limited Steam Passenger Set, *02*		870
_____31705	50th Anniversary Hudson Passenger Set, *02*		910
_____31706	UP Burro Crane Set, *02*		210
_____31707	C&O Diesel Freight Set, *03*		280
31708	Postwar "1805" Marines Missile Launch Train, *03*		400
_____31710	BN Diesel Coal Train, RailSounds, *03*		690

		Exc	Mint
31711	Postwar "1563W" Wabash Diesel Freight Set, RailSounds, 03		570___
31712	UP Alco PA Diesel Passenger Set, RailSounds, 03		1495___
31713	Southern Crescent Limited Steam Passenger Set, RailSounds, 03		1195___
31714	Amtrak Acela Diesel Passenger Set, RailSounds, 04–05		2000___
31715	Fire Rescue Steam Freight Set, 02		296___
31716	Fire Rescue Steam Freight Set, 03		275___
31717	CP Rail Snow Removal Train, 03		255___
31718	SP "Oil Can" Tank Train Freight Set, 03		1600___
31719	Western Maryland Fireball Diesel Freight Set, 04		290___
31720	FEC Champion Diesel Passenger Set, RailSounds, 04		900___
31721	Postwar "13138" Majestic Electric Freight Set, RailSounds, 04		580___
31724	Nabisco 3-car Passenger Set, 03		110___
31727	Postwar "2291W" Rio Grande Diesel Freight Set, RailSounds, 04		640___
31728	Elvis "He Dared to Rock" Steam Freight Set, 04		325___
31730	Norman Rockwell Boxcar 4-pack, 05		95___
31733	Jones & Laughlin Steel Slag Train, 05		250___
31734	Chessie Steam Special Passenger Set, TMCC, 05		405___
31735	Chessie Diesel Freight Set, TMCC, 05–06		670___
31736	CP Diesel Grain Train, TMCC, 05		700___
31737	Napa Valley Wine Train, TMCC, 05		900___
31739	Postwar "13150" Hudson Steam Freight Set, Super 0, 05		940___
31740	Postwar "2519W" Virginian Diesel Freight Set, TMCC, 05–07		620___
31742	Postwar "2544W" Santa Fe Super Chief Diesel Passenger Set, 05		700___
31746	GN Mountain Mover Steam Freight Set, 12–13		430___
31747	Pennsylvania Electric Ballast Train, TMCC, 06		550___
31748	Santa Fe U28CG Diesel Freight Set (std 0), TMCC, 06–07		770___
31749	Pennsylvania Diesel Coal Train, TMCC, 06		770___
31750	NYC Hotbox Reefer Steam Freight Set, TMCC, 06–07		530___
31751	New York City Transit Authority R27 Subway Train, CC, 07		700___
31752	B&O Diesel Freight Set, TMCC, 06–07		740___
31753	GN Diesel Freight Set, TMCC, 06–08		740___
31754	Postwar "2545WS" N&W Space Freight Set, TMCC, 06–07		960___
31755	Texas Special Diesel Passenger Set, CC, 07–08		1280___
31757	Postwar "2289WS" Berkshire Freight Set, CC, 07		750___
31758	Postwar "2270W" Jersey Central Diesel Passenger Car Set, CC, 08		750___
31760	CSX SD40-2 Diesel Husky Stack Car Set, CC, 07–08		770___
31765	Postwar "11268" C&O Diesel Freight Set, 08		580___
31767	Bethlehem Steel Rolling Stock Set, K-Line, 06		100___
31768	B&O Rolling Stock Set, K-Line, 06		100___
31772	Conrail LionMaster Diesel Freight Set, CC, 08–09		535___
31773	NS Dash 9 Diesel TankTrain Set, CC, 08		785___
31774	AEC Burro Crane Set, traditional, 09–11		260___

		Exc	Mint
____31775	"1562" Burlington GP Passenger Set, *08*		470
31776	"2219W" Lackawanna Train Master Freight Set, *08*		415
____31777	"2124W" GG1 Passenger Set, *08*		470
____31778	"1484WS" Steam Passenger Set, *08*		610
____31779	Amtrak HHP-8 Amfleet Passenger Set, CC, *09*		500
31782	ATSF Crane Car and Boom Car, CC (std O), *09–10*		560
____31783	BNSF Ice Cold Express Diesel Freight Set, CC, *10*		1000
____31784	No. 1593 UP Work Train Set, *09*		470
____31787	CN SD70M-2 Diesel Coal Train, CC, *09*		800
____31790	PRR GG1 Passenger Set, *10*		500
____31791	NYC LionMaster Diesel Freight Set, CC, *10*		700
31793	White Pass & Yukon Freight Car Add-on 3-pack, *10–11, 13*		195
31795	Pere Marquette Freight Car 3-pack (std O), *10–11*		210
____31796	Feather Route Freight Car 3-pack (std O), *10–11*		210
____31797	New York City Transit R16 Subway Set, CC, *10*		800
____31799	GN Empire Steam Freight Express Set, *10*		430
____31901	Christmas Steam Freight Set, *02*		145
____31902	PRR K4 Freight Set, *01–02*		580
____31904	C&O Steam Freight Set, RailSounds, *01*		400
____31905	NH Diesel Freight Set, CC, *01*		660
____31907	PRR Atlantic Freight Set, *01 u*		400
____31908	Reading Hobo Express Freight Set, *01 u*		365
____31909	Santa Fe Shell Tank Car Freight Set, *01 u*		320
____31910	Soo Line Diesel Freight Set, *01 u*		350
____31911	Snap-On Anniversary Steam Freight Set, *00 u*		600
____31913	PRR Flyer Steam Freight Set, *01*		145
____31914	NYC Flyer Steam Freight Set, RailSounds, *01–02*		170
____31915	Chessie GP38 Diesel Freight Set, *01–02*		155
____31916	Santa Fe Steam Freight Set, *01*		300
____31918	C&O Steam Freight Set, SignalSounds, *01*		315
____31919	T&P Steam Passenger Set, RailSounds, *01*		210
____31920	L.L. Bean Freight Set, *01 u*		260
____31922	Snap-On Tool Diesel Freight Set, *01 u*		352
____31923	PRR Flyer Freight Set, *01 u*		130
____31924	Union Pacific RS3 Diesel Freight Set, *02*		95
____31926	Area 51 FA Diesel Freight Set, *02*		160
____31928	Great Train Robbery Set, *02*		180
____31931	Ballyhoo Brothers Circus Train, *02*		190
____31932	NYC Limited Passenger Set, RailSounds, *02*		285
____31933	Santa Fe Steam Freight Set, RailSounds, *02*		320
31934	Lionel 20th Century Express Steam Freight Set, *00 u*		285
____31936	Pennsylvania Flyer Steam Freight Set, *03–05*		190
____31938	Southern Diesel Freight Set, *03–04*		160
____31939	Great Train Robbery Steam Freight Set, *03*		185
____31940	NYC Flyer Steam Freight Set, RailSounds, *03*		225
____31941	Winter Wonderland Railroad Christmas Train, *03*		150
____31942	Norman Rockwell Christmas Train, *03*		330
31944	NYC Limited Diesel Passenger Set, RailSounds, *03*		250

		Exc	Mint
31945	Santa Fe Steam Super Freight Set, RailSounds, *03*		350____
31946	Disney Christmas Steam Train, *04–05*		310____
31947	World of Disney Steam Freight Set, *03*		215____
31950	Kraft Holiday UP RS3 Diesel Freight Set, *02 u*		149____
31952	Great Northern Glacier Route Diesel Freight Set, *03–04*		110____
31953	"Riding the Rails" Hobo Train Set, *03–04*		225____
31956	Thomas the Tank Engine Set, *04–07*		195____
31958	Santa Fe Flyer Steam Freight Set, RailSounds, *04*		205____
31960	Polar Express Steam Passenger Set, *04–13*		420____
31961	Bloomingdale's Pennsylvania Flyer Steam Freight Set, *02 u*		159____
31962	Nickel Plate Road Super Freight Set, RailSounds, *04*		350____
31963	Southern Pacific Overnight Steam Freight Set, *04*		340____
31966	Holiday Tradition Steam Freight Set, *04–05*		210____
31969	NYC Flyer Steam Freight Set, RailSounds, *04*		205____
31976	Yukon Special Diesel Freight Set, *05*		225____
31977	New York Central Flyer Steam Freight Set, *05*		250____
31985	Santa Fe Steam Fast Freight Set, TrainSounds, *05*		320____
31987	Mickey's Holiday Express Train, *04*		280____
31989	UP Overland Freight Express Set, *04*		880____
31990	Copper Range Steam Freight Mine Set, *05*		175____
31993	NS Black Diamond Diesel Freight Set, TMCC, *05*		500____
32900	DC Billboard, *99*		24____
32902	Construction Zone Signs, set of 6, *99–17*		10____
32904	Hellgate Bridge, *99*	235	415____
32905	Irvington Factory, *99–00*		295____
32910	Rotary Coal Tipple with bathtub gondola, *02*		442____
32919	Animated Maiden Rescue, *99*		65____
32920	Animated Pylon with airplane, *99*		130____
32921	Electric Coaling Station, *99–01*		125____
32922	Highway Barrels, set of 6, *99–17*		10____
32923	Accessory Transformer, *99–03, 06–16*		46____
32929	Icing Station with Santa, *99*		90____
32930	Power Supply Set with ZW controller and 2 power supplies, *99–02, 06–09*	240	425____
32933	Christmas Stocking Hanger Set, 4-piece, *99–00*		50____
32934	Stocking Hanger, gondola, *99–00*		15____
32935	Stocking Hanger, boxcar, *99–00*		15____
32960	Hindenburger Cafe, *99*		195____
32961	Route 66 UFO Cafe, *99*		200____
32987	Hobo Campfire, *99–00*	25	45____
32988	Postwar "192" Railroad Control Tower, *99–00*		75____
32989	Postwar "464" Sawmill, *99–00*		75____
32990	Linex Oil Derrick, *99–00*		55____
32991	WLLC Radio Station, *99*		75____
32996	Postwar "362" Barrel Loader, *00*		125____
32997	Aluminum Rico Station, *00*		300____
32998	Hobby Shop, *99–00*		300____
32999	Hellgate Bridge, *99–00*		375____
33000	GP9 Diesel "3000," RailScope video camera system, *88–90*	125	170____

			Exc	Mint
____	33002	RailScope Television Monitor, *88–90*	45	70
____	34102	Amtrak Shelter, *04–08*		25
____	34108	Lionelville Suburban House, *03*		20
____	34109	Lionelville Large Suburban House, *03*		15
____	34110	Lionelville Estate House, *03*		30
____	34111	Lionelville Deluxe Fieldstone House, *03*		17
____	34112	Lionelville Fieldstone House, *03*		17
____	34113	Lionelville Large Suburban House, *03*		17
____	34114	Late Illuminated Station and Terrace, red trim, *03*		475
____	34117	Early Illuminated Station and Terrace, green trim, *03*		475
____	34120	TMCC Direct Lockon, *04–16*		50
____	34121	Lionelville Bungalow, *04*		20
____	34122	Lionelville Bungalow with garage, *04*		20
____	34123	Lionelville Bungalow with addition, *04*		20
____	34124	Lionelville Anastasia's Bakery, *04*		20
____	34125	Lionelville Cotton's Candy, *04*		20
____	34126	Lionelville Market, *04*		20
____	34127	Lionelville O'Grady's Tavern, *04*		22
____	34128	Lionelville Pharmacy, *04*		15
____	34129	Lionelville Kiddie City Toy Store, *04*		20
____	34130	Lionelville Jim's 5&10, *04*		25
____	34131	Lionelville Al's Hardware, *04*		30
____	34144	Santa Fe Scrap Yard, *05–06*		80
____	34145	New Haven Scrap Yard, *06*		100
____	34149	Sly Fox and the Hunter, *05–07*		80
____	34150	Reading Room, *05–06*		70
____	34158	Ring Toss Midway Game, *05–06*		20
____	34159	Camel Race Midway Game, *05–06*		20
____	34162	Operating Oil Pump, *04–09*		53
____	34163	Speeder Shed, *04–06*		30
____	34164	Nutcracker Operating Gateman, *05–08*		80
____	34190	Carousel, *04–06*		165
____	34191	Hobo Depot, *04–05*		70
____	34192	Operating Lumberjacks, *04–06*		60
____	34193	UPS Animated Billboard, *04*		30
____	34194	UPS Package Station, *05*		120
____	34195	UPS People Pack, *06–09, 11*		27
____	34210	TMCC Direct Lockon, *09*		52
____	34500	Rio Grande FT Diesel "5484," traditional, *06*		245
____	34501	Southern FT Diesel "4102," traditional, *06*		400
____	34504	B&O F3 Diesel A Unit "2368," nonpowered, *06–07*		200
____	34505	B&O E7 Diesel AA Set, CC, *07*		700
____	34508	PRR E7 Diesel AA Set, CC, *07*		700
____	34509	PRR E7 Diesel B Unit, nonpowered (std O), *07*		170
____	34510	PRR E7 Diesel B Unit, powered, CC, *07*		300
____	34511	NYC F7 Diesel ABA Set, CC, *07–08*		900
____	34512	NYC F7 Diesel B Unit "2439," powered, CC, *07–08*		300
____	34513	WP F7 Diesel ABA Set, CC, *07–08*		900
____	34514	WP F7 Diesel B Unit "918C," powered, CC, *07–08*		300
____	34515	NYC F7 Diesel Breakdown B Unit "2440," RailSounds, *07*		270

Exc Mint

		Exc	Mint
34518	PRR E7 Diesel Breakdown B Unit, RailSounds, *07*	270	___
34519	NYC Sharknose RF-16 Diesel AA Set, CC, *07–08*	630	___
34520	NYC Sharknose Diesel B Unit "3818," nonpowered (std O), *07–08*	160	___
34521	Santa Fe F3 Diesel A Unit "17," traditional, *07*	265	___
34522	Santa Fe F3 Diesel B Unit "17," nonpowered (std O), *07*	150	___
34544	ATSF F3 Diesel B Unit, CC, *08*	270	___
34545	D&RGW F3 Diesel B Unit, CC, *08*	270	___
34546	Southern F3 Diesel B Unit, CC, *08*	270	___
34547	Texas Special F3 Diesel B Unit, CC, *08*	270	___
34559	Archive New Haven F3 Diesel AA Set, *10*	500	___
34564	SP Alco PA Diesel AA Set, CC, *10–11*	750	___
34567	SP Alco PB B Unit, CC, *10–11*	400	___
34568	ATSF Alco PA AA Diesel Set, CC, *11*	750	___
34569	ATSF Alco PB Diesel, CC, *11*	400	___
34570	B&O FA Diesel AA Set, CC, *10*	650	___
34573	Postwar Scale ATSF F3 AA Diesel Set, CC, *11*	700	___
34576	Postwar Scale NYC F3 AA Diesel Set, CC, *11*	700	___
34579	Postwar Scale ATSF F3 B Unit, CC, *11*	380	___
34580	Postwar Scale NYC F3 B Unit, CC, *11*	380	___
34581	Postwar "2331" Virginian Train Master Diesel, CC, *10*	495	___
34582	Postwar "2373" CP F3 Diesel AA Set, CC, *10*	700	___
34585	Postwar "2375" CP F3 B Unit, CC, *10*	380	___
34586	Postwar "2378" MILW F3 Diesel AB Set, CC, *10*	700	___
34589	Postwar "2377" MILW F3 A, powered, CC, *10*	425	___
34594	UP Alco PA AA Diesel Set, CC, *11*	750	___
34597	UP Alco PB Diesel, CC, *11*	400	___
34600	SP GP30 Diesel "5010," CC, *11*	500	___
34601	SP GP30 Diesel "5012," CC, *11*	500	___
34602	SP GP30 Diesel "5014," *11*	380	___
34603	SP GP30 Diesel "5017," nonpowered, *11*	240	___
34604	Conrail GP30 Diesel "2178," CC, *11*	500	___
34605	Conrail GP30 Diesel "2180," CC, *11*	500	___
34606	Conrail GP30 Diesel "2182," *11*	380	___
34607	Conrail GP30 Diesel "2185," nonpowered, *11*	240	___
34608	Lionelville & Western GP30 Diesel "1100," CC, *11*	450	___
34609	Lionelville & Western GP30 Diesel "1103," CC, *11*	450	___
34610	Lionelville & Western GP30 Diesel "1107," *11*	330	___
34611	Lionelville & Western GP30 Diesel "1112," nonpowered, *11*	190	___
34612	NS SD70M-2 Diesel "2658," CC, *11*	550	___
34613	NS SD70M-2 Diesel "2663," CC, *11*	550	___
34614	CN SD70M-2 Diesel "8020," CC, *11*	550	___
34615	CN SD70M-2 Diesel "8024," CC, *11*	550	___
34616	FEC SD70M-2 Diesel "101," CC, *11*	550	___
34617	FEC SD70M-2 Diesel "103," CC, *11*	550	___
34618	George Bush SD70ACe Diesel "4141," CC, *11*	550	___
34619	NH SD70ACe Diesel "8696," CC, *11*	550	___
34620	NH SD70ACe Diesel "8699," CC, *11*	550	___
34623	Texas Special SD70ACe Diesel "6340," CC, *11*	550	___
34624	Texas Special SD70ACe Diesel "6344," CC, *11*	550	___

		Exc Mint
____34625	NP F3 AA Diesel Set, CC, *11*	700
____34628	NP F3 Diesel B Unit "6005C," CC, *11*	380
____34629	NP F3 Diesel B Unit "6006C," nonpowered, *11*	240
____34630	Frisco F3 AA Diesel Set, CC, *11*	700
____34633	Frisco F3 Diesel B Unit, CC, *11*	380
____34634	Frisco F3 Diesel B Unit, nonpowered, *11*	260
____34635	ATSF F3 AA Diesel Set, CC, *11*	700
____34638	ATSF F3 Diesel B Unit, CC, *11*	380
____34639	ATSF F3 Diesel B Unit, nonpowered, *11*	240
____34640	GTW F3 AA Diesel Set, CC, *11*	700
____34643	GTW F3 Diesel B Unit, CC, *11*	380
____34644	GTW F3 Diesel B Unit, nonpowered, *11*	260
____34645	CN F3 AA Diesel Set, CC, *11*	700
____34648	CN F3 Diesel B Unit, CC, *11*	380
____34649	CN F3 Diesel B Unit, nonpowered, *11*	260
____34650	MILW DD35A Diesel "1535," CC, *11*	600
____34651	MILW DD35A Diesel "1537," nonpowered, *11*	440
____34662	RI GP9 Diesel "1331," CC, *12–13*	480
____34663	RI GP9 Diesel "1327," CC, *12–13*	480
____34664	GN GP9 Diesel "688," CC, *12–13*	480
____34665	GN GP9 Diesel "695," CC, *12–13*	480
____34666	L&N GP9 Diesel "504," CC, *12–13*	480
____34667	L&N GP9 Diesel "525," CC, *12–13*	480
____34668	CN GP90 Diesel "4463," CC, *12*	480
____34669	CN GP90 Diesel "4455," CC, *12*	480
____34670	C&O GP9 Diesel "6240," CC, *12–13*	480
____34671	C&O GP9 Diesel "6243," CC, *12*	480
____34672	PRR Baldwin Centipede Diesel AA, CC, *12–13*	2200
____34673	UP Baldwin Centipede Diesel AA, CC, *12*	2200
34676	PRR Baldwin Centipede Diesel "5821," CC, *12–14*	
____		1100
34677	Seaboard Baldwin Centipede Diesel "4503," CC, *12–14*	
____		1100
34680	NdeM Baldwin Centipede Diesel "6402," CC, *12–14*	
____		1100
____34681	UP GP9 Diesel "256," CC, *12*	480
____34682	UP GP9 Diesel "261," CC, *12*	480
____34683	PRR Baldwin Centipede Diesel AA, CC, *12–13*	2200
____34686	Baldwin Demonstrator Centipede AA, CC, *12*	2200
____34689	WM F7 AA Diesel Set, CC, *12–13*	730
____34692	WM F7 B Unit "410," CC, *12–13*	400
____34693	WM F7 B Unit, *12–13*	250
____34694	L&N F7 AA Diesel Set, CC, *12*	730
____34697	L&N F7 B Unit "900," CC, *12–13*	400
____34698	L&N F7 B Unit, *12–13*	250
____34701	PRR Baldwin RF-16 Diesel AA Set, CC, *12–14*	730
____34704	PRR Baldwin RF-16 Diesel B Unit, CC, *12–14*	400
34705	PRR Baldwin RF-16 Diesel B Unit, nonpowered, *12–14*	
____		250
____34731	NH Alco RS-11 Diesel "1413," nonpowered, *12*	240
____34732	LV Alco RS-11 Diesel "7640," CC, *12*	480
____34733	LV Alco RS-11 Diesel "7642," CC, *12*	480
____34734	LV Alco RS-11 Diesel "7643," nonpowered, *12*	240
____34735	ATSF GP9 Diesel "726," CC, *12*	480
____34736	ATSF GP9 Diesel "741," CC, *12*	480

Exc Mint

34737	NP GP9 Diesel "202," CC, *12*	480____
34738	NP GP9 Diesel "317," CC, *12–13*	480____
34739	RI GP9 Diesel "1325," nonpowered, *12*	240____
34740	GN GP9 Diesel "668," nonpowered, *12*	240____
34741	L&N GP9 Diesel "531," nonpowered, *12*	240____
34742	CN GP90 Diesel "4527," nonpowered, *12*	240____
34743	C&O GP9 Diesel "6249," nonpowered, *12*	240____
34744	UP GP9 Diesel "268," nonpowered, *12*	240____
34745	Monon Alco C-420 Diesel "509," CC, *12–13*	530____
34746	Monon Alco C-420 Diesel "512," CC, *12–13*	530____
34747	Monon Alco C-420 Diesel "514," nonpowered, *12–13*	260____
34748	LV Alco C-420 Diesel "404," CC, *12*	530____
34749	LV Alco C-420 Diesel "412," CC, *12*	530____
34750	LV Alco C-420 Diesel "414," nonpowered, *12*	260____
34754	Alaska Alco C-420 Diesel "1210," CC, *12*	530____
34755	Alaska Alco C-420 Diesel "1214," CC, *12*	530____
34756	Alaska Alco C-420 Diesel "1217," nonpowered, *12*	260____
34757	Seaboard Alco C-420 Diesel "127," CC, *12–13*	530____
34758	Seaboard Alco C-420 Diesel "129," CC, *12–13*	530____
34759	Seaboard Alco C-420 Diesel "134," nonpowered, *12–13*	260____
34760	NKP Alco C-420 Diesel "578," CC, *12–13*	530____
34761	NKP Alco C-420 Diesel "575," CC, *12–13*	530____
34762	NKP Alco C-420 Diesel "572," nonpowered, *12–13*	260____
34763	CNJ Scale NW2 Diesel Switcher "1060," CC, *12*	470____
34764	CNJ Scale NW2 Diesel Switcher "1061," CC, *12*	470____
34765	KCS Scale NW2 Diesel Switcher "1221," CC, *12*	470____
34766	KCS Scale NW2 Diesel Switcher "1224," CC, *12*	470____
34767	L&N Scale NW2 Diesel Switcher "2203," CC, *12*	470____
34768	L&N Scale NW2 Diesel Switcher "2206," CC, *12*	470____
34769	MKT Scale NW2 Diesel Switcher "8," CC, *12*	470____
34770	MKT Scale NW2 Diesel Switcher "12," CC, *12*	470____
34771	Reading Scale NW2 Diesel Switcher "102," CC, *12*	470____
34772	Reading Scale NW2 Diesel Switcher "104," CC, *12*	470____
34773	PRR Scale NW2 Diesel Switcher "9163," CC, *12*	470____
34774	PRR Scale NW2 Diesel Switcher "9171," CC, *12*	470____
34775	N&W SD40-2 Diesel "6106," nonpowered, *12–13*	240____
34776	N&W SD40-2 Diesel "6121," CC, *12–13*	530____
34777	N&W SD40-2 Diesel "6109," CC, *12–14*	530____
34778	CSX SD40-2 Diesel "8023," nonpowered, *12–13*	240____
34779	CSX SD40-2 Diesel "8028," CC, *12–13*	530____
34780	CSX SD40-2 Diesel "8033," CC, *12–13*	530____
34781	BN SD40-2 Diesel "7140," nonpowered, *12–13*	240____
34782	BN SD40-2 Diesel "7153," CC, *12–13*	530____
34783	BN SD40-2 Diesel "7162," CC, *12–13*	530____
34784	Frisco SD40-2 Diesel "957," CC, *12–13*	530____
34785	Frisco SD40-2 Diesel "950," nonpowered, *12–13*	240____
34786	Frisco SD40-2 Diesel "952," CC, *12–13*	530____
34787	C&NW SD40-2 Diesel "6816," nonpowered, *12–13*	240____

Exc Mint

		Exc	Mint
____34788	C&NW SD40-2 Diesel "6820," CC, *12–13*		530
____34789	C&NW SD40-2 Diesel "6832," CC, *12–13*		530
____34790	MKT SD40-2 Diesel "602," nonpowered, *12–13*		240
____34791	MKT SD40-2 Diesel "609," CC, *12–13*		530
____34792	MKT SD40-2 Diesel "620," CC, *12–13*		530
____35100	NYC Vista Dome Car "7012," *07–09*		45
____35101	NYC Baggage Car "5028," *07*		40
____35102	Santa Fe El Capitan Streamliner Diner, *07*		65
35124	Alton Limited Madison Passenger Car 4-pack, *08–10*		240
____35128	ATSF El Capitan Baggage Car "2103," *08*		70
____35129	ATSF El Capitan Vista Dome Car "3153," *08*		70
35130	Polar Express Disappearing Hobo Car, *08–14, 16–17*		75
35133	MTA Metro-North M-7 Commuter Add-on 2-pack, *07–08*		85
____35134	North Pole Central Vista Dome Car, *08*		45
____35135	North Pole Central Diner, *08–10*		45
____35167	PRR Diner "2044," *10*		52
____35168	PRR Coach "4046," *09*		52
____35173	North Pole Central Blitzen Coach, *09*		45
____35174	MTA LIRR M-7 Add-on 2-pack, *09*		98
____35184	Western & Atlantic Baggage Car, *09*		60
____35185	Great Western Passenger Car 2-pack, *09*		100
____35193	PRR Streamliner 4-pack, *10–11*		250
____35200	Strasburg Observation Car, *10*		60
____35205	D&RGW Pikes Peak Add-on Coach, *10–11*		70
____35211	Strasburg Passenger Car Add-on 2-pack, *10*		100
____35214	Rio Grande Winter Park Diner, *11*		70
____35219	Hallow's Eve Express Passenger Car 2-pack, *11*		120
____35229	Hogwarts Express Dementors Coach, *11–15*		60
____35239	NJ Transit 2-pack Passenger Car Add-on, *11–14*		100
35247	Grand Central Express Passenger Car 2-pack, *12–13*		140
____35250	North Pole Coach 2-pack, *12–13*		120
35256	Hallow's Eve Express Passenger Car 2-pack #2, *12*		120
____35257	ATSF Vista Dome, *12*		70
____35258	ATSF Baggage Car, *12–13*		70
____35259	LIRR Passenger Car 2-pack, *12–15*		110
____35281	ATSF Super Chief Diner "1495," *13*		70
____35282	LIRR Jamaica Coach, *13–15*		60
____35283	CP Baggage Car and Diner 2-pack, *13*		130
____35286	Peanuts Coach 3-pack, *13*		165
35290	Polar Express Passenger Car Add-on 2-pack, *13–14, 16*		150
35293	Angela Trotta Thomas "Toyland Express" Boxcar, *13*		45
____35294	Polar Express Snow Tower, *13–14*		28
____35295	Christmas Billboard Set, *13–14, 16*		13
35403	NYC 20th Century Limited 18" Aluminum Passenger Car 4-pack (std O), *08*		625
35408	NYC 20th Century Limited 18" Aluminum Passenger Car 2-pack (std O), *08*		325
35411	NYC 20th Century Limited Diner, StationSounds (std O), *08*		325

Exc Mint

		Exc Mint
35412	Lenny Dean Passenger Coach, *08*	100____
35413	LL Streamliner Car 2-pack, *08*	270____
35415	UP 18" Streamliner Car 4-pack (std O), *08*	625____
35423	UP 18" Streamliner Car 2-pack (std O), *08*	325____
35430	Amtrak Coach	45____
35431	Amtrak Coach	45____
35432	Amtrak Coach	45____
35433	Amfleet Phase IVB Coach 2-pack (std O), *10*	140____
35445	SP Shasta Daylight 18" Passenger Car 4-pack (std O), *11*	640____
35446	SP Shasta Daylight 18" Passenger Car 2-pack (std O), *11*	320____
35454	Amfleet Cab Control End Car (std O), *10*	250____
35473	Amfleet Capstone Coach 3-pack (std O), *10*	180____
35481	NYC Add-on Passenger Car "M-498," *11*	120____
35490	Alaska Budd RDC Combination Car "702," nonpowered, *11*	130____
35497	RI Budd RDC Combination Car "751," nonpowered, *11*	130____
35498	RI Budd RDC Coach "750," nonpowered, *11*	130____
35499	Alaska Budd RDC Coach "712," nonpowered, *11*	130____
36000	Route 66 Flatcar with 2 red sedans, *98*	44____
36001	Route 66 Flatcar with 2 wagons, *98*	42____
36002	Pratt's Hollow Passenger Car 4-pack, *98*	445____
36006	Uranium Flatcar "6508," *99*	60____
36016	Flatcar with propellers, *98*	45____
36020	Flatcar "TT-6424" with auto frames, *99*	32____
36021	Alaska Flatcar "6424" with airplane, *99*	44____
36024	J.B. Hunt Flatcar "64245" with trailer, *99*	44____
36025	J.B. Hunt Flatcar "64246" with trailer, *99*	50____
36026	Flatcar with J.B. Hunt trailers 2-pack, *99*	85____
36027	Tredegar Iron Works Flatcar with cannon, *99*	45____
36028	Heavy Artillery Flatcar with cannon, *99*	45____
36029	SP Auto Carrier "516712," *99*	44____
36030	Troublesome Truck #1, *99*	35____
36031	Troublesome Truck #2, *99*	35____
36032	Christmas Gondola "6462" with presents, *99*	35____
36036	C&O Gondola, *99*	20____
36038	Construction Zone Gondola, *99 u*	NRS____
36040	Bethlehem Flatcar with block (SSS), *99*	75____
36041	Bethlehem Ore Car (SSS), *99*	40____
36043	Custom Consist Flatcar with pickup truck, *99*	40____
36044	Custom Consist Flatcar with dragster, *99*	40____
36045	Flatcar with dragster, *04*	30____
36046	Flatcar with custom truck, *04*	30____
36047	Construction Zone Gondola, *99 u*	NRS____
36048	Construction Zone Gondola, *99 u*	NRS____
36054	Archaeological Expedition Gondola with eggs, *00 u*	55____
36055	Flatcar with dragster, *01 u*	30____
36056	Flatcar with roadster, *01 u*	30____
36059	"Season's Greetings" Gondola, *99 u*	50____
36062	NYC 6462 Gondola, *99–00*	22____
36063	Conrail Gondola "604768," *99–00*	20____
36064	Billboard Flatcar "6424," *00*	41____

		Exc	Mint
___36065	Wabash Flatcar "25536" with trailer, *00*		35
___36066	Christmas Gondola with presents, *00*		32
36067	King Auto Sales Flatcar "6424" with pink Cadillac, *00*		
___			40
___36068	Pine Peak Tree Transport Gondola, *00*		NRS
___36079	Service Station Ltd. Flatcar with trailer, *00*		34
___36082	Whirlpool Flatcar with trailer, *00 u*		NRS
___36083	Santa Fe Gondola "168998," *01*		17
___36084	Grand Trunk Western Coil Car, *00*		32
___36085	FEC Coil Car, *00*		29
___36086	SP Flatcar with trailer, *01*		35
___36087	Flatcar "6424" with wooden whistle, *01*		25
___36088	Allis Chalmers Condenser Car "6519," *00*		43
___36089	Frisco Flatcar with airplane, *00*		35
___36090	TT Flatcar "6424" with Pepsi truck, *01*		44
36091	Maersk Flatcar "250129" with die-cast tractors, *00*		
___			55
36092	Maersk Flatcar "250130" with die-cast frames, *00*		
___			55
___36093	Soo TT Auto Carrier "906760," *00*		49
___36094	PC F9 Well Car "768122," *01*		41
___36095	Christmas Chase Gondola, *01*		37
___36098	PRR Gondola "385186," *01*		20
___36099	NYC Flatcar with stakes and bulkheads, *01*		25
___36104	Area 51 3-D Tank Car, *07*		60
___36108	Candy Cane 1-D Tank Car, *07*		60
___36112	NP 3-D Tank Car, *08*		35
___36113	IC 1-D Tank Car, *08*		35
___36114	ART Wood-sided Reefer, *08*		35
___36117	Lionel Lines 2-D Tank Car, *08*		50
___36118	NYC Pastel Stock Car "63561," *08–09*		55
___36128	Texas & Pacific 3-D Tank Car, *09*		40
___36129	British Columbia 1-D Tank Car, *09*		40
___36131	Lackawanna Wood-sided Reefer "7000," *09–10*		40
___36145	Philadelphia Quartz 3-D Tank Car "606," *10*		40
___36146	Cities Service 1-D Tank Car "11800," *10*		40
___36149	Strasburg Wood-sided Reefer "105," *10*		55
___36151	Grave's Blood Bank Tank Car, *10*		50
___36156	Pennsylvania Power & Light 1-D Tank Car, *10*		40
___36162	Diamond Chemicals 3-D Tank Car, *11*		40
___36163	Celanese 2-D Tank Car, *11–12*		40
___36166	Polar Express Reefer, *11–12*		55
___36169	Coca-Cola 3-D Tank Car, *11*		55
___36170	Partridge in a Pear Tree Reefer, *11–13*		55
___36172	Bubble Yum 1-D Tank Car, *11*		55
___36173	Santa's Flyer Hot Cocoa 3-D Tank Car, *11*		40
___36176	C&O 1-D Tank Car, *13*		43
___36177	WP 3-D Tank Car, *12*		40
___36178	Frisco 2-D Tank Car, *12–13*		40
___36182	Eggnog Unibody 1-D Tank Car, *12*		70
___36191	GN Waffle-sided Boxcar, *13*		43
___36195	PRR Flatcar with patrol helicopter, *13*		60
___36200	Quaker Life Cereal Boxcar, *00*		480
___36203	Whirlpool Boxcar, *00 u*		120
___36205	eBay Boxcar, *00*		270

		Exc	Mint
36206	REA Boxcar, *01*	25	___
36207	Vapor Records Christmas Boxcar, *01*	78	___
36208	Father's Day Boxcar, *00*	35	___
36210	Burlington Hi-Cube Boxcar "19825," *01*	40	___
36211	NP Hi-Cube Boxcar "659999," *01*	33	___
36212	Lionel Employee Christmas Boxcar, *00 u*	410	___
36213	Vapor Records Christmas Boxcar, *00*	45	___
36215	Train Station 25th Anniversary Boxcar, *00 u*	48	___
36218	Snap-On Boxcar, *00 u*	140	___
36219	UP Boxcar "183518," *02*	78	___
36220	Pioneer Seed Boxcar, *00 u*	NRS	___
36221	PRR Boxcar "569356," *01*	20	___
36222	NYC Boxcar "162440," *01*	20	___
36223	Chessie System Boxcar, *01*	20	___
36224	Santa Fe Boxcar "16263," *01*	20	___
36225	C&O Boxcar "250549," *01*	20	___
36226	E-Hobbies Boxcar, *01 u*	200	___
36227	Monopoly Community Chest Boxcar, *00 u*	50	___
36228	Lionel Visitor Center Boxcar, *01 u*	34	___
36229	Island Trains 20th Anniversary Boxcar, *01 u*	29	___
36232	Farmall Boxcar, *01 u*	NRS	___
36236	TM Books "I Love Lionel" Boxcar "7474-1," *01 u*	43	___
36238	Snap-On Tool Team ASE Racing Boxcar, *01 u*	NRS	___
36239	L.L. Bean Boxcar, *01 u*	120	___
36240	Do It Best Boxcar, *01 u*	100	___
36242	Erie-Lackawanna Boxcar "73113," *02*	24	___
36243	Christmas Boxcar "2002," *02*	31	___
36244	Teddy Bear Centennial Boxcar, *02*	36	___
36245	Lionel 20th Century Boxcar "1900-1925," *00 u*	30	___
36246	Lionel 20th Century Boxcar "1926-1950," *00 u*	30	___
36247	Lionel 20th Century Boxcar "1951-1975," *00 u*	30	___
36248	Lionel 20th Century Boxcar "1976-2000," *00 u*	30	___
36253	Christmas Boxcar (O), *03*	32	___
36254	Goofy Hi-Cube Boxcar, *03*	37	___
36255	Donald Duck Hi-Cube Boxcar, *03*	40	___
36256	GN Boxcar "6341," *03*	23	___
36261	PRR Boxcar, *03–05*	15	___
36262	Southern Central of Georgia Boxcar, *03 04*	20	___
36264	Santa Fe Boxcar "600196, *02*	18	___
36265	Angela Trotta Thomas "Window Wishing" Boxcar, *02*	38	___
36267	Mickey Mouse Hi-Cube Boxcar, *03*	50	___
36270	Angela Trotta Thomas "Home for the Holidays" Boxcar, *02–03*	30	___
36272	New Haven Boxcar "6501," *04*	20	___
36273	Railbox Hi-Cube Boxcar "15000," *04*	21	___
36275	Christmas Boxcar, *04*	35	___
36276	Angela Trotta Thomas "Tis the Season" Boxcar, *04*	34	___
36277	Pluto Hi-Cube Boxcar, *04–05*	50	___
36278	Winnie the Pooh Hi-Cube Boxcar, *04–05*	50	___
36281	B&O Boxcar, *04*	35	___
36291	Simpsons Boxcar, *04–05*	44	___
36294	UP Hi-Cube Boxcar, traditional, *05*	27	___
36295	CN Boxcar, traditional, *05*	27	___

		Exc	Mint
____36296	2005 Holiday Boxcar, *05*		48
36297	Angela Trotta Thomas "Christmas Eve" Boxcar, *05*		
____			48
____36299	Hammacher Schlemmer Music Boxcar, *04*		65
____36305	eBay Boxcar, *00 u*		120
____36500	Western Pacific Caboose "36500," *04*		23
____36501	D&RGW Caboose "36501," *04*		22
____36502	Reading Caboose "36502," *04*		25
____36515	North Pole Central Lines Caboose "36515," *04*		36
____36519	Lionel Lines Caboose, *04*		22
____36520	Santa Fe Caboose "36520," *04*		22
____36525	CSX Work Caboose, lighted, *05*		35
____36526	Pennsylvania Work Caboose, traditional, *05*		27
____36527	Santa Fe Work Caboose, traditional, *05*		28
36528	Chesapeake & Ohio Work Caboose, traditional, *05*		
____			40
36529	North Pole Central Work Caboose with presents, traditional, *05*		
____			38
____36530	Pennsylvania Caboose, traditional, *05*		33
____36531	Erie Caboose "C150," traditional, *05*		33
____36532	SP Caboose "1097," traditional, *05*		48
____36533	Reading Caboose "92803," traditional, *05*		33
____36534	NYC Center Cupola Caboose, traditional, *05*		40
____36535	LL Center Cupola Caboose, traditional, *05*		28
____36536	Southern Center Cupola Caboose, traditional, *05*		40
____36544	Alaska Caboose, *05*		35
____36547	Bethlehem Steel Transfer Caboose, traditional, *05*		40
____36548	Transylvania RR Work Caboose, traditional, *05*		45
____36550	Halloween Transfer Caboose, traditional, *06–07*		45
____36551	Christmas Caboose, *06*		45
____36552	U.S. Steel Work Caboose, traditional, *06–07*		45
____36553	NYC Caboose, *08*		20
____36554	SP Work Caboose, traditional, *06*		45
____36555	Pennsylvania Transfer Caboose, *06*		45
____36556	Lionel Lines Work Caboose, *06–07*		30
____36557	Rio Grande Work Caboose, traditional, *06*		29
36558	Virginian Center Cupola Caboose "316," traditional, *06*		
____			45
36559	WM Center Cupola Caboose "1863," traditional, *06*		
____			45
36560	C&O Center Cupola Caboose "90876," traditional, *06*		
____			45
36562	Army Transportation Work Caboose, traditional, *06*		
____			45
____36563	Reading Work Caboose, traditional, *06*		45
____36565	UP SP-type Caboose, traditional, *06*		48
____36566	NYC SP-type Caboose, traditional, *06*		48
____36567	GN SP-type Caboose, traditional, *06*		48
____36571	PRR Caboose, *08*		20
36580	B&O Center Cupola Caboose "C2047," traditional, *05*		
____			40
____36582	C&O Caboose, *05*		22
____36583	Holiday Caboose, *07*		50
____36587	SP Caboose "1121," *07–09*		40
____36589	PRR Work Caboose, *07*		40
____36590	UP Work Caboose, *07*		45

		Exc Mint
36591	Southern Caboose "X99," *08*	45____
36592	Santa Fe Caboose "999471," *06*	48____
36593	NYC Caboose, *06*	48____
36601	UP Caboose, *06*	48____
36602	UPS Centennial Caboose, *06*	45____
36604	Pennsylvania Caboose, *06*	25____
36607	K-Line Caboose, *06*	40____
36611	Conrail Caboose "19674," *07*	40____
36612	Alaska Caboose "1080," *07*	40____
36613	NYC Caboose, *07*	30____
36622	C&O Caboose "C-1838," *08–09*	40____
36623	ATSF Caboose, *07–09*	40____
36624	Lionel Lines Caboose, *08–09*	40____
36625	B&M Caboose, *08*	50____
36626	Erie Caboose "C101," *08–09*	45____
36634	Holiday Porthole Caboose, green, *08*	50____
36646	Monopoly Caboose, *10*	48____
36647	Strasburg Caboose, *10*	48____
36649	Pennsylvania Power & Light Work Caboose, *10*	45____
36657	Western & Atlantic Caboose, *10–11*	48____
36659	PRR Illuminated Porthole Caboose, *11*	35____
36668	CSX Illuminated Square Window Caboose, *10*	35____
36672	NS Caboose, *11*	25____
36674	Polar Caboose, *11–12*	53____
36701	Baldwin Locomotive Works Operating Welding Car "36701," *02*	60____
36702	Bosco Operating Milk Car with platform, *02*	115____
36703	Circus Horse Car with corral, *06*	150____
36704	Animated Reindeer Stock Car and Corral, *02*	145____
36718	AEC Security Caboose, *02*	45____
36719	Lionel Lion Bobbing Head Car, *02*	20____
36720	Aladdin Aquarium Car, *03*	40____
36721	101 Dalmatians Animated Gondola, *03*	45____
36722	Peter Pan Bobbing Head Boxcar, *03*	45____
36726	Santa Fe Searchlight Car "36726," *03*	50____
36727	Weyerhaeuser Moe & Joe Flatcar, *03*	65____
36728	SP Walking Brakeman Boxcar 163143," *03*	42____
36729	Lionel Lines Animated Caboose, *04–05*	68____
36730	U.S. Army Missile Launch Sound Car "44," *03*	175____
36731	Motorized Aquarium Car "3435," *03*	83____
36732	C&NW Jumping Hobo Car, *03*	41____
36733	Christmas Music Boxcar, *03*	45____
36734	Santa Fe Operating Searchlight Car "20611," *02*	25____
36735	WP Ice Car "7045," *02*	55____
36736	D&RGW Stock Car "39268," RailSounds, *04*	45____
36738	T&P Poultry Dispatch Car "36738," *02*	50____
36739	Postwar "3461" Lionel Lines Log Dump Car, *03*	50____
36740	Postwar "3469" Lionel Lines Coal Dump Car, *03*	49____
36743	Santa Claus Bobbing Head Boxcar, *03*	40____
36744	Little Mermaid Aquarium Car, *03*	55____
36745	Toy Story Animated Gondola, *03*	70____
36753	LFD Firecar with ladder, *02*	60____
36757	Southern Searchlight Car, *03–04*	NRS____
36758	Patriotic Lighted Boxcar, *02*	60____

No.	Description	Exc	Mint
36760	B&O Sentinel Operating Brakeman Boxcar "3424," Archive Collection, 02		65
36761	Wellspring Capital Management Lighted Boxcar, 02 u		220
36764	West Side Lumber Log Dump Car "36764," 03		55
36765	Alaska Coal Dump Car "401," 03		50
36766	Erie Chase Gondola, 03		50
36767	Santa's Radar Tracking Car, 03		40
36769	Fourth of July Lighted Boxcar, 03		70
36770	American Refrigerator Transit Ice Car "23701," 04		42
36771	CN Barrel Car "74208," 04		48
36772	Spokane, Portland & Seattle Log Dump Car "36772," 04		46
36773	Jersey Central Coal Dump Car "92926," 04		45
36774	PRR Moe & Joe Lumber Flatcar, 04		50
36775	Santa Fe Animated Caboose "999010," 05		75
36776	Santa Fe Walking Brakeman Car "19938," 04		43
36778	C&O Searchlight Car "216614," 04		30
36780	Sea-Monkeys Motorized Aquarium Car, 04		45
36781	Finding Nemo Aquarium Car, 04		50
36782	Goofy and Pete Jumping Boxcar, 05		70
36783	Disney Operating Boxcar, 04–05		65
36784	Monsters Inc. Bobbing Head Boxcar, 04		40
36786	Postwar "3494-150" MP Operating Boxcar, 03		40
36787	MOW Remote Control Searchlight Car, 04		45
36788	Lionel Lines Tender, TrainSounds, 04		75
36789	Railbox Boxcar, TrainSounds, 04–05		105
36790	Christmas Music Boxcar, 04		70
36793	Pennsylvania Derrick Car, 03		22
36794	NYC Log Dump Car, 03		25
36795	Southern Coal Dump Car, 03		25
36796	GN Searchlight Car, 03		24
36797	"Operation Iraqi Freedom" Minuteman Car, 03		45
36803	Santa Animated Caboose, 06		75
36804	Candy Cane Dump Car, 06		80
36805	Reindeer Jumping Boxcar, 06		70
36809	NYC Derrick Car, 07–08		35
36810	PRR Searchlight Car, 07		35
36811	UP Dump Coal Dump Car, 07		35
36812	British Columbia Log Dump Car, 07–08		35
36813	State of Maine Brakeman Car, 08		80
36814	D&RGW Animated Caboose "01415," 07–09		80
36815	Santa Fe Moe & Joe Flatcar, 07–08		80
36816	Virginian Coal Dump Car, 08		80
36818	U.S. Steel Searchlight Car, 07–08		75
36821	"Naughty or Nice" Dump Car, 07		80
36823	Halloween SpookySmoke Boxcar, 07		115
36824	AlienSmoke Boxcar, 07		110
36829	Alien Radioactive Car, 07		70
36830	Trick or Treat Aquarium Car, 07		75
36831	MOW Welding Car, 07–08		75
36833	Christmas Music Boxcar, 07		65
36834	Santa Fe Transparent Instruction Car, 07–08		65
36838	Lionel Power Co. Voltmeter Car, K-Line, 06		75

		Mint
36839	Operating Milk Car with platform, K-Line, *06*	140____
36841	Visitor Center 15th Anniversary Lighted Boxcar, *06*	70____
36847	Polar Express Tender, TrainSounds, *08–14*	130____
36848	Candy Cane Dump Car, *07*	80____
36849	Tell-Tale Reindeer Car, *07*	53____
36850	Santa and Snowman Boxcar, *07*	75____
36851	Generator Car with Christmas tree, *07*	75____
36853	U.S. Army Exploding Boxcar, *08*	60____
36855	GW Horse Car and Corral, *08*	160____
36856	W&ARR Sheriff and Outlaw Car, *08*	75____
36857	Bobbing Ghost Boxcar, *08*	65____
36859	Lionel Lines Aquarium Car, *08*	80____
36861	PRR Poultry Dispatch Car, *08–09*	80____
36863	Alien Security Car, *08*	80____
36864	Bethlehem Steel Searchlight Car, *08*	40____
36866	WP Coal Dump Car "52369," *08*	40____
36868	NH Barrel Ramp Car, *08*	40____
36869	Bobbing Santa Boxcar, *08*	65____
36870	Postwar "6812" Track Maintenance Car, *08*	65____
36874	PRR Searchlight Car, *09*	35____
36875	Polar Express Coach, sound, *08–14, 16*	132____
36878	NYC Track Cleaning Car, *08*	150____
36879	REA Ice Car "1221," *08*	65____
36880	Koi Fish Aquarium Car, *10*	75____
36881	Christmas Music Boxcar, *08*	70____
36887	Great Western Animated Gondola, *08–09*	65____
36888	Casper Aquarium Car, *09–10*	90____
36889	PRR Barrel Ramp Car, *09–10*	46____
36893	UP Transparent Instruction Car "195220," *09–10*	75____
36896	Christmas Music Boxcar, *09*	80____
36897	Pennsylvania Power & Light Coal Dump Car, *09–10*	46____
36898	Wisconsin Central Log Dump Car, *09*	46____
36900	Depressed Center Flatcar with backshop load, *99*	115____
36913	Allied Chemical 1-D Tank Car 2-pack, *00*	150____
36914	Allied Chemical 1-D Tank Car "68075," die-cast, white, *00*	90____
36915	Allied Chemical 1-D Tank Car "68076," die-cast, white, *00*	90____
36916	Allied Chemical 1-D Tank Car 2-pack, *00*	175____
36917	Allied Chemical 1-D Tank Car "65124," die-cast, black, *00*	95____
36918	Allied Chemical 1-D Tank Car "65125," die-cast, black, *00*	90____
36927	B&O DC Hopper 6-pack, "435040-45," *01*	520____
36935	Maersk Maxi-Stack Car 2-pack, "250131-32," *00*	135____
36937	SP Maxi-Stack Car "513957," *02*	65____
36998	Gingerbread Man Gateman, *12–13*	80____
37001	No. 3444 Erie Animated Gondola, *09*	70____
37002	Operating Plutonium Car 2-pack, *10–11*	140____
37003	PRR Jet Snow Blower "491252," *09–10*	138____
37004	Area 51 Searchlight Car, *09*	46____
37006	Lionel Flatcar with operating LCD billboard, *09*	180____

		Exc	Mint
____37009	Smoking Mount St. Helens Boxcar, *10–11*		125
____37010	Pennsylvania Power & Light Searchlight Car, *10*		46
____37011	B&M Operating Milk Car with platform, *10*		155
____37012	GN Jumping Hobo Boxcar, *10*		75
____37015	Jack-o-Lantern Flatcar, *11–13*		75
____37016	Radioactive Plutonium Flatcar, *11*		70
____37017	Plutonium Boom Car, *11*		70
____37022	ATSF Blinking Billboard, *12*		25
____37032	Postwar "3562" Operating Barrel Car, *11*		75
____37033	Casper Animated Gondola, *11*		70
____37035	Santa's Operating Snow Globe Car, *11*		75
____37036	Halloween Operating Globe Car, *11*		78
____37038	Halloween Searchlight Car, *12–13*		45
____37039	Minuteman Searchlight Car, *11*		45
____37040	UP Derrick Car, *11–12*		46
____37041	Pennsylvania Power & Light Coal Dump Car, *11*		80
____37042	IC Coal Dump Car, *11*		46
____37043	Seaboard Log Dump Car, *11*		46
____37044	CP Rail Log Dump Car, *11, 13*		80
____37045	Beatles Yellow Submarine Aquarium Car, *11*		85
____37047	Santa's Flyer Animated Gondola, *11*		55
____37053	EL Derrick Car, *12*		45
____37054	CSX Coal Dump Car, *12*		46
____37055	SP Log Dump Car, *12*		46
____37056	Zombie Aquarium Car, *12*		80
____37057	Bethlehem Steel Culvert Car, *12*		65
____37058	Ghost Globe Halloween Car, *12–15*		80
____37059	Christmas Snow Globe Car, *12*		85
____37060	LIRR Derrick Car, *13–14*		50
____37061	UP Railroad Speeder, CC, *12–14*		150
____37062	NS Railroad Speeder, CC, *12–14*		150
____37063	PRR Railroad Speeder, CC, *12–14, 16*		150
____37064	CSX Railroad Speeder, CC, *12–14*		150
____37065	BNSF Railroad Speeder, CC, *12–14*		150
____37066	MOW Railroad Speeder, CC, *12–14*		150
____37067	NYC Railroad Speeder, CC, *12–14*		150
____37068	CN Railroad Speeder, CC, *12–14*		150
____37069	Strasburg RR Crane Car, *12*		65
37070	Gingerbread Man and Santa Animated Gondola, *12*		55
____37071	MOW Searchlight Car, *12*		46
____37073	U.S. Marine Corps Cannon Car, *12*		75
____37075	Boy Scouts of America Crane Car, *13*		75
____37076	Bethlehem Steel Coal Dump Car, *13*		50
____37078	RI Searchlight Car, *13*		50
____37079	Santa Fe Derrick Car, *13*		50
____37081	Peanuts Pumpkin Jack-O-Lantern Car, *13*		85
37082	Peanuts Animated Trick or Treat Chase Gondola, *14–16*		75
____37083	Strasburg Coal Dump Car, *13*		50
____37084	PRR Cop and Hobo Animated Gondola, *13*		65
____37085	BN Log Dump Car, *13*		50
____37086	Lionelville Aquarium Co. Aquarium Car, *13*		80
____37087	NH Walking Brakeman Car, *13–14*		75
____37089	Santa's List Snow Globe Car, *13*		90

		Exc	Mint
37090	Polar Express Searchlight Car, *13*		60____
37094	Wizard of Oz Aquarium Car, *13–15*		85____
37095	North Pole Sleigh Repair Welding Car, *13*		85____
37097	Where the Wild Things Are Aquarium Car, *13–15*		85____
37099	North Pole Central EV Caboose "2510" (std O), *13*		95____
37100	Barrel Loader Building, *12–14*		43____
37101	Smiley Water Tower, *12–14*		23____
37102	Watchman Shanty, *12–14*		30____
37103	O31 Curved Track (FasTrack), *13–14, 16*		5____
37110	FasTrack Terminal, LionChief, *14–16*		9____
37112	Helicopter 2-pack, *13–17*		35____
37115	Pedestrian Walkover, green, *16–17*		55____
37120	Railroad Crossing Signs, *13–17*		10____
37121	Christmas Station Platform, *13*		25____
37122	Santa Fe Blinking Billboard, *13*		25____
37123	Weyerhaeuser Timber Operating Sawmill, *12–13*		140____
37124	West Side Lumber Operating Sawmill, *12–13*		140____
37125	Legacy Writable Utility Mobile, *12–16*		20____
37127	Angela Trotta Thomas Gallery, *12*		75____
37129	Boy Scouts of America Girder Bridge, *13*		23____
37130	Boy Scouts of America Covered Bridge, *13*		60____
37139	Tis the Season Accessories, *12–13*		310____
37140	All Aboard Accessories, *12–13*		65____
37141	Rail Yard Accessories, *12–13*		277____
37142	Welcome Home Accessories, *12–13*		154____
37146	Legacy PowerMaster, *12–16*		100____
37147	CAB-1L/Base-1L Command Set, *12–16*		250____
37149	FasTrack Modular Layout Straight Section Kit, *13*		200____
37150	FasTrack Modular Layout Template, *13–16*		30____
37151	Christmas Classic Street Lamps, *14, 16–17*		40____
37152	Operating Coaling Station, *13–14*		180____
37153	FasTrack Modular Layout 45-Degree Reversible Corner Kit, *13*		225____
37154	FasTrack Modular Layout 45-Degree Corner Kit, *13*		225____
37155	CAB-1L Remote Controller, *12–16*		150____
37156	Base-1L, *12–16*		125____
37158	Hershey's Water Tower, *13*		30____
37159	Peanuts Figure Pack, *13–15*		30____
37160	Strasburg Girder Bridge, *13*		21____
37161	Container 4-pack, *13*		40____
37162	Lionelville Water Tower, *13*		25____
37163	LIRR Girder Bridge, *13*		21____
37164	NS Girder Bridge, *13*		21____
37165	CP Water Tower, *13*		25____
37166	Crossing Shanty, *13–14, 16*		25____
37167	Freight Platform, *13*		30____
37169	Peanuts Psychiatric Booth, *13–16*		40____
37172	Gooseneck Lamp 2-pack, *13–14, 15–17*		34____
37173	Globe Lamp 3-pack, *13–14, 16–17*		25____
37174	Classic Street Lamp 3-pack, black, *13–14, 16–17*		40____
37176	Santa Fe Shanty, *13*		25____

		Exc	Mint
37183	Polar Express 10th Anniversary Pewter Snowman and Children Figure Pack, *13–14, 16–17*		37
37184	Christmas Half Covered Bridge, *13*		43
37185	Christmas Railroad Signs, *13–14, 16–17*		10
37187	Kris Kringle's Kloseout Shop, *13*		50
37191	36-watt Power Supply, LionChief, *14*		36
37195	Grand Central Terminal 100th Anniversary, *13–15*		280
37196	Christmas Extension Bridge, *13, 16–17*		15
37197	North Pole Central Girder Bridge, *13–14, 16–17*		30
37530	Santa Animated Caboose, *11*		80
37807	Station Platform, *10–15*		23
37808	Sunoco Spherical Oil Tank, *10–11*		100
37810	Curved O Gauge Tunnel, *11–17*		65
37813	Christmas Tractor and Trailer with trees, *10*		27
37814	Christmas Crossing Shanty, *10–14*		30
37816	Rockville Bridge, *11–12*		700
37820	Lionel Auto Loader Cars 4-pack, *12–13, 16–17*		25
37821	Smoke Fluid Loader, *11*		250
37826	Classic Travel Billboard Set, *11–14*		13
37827	Coca-Cola Covered Bridge, *11*		45
37828	Vintage Boy Scouts Figure Pack, *11–14*		30
37829	Polar Express Station Platform, *11–17*		40
37831	NJ Transit Blinking Light Water Tower, *11–12*		30
37834	Lionel Boat 4-pack, *11–17*		25
37836	Monopoly Auto 4-pack, *12*		25
37837	Polar Express Straight Tunnel, *12–14*		80
37840	Santa Fe Diorama, *12–17*		15
37841	Premium Smoke Fluid, *12–16*		7
37842	CN Tractor with piggyback trailer, *12, 15*		90
37846	PRR Tractor Trailer, *12*		90
37847	SP Tractor Trailer, *12*		90
37848	IC Tractor Trailer, *12*		90
37849	ATSF Tractor Trailer, *12*		90
37850	REA Tractor Trailer, *12*		90
37851	Scale Telephone Poles, *12–17*		37
37852	Christmas People Pack, *12–14, 16–17*		25
37853	Alien Billboard, *13, 15*		13
37854	Classic Christmas Billboard, *12*		11
37855	Lionel Airplane 2-pack, *12–17*		37
37900	Silver Truss Bridge, *11*		70
37901	Lehigh Valley Tugboat, *10*		270
37902	Illuminated Barge, *10*		180
37903	Cell Tower, *10–16*		70
37904	Boy Scouts Billboard Set, *10*		13
37907	Christmas Street Lamps with wreaths, *10–14*		30
37909	North Pole Central Jet Snowblower, *11–14*		138
37910	Operating Lighthouse, *10*		180
37911	D&RGW Blinking Light Water Tower, *10–11*		30
37912	Lighted Coaling Tower, *10–15*		180
37913	Hopper Shed, *10–15*		35
37914	Illuminated Work House, *10–17*		40
37916	Beige Brick Suburban House, *10*		80
37917	Red Brick Suburban House, *10*		80
37919	Operating Sawmill, *10*		130

Exc Mint

		Exc	Mint
37920	Bascule Bridge, *10*	350	____
37921	ZW-L Transformer, *11–16*	900	____
37923	Coca-Cola Blinking Light Water Tower, *11*	28	____
37928	Passenger Station, sounds, *11*	90	____
37929	Coca-Cola Diner, *11, 13*	75	____
37930	Rotary Aircraft Beacon, *11–12*	81	____
37933	MG Switch Tower, *11–13*	300	____
37935	Operating Track Gang, *11*	100	____
37939	Scale Telephone Poles, *11–17*	43	____
37940	PRR Hobo Hotel, *12*	150	____
37941	House Under Construction, *11*	90	____
37942	Christmas Hobo Hotel, *12–13*	150	____
37944	Weathered 50,000-gallon Water Tank, *11–12*	170	____
37946	House Under Construction #2, *12–13*	90	____
37947	GW-180 180-watt Transformer, *12–17*	280	____
37948	Boy Scouts Flagpole with lights, *11*	30	____
37951	Postwar "342" Culvert Loader, *11*	165	____
37952	Postwar "345" Culvert Unloader, *11*	190	____
37953	Jacobs Pharmacy, *11*	50	____
37954	Halloween Station Platform, *11–13*	35	____
37955	Sodor Station Platform, *11–15*	35	____
37957	Deluxe Holiday House, *11*	85	____
37958	SP Scrap Yard, *11–14*	110	____
37959	Midway Basketball Shot Game, *11–13*	21	____
37960	Burning Switch Tower, *11–13*	100	____
37961	NYC Scrap Yard, *11–13*	110	____
37962	NJ Transit Station Platform, *11*	37	____
37964	Archive Operating Freight Terminal, *11–14*	150	____
37965	Christmas Operating Freight Terminal, *11–14, 16–17*	150	____
37966	Lionel Cylindrical Oil Tank, *11–17*	100	____
37967	Boy Scouts Troop Cabin, *12–13*	80	____
37971	Bethlehem Steel Culvert Loader, *11*	165	____
37972	Bethlehem Steel Culvert Unloader, *11*	190	____
37973	Coca-Cola Station Platform, *12*	37	____
37975	PFE Operating Freight Terminal, *11–16*	150	____
37977	Hooker Tank Car Accident, *11–17*	130	____
37978	Deluxe Suburban House, *11–13*	80	____
37979	Rotary Coal Tipple, *12*	540	____
37980	Operating Coal Conveyor, *12*	90	____
37984	Santa's Repair Work House, *12–14*	40	____
37985	Operating Wind Turbine, *12–15*	75	____
37986	NJ Transit Blinking Billboard, *12–13*	28	____
37989	Sodor Train Shed, *12–16*	60	____
37992	Coca-Cola Blinking Light Billboard, *10–11*	28	____
37993	Snoopy and the Red Baron Animated Pylon, *12*	160	____
37994	Deluxe Holiday House #2, *12–14*	120	____
37995	Illuminated Scale Telephone Poles, *12–17*	50	____
37996	Postwar 192 Control Tower, *12*	70	____
37997	Christmas Lawn Figure Pack, *12–14, 16–17*	25	____
37998	Halloween Haunted Passenger Station, *12–13, 15*	75	____
38004	Virginian 4-6-0 10-wheel Locomotive "203," CC, *01–02*	570	____

		Exc	Mint
38005	Long Island 4-6-0 10-wheel Locomotive "138," CC, _01–02_		510
38007	UP Auxiliary tender, black, CC, _01_		200
38008	UP Auxiliary tender, gray, CC, _01_		205
38009	D&RGW 4-6-6-4 Challenger Locomotive "3803," CC, _01_		1550
38010	Clinchfield 4-6-6-4 Challenger Locomotive "673," CC, _01_		1400
38012	Wheeling & Lake Erie 2-6-6-2 Locomotive "8005," CC, _01_		610
38013	D&H 4-6-6-4 Challenger Locomotive "1527," CC, _01_		720
38014	D&RGW 4-6-6-4 Challenger Locomotive "3800," CC, _01_		710
38015	NYC 4-6-4 Hudson Locomotive "773," CC, _01_		900
38016	Southern 0-8-0 Yard Goat Locomotive "6536," CC, _01–02, 05_		530
38017	CN 2-6-0 Mogul Locomotive "86," CC, _03, 05_		600
38018	Wabash 2-6-0 Mogul Locomotive "826," CC, _03_		485
38019	B&M 2-6-0 Mogul Locomotive "1455," CC, _03, 05_		600
38020	PRR 4-4-4-4 T1 Duplex Locomotive "5514," _02–03_		630
38021	WP 4-6-6-4 Challenger Locomotive "402," CC, _02_		650
38022	WM 4-6-6-4 Challenger Locomotive "1206," CC, _02_		690
38023	UP 4-6-6-4 Challenger Locomotive "3976," CC, _02_		620
38024	PRR 6-4-4-6 S-1 Duplex Locomotive "6100," TMCC, _03_		1000
38025	PRR 4-6-2 K4 Pacific Locomotive "1361," CC, _02_		950
38026	N&W 4-8-4 J Class Northern Locomotive "606," CC, _02_		1450
38027	Meadow River Lumber Heisler Geared Locomotive "6," CC, _03_		880
38028	PRR 6-8-6 S2 Steam Turbine Locomotive, _01_		650
38029	UP 4-12-2 Locomotive "9000," CC, _03_		570
38030	Santa Fe 2-8-8-2 Locomotive "1795," CC, _03_		920
38031	SP 2-8-8-4 AC-9 Locomotive "3809," CC, _04_		1100
38032	Virginian 2-8-8-2 Locomotive "741," CC, _03_		928
38036	Long Island 2-8-0 Consolidation Locomotive, _01_		500
38037	PRR Reading Seashore 2-8-0 Consolidation Locomotive "6072," CC, _01_		495
38038	D&RGW Auxiliary Water Tender, _01_		230
38039	Clinchfield Auxiliary Water Tender, _01_		220
38040	LV 4-6-0 Camelback Locomotive, _01_		405
38042	C&NW 4-6-0 10-wheel Locomotive "361," CC, _02_		450
38043	Frisco 4-6-0 10-wheel Locomotive "719," CC, _02_		525
38044	PRR 4-6-2 K4 Pacific Locomotive "5385," CC, _02_		920
38045	NYC Hudson J-3a 4-6-4 Locomotive "5418," CC, _03_		495
38046	GN 0-8-0 Locomotive "815," CC, _02_		530
38047	N&W 0-8-0 Locomotive "266," CC, _02_		550
38048	NPR 0-8-0 Locomotive "303," CC, _02_		530
38049	N&W 2-6-6-4 Locomotive "1234," CC, _02_		690

		Exc	Mint
38050	Nickel Plate 2-8-4 Berkshire Locomotive "779," CC, *03*		925___
38051	Erie 2-8-4 Berkshire Locomotive "3315," CC, *03*		810___
38052	Pere Marquette 2-8-4 Berkshire Locomotive "1225," CC, *03*		1000___
38053	NYC 4-8-2 Mohawk L-2a Locomotive "2793," CC, *03*		915___
38055	Santa Fe 4-8-4 Northern Locomotive "3751" CC, *04*		1100___
38056	PRR 4-8-2 Mountain M1a Locomotive "6759," CC, *03*		850___
38057	Weyerhaeuser Shay Locomotive, CC, *03*		1000___
38058	C&O 2-8-8-2 H7 Locomotive "1580," CC, *04*		1200___
38060	UP 2-8-8-2 H7 Locomotive "3590," CC, *04*		1200___
38061	Cass Scenic Heisler Geared Locomotive "6," CC, *03*		940___
38062	Lionel Lines 4-6-2 Pacific Locomotive "8062," CC, *02–03*		275___
38065	UP 2-8-8-2 Mallet Locomotive "3672," CC, *02*		1002___
38066	Elk River Shay Locomotive, CC, *03*		1000___
38067	MILW 4-6-2 Pacific Locomotive "6316," CC, *03*		300___
38068	WM 4-6-2 Pacific Locomotive "204," CC, *03*		300___
38069	Erie Hudson Locomotive, whistle, *05*		150___
38070	C&O 4-6-2 Pacific Locomotive "489," CC, *04*		300___
38071	SP Cab Forward AC-12 Locomotive "4294," CC, *05*		1550___
38075	UP 4-8-8-4 Big Boy Locomotive "4024," LionMaster, *03*		800___
38076	C&O 2-8-4 Berkshire Locomotive "2699," CC, *04*		860___
38077	Virginian 2-8-4 Berkshire Locomotive "508," CC, *04*		1000___
38079	SP 4-8-4 Northern GS-2 Locomotive "4410" CC, *04*		980___
38080	WP 4-8-4 Northern GS-64 Locomotive "485" CC, *04*		1000___
38081	C&O 2-6-6-6 Allegheny Locomotive "1650," CC, *05–07*		1700___
38082	Pennsylvania 2-8-8-2 Y3 Locomotive "374," CC, *04*		1000___
38083	N&W 2-8-8-2 Y3 Locomotive "2009," CC, *04*		910___
38085	NYC 4-6-4 Hudson J-3a Locomotive 5422," CC, *03*		495___
38086	B&A 4-6-4 Hudson Locomotive "607," CC, *03*		495___
38087	Nickel Plate 2-8-4 Berkshire Locomotive, RailSounds, *05*		190___
38088	NYC 2-6-0 Mogul Locomotive "1924," CC, *03, 05*		600___
38089	Pennsylvania 4-6-2 Pacific Locomotive "3678," CC, *04*		300___
38090	Clinchfield 4-6-6-4 Challenger Locomotive "672" CC, *04*		640___
38091	NP 4-6-6-4 Challenger Locomotive "5121" CC, *04*		660___
38092	Pickering Lumber Heisler Locomotive "5," CC, *04*		1000___
38093	UP 4-6-6-4 Challenger Locomotive "3980," CC, *04*		700___
38094	MILW Hiawatha 4-4-2 Atlantic Locomotive, CC, *06*		950___

		Exc	Mint
38095	N&W 4-8-4 J Class Locomotive "611," CC, 05–06		1250
38100	Texas Special F3 Diesel AB Set, 99		930
38103	Texas Special F3 Diesel "2245," 99		510
38114	ATSF FT Diesel B Unit, 99–00		170
38115	NYC FT Diesel B Unit "2403," nonpowered, 99–00		130
38116	B&O FT Diesel B Unit, 99–00		130
38144	C&O F3 Diesel AA Set"7019, 7021," 00		700
38147	GN Alco FA2 AA Diesel Set, CC, 02		405
38150	Platinum Ghost "2333," 99		495
38153	"Spirit of the Century" F3 Diesel AA Set, 99		800
38160	Pennsylvania Alco FB2 Diesel, 02		125
38161	MKT Alco FB2 Diesel, 02		125
38162	Burlington FT Diesel B Unit, 01		NRS
38167	Burlington FT Diesel AA Set, 01		225
38176	Pennsylvania Alco FA2 AA Diesel Set, CC, 02		405
38182	MKT Alco FA2 AA Diesel Set, CC, 02		360
38188	Southern F3 Diesel ABA Set, 00		557
38194	GN Alco FB2 Diesel, 02		125
38195	Santa Fe FT Diesel A Unit "170," 00		125
38196	Santa Fe FT Diesel A Unit "171," 00		175
38197	SP F3 Diesel ABA Set, 00		640
38202	Wild West Handcar, 10		75
38203	Holly Jolly Trolley 2-car Set, 10		160
38204	ATSF FT B Unit, nonpowered, 10		120
38210	PRR Alco Diesel AA Set, CC, 10		400
38214	Rio Grande Ski Train FT B Unit, nonpowered, 11		120
38215	ATSF FT Diesel "165," RailSounds, 10–11		280
38216	Rio Grande Ski Train FT A Unit, nonpowered, 11		120
38219	Texan FT B Unit Diesel, nonpowered, 11, 13–14		120
38221	CNJ Alco AA Diesel Set, 11		300
38224	Alaska Alco AA Diesel Set, 11		300
38234	Classic PRR GG1 Electric Locomotive "4866," 12		330
38235	Classic PC GG1 Electric Locomotive "4840," 12		330
38240	Elf Gang Car, 12		120
38241	MOW Gang Car, 12–13		120
38300	Postwar "2331" Virginian Train Master Diesel, 08	190	210
38303	Postwar "2340" GG1 Electric Locomotive, 08		280
38305	Postwar "2338" Milwaukee Road GP7 Diesel, 08		220
38308	Postwar 2146WS Berkshire Passenger Set, 12		460
38310	"2185W" NYC F3 Diesel Freight Set, 09		600
38311	"2276W" B&O RDC Commuter Set, 09		470
38312	"2343" Santa Fe F3 Diesel AA Set, 09		500
38313	B&O Budd RDC 2-pack, 09		350
38323	Postwar "2348" M&StL GP9 Diesel, CC, 10		390
38324	Postwar 2507W NH F3 Diesel Freight Set, 10		600
38328	Postwar 1623W NP GP9 Diesel Freight Set, 10		750
38329	Postwar 2261W Freight Hauler Set, 10		610
38334	Postwar 11288 Orbitor Diesel Freight Set, 10		500
38338	Postwar 2129WS Berkshire Freight Set, 12		550
38339	Postwar 2505W Virginian Rectifier Freight Set, 10		470
38340	Postwar 1587S Girl's Steam Freight Set, 10		580
38342	Postwar 1619W Santa Fe Freight Set, 10–11		470

		Exc	Mint
38348	Postwar "2339" Transparent Wabash GP7 Diesel, *11*	290	___
38349	Postwar 12885-500 C&O GP7 Freight Set, *11–12*	600	___
38351	Postwar Archive UP GP7 Diesel, *11*	290	___
38353	Postwar X-628 Promotional U.S. Navy Diesel Freight Set, *12–14*	600	___
38354	Postwar 1464W UP Anniversary Alco Diesel Passenger Set, *12–14*	460	___
38357	Postwar 221 U.S. Marine Corps Alco Diesel A Unit, *12–14*	300	___
38358	Postwar 2239 IC F3 Freight Set, *12–14*	600	___
38365	Archive ATSF Black Bonnet F3 AA Diesel Set, *12–14*	500	___
38368	Archive NYC Red Lightning F3 AA Diesel Set, *12–14*	500	___
38371	Postwar 2031 RI Alco Diesel AA Set, *12–13*	400	___
38374	Postwar 221 U.S. Marine Corps Alco Diesel B Unit, *12–14*	120	___
38377	Postwar 2363T F3 A Unit, nonpowered, *12–14*	170	___
38379	Archive ATSF Black Bonnet F3 B Unit, *12–14*	170	___
38380	Archive NYC Red Lightning F3 B Unit, *12–14*	170	___
38386	Postwar "2367" Wabash F3 Diesel AB Units, *12–14*	500	___
38388	Postwar "2367" Wabash F3 Diesel A Unit, nonpowered, *12–14*	170	___
38389	Postwar "2362" UP F3 Diesel AA Set, *14*	460	___
38392	Postwar "2362" F3 Diesel B Unit, nonpowered, *14*	170	___
38393	PRR Round-roof Boxcar "76648" (std O), *14*	80	___
38401	NYC M-497 Jet-Powered Rail Car, *10*	300	___
38402	Amtrak HHP-8 Electric Locomotive, RailSounds, *10*	400	___
38403	B&O CSX Heritage AC6000 Diesel "6607," CC, *11*	550	___
38404	B&O CSX Heritage AC6000 Diesel "7812," CC, *11*	550	___
38405	Chessie System CSX Heritage AC6000 Diesel, CC, *11–14*	550	___
38406	Chessie System CSX Heritage AC6000 Diesel, CC, *11–14*	550	___
38407	WM CSX Heritage AC6000 Diesel "2652," CC, *11*	550	___
38408	WM CSX Heritage AC6000 Diesel "2659," CC, *11*	550	___
38409	Clinchfield CSX Heritage AC6000 Diesel, CC, *11–13*	550	___
38410	Clinchfield CSX Heritage AC6000 Diesel, CC, *11–14*	550	___
38411	Family Lines CSX Heritage AC6000 Diesel "4825," CC, *11*	550	___
38412	Family Lines CSX Heritage AC6000 Diesel "4837," CC, *11*	550	___
38413	CSX Heritage AC6000 Diesel "607," CC, *11–13*	550	___
38414	CSX Heritage AC6000 Diesel "654," CC, *11–13*	550	___
38415	PRR U28C Diesel "6531," CC, *11–12*	530	___
38416	PRR U28C Diesel "6534," CC, *11–12*	530	___
38417	BN Bicentennial U30C Diesel "1776," CC, *11*	530	___
38418	BN Bicentennial U30C Diesel "1777," CC, *11*	530	___
38419	UP U30C Diesel "2918," CC, *11–12*	530	___
38420	UP U30C Diesel "2897," CC, *11–12*	530	___
38421	NP U33C Diesel "3305," CC, *11–12*	530	___

		Exc Mint
38422	NP U33C Diesel "3307," CC, *11–12*	530
38423	Southern U30C Diesel "3801," CC, *11–12*	530
38424	Southern U30C Diesel "3804," CC, *11–12*	530
38425	RI Budd RDC Jet Car, *11*	330
38428	Alaska Budd RDC Coach, *11*	300
38429	NYC Budd RDC M-497 Jet Car, *11*	330
38432	MKT H16-44 Diesel "1591," CC, *11*	500
38433	MKT H16-44 Diesel "1731," CC, *11*	500
38434	MKT H16-44 Diesel "1732," *11*	380
38435	MKT H16-44 Diesel "1733," nonpowered, *11*	240
38436	LIRR H-16-44 Diesel "1501," CC, *11*	500
38437	LIRR H-16-44 Diesel "1504," CC, *11*	500
38438	LIRR H-16-44 Diesel "1507," *11*	380
38439	LIRR H-16-44 Diesel "1509," nonpowered, *11*	240
38440	UP H-16-44 Diesel "1341," CC, *11*	500
38441	UP H-16-44 Diesel "1342," CC, *11*	500
38442	UP H-16-44 Diesel "1343," *11*	380
38443	UP H-16-44 Diesel "1344," nonpowered, *11*	240
38444	PRR H16-44 Diesel "8807," CC, *11*	500
38445	PRR H16-44 Diesel "8810," CC, *11*	500
38446	PRR H16-44 Diesel "8812," *11*	380
38447	PRR H16-44 Diesel "8815," nonpowered, *11*	240
38452	PC Alco RS-11 Diesel "7605," CC, *12*	480
38453	PC Alco RS-11 Diesel "7608," CC, *12*	480
38454	PRR Alco RS-11 Diesel "9622," CC, *12*	480
38455	PC Alco RS-11 Diesel "7625," nonpowered, *12*	240
38456	N&W Alco RS-11 Diesel "308," CC, *12–13*	480
38457	N&W Alco RS-11 Diesel "318," CC, *12*	480
38458	PRR Alco RS-11 Diesel "8631," CC, *12*	480
38459	N&W Alco RS-11 Diesel "330," nonpowered, *12*	240
38460	NKP Alco RS-11 Diesel "855," CC, *12*	480
38461	NKP Alco RS-11 Diesel "859," CC, *12*	480
38462	PRR Alco RS-11 Diesel "8639," nonpowered, *12*	240
38463	NKP Alco RS-11 Diesel "863," nonpowered, *12*	240
38464	Alaska Alco RS-11 Diesel "3602," CC, *12*	480
38465	Alaska Alco RS-11 Diesel "3604," CC, *12*	480
38466	NH Alco RS-11 Diesel "1403," CC, *12*	480
38467	Alaska Alco RS-11 Diesel "3607," nonpowered, *12*	240
38468	Seaboard Alco RS-11 Diesel "101," CC, *12–13*	480
38469	Seaboard Alco RS-11 Diesel "102," CC, *12*	480
38470	NH Alco RS-11 Diesel "1405," CC, *12*	480
38471	Seaboard Alco RS-11 Diesel "104," nonpowered, *12*	240
38472	C&O Alco S2 Diesel Switcher "5001," CC, *11*	470
38473	C&O Alco S2 Diesel Switcher "5505," CC, *11*	480
38474	C&O Alco S2 Diesel Switcher "5020," *11*	360
38475	C&O Alco S2 Diesel Switcher "5027," nonpowered, *11*	220
38476	CN Alco S2 Diesel Switcher "7946," CC, *11*	480
38477	CN Alco S2 Diesel Switcher "7949," CC, *11*	480
38478	CN Alco S2 Diesel Switcher "7951," *11*	360
38479	CN Alco S2 Diesel Switcher "7954," *11*	360
38480	NYC Alco S2 Diesel Switcher "8504," CC, *11*	480
38481	NYC Alco S2 Diesel Switcher "8507," CC, *11*	480

		Exc Mint
38482	NYC Alco S2 Diesel Switcher "8514," *11*	360____
38483	NYC Alco S2 Diesel Switcher "8521," nonpowered, *11*	220____
38484	Southern Alco S2 Diesel Switcher "2209," CC, *11*	480____
38485	Southern Alco S2 Diesel Switcher "2211," CC, *11*	480____
38486	Southern Alco S2 Diesel Switcher "2215," *11*	360____
38487	Southern Alco S2 Diesel Switcher "2218," nonpowered, *11*	220____
38488	Mopac Alco S2 Diesel Switcher "9108," CC, *11*	480____
38489	Mopac Alco S2 Diesel Switcher "9113," CC, *11*	480____
38490	Mopac Alco S2 Diesel Switcher "9116," *11*	360____
38491	Mopac Alco S2 Diesel Switcher "9131," nonpowered, *11*	220____
38493	ATSF Early Era Inspection Vehicle, CC, *12*	150____
38494	CP DD35 Diesel "9864," CC, *12*	600____
38495	CP DD35 Diesel "9868," nonpowered, *12*	440____
38496	SP DD35A Diesel "9903," CC, *11*	600____
38497	SP DD35A Diesel "9914," nonpowered, *11*	440____
38498	PRR DD35A Diesel "2380," CC, *11*	600____
38499	PRR DD35A Diesel "2383," nonpowered, *11*	440____
38505	CSX GP-38 Diesel, *11*	140____
38521	PRR GG1 Electric "4839," *11*	330____
38522	Amtrak GG1 Electric "926," *11*	330____
38524	NYC GP35 Diesel "6131," CC, *12*	500____
38525	NYC GP35 Diesel "6138," CC, *12*	500____
38526	NYC GP35 Diesel "6147," nonpowered, *12*	260____
38527	UP GP35 Diesel "742," CC, *12*	500____
38528	UP GP35 Diesel "753," CC, *12*	500____
38529	UP GP35 Diesel "760," nonpowered, *12*	260____
38530	SP GP35 Diesel "7465," CC, *12*	500____
38531	SP GP35 Diesel "7474," CC, *12*	500____
38532	SP GP35 Diesel "7481," nonpowered, *12*	260____
38533	CP GP35 Diesel "5014," CC, *12*	500____
38534	CP GP35 Diesel "5018," CC, *12*	500____
38535	CP GP35 Diesel "5023," nonpowered, *12*	260____
38536	PRR GP35 Diesel "2297," CC, *12*	500____
38537	PRR GP35 Diesel "2302," CC, *12*	500____
38538	PRR GP35 Diesel "2305," nonpowered, *12*	260____
38539	N&W Alco RS-11 Diesel "308," CC, *12*	480____
38539	Conrail GP35 Diesel "2297," CC, *12*	500____
38540	Conrail GP35 Diesel "2302," CC, *12*	500____
38541	Conrail GP35 Diesel "2305," nonpowered, *12*	260____
38542	Milwaukee Road GP35 Diesel "361," CC, *12*	500____
38543	Milwaukee Road GP35 Diesel "363," CC, *12*	500____
38544	Milwaukee Road GP35 Diesel "366," nonpowered, *12*	260____
38545	Pacific Harbor Line Genset Switcher "31," CC, *11*	800____
38546	KCS Genset Switcher "1404," CC, *11–12*	800____
38547	Santa Fe Genset Switcher "9910," CC, *11*	800____
38548	EL GP35 Diesel "2555," CC, *12*	500____
38549	EL GP35 Diesel "2558," CC, *12*	500____
38550	EL GP35 Diesel "2561," nonpowered, *12*	260____
38558	D&H Baldwin RF-16 Diesel AA Set, CC, *12*	730____
38561	D&H Baldwin RF-16 Diesel B Unit, CC, *12*	400____

		Exc	Mint
38562	D&H Baldwin RF-16 Diesel B Unit, nonpowered, 12		250
38563	B&O Baldwin RF-16 Diesel AA Set, CC, 12–14		730
38566	B&O Baldwin RF-16 Diesel B Unit, CC, 12–14		400
38567	B&O Baldwin RF-16 Diesel B Unit, nonpowered, 12–14		250
38568	NYC Baldwin RF-16 Diesel AA Set "3806-3808," CC, 12–14		730
38571	NYC Baldwin RF-16 Diesel B Unit, CC, 12–14		400
38572	NYC Baldwin RF-16 Diesel B Unit, nonpowered, 12–14		250
38573	SP Baldwin RF-16 Diesel AA Set, CC, 12–14		730
38576	SP Baldwin RF-16 Diesel B Unit, CC, 12–14		400
38577	SP Baldwin RF-16 Diesel B Unit, nonpowered, 12–14		250
38579	ATSF GP9 Diesel "744," nonpowered, 12		240
38580	NP GP9 Diesel "324," nonpowered, 12		240
38581	CSX SD80MAC Diesel "809," CC, 12–13		530
38582	CSX SD80MAC Diesel "812," CC, 12		530
38583	CSX SD80MAC Diesel "804," nonpowered, 12		260
38584	NS SD80MAC Diesel "7207," CC, 12		530
38585	NS SD80MAC Diesel "7203," CC, 12		530
38586	NS SD80MAC Diesel "7209," nonpowered, 12		260
38587	Conrail SD80MAC Diesel "4126," CC, 12		530
38588	Conrail SD80MAC Diesel "4129," CC, 12		530
38589	Conrail SD80MAC Diesel "4103," nonpowered, 12		260
38593	UP NW2 Diesel Switcher Locomotive "1028," CC, 12		470
38594	UP NW2 Diesel Switcher Locomotive "1043," CC, 12		470
38595	CB&Q Scale NW2 Diesel Switcher "9227," CC, 12		470
38596	CB&Q Scale NW2 Diesel Switcher "9245," CC, 12		470
38597	CB&Q F3 AA Diesel Set"9962A-9962C," CC, 12–13		730
38600	UP 0-6-0 Dockside Switcher "87," traditional, 07–09		110
38601	Lionel Lines 0-6-0 Dockside Switcher, traditional, 07–09		110
38605	PRR 0-4-0 Locomotive "94," traditional, 07		170
38606	SP 0-4-0 Locomotive "71," traditional, 07–08		170
38607	Southern 2-8-4 Berkshire Locomotive "2718," RailSounds, 07–08		175
38608	LL 2-8-2 Mikado Locomotive "57," RailSounds, 07		260
38609	NYC 2-8-2 Mikado Locomotive "1843," CC, 07		370
38610	NKP 2-8-4 Berkshire Locomotive "779," CC, 07–08		370
38619	Santa Fe 4-6-2 Pacific Locomotive "2037," traditional, K-Line, 06		260
38620	B&O Porter Locomotive "16," traditional, K-Line, 06		100
38621	4-6-2 Pacific Locomotive, traditional, K-Line, 06		260
38626	Holiday 2-8-2 Mikado Locomotive "25," green, RailSounds, 08		260

		Exc	Mint
38627	GN 4-4-2 Atlantic Locomotive "1702," traditional, *08–09*		110____
38630	U.S. Army 0-6-0 Dockside Switcher "486," traditional, *08–09*		110____
38634	NYC 4-6-4 Hudson Locomotive "5417," TrainSounds, *07*		200____
38635	C&O 4-6-4 Hudson Locomotive "309," TrainSounds, *08*		200____
38636	ATSF 4-6-4 Hudson Locomotive "3459," TrainSounds, *07*		200____
38637	LL 4-6-4 Hudson Locomotive "5242," TrainSounds, *08*		200____
38638	UP 4-6-2 Pacific Locomotive "2888," RailSounds, *08*		300____
38639	Erie 4-6-2 Pacific Locomotive "2939," RailSounds, *08*		300____
38640	Southern 4-6-2 Pacific Locomotive "1317," RailSounds, *08*		300____
38641	B&M 4-6-2 Pacific Locomotive "3713," RailSounds, *08*		300____
38642	PRR 4-6-2 Pacific Locomotive "5385," RailSounds, *08*		300____
38643	Alaska Mikado 2-8-2 Locomotive "701," CC, *08–09*		280____
38644	T&P Mikado 2-8-2 Locomotive "810," CC, *08–09*		400____
38649	Christmas 4-6-4 Hudson Locomotive, traditional, *08*		220____
38651	Lionel Lines 0-8-0 Locomotive "100," traditional, *08–09*		120____
38654	Bethlehem Steel 0-4-0 Locomotive, traditional, *08–09*		170____
38657	Alton Limited Pacific 4-6-2 Locomotive "659," traditional, *08*		300____
38658	W&ARR 4-4-0 General "1892," TrainSounds, *08–09*		165____
38664	LL 4-4-2 Atlantic Locomotive "1058," traditional, *08–09*		110____
38671	Santa Flyer 4-6-0 Locomotive, *09*		200____
38677	Strasburg 0-6-0 Dockside Switcher "1252," *10*		130____
38678	Monopoly Hudson Locomotive, TrainSounds, *10*		240____
38679	ATSF 0-4-0 Switcher "1387," *10–11*		190____
38684	Pennsylvania Power & Light Docksider Switcher, *10*		110____
38687	Western & Atlantic 0-4-0 Locomotive "1897," *10–11*		190____
38691	North Pole Central Santa Flyer "2," *10–11*		190____
38692	Angela Trotta Thomas Signature Express, *10–11*		190____
38700	CB&Q F3 B Unit "9962B," CC, *12–13*		400____
38701	CB&Q F3 B Unit, *12–13*		250____
38702	D&RGW F3 AA Diesel Set"5531-5533," CC, *12–14*		730____
38705	D&RGW F3 B Unit "5532," CC, *12–14*		400____
38706	D&RGW F3 B Unit, *12–14*		250____
38707	WP F3 AB Diesel Set"803A-803B," CC, *12–14*		730____
38710	WP F3 A Unit, nonpowered, *12–14*		380____
38711	WP F3 B Unit "803C," CC, *12–14*		400____
38712	Wabash F7 AA Diesel Set"1102A-1102C," CC, *12–13*		730____

		Exc Mint
___38715	Wabash F7 B Unit "1102B," CC, *12–13*	400
___38716	Wabash F7 B Unit, *12–13*	250
___38717	Milwaukee Road F7 AA Diesel SetCC, *12*	730
___38720	Milwaukee Road F7 B Unit "109B," CC, *12*	400
___38721	Milwaukee Road F7 B Unit, *12*	250
___38722	Grand Trunk SD80MAC Diesel "9085," CC, *12*	530
___38723	Grand Trunk SD80MAC Diesel "9088," CC, *12*	530
38724	Grand Trunk SD80MAC Diesel "9079," nonpowered, *12*	260
___38725	CB&Q SD80MAC Diesel "9654," CC, *12*	530
___38726	CB&Q SD80MAC Diesel "9651," CC, *12*	530
___38727	CB&Q SD80MAC Diesel "9660," nonpowered, *12*	260
___38728	PRR SD80MAC Diesel "9942," CC, *12*	530
___38729	PRR SD80MAC Diesel "9945," CC, *12*	530
38730	PRR SD80MAC Diesel "9947," nonpowered, *12–13*	260
38731	Polar SD80MAC Diesel, CC, *12*	530
38732	CB&Q BNSF Heritage SD70ACe Diesel "1848," CC, *12–13*	530
38733	CB&Q BNSF Heritage SD70ACe Diesel "1852," CC, *12–13*	530
38734	CB&Q BNSF Heritage SD70ACe Diesel "1856," nonpowered, *12–13*	260
38735	ATSF BNSF Heritage SD70ACe Diesel "1996," CC, *12–13*	530
38736	ATSF BNSF Heritage SD70ACe Diesel "1997," CC, *12–13*	530
38737	ATSF BNSF Heritage SD70ACe Diesel "1999," nonpowered, *12–13*	260
38738	Frisco BNSF Heritage SD70ACe Diesel "1876," CC, *12–13*	530
38739	Frisco BNSF Heritage SD70ACe Diesel "1896," CC, *12–14*	530
38740	Frisco BNSF Heritage SD70ACe Diesel "1916," nonpowered, *12–13*	260
38741	BN BNSF Heritage SD70ACe Diesel "1970," CC, *12–13*	530
38742	BN BNSF Heritage SD70ACe Diesel "1975," CC, *12–13*	530
38743	BN BNSF Heritage SD70ACe Diesel "1980," nonpowered, *12–13*	260
38744	GN BNSF Heritage SD70ACe Diesel "1889," CC, *12–13*	530
38745	GN BNSF Heritage SD70ACe Diesel "1891," CC, *12–13*	530
38746	GN BNSF Heritage SD70ACe Diesel "1893," nonpowered, *12–13*	260
38747	NP BNSF Heritage SD70ACe Diesel "1870," CC, *12–13*	530
38748	NP BNSF Heritage SD70ACe Diesel "1872," CC, *12–13*	530
38749	NP BNSF Heritage SD70ACe Diesel "1875," nonpowered, *12–13*	260
38750	EMD Demonstrator SD70ACe Diesel "2012," CC, *12–13*	530
___38751	CNJ F3 AA Diesel Set, CC, *13–14*	730
___38752	Vision Centipede AA Pilot Diesels, CC, *13*	2200

		Exc	Mint
38754	C&NW F7 AA Diesel Set, CC, 13–14		730____
38757	SP F7 AA Diesel Set, CC, 13–14		730____
38760	CNJ F3 B Unit, CC, 13–14		400____
38761	CNJ F3 B Unit, 13–14		250____
38762	C&NW F7 B Unit "410," CC, 13–14		400____
38763	C&NW F7 B Unit, 13–14		250____
38764	SP F7 B Unit "8219," CC, 13		400____
38765	SP F7 B Unit, 13		250____
38768	N&W GP35 Diesel "1306," CC, 13–14		500____
38769	N&W GP35 Diesel "1308," nonpowered, 13–14		260____
38770	RI GP35 Diesel "307," CC, 13–14		500____
38771	RI GP35 Diesel "309," CC, 13–14		500____
38772	RI GP35 Diesel "323," nonpowered, 13–14		260____
38773	WP GP35 Diesel "3002," CC, 13–14		500____
38774	WP GP35 Diesel "3009," CC, 13–14		500____
38775	WP GP35 Diesel "3014," nonpowered, 13–14		260____
38778	C&NW RS3 Diesel "1621," LionChief, 14–16		330____
38779	NYC RS3 Diesel "8244," LionChief, 14–16		330____
38782	C&BQ GP35 Diesel "990," CC, 13		500____
38783	C&BQ GP35 Diesel "996," nonpowered, 13		500____
38784	CN GP35 Diesel "4000," CC, 13		500____
38785	CN GP35 Diesel "4005," CC, 13		500____
38786	CN GP35 Diesel "4001," nonpowered, 13		260____
38787	D&RGW GP35 Diesel "3031," CC, 13		500____
38788	D&RGW GP35 Diesel "3034," CC, 13		500____
38789	D&RGW GP35 Diesel "3038," nonpowered, 13		260____
38790	DT&I GP35 Diesel "351," CC, 13		500____
38791	DT&I GP35 Diesel "353," CC, 13		500____
38792	DT&I GP35 Diesel "355," nonpowered, 13		260____
38794	GN GP35 Diesel "3018," CC, 13–14		500____
38795	GN GP35 Diesel "3036," nonpowered, 13–14		260____
38796	Chessie System GP35 Diesel "1125," CC, 13		500____
38797	Chessie System GP35 Diesel "1128," CC, 13		500____
38798	Chessie System GP35 Diesel "1113," nonpowered, 13		260____
38799	N&W GP35 Diesel "1302," CC, 13–14		500____
38800	B&M Early Era Inspection Vehicle, CC, 12		150____
38801	KCS Trackmobile, CC, 12–13		300____
38802	North Pole Central Trackmobile, CC, 12		300____
38803	MOW Trackmobile, CC, 12		300____
38804	LIRR Trackmobile, CC, 12		300____
38805	Conrail Trackmobile, CC, 12		300____
38806	NS Trackmobile, CC, 12		300____
38807	NP Trackmobile, CC, 12–13		300____
38808	Chessie System Trackmobile, CC, 12		300____
38809	CN Trackmobile, CC, 12		300____
38810	PRR Early Era Inspection Vehicle, CC, 12		150____
38811	D&RGW Early Era Inspection Vehicle, CC, 12		150____
38812	SP Early Era Inspection Vehicle, CC, 12–13		150____
38813	C&O Early Era Inspection Vehicle, CC, 12–13		150____
38814	Milwaukee Road Early Era Inspection Vehicle, CC, 12		150____
38815	Transylvania Early Era Inspection Vehicle, CC, 12		150____
38816	PRR RS3 Diesel "5620," LionChief, 14–16		330____
38819	D&RGW RS3 Diesel "5202," LionChief, 14–16		330____

		Exc	Mint
____38821	AT&SF GP7 Diesel "2656," LionChief, *14–15*		330
____38824	NP GP7 Diesel "563," LionChief, *14–15*		330
____38825	UP GP7 Diesel "121," LionChief, *14–15*		330
____38827	CB&Q GP7 Diesel "1596," LionChief, *14–15*		330
____38848	Christmas Pioneer Zephyr Set, CC, *13–14*		1100
____38853	Santa and Mrs. Claus Handcar, *13*		90
____38855	GN GP35 Diesel "2519," CC, *13–14*		500
____38856	CB&Q Mark Twain Zephyr, CC, *13–14*		1100
____38860	CB&Q Pioneer Zephyr, CC, *13–14*		1100
____38864	Lionel Lines Zephyr, CC, *13–14*		1100
____38865	L&N GP35 Diesel "1105," CC, *13*		500
____38866	L&N GP35 Diesel "1109," CC, *13*		500
____38867	L&N GP35 Diesel "1114," nonpowered, *13*		260
____38868	C&BQ GP35 Diesel "978," CC, *13*		500
____38874	B&O GP9 Diesel "6448," CC, *13–14*		480
____38875	B&O GP9 Diesel "6456," CC, *13–14*		480
____38876	B&O GP9 Diesel "6461," nonpowered, *13–14*		240
____38877	B&M GP9 Diesel "1705," CC, *13*		480
____38878	B&M GP9 Diesel "1714," CC, *13*		480
____38879	B&M GP9 Diesel "1722," nonpowered, *13*		240
____38883	C&NW GP9 Diesel "701," CC, *13*		480
____38884	C&NW GP9 Diesel "704," CC, *13*		480
____38885	C&NW GP9 Diesel "712," nonpowered, *13*		240
____38886	Erie GP9 Diesel "1260," CC, *13*		480
____38887	Erie GP9 Diesel "1263," CC, *13*		480
____38888	Erie GP9 Diesel "1265," nonpowered, *13*		240
____38889	Nickel Plate Road GP9 Diesel "514," CC, *13*		480
____38890	Nickel Plate Road GP9 Diesel "452," CC, *13*		480
38891 ____	Nickel Plate Road GP9 Diesel "457," nonpowered, *13*		240
____38892	SP GP9 Diesel "3411," CC, *13*		480
____38893	SP GP9 Diesel "3415," CC, *13*		480
____38894	SP GP9 Diesel "3419," nonpowered, *13*		240
____38895	Wabash GP9 Diesel "484," CC, *13*		480
____38896	Wabash GP9 Diesel "488," CC, *13*		480
____38897	Wabash GP9 Diesel "491," nonpowered, *13*		240
____38918	Chessie System SD40-2 Diesel "7609," CC, *13*		530
____38919	Chessie System SD40-2 Diesel "7611," CC, *13*		530
38920 ____	Chessie System SD40-2 Diesel "7614," nonpowered, *13*		240
____38921	SP SD40T-2 Diesel Locomotive "8322," CC, *13*		530
____38922	SP SD40T-2 Diesel Locomotive "8326," CC, *13*		530
____38923	SP SD40T-2 Diesel, nonpowered, *13*		260
____38924	B&O SD40-2 Diesel "7602," CC, *13*		530
____38925	B&O SD40-2 Diesel "7607," CC, *13*		530
____38926	B&O SD40-2 Diesel "7611," nonpowered, *13*		240
____38933	Conrail SD40-2 Diesel "6424," CC, *13*		530
____38934	Conrail SD40-2 Diesel "6437," CC, *13*		530
____38935	Conrail SD40-2 Diesel "6468," nonpowered, *13*		240
____38936	UP SD40-2 Diesel "2929," CC, *13*		530
____38937	UP SD40-2 Diesel "2932," CC, *13*		530
____38938	UP SD40-2 Diesel "2947," nonpowered, *13*		240
____38939	NS SD40-2 Diesel "3355," CC, *13*		530
____38940	NS SD40-2 Diesel "3365," CC, *13*		530
____38941	NS SD40-2 Diesel "3379," nonpowered, *13*		240

38942	Central of Georgia NS Heritage ES44AC Diesel, CC, *12*	550____
38943	Central of Georgia NS Heritage ES44AC Diesel, CC, *12*	550____
38944	Central of Georgia NS Heritage ES44AC Diesel, nonpowered, *12*	280____
38945	Conrail NS Heritage ES44AC Diesel, CC, *12*	550____
38946	Conrail NS Heritage ES44AC Diesel, CC, *12*	550____
38947	Conrail NS Heritage ES44AC Diesel, nonpowered, *12*	280____
38948	Interstate NS Heritage ES44AC Diesel Locomotive "8105," CC, *12*	550____
38949	Interstate NS Heritage ES44AC Diesel, CC, *12*	550____
38950	Interstate NS Heritage ES44AC Diesel, nonpowered, *12*	280____
38951	LV NS Heritage ES44AC Diesel, CC, *12*	550____
38952	LV NS Heritage ES44AC Diesel, CC, *12*	550____
38953	LV NS Heritage ES44AC Diesel, nonpowered, *12*	280____
38954	Nickel Plate Road NS Heritage ES44AC Diesel, CC, *12*	550____
38955	Nickel Plate Road NS Heritage ES44AC Diesel, CC, *12*	550____
38956	Nickel Plate Road NS Heritage ES44AC Diesel, nonpowered, *12*	280____
38957	N&W NS Heritage ES44AC Diesel, CC, *12*	550____
38958	N&W NS Heritage ES44AC Diesel, CC, *12*	550____
38959	N&W NS Heritage ES44AC Diesel, nonpowered, *12*	280____
38960	PRR NS Heritage ES44AC Diesel, CC, *12*	550____
38961	PRR NS Heritage ES44AC Diesel, CC, *12*	550____
38962	PRR NS Heritage ES44AC Diesel, nonpowered, *12*	280____
38963	Southern NS Heritage ES44AC Diesel, CC, *12*	550____
38964	Southern NS Heritage ES44AC Diesel, CC, *12*	550____
38965	Southern NS Heritage ES44AC Diesel, nonpowered, *12*	280____
38966	NS Heritage ES44AC Diesel, CC, *12*	550____
38967	NS Heritage ES44AC Diesel, CC, *12*	550____
38968	NS Heritage ES44AC Diesel, nonpowered, *12*	280____
38969	North Pole Central GP35 Diesel "2525," CC, *13*	500____
38970	North Pole Central GP35 Diesel "2512," CC, *13*	500____
38971	North Pole Central GP35 Diesel "2513," nonpowered, *13*	260____
38972	Reading GP35 Diesel "3625," CC, *13*	500____
38973	Reading GP35 Diesel "3630," CC, *13*	500____
38974	Reading GP35 Diesel "3633," nonpowered, *13*	260____
38975	AT&SF GP35 Diesel "3312," CC, *13*	500____
38976	AT&SF GP35 Diesel "3318," CC, *13*	500____
38977	AT&SF GP35 Diesel "3329," nonpowered, *13*	260____
38978	Alaska GP35 Diesel "2501," CC, *13*	500____
38979	Alaska GP35 Diesel "2503," CC, *13*	500____
38980	Alaska GP35 Diesel "2502," nonpowered, *13*	260____
38981	B&O GP35 Diesel "2506," CC, *13-14*	500____
38982	B&O GP35 Diesel "2511," CC, *13-14*	500____
38983	B&O GP35 Diesel "2517," nonpowered, *13-14*	260____
38984	C&O GP35 Diesel "3515," CC, *13-14*	500____

38985	C&O GP35 Diesel "3521," CC, *13-14*	500
38986	C&O GP35 Diesel "3526," nonpowered, *13-14*	260
38987	MP GP35 Diesel "603," CC, *13*	500
38988	MP GP35 Diesel "607," CC, *13*	500
38989	MP GP35 Diesel "611," nonpowered, *13*	260
38990	GM&O GP35 Diesel "603," CC, *13-14*	500
38991	GM&O GP35 Diesel "607," CC, *13-14*	500
38992	GM&O GP35 Diesel "611," nonpowered, *13-14*	260
38993	WM GP35 Diesel "3576," CC, *13*	500
38994	WM GP35 Diesel "3578," CC, *13*	500
38995	WM GP35 Diesel "3580," nonpowered, *13*	260
38996	CSX GP35 Diesel "4355," CC, *13*	500
38997	CSX GP35 Diesel "4363," CC, *13*	500
38998	CSX GP35 Diesel "4390," nonpowered, *13*	260
38999	NS GP35 Diesel "2916," CC, *13*	500
39008	PRR Heavyweight Passenger Car 4-pack, *00*	225
39009	PRR Indian Rock Heavyweight Combination Car, *00*	50
39010	PRR Andrew Carnegie Heavyweight Passenger Coach, *00*	60
39011	PRR Solomon P. Chase Heavyweight Passenger Coach, *00*	60
39012	PRR Skyline View Heavyweight Observation Car, *00*	50
39013	B&O Heavyweight Passenger Car 4-pack, *00*	400
39016	B&O Heavyweight Passenger Car 4-pack, *00*	200
39017	B&O Harper's Ferry Heavyweight Combination Car, *00*	50
39018	B&O Youngstown Heavyweight Passenger Coach, *00*	50
39019	B&O New Castle Heavyweight Passenger Coach, *00*	50
39020	B&O Chicago Heavyweight Observation Car, *00*	50
39028	LL Heavyweight Passenger Car 3-pack, *00*	195
39029	LL Irvington Heavyweight Coach "2625," *00*	60
39030	LL Madison Heavyweight Coach "2627," *00*	60
39031	LL Manhattan Heavyweight Coach "2628," *00*	60
39032	UP Madison Passenger Car 4-pack, *00*	275
39038	SP Madison Baggage Car "6015," *01*	NRS
39039	SP Madison Coach Car "1978," *01*	NRS
39040	SP Madison Coach "1975," *01*	NRS
39041	SP Madison Observation Car "2951," *01*	NRS
39042	N&W Heavyweight Passenger Car 4-pack, *00*	325
39047	B&O Heavyweight Passenger Car 2-pack, *01*	160
39050	PRR Heavyweight Passenger Car 2-pack, *01*	215
39053	Alaska Streamliner Car 2-pack, *01*	90
39056	NYC Streamliner Car 2-pack, *01*	75
39059	Santa Fe Streamliner Car 2-pack, *01*	100
39062	B&O Streamliner Car 2-pack, *01*	75
39065	PRR Streamliner Car 4-pack, *01*	165
39082	Blue Comet Heavyweight Passenger Car 2-pack, *02*	325
39085	"Freedom Train" Heavyweight Passenger Car 3-pack, *03*	260
39092	PRR Streamliner Car 2-pack, *01*	70

39099	Alton Limited Heavyweight Passenger Car 2-pack, *03*	230____
39100	William Penn Congressional Coach, *00*	115____
39101	Molly Pitcher Congressional Coach, *00*	100____
39102	Betsy Ross Congressional Vista Dome Car, *00*	100____
39103	Alexander Hamilton Congressional Observation Car, *00*	100____
39104	Phoebe Snow Car, StationSounds, *99*	255____
39105	Milwaukee Road Hiawatha Car, StationSounds, *99*	235____
39106	CP Aluminum Passenger Car 2-pack, *00*	185____
39107	CP Blair Manor Aluminum Passenger Coach "2553," *00*	115____
39108	CP Craig Manor Aluminum Passenger Coach "2554," *00*	110____
39109	"Spirit of the Century" Aluminum Passenger Car 4-pack, *99*	520____
39110	"Spirit of the Century" Full Vista Dome Car, *99–00*	100____
39111	"Spirit of the Century" Full Vista Dome Car, *99–00*	100____
39112	"Spirit of the Century" Full Vista Dome Car, *99–00*	100____
39113	"Spirit of the Century" Skytop Observation Car, *99–00*	100____
39118	Texas Special Garland Aluminum Passenger Coach "1203," StationSounds, *99–00*	220____
39119	Southern Aluminum Passenger Car 4-pack, *00*	350____
39120	Southern Grand Junction Aluminum Passenger/ Baggage Car, *00*	280____
39121	Southern Charlottesville Aluminum Passenger Coach "812," *00*	90____
39122	Southern Roanoke Aluminum Passenger Coach "814," *00*	250____
39123	Southern Memphis Aluminum Observation Car "1152," *00*	90____
39124	Amtrak Superliner Aluminum Passenger Car 4-pack, *02*	405____
39129	Santa Fe Superliner Aluminum Passenger Car 4-pack, *02*	305____
39141	RI Aluminum Passenger Car 4-pack, *01*	400____
39146	UP Aluminum Passenger Car 4-pack, *01*	285____
39151	CP Aluminum Passenger Car 2-pack, *01*	315____
39154	PRR Congressional Aluminum Passenger Car 2-pack, *02*	195____
39155	PRR Congressional Baggage Car, *02*	105____
39156	PRR Robert Morris Congressional Coach, *02*	100____
39157	Southern Aluminum Passenger Car 2-pack, *01*	290____
39160	KCS Aluminum Passenger Car 2-pack, *01*	260____
39163	Erie-Lack. Aluminum Passenger Car 2-pack, *01*	230____
39166	Texas Special Aluminum Passenger Car 2-pack, *01*	430____
39169	ACL Aluminum Passenger Car 4-pack, *01*	360____
39179	NP Aluminum Passenger Car 2-pack, *02*	305____
39182	WP Aluminum Passenger Car 2-pack, *02*	280____
39185	Rio Grande Aluminum Passenger Car 2-pack, *02*	290____
39194	UP Aluminum Passenger Car 2-pack, *02*	220____

	39197	CP Aluminum Passenger Coach, StationSounds, *02*	225
	39198	PRR Aluminum Passenger Coach, StationSounds, *02*	210
39200		Hellgate Bridge Boxcar #2 "1900-2000," *00 u*	55
39202		Lionel Centennial Boxcar "1900-2000," *00*	46
39203		Postwar "6464" Series X, 3 cars, *01*	115
39204		New Haven Boxcar "6464-725," *01*	44
39205		Alaska Boxcar "6464-825," *01*	55
39206		NYC Boxcar "6464-900," *01*	40
39207		UP Boxcar "508500," red, *00*	50
39208		UP Boxcar "903658," silver, *00*	42
39209		UP Boxcar "500200," yellow, *00*	40
39210		6530 Fire Fighting Car, *00*	37
39211		Postwar "6464" Boxcar 3-pack #2, *00*	85
39212		Postwar "6464" SP&S Boxcar, *00*	NRS
39213		Postwar "6464" Wabash Boxcar, *00*	NRS
	39214	Postwar "6464" Kansas, Oklahoma & Gulf Boxcar, *00*	NRS
39216		PRR DD Boxcar "47211," *01*	46
39220		B&LE Heavyweight Boxcar "82101," *01*	41
39221		L&N Heavyweight Boxcar "109829," *01*	41
39222		Conrail Heavyweight Boxcar "269198," *01*	44
39223		Postwar "6464" Archive Boxcar Set, 3-pack, *02*	125
39227		Postwar "6468" Automobile Boxcar 3-pack, *01*	95
39229		B&O DD Boxcar, *01*	40
39236		WP Boxcar "6464-250," *01*	55
39238		Elvis Boxcar, *03*	36
39239		P&LE Boxcar "22300, *02*	35
39240		Pennsylvania Boxcar "118747," *02*	32
39241		PC Boxcar "252455," *02*	28
	39242	Postwar "6464" Boxcar 3-pack #1, Archive Collection, *03–04*	80
39243		Soo Line Boxcar, Archive Collection	35
39247		NYC DD Boxcar "6468," *02–03*	32
39248		Lackawanna DD Boxcar with hobo, *03*	45
39250		Campbell's Kids Centennial Boxcar, *03–04*	40
39252		Lenny Dean 60th Anniversary Boxcar, *04*	38
	39253	No. 6464 Boxcar 3-pack #2, Archive Collection, *04*	100
39257		WP Boxcar "6464-100," boys set add-on, *03*	50
39258		Elvis Presley "All Shook Up" Boxcar, *03–04*	40
39259		Buick Centennial Boxcar, *03*	35
39260		New Haven Boxcar, *04*	40
	39262	Elvis Presley "Elvis Has Left the Building" Boxcar, *04*	38
39263		M&StL Boxcar, Postwar Celebration Series, *05*	35
	39267	No. 6464 Boxcar 3-pack #3, Archive Collection, *05*	100
39271		State of Maine Boxcar, *04*	35
	39273	No. 6464 Boxcar 3-pack #4, Archive Collection, *06*	100
39281		Florida State University Boxcar, *07*	48
39282		Purdue University Boxcar, *08*	50
39283		University of Virginia Boxcar, *08*	50
39284		Penn State University Boxcar, *06–07*	45

		Exc	Mint
39285	U.S. Military Academy at West Point Boxcar, *08*	50	___
39286	University of Illinois Boxcar, *06–07*	45	___
39287	University of Alabama Boxcar, *06–07*	45	___
39289	University of Oklahoma Boxcar, *06–08*	50	___
39290	Postwar "6464" Boxcar 2-pack, rare variations, *08*	100	___
39291	University of Michigan Boxcar, *06–07*	45	___
39292	Monopoly Boxcar 3-pack, *08*	135	___
39296	UPS Centennial Boxcar #3, *08–09*	55	___
39297	Macy's Parade Boxcar, *07*	55	___
39298	Monopoly Boxcar 3-pack #2, *08*	145	___
39299	Lenny Dean Commemorative Boxcar, *08*	50	___
39302	University of Maryland Boxcar, *08*	50	___
39303	Villanova University Boxcar, *08*	50	___
39304	Auburn University Boxcar, *08*	50	___
39308	CP Rail "6565" Boxcar "58700," *08–10*	55	___
39309	Macy's Parade Boxcar, *08*	50	___
39310	Monopoly Boxcar 3-pack #3, *09–10*	165	___
39316	New Haven Automobile Boxcar, *09–10*	60	___
39317	Wizard of Oz Boxcar #1, *09–10*	60	___
39318	Wizard of Oz Boxcar #2, *09–10*	60	___
39319	Boy Scouts "Scout Law" Add-on Boxcar, *10*	60	___
39321	Lionel Art Boxcar 2-pack, *10*	116	___
39325	Macy's Parade Boxcar, *09*	45	___
39326	UPS Centennial Boxcar #4, *10–11*	60	___
39328	Monopoly Boxcar 3-pack #4, *10–11*	190	___
39332	Holiday Boxcar, *10*	60	___
39334	Coca-Cola Christmas Boxcar, *10*	68	___
39335	Thomas Kinkade Boxcar, *10, 12*	60	___
39336	Angela Trotta Thomas "My Turn Yet, Dad?" Boxcar, *10*	60	___
39337	George Washington Boxcar, *11–12*	60	___
39338	Abraham Lincoln Boxcar, *11–12*	60	___
39339	Theodore Roosevelt Boxcar, *11–12*	60	___
39340	Thomas Jefferson Boxcar, *11–12*	60	___
39342	Strasburg Boxcar, *11*	55	___
39343	New Jersey Central Boxcar, *10*	45	___
39344	Monopoly Boxcar 3-pack #5, *11–12*	165	___
39345	Monopoly Tennessee Avenue Boxcar, *11*	55	___
39346	Monopoly Atlantic Avenue Boxcar, *11*	55	___
39347	Monopoly Illinois Avenue Boxcar, *11*	55	___
39348	Lionel NASCAR Collectables Boxcar, *11–12*	60	___
39350	Thomas Kinkade "All Aboard for Christmas" Boxcar, *12–13*	60	___
39351	Peanuts Thanksgiving Boxcar, *12*	70	___
39354	Monopoly North Carolina Avenue Boxcar, *12*	70	___
39358	Boy Scouts "Prepared for Life" Boxcar, *12*	60	___
39359	Thanksgiving Boxcar, *12*	60	___
39360	Boy Scouts Cub Scout Boxcar, *12–13*	60	___
39361	Coca-Cola Polar Bear Boxcar, *14*	70	___
39362	Thomas Kinkade "Emerald City" Boxcar, *12–15*	75	___
39363	Peanuts Halloween Boxcar, *12*	65	___
39364	Christmas Boxcar, *13*	60	___
39376	Monopoly Boxcar 2-pack, States and Vermont Avenues, *13–15*	140	___

		Exc	Mint
39379	Monopoly Boxcar 2-pack, Mediterranean and St. James Avenues, *13–15*		140
39383	Prewar "2719" Boxcar, *13*		65
39385	U.S. Navy 1-D Tank Car, *13–15*		70
39386	U.S. Marines 1-D Tank Car, *13–15*		70
39387	U.S. Air Force 1-D Tank Car, *13–15*		70
39388	U.S. National Guard 1-D Tank Car, *13–16*		70
39389	U.S. Coast Guard 1-D Tank Car, *13–16*		70
39391	U.S. Army Flatcar, *13–16*		70
39392	U.S. Navy Flatcar, *13–16*		70
39393	U.S. Marines Flatcar, *13–16*		70
39394	U.S. Air Force Flatcar, *13–16*		70
39395	U.S. National Guard Flatcar, *13–16*		70
39396	U.S. Coast Guard Flatcar, *13–16*		70
39398	Santa's Flyer Reefer, *13*		43
39399	U.S. Army 1-D Tank Car, *13–15*		70
39400	Republic Steel Slag Car 3-pack (std O), *04*		100
39404	Republic Steel Hot Metal Car 3-pack (std O), *04*		130
39411	Jones & Laughline Hot Metal Car 3-pack (std O), *05*		190
39423	Postwar "3460" LL Flatcar with trailers, *05*		45
39424	U.S. Steel 16-wheel Flatcar with girders, *05*		70
39425	Hood's Flatcar with milk container, traditional, *05*		55
39426	Nestle Nesquik Flatcar with milk container, traditional, *05*		55
39428	Bethlehem Steel Slag Car #4 (std O), *05*		60
39429	Bethlehem Steel Hot Metal Car #8 (std O), *05*		70
39430	Youngstown Sheet & Tube Slag Car #7 (std O), *05*		60
39431	Youngstown Sheet & Tube Hot Metal Car #11 (std O), *05*		70
39435	Postwar "6477" Flatcar with pipes, *06*		50
39436	Postwar "6262" Wheel Car, *06*		50
39437	Supplee Flatcar with milk container, *06*		60
39439	6827 Flatcar with P&H power shovel, *04*		50
39440	6828 Flatcar with P&H truck crane, *04*		50
39443	U.S. Steel Slag Car 3-pack #2 (std O), *06*		170
39447	Postwar "6561" LL Cable Reel Car, Archive Collection, *06–07*		55
39450	Postwar "6414" Evans Auto Loader, Archive Collection, *06*		70
39452	White Bros. Flatcar with milk container, *07*		60
39457	Postwar "6175" Flatcar with rocket, *08*		55
39458	Postwar "6844" Flatcar with missiles, *08*		55
39463	Postwar "6430" Flatcar with trailers, *08*		55
39468	Allis-Chalmers Car "52369," *08–09*		60
39469	Christmas Egg Nog Barrel Car, *08*		50
39470	UP Well Car "147128," *08*		65
39471	Postwar "6264" Flatcar, *08*		60
39472	ATSF Culvert Gondola, *08*		60
39473	Play-Doh Vat Car, *08*		55
39475	UPS Flatcar with trailer, *08*		65
39476	Bethlehem Steel 16-wheel Flatcar, *08*		75
39477	Christmas Flatcar with reindeer trailers, *08*		60
39478	Postwar "6475" Pickles Vat Car, *08*		55

		Exc	Mint
39479	Postwar "6404" Flatcar with brown automobile, *08*		50____
39480	Western & Atlantic Cannon Flatcar, *09*		60____
39482	CSX WM Track Maintenance Car "6812," *11*		65____
39483	CSX P&LE Gondola "69812," *11*		65____
39484	Cocoa Marsh Vat Car, *10–12*		60____
39486	Deep Sea Challenger Submarine Car, *11*		60____
39488	Reese's Vat Car, *10*		60____
39490	Western & Atlantic Cannonball Flatcar, *10*		55____
39497	Christmas Reindeer Stock Car, *10–11*		60____
39498	CNJ Gondola with culvert pipes, *11*		55____
39499	Alaska Oil Barrel Ramp Car, *11*		50____
39502	Monongahela NS Heritage ES44AC Diesel, nonpowered, *13*		280____
39530	PRR 1955 Pickup Truck, CC, *13*		180____
39531	UP 1955 Pickup Truck, CC, *13*		180____
39532	ATSF 1955 Pickup Truck, CC, *13–14*		180____
39533	CP 1955 Pickup Truck, CC, *13–14*		180____
39534	D&RGW 1955 Pickup Truck, CC, *13*		180____
39535	GN 1955 Pickup Truck, CC, *13*		180____
39536	MKT 1955 Pickup Truck, CC, *13–14*		180____
39537	NYC 1955 Pickup Truck, CC, *13*		180____
39538	Nickel Plate Road 1955 Pickup Truck, CC, *13*		180____
39539	NP1955 Pickup Truck, CC, *13–14*		180____
39540	Southern 1955 Pickup Truck, CC, *13*		180____
39541	SP 1955 Pickup Truck, CC, *13–14*		180____
39542	Weyerhaueser 1955 Pickup Truck, CC, *13–14*		180____
39543	Texas Special F3 B Unit, *13–14*		230____
39544	Texas Special F3 B Unit, CC, *13–14*		380____
39547	PRR F3 B Unit, *13–14*		230____
39548	PRR F3 B Unit, CC, *13–14*		380____
39554	NS GP35 Diesel "3918," CC, *13*		500____
39555	NS GP35 Diesel "2915," nonpowered, *13*		260____
39556	CP GP35 Diesel "5004," CC, *13–14*		500____
39557	CP GP35 Diesel "5007," CC, *13–14*		500____
39558	CP GP35 Diesel "5009," nonpowered, *13–14*		260____
39562	BN GP35 Diesel "2533," CC, *13–14*		500____
39563	BN GP35 Diesel "2509," CC, *13–14*		500____
39564	BN GP35 Diesel "2523," nonpowered, *13–14*		260____
39565	ATSF Dash-9 Diesel "612," CC, *13*		530____
39566	ATSF Dash-9 Diesel "623," CC, *13*		530____
39567	ATSF Dash-9 Diesel "631," nonpowered, *13*		260____
39568	BC Rail Dash-9 Diesel "4641," CC, *13*		530____
39569	BC Rail Dash-9 Diesel "4647," CC, *13*		530____
39570	BC Rail Dash-9 Diesel "4652," nonpowered, *13*		260____
39571	BNSF Dash-9 Diesel "4023," CC, *13*		530____
39572	BNSF Dash-9 Diesel "4037," CC, *13*		530____
39573	BNSF Dash-9 Diesel "4046," nonpowered, *13*		260____
39574	C&NW Dash-9 Diesel "8605," CC, *13*		530____
39575	C&NW Dash-9 Diesel "8610," CC, *13*		530____
39576	C&NW Dash-9 Diesel "8622," nonpowered, *13*		260____
39577	SP Dash-9 Diesel "8112," CC, *13*		530____
39578	SP Dash-9 Diesel "8123," CC, *13*		530____
39579	SP Dash-9 Diesel "8129," nonpowered, *13*		260____
39580	UP Dash-9 Diesel "9599," CC, *13*		530____

_____	**39581** UP Dash-9 Diesel "9714," CC, _13_	530
_____	**39582** UP Dash-9 Diesel "9717," nonpowered, _13_	260
_____	**39583** CSX Dash-9 Diesel "9036," CC, _13_	530
_____	**39584** CSX Dash-9 Diesel "9048," CC, _13_	530
_____	**39585** CSX Dash-9 Diesel "9051," nonpowered, _13_	260
_____	**39586** NS Dash-9 Diesel "9310," CC, _13_	530
_____	**39587** NS Dash-9 Diesel "9322," CC, _13_	530
_____	**39588** NS Dash-9 Diesel "9334," nonpowered, _13_	260
_____	**39589** CN Dash-9 Diesel "2534," CC, _13_	530
_____	**39590** CN Dash-9 Diesel "2547," CC, _13_	530
_____	**39591** CN Dash-9 Diesel "2570," nonpowered, _13_	260
_____	**39592** CNJ NS Heritage SD70ACe Diesel "1071," CC, _13_	530
_____	**39593** CNJ NS Heritage SD70ACe Diesel "1831," CC, _13_	530
_____	**39594** CNJ NS Heritage SD70ACe Diesel "1834," nonpowered, _13_	260
_____	**39595** DL&W NS Heritage SD70ACe Diesel "1074," CC, _13_	530
_____	**39596** DL&W NS Heritage SD70ACe Diesel "1853," CC, _13_	530
_____	**39597** DL&W NS Heritage SD70ACe Diesel "1856," nonpowered, _13_	260
_____	**39598** Monongahela NS Heritage ES44AC Diesel "8025," CC, _12_	550
_____	**39599** Monongahela NS Heritage ES44AC Diesel "1901," CC, _12_	550
_____	**39600** PRR E8 AA Diesel Set, CC, _13_	930
_____	**39603** B&O E9 AA Diesel Set, CC, _13_	930
_____	**39606** FEC E9 AA Diesel Set, CC, _13_	930
_____	**39609** SP E9 AA Diesel Set, CC, _13_	930
_____	**39612** SP E9 AA Diesel Set, CC, _13_	930
_____	**39612** UP E9 AA Diesel Set, CC, _13_	930
_____	**39615** CB&Q E9 AA Diesel Set, CC, _13_	930
_____	**39618** MILW E9 AA Diesel Set, CC, _13_	930
_____	**39621** KCS E9 AA Diesel Set, CC, _13_	930
_____	**39624** Erie NS Heritage SD70ACe Diesel "1068," CC, _13_	530
_____	**39625** Erie NS Heritage SD70ACe Diesel "1832," CC, _13_	530
_____	**39626** Erie NS Heritage SD70ACe Diesel "1835," nonpowered, _13_	260
_____	**39627** Illinois Terminal NS Heritage SD70ACe Diesel "1072," CC, _13_	530
_____	**39628** Illinois Terminal NS Heritage SD70ACe Diesel "1896," CC, _13_	530
_____	**39629** Illinois Terminal NS Heritage SD70ACe Diesel "1899," nonpowered, _13_	260
_____	**39630** NYC NS Heritage SD70ACe Diesel "1066," CC, _13_	530
_____	**39631** NYC NS Heritage SD70ACe Diesel "1831," CC, _13_	530
_____	**39632** NYC NS Heritage SD70ACe Diesel "1834," nonpowered, _13_	260
_____	**39633** Reading NS Heritage SD70ACe Diesel "1067," CC, _13_	530
_____	**39634** Reading NS Heritage SD70ACe Diesel "1833," CC, _13_	530
_____	**39635** Reading NS Heritage SD70ACe Diesel "1836," nonpowered, _13_	260

		Exc	Mint
39636	Savannah & Atlanta NS Heritage SD70ACe Diesel "1065," CC, *13*		530____
39637	Savannah & Atlanta NS Heritage SD70ACe Diesel "1915," CC, *13*		530____
39638	Savannah & Atlanta NS Heritage SD70ACe Diesel "1918," nonpowered, *13*		260____
39639	Virginian NS Heritage SD70ACe Diesel "1069," CC, *13*		530____
39640	Virginian NS Heritage SD70ACe Diesel "1907," CC, *13*		530____
39641	Virginian NS Heritage SD70ACe Diesel "1910," nonpowered, *13*		260____
39642	Wabash NS Heritage SD70ACe Diesel "1070," CC, *13*		530____
39643	Wabash NS Heritage SD70ACe Diesel "1877," CC, *13*		530____
39644	Wabash NS Heritage SD70ACe Diesel "1880," nonpowered, *13*		260____
39645	PC NS Heritage SD70ACe Diesel "1073," CC, *13*		530____
39646	PC NS Heritage SD70ACe Diesel "1968," CC, *13*		530____
39647	PC NS Heritage SD70ACe Diesel "1971," nonpowered, *13*		260____
51008	Burlington Pioneer Zephyr Diesel Passenger Set, RailSounds, *04*		875____
51009	Prewar "269E" Steam Freight Set, TrainSounds, *06*		630____
51010	Prewar "246E" Steam Passenger Set, TrainSounds, *07–08*		630____
51012	Christmas Tinplate Freight Set, *08*		675____
51014	Prewar "291W" Red Comet Passenger Car Set, *08*		675____
51220	NYC Imperial Castle Passenger Coach, *93 u*		500____
51221	NYC Niagara County Passenger Coach, *93 u*		500____
51222	NYC Cascade Glory Passenger Coach, *93 u*		500____
51223	NYC City of Detroit Passenger Coach, *93 u*		500____
51224	NYC Imperial Falls Passenger Coach, *93 u*		500____
51225	NYC Westchester County Passenger Coach, *93 u*		500____
51226	NYC Cascade Grotto Passenger Coach, *93 u*		500____
51227	NYC City of Indianapolis Passenger Coach, *93 u*		500____
51228	NYC Manhattan Island Observation Car, *93 u*		500____
51229	NYC Diner "680," *93 u*		500____
51230	NYC Baggage Car "5017," *93 u*		500____
51231	NYC Century Club Passenger Coach, *93 u*		500____
51232	NYC Thousand Islands Observation Car, *93 u*		500____
51233	NYC Diner "684," *93 u*		500____
51234	NYC Baggage Car "5020," *93 u*		500____
51235	NYC Century Tavern Passenger Coach, *93 u*		500____
51236	NYC City of Toledo Passenger Coach, *93 u*		500____
51237	NYC Imperial Mansion Passenger Coach, *93 u*		500____
51238	NYC Imperial Palace Passenger Coach, *93 u*		500____
51239	NYC Cascade Spirit Passenger Coach, *93 u*		500____
51240	NYC Diner "681," *93 u*		500____
51241	NYC City of Chicago Passenger Coach, *93 u*		500____
51242	NYC Imperial Garden Passenger Coach, *93 u*		500____
51243	NYC Imperial Fountain Passenger Coach, *93 u*		500____
51244	NYC Cascade Valley Passenger Coach, *93 u*		500____

		Exc	Mint
___**51245**	NYC Diner "685," *93 u*		500
___**51300**	Shell Semi-Scale 1-D Tank Car "8124," *91*	50	135
___**51301**	Lackawanna Semi-Scale Reefer "7000," *92*	119	161
___**51401**	PRR Semi-Scale Boxcar "100800," *91*	84	128
___**51402**	C&O Semi-Scale Stock Car "95250," *92*	98	138
___**51501**	B&O Semi-Scale Hopper "532000," *91*	78	108
___**51502**	LL Steel Die-cast Ore Car "6486-3" (SSS), *96*		80
___**51503**	LL Steel Die-cast Ore Car "6486-1" (SSS), *96*		80
___**51504**	LL Steel Die-cast Ore Car "6486-2" (SSS), *96*		70
51600	NYC Depressed Center Flatcar with transformer		
___	"6418," *96*		105
___**51701**	NYC Semi-Scale Caboose "19400," *91*	84	123
___**51702**	PRR N-8 Caboose "478039," *91–92*	300	385
___**52054**	Carail Boxcar, *94 u*		300
___**52066**	Trainmaster Tractor and Trailer, *94 u*		120
___**52069**	Carail Tractor and Trailer, *94 u*		70
___**52070**	Knoebel's Boxcar #1, *95 u*		92
___**52075**	United Auto Workers Boxcar, *95 u*		90
___**52082**	Steamtown Lackawanna Boxcar, *95 u*		90
___**52132**	Knoebel's Boxcar #2, *99 u*		90
___**52133**	Knoebel's Boxcar #3, *98 u*		100
___**52134**	Knoebel's Boxcar #4, *00 u*		95
___**52136A**	Christmas Special Tractor and Trailer, *97*		NRS
___**52136B**	Frisco Special Tractor and Trailer, *98*		NRS
___**52137**	Red Wing Shoes Boot Oil Tank Car, *98*		65
___**52141**	Zep Manufacturing Boxcar, *96*		100
___**52158**	Monopoly Mint Car "M-0539," *98*		340
52159	Monopoly Depressed Center Flatcar with		
___	transformer, *98*		95
___**52160**	Monopoly Water Works Tank Car, *98*		105
___**52161**	Monopoly SP-type Caboose "M-1006," *98*		55
___**52168**	Carail Flatcar with Trailer "17455," *99 u*		100
52169	Zep Manufacturing Flatcar with trailer "62734,"		
___	*99 u*		88
___**52181**	Monopoly Set #2, 4-pack, *99*		295
___**52182**	Monopoly Railroads Boxcar "M0636," *99 u*		78
___**52183**	Monopoly Jail Car "M-1131," *99*		75
___**52184**	Monopoly Free Parking Flatcar with 2 autos, *99*		60
___**52185**	Monopoly Chance Gondola "M-0893," *99*		50
___**52187**	Madison Hardware Flatcar with 2 trailers, *99*		98
52188	Carail Aquarium with 2 autos, 25th Anniversary,		
___	*99*		95
___**52189**	Monopoly 4-6-4 Hudson Locomotive, *99*		550
___**52207**	Lionel Lines SD40 Diesel, traditional, *00*		600
___**52208**	Lionel Lines Extended Vision Caboose, *00 u*		200
___**52218**	Monopoly 4-4-2 Steam Freight Set, *00 u*		388
52219	Monopoly 4-6-4 Hudson Locomotive, bronze,		
___	*00 u*		530
___**52224A**	SP Flatcar with Navajo tractor and trailer, *01*		25
52224B	SP Flatcar with Trailer Flatcar Service tractor and		
___	trailer, *01*		25
52225	Monopoly 4-6-4 Hudson Locomotive, pewter,		
___	*01 u*		495
___**52231**	British Columbia 1-D Tank Car, *00 u*		65
52249	Knoebel's Amusement Park 75th Anniversary		
___	Boxcar, *01 u*		89

		Exc	Mint
52262	Plasticville Boxcar, *01 u*	120	___
52282	Western Pacific Feather Boxcar, red, *03*	365	___
52315/20	PRR FM Diesel and Caboose, *04 u*	440	___
52330	B&O Museum Fundraiser Boxcar, *03 u*	100	___
52371	NYC Flatcar with tanker trailer, *05 u*	150	___
62162	Postwar "262" Automatic Crossing Gate and Signal, *99–14*	60	___
62180	Railroad Signs, set of 14, *99–04, 08–17*	10	___
62181	Telephone Pole Set, *99–04, 08–17*	10	___
62283	Die-cast Illuminated Bumpers, *99–17*	27	___
62709	Rico Station Kit, *99–00*	46	___
62716	Short Extension Bridge, *99–03, 07–17*	15	___
62900	Lockon, *99–13*	3	___
62901	Ives Track Clips, 12 pieces (O27), *99–10, 13–16*	5	___
62905	Lockon with wires, *99–10, 13–14*	7	___
62909	Smoke Fluid, *99–12*	7	___
62927	Lubrication/Maintenance Set, *99–17*	25	___
62985	The Lionel Train Book, *99–03*	12	___
65014	Half Curved Track (O27), *99–16*	1	___
65019	Half Straight Track (O27), *99–16*	1	___
65020	90-degree Crossover (O27), *99–16*	11	___
65021	27" Manual Switch, left hand (O27), *99–16*	17	___
65022	27" Manual Switch, right hand (O27), *99–16*	18	___
65023	45-degree Crossover (O27), *99–16*	11	___
65024	35" Straight Track (O27), *99–16*	5	___
65033	27" Diameter Curved Track (O27), *99–16*	2	___
65038	9" Straight Track (O27), *99–16*	2	___
65041	Insulator Pins, dozen (O27), *99–04, 06, 13–14*	3	___
65042	Steel Pins, dozen (O27), *99–04, 06–09, 13–14*	3	___
65049	42" Diameter Curved Track (O27), *99–16*	3	___
65113	54" Diameter Curved Track (O27), *99–16*	3	___
65121	27" Path Remote Switch, left hand (O27), *99–14*	43	___
65122	27" Path Remote Switch, right hand (O27), *99–14*	43	___
65149	Uncoupling Track (O27), *99–14*	12	___
65165	72" Path Remote Switch, right hand (O), *99–14*	125	___
65166	72" Path Remote Switch, left hand (O), *99–14*	125	___
65167	42" Remote Switch, right hand (O27), *99–14*	25	___
65168	42" Remote Switch, left hand (O27), *99–14*	25	___
65500	10" Straight Track (O), *99–16*	2	___
65501	31" Diameter Curved Track (O), *99–16*	2	___
65504	Half Curved Track (O), *99–16*	2	___
65505	Half Straight Track (O), *99–16*	2	___
65514	Half Curved Track (O27), *99–03*	3	___
65523	40" Straight Track (O), *99–16*	7	___
65530	Remote Control Track (O), *99–16*	38	___
65540	90-degree Crossover (O), *99–14*	16	___
65543	Insulator Pins, dozen (O), *99–16*	3	___
65545	45-degree Crossover (O), *99–14*	27	___
65551	Steel Pins, dozen (O), *99–16*	3	___
65554	54" Diameter Curved Track (O), *99–16*	4	___
65572	72" Diameter Curved Track (O), *99–16*	5	___
81000	BNSF Waffle-sided Boxcar "496464," *14–15*	50	___
81001	SP&S Flatcar with bulkheads, *14–16*	50	___
81002	UP 3-D Tank Car, *14–15*	50	___

		Exc	Mint
____81003	CP Bilevel Auto Carrier, *14–16*		50
81004	B&O Depressed-Center Flatcar with transformer,		
____	*14–15*		50
____81005	Maine Central 2-bay Hopper "1005," *14–16*		50
____81006	PRR Hi-Cube Boxcar "31010," *14–16*		50
____81007	Seaboard Waffle-sided Boxcar "25335," *14–16*		50
____81008	Central of Georgia Boxcar "5818," *14–17*		50
____81009	Southern 2-D Tank Car "951005," *14–16*		50
____81010	FEC Gondola "6121" with reels, *14–16*		50
____81011	PFE Reefer "33280," *14–16*		50
____81012	T&P 1-D Tank Car, *14–16*		50
____81013	Frisco Boxcar "700117," *14–16*		50
____81014	D&RGW Ore Car "31101," *14–15*		50
____81015	B&M Reefer "1878," *14–16*		50
____81016	Coaling Station, *14, 16–17*		110
____81017	Barrel Loading Building, *14–16–17*		43
____81018	Shell Vat Car, *17*		80
____81019	Short Tunnel, *14–16–17*		45
____81021	B&M Paul Revere GP9 Diesel Freight Set, *14–15*		500
81023	Jersey Central Yard Boss 0-4-0 Steam Freight		
____	Set, *14–15*		500
____81024	Christmas Train Set, *02–04*		150
81025	Lackawanna Pocono Berkshire Steam Freight		
____	Set, *14–15*		480
____81027	Thomas the Tank Engine Set, *01–04*		120
____81028	Marquette GP38 Diesel Freight Set, *14–15*		430
81029	C&NW Windy City GP38 Diesel Freight Set,		
____	*14–15*		400
____81030	UP Gold Coast Flyer Steam Freight Set, *14–15*		430
____81031	Dinosaur Diesel Freight Set, LionChief, *14–16*		175
____81038	MILW Heavy Mikado Locomotive "8693" CC, *15*		1300
____81063	Classic Automatic Gateman, *14–17*		95
____81064	Construction Zone Signs #2, *14–17*		10
81066	Milwaukee Road Double-sheathed Boxcar		
____	"8775" (std O), *14*		80
____81067	Monopoly Aquarium Car, *14–15*		85
81073	Monopoly Boxcar 2-pack, Ventnor and Indiana		
____	Avenues, *14–15*		135
81076	Pennsylvania Salt 8,000-gallon 1-D Tank Car		
____	"4724" (std O), *14*		73
81077	Pere Marquette 8,000-gallon 1-D Tank Car		
____	"71710" (std O), *14*		73
81078	NYC 8,000-gallon 1-D Tank Car "107898"		
____	(std O), *14*		73
81079	NKP 8,000-gallon 1-D Tank Car "50277"		
____	(std O), *14*		73
81080	BN 8,000-gallon 1-D Tank Car "977100"		
____	(std O), *14*		73
____81081	Alaska Steel-sided Reefer "10806" (std O), *14*		80
____81090	NS Hi-Cube Boxcar 2-pack (std O), *14–15*		190
81094	Conrail "Big Blue" High-Cube Boxcar Diesel		
____	Freight Set, CC, *14*		970
____81095	Conrail Hi-Cube Boxcar 2-pack (std O), *14–16*		190
81101	Polar Express 10th Anniversary Steam Passenger		
____	Set, LionChief, *14–15*		430
____81113	SP 50' DD Boxcar "214051" (std O), *14–15*		75

		Exc	Mint
81122	Christmas Inspection Truck, *15*		180____
81134	BN SD70MAC Diesel "9424," CC, *14*		550____
81135	BN SD70MAC Diesel "9431," CC, *14*		550____
81137	BNSF SD70MAC Diesel "9858," CC, *14*		550____
81138	BNSF SD70MAC Diesel "9860," CC, *14*		550____
81141	Conrail SD70MAC Diesel "4138," CC, *14*		550____
81142	PFE Steel-sided Reefers 3-pack (std O), *14*		300____
81144	CSX SD70MAC Diesel "781," CC, *14*		550____
81147	KCS SD7CMAC Diesel "3950," CC, *14*		550____
81148	KCS SD7CMAC Diesel "3953," CC, *14*		550____
81151	Alaska SD7CMAC Diesel "4002," CC, *14*		550____
81152	Alaska SD7CMAC Diesel "4005," CC, *14*		550____
81153	CSX SD70MAC Diesel "778," CC, *14*		550____
81154	UP ES44AC Diesel "7361," CC, *14*		550____
81155	UP ES44AC Diesel "7388," CC, *14*		550____
81160	CSX ES44AC Diesel "937," CC, *14*		550____
81161	CSX ES44AC Diesel "944," CC, *14*		550____
81169	Iowa Interstate ES44AC Diesel "504," CC, *14*		550____
81170	Iowa Interstate ES44AC Diesel "507," CC, *14*		550____
81171	Ferromex ES44AC Diesel "4617," CC, *14*		550____
81172	Ferromex ES44AC Diesel "4626," CC, *14*		550____
81176	CN ES44AC Diesel "2812," CC, *14*		550____
81177	CN ES44AC Diesel "2818," CC, *14*		550____
81179	2-8-2 Heavy Mikado Pilot Locomotive, CC, *14*		1300____
81180	2-8-2 Heavy Mikado Locomotive, CC, *15*		1300____
81181	Southern 2-8-2 Heavy Mikado Locomotive "4866," CC, *15*		1300____
81182	L&N 2-8-2 Heavy Mikado Locomotive "1757," CC, *14*		1300____
81183	MP 2-8-2 Heavy Mikado Locomotive "1496," CC, *14*		1300____
81184	P&WV 2-8-2 Heavy Mikado Locomotive "1152," CC, *14*		1300____
81185	CNJ 2-8-2 Heavy Mikado Locomotive "845," CC, *14*		1300____
81186	Frisco 2-8-2 Heavy Mikado Locomotive "4126," CC, *14*		1300____
81187	C&IM 2-8-2 Heavy Mikado Locomotive "551," CC, *14*		1300____
81188	NYC 2-8-2 Heavy Mikado Locomotive "9506," CC, *14*		1300____
81189	CB&Q 2-8-2 Heavy Mikado Locomotive "5509," CC, *15*		1300____
81190	WP 2-8-2 Heavy Mikado Locomotive "334," CC, *15*		1300____
81191	Erie 2-8-2 Heavy Mikado Locomotive "3207," CC, *15*		1300____
81192	GN 2-8-2 Heavy Mikado Locomotive "3148," CC, *14*		1300____
81193	Wheeling & Lake Erie 2-8-2 Heavy Mikado Locomotive "6012," CC, *15*		1300____
81194	NKP 2-8-2 Heavy Mikado Locomotive "689," CC, *15*		1300____
81195	PRR Boxcar, *14–15*		70____
81196	Timken Boxcar, *14–15*		70____
81197	Santa Fe Boxcar, *14–15*		70____

			Exc Mint
___	**81198**	GN Boxcar, *14–16*	70
___	**81199**	PRR 1-D Tank Car, *14–15*	70
___	**81200**	Timken 1-D Tank Car, *14–16*	70
___	**81201**	GN 1-D Tank Car, *14–16*	70
___	**81202**	Santa Fe 1-D Tank Car, *14–15*	70
___	**81203**	PRR Flatcar, *14–15*	70
___	**81204**	Santa Fe Flatcar, *14–16*	70
___	**81205**	Timken Flatcar, *14–16*	70
___	**81206**	GN Flatcar, *14–16*	70
___	**81207**	CP H-24-66 Train Master Diesel "8900," CC, *14*	550
___	**81208**	CP H-24-66 Train Master Diesel "8903," CC, *14*	550
___	**81209**	CNJ H-24-66 Train Master Diesel "2401," CC, *14*	550
___	**81210**	CNJ H-24-66 Train Master Diesel "2406," CC, *14*	550
___	**81211**	Reading H-24-66 Train Master Diesel "801," CC, *14*	550
___	**81212**	Reading H-24-66 Train Master Diesel "804," CC, *14*	550
___	**81213**	SP H-24-66 Train Master Diesel "4803," CC, *14*	550
___	**81214**	SP H-24-66 Train Master Diesel "4809," CC, *14*	550
___	**81215**	Southern H-24-66 Train Master Diesel "6300," CC, *14*	550
___	**81216**	Southern H-24-66 Train Master Diesel "6303," CC, *14*	550
___	**81217**	N&W H-24-66 Train Master Diesel "151," CC, *14*	550
___	**81218**	N&W H-24-66 Train Master Diesel "164," CC, *14*	550
___	**81219**	Santa Fe E8 Diesel AA Set"84/85," CC, *14*	930
___	**81222**	PC E8 Diesel AA Set"4289/4325," CC, *14*	930
___	**81225**	RI E8 Diesel AA Set"647/648," CC, *14*	930
___	**81228**	C&O E8 Diesel AA Set"4027/4028," CC, *14*	930
___	**81231**	Erie E8 Diesel AA Set"822/823," CC, *14*	930
___	**81234**	MKT E8 Diesel AA Set"131/132," CC, *14*	930
___	**81237**	SAL E8 Diesel AA Set"3051/3055," CC, *14*	930
___	**81240**	Wabash E8 Diesel AA Set"1007/1011," CC, *14*	930
___	**81243**	Pilot M1a 4-8-2 Locomotive, CC, *14*	1500
___	**81245**	PRR M1a 4-8-2 Locomotive "6671," CC, *14*	1500
___	**81246**	PRR M1a 4-8-2 Locomotive "6764," CC, *14*	1500
___	**81247**	PRR M1a Coal Hauler Twin-hopper Steam Freight Set, CC, *14*	1800
___	**81248**	10" Girder Bridge Track, *14–17*	25
___	**81249**	Christmas Girder Bridge Track, *14, 16–17*	25
___	**81250**	FasTrack O-96 Curve, *14*	7
___	**81251**	FasTrack O-31 Manual Switch, right-hand, *14–16*	50
___	**81252**	FasTrack O-31 Manual Switch, left-hand, *14–16*	50
___	**81253**	FasTrack O-31 Remote Switch, right-hand, *14–16*	110
___	**81254**	FasTrack O-31 Remote Switch, left-hand, *14–16*	110
___	**81256**	Personalized Birthday Message Boxcar, *14–15*	85
___	**81257**	Amtrak Water Tower, *14–17*	35
___	**81259**	PRR Broadway Limited Steam Passenger Set, *14*	370
___	**81261**	NYC Early Bird Special Steam Freight Set, *16–17*	380
___	**81262**	UP Steam Freight Set, LionChief, *15*	400
___	**81263**	CNJ Diesel Passenger Set, LionChief, *14–16*	390
___	**81264**	Western Union Telegraph Steam Freight Set, *14–16*	390

		Exc	Mint
81266	Amtrak FT Diesel Passenger Set, LionChief, *14–15*	460	___
81269	PRR Allegheny Hauler Steam Freight Set, *16–17*	420	___
81270	Bethlehem Steel Steam Work Train, LionChief, *15*	340	___
81279	Albert Hall European Steam Passenger Set, LionChief, *14–15*	430	___
81280	Victorian Christmas Steam Passenger Set, *14*	400	___
81284	Frosty the Snowman Steam Freight Set, LionChief, *14–15*	320	___
81286	Lionel Junction "Little Steam" Freight Set, *14–15*	175	___
81287	Lionel Junction UP Steam Freight Set, *14–15*	175	___
81288	Pet Shop Diesel Freight Set, *14–16*	175	___
81290	Thomas Kinkade Holiday Covered Bridge, *14*	70	___
81292	Valley Central 1-D Tank Car "45003," *14–17*	45	___
81294	LCS Sensor Track, *13–16*	95	___
81295	AT&SF 2-8-2 Locomotive "3158," LionChief, *14–16*	430	___
81296	GN 2-8-2 Locomotive "3123," LionChief, *14–15*	430	___
81297	PRR 2-8-2 Locomotive "9633," LionChief, *14–15*	430	___
82678	Angela Trotta Thomas Christmas Boxcar, *16*	85	___
81299	Chessie System 2-8-2 Locomotive "2103," LionChief, *14–15*	430	___
81301	NYC 4-6-4 Locomotive "5421," LionChief, *14–15*	430	___
81302	C&O 4-6-4 Locomotive "308," LionChief, *14–17*	430	___
81303	UP 4-6-4 Locomotive "674," LionChief, *14–17*	430	___
81304	CN 4-6-4 Locomotive "5702," LionChief, *14–17*	430	___
81307	B&O 4-6-2 Locomotive "5307," LionChief, *14–17*	430	___
81308	CP 4-6-2 Locomotive "2469," LionChief, *14–17*	430	___
81309	SP 4-6-2 Locomotive "3106," LionChief, *14–17*	430	___
81311	Alaska 4-6-2 Locomotive "652," LionChief, *14–17*	430	___
81313	FasTrack Power Lockon, *15–17*	23	___
81314	FasTrack Power Block Lockon, *15–17*	40	___
81315	Coaling Station, *15–17*	160	___
81316	Personalized Christmas Message Boxcar, *15*	80	___
81317	FasTrack Accessory Activator Track Pack, *15–17*	24	___
81325	LCS WiFi Module, *13–16*	180	___
81326	LCS Serial Converter #2, *14–16*	50	___
81331	Iron Arry Locomotive with Remote, LionChief, *14–15*	140	___
81332	Iron Bert Locomotive with Remote, LionChief, *14–15*	140	___
81373	Candy Cane Flatcar with bulkheads, *15*	60	___
81395	Thomas Kinkade Christmas Passenger Set, LionChief, *14–15*	380	___
81419	Alien Ooze 1-D Tank Car, *14–15*	65	___
81420	PRR Truss-rod Gondola with tarp, *14–16*	65	___
81422	NS Water Tower, *14*	31	___
81423	Sodor Coal and Scrap Cars 2-pack, *14–16*	70	___
81424	Sodor Crane Car and Work Caboose 2-pack, *14*	70	___
81425	Frosty the Snowman Passenger Station, *14*	65	___
81426	Frosty the Snowman Animated Gondola, *14*	75	___
81427	Frosty the Snowman Aquarium Car, *14*	85	___
81428	Frosty the Snowman Boxcar, *14*	65	___
81430	Lionelville Shanty, *14*	22	___
81432	PRR Girder Bridge, *14–15*	21	___

		Exc	Mint
____81433	PRR Crossing Shanty, *14*		22
____81434	Pennsylvania Station Platform, *14–15*		23
____81435	N&W NS Heritage Quad Hopper with coal, *14–15*		60
____81436	Intermodal Container 4-pack, *14*		43
____81437	York Peppermint Patty Vat Car, *14–15*		70
____81439	Halloween Pumpkinheads Handcar, *14–16*		90
____81440	Western Union Handcar, *14–16*		100
____81441	North Pole Central Snowplow, CC, *16–17*		280
____81442	PRR Rotary Snowplow "1442," CC, *16*		280
____81443	D&RGW Rotary Snowplow "443," CC, *16*		280
____81444	PRR Tie-Jector, CC, *14–16*		200
____81445	MOW Tie-Jector, CC, *14–16*		200
____81446	Santa Fe Tie-Jector, CC, *14–16*		200
____81447	NS Tie-Jector, CC, *14–16*		200
____81448	Amtrak Tie-Jector, CC, *14–16*		200
____81449	Zombie Motorized Trolley, *14*		100
____81450	Polar Express Trolley, *14*		110
____81451	St. Louis Motorized Trolley, *14*		100
81452	Neil Young Texas Special F3 AA Diesels, CC, *13–14*		650
____81453	Neil Young PRR F3 AA Diesels, CC, *13–14*		650
81462	PRR Broadway Limited Add-on Baggage Car, *14–17*		70
____81463	CNJ Water Tower, *14–17*		31
____81464	CNJ Montclair Add-on Passenger Car, *14–16*		60
____81465	SP Flatcar with piggyback trailers, *14–16*		75
____81466	BN Maxi-Stack Pair, *14–16*		140
____81469	GN Bilevel Stock Car "65385," *14–17*		65
____81470	DC Comics Batman Phantom Train, *16–17*		400
81475	DC Comics Batman M7 Subway Set, LionChief, *14–15*		370
____81479	Batman Add-on M7 Subway Car 2-pack, *14–15*		140
81480	John Deere RS-3 Diesel Freight Set, LionChief, *14–16*		320
____81486	NYC Patrol Flatcar with helicopter, *14–15*		65
____81487	Ronald Reagan Presidential Boxcar, *14–15*		70
____81488	Andrew Jackson Presidential Boxcar, *14–16*		70
____81489	Warren G. Harding Presidential Boxcar, *14–16*		70
81490	Dwight D. Eisenhower Presidential Boxcar, *14–16*		70
____81491	Jersey Central Coal Dump Car, *14–15*		65
____81492	Strasburg RR Searchlight Car, *14*		50
____81493	U.S.A.F. Missile Carrying Car, *15–16*		65
____81494	Santa's Sleigh Rocket Fuel Tank Car, *16*		65
____81495	40-watt Power Supply, *15–17*		70
____81499	LCS Power Supply with DB9 cable, *13–16*		37
____81500	LCS Sensor Track 1' Cable, *13–16*		14
____81501	LCS Sensor Track 3' Cable, *13–16*		15
____81502	LCS Sensor Track 10' Cable, *13–16*		19
____81503	LCS Sensor Track 20' Cable, *13–16*		19
____81504	Ann Arbor FA-2 Diesel AA Set "53/53A," CC, *14*		750
____81507	B&O FA-2 Diesel AA Set "817/827," CC, *14–15*		750
____81510	Erie FA-2 Diesel AA Set "736A/736D," CC, *14–15*		750
____81513	MKT FA-2 Diesel AA Set "331A/331C," CC, *14*		750
____81516	NYC FA-2 Diesel AA Set "1075/1078," CC, *14–15*		750

		Exc	Mint
81519	PRR FA-2 Diesel AA Set "9608/9609," CC, *14–15*		750____
81522	Ann Arbor FB2 Diesel "53B," CC, *14*		450____
81523	B&O FB2 Diesel "817B," CC, *14–15*		450____
81524	Erie FB2 Diesel "736B," CC, *14–15*		450____
81525	MKT FB2 Diesel "331B," CC, *14*		450____
81526	NYC FB2 Diesel "3327," CC, *14–15*		450____
81527	PRR FB2 Diesel "9608B," CC, *14*		450____
81528	Ann Arbor FB2 Diesel, nonpowered, *14*		350____
81529	B&O FB2 Diesel, nonpowered, *14–15*		350____
81530	Erie FB2 Diesel, nonpowered, *14–15*		350____
81531	MKT FB2 Diesel, nonpowered, *14*		350____
81532	NYC FB2 Diesel, nonpowered, *14–15*		350____
81533	PRR FB2 Diesel, nonpowered, *14–15*		350____
81534	Christmas Toys Stock Car, *14*		70____
81545	Operation Eagle Missile Launcher Car, CC, *15*		350____
81546	Operation Eagle Sound Car, CC, *15*		240____
81568	4th of July Parade Boxcar, *14–16*		80____
81596	Weathered UP 4-12-2 Locomotive "9000," CC, *13*		1400____
81597	Weathered B&O RF-16 Sharknose AA Diesels "855-857," CC, *13*		830____
81600	Weathered PRR RF-16 Sharknose AA Diesels "2020A-2021A," CC, *13*		830____
81603	72-watt Power Supply, LionChief, *14–17*		55____
81605	Santa Fe PS-1 Boxcar 5-pack (std O), *14*		380____
81615	UP 1-D Tank Car, *14*		45____
81617	Pet Shop 1-D Tank Car, *14–16*		45____
81619	Reading PS-1 Boxcar "109448" (std O), *14*		80____
81620	Zombie Figure Pack, *14–15*		23____
81621	John Deere Billboard Set, *15*		25____
81622	John Deere Water Tower, *15*		40____
81625	Amtrak Add-on Baggage Car, *14–16*		85____
81626	Barrel Shed, *14–16*		35____
81627	Christmas Hopper Shed, *14, 16–17*		45____
81628	Grain Elevator, *15*		80____
81629	Lumber Shed Kit, *14–17*		35____
81635	Water Tower, *14*		35____
81639	LCS Accessory Switch Controller #2, *14–16*		120____
81640	LCS Block Power Controller #2, *14–16*		120____
81644	Chessie System Baby Madison Passenger Car 3-pack, *14–16*		270____
81649	SP Baby Madison Passenger Car 3-pack, *14–16*		270____
81654	Philadelphia Energy Solutions 1-D Tank Car "0765," *15–17*		60____
81662	FasTrack O-31 Quarter Curved Track, *14, 16*		5____
81668	Philadelphia Energy Solutions 1-D Tank Car "0771," *15–16*		60____
81680	Dinosaur 1-D Tank Car, *14–16*		45____
81686	PRR GL-a 2-bay Hopper 3-pack (std O), *14*		220____
81687	LV GL-a 2-bay Hopper 2-pack (std O), *14–15*		146____
81688	CB&Q GL-a 2-bay Hopper 3-pack (std O), *14–16*		220____
81689	C&O GL-a 2-bay Hopper 3-pack (std O), *14–16*		220____
81693	Aerial Target Launcher, *15–16*		90____
81699	Polar Express Scale Twin Hopper, *15*		80____
81703	Santa Fe Hi-Cube Boxcar 2-pack (std O), *14–16*		190____

		Exc	Mint
____81704	Grand Trunk Hi-Cube Boxcar 2-pack (std O), *14–16*		190
81705	Milwaukee Road Hi-Cube Boxcar 2-pack (std O), *14–16*		190
____**81706**	Frisco Hi-Cube Boxcar 2-pack (std O), *14–16*		190
____**81707**	NYC Hi-Cube Boxcar 2-pack (std O), *14–16*		190
____**81708**	Santa Fe Hi-Cube Boxcar "36715" (std O), *14–15*		95
81710	Milwaukee Road Hi-Cube Boxcar "4980" (std O), *14–15*		95
____**81711**	Frisco Hi-Cube Boxcar "9125" (std O), *14–15*		95
____**81712**	NYC Hi-Cube Boxcar "67282" (std O), *14–15*		95
81723	Postwar "3413" Mercury Capsule Launcher Car, *15*		80
____**81725**	UP Operating Merchandise Car, *14–15*		80
____**81726**	REA Operating Merchandise Car, *14–15*		80
____**81729**	Great Western Passenger Car Add-on 2-pack, *14*		130
____**81733**	Christmas Boxcar, *14*		65
____**81734**	FasTrack Oval Track and Power Pack, *14–17*		200
____**81735**	FasTrack Figure-8 Track and Power Pack, *14–17*		250
____**81736**	Classic Lionel Catalogs Billboard Pack, *14–15*		13
____**81737**	Passenger Station, *14–15*		60
____**81738**	Lionel Auto Loader Cars 4-pack, *14–15, 17*		25
81739	Santa Fe Baby Madison Passenger Car 3-pack, *14–16*		270
____**81744**	CP Baby Madison Passenger Car 3-pack, *14–16*		270
81749	Pullman Baby Madison Passenger Car 3-pack, *14–16*		270
81754	NYC Baby Madison Passenger Car 3-pack, *14–16*		270
____**81759**	NYC Coach/Diner 2-pack, *14–16*		180
____**81760**	NYC Coach/Baggage Car 2-pack, *14–16*		180
81763	Pullman Baby Madison Passenger Car 3-pack, *14–16*		180
____**81764**	Pullman Coach/Baggage Car 2-pack, *14, 16*		180
____**81768**	Chessie System Coach/Diner 2-pack, *14–16*		180
81769	Chessie System Coach/Baggage Car 2-pack, *14–16*		180
____**81773**	SP Coach/Diner 2-pack, *14–16*		180
____**81774**	SP Coach/Baggage Car 2-pack, *14–16*		180
____**81778**	Santa Fe Coach/Diner 2-pack, *14–16*		180
____**81779**	Santa Fe Coach/Baggage Car 2-pack, *14–16*		180
____**81783**	CP Coach/Diner 2-pack, *14–16*		180
____**81784**	CP Coach/Baggage Car 2-pack, *14–16*		180
____**81789**	NH GL-a 2-bay Hopper 2-pack (std O), *14–16*		146
81793	Berwind GL-a 2-bay Hopper 3-pack (std O), *14–15*		220
81800	Southern 18" Aluminum Observation/Coach Car, 2-pack (std O), *14*		320
81801	Southern 18" Aluminum Combination/Vista Dome Car, 2-pack (std O), *14*		320
____**81806**	PRR N5b Caboose "477814" (std O), *14*		95
____**81807**	Conrail N5b Caboose "22882" (std O), *14–15*		95
____**81808**	PC N5b Caboose "22802" (std O), *14–16*		95
____**81809**	LIRR N5b Caboose "2" (std O), *14–15*		95
____**81810**	Lionel Lines N5b Caboose "1402" (std O), *14–16*		95
____**81811**	Polar Express N5b Caboose, *16*		95

		Exc	Mint
81812	RI 18" Aluminum Observation/Coach Car, 2-pack (std O), *14*	320	
81813	RI 18" Aluminum Combination/Vista Dome Car, 2-pack (std O), *14*	320	
81818	C&O 18" Aluminum Observation/Coach Car, 2-pack (std O), *14*	320	
81819	C&O 18" Aluminum Combination/Vista Dome Car, 2-pack (std O), *14*	320	
81824	P&WV GL-a 2-bay Hopper 2-pack (std O), *14–16*	146	
81827	PC Round-roof Boxcar "100104" (std O), *14*	80	
81828	GN Round-roof Boxcar "5885" (std O), *14*	80	
81829	WP Round-roof Boxcar "10211" (std O), *14*	80	
81830	MKT 18" Aluminum Observation/Coach Car, 2-pack (std O), *14*	320	
81831	MKT 18" Aluminum Baggage/Diner Car, 2-pack (std O), *14*	320	
81836	Erie Double-sheathed Boxcar "71107" (std O), *14–15*	80	
81837	Frisco Double-sheathed Boxcar "128528" (std O), *14–15*	80	
81838	CNJ Double-sheathed Boxcar "14014" (std O), *14–15*	80	
81839	Pacific Fright Express Steel-sided Reefer (std O), *14*	80	
81840	UP Ca-4 Caboose with smoke "3880" (std O), *14*	90	
81841	UP MOW Caboose "903224" (std O), *14*	90	
81842	Wabash 18" Aluminum Dome-Observation/Coach Car, 2-pack (std O), *14*	320	
81843	Wabash 18" Aluminum Combination/Vista Dome Car, 2-pack (std O), *14*	320	
81858	PRR GL-a 2-bay Hopper 3-pack (std O), *14*	220	
81862	FasTrack O-31 Curved Track 4-pack, *14, 16*	22	
81866	RI 18" Aluminum Baggage/Diner Car, 2-pack (std O), *14*	320	
81869	C&O 18" Aluminum Baggage/Diner Car, 2-pack (std O), *14*	320	
81871	Loggers Figure Pack, *16–17*	30	
81872	Wabash 18" Aluminum Baggage/Diner Car, 2-pack (std O), *14*	320	
81875	MKT 18" Aluminum Combination/Vista Dome Car, 2-pack (std O), *14*	320	
81878	Southern 18" Aluminum Baggage/Diner Car, 2-pack (std O), *14*	320	
81881	SP Crane Car, CC, *14–16*	500	
81882	DT&I Crane Car, CC, *14–16*	500	
81883	CSX Crane Car, CC, *14–16*	500	
81884	Bethlehem Steel Crane Car, CC, *14*	500	
81885	MOW Crane Car, CC, *14–16*	500	
81886	SP Boom Car, RailSounds, CC, *14–16*	240	
81887	DT&I Boom Car, RailSounds, CC, *14–16*	240	
81888	CSX Boom Car, RailSounds, CC, *14–16*	240	
81889	MOW Boom Car, RailSounds, CC, *14–16*	240	
81890	Bethlehem Steel Boom Car, RailSounds, CC, *14*	240	
81891	BNSF 52' Gondola "523300" with 3-piece covers (std O), *14*	80	
81892	Bethlehem Steel 52' Gondola "303022" with 3-piece covers (std O), *14*	80	

81893	GTW 52' Gondola "145391" with 3-piece covers (std O), *14*	80
81894	CSX 52' Gondola "709190" with 3-piece covers (std O), *14*	80
81895	North Pole Central 52' Gondola "128925" with 3-piece covers (std O), *14*	80
81896	NYC PS-5 Flatcar "506266" with piggyback trailers (std O), *14*	100
81897	Milwaukee Road PS-5 Flatcar "64660" with piggyback trailers (std O), *14*	100
81898	Lionel PS-5 Flatcar with piggyback trailers (std O), *14*	100
81899	CP PS-5 Flatcar "301000" with piggyback trailers (std O), *14*	100
81900	UP PS-5 Flatcar "258255" with piggyback trailers (std O), *14*	100
81901	NYC Tractor and Piggyback Trailer, *14, 17*	90
81902	Milwaukee Road Tractor and Piggyback Trailer, *14*	90
81903	Lionel Tractor and Piggyback Trailer, *14*	90
81904	CP Tractor and Piggyback Trailer, *14–15, 17*	90
81905	UP Tractor and Piggyback Trailer, *14*	90
81908	PFE Steel-sided Reefers 3-pack (std O), *14*	240
81912	New York Yankees Boxcar, *14*	70
81913	St. Louis Cardinals Boxcar, *14*	70
81914	Oakland Athletics Boxcar, *14*	70
81915	San Francisco Giants Boxcar, *14*	70
81916	Boston Red Sox Boxcar, *14*	70
81917	Los Angeles Dodgers Boxcar, *14*	70
81918	Cincinnati Reds Boxcar, *14*	70
81919	San Diego Padres Boxcar, *14*	70
81920	Detroit Tigers Boxcar, *14*	70
81921	Atlanta Braves Boxcar, *14*	70
81922	Baltimore Orioles Boxcar, *14*	70
81923	Minnesota Twins Boxcar, *14*	70
81924	Chicago White Sox Boxcar, *14*	70
81925	Chicago Cubs Boxcar, *14*	70
81926	Philadelphia Phillies Boxcar, *14*	70
81927	Cleveland Indians Boxcar, *14*	70
81928	New York Mets Boxcar, *14*	70
81929	Toronto Blue Jays Boxcar, *14*	70
81930	Miami Marlins Boxcar, *14*	70
81931	Angels Baseball Boxcar, *14*	70
81932	Pittsburgh Pirates Boxcar, *14*	70
81933	Texas Rangers Boxcar, *14*	70
81934	Milwaukee Brewers Boxcar, *14*	70
81935	Houston Astros Boxcar, *14*	70
81936	Colorado Rockies Boxcar, *14*	70
81937	Tampa Bay Rays Boxcar, *14*	70
81938	Seattle Mariners Boxcar, *14*	70
81939	Washington Nationals Boxcar, *14*	70
81940	Arizona Diamondbacks Boxcar, *14*	70
81941	Kansas City Royals Boxcar, *14*	70
81944	Rotary Beacon, yellow, *14–16*	85
81945	Polar Express Scale Coach, *14*	210

		Exc	Mint
81946	FasTrack O-36 Remote Switch, right-hand, *14–16*		110____
81947	FasTrack O-36 Remote Switch, left-hand, *14–16*		110____
81948	FasTrack O-48 Remote Switch, right-hand, *14–16*		120____
81949	FasTrack O-48 Remote Switch, left-hand, *14–16*		120____
81950	FasTrack O-60 Remote Switch, right-hand, *14–16*		120____
81951	FasTrack O-60 Remote Switch, left-hand, *14–16*		120____
81952	FasTrack O-72 Remote Switch, right-hand, *14–16*		120____
81953	FasTrack O-72 Remote Switch, left-hand, *14–16*		120____
81954	FasTrack O-72 Remote Switch, wye, *14–16*		120____
81968	Halloween Pacific Fright Express Caboose (std O), *14*		90____
81969	PRR 18" Aluminum Parlor/Coach Car, 2-pack (std O), *14–15*		320____
81972	B&O 18" Aluminum Baggage/Sleeper Car, 2-pack (std O), *14*		320____
81975	SP 18" Aluminum Sleeper/Coach Car, 2-pack (std O), *14–15*		320____
81978	UP 18" Aluminum Sleeper/Coach Car, 2-pack (std O), *14–15*		320____
81981	KCS 18" Aluminum Sleeper/Coach Car, 2-pack (std O), *14*		320____
81984	Postwar "1887" Christmas Flatcar with reindeer, *14*		70____
81985	Postwar "6428" Christmas Mail Car, *14*		60____
81986	Christmas Wish 1-D Tank Car, *14*		60____
81987	Angela Trotta Thomas "Santa's Letter" Boxcar, *14*		65____
81988	Angela Trotta Thomas Christmas Billboard Pack, *14*		15____
81990	Christmas Gondola with reindeer feed vats, *14*		65____
81992	Santa Claus Bobbing Head Boxcar, *14*		65____
81993	North Pole Central Santa Finder Searchlight Car, *14*		55____
81999	PRR Gondola with Christmas gifts and trees, *14*		65____
82000	PRR Christmas Crane Car, *14*		75____
82001	Merry & Bright Hot Cocoa Car, *14*		70____
82002	Old St. Nick Operating Billboard, *14, 16*		60____
82003	Christmas Blinking Water Tower, *14*		35____
82005	Christmas Wreath Clock Tower, *14, 16–17*		43____
82008	Bungalow House, *15–17*		80____
82009	Suburban House, *15–16*		80____
82010	Joe's Bait & Tackle Shop, *15–16*		65____
82011	Keystone Cafe, *15–16*		80____
82012	Single Floodlight Tower, *15–17*		75____
82013	Double Floodlight Tower, *15–17*		90____
82014	Postwar "192" Control Tower, *15–16*		100____
82015	Wind Turbine, *15–17*		80____
82016	Oil Pump, *15–17*		60____
82017	Lionel Art Operating Billboard, *15–17*		70____
82018	Track Gang, *15–16*		100____
82020	Burning Switch Tower, *15–17*		130____
82021	Bascule Bridge, *15*		450____
82022	Lionel Steel Gantry Crane, CC, *15–17*		400____

____ 82023	Operating Sawmill, CC, *15–17*	350
____ 82024	Postwar "164" Log Loader, *15*	340
____ 82026	Postwar "497" Coaling Station, *15–17*	300
____ 82028	Postwar "352" Icing Station, *15–17*	150
____ 82029	Culvert Loader, CC, *15–17*	300
____ 82030	Culvert Unloader, CC, *15–17*	300
____ 82033	MOW Trackside Crane, CC, *16–17*	600
____ 82034	Loading Station, *16*	350
____ 82035	Work House, crane sounds, *16–17*	150
____ 82036	Luxury Diner, *15–17*	80
____ 82038	8" Female Pigtail Power Cable, *16–17*	10
____ 82039	36" Male Pigtail Power Cable, *16–17*	11
____ 82043	Plug-n-play Power Cable Extension, *16–17*	16
____ 82045	Plug-n-play Control Cable Extension, *16–17*	20
____ 82046	36" Power Tap Cable, *16–17*	16
____ 82047	Lionel Lines Log Dump Car, *15–16*	65
____ 82048	AT&SF Ice Car, *15–17*	75
____ 82049	Santa's Work Shoppe Log Dump Car, *16*	65
____ 82050	Santa's Work Shoppe Sawmill, *16–17*	240
____ 82051	North Pole Central Icing Station, *16–17*	150
____ 82052	PFE Ice Car, *15–17*	75
____ 82053	North Pole Central Icing Car, *16–17*	75
____ 82054	Weyerhaeuser Log Dump Car, *15–17*	65
____ 82055	Bethlehem Steel Trackside Crane, CC, *16–17*	600
____ 82064	Halloween Operating Billboard, *15–17*	80
____ 82066	PRR Log Dump Car, *15*	65
____ 82067	Lionel Lines Coal Dump Car, *15–17*	65
____ 82068	NS Coal Dump Car, *15*	65
____ 82069	Conrail Coal Dump Car, *15–17*	65
____ 82072	Philadelphia Quartz Hopper "755," *15–17*	50
____ 82073	CN Ore Car, *15–17*	50
____ 82074	SP 1-D Tank Car, *15–17*	50
____ 82075	NYC Waffle-sided Boxcar, *15–17*	50
____ 82076	Chessie System Gondola with containers, *16–17*	50
____ 82077	D&H Hi-Cube Boxcar, *16*	50
____ 82078	NP 1-D Tank Car, *16*	50
____ 82079	UP Wood-sided Reefer, *16*	50
____ 82080	C&NW 3-D Tank Car, *16–17*	50
____ 82081	CSX Auto Carrier, *16–17*	50
____ 82082	NS Flatcar with pipes, *16–17*	50
____ 82083	Central of Georgia Gondola with cable reels, *16*	50
____ 82084	Virginian Boxcar, *16–17*	50
____ 82085	AT&SF Waffle-sided Boxcar, *16–17*	50
____ 82086	MKT Reefer, *16*	50
____ 82087	WP Depressed Flatcar with generator, *16–17*	50
____ 82088	Log Pack, *16–17*	10
____ 82091	PRR Tie Work Car "82091," *14–16*	75
____ 82092	MOW Tie Work Car "77," *14–16*	75
____ 82093	AT&SF Tie Work Car "82093," *14–16*	75
____ 82094	NS Tie Work Car "51," *14–16*	75
____ 82095	Amtrak Tie Work Car "67," *14–16*	75
____ 82096	Lionel Steel Culvert Gondola, *15–16*	65
____ 82097	Bucyrus-Erie Gantry Crane, CC, *15–17*	400
____ 82098	Bucyrus-Erie Culvert Gondola, *15*	65

		Exc	Mint
82099	Zombie Apocalypse Survivors GP38 Diesel Freight Set, LionChief, *15*		440____
82100	Polar Express Hero Boy's Home, *16–17*		90____
82101	Postwar "6512" Mercury Capsule Astronaut Car, *15–16*		80____
82102	Lumberjacks, *15–16*		65____
82103	Playground Swing, *15–16*		75____
82104	Playground Playtime, *15–16*		100____
82105	Tire Swing, *15–16*		100____
82106	Pony Ride, *15–17*		75____
82107	Tug-of-War, *15–17*		65____
82108	Hobo Campfire, *15*		100____
82110	Extended Truss Bridge, *15–17*		300____
82111	Lionel Industrial Coal 2-bay Hopper "28111," *15–17*		60____
82112	B&M Alco S2 Diesel Switcher "1260," CC, *15*		650____
82113	B&M Alco S2 Diesel Switcher "1263," CC, *15*		650____
82114	CB&Q Alco S2 Diesel Switcher "9306," CC, *15*		650____
82115	CB&Q Alco S2 Diesel Switcher "9308," CC, *15*		650____
82116	CP Alco S2 Diesel Switcher "7020," CC, *15*		650____
82117	CP Alco S2 Diesel Switcher "7024," CC, *15*		650____
82118	GM&O Alco S2 Diesel Switcher "1001," CC, *15*		650____
82119	GM&O Alco S2 Diesel Switcher "1007," CC, *15*		650____
82120	GN Alco S2 Diesel Switcher "2," CC, *15*		650____
82121	GN Alco S2 Diesel Switcher "5," CC, *15*		650____
82122	PRR Alco S2 Diesel Switcher "5648," CC, *15*		650____
82123	PRR Alco S2 Diesel Switcher "5652," CC, *15*		650____
82124	South Buffalo Alco S2 Diesel Switcher "102," CC, *15*		650____
82125	South Buffalo Alco S2 Diesel Switcher "104," CC, *15*		650____
82126	UP Alco S2 Diesel Switcher "1111," CC, *15*		650____
82127	UP Alco S2 Diesel Switcher "1138," CC, *15*		650____
82128	C&O GP30 Diesel Locomotive "3011," CC, *15*		650____
82129	C&O GP30 Diesel Locomotive "3018," CC, *15*		650____
82130	EMD Demonstrator GP30 Diesel Locomotive "1962," CC, *15*		650____
82131	TP&W GP30 Diesel Locomotive "700," CC, *15*		650____
82132	PC GP30 Diesel Locomotive "2202," CC, *15*		650____
82133	PC GP30 Diesel Locomotive "2246," CC, *15*		650____
82134	GM&O GP30 Diesel Locomotive "501," CC, *15*		650____
82135	GM&O GP30 Diesel Locomotive "521," CC, *15*		650____
82136	N&W GP30 Diesel Locomotive "522," black, CC, *15*		650____
82137	N&W GP30 Diesel Locomotive "542," blue, CC, *15*		650____
82138	MILW GP30 Diesel Locomotive "344," CC, *15*		650____
82139	MILW GP30 Diesel Locomotive "350," CC, *15*		650____
82140	Southern GP30 Diesel Locomotive "2594," CC, *15*		650____
82141	Southern GP30 Diesel Locomotive "2601," CC, *15*		650____
82142	UP GP30 Diesel Locomotive "803" CC, *15*		650____
82143	UP GP30 Diesel Locomotive "830," CC, *15*		650____
82146	Soo Line PS-1 Boxcar "45025," *15*		80____
82147	N&W PS-1 Boxcar "44292," *15*		80____

		Exc Mint
___ 82148	GB&W PS-1 Boxcar "777," *15*	80
82150	Duluth, South Shore & Atlantic PS-1 Boxcar "15091," *15*	80
82163	B&O NW2 Diesel Locomotive "9555," LionChief, *15–16*	300
82164	BN NW2 Diesel Locomotive "546," LionChief, *15–16*	300
82165	CB&Q NW2 Diesel Locomotive "9412A," LionChief, *15–16*	300
82166	Southern NW2 Diesel Locomotive "2401A," LionChief, *15–16*	300
82171	BNSF GP20 Diesel Locomotive "2050," LionChief, *15–17*	340
82172	NYC GP20 Diesel Locomotive "2102," LionChief, *15–17*	340
82173	NS GP20 Diesel Locomotive "10," LionChief, *15–17*	340
82174	NYS&W GP20 Diesel Locomotive "1800," LionChief, *15–17*	340
82175	Virginian Rectifier Locomotive "135," LionChief, *15–17*	340
82176	N&W Rectifier Locomotive "235," LionChief, *15–17*	340
___ 82177	NH Rectifier Locomotive "306," LionChief, *15–17*	340
82178	Conrail Rectifier Locomotive "4605," LionChief, *15–17*	340
82179	PRR Rectifier Locomotive "4466," LionChief, *15–17*	340
___ 82184	PRR B6sb 0-4-0 Locomotive "1670," CC, *15*	700
___ 82185	D&RGW Bicentennial Gondola with canisters, *16*	50
___ 82186	Patriot Chemicals 1-D Tank Car "2015," *15*	60
___ 82187	Bethlehem Steel Water Tower, *15*	35
___ 82188	Metro-North M7 Subway Set, LionChief, *15*	350
___ 82196	Metro-North Add-on 2-pack, *15*	130
___ 82202	UP Big Boy Commemorative CA-4 Caboose, *15*	95
___ 82203	Remote Control Box, *15–17*	25
82205	BNSF Golden Swoosh ES44AC Diesel Locomotive "7695," CC, *15*	650
___ 82206	N&W 2-6-6-4 Locomotive "1218," CC, *16*	1000
82207	Iowa Interstate/Rock Island ES44AC Diesel Locomotive "513," CC, *15*	650
___ 82208	N&W 2-6-6-4 Locomotive "1212," CC, *16*	1000
___ 82209	NS ES44AC Diesel Locomotive "8056," CC, *15*	650
___ 82210	NS ES44AC Diesel Locomotive "8065," CC, *15*	650
___ 82213	KCS ES44AC Diesel Locomotive "4696," CC, *15*	650
___ 82214	KCS ES44AC Diesel Locomotive "4685," CC, *15*	650
___ 82215	AT&SF ES44AC Diesel Locomotive "440," CC, *15*	650
___ 82216	AT&SF ES44AC Diesel Locomotive "444," CC, *15*	650
___ 82218	FEC ES44AC Diesel Locomotive "802," CC, *15*	650
___ 82219	FEC ES44AC Diesel Locomotive "804," CC, *15*	650
82220	SP Alco PA AA Diesel Locomotive Set "6006, 6015," CC, *15*	1000
82223	D&RGW Alco PA AA Diesel Locomotive Set "6001, 6003," CC, *15*	1000
82226	LV Alco PA AA Diesel Locomotive Set "601, 602," CC, *15*	1000

Exc Mint

82229	MP Alco PA AA Diesel Locomotive Set "8018, 8018," CC, *15*	1000	
82232	NKP Alco PA AA Diesel Locomotive Set "190, 189," CC, *15*	1000	
82235	PRR Alco PA AA Diesel Locomotive Set "5070A, 5071A," CC, *15*	1000	
82238	Southern Alco PA AA Diesel Locomotive Set "6900, 6901," CC, *15*	1000	
82241	Wabash Alco PA AA Diesel Locomotive Set "1020, 1020A," CC, *15*	1000	
82244	SP Alco PB Diesel Locomotive, CC, *15*	530	
82245	B&O 2-6-6-4 Locomotive "7620," CC, *16*	1000	
82246	D&RGW Alco PB Diesel Locomotive, CC, *15*	530	
82247	AT&SF 2-6-6-4 Locomotive "1798," CC, *16*	1000	
82248	LV Alco PB Diesel Locomotive, CC, *15*	530	
82249	Bethlehem Steel Boom Car, *15*	55	
82250	MP Alco PB Diesel Locomotive, CC, *15*	530	
82251	Zombie Animated Gondola, *15*	75	
82252	Nickel Plate Road Alco PB Diesel Locomotive, CC, *15*	530	
82253	John Deere 1-D Tank Car, *15*	65	
82254	PRR Alco PB Diesel Locomotive, CC, *15*	530	
82256	Southern Alco PB Diesel Locomotive, CC, *15*	530	
82258	Wabash Alco PB Diesel Locomotive, CC, *15*	530	
82260	PC 50' DD Boxcar "267210" (std O), *16–17*	80	
82261	Frisco 50' DD Boxcar "7002" (std O), *16–17*	80	
82263	PRR Scrapyard, *16–17*	130	
82265	MOW Welding Car, *15–16*	80	
82266	CN 4-6-0 Steam Locomotive "1158," CC, *15*	900	
82267	C&NW 4-6-0 Steam Locomotive "1385," CC, *15*	900	
82268	Frisco 4-6-0 Steam Locomotive "633," CC, *15*	900	
82269	NP 4-6-0 Steam Locomotive "1382," CC, *15*	900	
82270	SP 4-6-0 Steam Locomotive "2353," CC, *15*	900	
82271	NYC 4-6-0 Steam Locomotive "1258," CC, *15*	900	
82272	NH 4-6-0 Steam Locomotive "816," CC, *15*	900	
82273	ACL 4-6-0 Steam Locomotive "1031," CC, *15*	900	
82274	Chessie SD40 Diesel Locomotive "7500," CC, *15*	650	
82275	Chessie SD40 Diesel Locomotive "7593," CC, *15*	650	
82276	BN SD40 Diesel Locomotive "6314," CC, *15*	650	
82277	BN SD40 Diesel Locomotive "6320," CC, *15*	650	
82278	GT SD40 Diesel Locomotive "5922," CC, *15*	650	
82279	GT SD40 Diesel Locomotive "5927," CC, *15*	650	
82280	MP SD40 Diesel Locomotive "3007," CC, *15*	650	
82281	MP SD40 Diesel Locomotive "3014," CC, *15*	650	
82282	Conrail SD40 Diesel Locomotive "6308," CC, *15*	650	
82283	Conrail SD40 Diesel Locomotive "6350," CC, *15*	650	
82284	Conrail SD40 Diesel Locomotive "6300," CC, *15*	650	
82285	SP SD40 Diesel Locomotive "8402," CC, *15*	650	
82286	SP SD40 Diesel Locomotive "8451," CC, *15*	650	
82287	SP Daylight SD40 Diesel Locomotive "7342," CC, *15*	650	
82288	Clinchfield SD40 Diesel Locomotive "3000," CC, *15*	650	
82289	Clinchfield SD40 Diesel Locomotive "3006," CC, *15*	650	

		Exc	Mint
82290	AT&SF FT AA Diesel Locomotive Set, LionChief, *15–17*		500
82293	ACL FT AA Diesel Locomotive Set, LionChief, *15–17*		500
82296	Erie FT AA Diesel Locomotive Set, LionChief, *15–17*		500
82299	D&RGW FT AA Diesel Locomotive Set, LionChief, *15–17*		500
82302	AT&SF FT B Unit, LionChief, *15–17*		280
82303	ACL FT B Unit, LionChief, *15–17*		280
82304	Erie FT B Unit, LionChief, *15–17*		280
82305	D&RGW FT B Unit, LionChief, *15–17*		280
82307	PRR B6sb 0-4-0 Locomotive "5244," CC, *15*		700
82308	PRR B6sb 0-4-0 Locomotive "3233," CC, *15*		700
82309	PRR-Reading Seashore Lines B6sb 0-4-0 Locomotive "6096," CC, *15*		700
82310	LIRR B6sb 0-4-0 Locomotive "2015," CC, *15*		700
82311	Polar RR B6sb 0-4-0 Locomotive "2515," CC, *15*		700
82312	UP ACF 40-ton Stock Car "48133," *15*		80
82313	GN ACF 40-ton Stock Car "55989," *15*		80
82314	MILW ACF 40-ton Stock Car "104954," *15*		80
82315	NP ACF 40-ton Stock Car "84161," *15*		80
82316	NKP ACF 40-ton Stock Car "42040," *15*		80
82324	Chessie Diesel Freight Set, LionChief, *15*		400
82330	U.S.A.F. Minuteman Missile Launcher Car, CC, *15*		350
82331	U.S.A.F. Missile Launch Sound Car, CC, *15*		240
82333	Illuminated Hopper Shed, *15–17*		45
82334	Ulysses S. Grant Presidential Boxcar, *15*		70
82335	Franklin D. Roosevelt Presidential Boxcar, *15*		70
82340	N&W Y6b 2-8-8-2 Steam Locomotive "2171," CC, *15*		2000
82341	N&W Y6b 2-8-8-2 Steam Locomotive "2175," CC, *15*		2000
82342	N&W Y6b 2-8-8-2 Steam Locomotive "2195," CC, *15*		2000
82343	Lionel Steel Welding Car, *15*		80
82344	WM Wood Chip Hopper "2945," *15–16*		65
82349	Friday the 13th Jason Voorhees Boxcar, *16*		85
82394	UP Auxiliary Water Tender "907853," CC, *15*		380
82395	UP Auxiliary Water Tender "907856," CC, *15*		380
82396	UP Commemorative Auxiliary Water Tender "809," CC, *15*		380
82410	Virginian 2-bay Hopper "13168," *16–17*		60
82411	N&W 2-bay Hopper "113733," *15–17*		60
82412	Reading Birney Trolley, *15*		100
82413	Lionel Transit Birney Trolley, *15*		100
82414	CNJ 4-6-0 Camelback Locomotive "777," LionChief, *15–16*		440
82415	DL&W 4-6-0 Camelback Locomotive "1035," LionChief, *15–17*		440
82416	LV 4-6-0 Camelback Locomotive "1602," LionChief, *15–17*		440
82417	Philadelphia & Reading 4-6-0 Camelback Locomotive "675," LionChief, *15–17*		440
82418	Erie 4-6-0 Camelback Locomotive "861," LionChief, *15–17*		440

		Exc	Mint
82419	UP 8-door Hi-Cube Boxcar, *16*	100	___
82420	SP 8-door Hi-Cube Boxcar, *16*	100	___
82421	B&O 8-door Hi-Cube Boxcar, *16*	100	___
82422	PRR 8-door Hi-Cube Boxcar, *16*	100	___
82423	C&NW 8-door Hi-Cube Boxcar, *16*	100	___
82424	Chessie 8-door Hi-Cube Boxcar, *16*	100	___
82425	PC 8-door Hi-Cube Boxcar, *16*	100	___
82426	RI 8-door Hi-Cube Boxcar, *16*	100	___
82427	Patriot U36B Diesel Freight Set, LionChief, *15–17*	360	___
82436	Pennsylvania Keystone GP38 Diesel Freight Set, LionChief, *15*	450	___
82442	Five-Star General Old-Time Steam Set, LionChief, *17*	400	___
82447	Sheriff & Outlaw Car, *17*	80	___
82453	Amtrak F40PH Diesel Phase II "200," CC, *16*	550	___
82454	Amtrak F40PH Diesel Phase II "207," CC, *16*	550	___
82455	Amtrak F40PH Diesel Phase III "364," CC, *16*	550	___
82456	Amtrak F40PH Diesel Phase III "388," CC, *16*	550	___
82460	CSX F40PH Diesel "9998," CC, *16*	550	___
82461	CSX F40PH Diesel "9999," CC, *16*	550	___
82473	N&W Early Era Inspection Vehicle, CC, *15*	200	___
82474	BN Early Era Inspection Vehicle, CC, *15*	200	___
82475	Bethlehem Steel Early Era Inspection Vehicle, CC, *15*	200	___
82476	NH Early Era Inspection Vehicle, CC, *15*	200	___
82477	Virginian Early Era Inspection Vehicle, CC, *15*	200	___
82478	Reading Early Era Inspection Vehicle, CC, *15*	200	___
82486	Weathered Virginian USRA Y-3 2-8-8-2 Locomotive "737," CC, *14*	1450	___
82487	Weathered AT&SF USRA Y-3 2-8-8-2 Locomotive "1797," CC, *14*	1450	___
82488	Weathered N&W USRA Y-3 2-8-8-2 Locomotive "2029," CC, *14*	1450	___
82489	MILW 18" Aluminum Coach/Dining Car 2-pack, *14*	320	___
82489	MILW Olympian 18" Aluminum Passenger Car 2-pack, *14–15*	320	___
82494	Turbo Missile Launch Flatcar, *15*	60	___
82495	D&RGW Scrapyard, *16–17*	130	___
82498	Polar Express Mail Car, *16–17*	70	___
82500	Polar Express Covered Bridge, *15*	70	___
82501	Providence & Worcester 89' Auto Carrier "190091," *15–16*	110	___
82502	C&NW 89' Auto Carrier "962255," *15–16*	110	___
82503	Chessie 89' Auto Carrier "255798," *15–16*	110	___
82504	TFM 89' Auto Carrier "987408," *15–16*	110	___
82505	BNSF 89' Auto Carrier "212878," *15–16*	110	___
82506	UP 89' Auto Carrier "992579," *15–16*	110	___
82508	NYC Milk Car "6589" (std O), *16*	80	___
82510	Polar Express Aquarium Car, *16*	85	___
82512	Polar Express Work Caboose with presents, *15*	85	___
82514	Polar Express Reindeer Stock Car, *15*	90	___
82518	Moon Pie Boxcar, *15*	85	___
82528	NYC Empire State Express Steam Passenger Set, CC, *15*	1950	___

		Exc	Mint
82534	NYC J3a 4-6-4 Hudson Locomotive "5429," tender, *15*		1500
82535	NYC J3a 4-6-4 Hudson Locomotive "5426," tender, *15*		1500
82536	NYC J3a 4-6-4 Hudson Locomotive "5429," tender, *15*		1500
82537	NYC J3a 4-6-4 Hudson Locomotive "5426," tender, *15*		1500
82543	Postwar "943" Exploding Ammunition Dump, *15–16*		50
82544	Missile Firing Range, *15–16*		65
82545	Santa's Helper Steam Freight Set, *16–17*		340
82550	Wabash 21" Streamlined Passenger Car 4-pack, *15*		600
82555	Wabash 21" Streamlined Passenger Car 2-pack, *15*		300
82558	Southern 21" Streamlined Passenger Car 4-pack, *15*		600
82563	Southern 21" Streamlined Passenger Car 4-pack, *15*		300
82566	RI 21" Streamlined Passenger Car 4-pack, *15*		600
82571	RI 21" Streamlined Passenger Car 4-pack, *15*		300
82574	Texas Special 21" Streamlined Passenger Car 4-pack, *15*		600
82579	Texas Special 21" Streamlined Passenger Car 4-pack, *15*		300
82582	C&O 21" Streamlined Passenger Car 4-pack, *15*		600
82587	C&O 21" Streamlined Passenger Car 4-pack, *15*		300
82590	Amtrak 21" Passenger Car 4-pack, *16*		600
82595	Amtrak 21" Passenger Car 2-pack, *16*		300
82598	NYC Empire State Passenger Car Add-on 2-pack, *15*		300
82611	PRR GL-a 2-bay Hopper 3-pack, *15*		220
82621	Buffalo Creek Flour PS-1 Boxcar "2366," *15*		80
82622	U.S. Army PS-1 Boxcar "26875, *15*		80
82623	West India Fruit & Steamship Co. PS-1 Boxcar "321," *15*		80
82624	Linde Air Products PS-1 Boxcar "3019," *15*		80
82625	Air Reduction Products PS-1 Boxcar "100," *15*		80
82629	PRR N5b Caboose "478883," *15–16*		95
82630	PRR N5b Caboose with trainphone antenna, *15–16*		95
82631	B&M N5b Caboose "C-16," *15–16*		95
82639	MILW Milk Car "370" (std O), *16*		80
82640	UTLX 30,000-Gallon 1-D Tank Car 3-pack, *15*		250
82644	Philadelphia Energy Solutions 1-D Tank Car 3-pack, *15*		250
82648	Midwest Ethanol Transport 1-D Tank Car 3-pack, *15*		250
82652	Global Ethanol Transport 1-D Tank Car 3-pack, *15*		250
82656	Conrail 60' Boxcar "216010," *15–17*		90
82657	WM 60' Boxcar "38020," *15–17*		90
82658	BN 60' Boxcar "355145," *15–17*		90
82659	RI 60' Boxcar "33825," *15–17*		90
82660	N&W 60' Boxcar "600949," *15–17*		90
82661	P&LE PS-5 Gondola and PS-4 Flatcar, *15–16*		175

		Exc	Mint
82664	B&LE PS-5 Gondola and PS-4 Flatcar, *15–16*		175____
82667	DT&I PS-5 Gondola and PS-4 Flatcar, *15–16*		175____
82670	Conrail PS-5 Gondola and PS-4 Flatcar, *15–16*		175____
82674	UP Bathtub Gondola 2-pack, *15*		140____
82677	Strasburg 3-D Tank Car, *16*		656____
82683	Batman and Flash Justice League Boxcar 2-pack, *15–16*		170____
82684	Superman and Green Lantern Justice League Boxcar 2-pack, *15–16*		170____
82685	New York Giants Cooperstown Boxcar, *15*		85____
82686	Washington Senators Cooperstown Boxcar, *15*		85____
82687	Detroit Tigers Cooperstown Boxcar, *15*		85____
82688	Pittsburgh Pirates Cooperstown Boxcar, *15*		85____
82689	Operation Eagle Missile Carrying Car, *15–17*		65____
82690	Coca-Cola Anniversary Bottle Boxcar, *15*		90____
82691	Christmas Boxcar, *15*		75____
82693	Santa's Helper Crane, *15*		85____
82694	UP LionMaster 4-6-6-4 Challenger Locomotive "3985," CC, *15*		1000____
82695	UP LionMaster 4-6-6-4 Challenger Locomotive "3977," CC, *15*		1000____
82696	UP LionMaster 4-6-6-4 Challenger Locomotive "3989," CC, *15*		1000____
82697	D&RGW LionMaster 4-6-6-4 Challenger Locomotive "3803," CC, *15*		1000____
82698	WM LionMaster 4-6-6-4 Challenger Locomotive "1201," CC, *15*		1000____
82699	Angela Trotta Thomas Lionelville Christmas Boxcar, *15*		75____
82701	Escaping Snowmen Handcar, *15*		90____
82702	Ontario Northland PS-4 Flatcar with covered load, *15*		90____
82703	BN PS-4 Flatcar with covered load, *15*		90____
82704	D&RGW PS-4 Flatcar with covered load, *15*		90____
82705	Reading PS-4 Flatcar with covered load, *15*		90____
82706	Southern PS-4 Flatcar with covered load, *15*		90____
82708	Christmas Gingerbread Shanty, *16–17*		40____
82709	PRR Silver & Gold Ore Car 2-pack, *16–17*		130____
82710	PRR Ice Breaker Tunnel Car, *16–17*		65____
82711	Santa's Favorites Transparent Gift Car, *16*		85____
82713	Christmas Music Boxcar, *15*		80____
82716	Mickey's Holiday to Remember Freight Set, *16*		400____
82717	W. E. Disney Girder Bridge, *16–17*		33____
82718	Disney Villains Hi-Cube Boxcar 2-pack, *16–17*		160____
82721	Dumbo 75th Anniversary Boxcar, *16–17*		85____
82726	Postwar Alco FA Diesel Green Passenger Set, *17*		550____
82734	New York Yankees Cooperstown Boxcar, *15*		85____
82736	North Pole Central Water Tower, *15*		40____
82737	Coca-Cola Santa Boxcar, *15*		85____
82739	North Pole Central Boxcar, *16–17*		80____
82740	Winter Wonderland Aquarium Car, *15*		95____
82741	Christmas Tinsel Vat Car, *16*		70____
82742	Candy Mountain Christmas Quad Hopper, *16–17*		65____
82743	Santa's Reindeer Station Platform, *15*		50____
82744	Santa Claus Automatic Gateman, *16–17*		100____
82745	Christmas Cocoa Barrel Shed, *15*		50____

		Exc Mint
____82746	Christmas Floodlight Tower, 16	75
____82747	Christmas Red Arch Under Bridge, 16	30
____82748	Silver Bell Casting Co. Hopper, 15	70
____82749	PRR GG1 Electric "4935," CC, 16	1400
____82751	PRR GG1 Electric "4913," CC, 16	1400
____82752	PRR GG1 Electric "4877," CC, 16	1400
____82754	PC GG1 Electric "4828," CC, 16	1400
____82755	Amtrak GG1 Electric "926," CC, 16	1400
____82757	CP SD90MAC Diesel "9116," CC, 16	650
____82758	CP SD90MAC Diesel "9130," CC, 16	650
____82759	NS SD90MAC Diesel "7230," CC, 16	650
____82760	NS SD90MAC Diesel "7245," CC, 16	650
____82761	UP SD90MAC Diesel "8130," CC, 16	650
____82762	UP SD90MAC Diesel "8133," CC, 16	650
____82763	UP SD90MAC Diesel "8025," CC, 16	650
____82764	UP SD90MAC Diesel "8055," CC, 16	650
____82765	Indiana SD90MAC Diesel "9003," CC, 16	650
____82766	Indiana SD90MAC Diesel "9006," CC, 16	650
____82767	C&O 2-6-6-6 Locomotive "1601," CC, 16	2200
____82768	C&O 2-6-6-6 Locomotive "1604," CC, 16	2200
____82769	C&O 2-6-6-6 Locomotive "1608," CC, 16	2200
____82770	Virginian 2-6-6-6 Locomotive "906," CC, 16	2200
____82825	CP GP38 Diesel Locomotive "3019," 16–17	340
____82826	CSX GP38 Diesel Locomotive "2145," 16–17	340
____82827	SP GP38 Diesel Locomotive "4846," 16–17	340
____82828	UP GP38 Diesel Locomotive "905," 16–17	340
____82840	AT&SF PS-4 Flatcar with trailer (std O), 16	110
____82841	E-L PS-4 Flatcar with trailer (std O), 16	110
____82842	GN PS-4 Flatcar with trailer (std O), 16	110
____82843	WM PS-4 Flatcar with trailer (std O), 16	110
____82844	PRR PS-4 Flatcar with trailer (std O), 16	110
____82845	B&O Truck with 40' trailer, 16	90
____82846	MILW Truck with 40' trailer, 16–17	90
____82847	MKT Truck with 40' trailer, 16–17	90
____82848	Logging Disconnect with load, 16	65
____82849	Logging Disconnect with load 2-pack, 16	125
____82850	MILW 40' Flatcar with lumber (std O), 16–17	90
____82851	NP 40' Flatcar with lumber (std O), 16–17	90
82852____	Meadow River 40' Flatcar with lumber (std O), 16–17	90
____82853	Pickering 40' Flatcar with lumber (std O), 16–17	90
____82854	PRR 40' Flatcar with lumber (std O), 16	90
____82855	ADM Unibody Tank Car "190516" (std O), 16	75
____82856	GATX Unibody Tank Car "4415" (std O), 16	75
____82857	AFPX Unibody Tank Car "413303" (std O), 16	75
____82858	Shell Unibody Tank Car "82858" (std O), 16	85
____82859	Engelhard Unibody Tank Car "24586" (std O), 16	75
____82860	PC PS-5 Gondola "557065" (std O), 16	90
____82861	E-L PS-5 Gondola "14552" (std O), 16	90
____82862	Frisco PS-5 Gondola "61442" (std O), 16	90
____82863	CB&Q PS-5 Gondola "82050" (std O), 16	90
____82864	NYC PS-5 Gondola "712603" (std O), 16	90
____82865	PRR N5b Caboose "5017" (std O), 16	90
____82866	PRR N5b Caboose "477746" (std O), 16	90
____82867	PRR N5b Caboose "477625" (std O), 16	90

		Exc	Mint
82868	NH N5 Caboose "C-507" (std O), *16*	90____	
82870	Loading Ramp, *16–17*	25____	
82872	Loader/Unloader Workers Figure Pack, *16–17*	30____	
82873	Loggers Cabin, sound, *16*	140____	
82874	Early Intermodal Work House, sound, *16–17*	130____	
82877	Thomas Kinkade Polar Express Boxcar, *16*	85____	
82878	Smithsonian Boxcar, *16*	85____	
82879	Coca-Cola Christmas Boxcar, *16–17*	85____	
82883	Legacy 360-watt PowerMaster, *16*	220____	
82884	Wabash 21" Streamlined Dining Car, StationSounds, *15*	300____	
82885	Southern 21" Streamlined Dining Car, StationSounds, *15*	300____	
82886	RI 21" Streamlined Dining Car, StationSounds, *15*	300____	
82887	Texas Special 21" Streamlined Dining Car, StationSounds, *15*	300____	
82888	C&O 21" Streamlined Dining Car, StationSounds, *15*	300____	
82889	Amtrak 21" Diner, StationSounds, *16*	300____	
82890	NYC Empire State Express Diner, StationSounds, *15*	300____	
82906	Pluto Walking Brakeman Car, *16–17*	100____	
82908	Mickey's Christmas Shanty, *16–17*	50____	
82913	Winnie the Pooh Boxcar, *16–17*	85____	
82914	Disney Aquarium Car, *16–17*	85____	
82917	Disney Station Platform, *17*	55____	
82921	Evil Queen Hi-Cube Boxcar, *17*	80____	
82922	Scar Hi-Cube Boxcar, *17*	80____	
82925	Scrooge McDuck Mint Car, *17*	80____	
82942	James Monroe Presidential Boxcar, *16*	70____	
82943	John F. Kennedy Presidential Boxcar, *16*	70____	
82944	Herbert Hoover Presidential Boxcar, *16*	70____	
82945	James Madison Presidential Boxcar, *16*	70____	
82947	Wonder Woman/Green Arrow Boxcar 2-pack, *16*	170____	
82950	Aquaman/Martian Manhunter Boxcar 2-pack, *16*	170____	
82953	Joker/Lex Luthor Boxcar 2-pack, *16*	170____	
82954	Lionel Christmas Boxcar, *16*	65____	
82958	Christmas Floodlight, *17*	75____	
82960	NYC 2-8-2 Steam Locomotive "1548," *16–17*	430____	
82961	UP 2-8-2 Steam Locomotive "2537," *16–17*	430____	
82962	Southern 2-8-2 Steam Locomotive "4501," *16–17*	430____	
82963	Rio Grande 2-8-2 Steam Locomotive "1208," *16–17*	430____	
82964	MILW 4-6-4 Steam Locomotive "125," *16–17*	430____	
82965	AT&SF 4-6-4 Steam Locomotive "3450," *16–17*	430____	
82966	DL&W 4-6-4 Steam Locomotive "1151," *16–17*	430____	
82967	CB&Q 4-6-4 Steam Locomotive "3007," *16–17*	430____	
82968	LL 4-6-2 Steam Locomotive "462," *16–17*	430____	
82969	WM 4-6-2 Steam Locomotive "202," *16–17*	430____	
82970	Reading & Northern 4-6-2 Locomotive "425," *16–17*	450____	
82971	C&NW 4-6-2 Steam Locomotive "600," *16–17*	300____	
82972	Lionel Junction PRR Diesel Freight Set, *16–17*	175____	
82973	PRR A5 0-4-0 Locomotive "3891," *16–17*	450____	

		Exc	Mint
____82974	SP A5 0-4-0 Locomotive "1040," *16–17*		450
____82975	B&O A5 0-4-0 Locomotive "317," *16–17*		450
82976	Bethlehem Steel A5 0-4-0 Locomotive "140," LionChief, *16–17*		450
82982	Christmas Express Steam Freight Set, LionChief, *17*		320
____82984	NYC RS-3 Diesel Freight Set, *16–17*		260
____82992	115th Anniversary Boxcar, *16*		85
83002	PRR Broadway Limited 21" Diner 2-pack, StationSounds, *16*		450
____83003	PC 21" StationSounds Diner "4552," *16*		300
____83006	UP 21" Excursion Diner, StationSounds, *16*		300
83007	PRR Broadway Limited 21" Passenger Car 2-pack, *16*		300
____83010	PC 21" Passenger Car 2-pack, *16*		300
____83019	UP 21" Excursion Passenger Car 2-pack, *16*		300
83022	PRR Broadway Limited 21" Passenger Car 4-pack, *16*		600
____83027	PC 21" Passenger Car 4-pack, *16*		600
____83042	UP 21" Excursion Passenger Car 4-pack, *16*		675
____83063	AT&SF Super Chief Boxcar "143093," *16–17*		50
____83071	Universal Remote, *16–17*		50
83072	PRR "Keystone Special" Steam Freight Set, LionChief, *17*		300
____83080	Rio Grande 0-4-0 Switcher Freight Set, *16–17*		300
____83092	Steel City Switcher Freight Set, CC, *16*		1300
____83102	SP 21" Passenger Car 4-pack, *16*		600
____83107	SP 21" Passenger Car 2-pack, *16*		300
____83110	SP 21" Diner "290," StationSounds, *16*		300
83111	American Freedom Train 21" Passenger Car 4-pack, *16–17*		675
83116	American Freedom Train 21" Passenger Car 2-pack, *16–17*		300
____83119	American Freedom Train 21" Crew Car, *16–17*		300
83120	CSX Office Car Special 21" Passenger Car 4-pack, *16–17*		600
83125	CSX Office Car Special 21" Passenger Car 2-pack, *16–17*		300
83128	CSX Office Car Special 21" Diner, StationSounds, *16–17*		300
____83147	Lighted Yard Tower, *16*		60
____83148	Christmas Express Boxcar, *16–17*		53
____83157	Smithsonian Air & Space Boxcar 2-pack, *16*		170
____83162	Nightmare on Elm Street Boxcar, *16*		85
____83163	Thomas Kinkade Christmas Boxcar, *16–17*		85
____83164	Frosty the Snowman 1-D Tank Car, *16–17*		60
____83165	PRR GG1 Electric "4899," CC, *16*		1400
____83166	PRR GG1 Electric "4800," CC, *16*		1400
____83167	Conrail Bicentennial GG1 Electric "4800," CC, *16*		1400
____83168	Iron Workers Figure Pack, *16*		30
____83169	NYC Flatcar with piggyback trailers, *16–17*		75
____83170	Steel Mill Structure, sound, *16–17*		130
____83171	MOW Workers Figure Pack, *16–17*		30
____83172	MOW Work Structure, sound, *16–17*		130
____83173	Single Signal Bridge, *16–17*		80
____83174	Double Signal Bridge, *16–17*		100

Exc Mint

		Exc	Mint
83175	Christmas Music Boxcar, *16*	80	____
83176	Lionel Lines Christmas Caboose, *16–17*	75	____
83177	Angela Trotta Thomas Caboose, *16–17*	80	____
83178	Coca-Cola Caboose, *16*	75	____
83179	Conrail Caboose "23878," *16–17*	75	____
83180	PRR Caboose "477100," *16–17*	7	____
83181	AT&SF Caboose "999316," *16–17*	75	____
83182	ACL Caboose "0634," *16–17*	75	____
83183	Erie Caboose "C226," *16–17*	75	____
83184	UP Caboose "25214," *16–17*	75	____
83185	Polar Express Elves Figure Set, *16–17*	33	____
83186	NYC Caboose "21777," *16*	75	____
83190	Moon Pie 1-D Tank Car, *16–17*	75	____
83191	Lionel Christmas 1-D Tank Car, *16*	85	____
83192	Smithsonian Dinosaur Aquarium Car, *16–17*	85	____
83193	SP GS-4 4-8-4 Locomotive "4449," CC, *16*	1700	____
83194	SP GS-4 4-8-4 Locomotive "4449," CC, *16*	1700	____
83195	SP GS-4 4-8-4 Locomotive "4443," CC, *16*	1700	____
83196	SP GS-4 4-8-4 Locomotive "4444," CC, *16*	1700	____
83197	American Freedom Train GS-4 4-8-4 Locomotive, CC, *16*	1700	____
83198	Reading T1 4-8-4 Locomotive "2100," CC, *16*	1700	____
83199	Reading T1 4-8-4 Locomotive "2119," CC, *16*	1700	____
83200	Reading T1 4-8-4 Locomotive "2102," CC, *16*	1700	____
83201	Reading T1 4-8-4 Locomotive "2124," CC, *16*	1700	____
83202	American Freedom Train T1 4-8-4 Locomotive, CC, *16*	1700	____
83203	Chessie T1 4-8-4 Locomotive "2101," CC, *16*	1700	____
83204	B&O 0-8-0 Locomotive "1695," CC, *16*	900	____
83205	GTW 0-8-0 Locomotive "8380," CC, *16*	900	____
83206	Indiana Harbor Belt 0-8-0 Locomotive "312," CC, *16*	900	____
83208	Wabash 0-8-0 Locomotive "1526," CC, *16*	900	____
83209	Terminal Railroad 0-8-0 Locomotive, CC, *16*	900	____
83214	North Pole Central 4-6-2 Locomotive "1225," *16–17*	430	____
83215	Transformer 2-pack, *16–17*	15	____
83223	Steel I-Beam 12-pack, *16–17*	15	____
83230	Amtrak Metal Girder Bridge, *16–17*	43	____
83231	Polar Express Metal Girder Bridge, *16–17*	43	____
83232	Bethlehem Steel Metal Girder Bridge, *16–17*	43	____
83233	CSX Metal Girder Bridge, *16–17*	37	____
83234	John Deere Plastic Girder Bridge, *16–17*	33	____
83238	John Deere Flatcar with spreaders, *16–17*	80	____
83239	Polar Express Bells Mint Car, *16–17*	80	____
83240	Shell Operating Oil Derrick, *16*	120	____
83241	Shell Oil Storage Tank with Light, *16*	85	____
83242	Shell 1-D Tank Car, *16*	75	____
83243	Shell 3-D Tank Car, *16–17*	75	____
83244	Shell Elevated Oil Tank, *17*	100	____
83246	Shell Boxcar, *16*	85	____
83247	Shell Billboard Pack, *16–17*	25	____
83248	"It's a Boy" Boxcar, *16*	90	____
83249	Polar Express Combination Car, *16–17*	70	____
83250	"It's a Girl" Boxcar, *16*	90	____

Exc Mint

			Exc	Mint
____83251	Poultry Dispatch Sweep Car, *16*			120
____83252	Gold Medal Milk Car with platform, *17*			180
____83253	D&RGW Searchlight Car, *16–17*			63
____83254	Western Union Animated Gondola, *16–17*			70
____83256	GN Horse Transport, *16*			80
____83257	Bobbing Werewolf Boxcar, *16–17*			75
____83258	CP Boom Car, *16*			63
____83266	Lionel Junction Santa Fe Steam Freight Set, *16*			175
____83275	Sugar Cookie Scented Smoke Fluid, *17*			7
____83276	Peppermint Scented Smoke Fluid, *17*			7
____83277	Pine Scented Smoke Fluid, *17*			7
____83278	Hot Chocolate Scented Smoke Fluid, *17*			7
____83279	Wood Stove Scented Smoke Fluid, *17*			7
____83280	Unscented Smoke Fluid, *17*			7
____83284	Peekaboo Reindeer Operating Boxcar, *16–17*			75
____83286	John Deere Steam Freight Set, *16–17*			400
____83291	Christmas Half-covered Bridge, *16–17*			70
____83292	Christmas Cookies & Candies Store, *16–17*			85
____83304	North Pole Elves Work Shanty, *16*			40
____83305	Illuminated Winter Covered Bridge, *16–17*			80
____83308	North Pole Central Tank Car "122416," *16–17*			75
____83311	Santa's Favorites Egg Nog Reefer, *16–17*			65
____83312	Santa's Cookies Vat Car, *16–17*			70
83313 ____	Reindeer Express Agency Flatcar with trailer, *16–17*			70
____83315	Christmas Toys Stock Car, *16–17*			70
____83316	Santa's Sleigh Aquarium Car, *16–17*			80
____83317	BNSF 65' Mill Gondola "518357" (std O), *17*			80
____83318	C&NW 65' Mill Gondola "342036" (std O), *17*			80
____83319	CSX 65' Mill Gondola "491600" (std O), *17*			80
____83320	NS 65' Mill Gondola "195015" (std O), *17*			80
____83321	SP 65' Mill Gondola "365117" (std O), *17*			80
____83322	UP 65' Mill Gondola "96257" (std O), *17*			80
____83340	Boxcar Children Boxcar, *16*			85
____83347	ACL USRA Double-sheathed Boxcar, *16*			85
____83348	B&M USRA Double-sheathed Boxcar, *16*			85
____83349	RI USRA Double-sheathed Boxcar, *16*			85
83350 ____	Northwestern Pacific USRA Double-sheathed Boxcar, *16*			85
____83351	Wabash USRA Double-sheathed Boxcar, *16*			85
____83352	Polar Express USRA Double-sheathed Boxcar, *16*			95
____83353	D&RGW Flatcar with snowplow (std O), *16*			95
____83354	NYC Flatcar with snowplow (std O), *16*			95
____83355	UP Flatcar with snowplow (std O), *16*			95
____83356	MOW Flatcar with Snowplow (std O), *16*			95
____83357	Reading NE-style Caboose "92882" (std O), *16*			90
____83358	Reading NE-style Caboose "92902" (std O), *16*			90
83359 ____	Reading & Northern NE-style Caboose "92884" (std O), *16*			90
____83360	C&O NE-style Caboose "90352" (std O), *16*			90
____83361	N&W NE-style Caboose "500830" (std O), *16*			90
____83362	WM NE-style Caboose "1887" (std O), *16*			90
____83368	EL SD45 Diesel Locomotive "3607," CC, *16*			650
____83369	EL SD45 Diesel Locomotive "3618," CC, *16*			650

83370	EL Bicentennial SD45 Diesel Locomotive "3632," CC, *16*	650_____
83371	GN "Hustle Muscle" SD45 Diesel Locomotive "400," CC, *16*	650_____
83372	GN SD45 Diesel Locomotive "402," CC, *16*	650_____
83373	GN SD45 Diesel Locomotive "407," CC, *16*	650_____
83374	PC SD45 Diesel Locomotive "6235," CC, *16*	650_____
83375	PC SD45 Diesel Locomotive "6237," CC, *16*	650_____
83376	Southern SD45 Diesel Locomotive "3137," CC, *16*	650_____
83377	Southern SD45 Diesel Locomotive "3156," CC, *16*	650_____
83378	SP SD45 Diesel Locomotive "8801," CC, *16*	650_____
83379	SP SD45 Diesel Locomotive "8820," CC, *16*	650_____
83380	UP SD45 Diesel Locomotive "1," CC, *16*	650_____
83381	UP SD45 Diesel Locomotive "21," CC, *16*	650_____
83382	AT&SF NW2 Diesel Locomotive "2405," CC, *16*	500_____
83383	B&M NW2 Diesel Locomotive "1200," CC, *16*	500_____
83384	B&O NW2 Diesel Locomotive "9527," CC, *16*	500_____
83385	CSX NW2 Diesel Locomotive "9565," CC, *16*	500_____
83387	NYO&W NW2 Diesel Locomotive "116," CC, *16*	500_____
83388	PRR NW2 Diesel Locomotive "9171," CC, *16*	500_____
83389	Philadelphia, Bethlehem & New England NW2 Diesel Locomotive "27," CC, *16*	500_____
83390	SP NW2 Diesel Locomotive "1423," CC, *16*	500_____
83391	SP&S NW2 Diesel Locomotive "41," CC, *16*	500_____
83392	Union NW2 Diesel Locomotive "555," CC, *16*	500_____
83393	UP NW2 Diesel Locomotive "1011," CC, *16*	500_____
83395	AC&Y H16-44 Diesel "201," CC, *16*	550_____
83396	AC&Y H16-44 Diesel "202," CC, *16*	550_____
83397	AT&SF H16-44 Diesel "2801," CC, *16*	550_____
83398	AT&SF H16-44 Diesel "2807," CC, *16*	550_____
83399	B&O H16-44 Diesel "6705," CC, *16*	550_____
83400	B&O H16-44 Diesel "6708," CC, *16*	550_____
83401	MILW H16-44 Diesel "402," CC, *16*	550_____
83402	MILW H16-44 Diesel "404," CC, *16*	550_____
83403	DL&W H16-44 Diesel "931," CC, *16*	550_____
83404	DL&W H16-44 Diesel "934," CC, *16*	550_____
83405	Southern H16-44 Diesel "6547," CC, *16*	550_____
83406	Southern H16-44 Diesel "6550," CC, *16*	550_____
83426	Johnstown Birney Trolley, *16*	100_____
83434	Polar Express Passenger Station, *16–17*	90_____
83435	World War II Pylon, *17*	160_____
83437	Polar Express Conductor Announcement Car, *16–17*	110_____
83438	Miller Coors Operating Billboard, *17*	80_____
83440	Rico Station Kit, *16–17*	60_____
83442	Bungalow House, *17*	90_____
83443	Suburban House, *17*	100_____
83444	Illuminated Station Platform, *16–17*	43_____
83445	Smithsonian Old St. Nick Boxcar, *16–17*	85_____
83455	Polar Express Operating Billboard, *16–17*	85_____
83462	Bethlehem Steel Slag Car 3-pack, *16*	240_____
83466	U.S. Steel Slag Car 3-pack (std O), *16*	240_____
83470	Slag Car 3-pack (std O), *16*	240_____

			Mint
___	83474	Weathered Slag Car 3-pack (std O), *16*	240
___	83478	Bethlehem Steel Hot Metal Car 2-pack, *16*	200
___	83481	U.S. Steel Hot Metal Car 2-pack (std O), *16*	200
___	83484	Hot Metal Car 2-pack (std O), *16*	200
___	83487	Weathered Hot Metal Car 2-pack (std O), *16*	200
___	83490	Lighted Coaling Tower, *16*	180
___	83491	Boston Red Sox Cooperstown Boxcar, *16*	85
___	83492	St. Louis Cardinals Cooperstown Boxcar, *16*	85
___	83493	Philadelphia Phillies Cooperstown Boxcar, *16*	85
___	83494	Baltimore Orioles Cooperstown Boxcar, *16*	85
___	83496	Station Platform, *16–17*	40
___	83497	National Train Day Boxcar, *16–17*	85
___	83503	Thomas with remote, *16–17*	120
___	83504	Birthday Thomas with remote, *16–17*	120
___	83510	Thomas Passenger Set, LionChief, *16–17*	200
___	83512	Thomas & Friends Christmas Freight Set, *16–17*	200
___	83518	PRR Boxcar "83518" (std O), *16*	100
___	83519	REA SensorCar Steel Reefer "7844" (std O), *16*	130
___	83520	North Pole Central Flatcar with snowplow, *16*	95
___	83527	AT&SF PS-1 Boxcar "142501," sound (std O), *16*	130
___	83528	BAR PS-1 Boxcar "5149," sound (std O), *16*	130
___	83529	B&O PS-1 Boxcar "467931," sound (std O), *16*	130
___	83530	BN PS-1 Boxcar "132909," sound (std O), *16*	130
___	83531	C&NW PS-1 Boxcar "5," sound (std O), *16*	130
___	83532	NYC PS-1 Boxcar "175001," sound (std O), *16*	130
___	83533	PRR PS-1 Boxcar "47005," sound (std O), *16*	130
___	83534	UP PS-1 Boxcar "196883," sound (std O), *16*	130
___	83535	PRR GL-a 2-bay Hopper 3-pack #1 (std O), *16*	220
___	83539	PRR GL-a 2-bay Hopper 3-pack #2 (std O), *16*	220
___	83544	PRR N5b Caboose "477797" (std O), *16*	95
___	83545	PFE Reefer 3-pack (std O), *16*	170
___	83549	AT&SF Reefer 3-pack (std O), *16*	300
___	83553	Heisler Log Train Set, CC, *16*	1450
___	83555	Red Logging Disconnect Caboose "1" (std O), *16*	40
___	83556	Brown Logging Disconnect Caboose "6" (std O), *16*	40
___	83557	Logging Disconnect Boxcar (std O), *16*	40
___	83558	Logging Disconnect Flatcar (std O), *16*	35
___	83559	Logging Disconnect Gondola (std O), *16*	40
___	83560	Logging Disconnect Tank Car (std O), *16*	40
___	83561	ATSF Express 50' DD Boxcar "1342" (std O), *16–17*	80
___	83562	CNJ PS-1 Express Boxcar "22487" (std O), *16–17*	80
___	83563	C&EI PS-1 Express Boxcar "2" (std O), *16–17*	80
___	83564	GN PS-1 Express Boxcar "2538" (std O), *16–17*	80
___	83565	KCS PS-1 Express Boxcar "400" (std O), *16–17*	80
___	83566	SP PS-1 Express Boxcar "5712" (std O), *16–17*	80
___	83567	T&P PS-1 Express Boxcar "1721" (std O), *16–17*	80
___	83568	C&S Grain-door PS-1 Boxcar "1650" (std O), *16–17*	80
___	83569	CP Grain-door PS-1 Boxcar "260293" (std O), *16–17*	80
___	83570	GN Grain-door PS-1 Boxcar "18119" (std O), *16–17*	80

Exc Mint

83571	CGW Grain-door PS-1 Boxcar "5450" (std O), *16–17*	80____
83572	IC Grain-door PS-1 Boxcar "19000" (std O), *16–17*	80____
83573	MKT Grain-door PS-1 Boxcar "92463" (std O), *16–17*	80____
83574	UP CA-4 Caboose "3824" (std O), *16*	90____
83575	UP CA-4 Caboose "25121" (std O), *16*	90____
83576	B&O Milk Car "847" (std O), *16–17*	80____
83577	Supplee Milk Car "7" (std O), *16–17*	80____
83579	Rutland Milk Car "351" (std O), *16–17*	80____
83580	BAR State of Maine 40' Trailer, 2-pack, *16–17*	65____
83581	C&NW 40' Trailer, 2-pack, *16–17*	65____
83582	PFE 40' Trailer, 2-pack, *16–17*	65____
83583	PC 40' Trailer, 2-pack, *16–17*	65____
83584	SP 40' Trailer, 2-pack, *16–17*	65____
83585	UP 40' Trailer, 2-pack, *16–17*	65____
83586	PRR Broadway Limited 21" Passenger Car 2-pack #2 (std O), *16*	300____
83587	Hood Milk Car "807" (std O), *16–17*	80____
83589	American Freedom Train Add-On 2-pack #2, *16–17*	300____
83592	American Freedom Train Add-On 2-pack #3, *16–17*	300____
83595	Conrail Office Car Special Diesel Passenger Set, CC, *17*	1250____
83601	Conrail Office Car Special Add-on 2-pack, *17*	310____
83604	Conrail Office Car Special 21" Dome Car "55," StationSounds, *17*	320____
83605	Presidents 2-8-2 Mikado Locomotive "1789," *16–17*	430____
83606	Halloween 2-8-2 Mikado Locomotive "1031," *16–17*	430____
83607	USRA2-8-2 Mikado Locomotive "4500," *16–17*	430____
83608	B&O 2-8-2 Mikado Locomotive "4500," *16–17*	430____
83609	C&O 2-8-2 Mikado Locomotive "1067," *16–17*	430____
83610	MKT 2-8-2 Mikado Locomotive "851," *16–17*	430____
83611	NYC Empire State Express 21" Coach 4-pack #2, *17*	620____
83616	NYC Empire State Express 21" Combine/ Observation Car 2-pack #2, *17*	310____
83619	NYC Empire State Express 21" Diner #2, StationSounds, *17*	310____
83620	Hogwarts Express Passenger Set, *16–17*	400____
83624	UP Sherman Hill Scout RS-3 Freight Set, *16–17*	500____
83633	Alaska Gold Mint Car, *17*	70____
83634	Keystone Smoke Fluid Loader, *16–17*	350____
83635	North American Smoke Fluid Loader, *16–17*	350____
83637	Mets-Phillies Mascot Aquarium Car, *16*	85____
83645	Polar Express Boxcar 2-pack, *16–17*	170____
83648	New York Yankees Subway Set, *16*	390____
83653	21" Passenger Car Figure Pack, *16–17*	30____
83655	Hamm's Heritage Beer Wood-sided Reefer, *16–17*	80____
83656	Coors Heritage Beer Wood-sided Reefer, *16–17*	80____
83657	Miller Heritage Beer Wood-sided Reefer, *16–17*	80____

			Mint
____	83658	Lionelville School Kit, *16–17*	60
____	83659	PRR Keystone Special Steam Freight Set, *16–17*	280
____	83688	Trackside Railroad Details Pack, *16*	25
	83689	Angela Trotta Thomas Christmas Covered Bridge,	
____		*17*	70
____	83690	Company Row House, blue, *16–17*	60
____	83691	Company Row House, yellow, *16–17*	60
____	83692	Company Row House, white, *16–17*	60
____	83693	Company Row House, red, *16–17*	60
	83696	NYC "Pacemaker" Lionel Junction Diesel Freight	
____		Set, *17*	175
	83701	Alaska Gold Mine 0-4-0 Steam Freight Set,	
____		LionChief, *17*	320
	83716	BNSF RS-3 Diesel Scout Freight Set, LionChief,	
____		*17*	280
____	83733	Lighted Aquarius Hi-Cube Boxcar, *17*	90
____	83734	Lighted Pegasus Hi-Cube Boxcar, *17*	90
____	83745	Lionelville Hospital Kit, *17*	80
____	83752	W&A Horse Car and Corral, *17*	180
____	83762	Personalized Christmas Boxcar, *16*	90
____	83763	Personalized Holiday Boxcar, *16*	90
____	83764	Happy Birthday Boxcar, *16*	90
____	83765	Anniversary Boxcar, *16–17*	90
____	83766	Personalized Polar Express Baggage Car, *16–17*	95
____	83779	Pearl Harbor 75th Anniversary Boxcar, *16–17*	85
____	83783	Rosie the Riveter Boxcar, *17*	85
____	83784	Heavies and Little Friends Boxcar, *17*	85
____	83785	Doolittle Raid Boxcar, *16–17*	85
____	83786	D-Day Boxcar, *17*	85
____	83788	Uncle Sam "Enlist Now" Boxcar, *16–17*	85
____	83790	Mickey Mouse Happy Holidays Boxcar, *17*	85
____	83791	Donald Duck Happy Holidays Boxcar, *17*	85
____	83792	Goofy Happy Holidays Boxcar, *17*	85
____	83796	100th Anniversary Moon Pie Boxcar, *17*	85
____	83800	Happy Thanksgiving Boxcar, *17*	80
____	83801	Happy Hanukkah Boxcar, *17*	80
____	83802	Disney Happy Halloween Boxcar, *17*	85
____	83913	Personalized Halloween Boxcar, *17*	95
____	83923	Angela Trotta Thomas Santa's Cookies Boxcar, *17*	85
____	83925	Frosty the Snowman Boxcar, *17*	85
____	83926	Personalized Polar Express Boxcar, *17*	95
____	83927	Lionel Smoke Fluid 1-D Tank Car, *17*	75
____	83928	Lionel Paint 1-D Tank Car, *17*	75
____	83929	Lionel Hydraulic Oil 1-D Tank Car, *17*	75
____	83943	Polar Express Boxcar, *17*	85
____	83944	John Deere Boxcar, *17*	85
____	83945	Richard Nixon Presidential Boxcar, *17*	70
____	83946	Jimmy Carter Presidential Boxcar, *17*	70
____	83947	Woodrow Wilson Presidential Boxcar, *17*	70
____	83948	William Howard Taft Presidential Boxcar, *17*	70
____	83950	Personalized "It's A Boy" Boxcar, *17*	90
____	83951	Personalized "It's A Girl" Boxcar, *17*	90
____	83952	Minnie Mouse Happy Holidays Boxcar, *17*	85
	83964	Mickey Mouse Christmas Express Steam Freight	
____		Set, LionChief, *17*	420

		Exc	Mint
83972	Harry Potter Hogwarts Steam Passenger Set, LionChief, *17*		420____
83974	CSX Intermodal Set, LionChief, *17*		460____
83979	Mickey & Friends B337Express Steam Freight Set, LionChief, *17*		370____
83984	Pennsylvania Flyer 0-8-0 Steam Freight Set, LionChief, *17*		300____
84000	DETX Rotary Gondola 4-pack (std 0), *16–17*		280____
84005	CSX Rotary Gondola 4-pack (std 0), *16–17*		280____
84010	UP Rotary Gondola 4-pack (std 0), *16–17*		280____
84015	NS Rotary Gondola 4-pack (std 0), *16–17*		280____
84020	PPLX Rotary Gondola 4-pack (std 0), *16–17*		280____
84025	PPLX Rotary Gondola 2-pack (std 0), *16–17*		140____
84028	BNSF Rotary Gondola 4-pack (std 0), *16–17*		280____
84033	BNSF Rotary Gondola 2-pack (std 0), *16–17*		140____
84045	BN 21" Passenger Car 4-pack, *17*		620____
84050	BN 21" Coach 2-pack, *17*		310____
84053	BN 21" Diner, StationSounds, *17*		310____
84063	Weathered N&W Y6B 2-8-8-2 Locomotive "2186," CC, *16*		2200____
84069	B&M 2-6-0 Mogul Locomotive "1397," CC, *16*		700____
84070	CV 2-6-0 Mogul Locomotive "397," CC, *16*		700____
84071	DL&W 2-6-0 Mogul Locomotive "565," CC, *16*		700____
84072	Everett 2-6-0 Mogul Locomotive "11," CC, *16*		700____
84073	GT 2-6-0 Mogul Locomotive "713," CC, *16*		700____
84074	Rutland 2-6-0 Mogul Locomotive "145," CC, *16*		700____
84075	ACL E8 Diesel AA Set "544, 545," CC, *17*		1000____
84078	BN E8 Diesel AA Set "9935, 9940," CC, *17*		1000____
84081	Conrail E8 Diesel AA Set "4020, 4021," CC, *17*		1000____
84084	EMD Demonstrator E8 Diesel A Unit "950," CC, *17*		650____
84085	L&N E8 Diesel AA Set "796, 797," CC, *17*		1000____
84088	NYC E8 Diesel AA Set "4036, 4037," CC, *17*		1000____
84091	PRR E8 Diesel AA Set "5763, 5764," CC, *17*		1000____
84094	Arkansas & Missouri SD70ACe Diesel Locomotive "70," CC, *16*		650____
84095	Arkansas & Missouri SD70ACe Diesel Locomotive "71," CC, *16*		650____
84096	BNSF SD70ACe Diesel Locomotive "9372," CC, *16*		650____
84097	BNSF SD70ACe Diesel Locomotive "9385," CC, *16*		650____
84098	CN SD70ACe Diesel Locomotive "8100," CC, *16*		650____
84099	CN SD70ACe Diesel Locomotive "8102," CC, *16*		650____
84100	CSX SD70ACe Diesel Locomotive "4837," CC, *16*		650____
84101	CSX SD70ACe Diesel Locomotive "4843," CC, *16*		650____
84102	EMDX SD70ACe Diesel Locomotive "72," CC, *16*		650____
84103	EMDX SD70ACe Diesel Locomotive "73," CC, *16*		650____
84104	Montana Rail Link SD70ACe Diesel Locomotive "4309" CC, *16*		650____
84105	Montana Rail Link SD70ACe Diesel Locomotive "4312" CC, *16*		650____
84106	UP SD70ACe Diesel Locomotive "8360," CC, *16*		650____
84107	UP SD70ACe Diesel Locomotive "8415," CC, *16*		650____
84108	GN GP7 Diesel "601," *16–17*		330____
84109	L&N GP7 Diesel "405," *16–17*		330____

		Exc	Mint
___84110	Reading GP7 Diesel "619," *16–17*		330
___84111	WP GP7 Diesel "707," *16–17*		330
84112	Cotton Belt 50' DD Boxcar "47509" (std O), *16–17*		80
___84113	D&RGW 50' DD Boxcar "63689" (std O), *16–17*		80
___84114	Seaboard 50' DD Boxcar "10090" (std O), *16–17*		80
84115	PRR K4s 4-6-2 Pacific Locomotive "5385," CC, *16*		1300
84116	PRR K4s 4-6-2 Pacific Locomotive "5432," CC, *16*		1300
84117	Burlington Refrigerator Express 40' Steel Reefer "76060" (std O), *17*		85
___84118	BAR 40' Steel Reefer "7342" (std O), *17*		85
___84119	BN 40' Steel Reefer "70609" (std O), *17*		85
84120	Eastern States ERDX 40' Steel Reefer "10060" (std O), *17*		85
84121	National Car Co. 40' Steel Reefer "2430" (std O), *17*		85
___84122	FGE 40' Steel Reefer "41475" (std O), *17*		85
___84123	B&M PS-2CD Covered Hopper "5717" (std O), *17*		90
84124	L&N PS-2CD Covered Hopper "37399" (std O), *17*		90
84125	MILW PS-2CD Covered Hopper "98333" (std O), *17*		90
___84126	NP PS-2CD Covered Hopper "75675" (std O), *17*		90
84127	AT&SF PS-2CD Covered Hopper "304713" (std O), *17*		90
84128	TLDX Demonstrator PS-2CD Covered Hopper "91" (std O), *17*		90
___84129	AT&SF Wide Vision Caboose "999705" (std O), *17*		95
84130	BN Freedom Train Wide Vision Caboose "12618" (std O), *17*		95
___84131	BNSF Wide Vision Caboose "12584" (std O), *17*		95
___84132	CSX Wide Vision Caboose "903180" (std O), *17*		95
___84135	C&O Northeast Caboose "A918" (std O), *17*		90
___84137	Conrail Northeast Caboose "18866" (std O), *17*		90
84138	Pere Marquette Northeast Caboose "A909" (std O), *17*		90
84139	WM Northeast Caboose circle herald "1874" (std O), *17*		90
84140	WM Northeast Caboose circus herald "1882" (std O), *17*		90
___84141	WM USRA 2-bay Hopper 3-pack #1 (std O), *17*		220
___84145	WM USRA 2-bay Hopper 3-pack #2 (std O), *17*		220
___84149	Reading USRA 2-bay Hopper 3-pack (std O), *17*		220
___84153	B&O 1905 2-bay Hopper 3-pack (std O), *17*		220
84157	Bethlehem Steel 1905 2-bay Hopper 3-pack (std O), *17*		220
___84161	Logging Disconnect Stock Car, *17*		40
___84163	Logging Disconnect Christmas 4-pack (std O), *17*		160
84165	Logging Disconnect Dinner Train 4-pack (std O), *17*		160
___84166	Logging Disconnect, 1-pair, brown (std O), *17*		65
___84167	Logging Disconnect, 2-pair, brown (std O), *17*		125
___84226	American Freedom Train Add-On 2-pack #4, *17*		300
___84229	Conrail 21" Theater Inspection Car "9," *17*		340
___84230	NS 21" Theater Inspection Car Buena Vista, *17*		340

		Exc	Mint
84231	CSX 21" Theater Inspection Car Alabama, *17*	340	___
84232	UP 21" Theater Inspection Car Fox River, *17*	340	___
84237	Cass Scenic RR 3-Truck Shay Locomotive "6," CC, *17*	1500	___
84238	Elk River Lumber Co. 3-Truck Shay Locomotive "20," CC, *17*	1500	___
84239	WM 3-Truck Shay Locomotive "6," CC, *17*	1500	___
84240	West Side Lumber Co. 3-Truck Shay Locomotive "3," CC, *17*	1500	___
84248	SP AC-9 2-8-8-4 Locomotive "3800," CC, *17*	2000	___
84249	SP AC-9 2-8-8-4 Locomotive "3805," CC, *17*	2000	___
84250	SP AC-9 Daylight 2-8-8-4 Locomotive "3811," CC, *17*	2000	___
84251	AT&SF 2-8-4 Berkshire Locomotive "4103," *17*	450	___
84252	Nickel Plate Road 2-8-4 Berkshire Locomotive "767," *17*	450	___
84253	Pere Marquette 2-8-4 Berkshire Locomotive "1223," *17*	450	___
84254	IC 2-8-4 Berkshire Locomotive "8006," *17*	450	___
84255	Lionel Lines 2-8-4 Berkshire Locomotive "726," *17*	450	___
84256	AT&SF SD40 Diesel "5006," CC, *17*	650	___
84257	AT&SF SD40 Diesel "5018," CC, *17*	650	___
84258	UP SD40 Diesel "4057," CC, *17*	650	___
84259	UP SD40 Diesel "4062," CC, *17*	650	___
84260	CSX SD40 Diesel "4614," CC, *17*	650	___
84261	CSX SD40 Diesel "4621," CC, *17*	650	___
84262	PRR SD40 Diesel "6041," CC, *17*	650	___
84263	PRR SD40 Diesel "6089," CC, *17*	650	___
84264	Southern SD40 Diesel "3170," CC, *17*	650	___
84265	Southern SD40 Diesel "3200," CC, *17*	650	___
84267	SP SD40R Diesel "7372," CC, *17*	650	___
84268	WM SD40 Diesel "7547," CC, *17*	650	___
84269	WM SD40 Diesel "7549," CC, *17*	650	___
84296	SP Salad Bowl Express Diesel Freight Set, CC, *17*	900	___
84297	Logging Disconnect Steel Tank Car (std O), *17*	40	___
84303	Bucking Feed and Tack, *17*	85	___
84304	CB&Q Gondola with covers, *17*	55	___
84306	Illuminated John Deere Flagpole, *17*	60	___
84307	Illuminated Lionel Flagpole with flag, *17*	50	___
84308	Gray Half-Covered Bridge, *17*	60	___
84309	PRR Blinking Water Tower, *17*	45	___
84310	Modular Train Car Repair Facility, *16–17*	110	___
84312	Alaska RR Gondola with canisters, *17*	55	___
84315	Branchline Water Tank Kit, *16–17*	40	___
84317	Passenger Station, *17*	80	___
84318	Illuminated Station Platform, *17*	43	___
84327	Santa Fe Operating Billboard, *17*	70	___
84328	Polar Express Steam Passenger Set, LionChief, *17*	420	___
84330	Witches Brew 1-D Tank Car, *17*	70	___
84332	Halloween Boxcar, SpookySounds, *17*	80	___
84333	Strasburg RR Gondola with vats, *17*	65	___
84334	Strasburg Half-covered Bridge, *17*	60	___
84335	PRR Culvert Gondola "374200," *17*	65	___
84336	UP Log Car, *17*	65	___

		Exc	Mint
84337	MKT Wood-chip Hopper, *17*		65
84338	CSX Wood-chip Hopper, *17*		65
84339	SP Jumping Hobo Boxcar, *17*		80
84340	Santa and Snowman Operating Boxcar, *17*		90
84341	Tell-Tale Reindeer Car, *17*		80
84366	PRR Wood-chip Hopper, *17*		65
84367	Christmas Pylon, *17*		160
84369	NYC Welding Car "X939," *17*		80
84370	Polar Express Hopper with silver, *17*		70
84371	Mickey's Holiday Hopper with presents, *17*		70
84372	Christmas Station Platform, *17*		43
84374	Christmas Music Boxcar, *17*		80
84375	Christmas Boxcar, *17*		65
84376	Angela Trotta Thomas Signature Express Aquarium Car, *17*		85
84377	Christmas Peppermint 1-D Tank Car, *17*		60
84378	Santa's Choice Milk Car with platform, *17*		180
84383	Elevated Oil Tank, *17*		95
84388	Gray 10" Girder Bridge, *17*		25
84400	BN "Pulling for Freedom" SD60M Diesel "1991," CC, *17*		650
84401	BN SD60M Diesel "9200," CC, *17*		650
84402	BN SD60M Diesel "9225," CC, *17*		650
84403	Soo Line SD60M Diesel "6058," CC, *17*		650
84404	Soo Line SD60M Diesel "6061," CC, *17*		650
84405	Conrail SD60M Diesel "5504," CC, *17*		650
84406	Conrail SD60M Diesel "5510," CC, *17*		650
84407	CSX SD60M Diesel "8783," CC, *17*		650
84408	CSX SD60M Diesel "8784," CC, *17*		650
84409	NS SD60M Diesel "6808," CC, *17*		650
84410	NS SD60M Diesel "6815," CC, *17*		650
84411	UP SD60M Diesel "6165," CC, *17*		650
84412	UP SD60M Diesel "6187," CC, *17*		650
84413	B&O FA A-A Diesel Set, "814, 815," *17*		500
84416	GN FA A-A Diesel Set, "278A, 278B," *17*		500
84419	NH FA A-A Diesel Set, "417, 418," *17*		500
84422	UP FA A-A Diesel Set, "1616, 1617," *17*		500
84433	Polar Express 40' Scale Reefer "122517," *17*		90
84434	NS 30,000-gallon 1-D Tank Car 3-pack (std O), *16*		250
84438	NS 30,000-gallon 1-D Tank Car "362785" (std O), *16*		80
84439	UTLX 30,000-gallon 1-D Tank Car 3-pack (std O), *16*		250
84443	PESX 30,000-gallon 1-D Tank Car 3-pack (std O), *16*		250
84447	TILX 30,000-gallon 1-D Tank Car 3-pack (std O), *16*		250
84451	PRR Flatcar 6-pack, *17*		120
84452	AT&SF Flatcar 6-pack, *17*		120
84453	UP Flatcar 6-pack, *17*		120
84454	Trailer Train Flatcar 6-pack, *17*		120
84455	Assorted Flatcar 6-pack, *17*		120
84456	B&O Gondola 6-pack, *17*		120
84457	UP Gondola 6-pack, *17*		120

		Exc	Mint
84458	East Assorted Gondola 6-pack, *17*	120	___
84459	Midwest Assorted Gondola 6-pack, *17*	120	___
84460	West Assorted Gondola 6-pack, *17*	120	___
84462	2-Rail Conversion Kit, 50-ton Scale Trucks, *16–17*	20	___
84463	2-Rail Conversion Kit, 70-ton Scale Trucks, *16–17*	20	___
84465	B&O 2-8-2 Light Mikado Locomotive "4500," CC, *17*	1300	___
84466	GTW 2-8-2 Light Mikado Locomotive "3734," CC, *17*	1300	___
84467	Maine Central 2-8-2 Light Mikado Locomotive "624," CC, *17*	1300	___
84468	NYC 2-8-2 Light Mikado Locomotive "5187," CC, *17*	1300	___
84469	PRR 2-8-2 Light Mikado Locomotive "9630," CC, *17*	1300	___
84470	Southern 2-8-2 Light Mikado Locomotive "4758," CC, *17*	1300	___
84471	UP 2-8-2 Light Mikado Locomotive "2537," CC, *17*	1300	___
84480	John Deere Covered Bridge, *17*	70	___
84481	John Deere General Store, *17*	85	___
84482	John Deere Gondola with hay bales, *17*	75	___
84483	John Deere Grain Vat Car, *17*	75	___
84485	Disney Covered Bridge, *17*	70	___
84486	MILW NW2 Diesel Locomotive "1649," CC, *16*	500	___
84487	Donald Duck Holiday 1-D Tank Car, *17*	70	___
84489	Polar Express Covered Bridge, *17*	70	___
84490	NS First Responders Diesel Freight Set, LionChief, *17*	450	___
84496	Shell Service Station, *17*	150	___
84498	NS Fire Rescue Car, *17*	75	___
84499	Mickey Industrial Water Tower, *17*	100	___
84500	NS Unibody 1-D Tank Car "490112," *17*	75	___
84507	New York Central & Hudson River S2 Electric "3207," CC, *17*	800	___
84508	NYC S2 Electric "113," CC, *17*	800	___
84509	NYC S2 Electric "115," CC, *17*	800	___
84510	PC S2 Electric "4710," CC, *17*	800	___
84511	NYC "Lightning Stripe" S2 Electric "101," CC, *17*	800	___
84512	S2 Electric Scale Tinplate Freight Set, CC, *17*	1000	___
84525	Uptown Apartment Building, *17*	100	___
84526	Leuzure Marble Co. Warehouse, *17*	110	___
84529	NS Veterans Wide Vision Caboose "6920" (std O), *17*	95	___
84530	NS First Responders Wide Vision Caboose "9-1-1" (std O), *17*	95	___
84532	Nickel Plate Road 2-8-2 Light Mikado Locomotive "587," CC, *17*	1300	___
84538	NS 65' Mill Gondola "195029" (std O), *17*	80	___
84539	NS 65' Mill Gondola "195065" (std O), *17*	80	___
84553	Logging Disconnect Reindeer Train 4-pack A, *17*	160	___
84554	Logging Disconnect Reindeer Train 4-pack B, *17*	160	___
84555	Logging Disconnect Santa Claus Observation (std O), *17*	45	___

		Exc	Mint
84562	BN "Pulling for Freedom" SD60M Diesel "1991," LionChief, *17*		500
84563	BN SD60M Diesel "9215," LionChief, *17*		500
84564	Soo Line SD60M Diesel "6060," LionChief, *17*		500
84565	Conrail SD60M Diesel "5509," LionChief, *17*		500
84566	CSX SD60M Diesel "8757," LionChief, *17*		500
84567	NS SD60M Diesel "6810," LionChief, *17*		500
84568	UP SD60M Diesel "6170," LionChief, *17*		500
84570	First Responders EMT Boxcar, *17*		90
84571	First Responders Police Boxcar, *17*		90
84572	First Responders Fire Fighter Boxcar, *17*		90
84573	Happy Birthday Boxcar, *17*		90
84574	Personalized Merry Christmas Boxcar, *17*		90
84575	U.S. Army Boxcar, *17*		90
84576	U.S. Marine Boxcar, *17*		90
84577	U.S. Air Force Boxcar, *17*		90
84578	U.S. Navy Boxcar, *17*		90
84579	U.S. Coast Guard Boxcar, *17*		90
84580	From The Home Front Boxcar, blue, *17*		90
84581	From The Home Front Boxcar, green, *17*		90
84582	BNSF 65' Mill Gondola "518375" (std O), *17*		80
84583	BNSF 65' Mill Gondola "518392" (std O), *17*		80
84584	C&NW 65' Mill Gondola "342045" (std O), *17*		80
84585	C&NW 65' Mill Gondola "342049" (std O), *17*		80
84586	CSX 65' Mill Gondola "491616" (std O), *17*		80
84587	CSX 65' Mill Gondola "491638" (std O), *17*		80
84590	SP 65' Mill Gondola "365136" (std O), *17*		80
84591	SP 65' Mill Gondola "365142" (std O), *17*		80
84592	UP 65' Mill Gondola "96267" (std O), *17*		80
84593	UP 65' Mill Gondola "96281" (std O), *17*		80
99000	Keebler Elf Express Steam Freight Set, *99 u*		1150
99001	Mickey's Holiday Express Freight Set, *99 u*		170
99002	Looney Tunes Square Window Caboose, *99 u*		NRS
99006	Keebler Bulkhead Flatcar, *99 u*		NRS
99007	Smuckers Fudge 1-D Tank Car, *99 u*		90
99008	Mickey's Merry Christmas Boxcar, *99 u*		NRS
99009	Mickey's Holiday Express Square Window Caboose, *99 u*		NRS
99013	Case Cutlery Tank Car "1889," *00 u*		NRS
99014	Case Cutlery Gondola "1889," *00 u*		NRS
99015	Case Cutlery Boxcar "1889," *00 u*		NRS
99018	Case Cutlery Rolling Stock 3-pack, *00 u*		210
79C95204C	Sears Santa Fe Diesel Freight Set, *71 u*	150	165
79C9715C	Sears 4-unit Diesel Freight Set, *75 u*	50	65
79C9717C	Sears 7-unit Steam Freight Set, *75 u*	150	165
79N95223C	Sears 6-unit Diesel Freight Set, *74 u*	150	165
79N9552C	Sears 6-unit Steam Freight Set, *72 u*	150	165

Exc Mint

		Exc	Mint
79N9553C	Sears 6-unit Diesel Freight Set, *72 u*	150	165____
79N96178C	Sears 4-unit Steam Freight Set, *74 u*	50	65____
79N97082C	Sears Steam Freight Set, *70 u*		NRS____
79N97101C	Sears 5-unit Steam Freight Set, *72 u*	150	165____
79N98765C	Sears Logging Empire Set, *78 u*	100	115____
T1428RRODTS	Tony Stewart NASCAR Steam Freight Set, *12–14*		300____
T1828RRMMKB	Kyle Busch NASCAR Steam Freight Set, *12–14*		300____
T2428RRDUJG	Jeff Gordon NASCAR Steam Freight Set, *12–14*		300____
T4828RRLOJJ	Jimmy Johnson NASCAR Steam Freight Set, *12–14*		300____
T4828RRLOJJ	Dale Earnhardt Jr. NASCAR Steam Freight Set, *12–14*		300____
TX328RRGMDE	Dale Earnhardt NASCAR Steam Freight Set, *12–14*		300____
UCS	Remote Control Track (O), *70*	4	7____

Unnumbered Items

	Exc	Mint
Amtrak Passenger Car Set, *89, 89 u*	640	770____
B&A Hudson and Standard O Car Set, *86 u*	1500	1700____
Baltimore & Ohio Set, *94, 96*		NRS____
Black Cave Flyer Playmat, *82*		8____
Blue Comet Set, *78–80, 87 u*	560	620____
Burlington Texas Zephyr Set, *80, 80 u*	980	1150____
C&NW Passenger Car Set, *93*	385	460____
Cannonball Freight Playmat, *81–82*		8____
Chesapeake & Ohio Set, *95–96*		NRS____
Chessie System Special Set, *80, 86 u*	560	620____
Chicago & Alton Limited Set, *81, 86 u*	560	620____
Commando Assault Train Playmat, *83–84*		8____
D&RGW California Zephyr Set, *92, 93*		900____
Erie Set (FF 7), *93*	385	460____
Erie-Lackawanna Passenger Car Set, *93, 94*	940	980____
Favorite Food Freight Set, *81–82*	248	338____
Frisco Set (FF 5), *91*	405	425____
The General Set, *77–80*	240	285____
GN Empire Builder Set, *92, 93*	620	730____
Great Northern Set (FARR 3), *81, 81 u*	620	690____
IC City of New Orleans Set, *85, 87, 93*	885	1045____
Illinois Central Set, *91–92, 95*	255	285____
Jersey Central Set, *86*	345	370____
Joshua Lionel Cowen Set, *80, 80 u, 82*	540	580____
L.A.S.E.R. Playmat, *81–82*		8____
Lionel Lines Madison Car Set, *91, 93*	560	620____
Lionel Lines Set, *82–84 u, 86, 86–87 u, 94–95*	530	620____
Mickey Mouse Express Set, *77–78, 78 u*	1010	1700____
Milwaukee Road Set (FF 2), *87, 90 u*	380	405____
Mint Set, *79 u, 80–83, 84 u, 86 u, 87, 91 u, 93*	940	1073____
Missouri Pacific Set, *95*		390____
N&W Powhatan Arrow Passenger Car Set, *95*	370	445____
N&W Powhatan Arrow Set, *81, 81 u, 82 u, 91 u*	1450	1700____
New Haven Set, *94–95*		400____
New York Central Set, *89, 91*	240	270____

		Exc	Mint
____	Nickel Plate Road Set (FF 6), *92*	385	460
____	Northern Pacific Set, *90–92*	190	250
____	NYC 20th Century Limited Set, *83, 83 u, 95*	980	1150
____	Pennsylvania Set, *79–80, 79–80 u, 81 u, 83 u*	1200	1350
____	Pennsylvania Set, *87–90, 95*	240	270
____	Pennsylvania Set (FARR 5), *84–85, 89 u*	600	660
____	Pere Marquette Set, *93*	720	770
____	Rock Island & Peoria Set, *80–82*	240	315
____	Rocky Mountain Platform, *83–84*		8
____	Santa Fe Super Chief Set, *91, 91 u, 92 u, 93, 95*	1400	1700
____	Santa Fe Set (FARR 1), *79, 79 u*	460	580
____	Southern Crescent Limited Set, *77–78, 87 u*	540	650
____	Southern Pacific Daylight Diesel Set, *82–83, 82–83 u, 90 u*	2150	2300
____	Southern Set (FARR 4), *83, 83 u*	620	690
____	SP Daylight Steam Set, *90, 92, 93*	790	940
____	Spirit of '76 Set, *74–76*	570	690
____	Station Platform, *83–84*		8
____	Toys "R" Us Thunderball Freight Set, *75 u*		NRS
____	Union Pacific Set, *94*	430	500
____	Union Pacific Set (FARR 2), *80, 80 u*	540	580
____	UP Overland Route Set, *84, 92 u*	770	840
____	Wabash Set (FF 1), *86, 87*	755	905
____	Western Maryland Set (FF 4), *89*	345	405

		Retail
11-1001	No. 400E Locomotive, black, brass trim (std)	900____
11-1002	No. 400E Locomotive, gray, nickel trim (std)	900____
11-1003	No. 400E Locomotive, gray, brass trim (std)	900____
11-1005	No. 390 Locomotive, green	600____
11-1006	No. 400E Locomotive, crackele black, brass trim	900____
11-1008	No. 400E Lionel Lines Locomotive	900____
11-1009	No. 400E Locomotive, blue, brass trim	900____
11-1010	No. 385E Locomotive (std)	700____
11-1012	No. 1835E Locomotive, black, nickel trim	700____
11-1013	AF No. 4694 Warrior Passenger Set	1400____
11-1014	AF No. 4694 Iron Monarch Passenger Set	1250____
11-1015	No. 392E Locomotive, black, brass trim	800____
11-1016	No. 392E Locomotive, gray, nickel trim	800____
11-1017	No. 400E Locomotive, blue, nickel trim (std)	900____
11-1018	No. 7 Lionel Locomotive (std)	900____
11-1019	No. 6 Pennsylvania Locomotive (std)	900____
11-1020	American Flyer No. 4696 Locomotive	1000____
11-1021	No. 400E Presidential Locomotive (std)	1000____
11-1022	No. 400E Red Comet Locomotive (std)	1000____
11-1023	No. 400E Locomotive, blue, brass trim (std)	900____
11-1024	No. 400E Locomotive, black, brass trim (std)	900____
11-1025	No. 400E Lionel Lines Locomotive (std)	900____
11-1026	No. 400E Locomotive, pink (std)	1000____
11-1027	No. 400E Locomotive, state green (std)	1000____
11-1028	No. 400E Locomotive, black, brass trim (std)	1000____
11-1029	No. 6 NYC Locomotive (std)	900____
11-1030	No. 6 General Locomotive (std)	900____
11-1031	No. 6 Texas Locomotive (std)	950____
11-1038	No. 6 B&O Locomotive (std)	900____
11-1039	No. 6 Long Island Locomotive (std)	900____
11-1040	No. 6 Strasburg Locomotive (std)	900____
11-1041	No. 6 PRR Locomotive (std)	900____
11-1042	Great Northern Steam Locomotive (std)	1000____
11-1043	Lehigh Valley Steam Locomotive (std)	1000____
11-1044	NYC Steam Locomotive (std)	1000____
11-1045	PRR Steam Locomotive (std)	1000____
11-1046	No. 392E LL Locomotive, blue, nickel trim (std)	650____
11-1047	No. 392E LL Locomotive, blue, brass trim (std)	650____
11-1048	No. 390 LL Locomotive, black, brass trim (std)	650____
11-1049	No. 390 LL Locomotive, green, brass trim (std)	650____
11-1050	No. 390 LL Locomotive, gray, nickel trim (std)	650____
11-1051	No. 400E LL Locomotive, blue, nickel trim (std)	1000____
11-1052	No. 400E Locomotive, blue, brass trim (std)	1000____

____	**11-1053**	No. 400E Locomotive, black, brass trim (std)	1000
____	**11-1054**	No. 400E LL Locomotive, gray, nickel trim (std)	1000
____	**11-1055**	No. 400E UP Locomotive, yellow (std)	1000
____	**11-1056**	No. 400E NW Locomotive (std)	1000
____	**11-1057**	No. 392E LL Locomotive, black, brass trim (std)	900
____	**11-1058**	No. 392E Lionel Lines Locomotive (std)	900
____	**11-1059**	No. 392E LL Locomotive, gray, nickel trim (std)	900
____	**11-1060**	No. 392E PRR Locomotive (std)	900
____	**11-1061**	No. 392E Lehigh Valley Locomotive (std)	900
____	**11-2003**	No. 8E Electric Locomotive, olive green (std)	500
____	**11-2004**	No. 8E Electric Locomotive, dark olive green (std)	500
____	**11-2005**	No. 8E Electric Locomotive, orange (std)	500
____	**11-2006**	No. 8E Electric Locomotive, red/cream (std)	500
____	**11-2007**	American Flyer Presidential Passenger Set (std)	1800
____	**11-2008**	AF No. 4689 Presidential Locomotive, blue (std)	800
____	**11-2009**	Big Brute Electric Engine, zinc chromate	1500
____	**11-2010**	Big Brute Electric Engine, green	1500
____	**11-2015**	Super 381 Electric Engine, state green (std)	1300
____	**11-2016**	Super 381 MILW Electric Engine (std)	1300
____	**11-2017**	No. 408E Electric Locomotive (std)	900
____	**11-2018**	No. 408E Electric Locomotive, Mojave	900
____	**11-2019**	No. 408E Electric Locomotive, pink	900
____	**11-2020**	No. 9 Electric Locomotive, green	600
____	**11-2021**	No. 9 Electric Locomotive, orange	600
____	**11-2022**	No. 9 Electric Locomotive, gray, nickel trim	600
____	**11-2023**	No. 9 Electric Locomotive, dark green	600
____	**11-2024**	No. 8 Trolley (std)	530
____	**11-2025**	No. 9 Trolley (std)	650
____	**11-2026**	No. 8 Christmas Trolley (std)	570
____	**11-2027**	No. 381E Electric Locomotive, blue (std)	900
____	**11-2028**	No. 381E Electric Locomotive, brown (std)	900
____	**11-2029**	No. 381E Great Northern Electric Locomotive (std)	900
____	**11-2031**	No. 4689 President's Locomotive, red (std)	900
____	**11-2033**	Big Brute Electric Locomotive, brown (std)	1600
____	**11-2034**	Big Brute Electric Locomotive, orange (std)	1600
____	**11-2038**	Super 381 MILW Electric Locomotive (std)	1300
____	**11-2039**	Super 381 PRR Electric Locomotive (std)	1300
____	**11-2040**	Super 381 Electric Locomotive, two-tone brown (std)	1300
____	**11-2041**	Super 381 New Haven Electric Locomotive (std)	1300
____	**11-2042**	No. 408E LL Electric Locomotive, dark green (std)	950
____	**11-2043**	No. 408E LL Electric Locomotive, apple green (std)	950
____	**11-2044**	No. 408E LL Electric Locomotive, blue (std)	950
____	**11-2045**	No. 408E MILW Electric Locomotive (std)	950
____	**11-2046**	No. 408E GN Electric Locomotive (std)	950
____	**11-2047**	No. 318E LL Electric Locomotive, black (std)	500

11-2048	No. 318E LL Electric Locomotive, green (std)	500____
11-2049	No. 318E LL Electric Locomotive, gray (std)	500____
11-2050	No. 318E LL Electric Locomotive, brown (std)	500____
11-2051	No. 318E MILW Electric Locomotive (std)	500____
11-2052	No. 318E New Haven Electric Locomotive (std)	500____
11-5001	No. 384 Locomotive Passenger Set, black, brass trim	600____
11-5002	No. 384 Locomotive Christmas Freight Set (std)	600____
11-5003	No. 384 Locomotive LV Passenger Set (std)	600____
11-5004	No. 384 Locomotive NYC Freight Set	600____
11-5006	No. 384E Locomotive Girl's Passenger Set	600____
11-5007	No. 386 Freight Set (std)	600____
11-5008	No. 340E Coal Freight Set (std)	600____
11-5009	No. 342E Baby State Passenger Set (std)	600____
11-5010	No. 384E Blue Comet Passenger Set (std)	600____
11-5011	No. 386 Christmas Freight Set (std)	600____
11-5012	No. 342E Passenger Set (std)	600____
11-5013	No. 318E Christmas Freight Set (std)	600____
11-5014	No. 384E PRR Steam Passenger Set (std)	600____
11-5501	No. 263E Steam Christmas Freight Set	600____
11-5502	No. 263E Steam B&O Freight Set	600____
11-5505	No. 249E Christmas Steam Passenger Set	500____
11-5506	No. 299 Freight Set	450____
11-5507	No. 269E Distant Control Freight Set	500____
11-5508	Celebration Passenger Set	480____
11-5509	No. 269E Christmas Distant Control Freight Set	500____
11-5510	No. 269E Distant Control Freight Set	500____
11-6001	No. 263E Locomotive, black, brass trim	430____
11-6002	No. 263E Locomotive, blue	430____
11-6003	No. 277W Remote Control Work Train	680____
11-6004	Blue Comet Distant Control Passenger Set	650____
11-6005	No. 275W Distant Control Freight Set	600____
11-6006	UP Streamliner Passenger Set, silver	800____
11-6007	UP Streamliner Passenger Set, yellow	800____
11-6008	No. 249E Steam Passenger Set, black, brass trim	600____
11-6009	No. 249E Steam Passenger Set, blue	600____
11-6010	No. 249E Steam Passenger Set, gray, nickel trim	600____
11-6012	No. 260E Locomotive, black, brass trim	430____
11-6013	No. 255E Locomotive, gray, nickel trim	430____
11-6014	No. 255E Lionel Lines Locomotive	430____
11-6015	No. 279E Distant Control Passenger Set	750____
11-6016	No. 295E Distant Control Passenger Set	750____
11-6017	Hiawatha Distance Control Streamliner Set	900____
11-6018	Hiawatha Passenger Train Set	900____
11-6019	Hiawatha Distance Control Freight Set	900____
11-6020	UP City of Denver Passenger Set, green	590____
11-6021	UP City of Denver Passenger Set, yellow/brown	700____

____ **11-6022**	No. 262E Locomotive, black, brass trim	300
____ **11-6023**	No. 262E Locomotive, black, nickel trim	300
____ **11-6024**	No. 260E Locomotive, black, brass trim	450
____ **11-6025**	No. 214 Armored Motor Car Set	400
____ **11-6028**	No. 256 Electric Locomotive, orange	450
____ **11-6029**	No. 214 Armored Motor Car Set	400
____ **11-6030**	No. 295E Distant Control Passenger Set	750
____ **11-6031**	No. 279E NYC Distance Control Passenger Set	700
____ **11-6033**	No. 265E Commodore Vanderbilt Locomotive	430
____ **11-6036**	No. 263E Baby Blue Comet Locomotive	460
____ **11-6037**	Girls Freight Set	830
____ **11-6038**	No. 284E Distant Control Freight Set	700
____ **11-6039**	No. 616 Flying Yankee Passenger Set, black/chrome	590
____ **11-6040**	No. 616 Flying Yankee Passenger Set, red/chrome	590
____ **11-6041**	No. 616 Flying Yankee Passenger Set, green/chrome	590
____ **11-6046**	No. 279E Distant Control Passenger Set	700
____ **11-6047**	No. 264 Red Comet Locomotive	460
____ **11-6048**	No. 263E Baby Blue Comet Locomotive, brass trim	500
____ **11-6050**	No. 256 New Haven Electric Locomotive	500
____ **11-6051**	No. 256 Great Northern Electric Locomotive	500
____ **11-6052**	No. 263E Locomotive, black, nickel trim	500
____ **11-6053**	No. 263E Chessie Locomotive	500
____ **11-6054**	No. 263E Southern Locomotive	500
____ **11-6055**	Boys Freight Set	900
____ **11-6056**	No. 261E LL Locomotive and Tender	350
____ **11-6057**	No. 216E Locomotive and Tender	350
____ **11-6061**	No. 256 MILW Electric Locomotive	500
____ **11-6062**	No. 256 PRR Electric Locomotive	500
____ **11-6063**	No. 263E Lionel Lines Locomotive, orange/blue	500
____ **11-6064**	No. 263E Lionel Lines Locomotive, black, brass trim	500
____ **11-6065**	No. 263E Lionel Lines Locomotive, gray, nickel trim	500
____ **11-6066**	No. 263E Norfolk & Western Locomotive	500
____ **11-6067**	No. 263E UP Locomotive, yellow	500
____ **11-6068**	No. 214 Armored Motor Car Set, gray	400
____ **11-6069**	No. 214 Armored Motor Car Set, tan	400
____ **11-6070**	No. 263E Lionel Lines Locomotive, blue, brass trim	500
____ **11-6071**	No. 263E Lionel Lines Locomotive, blue, nickel trim	500
____ **11-30004**	No. 213 Cattle Car, cream/maroon (std)	130
____ **11-30005**	No. 213 Cattle Car, terra-cotta/green (std)	130
____ **11-30006**	No. 214 Boxcar, cream/orange (std)	130
____ **11-30007**	No. 214 Boxcar, yellow/brown (std)	130
____ **11-30008**	No. 214R Refrigerator Car, white/blue (std)	130
____ **11-30009**	No. 215 Tank Car, silver, nickel trim (std)	130
____ **11-30010**	No. 215 Tank Car, green, brass trim (std)	130
____ **11-30011**	No. 215 Tank Car, white (std)	130
____ **11-30012**	No. 216 Hopper Car, red (std)	130
____ **11-30013**	No. 217 Caboose, orange/maroon (std)	140

LIONEL CORPORATION TINPLATE

11-30014	No. 217 Caboose, red (std)	160____
11-30015	No. 513 Cattle Car, green/orange, brass trim (std)	100____
11-30016	No. 514 Boxcar, cream/orange (std)	120____
11-30017	No. 514R Refrigerator Car, ivory/peacock, brass trim (std)	120____
11-30018	No. 515 Tank Car, terra-cotta, brass trim (std)	100____
11-30019	No. 516 Hopper Car, red, brass trim (std)	120____
11-30020	No. 517 Caboose, pea green/red (std)	120____
11-30021	No. 212 Gondola, maroon (std)	110____
11-30022	No. 212 Gondola, pea green (std)	110____
11-30023	No. 513 Cattle Car, cream/maroon, nickel trim (std)	100____
11-30024	No. 514R Refrigerator Car, white/blue, nickel trim (std)	120____
11-30025	No. 515 Tank Car, silver, nickel trim (std)	100____
11-30026	No. 516 Hopper Car, red, nickel trim (std)	100____
11-30027	No. 517 Caboose, red, nickel trim (std)	120____
11-30028	No. 520 Floodlight Car, green, nickel trim (std)	130____
11-30029	No. 520 Floodlight Car, terra-cotta, brass trim (std)	130____
11-30030	No. 514R Christmas Refrigerator Car, (std)	100____
11-30031	No. 514 Christmas Boxcar (std)	100____
11-30032	No. 515 MTH/Lionel Tank Car (std)	100____
11-30033	No. 211 Flatcar, black, brass trim, with wood (std)	120____
11-30034	No. 211 Flatcar, black, nickel trim, with wood (std)	120____
11-30035	No. 218 Dump Car, Mojave, nickel trim (std)	140____
11-30036	No. 218 Dump Car, Mojave, brass trim (std)	140____
11-30037	No. 219 Crane Car, white (std)	200____
11-30038	No. 219 Crane Car, yellow, nickel trim (std)	200____
11-30039	No. 219 Crane Car, yellow (std)	380____
11-30042	No. 514 Boxcar, red/black (std)	100____
11-30043	No. 512 Gondola, peacock, brass trim (std)	80____
11-30044	No. 512 Gondola, green, nickel trim (std)	80____
11-30045	No. 514 Boxcar, yellow/brown (std)	120____
11-30046	No. 511 Flatcar, black, brass trim, with wood (std)	100____
11-30047	No. 511 Flatcar, black, nickel trim, with wood (std)	100____
11-30048	No. 216 Hopper Car, dark green (std)	130____
11-30050	No. 219 Crane Car, white, brass trim (std)	380____
11-30051	No. 514R NYC Refrigerator Car (std)	100____
11-30055	No. 212 Gondola, gray (std)	110____
11-30056	No. 213 Cattle Car, Mojave/maroon (std)	130____
11-30057	No. 213 Cattle Car, terra-cotta/maroon (std)	130____
11-30058	No. 214 Boxcar, terra-cotta/black, brass trim (std)	130____
11-30059	No. 214R Refrigerator Car, white/peacock, brass trim (std)	130____
11-30060	No. 214R Refrigerator Car, ivory/peacock, brass trim (std)	130____
11-30061	No. 215 Tank Car, silver, brass trim (std)	130____
11-30062	No. 215 Tank Car, silver, nickel trim (std)	130____
11-30063	No. 217 Caboose, olive green (std)	140____

____ **11-30064**	No. 217 Lionel Lines Caboose (std)	140
____ **11-30065**	No. 217 Caboose, pea green/red (std)	140
____ **11-30066**	No. 217 Caboose, red/peacock (std)	160
____ **11-30067**	No. 218 Dump Car, gray (std)	140
____ **11-30068**	No. 218 Dump Car, pea green (std)	140
____ **11-30069**	No. 218 Dump Car, peacock (std)	140
____ **11-30070**	No. 219 Crane Car, peacock/dark green (std)	200
____ **11-30071**	No. 219 Lionel Lines Crane Car (std)	380
____ **11-30072**	No. 220 Floodlight Car, green, nickel trim (std)	140
____ **11-30073**	No. 220 Floodlight Car, terra-cotta, brass trim (std)	140
____ **11-30074**	No. 513 Cattle Car, orange/pea green (std)	100
____ **11-30075**	No. 514 Christmas Boxcar (std)	100
____ **11-30076**	No. 514R Refrigerator Car, ivory/blue (std)	100
____ **11-30077**	No. 515 Tank Car, cream (std)	100
____ **11-30078**	No. 515 Tank Car, ivory (std)	100
____ **11-30079**	No. 515 Tank Car, orange (std)	100
____ **11-30080**	No. 516 Christmas Hopper Car (std)	120
____ **11-30081**	No. 516 Hopper Car, red (std)	120
____ **11-30082**	No. 517 Caboose, red/black (std)	120
____ **11-30083**	No. 520 Floodlight Car, green, nickel trim (std)	130
____ **11-30087**	No. 516 Hopper Car, red, brass trim (std)	100
____ **11-30088**	AF 4018 Automobile Car, white/blue	150
____ **11-30089**	AF 4020 Stock Car, blue	150
____ **11-30090**	AF 4006 Hopper Car, red	150
____ **11-30091**	AF 4017 Sand Car, green	150
____ **11-30092**	AF 4010 Tank Car, cream/blue	150
____ **11-30093**	AF 4022 Machine Car, orange	110
____ **11-30094**	AF 4021 Caboose, red	160
____ **11-30095**	AF 4018 Automobile Car, orange/maroon	130
____ **11-30096**	AF 4022 Machine Car, blue	110
____ **11-30097**	AF 4022 Machine Car, orange/green	110
____ **11-30098**	AF 4010 Tank Car, blue	130
____ **11-30099**	AF 4017 Sand Car, maroon	130
____ **11-30100**	AF 4006 Hopper Car, green	130
____ **11-30101**	AF 4020 Stock Car, cream/maroon	130
____ **11-30102**	AF 4021 Caboose, red/maroon	140
____ **11-30103**	AF 4021 Caboose, cream/red	140
____ **11-30104**	No. 215 Tank Car (std)	130
____ **11-30105**	No. 214R Refrigerator Car (std)	130
____ **11-30107**	No. 214R Altoona 36 Lager Refrigerator Car (std)	130
____ **11-30108**	No. 214R Budweiser Refrigerator Car (std)	140
____ **11-30109**	No. 214R Burp-oh Beer Refrigerator Car (std)	130
____ **11-30110**	No. 214R Hood's Dairy Refrigerator Car (std)	130
____ **11-30111**	No. 214R Old Reading Refrigerator Car (std)	130
____ **11-30112**	No. 214R Palisades Park Refrigerator Car (std)	130
____ **11-30113**	No. 214 Circus Boxcar (std)	130
____ **11-30114**	No. 214 M&M's Christmas Boxcar (std)	140

11-30115	No. 215 Budweiser Tank Car (std)	140____
11-30116	No. 215 Freedomland Tank Car (std)	130____
11-30117	No. 215 Gulf Tank Car (std)	130____
11-30118	No. 215 Tropicana Tank Car (std)	130____
11-30119	No. 513 UP Cattle Car (std)	100____
11-30120	No. 513 WM Cattle Car (std)	100____
11-30121	No. 514 B&O Boxcar (std)	100____
11-30122	No. 514 State of Maine Boxcar (std)	120____
11-30123	No. 514R PFE Refrigerator Car (std)	100____
11-30124	No. 514R Tropicana Refrigerator Car (std)	120____
11-30125	No. 515 Anheuser Busch Tank Car (std)	110____
11-30126	No. 515 Hooker Chemicals Tank Car (std)	100____
11-30127	No. 516 Blue Coal Hopper Car (std)	100____
11-30128	No. 516 Waddell Coal Hopper Car (std)	120____
11-30129	No. 517 Pennsylvania Caboose (std)	120____
11-30130	No. 517 Santa Fe Caboose (std)	140____
11-30131	No. 215 Lionel Lines Tank Car (std)	130____
11-30134	No. 515 Christmas Tank Car (std)	100____
11-30136	No. 214 Christmas Boxcar (std)	150____
11-30137	No. 214 UP Boxcar (std)	150____
11-30138	No. 214R Horlacher's Brewing Refrigerator Car (std)	150____
11-30139	No. 214R Coors Refrigerator Car (std)	140____
11-30140	No. 215 Keystone Gasoline Tank Car (std)	150____
11-30141	No. 215 Texaco Tank Car (std)	150____
11-30142	No. 216 Peabody Hopper Car (std)	130____
11-30143	No. 216 Pennsylvania Power & Light Hopper Car (std)	130____
11-30144	No. 213 Cattle Car (std)	130____
11-30146	No. 217 Jersey Central Caboose (std)	140____
11-30147	No. 214 Jersey Central Boxcar (std)	130____
11-30148	No. 214 U.S. Army Boxcar (std)	130____
11-30149	No. 215 MTH/Lionel Tank Car	130____
11-30150	No. 212 Lionel Lines Gondola (std)	130____
11-30151	No. 212 Circus Gondola (std)	130____
11-30152	No. 212 NYC Gondola (std)	130____
11-30153	No. 214 MKT Boxcar (std)	150____
11-30154	No. 214 NYC Boxcar (std)	150____
11-30155	No. 215 C&O Tank Car (std)	150____
11-30156	No. 215 Shell Tank Car (std)	150____
11-30157	No. 216 Hopper Car, red, brass trim (std)	150____
11-30158	No. 216 LV Hopper Car (std)	150____
11-30159	No. 217 Pennsylvania Caboose (std)	160____
11-30160	No. 219 B&O Crane Car (std)	220____
11-30161	No. 219 Crane Car, ivory/red (std)	400____
11-30162	No. 219 Lionel Lines Crane Car (std)	220____
11-30163	No. 219 Crane Car, red/silver (std)	400____
11-30164	No. 514R Christmas Refrigerator Car (std)	120____
11-30168	No. 515 PRR Tank Car (std)	120____

____ **11-30169**	No. 515 Texaco Tank Car (std)	120
____ **11-30170**	No. 515 Esso Tank Car (std)	120
____ **11-30180**	No. 219 Crane Car, black/cream (std)	220
____ **11-30182**	No. 217 NYC Illuminated Caboose (std)	160
____ **11-30185**	No. 212 Gondola, pea green (std)	150
____ **11-30193**	No. 514R Altoona Brewing Refrigerator Car (std)	120
____ **11-30194**	No. 514R PFE Refrigerator Car (std)	120
____ **11-30195**	No. 514R REA Refrigerator Car (std)	120
____ **11-30196**	No. 514R Robin Hood Beer Refrigerator Car (std)	120
____ **11-30197**	No. 514 UP Boxcar (std)	120
____ **11-30198**	No. 514 Santa Fe Boxcar (std)	120
____ **11-30199**	No. 514 PRR Boxcar (std)	120
____ **11-30200**	No. 514 B&O Boxcar (std)	120
____ **11-30201**	No. 215-3 Shell 3-D Tank Car (std)	150
____ **11-30202**	No. 215-3 Mazda Lamps 3-D Tank Car (std)	150
____ **11-30203**	No. 215-3 Celanese Chemicals 3-D Tank Car (std)	150
____ **11-30204**	No. 215-3 Clark Oil 3-D Tank Car (std)	150
____ **11-30205**	No. 215-2 Sterling Fuels 2-D Tank Car (std)	150
____ **11-30206**	No. 215-2 Philadelphia Quartz 2-D Tank Car (std)	150
____ **11-30207**	No. 215-2 Cook's Paints 2-D Tank Car (std)	150
____ **11-30208**	No. 215-2 Hercules 2-D Tank Car (std)	150
____ **11-30209**	No. 216-1 PRR Covered Hopper (std)	150
____ **11-30210**	No. 216-1 P&LE Covered Hopper (std)	150
____ **11-30211**	No. 216-1 Jack Frost Covered Hopper (std)	150
____ **11-30212**	No. 216-1 GE Lamps Covered Hopper (std)	150
____ **11-30213**	No. 212-1 PRR Covered Gondola Car (std)	150
____ **11-30214**	No. 212-1 Covered Gondola Car (std)	150
____ **11-30215**	No. 212-1 NYC Covered Gondola Car (std)	150
____ **11-30216**	No. 212-1 GN Covered Gondola Car (std)	150
____ **11-30217**	No. 211 Flatcar with wheel load (std)	150
____ **11-30218**	No. 211 Altoona Shops Flatcar with wheel load (std)	150
____ **11-30219**	No. 211 Baldwin Flatcar with wheel load (std)	150
____ **11-30220**	No. 211 Lima Flatcar with wheel load (std)	150
____ **11-30221**	No. 217-1 Chessie Bay Window Caboose (std)	160
____ **11-30222**	No. 217-1 UP Bay Window Caboose (std)	160
____ **11-30223**	No. 217-1 NYC Bay Window Caboose (std)	160
____ **11-30224**	No. 217-1 Long Island Bay Window Caboose (std)	160
____ **11-30225**	PRR Automobile Car (std)	150
____ **11-30226**	NYC Automobile Car (std)	150
____ **11-30227**	Shell Tank Car (std)	150
____ **11-30228**	Gulf Tank Car (std)	150
____ **11-30229**	Blue Coal Hopper (std)	150
____ **11-30230**	Waddell Coal Hopper (std)	150
____ **11030231**	NYC Caboose (std)	160
____ **11-30232**	PRR Caboose (std)	160
____ **11-30234**	No. 514 Boxcar (std)	120
____ **11-30235**	No. 514R Refrigerator Car (std)	120

11-30237	No. 217 LL Illuminated Caboose, orange (std)	160____
11-30238	No. 217 Lionel Illuminated Caboose, pea green (std)	160____
11-30239	No. 217 LL Illuminated Caboose, olive green (std)	160____
11-30240	No. 214R Refrigerator Car, white/blue (std)	150____
11-30241	No. 214R Refrigerator Car, ivory/peacock (std)	150____
11-30242	No. 514 Boxcar, 1923 catalog cover (std)	150____
11-30243	No. 514 Boxcar, 1924 catalog cover (std)	150____
11-30244	No. 514 Boxcar, 1925 catalog cover (std)	150____
11-30245	No. 514 Boxcar, 1926 catalog cover (std)	150____
11-30246	No. 212-1 UP Covered Gondola Car (std)	150____
11-30247	No. 212-1 Reading Covered Gondola Car (std)	150____
11-40001	Presidential Passenger Set, blue (std)	1200____
11-40002	No. 339 Pullman Car, green (std)	150____
11-40003	No. 332 Mail/Baggage Car, green (std)	150____
11-40004	No. 332 LV Ithaca Baggage Car	150____
11-40005	No. 339 LV Easton Passenger Coach	150____
11-40007	300 Series 3-Car Passenger Set, blue/silver (std)	400____
11-40009	3-Car State Passenger Set, green (std)	1200____
11-40010	Pennsylvania State Baggage Car, green (std)	400____
11-40011	Illinois State Coach, green (std)	400____
11-40012	Solarium State Car, green (std)	400____
11-40013	MILW 3-Car State Passenger Set (std)	1200____
11-40014	MILW State Baggage Car (std)	400____
11-40015	MILW State Passenger Coach (std)	400____
11-40016	MILW Solarium State Car (std)	400____
11-40017	3-Car Showroom Passenger Set, green (std)	1500____
11-40018	Showroom Passenger Coach, green (std)	500____
11-40019	3-Car Showroom Passenger Set, zinc chromate (std)	1500____
11-40020	Showroom Passenger Coach, zinc chromate (std)	500____
11-40021	3-Car Blue Comet Passenger Set (std)	1100____
11-40022	No. 432 Olbers Blue Comet Baggage Car (std)	380____
11-40023	No. 419 Tuttle Blue Comet Passenger Coach (std)	380____
11-40024	No. 4343 Diner Car	180____
11-40025	339 Series Passenger Car, pink	130____
11-40026	332 Series Baggage Car, pink	130____
11-40027	309 Series 3-Car State Passenger Set, brown (std)	1200____
11-40028	Pennsylvania State Baggage Car, brown (std)	400____
11-40029	Illinois State Passenger Coach, brown (std)	400____
11-40030	Solarium State Car, brown (std)	400____
11-40031	State 3-Car Passenger Set, blue (std)	1200____
11-40032	Pennsylvania State Baggage Car, blue (std)	400____
11-40033	Illinois State Passenger Coach, blue (std)	400____
11-40034	Solarium State Car, blue (std)	400____
11-40035	309 Series 3-Car Passenger Set, blue (std)	400____
11-40036	309 Series 3-Car Passenger Set, green (std)	400____
11-40037	309 Series 3-Car Passenger Set, red (std)	400____
11-40038	No. 309 Passenger Coach (std)	140____

____ **11-40039**	No. 310 Baggage Car (std)	140
____ **11-40040**	3-Car Blue Comet Passenger Set, nickel trim (std)	1100
____ **11-40041**	No. 432 Blue Comet Baggage Car, nickel trim (std)	380
____ **11-40042**	No. 423 Blue Comet Passenger Coach, nickel trim (std)	380
____ **11-40043**	3-Car Stephen Girard Set, brass trim	600
____ **11-40044**	No. 4427 Stephen Girard Baggage Car, brass trim	200
____ **11-40045**	No. 427 Stephen Girard Passenger Coach, brass trim	200
____ **11-40046**	3-Car Stephen Girard Set, nickel trim	600
____ **11-40047**	No. 4427 Stephen Girard Baggage Car, nickel trim	200
____ **11-40048**	No. 427 Stephen Girard Passenger Coach, nickel trim	200
____ **11-40049**	No. 418 3-Car Passenger Set, green, brass trim (std)	600
____ **11-40050**	No. 418 Diner, green, brass trim (std)	200
____ **11-40051**	No. 418 3-Car Passenger Set, orange, brass trim (std)	600
____ **11-40052**	No. 418 Diner, orange brass trim (std)	200
____ **11-40053**	No. 418 3-Car Passenger Set, Mojave, brass trim (std)	600
____ **11-40054**	No. 418 Diner, Mojave, brass trim (std)	200
____ **11-40055**	No. 418 3-Car Passenger Set, pink, brass trim (std)	600
____ **11-40056**	No. 418 Diner, pink, brass trim (std)	200
____ **11-40057**	Lionel 3-Car Pullman Passenger Set (std)	700
____ **11-40058**	Pennsylvania 3-Car Pullman Passenger Set (std)	700
____ **11-40059**	No. 332 Baggage Car (std)	140
____ **11-40060**	No. 339 Passenger Coach (std)	140
____ **11-40061**	Great Northern State 3-Car Passenger Set (std)	1200
____ **11-40062**	Great Northern State Baggage Car (std)	430
____ **11-40063**	Great Northern State Passenger Coach (std)	430
____ **11-40064**	Great Northern State Solarium Car (std)	430
____ **11-40065**	Presidential 3-Car Passenger Set (std)	1200
____ **11-40066**	Presidential Baggage Car (std)	430
____ **11-40067**	Presidential Passenger Coach (std)	430
____ **11-40068**	Red Comet 3-Car Passenger Set (std)	1140
____ **11-40069**	Red Comet Baggage Car (std)	400
____ **11-40070**	Red Comet Passenger Coach (std)	400
____ **11-40072**	President's Passenger Set, red (std)	1300
____ **11-40073**	No. 310 Baggage Car (std)	140
____ **11-40074**	No. 309 Passenger Coach (std)	140
____ **11-40076**	Green Comet 3-Car Passenger Set (std)	1140
____ **11-40077**	NYC 3-Car Passenger Set, brown (std)	700
____ **11-40078**	General 3-Car Pullman Passenger Set (std)	700
____ **11-40079**	Green Comet Baggage Car (std)	400
____ **11-40080**	Green Comet Passenger Coach (std)	400
____ **11-40081**	Showroom 3-Car Passenger Set, brown (std)	1600
____ **11-40082**	Showroom Passenger Coach, brown (std)	540
____ **11-40083**	Showroom 3-Car Passenger Set, orange (std)	1600
____ **11-40084**	Showroom Passenger Coach, orange (std)	540
____ **11-40095**	3-car B&O Pullman Passenger Set (std)	700
____ **11-40096**	3-car Long Island Pullman Passenger Set (std)	700
____ **11-40097**	3-car Strasburg Pullman Passenger Set (std)	700

LIONEL CORPORATION TINPLATE

Retail

11-40098	3-car PRR Pullman Passenger Set (std)	700____
11-40099	3-car MILW State Passenger Set (std)	1200____
11-40100	MILW State Solarium Car (std)	400____
11-40101	MILW State Passenger Coach (std)	400____
11-40102	MILW State Baggage Car (std)	400____
11-40103	3-car PRR State Passenger Set (std)	1200____
11-40104	PRR State Solarium Car (std)	400____
11-40105	PRR State Passenger Coach (std)	400____
11-40106	PRR State Baggage Car (std)	400____
11-40107	3-car State Passenger Set, two-tone brown (std)	1200____
11-40108	State Solarium Car, two-tone brown (std)	400____
11-40109	State Passenger Coach, two-tone brown (std)	400____
11-40110	State Baggage Car, two-tone brown (std)	400____
11-40111	3-car Great Northern Presidential Set (std)	1200____
11-40112	Great Northern Presidential Diner (std)	400____
11-40113	3-car Lehigh Valley Presidential Set (std)	1200____
11-40114	Lehigh Valley Presidential Diner (std)	400____
11-40115	3-car New Haven State Passenger Set (std)	1200____
11-40116	New Haven State Solarium Car (std)	400____
11-40117	New Haven State Passenger Coach (std)	400____
11-40118	New Haven State Baggage Car (std)	400____
11-60033	No. 607 Christmas Coach Passenger	90____
11-70002	No. 2814 Boxcar, cream/orange	80____
11-70003	No. 2814R Refrigerator Car, white/brown	80____
11-70004	No. 2814R Christmas Refrigerator Car	80____
11-70005	No. 2814R Refrigerator Car, Ivory/peacock	80____
11-70006	No. 2815 Tank Car, silver	90____
11-70007	No. 2815 Tank Car, orange, nickel trim	80____
11-70008	No. 2817 Caboose, red/green	90____
11-70009	No. 2815 Christmas Tank Car	80____
11-70010	No. 2813 Cattle Car, cream/maroon	80____
11-70011	No. 2812 Gondola, apple green	80____
11-70012	No. 2811 Flatcar, silver	70____
11-70013	No. 2816 Hopper Car, red	90____
11-70014	No. 2816 Hopper Car, olive green	80____
11-70015	No. 2820 Floodlight Car, terra-cotta	90____
11-70016	No. 2815 Sunoco Tank Car	80____
11-70017	No. 2810 Crane Car, terra-cotta/maroon	180____
11-70018	No. 2811 Flatcar, maroon	70____
11-70019	No. 2814R MTH/Lionel Refrigerator Car	90____
11-70024	No. 2814 Christmas Boxcar	80____
11-70025	No. 2814 Boxcar, cream/orange	80____
11-70026	No. 2814 Boxcar, orange/brown	80____
11-70027	No. 2814 Boxcar, white brown	80____
11-70028	No. 2816 Christmas Hopper Car	80____
11-70029	No. 2817 Caboose, red/brown	90____
11-70030	No. 2812 Gondola, dark orange	70____

Retail

11-70031	No. 813 Cattle Car, brown	80
11-70032	No. 2816 Hopper Car, black	80
11-70033	No. 2820 Floodlight Car, light green	90
11-70034	No. 2814R Refrigerator Car, white/brown	80
11-70035	No. 2651 Flatcar, green	60
11-70036	No. 2652 Gondola, red	60
11-70037	No. 2653 Hopper Car, black	60
11-70038	No. 2654 Shell Tank Car, yellow	60
11-70039	No. 2655 Boxcar, yellow/brown	60
11-70040	No. 2656 Cattle Car, red/brown	60
11-70041	No. 2657 Caboose, red/maroon	60
11-70042	No. 659 Dump Car, green	60
11-70043	No. 659 Dump Car, orange	60
11-70045	No. 2814 Boxcar, yellow/brown	90
11-70046	No. 2817 Caboose, red	100
11-70047	No. 2814 Christmas Boxcar	80
11-70048	No. 2815 Christmas Tank Car	90
11-70049	No. 2814R Refrigerator Car, silver frame	90
11-70050	No. 2814R Refrigerator Car, black frame	80
11-70051	No. 2817 Caboose, red/maroon	90
11-70052	No. 2654 Shell Tank Car, gray	60
11-70053	No. 2654 Shell Tank Car, black	60
11-70054	No. 2653 Hopper Car, green	60
11-70055	No. 2653 Hopper Car, red	60
11-70056	No. 2655 Boxcar, yellow/maroon	60
11-70057	No. 2655 Boxcar, yellow/brown	60
11-70058	No. 2656 Cattle Car, gray/red	60
11-70059	No. 2656 Cattle Car, burnt orange	60
11-70060	No. 659 Dump Car, blue	60
11-70061	No. 900 Ammunition Car, gray	60
11-70064	No. 2814R Hoods Dairy Refrigerator Car	80
11-70065	No. 2814R Isaly's Refrigerator Car	80
11-70066	No. 2814R Sheffield Farms Refrigerator Car	90
11-70067	No. 2814R Palisades Park Refrigerator Car	80
11-70068	No. 2654 UP Tank Car, yellow	60
11-70069	No. 2654 M&M's Tank Car	70
11-70070	No. 2654 Baker's Chocolate Tank Car	60
11-70071	No. 2654 Budweiser Tank Car	70
11-70072	No. 2655 Delaware & Hudson Boxcar	60
11-70073	No. 2655 Railbox Boxcar	60
11-70074	M&M's Christmas Boxcar	70
11-70076	No. 2654 LL Tank Car, orange/blue	70
11-70078	No. 900 Ammunition Car, green	60
11-70079	No. 2820 LL Floodlight Car, black/orange	120
11-70080	No. 2820 U.S. Army Air Corps Floodlight Car	120
11-70081	No. 2810 Crane Car, yellow/red	180
11-70082	No. 2810 Crane Car, white/red	180

11-70083	No. 2660 Crane Car, cream/red	100____
11-70084	No. 2660 Crane Car, terra-cotta/maroon	100____
11-70085	No. 2660 Crane Car, yellow/red	100____
11-70086	No. 2660 Crane Car, peacock/dark green	100____
11-70087	No. 2813 LL Cattle Car, cream/tuscan	90____
11-70088	No. 2813 LL Cattle Car, terra cotta/pea green	90____
11-70089	No. 2810 B&O Crane Car	180____
11-70091	No. 2815 LL Tank Car, cream, orange/blue	80____
11-70092	No. 2810 Crane Car, blue	180____
11-70095	No. 2820 LL Floodlight Car, black/peacock	120____
11-70096	No. 2814 Southern Boxcar	90____
11-70097	No. 2814 Chessie Boxcar	90____
11-70098	No. 2814 Blue Comet Boxcar, nickel trim	90____
11-70099	No. 2814 Blue Comet Boxcar, brass trim	90____
11-70102	No. 2654 Mobilgas Tank Car	70____
11-70103	No. 2654 Esso Tank Car	70____
11-70104	No. 2653 Blue Coal Hopper	70____
11-70105	No. 2653 Peabody Hopper	70____
11-70106	No. 2655 Altoona Brewing Boxcar	70____
11-70107	No. 2655 Hood's Grade A Milk Boxcar	70____
11-70108	No. 2655 LL Boxcar	70____
11-70109	No. 2657 LL Caboose, green/red	70____
11-70110	No. 2657 LL Caboose, orange/red	70____
11-70113	No. 2814 PRR Boxcar	90____
11-70114	No. 2814 ATSF Grand Canyon Boxcar	90____
11-70115	No. 2814 Long Island Boxcar	90____
11-70116	No. 2814 Alaska Boxcar	90____
11-70117	No. 2814R M. K. Goetz Brewing Refrigerator Car	90____
11-70118	No. 2814R Gerber Refrigerator Car	90____
11-70119	No. 2814R Roberts & Oake Meats Refrigerator Car	90____
11-70120	No. 2814R Sullivan's Packing Refrigerator Car	90____
11-70121	No. 2816 Western Maryland Coal Car	90____
11-70122	No. 2816 P&LE Coal Car	90____
11-70123	No. 2816 Waddell Mining Coal Car	90____
11-70124	No. 2816 Blue Coal Car	90____
11-70125	No. 2815 Clark Oil Tank Car	90____
11-70126	No. 2815 Celanese Chemicals Tank Car	90____
11-70127	No. 2815 Shell Tank Car	90____
11-70128	No. 2815 Cook's Paints Tank Car	90____
11-70129	No. 2817 C&O Caboose	100____
11-70130	No. 2817 Long Island Caboose	100____
11-70131	No. 2817 Southern Caboose	100____
11-70132	No. 2817 Jersey Central Caboose	100____
11-70133	No. 2814R Gerber Refrigerator Car	90____
11-70144	No. 2815 Shell Tank Car	90____
11-70154	No. 2814 ATSF Grand Canyon Boxcar	90____
11-70156	No. 2814R LL Refrigerator Car, orange/blue	90____

____	11-70157	No. 2814R LL Blue Comet Refrigerator Car	90
____	11-70158	No. 2817 Lionel Lines Caboose, orange/blue	100
____	11-70159	No. 2817 Lionel Lines Caboose, red/brown	100
____	11-70160	No. 2817 NYC Caboose	100
____	11-70161	No. 2817 Jersey Central Blue Comet Caboose	100
____	11-70164	No. 2814R LL Refrigerator Car, red/brown	90
____	11-80001	2600 Series 4-Car Blue Comet Passenger Set	430
____	11-80002	UP Articulated Baggage Car, silver	150
____	11-80003	UP Articulated Baggage Car, yellow	150
____	11-80004	UP Articulated Coach, silver	150
____	11-80005	UP Articulated Coach, yellow	150
____	11-80006	No. 2613 Series Pullman Coach, blue	110
____	11-80007	2600 Series 3-Car Passenger Set, red	300
____	11-80008	2600 Series 3-Car Passenger Set, green	300
____	11-80009	Milwaukee Road Articulated Baggage Car	150
____	11-80010	Milwaukee Road Articulated Coach	150
____	11-80011	Articulated Streamliner Baggage Car	150
____	11-80012	Articulated Streamliner Coach	150
____	11-80013	No. 2613 Series Pullman Coach, red	100
____	11-80014	No. 2613 Series Pullman Coach, green	100
____	11-80015	No. 605 Christmas Baggage Car	90
____	11-80016	710 Series 3-Car Passenger Set, blue	350
____	11-80017	No. 710 Series Baggage Car, blue	120
____	11-80018	No. 710 Series Passenger Coach, blue	120
____	11-80019	710 Series 3-Car Passenger Set, orange	350
____	11-80020	No. 710 Series Baggage Car, orange	120
____	11-80021	No. 710 Series Passenger Coach, orange	120
____	11-80022	710 Series 3-Car Passenger Set, red	350
____	11-80023	No. 710 Series Baggage Car, red	120
____	11-80024	No. 710 Series Passenger Coach, red	120
____	11-80025	No. 1695 3-Car Passenger Set, blue/silver	350
____	11-80026	No. 1685 Passenger Car, blue/silver	120
____	11-80027	1695 Series 3-Car Passenger Set, red/maroon	380
____	11-80028	No. 1695 Passenger Coach, red/maroon	130
____	11-80029	City of Denver Coach, yellow/green	110
____	11-80030	City of Denver Coach, green	110
____	11-80031	No. 605 Baggage Car	90
____	11-80032	No. 607 Passenger Coach	90
____	11-80034	No. 2613 NYC Pullman Car, LCCA 2012 Convention	100
____	11-80036	No. 605 Red Comet Baggage Car	90
____	11-80039	600 Series 3-Car Red Comet Passenger Set	270
____	11-80040	2600 Series 4-Car Blue Comet Passenger Set, brass trim	430
____	11-80041	No. 2613 Pullman Coach, brass trim	110
____	11-80042	Flying Yankee Chrome Coach	110
____	11-80047	710 Series 3-Car NH Passenger Set	400
____	11-80048	710 Series 3-Car GN Passenger Set	400

LIONEL CORPORATION TINPLATE

Retail

11-80049	2600 Series 4-Car Chessie Passenger Set	430____
11-80050	2600 Series 4-Car Southern Passenger Set	430____
11-80051	No. 2613 Chessie Pullman Coach	110____
11-80052	No. 2613 Southern Pullman Coach	110____
11-80053	No. 710 NH Baggage Car	140____
11-80054	No. 710 NH Passenger Coach	140____
11-80055	No. 710 GN Baggage Car	140____
11-80056	No. 710 GN Passenger Coach	140____
11-80059	710 Series 3-car MILW Passenger Set	400____
11-80060	No. 713 MILW Baggage Car	140____
11-80061	No. 710 MILW Passenger Coach	140____
11-80062	710 Series 3-car PRR Passenger Set	400____
11-80063	No. 713 PRR Baggage Car	140____
11-80064	No. 710 PRR Passenger Coach	140____
11-80065	2600 Series 4-car LL Passenger Set, blue, nickel trim	430____
11-80066	2600 Series 4-car LL Passenger Set, blue, brass trim	430____
11-80067	2600 Series 4-car LL Passenger Set, orange/blue	430____
11-80068	2600 Series 4-car NW Passenger Set	430____
11-80069	2600 Series 4-car UP Passenger Set, yellow	430____
11-90001	No. 300 Hellgate Bridge, green/cream	500____
11-90002	No. 300 Hellgate Bridge, silver/white	500____
11-90003	No. 092 Signal Tower, cream/red	70____
11-90006	No. 437 Switch Tower	280____
11-90007	No. 155 Freight Shed	330____
11-90008	No. 116 Passenger Station	400____
11-90009	No. 438 Signal Tower	150____
11-90010	No. 192 Villa Set	200____
11-90011	No. 191 Villa	70____
11-90012	No. 54 Street Lamp Set, green	45____
11-90013	No. 54 Street Lamp Set, red	45____
11-90014	No. 56 Gas Lamp Set, green	35____
11-90015	No. 56 Gas Lamp Set, maroon	35____
11-90016	No. 57 Corner Lamp Set, black	40____
11-90017	No. 57 Corner Lamp Set, red	35____
11-90018	No. 58 Lamp Set, single arc, cream	35____
11-90019	No. 58 Lamp Set, single arc, dark green	35____
11-90020	No. 59 Gooseneck Lamp Set, black	40____
11-90021	No. 59 Gooseneck Lamp Set, maroon	40____
11-90022	No. 1184 Bungalow (std)	200____
11-90023	No. 1184 Bungalow (std)	200____
11-90024	No. 1189 Villa (std)	300____
11-90025	No. 1191 Villa (std)	300____
11-90026	No.165 Magnetic Crane	300____
11-90027	No. 441 Weighing Station (std)	380____
11-90028	No. 69 Operating Warning Bell	50____
11-90029	No. 78 Automatic Control Signal (std)	70____
11-90030	No. 79 Flashing Railroad Signal	70____

LIONEL CORPORATION TINPLATE

_____	**11-90031** No. 80 Operating Semaphore	70
_____	**11-90032** No. 63 Lamp Post Set, aluminum	50
_____	**11-90033** No. 87 Railroad Crossing Signal	50
_____	**11-90034** No. 92 Floodlight Tower Set	160
_____	**11-90035** No. 94 High Tension Tower Set	150
_____	**11-90036** No. Automatic Block Signal (std)	70
_____	**11-90037** No. 163 Freight Accessory Set, green cart	100
_____	**11-90038** No. 163 Freight Accessory Set, orange cart	100
_____	**11-90039** No. 208 Tools and Chest, dark gray	80
_____	**11-90040** No. 208 Tools and Chest, silver	80
_____	**11-90041** No. 550 Miniature Figures	100
_____	**11-90042** No. 64 Lamp Post Set, light green	30
_____	**11-90043** No. 85 Race Car Set	700
_____	**11-90044** Straight Race Car Track Section	20
_____	**11-90045** Inside Curve Race Car Track Section	20
_____	**11-90046** Outside Curve Race Car Track Section	20
_____	**11-90047** No. 55 Airplane & No. 49 Airport Set with mat	800
_____	**11-90048** No. 49 Airport Mat	60
_____	**11-90049** No. 90 Flagpole	50
_____	**11-90050** No. 205 Merchandise Containers, 3 pieces (std)	130
_____	**11-90052** No. 442 Diner	160
_____	**11-90053** No. 43 Runabout Boat, red/white	450
_____	**11-90054** No. 44 Speed Boat	450
_____	**11-90055** No. 71 Telegraph Post Set, gray/red	80
_____	**11-90056** Teardrop Lamp Set, pea green	20
_____	**11-90057** No. 46 Crossing Gate	40
_____	**11-90058** Small Oil Drum Set	20
_____	**11-90060** No. 115 Passenger Station, beige/pea green	300
_____	**11-90061** No. 115 Passenger Station, cream, orange/blue	300
_____	**11-90062** No. 134 Lionel City Station with stop	330
_____	**11-90063** No. 444 Roundhouse Section	500
_____	**11-90064** No. 200 Turntable, red/black	200
_____	**11-90065** No. 89 Flagpole, blue base (std)	50
_____	**11-90066** No. 89 Flagpole, white base (std)	50
_____	**11-90067** No. 89 American Flag Pole, white base (std)	50
_____	**11-90068** Operating Industrial Crane	350
_____	**11-90069** Operating Industrial Crane, TCA 2010 Convention	350
_____	**11-90070** No. 552 Diner, orange/blue	200
_____	**11-90071** No. 552 Diner, white/blue	200
_____	**11-90072** No. 911 Country Estate, cream/red	140
_____	**11-90073** No. 911 Country Estate, red/green	140
_____	**11-90074** No. 912 Suburban Home, ivory/peacock	140
_____	**11-90075** No. 912 Suburban Home, mustard/green	140
_____	**11-90076** No. 913 Landscaped Bungalow, white/maroon	110
_____	**11-90077** No. 913 Landscaped Bungalow, light green/peacock	110
_____	**11-90078** AF No. 2050 Old Glory Flag Pole	100
_____	**11-90079** No. 43 Runabout Boat, orange/blue	400

11-90084	No. 57 Lamp Post Set, Lionel & American Flyer Aves.	40____
11-90085	No. 57 Lamp Post Set, orange, 21st St. & Fifth Ave.	40____
11-90086	AF No. 2013 Corner Lamp Set, yellow	40____
11-90087	No. 440 Signal Bridge and Control Panel, silver	300____
11-90088	No. 440 Signal Bridge and Control Panel, gray	300____
11-90089	No. 436 Power Station, cream	150____
11-90090	No. 436 Power Station, terra-cotta	150____
11-90094	No. 438 Signal Tower	160____
11-90095	No. 116 Passenger Station	400____
11-90096	No. 1184 Bungalow, gray/green	200____
11-90097	No. 1184 Bungalow, white/maroon	200____
11-90098	No. 1189 Villa (std)	300____
11-90099	No. 1191 Villa (std)	300____
11-90100	No. 442 Diner	160____
11-90101	No. 54 Lamp Post Set, pea green	45____
11-90102	No. 54 Lamp Post Set, state brown	45____
11-90103	No. 58 Lamp Post Set, peacock	35____
11-90104	No. 58 Lamp Post Set, orange	35____
11-90105	No. 59 Lamp Post Set, dark green	40____
11-90106	No. 59 Lamp Post Set, light green	40____
11-90107	No. 92 Floodlight Tower Set	170____
11-90108	No. 79 Flashing Signal	70____
11-90109	No. 69 Warning Signal	50____
11-90110	No. 94 High Tension Tower Set	170____
11-90111	No. 57 Corner Lamp Set, orange, Lionel	40____
11-90112	No. 57 Corner Lamp Set, blue, Lionel	40____
11-90113	No. 57 Corner Lamp Set, blue/yellow	40____
11-90114	No. 152 Operating Crossing Gate	40____
11-90115	No. 153 Operating Block Signal	40____
11-90116	No. 154 Highway Flashing Signal	40____
11-90117	No. 437 Switch Signal Tower, cream/orange	300____
11-90118	No. 437 Switch Signal Tower, terra-cotta/green	300____
11-90119	AF No. 4230 Roadside Flashing Signal	100____
11-90120	No. 200 Turntable, gray/green	200____
11-90121	No. 200 Turntable, orange/blue	200____
11-90122	No. 437 Switch Tower	280____
11-90123	No. 98 Coal Bunker	180____
11-90124	No. 550 Railroad Figure Set	100____
11-90125	No. 550 Railroad Figure Set	100____
11-90126	No. 205 3-piece Container Set, green (std)	130____
11-90127	No. 205 3-piece Container Set, black (std)	130____
11-90128	No. 205 3-piece Container Set, yellow (std)	130____
11-90129	No. 163 Freight Accessory Set, green/yellow	100____
11-90130	No. 163 Freight Accessory Set, peacock/orange	100____
11-99030	No. 25 Illuminated Track Bumpers (std)	60____

		Exc	Mint

Artrain

		Exc	Mint
9486	GTW "I Love Michigan" Boxcar, 87	155	305
17885	1-D Tank Car, 90	35	65
17891	GTW 20th Anniversary Boxcar, 91	40	75
19425	CSX Flatcar with "Art in Celebration" trailer, 96	40	80
52013	Norfolk Southern Flatcar with trailer, 92	115	230
52024	Conrail Auto Carrier, 93	45	90
52049	BN Gondola with coil covers, 94	30	55
52097	Chessie System Reefer, 95	20	35
52140	Union Pacific Bunk Car, 97	20	35
52165	SP Caboose "6256," 98	30	60
52197	Santa Fe GP38 Diesel, 99	125	245
52227	"Artistry in Space" Boxcar, 00	40	75
52255	30th Anniversary Flatcar with billboard, 01	50	100
52283	Paint Vat Car, 02	30	60
52331	Flatcar with "America's Railways" trailer, 03	75	150
52349	Hometown Art Museum Hopper, purple, 04	20	35
52350	"Native Views" 3-bay Hopper, 04	35	65
52411	"35 Years" 1-D Tank Car, 06	20	35

Carnegie Science Center

		Exc	Mint
25085	Miniature Railroad & Village Boxcar, 09	25	50
26750	Great Miniature Railroad & Village Boxcar, 99	40	80
36202	Great Miniature Railroad 80th Anniversary Boxcar, 00	55	110
36234	Great Miniature Railroad & Village Boxcar, 01	25	50
52277	Carnegie Science Center 10th Anniversary Boxcar, 02	30	60
52332	Miniature Railroad & Village Boxcar, 03	30	60
52362	Miniature Railroad & Village 50th Anniversary Boxcar, 04	25	50
52399	MRR&V Express Boxcar, 05	25	50
52432	Miniature Railroad & Village Boxcar, 06	25	50
52510	Miniature Railroad & Village Caboose, 08	25	50

Chicagoland Railroad Club

		Exc	Mint
52081	C&NW Boxcar "6464-555," 96	35	70
52101	BN Maxi-Stack Flatcar "64287" with containers, 97	40	80
52102	SF Extended Vision Caboose, red roof, 96	40	75
52103	SF Extended Vision Caboose, black roof, 96	40	75

CLUB CARS AND SPECIAL PRODUCTION

		Exc	Mint	
52120	Shedd Aquarium Car "3435-557," 98	50	100	____
52148	REA/Santa Fe Operating Boxcar, 99	35	70	____
52170	SP Operating Boxcar "52170-561," 99	35	65	____
52171	UP Operating Boxcar "52171-561," 99	35	65	____
52178	Burlington Operating Boxcar "52178-559," 00	35	70	____
52179	ACL Operating Boxcar "52179-560," 00	40	75	____
52215	C&NW 3-bay Cylindrical Hopper, 01	30	60	____
52216	C&NW Cylindrical Hopper, 02	30	60	____
52223	REA/Santa Fe Centennial Operating Boxcar, 00	35	65	____
52251	PRR Express Car, green, 01	35	65	____
52259	MP GP20 Diesel, traditional, 01	125	250	____
52292	PRR Express Car, tuscan red, 02	25	50	____
52327	City of Los Angeles Express Car, 04	35	65	____
52328	City of New Haven Express Car, 04	30	55	____
52363	City of New Orleans Express Car, 04	30	55	____
52364	City of New York Express Car, 04	35	65	____
52388	Great Northern Tool Car, 06	25	50	____
52389	Great Northern Crew Car, 06	25	50	____
52390	Great Northern Welding Caboose, 06	40	80	____
52391	Great Northern Racing Crew Car, 06	25	50	____
52426	City of San Francisco Express Car, 07	30	55	____
52427	Rock Island Rocket Express Car, 07	30	55	____
52475	Western Pacific UP Heritage Boxcar, 07	30	60	____

Classic Toy Trains

52126	MILW Boxcar "21027" with CTT Logo, 97	25	50	____

Dept. 56

16270	Heritage Village Boxcar "9796," 96	30	55	____
52096	Snow Village Boxcar "9756," 95	45	85	____
52139	Square Window Caboose "6256," 97	35	70	____
52157	Holly Brothers 3-D Tank Car, 98	45	85	____
52175	4-6-4 Hudson Locomotive, CC, 99	175	350	____
52199	4-bay Hopper "6756," 00	30	55	____
52254	"Happy Holidays" Gondola, 01	20	35	____

Eastwood Automobilia

16275	Radio Flyer Boxcar "16275," 96	25	50	____
16757	Johnny Lightning Auto Carrier "3435," 96	45	90	____
16985	Flatcar with 2 Ford vans, 97	25	50	____
52044	Vat Car, 95	15	30	____
52083	PRR Flatcar "21697" with tanker, 95	20	40	____
52130	Flatcar with Hot Wheels tanker, 97	30	60	____

Gadsden-Pacific Division
Toy Train Operating Museum

			Exc	Mint
____	17872	Anaconda Ore Car, 88	35	70
____	17878	Magma Ore Car, 89	30	55
____	17881	Phelps Dodge Ore Car, 90	20	40
____	17886	Cyprus Ore Car, 91	15	30
____	19961	Inspiration Consolidated Copper Ore Car, 92	15	30
____	52011	Tucson, Cornelia & Gila Bend Ore Car, 93	15	30
____	52027	Pinto Valley Mine Ore Car, 94	15	30
____	52071	Copper Basin Railway Ore Car, 95	15	30
____	52089	SMARRCO Ore Car, 96	10	25
____	52124	El Paso & Southwestern Ore Car, 97	20	40
____	52164	SP Ore Car, 98	20	35
____	52177	Arizona Southern Ore Car, 99	20	35
____	52213	BHP Copper Ore Car, 00	15	30
____	52248	Tombstone & Western Ore Car, 01	20	40
____	52279	Dragoon & Northern Ore Car, 02	25	50
____	52307	Twin Buttes Ore Car, 03	20	35
____	52358	AJO & Southwestern Ore Car, 04	25	45
____	52386	Ray & Gila Bend Ore Car, 05	24	45
____	52421	Calabasas, Tuscon & Northwestern Ore Car, 06	25	45
____	52473	Mascot & Western Ore Car, 07	45	90
____	52524	Tucson, Globe & Northern Ore Car, 08	20	40
____	52558	Port of Tucson Ore Car, 09	25	45
____	52579	Rosemont Copper Ore Car, 10	20	40
____	52588	ASARCO Ore Car, 11	20	40
____	58234	ASARCO Haden Smelter Ore Car, 15		45
____	58262	Union Pacific Ore Car, 16		45
____	58513	Freeport-McMoRan Ore Car, 12	20	40
____	58557	San Pedro & Southwestern Ore Car, 13	20	40
____	58583	Arizona Eastern Ore Car, 14	20	40

Houston Tinplate Operators Society

			Exc	Mint
____	8900	Sam Houston Mint Car, 00	60	120
____	8901	Miracle Petroleum 1-D Tank Car, 01	50	100
____	8902	USS Houston Submarine Car, 02	50	100
____	8903	Railway Express Boxcar, 03	50	100
____	8904	Lone Star Bay Window Caboose, 04	50	100
____	8999	Lone Star Aquarium Car, mermaid or trout, 99	50	100

Inland Empire Train Collectors Association

		Exc	Mint
1979	Boxcar, *79*	5	15 ____
1980	SP-type Caboose, *80*	5	15 ____
1981	Quad Hopper, *81*	5	15 ____
1982	3-D Tank Car, *82*	5	15 ____
1983	Reefer, *83*	5	15 ____
1986	Bunk Car, *86*	5	15 ____
7518	Carson City Mint Car, *84*	25	45 ____

Lionel Central Operating Lines

		Exc	Mint
1981	Boxcar, *81*	10	25 ____
1986	Work Caboose, shell only, *86*	5	15 ____
5724	Pennsylvania Bunk Car, *84*	20	40 ____
6508	Canadian Pacific Crane Car, *83*	20	40 ____
6907	NYC Wood-sided Caboose, *97*	25	50 ____
9184	Erie Bay Window Caboose, *82*	10	20 ____
9475	D&H "I Love NY" Boxcar, *85*	20	35 ____
16342	CSX Gondola with coil covers, *92*	10	20 ____
17221	NYC Boxcar, *95*	15	30 ____

Lionel Collectors Association of Canada

		Exc	Mint
5710	Canadian Pacific Reefer, *83*	110	215 ____
5714	Michigan Central Reefer, *85*	75	150 ____
6100	Ontario Northland Covered Quad Hopper, *82*	125	250 ____
8103	Toronto, Hamilton & Buffalo Boxcar, *81*	75	150 ____
8204	Algoma Central Boxcar, *82*	75	150 ____
8507/08	Canadian National F3 Diesel AA, shells only, *85*	200	400 ____
8912	Canada Southern Operating Hopper, *89*	50	95 ____
9413	Napierville Junction Boxcar, *80*	5	10 ____
9718	Canadian National Boxcar, *79*	10	20 ____
17893	BAOC 1-D Tank Car "914," *91*	60	120 ____
52004	Algoma Central Gondola "9215" with coil covers, *92*	45	90 ____
52005	Canadian National F3 Diesel B Unit "9517," *93*	15	30 ____
52006	Canadian Pacific Boxcar "930016" (std O), *93*	55	110 ____
52115	Wabash Lake Railway 2-tier Auto Carrier "9519," *98*		100 ____
52125	TH&B Gondola 2-pack, *99*	45	90 ____
86009	Canadian National Bunk Car, *86*	60	115 ____
87010	Canadian National Express Reefer, *87*	60	115 ____
88011	Canadian National Caboose (std O), *88*	250	500 ____
830005	Canadian National Boxcar, *83*	150	300 ____
840006	Canadian Wheat Board Covered Quad Hopper, *84*		165 ____
900013	Canadian National Flatcar with trailers, *90*	115	225 ____

Lionel Collectors Club of America

LCCA National Convention Cars

			Exc	Mint
____	6112	Commonwealth Edison Quad Hopper with coal, *83*	40	80
____	6323	Virginia Chemicals 1-D Tank Car, *86*	35	65
____	6567	Illinois Central Gulf Crane Car "100408," *85*	35	65
____	7403	LNAC Boxcar, *84*	10	25
____	9118	Corning Covered Quad Hopper, *74*	45	90
____	9155	Monsanto 1-D Tank Car, *75*	25	45
____	9159UP	UP Reefer, *10*	50	100
____	9212	Seaboard Coast Line Flatcar with trailers, *76*	15	30
____	9259	Southern Bay Window Caboose, *77*	15	40
____	9358	"Sands of Iowa" Covered Quad Hopper, *80*	20	35
____	9435	Central of Georgia Boxcar, *81*	15	30
____	9460	D&TS Automobile Boxcar, *82*	20	35
____	9701	Baltimore & Ohio Automobile Boxcar, *72*	85	170
____	9727	TA&G Boxcar, *73*	70	135
____	9728	Union Pacific Stock Car, *78*	10	25
____	9733	Airco Boxcar with tank car body, *79*	25	50
____	17870	East Camden & Highland Boxcar (std O), *87*	20	35
____	17873	Ashland Oil 3-D Tank Car, *88*	35	70
____	17876	Columbia, Newberry & Laurens Boxcar (std O), *89*	20	40
____	17880	D&RGW Wood-sided Caboose (std O), *90*	30	55
____	17887	Conrail Flatcar with Armstrong Tile trailer (std O), *91*	25	50
____	17888	Conrail Flatcar with Ford trailer (std O), *91*	40	80
____	17892	Conrail Flatcar with Armstrong and Ford Trailers (std O), *91*	70	140
____	17899	NASA Tank Car "190" (std O), *92*	25	50
____	27019	Imco PS-2 Covered Hopper, *09*	25	50
____	52023	D&TS 2-bay ACF Hopper "2601" (std O), *93*	20	40
____	52038	Southern Hopper "360794" with coal (std O), *94*	25	45
____	52074	Iowa Beef Packers Reefer "197095" (std O), *95*	15	30
____	52090	Pere Marquette DD Boxcar "71996" (std O), *96*	25	50
____	52110	CStPM&O Boxcar "71997" (std O), *97*	25	50
____	52151	Amtrak Baggage Boxcar "71998" (std O), *98*	35	65
____	52176	Fort Worth & Denver Boxcar "8277" (std O), *99*	30	55
____	52195	Double-stack Car with 2 containers, *00*	50	100
____	52244	Louisville & Nashville Horse Car "2001," *01*	25	50
____	52266	PRR "Coal Goes To War" Hopper "707025," *02*	45	85
____	52267	PRR "Coal Goes To War" Hopper "707026," *02*	45	90
____	52299	Las Vegas Mint Car, *03*	40	80
____	52343	MILW Milk Car, orange, *04*	80	160
____	52344	MILW Milk Car, blue, *04*	105	205
____	52393	MKT Speeder, yellow, nonpowered, *05*	10	20
____	52394	Frisco Speeder, red, powered, *05*	10	25

CLUB CARS AND SPECIAL PRODUCTION

		Exc	Mint
52395	Frisco Flatcar, silver, 05	10	25 ____
52396	Frisco Flatcar with 2 speeders, 05	65	125 ____
52412	UP Auxiliary Power Car, 06	30	55 ____
52455	C&NW/UP Tank Car, 07	55	110 ____
52491	PS-2 Covered Hopper 2-pack, 08	70	140 ____
52507	NYC Water Tower, 08	45	85 ____
52514	ATSF Mint Car with Gold, 09	140	275 ____
52543	BNSF Mechanical Reefer, 09	70	140 ____
52559	UP Cylindrical Hopper, 10	50	100 ____
52562	D&RGW Uranium Transport Mint Car, 10	115	230 ____
58254	Providence & Worcester Flatcar, 15	50	130 ____
58271	MP Maxi-Stack Container Car with containers, 16		100 ____
58509	Norfolk Southern Camouflage PS-1 Boxcar, 12	50	95 ____
58560	Southern Tennessean Boxcar, 13	45	90 ____
58576	Monon Operating Boxcar, 14	65	125 ____
72511	Alamo Mint Car, 11	75	150 ____
75511	Federal Reserve Mint Car, 11	100	200 ____

LCCA Meet Specials

		Exc	Mint
1130	Tender, 76	5	15 ____
6014-900	Frisco Boxcar (O27), 75	15	30 ____
6483	Jersey Central SP-type Caboose, 82	15	30 ____
9016	Chessie System Hopper (O27), 79	10	20 ____
9036	Mobilgas 1-D Tank Car (O27), 78	10	20 ____
9142	Republic Steel Gondola, green or blue, with canisters, 77	10	25 ____

Other LCCA Production

		Exc	Mint
4001	RJ Corman Boxcar, 99	40	80 ____
4002	RJ Corman Boxcar, 99	20	40 ____
6464-2002	Maddox Retirement Boxcar, 02	50	100 ____
8068	Rock Island GP20 Diesel, 80	60	120 ____
9739	D&RGW Boxcar, 78	10	25 ____
9771	Norfolk & Western Boxcar, 77	15	30 ____
14154	Water Tower with LCCA plaque, 04	45	90 ____
17174	Great Northern 3-bay Hopper, 03	10	25 ____
17234	Port Huron & Detroit Boxcar, 00	25	45 ____
17377	American Railway Express Reefer "302," 06	25	50 ____
17412	Gondola, blue, 02	15	30 ____
17895	LCCA Tractor, 91	10	20 ____
17896	Lancaster Lines Tractor, 91	15	30 ____
18090	D&RGW 4-6-2 Locomotive and Tender, 90	155	305 ____
18483	C&O Ballast Tamper, 07	40	75 ____
18490	UP Ballast Tamper, yellow, 06	65	125 ____
19998	"Seasons Greetings" Boxcar, 03	20	40 ____
26023	Flatcar with bulldozer, 04	30	55 ____
26024	Flatcar with scraper, 04	35	65 ____

CLUB CARS AND SPECIAL PRODUCTION

			Exc	Mint
____	**26049**	Speedboat Willie Flatcar with boat, *05*	25	45
____	**26132**	UP 1-D Tank Car, *06*	15	30
____	**26780**	Operating Giraffe Car, green or pink, *05*	35	70
____	**26791**	UP Chase Gondola, red, *03*	15	30
____	**26791**	Rio Grande Chase Gondola, black, *06*	15	30
____	**26795**	Mrs. O'Leary's Dairy Farm Stock Car, *07*	50	100
____	**26834**	"La Cosa Nostra Railway" Operating Ice Car, *07*	40	75
____	**29232**	Lenny the Lion Hi-Cube, signed by Lenny Dean, *98*	35	65
____	**52025**	Madison Hardware Tractor and Trailer, *93*	10	20
____	**52039**	"Track 29" Bumper, *94*	10	25
____	**52055**	SOVEX Tractor and Trailer, *94*	10	20
____	**52056**	Southern Tractor and Trailer, *94*	15	25
____	**52091**	Lenox Tractor and Trailer, *95*	5	15
____	**52092**	Iowa Interstate Tractor and Trailer, *95*	10	20
____	**52100**	Grand Rapids Station Platform, *98*	10	25
____	**52107**	On-track Pickup, orange, *96*	25	50
____	**52108**	On-track Van, blue, *96*	20	35
____	**52131**	Beechcraft Airplane, blue, *97*	10	25
____	**52138**	Beechcraft Airplane, orange, *97*	10	25
____	**52152**	Ben Franklin and Liberty Bell Reefer, *98*	60	120
____	**52153**	6414 Auto Set, 4-pack, *98*	35	70
____	**52206**	SD40 Diesel and Extended Vision Caboose, *00*	325	650
____	**52257**	"Season's Greetings" Gondola, *01*	20	35
____	**52273**	Flatcar with submarine, *02*	110	220
____	**52300**	Halloween General Train, *04*	180	360
____	**52348**	Halloween General Sheriff and Outlaw Car, *04*	60	115
____	**52405**	Halloween General Add-on Cars, *06*	80	160
____	**52406**	Halloween General Cannon, *08*	70	135
____	**52423**	New Haven Alco Diesel Passenger Set, *09*	255	510
____	**52468**	Postwar "2434" Passenger Coach, *09*	40	75
____	**52469**	Postwar "2432" Passenger Coach, *09*	40	75
____	**52528**	Burlington Alco Diesel Passenger Set, *09*	150	340
____	**52540**	Passenger Shelter, *09*	10	25
____	**52581**	Texas Special Milk Car, *10*	55	110
____	**52582**	Gondola with dinosaurs, *12*	25	45
____	**58217**	B&M Smoking Caboose, *15*		105
____	**58224**	Walking Brakeman Car, *15*		100
____	**58249**	Holiday Boxcar, *15*	20	80
____	**58251**	Maine Central Flatcar with trailers, *15*		100
____	**58272**	MKT Maxi-Stack Container Car with containers, *16*		100
____	**58526**	Texas Special Cow and Calf SW9 Switchers, *14*		375
____	**58532**	Lou Caponi Blue Coal Train, *14*	100	200
____	**58549**	Texas Special Diamonds Mint Car, *14*	40	75
____	**58561**	Southern Pelican Boxcar, *13*	35	70
____	**58584**	45th Anniversary Auto Rack Loader, *14*	60	120

Lionel Operating Train Society

LOTS National Convention Cars

		Exc	Mint	
303	Stauffer Chemical 1-D Tank Car, 85	105	210	___
3764	Kahn's Brine Tank Reefer, 81	45	85	___
6111	L&N Covered Quad Hopper, 83	20	40	___
6211	C&O Gondola with canisters, 86	45	90	___
9414	Cotton Belt Boxcar, 80	30	55	___
16812	Grand Trunk 2-bay ACF Hopper (std O), 96	30	60	___
16813	Pennsylvania Power & Light Hopper (std O), 97	40	80	___
17874	Milwaukee Road Log Dump Car "59629," 88	75	150	___
17875	Port Huron & Detroit Boxcar "1289," 89	25	50	___
17882	B&O DD Boxcar "298011" with ETD, 90	35	65	___
17890	CSX Auto Carrier "151161," 91	40	80	___
18890	Union Pacific RS3 Diesel "8805," 89	75	145	___
19960	Western Pacific Boxcar "1952" (std O), 92	35	65	___
38356	Dow Chemical 3-D Tank Car, 87	65	125	___
52014	BN TTUX Flatcar Set with N&W trailers, 93	105	205	___
52041	BN TTUX Flatcar Set with Conrail trailers, 94	45	85	___
52067	Burlington Operating Ice Car "50240," 95	30	60	___
52135	ATSF Reefer "22739," 98	30	55	___
52162	Gulf Mobile & Ohio DD Boxcar "24580," 99	35	65	___
52196	CP Maxi-Stack Flatcar "524115" with 2 containers, 00	50	95	___
52234	WM Well Car with transformer, 01	30	60	___
52261	Schlitz Beer Reefer "92132," 02	30	60	___
52281	PRR Operating Boxcar, 03	30	55	___
52342	Southern Stock Car, sound, 04	30	55	___
52346	D&H PS-2 Cement Hopper, 06	35	65	___
52347	SF SD80 MAC Diesel, TMCC, 04	175	350	___
52380/81	Virginian Coal Hopper, 05	25	50	___
52382	SF Extended View Caboose, 05	165	325	___
52425	SP&S Boxcar (std O), 07	45	90	___
52474	NYC Evans Auto Loader with 4 Studebakers, 08	40	80	___
52550	NC&StL Dixieland Boxcar, 09	40	75	___
52566	NH State of Maine Boxcar, 10	30	60	___
52580	Robin Hood Beer Double-sheathed Boxcar, 11	40	80	___
58223	Chicago Great Western Flatcar with Edelweiss Beer Trailers, 15		75	___
58508	Genesee Beer & Ale Double-sheathed Boxcar, 11	35	70	___
58553	UP Maxi-Stack Car with WP feather containers, 13	40	75	___
58575	H. J. Heinz Double-sheathed Boxcar, 14	35	70	___
80948	Michigan Central Boxcar, 82	115	230	___
83862	Cradle of Liberty Boxcar, 16		75	___
83863	Santa Fe Warbonnet Tank Car, 16		75	___
83872/3	D&RGW 2-car Ore Car Set, 17		110	___
121315	Pennsylvania Hi-Cube Boxcar, 84	175	345	___

CLUB CARS AND SPECIAL PRODUCTION

		Exc	Mint

LOTS Meet Specials

		Exc	Mint
52413	Saratoga Brewery Reefer, 06	30	60
52456	Alpenrose Dairy Milk Car, 07	50	95
52506	Studebaker Automobile Parts Boxcar, 08	40	75
52552	Radioactive Waste Removal Car, 09	45	85
58236	Tucker Automobile Parts Boxcar, 15		75

Other LOTS Production

		Exc	Mint
1223	Seattle & North Coast Hi-Cube Boxcar, 86	100	200
52042	BN TTUX Flatcar "637500C" with CN trailer, 94	30	60
52048	Canadian National Tractor and Trailer "197993," 94	20	35
52129	Lighted Billboard with Angela Trotta Thomas art, 97	15	30
52217	LOTS/LCCA 2000 Convention Billboard, 00	5	10
52260	National Aquarium in Baltimore Car, 01	55	110
52280	"More Precious than Gold" Mint Car, 02	45	90
52309	Patriotic Tank Car, 03	35	70
52359	Silver Anniversary Ore Car "1979," 04	20	40
52360	Silver Anniversary Ore Car "2004," 04	20	40
52419	Touring Layout Aquarium Car, 05	45	90
52477	Santa Fe Warbonnet Boxcar, 07	40	75
52523	Santa Fe Flatcar with trailer and tractor, 08	45	90
52553	Tennessee Aquarium Car, 09	35	65
52567	Santa Fe ACF 2-bay Hopper, 10	30	60
52590	Santa Fe Warbonnet Mint Car, 11	40	75
58228	Burlington Zephyr Double-sheathed Boxcar, 15		75
58535	Santa Fe ACF Transparent Boxcar, 12	40	75
58566	Virginia & Truckee Carson City Mint Car, 13	35	70
58593	Porter Locomotive Parts Boxcar, 14		70
58594/5	Santa Fe Crane and Work Caboose, 14		135

Lionel Century Club

		Exc	Mint
14532	PRR Sharknose Diesel AA Set, LCC II, 00	350	690
18053	2-8-4 Berkshire Locomotive "726," 97	360	705
18057	6-8-6PRR S2 Steam Turbine Locomotive "671," 98	290	570
18058	4-6-4 Hudson Locomotive "773," 97	375	735
18068	Tender for PRR Steam Turbine Locomotive "773," 99	105	210
18135	NYC F3 Diesel AA Set, 99	325	650
18178	NYC F3 Diesel B Unit, 99	115	230
18314	PRR GG1 Electric "2332," 97	280	560
18340	FM Train Master Set, LCC II, 00	450	900
24510	PRR Sharknose Diesel B Unit, LCC II, 00	100	200

CLUB CARS AND SPECIAL PRODUCTION

		Exc	Mint
28069	NYC 4-8-6 Niagara Locomotive "6024," CC, LCC II, 00	460	920 ____
29173	Empire State Express Passenger Car 4-pack, LCC II, 02	175	350 ____
29178	Empire State Express Passenger Car 2-pack, LCC II, 02	90	175 ____
29181	Empire State Express Diner, LCC II, 02	95	190 ____
29204	Boxcar "1900-2000," 96	165	330 ____
29226	Berkshire Boxcar, 97	75	145 ____
29227	GG1 Boxcar, 98	30	55 ____
29228	PRR Turbine Boxcar "671," 99	30	60 ____
29248	F3 Boxcar "2333," 99	35	65 ____
31716	Niagara Milk Train Set, LCC II, 00	150	300 ____
31726	PRR Sharknose Coal Train Set, LCC II, 00	90	180 ____
31731	Train Master Freight Train Set, LCC II, 00	90	180 ____
38000	NYC 4-6-4 Hudson Empire State Locomotive, LCC II, 02	495	990 ____
39201	Hudson Boxcar "773," 00	30	60 ____
39215	Niagara Boxcar, LCC II, 01	25	50 ____
39217	Boxcar, LCC II, 00	30	60 ____
39218	Gold Boxcar, LCC II, 00	45	85 ____
39237	M-10000 Boxcar, LCC II, 00	35	70 ____
39246	PRR Sharknose Boxcar, LCC II, 00	30	55 ____
39265	Fairbanks-Morse Train Master Boxcar, LCC II, 00	30	60 ____
39266	Empire State Boxcar, LCC II, 00	20	40 ____
51007	UP M-10000 4-car Passenger Set, LCC II, 00	485	970 ____
51249	UP Overland Route Sleeper Car, LCC II, 02	60	120 ____

Lionel Railroader Club

		Exc	Mint
780	Boxcar, 82	35	65 ____
781	Flatcar with trailers, 83	25	50 ____
782	1-D Tank Car, 85	25	45 ____
784	Covered Quad Hopper, 84	30	60 ____
11183	Lincoln Funeral Train	400	800 ____
11319	PRR Tuscan K4 Locomotive, CC	450	900 ____
11320	PRR Tuscan K4 Locomotive	375	750 ____
12875	Tractor and Trailer, 94	10	20 ____
12921	Illuminated Station Platform, 95	10	20 ____
14274	Water Tower, 07	10	20 ____
15034	50th Anniversary Mail Car, 10	25	50 ____
15035	Holiday Boxcar, 10	25	50 ____
16800	Ore Car, yellow, 86	35	70 ____
16801	Bunk Car, blue, 88	20	35 ____
16802	Tool Car, 89	25	35 ____
16803	Searchlight Car, 90	10	25 ____
16804	Bay Window Caboose, 91	15	30 ____

CLUB CARS AND SPECIAL PRODUCTION

			Exc	Mint
___	16839	Covered Bridge, 11	25	50
___	18680	4-6-4 Hudson Locomotive, 00	150	300
___	18684	4-6-2 Pacific Locomotive, 99	110	220
___	18818	GP38-2 Diesel, 92	100	115
___	19399	Christmas Boxcar, 13	30	60
___	19437	Flatcar with trailer, 97	30	55
___	19473	Operating Log Dump Car "3351," 99	20	40
___	19685	Western Union Dining Car, 02	20	40
___	19695	Western Union 1-D Tank Car, 03	10	20
___	19774	Porthole Caboose, 99	25	50
___	19775	Stock Car, 99	25	50
___	19924	Boxcar, 93	10	20
___	19930	Quad Hopper with coal, 94	10	20
___	19935	1-D Tank Car, 95	10	25
___	19940	Vat Car, 96	15	30
___	19953	6464 Boxcar, 97	20	35
___	19965	Aquarium Car "3435," 99	30	55
___	19966	Gondola "9820" (std O), 98	15	30
___	19978	Gold Membership Boxcar, 99	25	45
___	19991	Gold Membership Boxcar, 00	35	65
___	19992	Western Union Tool Car "3550," 00	25	50
___	19993	Gold Membership Boxcar, 01	35	65
___	19994	Western Union Passenger Car "1307," 01	30	60
___	19995	25th Anniversary Boxcar (std O), 01	25	50
___	24217	Animated Billboard, 08	15	30
___	25073	Holiday Boxcar, 09	20	50
___	25631	Lincoln Train Passenger Car 2-pack	150	300
___	25635	Red Passenger Car 3-pack, 12	210	420
___	25635	Red Arrow Diner, 12	70	140
___	26089	Western Union Gondola with handcar, 05	35	65
___	26165	Western Union Reefer, 04	15	30
___	26382	Flatcar with tractor and tanker, 08	30	60
___	26413	Commemorative 4-bay Hopper, 08	35	70
___	26636	"6830" 50th Anniversary Flatcar with submarine, 11	30	55
___	26637	"6640" 50th Anniversary USMC Missile Launching Car, 11	35	65
___	27940	"6469" Liquified Gas Tank Car, 13	25	50
___	27943	"6416" Boat Loader, 13	25	50
___	27944	"3413" Mercury Capsule Launch Car, 13	30	60
___	27945	"6460-60" LV Covered Quad Hopper, 13	30	55
___	28062	4-6-4 Hudson Locomotive, 00	575	1150
___	28571	GP9 Diesel, CC, 07	125	250
___	28665	Western Union 2-8-4 Berkshire Locomotive "665," 05	90	175
___	29200	Lionel Boxcar "9700," 96	20	40

CLUB CARS AND SPECIAL PRODUCTION

		Exc	Mint
29313	"3409" 50th Anniversary Helicopter Car, *11*	35	70 ____
29657	"6413" 50th Anniversary Mercury Capsule Car, *12*	30	55 ____
29658	"6465" 50th Anniversary Cities Service 2-D Car, *12*	25	50 ____
29931	Holiday Boxcar, *05*	10	25 ____
29939	30th Anniversary Boxcar, *06*	25	50 ____
29941	Holiday Boxcar, *06*	10	25 ____
29946	Holiday Boxcar, *07*	20	35 ____
29947	Commemorative Boxcar, *07*	15	30 ____
29957	Holiday Boxcar, *08*	25	50 ____
29977	Holiday Boxcar, *11*	30	60 ____
36521	Western Union Searchlight Caboose, *05*	15	30 ____
36769	4th of July Lighted Boxcar, *03*	35	70 ____
37968	Clock Tower with wreath, *11*	25	45 ____
39249	Holiday Boxcar, *03*	15	30 ____
39264	Holiday Boxcar, *04*	25	50 ____
39352	"6445" 50th Anniversary Fort Knox Mint Car, *12*	35	70 ____
39353	50th Anniversary Santa Fe Boxcar, *11*	30	55 ____
39496	"6475" 50th Anniversary Vat Car, *10*	30	60 ____
58613	Holiday Boxcar, *14*	30	90 ____
58632	1955 Maintenance of Way Truck, *13*	85	165 ____
81116	Polar Express Operating Billboard, *14*	30	60 ____
81117	Polar Express Flatcar with silver bell, *14*	25	45 ____

Lionel Railroad Club Milwaukee

		Exc	Mint
52116	MILW Flatcar "194797," black, with tractor and trailer, *97*	40	75 ____
52163	CMStP&P "Hiawatha" DD Automobile Boxcar, *98*	30	60 ____
52180	MILW Flatcar "194799," tuscan, with trailer, *99*	40	75 ____
52228	CMStP&P 1-D Water Tank Car "908309," *00*	25	50 ____
52229	MILW 1-D Diesel Fuel Tank Car "907797," *00*	25	50 ____
52230	1-D Tank Car 2-pack, *00*	70	140 ____
52246	CMStP&P "Olympian" Boxcar "194701," *01*	35	65 ____
52265	MILW/Zoological Society Aquarium Car "4701," orange, *02*	30	55 ____
52278	MILW/Zoological Society Aquarium Car "4702," blue, *03*	50	95 ____
52297	MILW Reefer "194703," yellow, *03*	35	65 ____
52298	MILW Flatcar "194704" with orange trailer, *04*	60	115 ____
52337	MILW/Zoological Society Motorized Aquarium Car, *04*	45	90 ____
52368	MILW Flatcar "472004," black, *05*	35	65 ____
52369	MILW Trailer Train Auto Carrier "194705," *05*	45	85 ____
52370	CMStP&P Milk Car "364," tan, *05*	40	80 ____
52387	CMStP&P Flatcar "194706," gray, *06*	25	50 ____
52400	MILW PS-2 2-bay Hopper "99607," orange, *06*	45	85 ____

CLUB CARS AND SPECIAL PRODUCTION

		Exc	Mint
___ 52401	MILW PS-2 2-bay Hopper "98809," yellow, 06	35	65
___ 52402	CMStP&P URTX Operating Ice Car "4706," 06	45	85
___ 52428	CMStP&P 0-4-0 Switcher and Caboose Set, 60th Anniversary, 06	140	275
___ 52429	CMStP&P 0-4-0 Switcher, 06	100	200
___ 52430	CMStP&P Offset Cupola Caboose, 06	35	70
___ 52458	MILW Stock Car "102721" (std O), 07	35	65
___ 52466	CMStP&P Stock Car "105254" (std O), 07	35	65
___ 52551	MILW "Big M" DD Boxcar "200947," yellow, 09	30	60
___ 52572	MILW Reiman Aquarium Car, 11	40	75
___ 52599	MILW 2-bay ACF Hopper, 12	30	60
___ 58263	Breast Cancer Awareness Boxcar, 16		80
___ 58563	CMStP&P Round-Roof Boxcar, 13	35	70
___ 58591	MILW Flatcar with auto frames, 14	30	60

Long Island Toy Train Locomotive Engineers

		Exc	Mint
___ 58520	Entenmann's Vat Car, 12	35	65
___ 58556	Flatcar with U.S. Navy airplane, 13	35	70
___ 58562	Entenmann's Quad Hopper, 14	40	75

Nassau Lionel Operating Engineers

		Exc	Mint
___ 8389	Long Island Boxcar, 89	50	100
___ 8390	Long Island Covered Quad Hopper, 90	50	100
___ 8391A	Long Island Bunk Car, 91	45	90
___ 8391B	Long Island Tool Car, 91	45	90
___ 8392	Long Island 1-D Tank Car, 92	55	105
___ 52007	Long Island RS3 Diesel "1552," 93	125	250
___ 52019	Long Island Boxcar, 93	35	65
___ 52020	Long Island Bay Window Caboose, 93	50	95
___ 52026	Long Island Flatcar "8394" with Grumman trailer, 94	235	465
___ 52061	Long Island Stern's Pickle Products Vat Car "8395," 95	100	200
___ 52072	Grumman Tractor, 94	40	75
___ 52076	Long Island Observation Car "8396," 96	175	350
___ 52112	Long Island Ronkonkoma Vista Dome Car "9783," 97	150	300
___ 52122	Meenan Oil 1-D Tank Car "8397" (std O), 97	30	60
___ 52123	Long Island Hicksville Diner Car "9883," 98	150	300
___ 52144	Long Island Flatcar with Grumman van, 99	50	95
___ 52145	Long Island Jamaica Passenger Coach, 99	150	300
___ 52145	Long Island Penn Station Passenger Coach, 99	150	300
___ 52166	Long Island Flatcar "8398" with Grumman trailer, 98	40	75
___ 52174	REA Baggage Car "0083," 00		400
___ 52186	Grucci Fireworks Boxcar, 00	35	70

CLUB CARS AND SPECIAL PRODUCTION

		Exc	Mint
52209	World's Fair Sleeper/Roomette Car "0183," *01*		170 ____
52232	Central RR of Long Island Boxcar, *01*	30	60 ____
52235	World's Fair Vista Dome Car "0283," *02*		NRS ____
52256	New York & Atlantic Boxcar "8302," *02*	30	60 ____
52263	World's Fair Combination Car "0383," *02*		NRS ____
52296	Long Island Flatcar with Republic tanker, *03*	40	80 ____
52329	New York & Atlantic Caboose, *04*	40	80 ____
52341	Long Island Flatcar with Pan Am trailer, *05*	45	85 ____
52365	Long Island Flatcar with Lilco transformer, *04*	70	135 ____
52420	Long Island 80th Anniversary Boxcar, *06*	25	45 ____
52480	Long Island Flatcar with pipes, *08*	25	50 ____
52489	Long Island Flatcar with P.C. Richard & Son trailer, *07*	35	65 ____
52555	Martha Clara Vineyards Vat Car, *09*	30	60 ____
52568	Flatcar with NY Islanders refrigerated trailer, *10*	30	60 ____
52586	Flatcar with Cradle of Aviation Museum trailer, *11*	25	50 ____
52592	Petland Discounts Aquarium Car, *11*	35	70 ____
58212	Cross Harbor Round-roof Boxcar, *15*		65 ____
58240	LIRR GLa Hopper, black, *16*		80 ____
58240	LIRR GLa Hopper, tuscan, *16*		80 ____
58266	Nathan's 100th Anniversary Reefer, *16*		65 ____
58500	Nassau County Firefighters Museum Tank Car, *12*	30	55 ____
58567	Nathan's Famous Reefer "83131," *13*	40	75 ____
58568	Nathan's Famous Reefer "83132," *13*	40	75 ____
58573	Long Island PS1 Boxcar "8312," *14*		80 ____
58581	Long Island Double-sheathed Boxcar, *14*		65 ____
	LIRR PS-2CD Scale Hopper, *17*		70 ____

Railroad Museum of Long Island

52416	RMLI 15th Anniversary LIRR Boxcar, *05*	85	170 ____
52433	Atlantis Marine World Aquarium Car, *06*	75	145 ____
52453	North Fork Bank Mint Car, *07*	45	90 ____
52497	LIRR Flatcar with Entenmann's trailer and tractor, *08*	55	110 ____
52498	Boeing Fairchild Container Car, *10*	40	75 ____
52548	RMLI "Celebrating 175 Years of Railroading" Boxcar, *09*	45	90 ____
52557	Entenmann's Operating Boxcar, *10*	45	90 ____
52570	Riverhead Building Supply Boxcar, *11*	30	60 ____
52571	Riverhead Visitor's Center Boxcar, *11*	30	60 ____
52577	King Kullen Boxcar, *11*	30	60 ____
52595	J. P. Holland Submarine Car, *12*	30	60 ____
58227	World's Fair Crew Car, *15*		75 ____
58259	Steam Up LIRR 39 Boxcar, *16*		85 ____
58521	Wonder Bread PS-2 Covered Hopper, *12*	30	60 ____

CLUB CARS AND SPECIAL PRODUCTION

		Exc	Mint
____ 58551	Flatcar with White Castle refrigerated trailer, 13	30	60
____ 58554	RCA Operating Radar Car, 13	30	60
____ 58555	Flatcar with produce trailers, 15		75
____ 58579	World's Fair Exhibit Car, 14		80
____ 58580	World's Fair Tool Car, 15		60

St. Louis Lionel Railroad Club

		Exc	Mint
____ 52099	MP Flatcar with St. Louis trailer, 96	35	65
____ 52104	St. Louis tractor and trailer, 96	10	20
____ 52117	Wabash Flatcar with REA tractor and trailer, 97	35	65
____ 52136A	Christmas Tractor and Trailer, 97		NRS
____ 52136B	Frisco Tractor and Trailer, 98		NRS
____ 52147	Frisco Campbell TOFC Flatcar, 98	40	75
____ 52150	Frisco Campbell TOFC Flatcar, 98	65	130
____ 52167	ATSF Flatcar "831999" with Navajo trailer, 99	40	75
____ 52190	IC Flatcar with trailers, 00	40	80
____ 52222	Cotton Belt Flatcar with SP tractor and trailer, 01	25	50
____ 52224A	SP Flatcar with Navajo tractor and trailer, 01	10	25
____ 52224B	SP Flatcar with service tractor and trailer, 01	10	25
____ 52258	UP Flatcar with UP tractor and trailer, 02	30	55
____ 52290	UP Flatcar with tractor trailer, 03	40	75
____ 52336	U.S. Army Flatcar with tanker truck, 04	65	125
____ 52371	NYC Flatcar with Fire Company tanker truck, 05	70	145
____ 52392	PRR Flatcar with Hood's Milk tanker truck, 06	50	100
____ 52440	U.S.M.C. Flatcar with tractor and trailer, 07	70	135
____ 52490	Silver Special Flatcar with USA tractor and trailer, 08	50	100
____ 52513	Frisco Flatcar with U.S.A.F. trailer, 09	60	120

Train Collectors Association

TCA National Convention Cars

		Exc	Mint
____ 511	St. Louis Baggage Car, 81	20	40
____ 2671-1968	TCA Tender, shell only, 68	30	55
____ 5734	REA Reefer, 85	25	50
____ 6315	Pittsburgh 1-D Tank Car, 72	30	60
____ 6436-1969	Open Quad Hopper, red, 69	35	65
____ 6464-1965	Pittsburgh Boxcar, blue, 65	125	210
____ 6464-1970	Chicago Boxcar, 70	45	85
____ 6464-1971	Disneyland Boxcar, 71	210	240
____ 6517-1966	Bay Window Caboose, 66	150	250
____ 6926	New Orleans Extended Vision Caboose, 86	20	40
____ 7205	Denver Combination Car, 82	25	50
____ 7206	Louisville Passenger Car, 83	30	55
____ 7212	Pittsburgh Passenger Car, 84	25	50

CLUB CARS AND SPECIAL PRODUCTION

		Exc	Mint	
7812	Houston Stock Car, 77	10	25	___
8476	4-6-4 Locomotive "5484," 85	155	310	___
9123	Dearborn 3-tier Auto Carrier, 73	20	35	___
9319	"Silver Jubilee" Mint Car, 79	65	130	___
9544	Chicago Observation Car, 80	25	50	___
9611	Boston Hi-Cube Boxcar, 78	10	25	___
9774	Orlando "Southern Belle" Boxcar, 75	15	35	___
9779	Philadelphia Boxcar "9700-1976," 76	20	35	___
9864	Seattle Reefer, 74	25	50	___
11737	TCA 40th Anniversary F3 Diesel ABA Set, 93	265	530	___
17879	Valley Forge Dining Car, 89	30	60	___
17883	New Georgia Passenger Car, 90	35	65	___
17898	Wabash Reefer "21596," 92	25	45	___
19211	Vermont Railway Flatcars (2) with 4 trailers, 08	80	160	___
52008	Bucyrus Erie Crane Car, 93	25	50	___
52035	Yorkrail GP9 Diesel "1750," shell only, 94	30	55	___
52036	TCA 40th Anniversary Bay Window Caboose, 94	20	40	___
52037	Yorkrail GP9 Diesel "1754," 94	75	150	___
52062	Skytop Observation Car, 95	180	360	___
52085	Full Vista Dome Car, 96	60	115	___
52106	City of Phoenix Diner, 97	50	100	___
52142	Massachusetts Central Maxi-Stack Flatcar "5100-01," 98	60	120	___
52143	City of Providence Passenger Car, 98	70	140	___
52146	Ocean Spray Reefer, 98	120	235	___
52155	City of San Francisco Baggage Car, 99	70	140	___
52191	City of Grand Rapids Aluminum Passenger Car, 00	70	135	___
52210	Rico Station, 00	15	30	___
52220	City of Chattanooga Vista Dome Car, 01	70	140	___
52221	Norfolk Southern Boxcar, 01	25	50	___
52274	City of Los Angeles Railway Post Office Car, 03	35	80	
52237	Lionel Gondola, yellow, 01	55	110	___
52238	Lionel Gondola, red, 01	55	110	___
52239	Lionel Gondola, silver, 01	55	110	___
52240	Lionel Gondola 3-pack, 01	55	110	___
52241	Lionel Gondola, black, 02	5	15	___
52242	Lionel Gondola, blue, 02	20	35	___
52250	City of Chicago Combination Car, 02	65	130	___
52272	Lionel Gondola, gold, 02	40	80	___
52276	California Gold Mint Car, 03	35	65	___
52333	Harmony Dairy Milk Car, 04	45	90	___
52338	Lionel 50th Anniversary Mint Car, 04	40	75	___
52339	50th Anniversary Convention Banquet Car with coin, 04	180	360	___
52340	Train Order Building, 04	45	90	___
52373	Montana Rail Link 2-car Set, 05	45	90	___

CLUB CARS AND SPECIAL PRODUCTION

			Exc	Mint
____	**52374**	Montana Rail Link 2-bay Hopper, *05*	25	50
____	**52375**	Montana Rail Link Flatcar with pulp-wood logs, *05*	25	50
____	**52376**	GN Reefer, *05*	30	60
____	**52403**	T&P Stock Car (std O), *06*	40	75
____	**52414**	Flatcar with 3 snowmobiles, *07*	40	80
____	**52481**	Ben & Jerry's Reefer, *08*	50	95
____	**52500**	ATSF Grand Canyon Reefer, *09*	30	60
____	**52508**	Celebrate America Mint Car, *09*	50	95
____	**58216**	NYC Merchants Despatch Reefer, *15*		90
____	**58258**	Made in the USA Boxcar, *16*		80
____	**58544**	St. Louis Reefer, *13*	45	85
____	**58547**	Cotton Belt Blue Streak Merchandise Boxcar, *13*	35	75
____	**58571**	Bethlehem Steel PS-1 Boxcar, *14*	40	80
____	**58572**	Reading Philadelphia Mint Car, *14*	40	80

TCA Museum-Related and Other Cars

			Exc	Mint
____	**1018-1979**	Mortgage Burning Hi-Cube Boxcar, *79*	20	35
____	**5731**	L&N Reefer, *90*	50	95
____	**7780**	TCA Museum Boxcar, *80*	10	25
____	**7781**	Hafner Boxcar, *81*	10	25
____	**7782**	Carlisle & Finch Boxcar, *82*	10	25
____	**7783**	Ives Boxcar, *83*	10	25
____	**7784**	Voltamp Boxcar, *84*	10	25
____	**7785**	Hoge Boxcar, *85*	10	25
____	**9771**	Norfolk & Western Boxcar, *77*	15	30
____	**16811**	Rutland Boxcar "5477096," *96*	20	35
____	**52045**	Pennsylvania Dutch Milk Car "61052," *94*	45	90
____	**52051**	Baltimore & Ohio Sentinel Boxcar "6464095," *95*	20	40
____	**52052**	TCA 40th Anniversary Boxcar, *94*	45	90
____	**52063**	NYC Pacemaker Boxcar "6464125," *95*	175	345
____	**52064**	Missouri Pacific Boxcar "6464150," *95*	185	370
____	**52065**	Pennsylvania Dutch Grain Operating Boxcar "9208," *96*	50	100
____	**52118**	Rio Grande Boxcar "5477097," *97*	30	55
____	**52119**	TCA Museum 20th Anniversary Boxcar, *97*	35	70
____	**52128**	Pennsylvania Dutch Pretzels Boxcar, *99*	40	80
____	**52172**	L&N "Share the Freedom" Boxcar "5477099," *99*	25	55
____	**52198**	Frisco Boxcar "5477000," *00*	25	45
____	**52215**	Museum Work Train Gondola with pipes, *03*	30	55
____	**52226**	Angela Trotta Thomas Boxcar "2000," *01*	50	100
____	**52243**	Museum Work Train 1-D Tank Car, *01*	25	50
____	**52271**	Museum Work Train Flatcar with wheel load, *02*	10	20
____	**52289**	National Toy Train Museum 25th Anniversary Bullion Car, *02*	40	75
____	**52295**	National Toy Train Museum Gondola with pipes, *03*	5	15

CLUB CARS AND SPECIAL PRODUCTION

		Exc	Mint
52310	Museum Work Train Boxcar, *04*	30	55 ____
52311	50th Anniversary Golden Express Freight Set, *04*	200	450 ____
52321	SP Trainmaster Locomotive, *04*	175	345 ____
52372	Museum Work Train Baggage Car, *05*	35	70 ____
52408	N&W Caboose, *06*	30	55 ____
52409	Museum Work Train Idler Caboose, *06*	35	70 ____
52437	Museum Work Train Crane Car, *07*	40	80 ____

TCA Bicentennial Special Set

		Exc	Mint
1973	Bicentennial Observation Car, *76*	25	50 ____
1974	Bicentennial Passenger Car, *76*	25	50 ____
1975	Bicentennial Passenger Car, *76*	25	50 ____
1976	Bicentennial U36B Diesel, *76*	85	165 ____

Atlantic Division

		Exc	Mint
1980	Atlantic Division Flatcar with trailers, *80*	20	35 ____
6101	Burlington Northern Covered Quad Hopper, *82*	20	35 ____
9186	Conrail N5c Caboose, *79*	15	30 ____
9193	Budweiser Vat Car, *84*	55	110 ____
9466	Wanamaker Boxcar, *83*	70	135 ____
9788	Lehigh Valley Boxcar, *78*	10	25 ____
58598	Philly Pretzel Factory Boxcar, *14*		40 ____
	Wawa Hoagiefest Boxcar, *17*		70 ____

Desert Division

		Exc	Mint
52088	Desert Division 25th Anniversary On-track Step Van, *96*	60	120 ____
52105	Superstition Mountain Operating Gondola "61997," *97*	40	80 ____
52442	Verde Canyon Boxcar, *07*	30	55 ____
52443	Grand Canyon Boxcar, *07*	30	55 ____
58222	Los Alamos Mint Car, *16*		80 ____
58226	Cumbres & Toltec Boxcar, *16*		80 ____
	Fred Harvey Boxcar, *17*		80 ____

Dixie Division

		Exc	Mint
27007/87	Dixie Division 20th Anniversary PS-1 Boxcar, *06*	40	80 ____
52127	Dixie Division 10th Anniversary Southern 3-bay Hopper, *98*	35	70 ____

Eastern Division

		Exc	Mint
52059	Clinchfield Quad Hopper "16413" with coal, *94*	55	110 ____

CLUB CARS AND SPECIAL PRODUCTION

Exc Mint

Eastern Division: Washington, Baltimore & Annapolis Chapter

		Exc	Mint
____ 9412	Richmond, Fredericksburg & Potomac Boxcar, *79*	10	25
____ 9740	Chessie System Boxcar, *76*	10	25
____ 9771	Norfolk & Western Boxcar, *78*	15	30
____ 9783	B&O Time-Saver Boxcar, *77*	15	30

Fort Pitt Division

____ 1984-30X	Heinz Ketchup Boxcar, *84*	250	500

Great Lakes Division

____ 1983	Churchill Downs Boxcar, *83*	100	200
____ 1983	Churchill Downs Reefer, *83*	125	250
____ 9740	Chessie System Boxcar, *76*	10	25

Great Lakes Division: Detroit-Toledo Chapter

____ 8957	Burlington Northern GP20 Diesel, *80*	115	230
____ 8958	Burlington Northern GP20 Diesel Dummy Unit, *80*	75	150
____ 9119	Detroit & Mackinac Covered Quad Hopper, *77*	10	20
____ 9272	New Haven Bay Window Caboose, *79*	10	20
____ 9401	Great Northern Boxcar, *78*	10	25
____ 9730	CP Rail Boxcar, *76*	10	25
____ 52000	Detroit-Toledo Division Flatcar with trailer, *92*	45	85

Great Lakes Division: Three Rivers Chapter

____ 9113	Norfolk & Western Quad Hopper, *76*	15	30

Great Lakes Division: Western Michigan Chapter

____ 9730	CP Rail Boxcar, *74*	10	25

Lake & Pines Division

____ 52018	3-M Boxcar, *93*	225	450

Lone Star Division

____ 7522	New Orleans Mint Car with coin, *86*	210	420
____ 52093	Lone Star Division Boxcar "6464696," *96*	15	30
____ 52585	Texas Special Mint Car, *11*	35	65
____ 58512	SP Daylight Mint Car, *12*	35	65
____ 58552	Texas Special Mint Car with silver bars, *12*	35	65

Lone Star Division: North Texas Chapter

____ 9739	D&RGW Boxcar, *76*	10	20

CLUB CARS AND SPECIAL PRODUCTION

Exc Mint

METCA

		Exc	Mint
10	Jersey Central F3 A Unit, shell only, *71*	10	25 ___
9272	New Haven Bay Window Caboose, *79*	10	25 ___
9754	New York Central Pacemaker Boxcar, *76*	15	30 ___
52485	New York Central Mint Car with copper load, *08*	60	120 ___
52486	Pennsylvania Mint Car, green, *09*	65	125 ___
52487	Pennsylvania Mint Car, tuscan, *09*	65	125 ___
52488	NYC Lightning Stripe Mint Car, *10*	30	60 ___
52574	Fort Knox 50th Anniversary Mint Car, *11*	50	100 ___
52583	B&O Capitol Dome Mint Car, *11*	50	100 ___
52596	LIRR Mint Car, *12*	50	100 ___
58033	Jersey Central Boxcar, *16*		80 ___
58174	Lehigh Valley Map Boxcar, *16*		80 ___
58280	REA Christmas Boxcar, *16*		80 ___
58523	Blue Comet Mint Car, *13*	35	70 ___
58243	Entenmann's Gondola with load, *15*		70 ___
58285	Brookside Milk Reefer, *17*		85 ___
58286	Riverside Milk Reefer, *17*		85 ___
58534	Jersey Central Mint Car, *13*	35	70 ___
58569	Erie Lackawanna Mint Car, *14*	35	70 ___

Midwest Division

		Exc	Mint
4	C&NW F3 Diesel A Unit, shell only, *77*	40	80 ___
5	Midwest Division Covered Quad Hopper, *78*	25	45 ___
1287	C&NW Reefer, *84*		NRS ___
7600	Frisco "Spirit of '76" N5c Caboose "00003," *76*	20	40 ___
9872	PFE Reefer "00006," *79*	205	410 ___

Midwest Division: Museum Express

		Exc	Mint
9264	ICG Covered Quad Hopper, *78*	10	25 ___
9289	C&NW N5c Caboose, *80*	25	45 ___
9785	Conrail Boxcar, *77*	20	35 ___
9786	C&NW Boxcar, *79*	10	20 ___

NETCA

		Exc	Mint
1203	Boston & Maine NW2 Diesel, shell only, *72*	35	65 ___
5710	Canadian Pacific Reefer, *82*	25	45 ___
5716	Vermont Central Reefer, *83*	15	30 ___
6124	Delaware & Hudson Covered Quad Hopper, *84*	15	30 ___
8051	Hood's Milk Boxcar, *86*	40	75 ___
9181	Boston & Maine N5c Caboose, *77*	20	35 ___
9400	Conrail Boxcar, tuscan or blue, *78*	10	25 ___
9415	Providence & Worcester Boxcar, *79*	20	35 ___
9423	NYNH&H Boxcar, *80*	15	30 ___
9445	Vermont Northern Boxcar, *81*	20	40 ___
9753	Maine Central Boxcar, *75*	20	35 ___

CLUB CARS AND SPECIAL PRODUCTION

			Exc	Mint
_____	9768	Boston & Maine Boxcar, 76	20	40
_____	9785	Conrail Boxcar, 78	10	25
_____	16911	B&M Flatcar with trailer, 95	75	150
_____	22677	B&M Baked Beans Boxcar, 10	25	45
_____	52001	B&M Quad Hopper with coal, 92	40	75
_____	52016	B&M Gondola with coil covers, 93	35	65
_____	52043	L.L. Bean Boxcar, 94	105	210
_____	52080	B&M Flatcar "91095" with trailer, 95	110	215
_____	52111	Ben & Jerry's Flatcar with trailer, 96	160	315
_____	52212	Berkshire Brewing Reefer, 00	80	155
_____	52236	Moxie Boxcar, 01	80	160
_____	52270	Jenney Manufacturing Tank Car, 02	75	150
_____	52306	NH Flatcar with New England Transportation trailer, 03	75	150
_____	52352	Poland Spring Boxcar, 04	65	130
_____	52379	CP Rail with W.B. Mason trailer, 05	40	75
_____	52383	Fisk Tire Boxcar, 05	55	110
_____	52397	D&H Flatcar with Vermont Railway trailer, 06	45	90
_____	52418	Indian Motocycle Boxcar, 06	95	190
_____	52434	New England Central Flatcar with Cabot's trailer, 07	50	95
_____	52448	Oilzum Tanker 2-car Set, 08	55	105
_____	52457	Cape Cod Potato Chip Boxcar, 07	50	95
_____	52484A	Cabot's Reefer, 08	125	250
_____	52484B	Bay State Beer Reefer, 09	45	90
_____	52589	B&M Flatcar with Howard Johnson trailer, 11	50	100
_____	58221	G. Fox & Co. Boxcar, 15		60
_____	58522	Grafton & Upton Flatcar with Spag's trailer, 12	45	90
_____		Warwick Ice Cream Reefer, 17		100

Ozark Division: Gateway Chapter

			Exc	Mint
_____	5700	Oppenheimer Reefer, 81	55	110
_____	9068	Reading Bobber Caboose, 76	10	20
_____	9601	Illinois Central Gulf Hi-Cube Boxcar, 77	10	20
_____	9767	Railbox Boxcar, 78	10	20
_____	52003	"Meet Me In St. Louis" Flatcar with trailer, 92	260	520

Pacific Northwest Division

			Exc	Mint
_____	52077	Great Northern Hi-Cube Boxcar "9695," 95	230	460

Rocky Mountain Division

			Exc	Mint
_____	1971-1976	Rocky Mountain Division Reefer, 76	40	75

Sacramento Sierra Chapter

		Exc	Mint	
6401	Virginian Bay Window Caboose, *84*	20	35	___
9301	U.S. Mail Operating Boxcar, *76*	20	40	___
9414	Cotton Belt Boxcar, *80*	20	35	___
9427	Bay Line Boxcar, *81*	15	30	___
9444	Louisiana Midland Boxcar, *82*	20	35	___
9452	Western Pacific Boxcar, *83*	20	35	___
9705	D&RGW Boxcar, *75*	20	40	___
9723	Western Pacific Boxcar, *73*	15	30	___
9726	Erie-Lackawanna Boxcar, *79*	10	25	___
9730	CP Rail Boxcar, *77*	15	30	___
9785	Conrail Boxcar, *78*	10	20	___

Southern Division

		Exc	Mint	
1976	FEC F3 Diesel ABA, shells only, *76*	140	275	___
1986	Southern Division Bunk Car, *86*	15	30	___
6111	L&N Covered Quad Hopper, *83*	10	20	___
9287	Southern N5c Caboose, *77*	10	20	___
9352	Trailer Train Flatcar with circus trailers, *80*	30	55	___
9403	Seaboard Coast Line Boxcar, *78*	10	20	___
9405	Chattahoochie Boxcar, *79*	10	20	___
9443	Florida East Coast Boxcar, *81*	10	25	___
9471	ACL Boxcar, *84*	10	25	___
9482	Norfolk & Southern Boxcar, *85*	10	25	___
16606	Southern Searchlight Car, *88*	10	25	___
19942	Southern Division 30th Anniversary Boxcar, *96*	10	20	___

Western Division

		Exc	Mint	
52275	Western Pacific Boxcar, *03*	55	105	___

Toy Train Operating Society

TTOS National Convention Cars

		Exc	Mint	
1984	Sacramento Northern Boxcar, *84*	45	85	___
1985	Snowbird Covered Quad Hopper, *85*	30	55	___
6017	SP-type Caboose, blue, *68*	125	210	___
6017	SP-type Caboose, brown, *69*	200	300	___
6057	SP-type Caboose, orange, *69*	125	210	___
6076	Santa Fe Hopper (O27), *70*	45	85	___
6167-1967	Hopper, olive drab with gold lettering, *67*	45	85	___
6257	SP-type Caboose, red, *69*	125	210	___
6476-1	LV Hopper, gray, *69*	40	75	___
6582	Portland Flatcar with wood, *86*	30	55	___
9326	Burlington Northern Bay Window Caboose, *82*	10	25	___
9347	Niagara Falls 3-D Tank Car, *79*	25	45	___

CLUB CARS AND SPECIAL PRODUCTION

			Exc	Mint
____	9355	Delaware & Hudson Bay Window Caboose, *82*	25	50
____	9361	C&NW Bay Window Caboose, *82*	30	55
____	9382	Florida East Coast Bay Window Caboose, *82*	35	70
____	9512	Summerdale Junction Passenger Car, *74*	30	55
____	9520	Phoenix Combination Car, *75*	20	35
____	9526	Snowbird Observation Car, *76*	25	50
____	9535	Columbus Baggage Car, *77*	35	50
____	9678	Hollywood Hi-Cube Boxcar, *78*	15	30
____	9868	Oklahoma City Reefer, *80*	25	45
____	9883	Phoenix Reefer, *83*	25	50
____	17871	NYC Flatcar "81487" with Kodak and Xerox trailers, *87*	110	215
____	17877	MKT 1-D Tank Car "3739469," *89*	35	70
____	17884	Columbus & Dayton Terminal Boxcar (std O), *90*	20	40
____	17889	SP Flatcar "15791" (std O) with trailer, *91*	35	65
____	19963	Union Equity 3-bay ACF Hopper "86892" (std O), *92*	20	40
____	52010	Weyerhaeuser DD Boxcar "838593" (std O), *93*	20	40
____	52029	Ford 1-D Tank Car "12" (027), *94*	20	40
____	52030	Ford Gondola "4023," *94*	15	30
____	52031	Ford Hopper "1458" (027), *94*	20	35
____	52057	Western Pacific Boxcar "64641995," *95*	25	50
____	52087	New Mexico Central Boxcar "64641996," *96*	30	55
____	52114	NYC Flatcar with Gleason and SASIB trailers, *97*	30	60
____	52149	Conrail Flatcar with Blum coal shovel, *98*	30	60
____	52192	SP Crane and Gondola Set, *00*	40	75
____	52193	SP Gondola "6060," *00*	25	50
____	52194	SP Crane Car "7111," *00*	20	35
____	52231	British Columbia 1-D Tank Car, *01*	10	25
____	52253	San Pedro Boxcar, *02*	20	35
____	52288	D&RGW Cookie Boxcar, *03*	10	20
____	52293	D&RGW 1-D Tank Car, *03*	20	40
____	52351	BNSF Icicle Reefer with ETD, *04*	30	60
____	52378	Las Vegas & Tonopah Boxcar, *05*	35	70
____	52410	SP Flatcar with 2 trailers, *06*	35	70
____	52441	Pennsylvania Operating Hopper, *07*	30	60
____	52445	Pennsylvania Boxcar, *07*	35	70
____	52545	Erie "6464" Boxcar, *09*	25	50
____	58257	50th Anniversary Mint Car, *16*		65
____	58333	Sierra Railroad Sierra Beer Boxcar, *13*	35	70
____	58535	Smokey Bear Gondola, *15*		55

TTOS Division Cars

		Exc	Mint	
52009	Sacramento Valley Division WP Boxcar, *93*	25	45	___
52040	Wolverine Division GTW Flatcar with tractor and trailer, *94*	25	50	___
52058	Central California Division Santa Fe Boxcar, *95*	20	40	___
52086	Canadian Division Pacific Great Eastern Boxcar, *96*	25	50	___
52113	Northeastern Division Genesee & Wyoming 3-bay Hopper, *97*	20	35	___
52264	New Mexico Division Durango & Silverton Operating Hopper, *02*	30	55	___

Other TTOS Production

		Exc	Mint	
1983	Phoenix 3-D Tank Car, *83*	50	100	___
17894	Southern Pacific Tractor, *91*	10	20	___
27148	BNSF "4427" PS2 Hopper, *06*	25	50	___
52021	Weyerhaeuser Tractor and Trailer, *93*	15	30	___
52022	Union Pacific Boxcar, *93*	200	400	___
52032	Ford 1-D Tank Car (O27) with Kughn inscription, *94*	50	95	___
52046	ACL Boxcar "16247," *94*	55	110	___
52053	Carail Boxcar, *94*	30	55	___
52068	Toy Train Parade Contadina Boxcar "16245," *94*	30	55	___
52078	Southern Pacific SD9 Diesel "5366," *96*	120	235	___
52079	Southern Pacific Bay Window Caboose, *96*	30	55	___
52084	Union Pacific I-Beam Flatcar "16380" with load, *95*	80	155	___
52384	Transparent Damage Control Boxcar, *03*	35	70	___
52451	Pennsylvania "X2454" Boxcar, *07*	90	175	___
52505	Forest Service/Smokey Bear Flatcar with airplane, *08*	25	45	___
52525	SP "X6454" Boxcar, *08*	25	50	___
52526	SP "X6454" Boxcar, *08*	45	90	___
52547	C&NW Reefer, *09*	30	50	___

TTOS Southwestern Division

		Exc	Mint	
19962	Southern Pacific 3-bay ACF Hopper "496035" (std O), *92*	35	65	___
52047	Cotton Belt Wood-sided Caboose (std O), smoke, *93–94*	35	70	___
52073	Pacific Fruit Express Reefer "459402" (std O), *95*	30	65	___
52098	National Bureau of Standards Boxcar (std O), *96*	20	45	___
52121	Mobilgas Tank Car "238" (std O), *97*	40	75	___
52154	Pacific Fruit Express Reefer "459403" (std O), *98*	25	55	___
52205	SP Overnight Merchandise Service Boxcar 5-pack, *00*	95	185	___
52287	Operating MX Missile Car, *02*	30	55	___

CLUB CARS AND SPECIAL PRODUCTION

		Exc	Mint
____ 52385	Ward Kimball Boxcar, 05	30	55
____ 52431	Operating MX Missile Car, 06	30	60
____ 52476	Life Savers Tank Car, 07	45	85
____ 52515	Life Savers Wild Cherry Tank Car, 08	40	75
____ 52565	Life Savers Pep O Mint Tank Car, 09	30	60
____ 52569	Life Savers Butter Rum Tank Car, 10	30	60
____ 52591	Life Savers Wint O Green Tank Car, 11	30	60
____ 58208	Life Savers Peppermint Tank Car, 14	30	60
____ 58548	Life Savers Bay Window Caboose, 13	40	80

Virginia Train Collectors

		Exc	Mint
____ 7679	Boxcar, 79	5	15
____ 7681	N5c Caboose, 81	10	25
____ 7682	Covered Quad Hopper, 82	10	25
____ 7683	Virginia Fruit Express Reefer, 83	10	25
____ 7684	Vitraco 3-D Tank Car, 84	10	25
____ 7685	Boxcar, 85	10	25
____ 7686	GP7 Diesel, 86	50	100
____ 7692-1	Baggage Car (027), 92	25	45
____ 7692-2	Combination Car (027), 92	25	45
____ 7692-3	Dining Car (027), 92	25	45
____ 7692-4	Passenger Car (027), 92	25	45
____ 7692-5	Vista Dome Car (027), 92	25	45
____ 7692-6	Passenger Car (027), 92	25	45
____ 7692-7	Observation Car (027), 92	25	45
____ 7696	20th Anniversary Station, 96	35	65
____ 52060	Tender "7694" with whistle, 94	35	70

Section 6
BOXES

For more information on determining the condition of a box and a description of box types, see pages 8 and 9.

		Good (P-5)	Exc (P-7)
022	Switch Controller	2	6 ____
022	Remote Control Switches, pair (with both inserts)	5	17 ____
022	Remote Control Switches, pair (yellow, with both inserts)	8	21 ____
022A	Remote Control Switches, pair (with both inserts)	12	33 ____
25	Bumper	3	6 ____
26	Bumper	2	6 ____
30	Water Tower	17	42 ____
35	Boulevard Lamp	5	16 ____
36	Operating Car Remote Control Set	5	14 ____
37	Uncoupling Track Set	4	8 ____
38	Operating Water Tower	24	100 ____
40	Hookup Wire, 8 reels (dealer box)	33	145 ____
41	U.S. Army Switcher	13	57 ____
42	Manual Switches	4	15 ____
42	Picatinny Arsenal Switcher	25	80 ____
44	U.S. Army Mobile Launcher	29	89 ____
44	U.S. Army Mobile Launcher (with orange sleeve)	30	123 ____
45	U.S. Marines Mobile Launcher	45	110 ____
45/45N	Automatic Gateman	6	23 ____
48	Super O Insulated Straight Track, 6 pieces (dealer box)	15	48 ____
49	Super O Insulated Curved Track, 6 pieces (dealer box)	15	43 ____
50	Section Gang Car (early classic)	11	45 ____
50	Section Gang Car (brown corrugated)	5	18 ____
50	Section Gang Car (orange picture)	15	41 ____
51	Navy Yard Switcher	25	66 ____
52	Fire Car	33	81 ____
53	Rio Grande Snowplow	35	85 ____
54	Ballast Tamper	19	42 ____
55	PRR Tie-Jector Car	15	44 ____
56	Lamp Post	5	17 ____
56	M&StL Mine Transport	38	130 ____
57	AEC Switcher	77	262 ____
58	Lamp Post	10	24 ____
58	Great Northern Rotary Snow Blower	78	216 ____
59	Minuteman Switcher	80	252 ____

BOXES

		Good (P-5)	Exc (P-7)
____ 60	Lionelville Rapid Transit Trolley (classic)	12	39
____ 60	Lionelville Rapid Transit Trolley (brown corrugated)	13	40
____ 64	Highway Lamp Post	4	24
____ 65	Handcar	13	88
____ 68	Executive Inspection Car	19	87
____ 69	Maintenance Car	18	74
____ 70	Yard Light	5	17
____ 71	Lamp Post	5	9
____ 75	Goose Neck Lamps	3	15
____ 76	Boulevard Street Lamps	5	30
____ 76	Boulevard Street Lamps (Hillside Checkerboard)	10	70
____ 89	Flagpole	6	26
____ 91	Circuit Breaker	15	45
____ 93	Water Tower	14	36
____ 97	Coal Elevator	14	65
____ 108	Trestle Set (overstamped)	10	40
____ 110	Graduated Trestle Set	1	6
____ 111	Elevated Trestle Set	5	27
____ 112	Remote Control Switches, pair (Super O)	10	25
____ 112LH	Remote Control Super O Switch, left-hand	8	21
____ 112RH	Remote Control Super O Switch, right-hand	7	18
____ 114	Newsstand with horn	9	33
____ 115	Passenger Station (113-1, Star Corp. stamped on box)	30	140
____ 118	Newsstand with whistle	9	37
____ 122	Lamp Assortment	23	100
____ 123	Lamp Assortment	10	100
____ 125	Whistle Shack	5	19
____ 128	Animated Newsstand	14	39
____ 130	60-degree Crossing (Super O)	3	10
____ 132	Passenger Station	13	32
____ 133	Passenger Station	10	25
____ 138	Water Tower	12	35
____ 140	Automatic Banjo Signal (classic)	4	13
____ 142	Manual Switches, pair (Super O)	5	15
____ 145	Automatic Gateman (brown corrugated)	8	21
____ 145	Automatic Gateman (cellophane), *66*	12	59
____ 148	Dwarf Trackside Signal	5	22
____ 150	Telegraph Pole Set	5	18
____ 151	Automatic Semaphore	4	10
____ 151	Automatic Semaphore (narrower box, earlier postwar)	16	37
____ 151	Automatic Semaphore (blister pack enclosure)	20	75
____ 152	Automatic Crossing Gate	3	13
____ 153	Automatic Block Control Signal	5	17

BOXES

		Good (P-5)	Exc (P-7)	
154	Automatic Highway Signal (cellophane)	5	23	____
154	Automatic Highway Signal (all other boxes)	3	10	____
155	Blinking Light Signal	8	43	____
156	Station Platform	19	45	____
157	Station Platform	9	27	____
160	Unloading Bin	21	110	____
161	Mail Pickup Set (with liner)	10	40	____
163	Single Target Block Signal (white box)	20	65	____
164	Log Loader	23	64	____
167	Whistle Controller	4	10	____
175	Rocket Launcher	22	66	____
175-50	Rocket, separate sale	75	190	____
175-50	Dealer Display Box, 6 rockets	75	468	____
182	Magnetic Crane	20	73	____
192	Operating Control Tower	35	143	____
193	Industrial Water Tower	13	51	____
195	Floodlight Tower	6	25	____
195	Floodlight Tower (cellophane)	5	30	____
195-75	Floodlight Extension, 8-bulb (classic)	6	47	____
195-75	Floodlight Extension, 8-bulb (white box)	6	55	____
197	Rotating Radar Antenna	9	40	____
197-15	Separate Sale Radar Head	33	115	____
199	Microwave Relay Tower	5	35	____
202	UP Alco Diesel A Unit	11	50	____
204	Santa Fe Alco AA Set (master carton)	89	215	____
204	Santa Fe Alco AA Set (P and T boxes)	20	124	____
204P	Santa Fe A Unit	18	45	____
204T	Santa Fe Diesel Dummy A Unit	19	42	____
208	Santa Fe Alco AA Set (master carton)	49	254	____
208	Santa Fe Alco AA Set (P and T boxes)	21	106	____
208P	Santa Fe Alco A Unit	18	78	____
208T	Santa Fe Alco Dummy A Unit	45	76	____
209	New Haven Alco AA Set (master carton)	104	369	____
209	New Haven Alco AA Set (P and T boxes)	50	298	____
209P	New Haven Alco A Unit	20	95	____
209T	New Haven Diesel Dummy A Unit	45	135	____
210	Texas Special Alco AA Set (P and T boxes)	12	50	____
210P	Texas Special Alco A Unit	9	25	____
210T	Texas Special Alco Dummy A Unit	19	40	____
211	Texas Special Alco AA Set (P and T boxes)	29	132	____
211P	Texas Special Alco A Unit (brown corrugated)	20	60	____
212P	USMC Alco Diesel A Unit	33	80	____
212T	USMC Diesel Dummy A Unit	136	467	____
214	Plate Girder Bridge (classic)	3	10	____
214	Plate Girder Bridge (Hillside orange picture)	9	28	____

BOXES

		Good (P-5)	Exc (P-7)
___ 216	Burlington Alco Diesel A Unit	15	93
___ 217	B&M Alco AB Set (C and P boxes)	32	148
___ 217C	B&M Alco B Unit	15	50
___ 217P	B&M Alco A Unit	18	44
___ 217-16	Sleeve for 217 and 218 outer boxes	38	85
___ 218	Santa Fe Alco AA Set (master carton)	19	98
___ 218C	Santa Fe Alco Diesel B Unit	20	45
___ 218P	Santa Fe Alco Diesel A Unit	18	54
___ 218T	Santa Fe Diesel Dummy A Unit	18	60
___ 220	Santa Fe Alco AA Set (P and T boxes)	17	93
___ 220T	Santa Fe Alco Dummy A Unit	20	115
___ 221	2-6-4 Locomotive	15	60
___ 221T	Tender	10	27
___ 221W	Whistling Tender	12	39
___ 223P	Santa Fe Alco A Unit	15	58
___ 224	2-6-2 Locomotive	17	46
___ 224	U.S. Navy Alco AB Set (C and P boxes)	26	128
___ 224P	U.S. Navy Alco A unit	40	210
___ 225	C & O Alco Diesel A Unit	12	64
___ 226	B&M Alco Diesel AB Set (C and P boxes)	24	100
___ 226P	B&M Alco Diesel A Unit	9	44
___ 228P	CN Alco Diesel A Unit	20	65
___ 229C	M&StL Alco B Unit	11	39
___ 229P	M&StL Alco A Unit (brown corrugated)	8	40
___ 230P	C&O Alco A Unit	14	64
___ 231P	Rock Island Alco A Unit	12	48
___ 233	2-4-2 Scout Locomotive	10	35
___ 234W	Whistle Tender	18	40
___ 235	2-4-2 Scout Locomotive	26	89
___ 236	2-4-2 Scout Locomotive	10	45
___ 237	2-4-2 Scout Locomotive	10	39
___ 243	2-4-2 Scout Locomotive	10	33
___ 243W	Tender	5	20
___ 244T	Tender (overstamped 1625T box)	23	79
___ 245	2-4-2 Scout Locomotive	15	60
___ 246	2-4-2 Scout Locomotive	13	39
___ 247	2-4-2 Scout Locomotive	13	35
___ 247T	Tender	5	37
___ 248	2-4-2 Scout Locomotive	9	35
___ 249	2-4-2 Scout Locomotive	18	48
___ 250	2-4-2 Scout Locomotive	10	30
___ 250T	Tender	8	27
___ 252	Crossing Gate	3	10
___ 253	Block Control Signal	5	14
___ 256	Illuminated Freight Station	11	35

BOXES

		Good (P-5)	Exc (P-7)
257	Freight Station with diesel horn	9	35 ____
260	Bumper (Hagerstown checkerboard)	5	21 ____
260	Bumper (all other boxes)	2	4 ____
262	Highway Crossing Gate	4	22 ____
264	Operating Forklift Platform	24	62 ____
282	Portal Gantry Crane	25	67 ____
299	Code Transmitter Beacon Set	10	61 ____
308	Railroad Sign Set	2	11 ____
309	Yard Sign Set	3	13 ____
310	Billboard Set	1	7 ____
313	Bascule Bridge	35	133 ____
314	Scale Model Girder Bridge	3	11 ____
315	Illuminated Trestle Bridge	24	88 ____
316	Trestle Bridge	5	15 ____
317	Trestle Bridge	8	25 ____
321	Trestle Bridge	5	14 ____
321-100	Trestle Bridge	7	20 ____
332	Arch-Under Trestle Bridge	5	17 ____
334	Operating Dispatching Board	10	42 ____
342	Culvert Loader	21	56 ____
345	Culvert Unloader	25	69 ____
350	Engine Transfer Table	13	59 ____
350-50	Transfer Table Extension	15	57 ____
352	Ice Depot	19	73 ____
353	Trackside Control Signal	3	14 ____
356	Operating Freight Station	8	37 ____
356-35	Baggage Trucks Set	10	46 ____
362	Barrel Loader	5	26 ____
362-78	Wooden Barrels	1	8 ____
364	Conveyor Lumber Loader	10	24 ____
365	Dispatching Station	15	38 ____
375	Turntable	26	84 ____
394	Rotary Beacon	7	22 ____
394-37	Rotating Beacon Cap	2	8 ____
395	Floodlight Tower	10	34 ____
397	Operating Coal Loader	11	35 ____
397	Operating Coal Loader (separate label on box)	10	40 ____
400	B&O Passenger Rail Diesel Car	28	54 ____
404	B&O Baggage-Mail Rail Diesel Car	32	91 ____
410	Billboard Blinker	3	10 ____
413	Countdown Control Panel	6	20 ____
415	Diesel Fueling Station	15	43 ____
419	Heliport Control Tower	22	133 ____
443	Missile Launching Platform	10	29 ____
445	Switch Tower	6	19 ____

BOXES

			Good (P-5)	Exc (P-7)
____	448	Missile Firing Range Set	15	50
____	450	Operating Signal Bridge	2	20
____	452	Overhead Gantry Signal	8	38
____	455	Operating Oil Derrick	17	70
____	456	Coal Ramp	18	49
____	460	Piggyback Transportation Set	16	40
____	460-150	Two Trailers	71	224
____	461	Platform with truck and trailer	10	45
____	462	Derrick Platform Set	50	172
____	464	Lumber Mill	9	43
____	465	Sound Dispatching Station	13	38
____	470	Missile Launching Platform	5	33
____	494	Rotary Beacon (classic)	5	25
____	497	Coaling Station	24	57
____	600	MKT NW2 Switcher	19	74
____	601	Seaboard NW2 Switcher	23	84
____	602	Seaboard NW2 Switcher	29	78
____	610	Erie NW2 Switcher	15	94
____	611	Jersey Central NW2 Switcher (overstamped 621 box)	50	124
____	613	UP NW2 Switcher	26	105
____	614	Alaska NW2 Switcher	32	124
____	616	Santa Fe NW2 Switcher	23	95
____	617	Santa Fe NW2 Switcher	30	134
____	621	Jersey Central NW2 Switcher	27	67
____	622	Santa Fe NW2 Switcher	44	100
____	623	Santa Fe NW2 Switcher	19	62
____	624	C&O NW2 Switcher	23	68
____	625	LV GE 44-ton Switcher	100	450
____	626	B&O GE 44-ton Switcher	42	145
____	628	Northern Pacific GE 44-ton Switcher	20	76
____	629	Burlington GE 44-ton Switcher	32	176
____	634	Santa Fe NW2 Switcher	26	113
____	637	2-6-4 Locomotive	14	55
____	637LTS	2-6-4 Locomotive and Tender (master carton)	40	188
____	646	4-6-4 Locomotive	29	58
____	665	4-6-4 Locomotive	19	52
____	665LTS	4-6-4 Locomotive and Tender (master carton)	45	280
____	671	6-8-6 Steam Turbine Locomotive	41	99
____	671R	6-8-6 Steam Turbine Locomotive	36	143
____	671W	Whistle Tender	14	54
____	671-75	Smoke Lamp, 12 volt	2	10
____	675	2-6-2 Locomotive (classic), *47–49*	24	66
____	675	2-6-2 Locomotive (brown corrugated), *52*	37	84
____	681	6-8-6 Steam Turbine Locomotive	28	111

BOXES

		Good (P-5)	Exc (P-7)	
681LTS	6-8-6 Steam Turbine Locomotive and Tender (master carton)	150	500	____
682	6-8-6 Steam Turbine Locomotive	52	141	____
682LTS	6-8-6 Steam Turbine Locomotive and Tender (master carton)	400	850	____
685	4-6-4 Hudson Locomotive	28	74	____
685LTS	4-6-4 Hudson Locomotive and Tender (master carton)	185	450	____
726	2-8-4 Berkshire Locomotive, *46*	63	184	____
726	2-8-4 Berkshire Locomotive (after 1946)	44	130	____
726RR	2-8-4 Berkshire Locomotive	23	63	____
736	2-8-4 Berkshire Locomotive, *50*	39	101	____
736	2-8-4 Berkshire Locomotive	24	69	____
736X	2-8-4 Berkshire Locomotive	33	118	____
736LTS	2-8-4 Berkshire Locomotive and Tender (master carton)	47	236	____
736W	Pennsylvania Tender	14	53	____
746	N&W 4-8-4 Locomotive	57	152	____
746LTS	N&W 4-8-4 Locomotive and Tender (master carton)	170	415	____
746W	N&W Whistle Tender	30	129	____
746WX	N&W Whistle Tender, long stripe	50	150	____
760	Curved Track	8	29	____
773	4-6-4 Hudson Locomotive, *50*	102	334	____
773	4-6-4 Hudson Locomotive, *64–66*	76	151	____
773LTS	4-6-4 Hudson Locomotive and Tender (master carton), *50*	100	542	____
773LTS	4-6-4 Hudson and Whistle Tender (master carton), *64–66*	65	342	____
773W	NYC Tender	19	89	____
810	Milwaukee Road Freight Set	75	450	____
920-2	Tunnel Portals	7	20	____
927	Lubricating Kit	2	9	____
928	Maintenance and Lubricating Kit	5	25	____
943	Ammo Dump	3	10	____
951	Farm Set	14	45	____
952	Figure Set	13	35	____
953	Figure Set	13	50	____
957	Figure Set	20	55	____
959	Barn Set	18	52	____
960	Barnyard Set	10	35	____
963	Frontier Set	15	75	____
965	Farm Set	15	55	____
966	Firehouse Set	15	55	____
969	Construction Set	8	45	____
970	Ticket Booth	7	40	____
972	Landscape Tree Assortment	10	35	____

BOXES

			Good (P-5)	Exc (P-7)
____	981	Freight Yard Set	11	35
____	983	Farm Set	15	46
____	984	Railroad Set	10	75
____	986	Farm Set	18	115
____	1000W	Steam Freight Set	49	95
____	1001	Diesel Freight Set	20	65
____	1001	2-4-2 Scout Locomotive	8	40
____	1001T	Tender	6	12
____	1002	Gondola	4	10
____	X1004	PRR Baby Ruth Boxcar	4	10
____	1005	Sunoco 1-D Tank Car	4	10
____	1007	LL SP-type Caboose	4	10
____	1009	Manumatic Track Section	10	35
____	1019	Remote Control Track Set (027)	10	20
____	1025	Illuminated Bumper (027)	3	8
____	1032	Transformer, 75 watts	2	7
____	1033	Transformer, 90 watts	4	11
____	1034	Transformer, 75 watts	2	8
____	1041	Transformer, 50 watts	3	11
____	1041	Transformer, 60 watts	6	17
____	1043	Transformer, 50 watts	5	15
____	1043-500	Transformer, 90 watts, ivory	15	75
____	1044	Transformer, 90 watts	5	13
____	1045	Operating Watchman	6	21
____	1047	Operating Switchman	31	103
____	1060	2-4-2 Locomotive (brown corrugated)	23	102
____	1107	Steam Freight Set	20	45
____	1109	Steam Freight Set	15	40
____	1110	2-4-2 Locomotive	5	24
____	1112	Scout Set	8	25
____	1113	Scout Set	15	45
____	1119	Scout Set	15	40
____	1120	2-4-2 Scout Locomotive	5	18
____	1121	027 Remote Control Switches, pair	3	12
____	1121LH	027 Remote Control Switch, left-hand	4	14
____	1121RH	027 Remote Control Switch, right-hand	4	19
____	1122	027 Remote Control Switches, pair	4	16
____	1130	2-4-2 Locomotive	10	29
____	1130T	Tender (classic)	5	16
____	1130T	Tender (orange perforated)	17	41
____	1130T-500	Tender, pink, from Girls Set	27	180
____	1232	Transformer, 75 watts, made for export	4	14
____	1407B	Steam Switcher Work Set	45	310
____	1417WS	Steam Work Train Set	40	145
____	1423W	Steam Freight Set	28	124

BOXES

		Good (P-5)	Exc (P-7)	
1425B	Steam Switcher Freight Set	70	212	___
1427WS	Steam Freight Set	10	35	___
1429WS	Steam Freight Set	47	150	___
1431	Steam Freight Set	15	50	___
1432W	O27 Steam Passenger Set	80	233	___
1435WS	Steam Freight Set	10	35	___
1447WS	Turbine Locomotive Set	33	150	___
1451WS	O27 Steam Freight Set	37	110	___
1453WS	O27 Steam Freight Set	28	83	___
1455WS	Steam Freight Set	30	70	___
1457B	Santa Fe Freight Set (marked "1457"), *49*	73	193	___
1457B	Santa Fe Freight Set, *50*	62	198	___
1459WS	Steam Freight Set	44	95	___
1463WS	Steam Freight Set	45	105	___
1464W	Union Pacific Diesel Passenger Set	128	399	___
1465	Steam Freight Set	32	76	___
1467W	Union Pacific Freight Set	50	135	___
1469WS	Steam Freight Set	25	70	___
1471	Steam Freight Set	25	70	___
1471WS	Steam Freight Set	20	53	___
1473WS	Steam Freight Set	20	80	___
1475	Steam Freight Set	15	40	___
1479WS	Steam Freight Set	16	54	___
1481WS	Steam Freight Set	28	80	___
1483WS	Steam Freight Set	35	113	___
1485WS	Steam Freight Set	24	65	___
1500	Steam Freight Set	15	65	___
1502WS	Steam Freight Set	238	558	___
1503WS	Steam Freight Set	30	67	___
1505WS	Steam Freight Set	36	93	___
1507WS	Steam Freight Set	34	93	___
1511S	Steam Freight Set	20	60	___
1513S	Steam Freight Set	35	115	___
1515WS	Steam Freight Set	39	119	___
1517W	Texas Special Freight Set	35	181	___
1519WS	Steam Freight Set	50	170	___
1520W	Texas Special Passenger Set	170	658	___
1521WS	Steam Work Train Set	77	268	___
1523	Diesel Freight Set	55	155	___
1525	Diesel Freight Set	35	80	___
1527	O27 Steam Work Train Set	45	175	___
1529	Pennsylvania Diesel Freight Set	92	250	___
1531W	Diesel Freight Set	30	92	___
1533WS	Steam Freight Set	28	65	___
1534W	Burlington Diesel Passenger Set	169	466	___

BOXES

		Good (P-5)	Exc (P-7)
____ 1535W	Diesel Freight Set	105	300
____ 1536W	Diesel Passenger Set	75	285
____ 1537WS	Steam Freight Set	25	50
____ 1538WS	Hudson Passenger Set	155	775
____ 1539W	Santa Fe Diesel Freight Set	88	250
____ 1542	Electric Freight Set	10	38
____ 1543	Lehigh Valley Freight Set	13	41
____ 1547S	Steam Freight Set	20	50
____ 1549	Steam Work Train Set	38	95
____ 1551W	Diesel Freight Set	10	55
____ 1552W	Diesel Passenger Set	70	285
____ 1553W	Diesel Freight Set	28	60
____ 1555WS	027 Steam Freight Set	30	71
____ 1557	Diesel Freight Set	30	88
____ 1559W	MILW Diesel Freight Set	35	90
____ 1562W	Burlington GP7 Diesel Passenger Set	30	100
____ 1569	UP Diesel Freight Set	28	55
____ 1571	LV Diesel Freight Set	30	65
____ 1573	Steam Freight Set	33	75
____ 1575	Diesel Freight Set	30	60
____ 1578S	Steam Passenger Set	200	494
____ 1581	Jersey Central Mixed Set	40	79
____ 1583WS	Steam Freight Set	30	70
____ 1585W	Diesel Freight Set	30	75
____ 1586	Diesel Passenger Set	30	90
____ 1587S	Girls Train Set	430	1207
____ 1589WS	027 Steam Freight Set	45	180
____ 1590	Steam Freight Set	33	60
____ 1591	USMC Military Set	113	633
____ 1593	UP Diesel Work Train Set	35	90
____ 1599W	Texas Special Freight Set	39	106
____ 1600	Diesel Passenger Set	180	590
____ 1601W	Wabash GP7 Diesel Set	43	310
____ 1603WS	Steam Freight Set	45	110
____ 1605W	Santa Fe Diesel Freight Set	50	145
____ 1607WS	Steam Work Train Set	18	40
____ 1608W	New Haven Passenger Set	76	559
____ 1609W	Steam Freight Set	40	85
____ 1611	027 Alaska Diesel Freight Set	78	220
____ 1612	027 General Set	40	140
____ 1613S	Steam Freight Set	35	110
____ 1615	B&M Diesel Freight Set	20	50
____ 1615	0-4-0 Locomotive	15	46
____ 1615LTS	0-4-0 Locomotive and Tender (master carton)	29	113
____ 1615T	Tender	7	64

BOXES

		Good (P-5)	Exc (P-7)	
1619W	Santa Fe Diesel Freight Set	45	125	____
1621WS	O27 Steam Freight Set (brown corrugated)	95	275	____
1621WS	O27 Steam Freight Set (suitcase)	40	125	____
1623W	NP Diesel Freight Set	50	165	____
1625	0-4-0 Locomotive	23	100	____
1625T	Tender	18	114	____
1625WS	Steam Freight Set	41	140	____
1629WS	C&O Diesel Freight Set	20	115	____
1631WS	O27 Steam Freight Set	25	75	____
1633	U.S. Navy Diesel Freight Set	108	369	____
1637	Santa Fe Diesel Freight Set	20	50	____
1640-100	Presidential Kit	19	56	____
1643	C&O Diesel Freight Set	20	55	____
1647	U.S. Marines Military Set	40	90	____
1648	Steam Freight Set	8	23	____
1649	Santa Fe Steam Freight Set	20	60	____
1650	Steam Military Set	43	85	____
1651	Passenger Train Set	39	122	____
1654	2-4-2 Locomotive	5	28	____
1655	2-4-2 Locomotive	10	40	____
1656	0-4-0 Locomotive	26	133	____
1656LTS	4-4-0 Locomotive and Tender (master carton)	50	225	____
1665	0-4-0 Locomotive	30	173	____
1666	2-6-2 Locomotive	15	45	____
1682T	Tender	5	22	____
1800	General Gift Pack	20	115	____
1809	Western Gift Pack	8	60	____
1862	4-4-0 Civil War General Locomotive	25	88	____
1862T	Tender	15	60	____
1865	Western & Atlantic Coach	10	46	____
1866	Western & Atlantic Mail-Baggage Car	10	45	____
1872	4-4-0 Civil War General Locomotive	35	100	____
1872LTS	4-4-0 Locomotive and Tender (master carton)	115	400	____
1872T	Tender	18	41	____
1875	Western & Atlantic Coach	38	183	____
1875W	Western & Atlantic Coach, whistle	15	91	____
1876	Western & Atlantic Baggage Car	13	70	____
1877	Flatcar with fence and horses	8	40	____
2001	Track Make-up Kit (O27)	800	2000	____
2002	Track Make-up Kit (O27)	700	1500	____
2016	2-6-4 Locomotive	7	30	____
2018	2-6-4 Locomotive	8	32	____
2020	6-8-6 Steam Turbine Locomotive	22	73	____
2020W	Tender	11	72	____
2023	Union Pacific Alco AA Set (master carton), *50*	35	108	____

	BOXES		Good (P-5)	Exc (P-7)
____	2023	Union Pacific Alco AA Set (master carton), *51*	30	105
____	2025	2-6-2 or 2-6-4 Locomotive	13	50
____	2026	2-6-2 or 2-6-4 Locomotive	10	60
____	2028	Pennsylvania GP7 Diesel	25	88
____	2029	2-6-4 Locomotive	12	47
____	2031	Rock Island Alco AA Set (master carton), *52*	58	144
____	2032	Erie Alco AA Set (master carton)	34	111
____	2033	Uinion Pacific Alco AA Set (master carton)	36	94
____	2034	2-4-2 Scout Locomotive	6	53
____	2035	2-6-4 Locomotive	17	75
____	2036	2-6-4 Locomotive	9	58
____	2036LTS	2-6-4 Locomotive and Tender (master carton)	450	1294
____	2037	2-6-4 Locomotive (brown corrugated)	12	33
____	2037-500	2-6-4 Locomotive, pink, from Girls Set	54	250
____	2046	4-6-4 Locomotive	34	77
____	2046LTS	4-6-4 Locomotive and Tender (master carton)	90	250
____	2046T	Lionel Lines Tender, for export	23	77
____	2046W	Lionel Lines Tender (early classic, with liner)	19	44
____	2046W	Lionel Lines Tender (marked "2046")	16	72
____	2046W	Pennsylvania Tender	30	130
____	2046W-50	Pennsylvania Tender	10	55
____	2055	4-6-4 Locomotive	22	74
____	2055LTS	4-6-4 Locomotive and Tender (master carton)	50	245
____	2056	4-6-4 Locomotive	18	53
____	2065	4-6-4 Locomotive	20	47
____	2103W	Steam Freight Set	25	90
____	2105WS	Steam Freight Set	65	130
____	2113WS	Steam Freight Set	28	213
____	2121WS	Steam Freight Set	45	255
____	2124W	GG1 Passenger Set	144	1457
____	2126WS	Steam Turbine Passenger Set	60	871
____	2136WS	Steam Passenger Set	40	90
____	2139W	GG1 Freight Set	152	919
____	2140WS	Steam Turbine Passenger Set	60	816
____	2141WS	Steam Turbine Freight Set	40	180
____	2146W	Berkshire Passenger Set	75	278
____	2148WS	Hudson Passenger Set	232	1688
____	2149	Santa Fe Diesel Freight Set	105	435
____	2151W	F3 Freight Set	113	280
____	2153WS	Steam Freight Set	60	195
____	2155WS	Berkshire Freight Set	25	162
____	2159W	GG1 Freight Set	134	568
____	2161W	Santa Fe Twin Diesel Freight Set	42	150
____	2163WS	Steam Freight Set	45	160
____	2165WS	Steam Freight Set	50	125

BOXES

		Good (P-5)	Exc (P-7)	
2167WS	Steam Freight Set	34	146	____
2171W	NYC Diesel Freight Set	30	90	____
2173WS	Steam Freight Set	85	145	____
2175W	Santa Fe Diesel Freight Set	49	183	____
2177WS	Steam Freight Set	15	52	____
2179WS	Steam Freight Set	20	75	____
2183WS	Steam Freight Set	43	90	____
2185W	NYC Diesel Freight Set	55	100	____
2187WS	Steam Freight Set	25	60	____
2190W	Santa Fe Diesel Passenger Set	30	103	____
2191W	Santa Fe Diesel Freight Set	43	172	____
2193W	NYC Diesel Freight Set	47	93	____
2201WS	Steam Freight Set	43	90	____
2203WS	Steam Freight Set	92	330	____
2205WS	Steam Freight Set	30	75	____
2207W	Santa Fe Diesel Freight Set	38	152	____
2209W	NYC Diesel Freight Set	41	80	____
2211WS	Steam Freight Set	30	75	____
2213WS	Steam Freight Set	33	70	____
2217WS	Steam Turbine Freight Set	71	167	____
2219W	Diesel Freight Set	92	375	____
2221WS	Steam Freight Set	36	132	____
2222WS	Hudson Passenger Set	109	786	____
2223W	Lackawanna FM Freight Set	202	510	____
2225T	Tender	20	100	____
2225WS	Steam Freight Set	30	170	____
2226W	Tender	40	115	____
2226WX	Lionel Lines Tender	50	130	____
2227W	Santa Fe Diesel Freight Set	88	328	____
2231W	Southern Diesel Freight Set	65	210	____
2234W	Santa Fe Passenger Set	67	365	____
2235W	Milwaukee Road Diesel Freight Set	60	175	____
2237WS	Steam Freight Set	60	170	____
2239W	Illinois Central Freight Set	130	375	____
2240	Wabash F3 AB Set (C and P boxes)	56	310	____
2240	Wabash F3 AB Set (master carton)	107	775	____
2240C	Wabash F3 B Unit	40	120	____
2240P	Wabash F3 A Unit	39	106	____
2241WS	Steam Freight Set	20	60	____
2242	New Haven F3 AB Set (C and P boxes)	73	600	____
2242	New Haven F3 AB Set (master carton)	300	1025	____
2242C	New Haven F3 B Unit	105	420	____
2242P	New Haven F3 A Unit	163	400	____
2243	Santa Fe F3 AB Set (C and P boxes)	24	95	____
2243	Santa Fe F3 AB Set (master carton)	38	126	____

BOXES

		Good (P-5)	Exc (P-7)
___ 2243C	Santa Fe F3 B Unit	25	70
___ 2243P	Santa Fe F3 A Unit	35	110
___ 2243W	Diesel Freight Set	30	85
___ 2244W	Wabash Passenger Set	223	899
___ 2245	Texas Special F3 AB Set (C and P boxes)	54	255
___ 2245	Texas Special F3 AB Set (master carton)	300	800
___ 2245C	Texas Special F3 B Unit	35	111
___ 2245P	Texas Special F3 A Unit	26	83
___ 2247W	Wabash F3 Diesel Freight Set	80	280
___ 2251W	Diesel Freight Set	35	170
___ 2254W	Pennsylvania GG1 Passenger Set, 55	203	1266
___ 2255W	Diesel Work Train Set	34	169
___ 2257	SP-type Caboose	4	16
___ 2257WS	Steam Freight Set	28	131
___ 2259W	New Haven Electric Freight Set	38	171
___ 2261WS	Steam Freight Set	30	90
___ 2263W	New Haven Freight Set	40	210
___ 2265WS	Steam Freight Set	27	117
___ 2267W	Diesel Freight Set	57	250
___ 2269W	B&O Diesel Freight Set	120	712
___ 2270W	Jersey Central Passenger Set	167	1130
___ 2271W	Pennsylvania GG1 Freight Set	23	385
___ 2273W	Milwaukee Road Diesel Freight Set	93	670
___ 2274W	Pennsylvania Passenger Set	230	738
___ 2275W	Wabash GP7 Freight Set	70	130
___ 2276W	Budd Passenger Set	25	318
___ 2277WS	Work Train Set	20	170
___ 2283W	Steam Freight Set	20	125
___ 2289WS	Berkshire Super O Freight Set	46	206
___ 2291W	Rio Grande Diesel Freight Set	129	594
___ 2292WS	Steam Passenger Set	109	979
___ 2293W	Pennsylvania GG1 Freight Set	156	1035
___ 2295WS	N&W Steam Freight Set	154	1038
___ 2296W	Canadian Pacific Passenger Set	258	1306
___ 2297WS	N&W Steam Freight Set	99	625
___ 2321	Lackawanna FM Train Master Diesel	47	115
___ 2322	Virginian FM Train Master Diesel	30	102
___ 2328	Burlington GP7 Diesel	33	101
___ 2329	Virginian Electric Locomotive	53	251
___ 2330	Pennsylvania GG1 Electric Locomotive	69	290
___ 2331	Virginian FM Train Master Diesel	33	117
___ 2332	Pennsylvania GG1 Electric Locomotive	32	94
___ 2332-275	Pennsylvania GG1 Electric Locomotive	73	227
___ 2333	NYC F3 AA Set (master carton)	45	122
___ 2333	NYC F3 AA Set (P and T boxes)	38	180

BOXES

		Good (P-5)	Exc (P-7)	
2333P	NYC F3 A Unit (brown corrugated)	25	85	____
2333	Santa Fe F3 AA Set (master carton)	55	168	____
2333	Santa Fe F3 AA Set (P and T boxes)	35	92	____
2333T	Santa Fe F3 Dummy A Unit	25	60	____
2333P	Santa Fe F3 A Unit	17	63	____
2337	Wabash GP7 Diesel, *58*	28	213	____
2338	MILW GP7 Diesel (classic)	23	135	____
2338	MILW GP7 Diesel (brown corrugated)	10	59	____
2338	MILW GP7 Diesel (brown corrugated marked "2338X")	25	109	____
2339	Wabash GP7 Diesel, *57*	21	114	____
2340-10	Pennsylvania GG1 Electric, tuscan	75	205	____
2340-25	Pennsylvania GG1 Electric, green, gold stripes	31	169	____
2341	Jersey Central FM Train Master Diesel	169	797	____
2343	Santa Fe F3 AA Set (master carton)	45	104	____
2343	Santa Fe F3 AA Set (P and T boxes)	40	147	____
2343C	Santa Fe F3 B Unit	22	74	____
2343P	Santa Fe F3 A Unit	19	54	____
2343T	Santa Fe F3 Dummy Unit	23	82	____
2344	NYC F3 AA Set (master carton)	83	211	____
2344	NYC F3 AA Set (P and T boxes)	60	195	____
2344C	NYC F3 B Unit	41	79	____
2344P	NYC F3 A Unit	47	177	____
2344T	NYC F3 Dummy Unit	33	166	____
2345	Western Pacific F3 AA Set (master carton)	175	475	____
2345	Western Pacific F3 AA Set (P and T boxes, brown corrugated)	50	304	____
2345P	Western Pacific F3 A Unit	40	90	____
2345T	Western Pacific F3 Dummy A Unit	80	235	____
2346	B&M GP9 Diesel	29	132	____
2347	C&O GP9 Diesel	450	1200	____
2348	M&StL GP9 Diesel	37	142	____
2349	Northern Pacific GP9 Diesel	64	194	____
2349-12	Sleeve for 2349 and 2359 outer boxes	17	101	____
2350	New Haven EP-5 Electric Locomotive	35	105	____
2351	Milwaukee Road EP-5 Electric Locomotive	34	127	____
2352	Pennsylvania EP-5 Electric Locomotive	50	195	____
2353	Santa Fe F3 AA Set (master carton)	68	223	____
2353	Santa Fe F3 AA Set (P and T boxes)	40	138	____
2353P	Santa Fe F3 A Unit (brown corrugated)	24	60	____
2353T	Santa Fe F3 Dummy Unit	33	120	____
2354	NYC F3 AA Set (master carton)	31	295	____
2354P	NYC F3 A Unit (brown corrugated)	58	146	____
2354T	NYC F3 Dummy Unit	38	118	____
2355	Western Pacific F3 AA Set (master carton)	97	253	____
2355	Western Pacific F3 AA Set (P and T boxes)	60	322	____

BOXES

			Good (P-5)	Exc (P-7)
____	2355P	Western Pacific F3 A Unit	50	181
____	2355T	Western Pacific F3 Dummy A Unit	40	112
____	2356	Southern F3 AA Set (master carton)	84	422
____	2356C	Southern F3 B Unit	41	244
____	2356P	Southern F3 A Unit	44	98
____	2356T	Southern F3 Dummy Unit	56	265
____	2357	SP-type Caboose	4	13
____	2358	Great Northern EP-5 Electric Locomotive	72	212
____	2359	Boston & Maine GP9 Diesel	19	98
____	2360-10	Pennsylvania GG1 Electric Locomotive, tuscan	71	227
____	2360-25	Pennsylvania GG1 Electric Locomotive, green	39	207
____	2363	Illinois Central F3 AB Set (master carton)	183	671
____	2363	Illinois Central F3 AB Set (C and P boxes)	94	368
____	2363C	Illinois Central F3 B Unit	90	167
____	2363P	Illinois Central F3 A Unit	28	101
____	2365	C&O GP7 Diesel	15	59
____	2367C	Wabash F3 B Unit	24	317
____	2367P	Wabash F3 A Unit	38	130
____	2368	B&O F3 AB Set (master carton)	200	884
____	2368C	B&O F3 B Unit	53	262
____	2368P	B&O F3 A Unit	28	214
____	2373	CP F3 AA Set (P and T boxes)	168	495
____	2373P	CP F3 A Unit	55	167
____	2373T	CP F3 Dummy A Unit	55	168
____	2378	Milwaukee Road F3 AB Set (master carton)	169	867
____	2378C	Milwaukee Road F3 B Unit	85	264
____	2378P	Milwaukee Road F3 A Unit	64	224
____	2379C	Rio Grande F3 B Unit	48	171
____	2379P	Rio Grande F3 A Unit	60	157
____	2383	Santa Fe F3 AA Units (master carton)	55	206
____	2383P	Santa Fe F3 A Unit	17	74
____	2383T	Santa Fe F3 Dummy Unit	32	73
____	2400	Maplewood Pullman Car	19	77
____	2401	Hillside Observation Car	18	51
____	2402	Chatham Pullman Car	18	65
____	2403B	Tender with bell	18	102
____	2404	Santa Fe Vista Dome Car	18	54
____	2405	Santa Fe Pullman Car	17	52
____	2406	Santa Fe Observation Car	16	46
____	2408	Santa Fe Vista Dome Car	15	48
____	2409	Santa Fe Pullman Car	15	55
____	2410	Santa Fe Observation Car	14	56
____	2411	Lionel Lines Flatcar	10	37
____	2412	Santa Fe Vista Dome Car	19	61
____	2414	Santa Fe Pullman Car	17	53

BOXES

		Good (P-5)	Exc (P-7)	
2416	Santa Fe Observation Car (orange perforated)	15	100	____
2416	Santa Fe Observation Car (orange picture)	15	53	____
2419	DL&W Work Caboose	14	43	____
2420	DL&W Work Caboose with searchlight	25	57	____
2421	Maplewood Pullman Car	13	45	____
2422	Chatham Pullman Car	15	43	____
2423	Hillside Observation Car	13	43	____
2426W	Hudson Tender (early classic)	76	248	____
2426W	Hudson Tender (middle classic)	55	209	____
2429	Livingston Pullman Car	19	69	____
2430	Pullman Car, blue	12	36	____
2431	Observation Car, blue	12	36	____
2432	Clifton Vista Dome Car	16	43	____
2434	Newark Pullman Car	15	39	____
2435	Elizabeth Pullman Car	21	53	____
2436	Mooseheart Observation Car	16	37	____
2436	Mooseheart Observation Car (classic)	9	33	____
2440	Pullman Car, green	8	30	____
2441	Observation Car, green	8	30	____
2442	Pullman Car, brown	8	30	____
2442	Clifton Vista Dome Car	17	54	____
2443	Observation Car, brown	9	30	____
2444	Newark Pullman Car	15	50	____
2445	Elizabeth Pullman Car	25	104	____
2446	Summit Observation Car	15	46	____
2452	Pennsylvania Gondola	11	28	____
2452X	Pennsylvania Gondola	5	15	____
X2454	Pennsylvania Boxcar (marked "Box Car")	16	30	____
X2454	Pennsylvania Boxcar (marked "Merchandise Car")	20	66	____
2456	Lehigh Valley Hopper	6	16	____
2457	Pennsylvania N5-type Caboose	7	25	____
2458	Pennsylvania Automobile Boxcar	9	35	____
2460	Bucyrus Erie Crane Car (box with toy logo)	12	52	____
2460	Bucyrus Erie Crane Car (box without toy logo)	23	70	____
2461	Transformer Car	13	50	____
2465	Sunoco 2-D Tank Car	3	15	____
2466T	Tender	5	26	____
2466W	Tender	14	39	____
2466WX	Tender	15	40	____
2472	PRR N5-type Caboose	3	12	____
2481	Plainfield Pullman Car	35	160	____
2482	Westfield Pullman Car	37	158	____
2483	Livingston Observation Car	37	192	____
2501W	M&StL Diesel Freight Set	24	243	____
2503WS	Super O Steam Freight Set	30	70	____

BOXES

			Good (P-5)	Exc (P-7)
_____	2505W	Super O Electric Freight Set	60	272
_____	2507W	New Haven Diesel Freight Set	44	524
_____	2509WS	Super O Steam Freight Set	23	224
_____	2511W	Pennsylvania Electric Work Set	49	248
_____	2513W	Virginian Rectifier Set	37	399
_____	2515WS	Super O Steam Freight Set	165	565
_____	2517W	Rio Grande Diesel Freight Set	85	185
_____	2518W	Pennsylvania Electric Passenger Set	72	863
_____	2519W	Virginian Train Master Super O Freight Set	32	523
_____	2521	President McKinley Observation Car	22	77
_____	2521WS	Super O Steam Freight Set	25	110
_____	2522	President Harrison Vista Dome Car	24	97
_____	2523	President Garfield Pullman Car	27	76
_____	2523W	Santa Fe Super O Freight Set	30	319
_____	2525WS	Super O Steam Work Train Set	213	562
_____	2526W	Santa Fe Passenger Set	33	530
_____	2527	Missile Launcher Set, yellow	29	101
_____	2528WS	Super O General Set	35	167
_____	2530	REA Baggage Car	21	113
_____	2530	REA Baggage Car (orange perforated)	118	411
_____	2531	Silver Dawn Observation Car	21	51
_____	2531WS	Super O Steam Freight Set	55	124
_____	2532	Silver Range Vista Dome Car	16	55
_____	2533	Silver Cloud Pullman Car	22	62
_____	2533W	Super O GN Electric Freight Set	120	540
_____	2534	Silver Bluff Pullman Car	20	50
_____	2535WS	Steam Freight Set	45	210
_____	2537W	New Haven Freight Set	39	352
_____	2541	Alexander Hamilton Observation Car	25	66
_____	2541W	Santa Fe Super O Freight Set	149	650
_____	2542	Betsy Ross Vista Dome Car	23	73
_____	2543	William Penn Pullman Car	22	78
_____	2543WS	Berkshire Freight Set	113	475
_____	2544	Molly Pitcher Pullman Car	25	78
_____	2544W	Santa Fe Passenger Set	104	999
_____	2545WS	Super O Military Set	110	1000
_____	2549W	Super O Military Set	23	90
_____	2550	B&O Baggage-Mail Rail Diesel Car	45	187
_____	2551	Banff Park Observation Car	28	103
_____	2551W	GN Electric Set	120	624
_____	2552	Skyline 500 Vista Dome Car	33	101
_____	2553	Blair Manor Pullman Car	62	167
_____	2553WS	Berkshire Freight Set	65	289
_____	2554	Craig Manor Pullman Car	69	163
_____	2555	Sunoco 1-D Tank Car	10	46

BOXES

		Good (P-5)	Exc (P-7)	
2555	Sunoco 1-D Tank Car (overstamped 2755 box)	22	93	____
2559	B&O Passenger Rail Diesel Car	31	112	____
2560	Lionel Lines Crane Car	16	64	____
2561	Vista Valley Observation Car	38	125	____
2561	Vista Valley Observation Car (orange perforated)	88	173	____
2562	Regal Pass Observation Car	33	125	____
2562	Regal Pass Observation Car (orange perforated)	68	173	____
2563	Indian Falls Pullman Car	39	128	____
2570	Super O Santa Fe Work Train Set	40	240	____
2572	Boston & Maine Military Set	27	155	____
2574	Santa Fe Military Set	85	305	____
2625	Irvington Pullman Car	40	150	____
2627	Madison Pullman Car	24	93	____
2628	Manhattan Pullman Car	27	101	____
2671T	Pennsylvania Tender, for export	17	63	____
2671W	Pennsylvania Tender	20	75	____
2671WX	Lionel Lines Tender	23	59	____
2755	Sunoco 1-D Tank Car	17	65	____
2758	PRR Automobile Boxcar	8	32	____
2855	Sunoco 1-D Tank Car	29	136	____
3330	Flatcar with submarine kit	17	68	____
3330-100	Operating Submarine Kit, separate sale	47	194	____
3349	Turbo Missile Launch Car	6	25	____
3356	Operating Horse Car and Corral Set (classic)	13	62	____
3356	Operating Horse Car and Corral Set (orange picture)	23	88	____
3356-2	Horse Car	71	451	____
3356-100	Black Horses (classic)	4	15	____
3356-100	Black Horses (white box)	8	23	____
3356-150	Horse Car Corral	65	770	____
3357	Hydraulic Maintenance Car	11	36	____
3357-27	Trestle Components for Cop and Hobo Car	10	25	____
3359	Lionel Lines Twin-bin Coal Dump Car	14	44	____
3360	Operating Burro Crane	19	79	____
3361	Operating Log Dump Car	5	23	____
3361X	Operating Log Dump Car	5	23	____
3362	Helium Tank Unloading Car	17	42	____
3362/3364	Operating Unloading Car (Hagerstown checkerboard)	20	50	____
3364	Log Unloading Car	9	33	____
3366	Circus Car Corral Set	42	152	____
3366-100	White Horses	8	38	____
3370	W&A Outlaw Car	9	38	____
3376	Bronx Zoo Car	15	42	____
3376-160	Bronx Zoo Car, green	14	53	____
3410	Helicopter Car	18	80	____

BOXES

			Good (P-5)	Exc (P-7)
____	3413	Mercury Capsule Car	13	68
____	3419	Helicopter Car	15	48
____	3424	Wabash Operating Boxcar	23	62
____	3424-75	Low Bridge Signal (marked "3424-75" or overstamped on 3424-100 box)	103	288
____	3424-100	Low Bridge Signal	4	14
____	3428	U.S. Mail Operating Boxcar	9	43
____	3434	Poultry Dispatch Car	17	64
____	3435	Traveling Aquarium Car	38	132
____	3444	Erie Operating Gondola	11	28
____	3451	Operating Log Dump Car	7	32
____	3454	PRR Operating Merchandise Car	33	122
____	3456	N&W Operating Hopper	19	52
____	3459	LL Operating Coal Dump Car (no toymaker's logo)	29	77
____	3459	LL Operating Coal Dump Car (toymaker's logo)	18	74
____	3461	LL Operating Log Car	10	25
____	3461X	Automatic Lumber Car	28	63
____	3461X-25	Lionel Lines Operating Log Car, green	10	25
____	3462	Automatic Milk Car	13	50
____	3464	NYC Operating Boxcar	4	17
____	3469	LL Operating Coal Dump Car	18	47
____	3469X	LL Operating Coal Dump Car	8	20
____	3470	Target Launching Car	16	41
____	3472	Automatic Milk Car	13	37
____	3474	Western Pacific Operating Boxcar	8	64
____	3482	Automatic Milk Car	13	39
____	3484	Pennsylvania Operating Boxcar	9	27
____	3484-25	ATSF Operating Boxcar	7	40
____	3494	NYC Operating Boxcar	17	46
____	3494-150	Missouri Pacific Operating Boxcar	13	47
____	3494-275	State of Maine Operating Boxcar	16	48
____	3494-550	Monon Operating Boxcar	46	194
____	3494-625	Soo Operating Boxcar	54	189
____	3509	Satellite Launching Car	15	62
____	3512	Fireman and Ladder Car	17	76
____	3519	Satellite Launching Car	13	39
____	3520	Searchlight Car	9	36
____	3530	GM Generator Car	15	54
____	3530-50	Searchlight with pole and base, separate sale	46	93
____	3535	Security Car with searchlight	14	51
____	3540	Operating Radar Car	24	74
____	3545	Operating TV Monitor Car	21	73
____	3559	Operating Coal Dump Car	14	40
____	3562-1	ATSF Operating Barrel Car	29	105
____	3562-25	ATSF Operating Barrel Car, gray	18	41

BOXES

		Good (P-5)	Exc (P-7)	
3562-50	ATSF Operating Barrel Car, yellow	19	55	___
3562-75	ATSF Operating Barrel Car, orange	24	55	___
3619	Helicopter Reconnaissance Car	13	51	___
3620	Searchlight Car	11	30	___
3650	Extension Searchlight Car	11	34	___
3656	Operating Cattle Car	13	57	___
3656	Stockyard with cattle (set box with car box)	16	76	___
3656-9	Cattle (marked "3656" on 4 sides, unnumbered tuck flaps)	8	19	___
3656-9	Cattle (marked "3656" on 4 sides, "3656-44" on 1 tuck flap)	3	12	___
3656-9	Cattle (marked "3656-34" on 4 sides, "3656-44" on 1 tuck flap)	3	10	___
3656-9	Cattle (marked "3656" on 4 sides, "3656-44" on 1 tuck flap, OPS markings)	10	25	___
3656-9	Cattle (unnumbered sides, marked "3656-44" on 1 tuck flap)	10	25	___
3656-9	Cattle (unnumbered sides, marked "3656-34" on 1 tuck flap)	13	35	___
3656-150	Corral Platform, separate sale	161	734	___
3662	Automatic Milk Car (classic), *55*	19	51	___
3662	Automatic Milk Car (orange picture), *64*	16	75	___
3662	Automatic Milk Car (white box), *66*	20	80	___
3665	Minuteman Operating Car	23	50	___
3672	Bosco Operating Milk Car	62	166	___
3820	USMC Operating Submarine Car	20	50	___
3830	Operating Submarine Car	20	49	___
3854	Automatic Merchandise Car	73	425	___
3927	Lionel Lines Track Cleaning Car	10	32	___
4109WS	Electronic Control Set	90	470	___
4357	SP-type Caboose, electronic	25	107	___
4452	PRR Gondola, electronic	29	98	___
4454	Baby Ruth PRR Boxcar, electronic	20	123	___
4457	PRR N5-type Caboose, tintype, electronic	20	79	___
4671W	Tender	27	148	___
5160	Viewing Stand	10	60	___
5459	LL Coal Dump Car, electronic	18	183	___
6001T	Tender	2	10	___
6002	NYC Gondola	2	7	___
6004	Baby Ruth PRR Boxcar	3	12	___
6007	Lionel Lines SP-type Caboose	2	9	___
6009	Remote Control Uncoupling Track	3	20	___
6012	Gondola	4	12	___
6014	Boxcar	3	14	___
6014-60	Frisco Boxcar, white (middle classic)	12	20	___
6014-60	Frisco Boxcar, white	6	21	___
6014-85	Bosco or Frisco Boxcar, orange (classic)	8	33	___

BOXES

		Good (P-5)	Exc (P-7)
____	**6014-100** Airex Boxcar, red	8	22
____	**6014-100** Airex Boxcar, red (orange perforated)	15	45
____	**6014-150** Wix Boxcar	30	201
____	**6014-335** Frisco Boxcar	6	26
____	**6014-410** Frisco Boxcar	16	76
____	**6015** Sunoco 1-D Tank Car	4	16
____	**6017** Lionel Lines SP-type Caboose	2	9
____	**6017-1** Caboose	10	28
____	**6017-50** U.S. Marine Corps SP-type Caboose (box marked "6017-60")	17	82
____	**6017-85** Lionel Lines SP-type Caboose, gray	8	29
____	**6017-100** B&M SP-type Caboose	16	58
____	**6017-185** ATSF SP-type Caboose	3	18
____	**6017-200** U.S. Navy SP-type Caboose	22	139
____	**6017-235** ATSF SP-type Caboose	8	29
____	**6019** Remote Control Track	2	6
____	**6020W** Tender	8	38
____	**6024** Nabisco Shredded Wheat Boxcar	5	21
____	**6024-60** RCA Whirlpool Boxcar	15	68
____	**6025** Gulf 1-D Tank Car (classic)	7	19
____	**6025-60** Gulf 1-D Tank Car	4	29
____	**6025-60** Gulf 1-D Tank Car (classic, overstamped 6024 box)	7	45
____	**6025-85** Gulf 1-D Tank Car (classic)	6	43
____	**6026T** Lionel Lines Tender	5	23
____	**6026W** Lionel Lines Tender	13	40
____	**6027** Alaska SP-type Caboose	50	274
____	**6029** Remote Control Uncoupling Track (classic)	5	16
____	**6029** Remote Control Uncoupling Track (orange picture)	7	25
____	**6032** Short Gondola	3	15
____	**X6034** Baby Ruth PRR Boxcar	2	13
____	**6035** Sunoco 1-D Tank Car	4	16
____	**6037** Lionel Lines SP-type Caboose	2	8
____	**6050** Lionel Savings Bank Boxcar	7	32
____	**6050-110** Swift Boxcar	7	28
____	**6057** Lionel Lines SP-type Caboose	4	26
____	**6059** M&StL SP-type Caboose	9	24
____	**6059-50** M&StL SP-type Caboose (Hagerstown checkerboard)	8	20
____	**6062** NYC Gondola	6	23
____	**6066T** Tender	7	20
____	**6110** 2-4-2 Locomotive	4	20
____	**6111-75** Flatcar with logs	12	51
____	**6111-110** Flatcar	18	68
____	**6112-1** Canister Car	10	50

BOXES

		Good (P-5)	Exc (P-7)	
6112-25	Canister Set	8	27	____
6112-85	Short Gondola (marked "Canister Car")	4	26	____
6112-135	Short Gondola (marked "Canister Car")	5	38	____
6119	DL&W Work Caboose, red	5	22	____
6119-25	DL&W Work Caboose, orange	7	25	____
6119-50	DL&W Work Caboose, brown	10	29	____
6119-75	DL&W Work Caboose	10	41	____
6119-100	DL&W Work Caboose (classic)	8	33	____
6119-100	DL&W Work Caboose (picture, perforated, or window)	9	94	____
6121	Flatcar with pipes	13	49	____
6121-60	Flatcar with pipes	14	82	____
6121-85	Flatcar with pipes (classic)	15	86	____
6130	ATSF Work Caboose (cellophane)	10	42	____
6130	ATSF Work Caboose (Hagerstown checkerboard)	11	40	____
6130	ATSF Work Caboose (all other boxes)	5	28	____
6149	Remote Control Uncoupling Track, *64–69*	7	11	____
6151	Flatcar with patrol truck	9	45	____
6162-60	Alaska Gondola	34	172	____
6162-110	NYC Gondola, blue (orange picture)	9	39	____
6162-110	NYC Gondola, red, separate sale (orange picture with label)	21	83	____
6167-85	Union Pacific SP-type Caboose	22	82	____
6175	Flatcar with rocket	9	39	____
6220	Santa Fe NW2 Switcher	23	92	____
6250	Seaboard NW2 Switcher	31	129	____
6257	SP-type Caboose	4	10	____
6257X	SP-type Caboose	13	37	____
6257-25	SP-type Caboose	2	9	____
6257-50	SP-type Caboose	6	13	____
6262	Flatcar with wheel load	6	35	____
6264	Flatcar with lumber, separate sale	33	133	____
6311	Flatcar with pipes	11	67	____
6315	Gulf 1-D Chemical Tank Car (classic)	16	38	____
6315	Gulf 1-D Chemical Tank Car (Hagerstown checkerboard)	24	48	____
6315-60	Gulf 1-D Chemical Tank Car (orange picture)	6	23	____
6342	NYC Gondola	22	144	____
6343	Barrel Ramp Car	11	41	____
6346	Alcoa Quad Hopper	12	37	____
6356	NYC Stock Car	7	27	____
6357	SP-type Caboose (classic)	3	12	____
6357	SP-type Caboose (orange perforated, overstamped)	18	84	____
6357-50	ATSF SP-type Caboose	122	442	____
6361	Timber Transport Car	14	41	____

BOXES

			Good (P-5)	Exc (P-7)
____	6361	Timber Transport Car (Hagerstown checkerboard)	16	64
____	6362	Truck Car	10	52
____	6376	LL Circus Stock Car	10	51
____	6401	Flatcar, gray	25	107
____	6403B	Tender with bell	22	63
____	6405	Flatcar with piggyback van	6	29
____	6407	Flatcar with rocket	118	323
____	6411	Flatcar with logs	5	26
____	6413	Mercury Capsule Carrying Car	21	61
____	6414	Evans Auto Loader (classic)	25	64
____	6414	Evans Auto Loader (orange picture)	29	101
____	6414	Evans Auto Loader (orange picture, overstamped 6416 box)	30	152
____	6414	Evans Auto Loader (orange perforated), 59	18	102
____	6414	Evans Auto Loader (cellophane), 66	24	104
____	6414-25	Four Automobiles, separate sale	155	608
____	6414-85	Evans Auto Loader (orange picture)	165	477
____	6415	Sunoco 3-D Tank Car (classic)	7	22
____	6415	Sunoco 3-D Tank Car (orange picture)	15	38
____	6415	Sunoco 3-D Tank Car (cellophane)	24	76
____	6415	Sunoco 3-D Tank Car (Hillside checkerboard)	21	42
____	6415	Sunoco 3-D Tank Car (orange picture with label)	45	109
____	6416	Boat Transport Car	25	112
____	6417	PRR N5c Porthole Caboose	4	16
____	6417-1	PRR N5c Porthole Caboose, without "New York Zone"	9	35
____	6417-25	Lionel Lines N5c Porthole Caboose	7	29
____	6417-50	Lehigh Valley N5c Porthole Caboose	22	86
____	6418	Machinery Car	17	62
____	6419	DL&W Work Caboose	9	38
____	6419-25	DL&W Work Caboose	5	23
____	6419-50	DL&W Work Caboose	9	40
____	6419-100	N&W Work Caboose	27	66
____	6420	DL&W Work Caboose with searchlight	11	41
____	6424	Twin Auto Flatcar	17	41
____	6424-60	Twin Auto Flatcar	10	40
____	6424-85	Twin Auto Flatcar	10	67
____	6424-110	Twin Auto Flatcar	25	79
____	6425	Gulf 3-D Tank Car	10	30
____	6427	Lionel Lines N5c Porthole Caboose	9	24
____	6427-60	Virginian N5c Porthole Caboose	46	160
____	6427-500	PRR N5c Porthole Caboose, sky blue, from Girls Set	32	106
____	6428	U.S. Mail Boxcar	13	48
____	6429	DL&W Work Caboose	36	173

BOXES

		Good (P-5)	Exc (P-7)	
6430	Flatcar with trailers	12	35	___
6431	Flatcar with vans and tractor (cellophane), *66*	40	161	___
6434	Poultry Dispatch Stock Car	13	47	___
6436	Lehigh Valley Open Quad Hopper, black	9	30	___
6436-25	Lehigh Valley Open Quad Hopper, maroon	8	31	___
6436-110	Lehigh Valley Open Quad Hopper, red	9	30	___
6436-500	Lehigh Valley Open Quad Hopper, lilac, from Girls Set	34	112	___
6436-1969	TCA Hopper (Hagerstown checkered)	10	48	___
6437	PRR N5c Porthole Caboose	5	17	___
6440	Flatcar with vans	13	40	___
6440	Green Pullman Car	9	37	___
6441	Green Observation Car	9	36	___
6442	Brown Pullman Car	9	39	___
6443	Brown Observation Car	9	36	___
6445	Fort Knox Gold Reserve Car	19	48	___
6446	N&W Covered Quad Hopper	10	27	___
6446	N&W Covered Quad Hopper (orange picture)	15	60	___
6446-25	N&W Covered Quad Hopper	11	33	___
6446-60	Lehigh Valley Covered Quad Hopper	86	367	___
6447	PRR N5c Porthole Caboose	42	258	___
6448	Exploding Target Range Boxcar	9	27	___
6452	Pennsylvania Gondola	3	18	___
X6454	Santa Fe, NYC, or Baby Ruth Boxcar	5	23	___
X6454	PRR Boxcar	7	23	___
X6454	PRR Boxcar (classic, overstamped 3464 box)	7	34	___
X6454	SP Boxcar	6	25	___
X6454	Erie Boxcar	7	31	___
6456	Lehigh Valley Short Hopper	6	19	___
6456-25	LV Short Hopper ("25" rubber-stamped on end flaps)	8	36	___
6456-75	Lehigh Valley Short Hopper	27	146	___
6457	SP-type Caboose	7	17	___
6460	Bucyrus Erie Crane Car	10	47	___
6460-25	Bucyrus Erie Crane Car, red cab	13	49	___
6461	Transformer Car	7	29	___
6462	NYC Gondola, black	4	14	___
6462-25	NYC Gondola, green	6	20	___
6462-75	NYC Gondola, red	4	19	___
6462-125	NYC Gondola, red plastic	5	18	___
6462-500	NYC Gondola, pink, from Girls Set	34	122	___
6463	Rocket Fuel 2-D Tank Car	11	36	___
6464-1	Western Pacific Boxcar	11	48	___
6464-25	Great Northern Boxcar	13	40	___
6464-50	M&StL Boxcar	15	41	___

BOXES

		Good (P-5)	Exc (P-7)
6464-50	M&StL Boxcar (overstamped with "S" and "Silver")	15	55
6464-75	Rock Island Boxcar	9	50
6464-100	Western Pacific Boxcar	25	68
6464-125	NYC Pacemaker Boxcar	15	62
6464-150	Missouri Pacific Boxcar	14	59
6464-175	Rock Island Boxcar	11	66
6464-175	Rock Island Boxcar (overstamped with "S" and "Silver")	15	75
6464-200	Pennsylvania Boxcar	10	64
6464-200	Pennsylvania Boxcar (Hagerstown checkerboard)	15	40
6464-225	SP Boxcar	13	36
6464-250	Western Pacific Boxcar (orange picture with label)	38	151
6464-250	Western Pacific Blue Feather Boxcar (classic for 6464-100), *54*	93	463
6464-250	Western Pacific Boxcar (cellophane)	23	88
6464-275	State of Maine Boxcar	15	67
6464-300	Rutland Boxcar, *55*	25	91
6464-325	B&O Sentinel Boxcar	64	199
6464-350	MKT Boxcar	28	138
6464-375	Central of Georgia Boxcar	17	48
6464-400	B&O Time-Saver Boxcar	13	37
6464-425	New Haven Boxcar (classic)	10	40
6464-425	New Haven Boxcar (Hagerstown)	10	43
6464-450	Great Northern Boxcar	13	47
6464-450	Great Northern Boxcar (cellophane)	15	57
6464-475	B&M Boxcar (classic)	11	36
6464-475	B&M Boxcar (orange picture)	15	125
6464-500	Timken Boxcar	15	67
6464-510	NYC Pacemaker Boxcar	70	306
6464-515	MKT Boxcar	75	233
6464-525	M&StL Boxcar	10	37
6464-650	D&RGW Boxcar (cellophane)	15	44
6464-700	Santa Fe Boxcar	19	58
6464-725	New Haven Boxcar (orange picture, "735" on box)	10	31
6464-725	New Haven Boxcar (Hagerstown checkerboard)	20	68
6464-825	Alaska Boxcar	45	189
6464-900	NYC Boxcar	8	30
6465	Gulf 2-D Tank Car, black (classic)	5	17
6465	Sunoco 2-D Tank Car (classic, overstamped 2465 box)	3	18
6465	Sunoco 2-D Tank Car (classic, overstamped 6555 box)	6	16
6465	Sunoco 2-D Tank Car (orange picture, 6464-900 label)	9	64

BOXES

		Good (P-5)	Exc (P-7)	
6465-60	Gulf 2-D Tank Car (classic)	5	23	____
6465-60	Sunoco 2-D Tank Car (classic)	3	16	____
6465-85	Lionel Lines 2-D Tank Car (orange perforated)	29	84	____
6465-110	Cities Service 2-D Tank Car (orange perforated)	16	49	____
6465-160	Lionel Lines Tank Car (orange picture)	46	153	____
6466T	Lionel Lines Tender	7	17	____
6466W	Lionel Lines Tender (with liner)	13	37	____
6466WX	Lionel Lines Tender (with liner)	16	40	____
6467	Miscellaneous Car	12	35	____
6468	B&O Auto Boxcar, tuscan (marked "X")	41	121	____
6468	B&O Auto Boxcar, blue	9	33	____
6468-25	NH Auto Boxcar	17	45	____
6469	Liquified Gas Tank Car	15	60	____
6470	Explosives Boxcar	12	34	____
6472	Refrigerator Car	7	19	____
6473	Horse Transport Car	11	36	____
6473	Horse Transport Car (end flaps half white, half orange)	30	104	____
6475	Pickles Vat Car (orange picture)	22	67	____
6476	Lehigh Valley Short Hopper	6	22	____
6476	Lehigh Valley Short Hopper (orange perforated)	14	44	____
6476-85	Lehigh Valley Short Hopper	15	58	____
6476-135	Lehigh Valley Short Hopper	8	26	____
6476-160	Lehigh Valley Short Hopper (Hagerstown checkerboard)	9	28	____
6477	Miscellaneous Car with pipes	10	49	____
6482	Refrigerator Car	7	39	____
6500	Flatcar with Bonanza airplane	100	236	____
6501	Flatcar with jet boat	27	55	____
6511	Flatcar with pipes	10	29	____
6512	Cherry Picker Car	12	38	____
6517	Lionel Lines Bay Window Caboose	14	37	____
6517-60	Bay Window Caboose (TCA)	30	111	____
6517-75	Erie Bay Window Caboose	56	239	____
6518	Transformer Car	17	55	____
6519	Allis-Chalmers Flatcar (classic)	20	111	____
6519	Allis-Chalmers Flatcar (orange perforated)	27	133	____
6520	Searchlight Car	14	48	____
6530	Firefighting Instruction Car	11	63	____
6536	M&StL Open Quad Hopper	19	65	____
6544	Missile Firing Car	22	64	____
6555	Sunoco 1-D Tank Car	12	23	____
6556	MKT Stock Car	52	191	____
6557	SP-type Smoking Caboose	21	91	____
6560	Bucyrus Erie Crane Car (Hagerstown checkerboard)	17	58	____

BOXES

			Good (P-5)	Exc (P-7)
_____	6560	Bucyrus Erie Crane Car (all other boxes)	11	38
_____	6560-25	Bucyrus Erie Crane Car, 8-wheel (with liner)	16	39
_____	6561	Cable Car, 2 reels	9	33
_____	6562-1	NYC Gondola, gray	6	21
_____	6562-25	NYC Gondola, red	5	20
_____	6562-50	NYC Gondola, black	6	21
_____	6572	REA Reefer (classic)	8	54
_____	6572	REA Reefer (orange picture)	10	29
_____	6636	Alaska Open Quad Hopper	14	49
_____	6646	Lionel Lines Stock Car	6	26
_____	6650	IRBM Rocket Launcher	9	36
_____	6654W	Whistle Tender	10	20
_____	6657	Rio Grande SP-type Caboose	21	93
_____	6660	Boom Car	8	51
_____	6670	Derrick Car	15	53
_____	6672	Santa Fe Refrigerator Car	7	22
_____	6736	Detroit & Mackinac Open Quad Hopper	15	58
_____	6800	Flatcar with airplane (classic)	16	70
_____	6800	Flatcar with airplane (orange perforated)	17	81
_____	6800-60	Airplane, separate sale	93	192
_____	6801	Flatcar with brown and white boat	7	39
_____	6801-50	Flatcar with yellow and white boat	10	47
_____	6801-60	Boat, separate sale	30	92
_____	6801-75	Flatcar with blue and white boat	11	38
_____	6802	Flatcar with girders (late classic)	9	31
_____	6802	Flatcar with girders (orange perforated)	25	55
_____	6803	Flatcar with USMC tank and sound truck	35	109
_____	6804	Flatcar with USMC trucks	19	79
_____	6805	Atomic Energy Disposal Flatcar	20	68
_____	6806	Flatcar with USMC trucks	31	82
_____	6807	Flatcar with boat	15	88
_____	6808	Flatcar with military units	18	62
_____	6809	Flatcar with USMC trucks	26	92
_____	6810	Flatcar with trailer	7	35
_____	6812	Track Maintenance Car	15	64
_____	6814	Rescue Caboose	18	64
_____	6816	Flatcar with Allis-Chalmers bulldozer	42	143
_____	6816-100	Allis-Chalmers bulldozer	125	410
_____	6817	Flatcar with Allis-Chalmers motor scraper	47	185
_____	6818	Flatcar with transformer	8	30
_____	6819	Flatcar with helicopter	7	72
_____	6820	Aerial Missile Transport Car with helicopter	71	257
_____	6821	Flatcar with crates	6	38
_____	6822	Searchlight Car	6	29
_____	6823	Flatcar with IRBM missiles	15	75

BOXES

		Good (P-5)	Exc (P-7)	
6825	Flatcar with arch trestle bridge	7	26	____
6826	Flatcar with Christmas trees	19	59	____
6827	Flatcar with Harnischfeger power shovel	28	80	____
6827-100	Harnischfeger Power Shovel	32	80	____
6828	Flatcar with Harnischfeger crane (cellophane, no crane kit box)	30	87	____
6828	Flatcar with Harnischfeger crane (orange picture, no crane kit box)	16	66	____
6828	Harnischfeger Crane Kit, used with flatcar	12	90	____
6828-100	Harnischfeger Crane, separate sale	41	153	____
6830	Flatcar with submarine	23	49	____
6844	Missile Carrying Car	16	64	____
11001	Steam Freight Set (advance catalog 1962)	7	23	____
11011	Diesel Freight Set	30	85	____
11201	Steam Freight Set	20	65	____
11212	Diesel Freight Set	60	110	____
11222	027 Steam Freight Set	25	70	____
11232	NH Diesel Freight Set	20	65	____
11242	Steam Freight Set	30	70	____
11268	Military Set	38	105	____
11278	Steam Freight Set	25	55	____
11288	Steam Freight Set	43	100	____
11331	Steam Freight Set	15	40	____
11375	027 Steam Freight Set	15	55	____
11415	Steam Freight Set (advance catalog 1963)	14	49	____
11420	Steam Freight Set	10	30	____
11440	Diesel Freight Set	15	70	____
11450	Steam Freight Set	30	65	____
11460	Steam Freight Set	15	30	____
11490	Santa Fe Passenger Set	48	100	____
11500	Steam Freight Set	50	110	____
11520	Steam Freight Set	45	95	____
11550	Steam Freight Set	20	55	____
11560	Texas Special Set	15	35	____
11590	Santa Fe Passenger Set	30	88	____
11710	Steam Freight Set	45	95	____
11750	Steam Freight Set	22	54	____
12710	Steam Freight Set	23	119	____
12730	Santa Fe Diesel Freight Set	75	193	____
12760	Berkshire Freight Set	175	400	____
12780	Santa Fe Passenger Set	200	588	____
12800	B&M Diesel Freight Set	25	75	____
12800X	B&M Diesel Freight Set	75	190	____
12820	Virginian Train Master Freight Set	88	285	____
12840	Steam Freight Set	40	250	____
12850	Diesel Freight Set	40	160	____

BOXES

			Good (P-5)	Exc (P-7)
____	**13008**	Super O Introductory Set	20	66
____	**13018**	Santa Fe Space-age Military Set	349	917
____	**13028**	Super O Space Set	160	300
____	**13048**	Super O Steam Freight Set	65	140
____	**13058**	Santa Fe Space-age Military Set	150	400
____	**13088**	Santa Fe Passenger Set	424	1053
____	**13098**	Steam Freight Set	120	275
____	**13118**	Berkshire Freight Set	75	330
____	**13128**	Santa Fe Space-age Military Set	250	650
____	**13150**	Hudson Freight Set	335	900
____	**A**	Transformer, 90 watts	10	20
____	**CO-1**	Track Clips, 100	5	15
____	**ECU-1**	Electronic Control Unit	15	153
____	**KW**	Transformer, 190 watts	6	22
____	**KW**	Transformer, 190 watts (yellow)	5	23
____	**LW**	Transformer, 125 watts	7	15
____	**R**	Transformer, 110 watts	8	15
____	**RCS**	Remote Control Track	6	17
____	**RW**	Transformer, 110 watts	6	17
____	**S**	Transformer, 80 watts	3	10
____	**SW**	Transformer, 130 watts	5	14
____	**TW**	Transformer, 175 watts	3	15
____	**UCS**	Remote Control Track (O)	2	7
____	**UTC**	Lockon	10	18
____	**VW**	Transformer, 150 watts	5	15
____	**ZW**	Transformer, 275 watts (classic)	13	46
____	**ZW**	Transformer, 275 watts (orange, with inserts)	12	43
____	**ZW**	Transformer, 275 watts (yellow, with inserts)	13	48

Section 7
SETS

		Exc
463W	Steam Freight Set, *45* (224, 2466W, 2458, 2452, 2555, 2457)	615 ____
1000W	027 Steam Freight Set, *55* (2016, 6026W, 6014, 6012, 6017)	320 ____
1001	027 Diesel Freight Set, *55* (610, 6012, 6014, 6017)	250 ____
1111	027 Scout Freight Set, *48* (1001, 1001T, 1002, 1005, 1007)	225 ____
1112	027 Scout Freight Set, *48* (1001 or 1101, 1001T, 1002, 1004, 1005, 1007)	250 ____
1113	027 Scout Freight Set, *50* (1120, 1001T, 1002, 1005, 1007)	115 ____
1115	027 Scout Freight Set, *49* (1110, 1001T, 1002, 1005, 1007)	190 ____
1117	027 Scout Freight Set, *49* (1110, 1001T, 1002, 1005, 1004, 1007)	150 ____
1119	027 Freight Scout Set, *51–52* (1110, 1001T, 1002, 1004, 1007)	160 ____
1400	027 Steam Passenger Set, *46* (221, 221T, two 2430, 2431)	600 ____
1400W	027 Steam Passenger Set, *46* (221, 221W, two 2430 2431)	720 ____
1401	027 Steam Freight Set, *46* (1654, 1654T, 2452X, 2465, 2472)	120 ____
1401W	027 Steam Freight Set, *46* (1654, 1654W, 2452X, 2465, 2472)	220 ____
1402	027 Steam Passenger Set, *46* (1666, 2466T, two 2440, 2441)	550 ____
1402W	027 Steam Passenger Set, *46* (1666, 2466W, two 2440, 2441)	550 ____
1403	027 Steam Freight Set, *46* (221, 221T, 2411, 2465, 2472)	400 ____
1403W	027 Steam Freight Set, *46* (221, 221W, 2411, 2465, 2472)	500 ____
1405	027 Steam Freight Set, *46* (1666, 2466T, 2452X, 2465, 2472)	145 ____
1405W	027 Steam Freight Set, *46* (1666, 2466W, 2452X, 2465, 2472)	280 ____
1407B	027 Steam Switcher Set, *46* (1665, 2403B, 2560, 2452X, 2419)	1370 ____
1409	027 Steam Freight Set, *46* (1666, 2466T, 3559, 2465, 3454, 2472)	425 ____
1409W	027 Steam Freight Set, *46* (1666, 2466W, 3559, 2465, 3454, 2472)	435 ____
1411W	027 Steam Freight Set, *46* (1666, 2466WX, 2452X, 2465, 2454, 2472)	250 ____
1413WS	027 Steam Freight Set, *46* (2020, 2466WX, 2452X, 2465, 2454, 2472)	350 ____
1415WS	027 Steam Freight Set, *46* (2020, 2020W, 3459, 3454, 2465, 2472)	530 ____
1417WS	027 Steam Work Train Set, *46* (2020, 2020W, 2465, 3451, 2560, 2419)	720 ____

		Exc
1419WS	027 Steam Freight Set, *46* (2020, 2020W, 3459, 2452X, 2560, 2419, 97)	880
1421WS	027 Steam Freight Set, *46* (2020, 2020W, 3451, 2465, 3454, 2472, 164)	1100
1423W	027 Steam Freight Set, *48–49* (1655, 6654W, 6452, 6465, 6257)	220
1425B	027 Steam Switcher Freight Set, *48* (1656, 2403B, 6456, 6465, 6257X)	825
1425B	027 Steam Switcher Freight Set, *49* (1656, 6403B, 6456, 6465, 6257)	825
1426WS	027 Steam Passenger Set, *48–49* (2026, 6466WX, two 6440, 6441)	560
1427WS	027 Steam Freight Set, *48* (2026, 6466WX, 6454, 6465, 6257)	275
1429WS	027 Steam Freight Set, *48* (2026, 6466WX, 3451, 6454, 6465, 6257)	225
1430WS	027 Steam Passenger Set, *48–49* (2025, 6466WX, 2400, 2401, 2402)	800
1431	027 Steam Freight Set, *47* (1654, 1654T, 2452X, 2465, 2472)	220
1431W	027 Steam Freight Set, *47* (1654, 1654W, 2452X, 2465, 2472)	160
1432	027 Steam Passenger Set, *47* (221, 221T, two 2430, 2431)	850
1432W	027 Steam Passenger Set, *47* (221, 221W, two 2430 2431)	795
1433	027 Steam Freight Set, *47* (221, 221T, 2411, 2465, 2457)	560
1433W	027 Steam Freight Set, *47* (221, 221 W, 2411, 2465, 2457)	375
1434WS	027 Steam Passenger Set, *47* (2025, 2466WX, two 2440, 2441)	555
1435WS	027 Steam Freight Set, *47* (2025, 2466WX, 2452X, 2454, 2457)	240
1437WS	027 Steam Freight Set, *47* (2025, 2466WX, 2452X, 2465, 2454, 2472)	590
1439WS	027 Steam Freight Set, *47* (2025, 2466WX, 3559, 2465, 3454, 2457)	470
1441WS	027 Steam Work Train Set, *47* (2020, 2020W, 2560, 2461, 3451, 2419)	1225
1443WS	027 Steam Freight Set, *47* (2020, 2020W, 3459, 3462, 2465, 2457)	400
1445WS	027 Steam Freight Set, *48* (2025, 6466WX, 6454, 3559, 6465, 6357)	325
1447WS	027 Steam Work Train Set, *48* (2020, 6020W, 3451, 2461, 2460, 6419)	460
1447WS	027 Steam Work Train Set, *49* (2020, 6020W, 6461, 3461, 2460, 6419)	475
1449WS	027 Steam Freight Set, *48* (2020, 6020W, 3462, 3459, 6411, 6465, 6357)	430
1451WS	027 Steam Freight Set, *49* (2026, 6466WX, 6462, 3464, 6257)	230
1453WS	027 Steam Freight Set, *49* (2026, 6466WX, 3464, 6465, 3461, 6357)	325
1455WS	027 Steam Freight Set, *49* (2025, 6466WX, 6462, 6465, 3472, 6357)	335

SETS

		Exc
1457B	027 Diesel Freight Set, *49–50* (6220, 3464, 6462, 6520, 6419)	540 ___
1459WS	027 Steam Freight Set, *49* (2020, 6020W, 6411, 3656, 6465, 3469, 6357)	1090 ___
1461S	027 Steam Freight Set, *50* (6110, 6001T, 6002, 6004, 6007)	175 ___
1463W	027 Steam Freight Set, *50* (2036, 6466W, 6462, 6465, 6257)	230 ___
1463WS	027 Freight Set, *51* (2026, 6466W, 6462, 6465, 6257)	175 ___
1464W	027 UP Diesel Passenger Set, *50* (2023 AA, 2481, 2482, 2483)	985 ___
1464W	027 UP Passenger Set, *51* (2023 AA, 2421, 2422, 2423)	865 ___
1464W	027 UP Passenger Set, *52–53* (2033 AA, 2421, 2422, 2423)	830 ___
1465	027 Steam Freight Set, *52* (2034, 6066T, 6032, 6035, 6037)	180 ___
1467W	027 UP Diesel Freight Set, *50–51* (2023 AA, 6656, 6465, 6456, 6357)	585 ___
1467W	027 Erie Diesel Freight Set, *52–53* (2032 AA, 6656, 6456, 6465, 6357)	760 ___
1469WS	027 Steam Freight Set, *50–51* (2035, 6466W, 6462, 6465, 6456, 6257)	270 ___
1471WS	027 Steam Freight Set, *50–51* (2035, 6466W, 3469, 6465, 6454, 3461, 6357)	415 ___
1473WS	027 Steam Freight Set, *50* (2046, 2046W, 3464, 6465, 6520, 6357)	560 ___
1475WS	027 Steam Freight Set, *50* (2046, 2046W, 3656, 3461, 6472, 3469, 6419)	615 ___
1477S	027 Steam Freight Set, *51–52* (2026, 6466T, 6012, 6014, 6017)	210 ___
1479WS	027 Steam Freight Set, *52* (2056, 2046W, 6462, 6465, 6456, 6257)	375 ___
1481WS	027 Steam Freight Set, *51* (2035, 6466W, 3464, 3472, 6465, 6462, 6357)	510 ___
1483WS	027 Steam Freight Set, *52* (2056, 2046W, 3472, 6462, 6465, 3474, 6357)	1010 ___
1484WS	027 Steam Passenger Set, *52* (2056, 2046W, 2421, 2422, 2423, 2429)	1270 ___
1485WS	027 Steam Freight Set, *52* (2025, 6466W, 6462, 6465, 6257)	235 ___
1500	027 Steam Freight Set, *53* (1130, 6066T, 6032, 6034, 6037)	170 ___
1500	027 Steam Freight Set, *54* (1130, 1130T, 6032, 6034, 6037)	125 ___
1501S	027 Steam Freight Set, *53* (2026, 6066T, 6032, 6035, 6037)	250 ___
1502WS	027 Steam Passenger Set, *53* (2055, 2046W, 2421, 2422, 2423)	750 ___
1503WS	027 Steam Freight Set, *53–54* (2055, 6026W, 6462, 6465, 6456, 6257)	390 ___
1505WS	027 Steam Freight Set, *53* (2046, 2046W, 6462, 6464-1, 6415, 6357)	595 ___
1507WS	027 Steam Freight Set, *53* (2046, 2046W, 6415, 6462, 3472, 6468, 6357)	450 ___

SETS

			Exc
1509WS	027 Steam Freight Set, *53* (2046, 2046W, 6456, 3520, 3469, 6460, 6419)		500
1511S	027 Steam Freight Set, *53* (2037, 6066T, 6032, 3474, 6035, 6037)		250
1513S	027 Steam Freight Set, *54–55* (2037, 6026T, 6012, 6014, 6015, 6017)		260
1515WS	027 Steam Freight Set, *54* (2065, 2046W, 6462, 6415, 6464-25, 6456-25, 6357)		340
1516WS	027 Passenger Set, *54* (2065, 2046W, 2434, 2432, 2436)		650
1517W	027 Diesel Freight Set, *54* (2245P/C AB, 6464-225, 6561, 6462-25, 6427)		1250
1519WS	027 Steam Freight Set, *54* (2065, 6026W, 6356, 6462-75, 3482, 3461-25, 6427)		450
1520W	027 Texas Special Passenger Set, *54* (2245P/C AB, 2432, 2435, 2436)		1700
1521WS	027 Steam Work Train Set, *54* (2065, 2046W, 3620, 6561, 6460, 3562, 6419)		690
1523	027 Diesel Work Train Set, *54* (6250, 6511, 6456-25, 6460-25, 6419-25)		615
1525	027 Diesel Freight Set, *55* (600, 6111, 6014, 6017)		165
1527	027 Steam Work Train Set, *55* (1615, 1615T, 6462-125, 6560, 6119)		500
1529	027 PRR Diesel Freight Set, *55* (2028, 6311, 6436, 6257)		650
1531W	027 Diesel Freight Set, *55* (2328, 6462-125, 6465, 6456 or 6456-25, 6257)		575
1533WS	027 Steam Freight Set, *55* (2055, 6026W, 3562-50, 6436, 6465, 6357)		465
1534W	027 Diesel Passenger Set, *55* (2328, 2432, 2434, 2436)		1000
1535W	027 Diesel Freight Set, *55* (2243P/2243C AB, 6462-125, 6436, 6464-50 or 6468X, 6257)		1650
1536W	027 Texas Special Passenger Set, *55* (2245P/C AB, two 2432, 2436)		1800
1537WS	027 Steam Freight Set, *55* (2065, 6026W, 3469, 6464-275, 3562-50, 6357)		500
1538WS	027 Steam Passenger Set, *55* (2065, 2046W, 2432, 2434, 2435, 2436)		900
1539W	027 Santa Fe Diesel Freight Set, *55* (2243P/C AB, 3620, 6446, 6561, 6560, 6419)		850
1541WS	027 Steam Freight Set, *55* (2065, 2046W, 3482, 6415, 3461-25, 3494-1, 6427)		600
1542	027 Electric Freight Set, *56* (520, 6014, 6012, 6017)		215
1543	027 Diesel Freight Set, *56* (627, 6121, 6112, 6017)		285
1545	027 Diesel Freight Set, *56* (628, 6424, 6014, 6025, 6257)		265
1547S	027 Steam Freight Set, *56* (2018, 6026T, 6121, 6112, 6014, 6257)		155
1549S	027 Steam Work Train Set, *56* (1615, 1615T, 6262, 6560, 6119-25)		980
1551W	027 Diesel Freight Set, *56* (621, 6362, 6425, 6562-25, 6257)		545

SETS

1552	027 Diesel Passenger Set, *56* (629, 2432, 2434, 2436)	840 ___
1553W	027 MILW Diesel Freight Set, *56* (2338, 6430, 6462-125, 6464-425, 6346, 6257)	565 ___
1555WS	027 Steam Freight Set, *56* (2018, 6026W, 3361, 6464-400, 6462-125, 6257)	280 ___
1557W	027 Diesel Work Train Set, *56* (621, 6436, 6511, 3620, 6560, 6119-25)	455 ___
1559W	027 MILW Diesel Freight Set, *56* (2338, 6414, 3562-50, 6362, 3494-275, 6357)	800 ___
1561WS	027 Steam Freight Set, *56* (2065, 6026W, 3424, 6262, 6562-25, 6430, 6257)	730 ___
1562W	027 Diesel Passenger Set, *56* (2328, two 2442, 2444, 2446)	2000 ___
1563W	027 Wabash Diesel Freight Set, *56* (2240P/C AB, 6467, 3562-50, 6414, 3620, 6357)	1570 ___
1565WS	027 Steam Freight Set, *56* (2065, 6026W, 3662, 3650, 6414, 6346, 6357)	535 ___
1567W	027 Santa Fe Diesel Freight Set, *56* (2243P/C AB, 3356, 3424, 6430, 6672, 6357)	1200 ___
1569	027 UP Diesel Freight Set, *57* (202, 6014, 6111, 6112, 6017)	220 ___
1571	027 LV Diesel Freight Set, *57* (625, 6424, 6476, 6121, 6112, 6017)	400 ___
1573	027 Steam Freight Set, *57* (250, 250T, 6112, 6025, 6476, 6464-425, 6017)	195 ___
1575	027 MP Diesel Freight Set, *57* (205P/T AA, 6121, 6112, 6111, 6560-25, 6119-100)	320 ___
1577S	027 Steam Freight Set, *57* (2018, 1130T, 6014, 6121, 6464-475, 6111, 6112, 6017)	235 ___
1578S	027 Steam Passenger Set, *57* (2018, 1130T, 2432, 2434, 2436)	500 ___
1579S	027 Steam Freight Set, *57* (2037, 1130T, 6476, 6121, 6468-25, 6111, 6112, 6025, 6017)	260 ___
1581	027 Jersey Central Diesel Freight Set, *57* (611, 6464-650, 6424, 6024, 6025, 6476, 6560-25, 6119-100)	495 ___
1583WS	027 Steam Freight Set, *57* (2037, 6026W, 6482, 6112, 6646, 6121, 6476, 6017)	260 ___
1585W	027 Seaboard Diesel Freight Set, *57* (602, 6014, 6111, 6464-525, 6025, 6121, 6112, 6476, 6024, 6017)	455 ___
1586	027 Santa Fe Diesel Passenger Set, *57* (204P/T AA, two 2432, 2436)	670 ___
1587S	027 Steam Freight Set (Girls Set), *57–58* (2037-500, 1130T-500, 6462-500, 6464-515, 6436-500, 6464-510, 6427-500)	3145 ___
1589WS	027 Steam Freight Set, *57* (2037, 6026W, 6424, 6464-450, 6025, 6024, 6111, 6112, 6017)	500 ___
1590	027 Steam Freight Set, *58* (249, 250T, 6014, 6151, 6112, 6017)	390 ___
1591	027 Military Set, *58* (212, 6803, 6809, 6807, 6017-50)	970 ___
1593	027 UP Diesel Work Set, *58* (613, 6476, 6818, 6660, 6112, 6119-100)	590 ___

			Exc
SETS			
1595	027 Military Set, *58*		
	(1625, 1625T, 6804, 6806, 6808, 6017-85)		2050
1597S	027 Steam Freight Set, *58*		
	(2018, 1130T, 6014, 6818, 6476, 6025, 6112, 6017)		355
1599	027 Texas Special Freight Set, *58*		
	(210P/T AA, 6801, 6014, 6424, 6112, 6465, 6017)		430
1600	027 Burlington Diesel Passenger Set, *58*		
	(216, 6572, 2432, 2436)		750
1601W	027 Wabash Diesel Freight Set, *58*		
	2337, 6800, 6464-425, 6801, 6810, 6017)		745
1603WS	027 Steam Freight Set, *58*		
	(2037, 6026W, 6424, 6014, 6818, 6112, 6017)		340
1605W	027 Santa Fe Diesel Freight Set, *58*		
	(208P/T AA, 6800, 6464-425, 6801, 6477, 6802, 6017)		900
1607WS	027 Steam Work Train Set, *58*		
	(2037, 6026W, 6465, 6818, 6464-425, 6660, 6112, 6119-100)		450
1608W	027 NH Diesel Passenger Set, *58*		
	(209P/T AA, two 2432, 2434, 2436)		1865
1609	027 Steam Freight Set, *59–60*		
	(246, 1130T, 6162-25, 6476, 6057)		145
1611	027 Alaska Diesel Freight Set, *59*		
	(614, 6825, 6162-60, 6465, 6027)		520
1612	027 General Set, *59–60*		
	(1862, 1862T, 1866, 1865)		300
1613S	027 B&O Steam Freight Set, *59*		
	(247, 247T, 6826, 6819, 6821, 6017)		345
1615	027 B&M Diesel Freight Set, *59*		
	(217P/C AB, 6800, 6464-475, 6812, 6825, 6017-100)		520
1617S	027 Steam Work Train Set, *59*		
	(2018, 1130T, 6816, 6536, 6812, 6670, 6119-100)		800
1619W	027 Santa Fe Diesel Freight Set, *59*		
	(218P/T AA, 6819, 6802, 6801, 6519, 6017-185)		450
1621WS	027 Steam Freight Set, *59*		
	(2037, 6026W, 6825, 6519, 6062, 6464-475, 6017)		340
1623W	027 NP Diesel Freight Set, *59*		
	(2349, 3512, 3435, 6424, 6062, 6017)		1600
1625WS	027 Steam Freight Set, *59*		
	(2037, 6026W, 6636, 3512, 6470, 6650, 6017)		400
1626W	027 Santa Fe Diesel Passenger Set, *59*		
	(208P/T AA, 3428, two 2412, 2416)		875
1627S	027 Steam Freight Set, *60*		
	(244, 244T, 6062, 6825, 6017)		185
1629	027 C&O Diesel Freight Set, *60*		
	(225, 6650, 6470, 6819, 6219)		305
1631WS	027 Steam Freight Set, *60*		
	(243, 243W, 6519, 6812, 6465, 6017)		275
1633	027 U.S. Navy Diesel Freight Set, *60*		
	(224P/C AB, 6544, 6830, 6820, 6017-200)		1185
1635WS	027 Steam Freight Set, *60*		
	(2037, 6026W or 243W, 6361, 6826, 6636, 6821, 6017)		400
1637W	027 Santa Fe Diesel Freight Set, *60*		
	(218P/T AA, 6475, 6175, 6464-475, 6801 or 6424-110, 6017-185)		610

Exc

		Exc	
1639WS	027 Steam Freight Set, *60* (2037, 6026W or 243W, 6816, 6817, 6812, 6530, 6560, 6119-100)	1250	
1640W	027 Santa Fe Diesel Passenger Set, *60* (218P/T AA, 3428, two 2412, 2416, 1640-100)	750	
1641	027 Steam Freight Set, *61* (246, 244T, 3362, 6162, 6057)	150	
1642	027 Steam Freight Set, *61* (244, 1130T, 3376, 6405, 6119)	225	
1643	027 C&O Diesel Freight Set, *61* (230, 3509, 6050, 6175, 6058)	395	
1644	027 General Set, *61* (1862, 1862T, 3370, 1866, 1865)	425	
1645	027 Diesel Freight Set, *61* (229, 3410, 6465-110, 6825, 6059)	250	
1646	027 Steam Freight Set, *61* (233, 233W, 6162, 6343, 6476, 6017)	325	
1647	027 U.S. Marines Military Set, *61* (45, 3665, 3519, 6830, 6448, 6814)	1055	
1648	027 Steam Freight Set, *61* (2037, 233W, 6062, 6465-110, 6519, 6476, 6017)	335	
1649	027 Santa Fe Diesel Freight Set, *61* (218P/C AB, 6343, 6445, 6475, 6405, 6017)	460	
1650	027 Steam Military Set, *61* (2037, 233W, 6544, 6470, 3330, 3419, 6017)	500	
1651	027 Santa Fe Diesel Passenger Set, *61* (218P/T or 220T AA, two 2412, 2414, 2416)	675	
1800	General Gift Pack, *59–60* (1862, 1862T, 1865, 1866, 1877, storybook)	385	
1805	027 Military Set (Land-Sea and Air Gift Pack), *60* (45, 3429, 3820, 6640, 6824)	1600	
1809	Western Gift Pack, *61* (244, 1130T, 3370, 3376, 1877, 6017)	300	
1810	Space Age Gift Pack, *61* (231, 3665, 3519, 3820, 6017)	1165	
2100	Steam Passenger Set, *46* (224, 2466T, two 2442, 2443)	550	
2100W	Steam Passenger Set, *46* (224, 2466W, two 2442, 2443)	640	
2101	Steam Freight Set, *46* (224, 2466T, 2555, 2452, 2457)	350	
2101W	Steam Freight Set, *46* (224, 2466W, 2555, 2452, 2457)	395	
2103W	Steam Freight Set, *46* (224, 2466W, 2458, 3559, 2555, 2457)	375	
2105WS	Steam Freight Set, *46* (671, 2466W, 2555, 2454, 2457)	445	
2110WS	Steam Passenger Set, *46* (671, 2466W, three 2625)	1875	
2111WS	Steam Freight Set, *46* (671, 2466W, 3459, 2411, 2460, 2420)	895	
2113WS	Steam Freight Set, *46* (726, 2426W, 2855, 3854, 2857)	1900	
2114WS	Steam Passenger Set, *46* (726, 2426W, three 2625)	2500	
2115WS	Steam Work Train Set, *46* (726, 2426W, 2458, 3451, 2460, 2420)	1325	

SETS

Set	Description	Exc
2120S	Steam Passenger Set, *47* (675, 2466T, two 2442, 2443)	500
2120WS	Steam Passenger Set, *47* (675, 2466WX, two 2442, 2443)	500
2121S	Steam Freight Set, *47* (675, 2466T, 2555, 2452, 2457)	400
2121WS	Steam Freight Set, *47* (675, 2466WX, 2555, 2452, 2457)	405
2123WS	Steam Freight Set, *47* (675, 2466WX, 2458, 3559, 2555, 2457)	450
2124W	PRR Electric Passenger Set, *47* (2332 GG-1 green, 2625 Irvington, 2625 Madison, 2625 Manhattan)	3200
2125WS	Steam Freight Set, *47* (671, 671W, 2411, 2454, 2452, 2457)	550
2126WS	Steam Passenger Set, *47* (671, 671W, 2625 Irvington, 2625 Madison, 2625 Manhattan)	1950
2127WS	Steam Work Train Set, *47* (671, 671W, 3459, 2461, 2460, 2420)	705
2129WS	Steam Freight Set, *47* (726, 2426W, 3854, 2411, 2855, 2457)	2250
2131WS	Steam Work Train Set, *47* (726, 2426W, 3462, 3451, 2460, 2420)	1200
2133W	Diesel Freight Set, *48* (2333P/T AA, 2458, 3459, 2555, 2357)	1350
2135WS	Steam Freight Set, *48* (675, 2466WX, 2456, 2411, 2357)	350
2135WS	Steam Freight Set, *49* (675, 6466WX, 6456, 6411, 6457)	345
2136WS	Steam Passenger Set, *48* (675, 2466WX, two 2442, 2443)	620
2136WS	Steam Passenger Set, *49* (675, 6466WX, two 6442, 6443)	640
2137WS	Steam Freight Set, *48* (675, 2466WX, 2458, 3459, 2456, 2357)	720
2139W	PRR Electric Freight Set, *49* (2332, 6456, 3464, 3461, 6457)	1360
2139W	PRR Electric Freight Set, *48* (2332, 2458, 3451, 2456, 2357)	1425
2140WS	Steam Passenger Set, *48–49* (671, 2671W, 2400, 2401, 2402)	1270
2141WS	Steam Freight Set, *48* (671, 2671W, 3451, 3462, 2456, 2357)	375
2143WS	Steam Work Train Set, *48* (671, 2671W, 3459, 2461, 2460, 2420)	795
2144W	PRR Electric Passenger Set, *48–49* (2332, 2625, 2627, 2628)	2065
2145WS	Steam Freight Set, *48* (726, 2426W, 3462, 2411, 2460, 2357)	815
2146WS	Steam Passenger Set, *48–49* (726, 2426W, 2625, 2627, 2628)	2000
2147WS	Steam Freight Set, *49* (675, 6466WX, 3472, 6465, 3469, 6457)	400
2148WS	Hudson Passenger Set, *50* (773, 2426W, 2625, 2627, 2628)	5550
2149B	Diesel Work Train Set, *49* (622, 6520, 3469, 2460, 6419)	690

SETS

Exc

2150WS	Steam Passenger Set, *50* (681, 2671W, 2421, 2422, 2423)	1000	___
2151W	Diesel Freight Set, *49* (2333P/T AA, 3464, 6555, 3469, 6520, 6457)	850	___
2153WS	Steam Work Train Set, *49* (671, 2671W, 3469, 6520, 2460, 6419)	620	___
2155WS	Steam Freight Set, *49* (726, 2426W, 6411, 3656, 2460, 6457)	795	___
2159W	Electric Freight Set, *50* (2330, 3464, 6462, 3461, 6456, 6457)	3000	___
2161W	Santa Fe Diesel Freight Set, *50* (2343P/T AA, 3469, 3464, 3461, 6520, 6457)	1520	___
2163WS	Steam Freight Set, *50* (736, 2671WX, 6472, 6462, 6555, 6457)	550	___
2163WS	Steam Freight Set, *51* (736, 2671WX, 6472, 6462, 6465, 6457)	600	___
2165WS	Steam Freight Set, *50* (736, 2671WX, 3472, 6456, 3461, 6457)	690	___
2167WS	Steam Freight Set, *50–51* (681, 2671W, 6462, 3464, 6457)	475	___
2169WS	Hudson Freight Set, *50* (773, 2426W, 3656, 6456, 3469, 6411, 6457)	2810	___
2171W	NYC Diesel Freight Set, *50* (2344P/T AA, 3469, 3464, 3461, 6520, 6457)	1100	___
2173WS	Steam Freight Set, *50* (681, 2671W, 3472, 6555, 3469, 6457)	595	___
2173WS	Steam Freight Set, *51* (681, 2671W, 3472, 6465, 3469, 6457)	515	___
2175W	Santa Fe Diesel Freight Set, *50* (2343P/T AA, 6456, 3464, 6555, 6462, 6457)	925	___
2175W	Santa Fe Diesel Freight Set, *51* (2343 AA, 6456, 3464, 6465, 6462, 6457)	935	___
2177WS	Steam Freight Set, *52* (675, 2046W, 6462, 6465, 6457)	235	___
2179WS	Steam Freight Set, *52* (671, 2046WX, 3464, 6465, 6462, 6457)	330	___
2183WS	Steam Freight Set, *52* (726, 2046W, 3464, 6462, 6465, 6457)	900	___
2185W	NYC Diesel Freight Set, *50* (2344P/T AA, 6456, 3464, 6555, 6462, 6457)	960	___
2185W	NYC Diesel Freight Set, *51* (2344 AA, 6456, 3464, 6465, 6462, 6457)	1050	___
2187WS	Steam Freight Set, *52* (671, 2046WX, 6462, 3472, 3469, 6456, 6457)	650	___
2189WS	Steam Freight Set, *52* (726, 2046W, 3520, 3656, 6462, 3461, 6457)	630	___
2190W	Santa Fe Diesel Passenger Set, *52* (2343P/T AA, 2531, 2532, 2533, 2534)	1900	___
2190W	Santa Fe Diesel Passenger Set, *53* (2353P/T AA, 2531, 2533, 2532, 2534)	1900	___
2191W	Santa Fe Diesel Freight Set, *52* (2343P/C/T ABA, 6462, 6656, 6456, 6457)	1350	___
2193W	NYC Diesel Freight Set, *52* (2344P/C/T ABA, 6462, 6656, 6456, 6457)	1040	___
2201WS	Steam Freight Set, *53* (685, 6026W, 6462, 6464-50, 6465, 6357)	365	___

2203WS Steam Freight Set, *53*
(681, 2046WX, 6415, 3520, 6464-25, 6417)   665

2205WS Steam Freight Set, *53*
(736, 2046W, 3484, 6415, 6468, 6456, 6417)   575

2207W Santa Fe Diesel Freight Set, *53*
(2353P/C/T ABA, 6462, 3484, 6415, 6417)   965

2209W NYC Diesel Freight Set, *53*
(2354P/C/T ABA, 6462, 3484, 6415, 6417)   1200

2211WS Steam Freight Set, *53*
(681, 2046WX, 3656, 6464-75, 3461, 6417)   740

2213WS Steam Freight Set, *53*
(736, 2046W, 3461, 3520, 3469, 6460, 6419)   650

2217WS Steam Freight Set, *54*
(682, 2046WX, 6464-175, 3562-25, 6356, 6417)   1000

2219W Diesel Freight Set, *54*
(2321, 6456-25, 6464-50, 6462-25, 6415, 6417)   1535

2221WS Steam Freight Set, *54*
(646, 2046W, 6468, 3620, 3469, 6456-25, 6417-25)   500

2222WS Steam Passenger Set, *54*
(646, 2046W, 2530, 2531, 2532)   1800

2223W Diesel Freight Set, *54*
(2321, 6464-100, 3461-25, 3482, 6462-125,
6417-50)   2085

2225WS Steam Work Train Set, *54*
(736, 2046W, 3461-25, 3562 or 3562-25, 3620,
6460, 6419)   1020

2227W Santa Fe Diesel Freight Set, *54*
(2353P/T AA, 3562-25, 6356, 6456-75, 6468,
6417-25)   1725

2229W NYC Freight Set, *54*
(2354P/T AA, 3562-25, 6356, 6456-75, 6468,
6417-25)   1300

2231W Southern Diesel Freight Set, *54*
(2356P/C/T ABA, 6511, 6561, 3482, 6415, 6417-25)   2610

2234W Santa Fe Diesel Passenger Set, *54*
(2353P/T AA, 2530, 2531, 2532, 2533)   1045

2235W MILW Diesel Freight Set, *55*
(2338, 6436-25, 6362, 6560, 6419)   575

2237WS Steam Freight Set, *55*
(665, 6026W, 3562-50, 6464-275, 6415, 6417)   380

2239W Illinois Central Diesel Freight Set, *55*
(2363P/C AB, 6672, 6464-125, 6414, 6517)   1700

2241WS Steam Freight Set, *55*
(646, 2046W, 3359, 6446, 3620, 6417)   535

2243W Diesel Freight Set, *55*
(2321, 3662, 6511, 6462-125, 6464-300, 6417)   1400

2244W Wabash Diesel Passenger Set, *55*
(2367P/C AB, 2530, 2531, 2533)   3650

2245WS Steam Freight Set, *55*
(682, 2046WX, 3562-25, 6436-25, 6561, 6560,
6419)   1150

2247W Wabash Diesel Freight Set, *55*
(2367P/C AB, 6462-125, 3662, 6464-150, 3361,
6517)   2200

2249WS Steam Freight Set, *55*
(736, 2046W, 6464-275, 6414, 3359, 3562-50,
6517)   1000

SETS

2251W Diesel Freight Set, *55*
(2331, 6464-275, 3562-50, 6414, 3359, 6517) — 2000 ____

2253W PRR Electric Freight Set, *55*
(2340-25, 3361, 6464-300, 3620, 6414, 6417) — 2700 ____

2254W PRR Electric Passenger Set, *55*
(2340, 2541, 2542, 2543, 2544) — 5500 ____

2255W Diesel Work Train Set, *56*
(601, 3424, 6362, 6560, 6119-25) — 725 ____

2257WS Steam Freight Set, *56*
(665, 2046, 3361, 6346, 6467, 6462-125, 6427) — 500 ____

2259W NH Electric Freight Set, *56*
(2350, 6464-425, 6430, 3650, 6511, 6427) — 775 ____

2261WS Steam Freight Set, *56*
(646, 2046W, 3562-50, 6414, 6436-25, 6376, 6417) — 570 ____

2263W NH Electric Freight Set, *56*
(2350, 3359, 6468-25, 6414, 3662, 6517) — 1000 ____

2265WS Steam Freight Set, *56*
(736, 2046W, 3620, 3424, 6430, 6467, 6517) — 675 ____

2267W Diesel Freight Set, *56*
(2331, 3562-50, 3359, 3361, 6560, 6419-50) — 1700 ____

2269W B&O Diesel Freight Set, *56*
(2368P/C AB, 3356, 6518, 6315, 3361, 6517) — 3200 ____

2270W Jersey Central Diesel Passenger Set, *56*
(2341, 2531, 2532, 2533) — 5000 ____

2271W PRR Electric Freight Set, *56*
(2360-25, 3424, 3662, 6414, 6418, 6417) — 2200 ____

2273W MILW Diesel Freight Set, *56*
(2378P/C AB, 342, 6342, 3562-50, 3662, 3359, 6517) — 3500 ____

2274W PRR Electric Passenger Set, *56*
(2360, 2541, 2542, 2543, 2544) — 2650 ____

2275W Wabash Diesel Freight Set, *57*
(2339, 3444, 6464-475, 6425, 6427) — 790 ____

2276W Budd RDC Set, *57*
(404, two 2559) — 2035 ____

2277WS Steam Work Train Set, *57*
(665, 2046W, 6446-25, 3650, 6560-25, 6119-75) — 585 ____

2279W NH Electric Freight Set, *57*
(2350, 3424, 6464-425, 6424, 6477, 6427) — 730 ____

2281W Santa Fe Diesel Freight Set, *57*
(2243P/C AB, 6464-150, 3361, 3562-75, 6560-25, 6119-75) — 1050 ____

2283WS Steam Freight Set, *57*
(646, 2046W, 3424, 3361, 6464-525, 6562-50, 6357) — 750 ____

2285W Diesel Freight Set, *57*
(2331, 6418, 6414, 6425, 3662, 6517) — 2000 ____

2287W MILW Electric Freight Set, *57*
(2351, 342, 6342, 6464-500, 3650, 6315, 6427) — 2000 ____

2289WS Super O Steam Freight Set, *57*
(736, 2046W, 3359, 3494-275, 3361, 6430, 6427) — 1105 ____

2291W Super O Rio Grande Diesel Freight Set, *57*
(2379P/C AB, 3562-75, 3530, 3444, 6464-525, 6657) — 1965 ____

2292WS Super O Steam Passenger Set, *57*
(646, 2046W, 2530, 2531, 2532, 2533) — 2000 ____

2293W Super O PRR Electric Freight Set, *57*
(2360, 3662, 3650, 6414, 6518, 6417) — 2400 ____

SETS

			Exc
___	**2295WS**	Super O Steam Freight Set, *57* (746, 746W, 342, 6342, 3530, 3361, 6560-25, 6419-100)	2290
___	**2296W**	Super O CP Diesel Passenger Set, *57* (2373P/T AA, 2551, 2552, 2553, 2554)	4670
___	**2297WS**	Super O Steam Freight Set, *57* (746, 746W, 264, 6264, 3356, 3662, 345, 6342, 6517)	2300
___	**2501W**	Super O Diesel Work Train Set, *58* (2348, 6464-525, 6802, 6560-25, 6119-100)	680
___	**2502W**	Super O Budd RDC Set, *58* (400, 2550, 2559)	2000
___	**2503WS**	Super O Steam Freight Set, *58* (665, 2046W, 3361, 6434, 6801, 6536, 6357)	525
___	**2505W**	Super O Electric Freight Set, *58* (2329, 6805, 6519, 6800, 6464-500, 6357)	1400
___	**2507W**	Super O Diesel Freight Set, *58* (2242P/C AB, 3444, 6464-425, 6424, 6468-25, 6357)	2000
___	**2509WS**	Super O Steam Freight Set, *58* (665, 2046W, 6414, 3650, 6464-475, 6805, 6357)	800
___	**2511W**	Super O Electric Work Set, *58* (2352, 3562-75, 3424, 3361, 6560-25, 6119-100)	1100
___	**2513W**	Super O Electric Freight Set, *58* (2329, 6556, 6425, 6414, 6434, 3359, 6427-60)	3000
___	**2515WS**	Super O Steam Freight Set, *58* (646, 2046W, 3662, 6424, 3444, 6800, 6427)	785
___	**2517W**	Super O Rio Grande Diesel Freight Set, *58* (2379P/C AB, 6519, 6805, 6434, 6800, 6657)	2550
___	**2518W**	Super O PRR Electric Passenger Set, *58* (2352, 2531, 2533, 2534)	1850
___	**2519W**	Super O Diesel Freight Set, *58* (2331, 6434, 3530, 6801, 6414, 6464-275, 6557)	1900
___	**2521WS**	Super O Steam Freight Set, *58* (746, 746W, 6805, 3361, 6430, 3356, 6424, 6557)	2000
___	**2523W**	Super O Santa Fe Diesel Freight Set, *58* (2383P/T AA, 264, 6264, 6434, 6800, 3662, 6517)	1300
___	**2525WS**	Super O Steam Work Train Set, *58* (746, 746W, 342, 345, 6519, 6518, 6560-25, 6419-100)	2300
___	**2526W**	Super O Santa Fe Diesel Passenger Set, *58* (2383P/T AA, 2530, 2531, two 2532)	1775
___	**2527**	Super O Missile Launcher Set, *59–60* (44, 3419, 6844, 6823, 6814, 943)	755
___	**2528WS**	Super O General Set, *59–61* (1872, 1872T, 1877, 1876, 1875W)	845
___	**2529W**	Super Electric Work Train Set, *59* (2329, 3512, 6819, 6812, 6560, 6119-25 or 6119-100)	1300
___	**2531WS**	Super O Steam Freight Set, *59* (637, 2046W, 3435, 6817, 6636, 6825, 6119-100)	1300
___	**2533W**	Super O GN Electric Freight Set, *59* (2358, 6650, 6414, 3444, 6470, 6357)	1910
___	**2535WS**	Super O Steam Freight Set, *59* (665, 2046W, 3434, 6823, 3672, 6812, 6357)	840
___	**2537W**	Super O NH Diesel Freight Set, *59* (2242P/C AB, 3435, 3650, 6464-275, 6819, 6427)	2500

SETS

		Exc	
2539WS	Super O Steam Freight Set, *59* (665, 2046W, 3361, 6464-825, 3512, 6812, 6357, 464)	1015	___
2541W	Super O Santa Fe Diesel Freight Set, *59* (2383P/T AA, 3356, 3512, 6519, 6816, 6427)	2400	___
2543WS	Super O Steam Freight Set, *59* (736, 2046W, 264, 6264, 3435, 6823, 6434, 6812, 6557)	1590	___
2544W	Super O Santa Fe Diesel Passenger Set, *59–60* (2383P/T AA, 2530, 2561, 2562, 2563)	1860	___
2545WS	Super O Military Set, *59* (746, 746W, 175, 6175, 6470, 3419, 6650, 3540, 6517)	3000	___
2547WS	Super O Steam Freight Set, *60* (637, 2046W, 3330, 6475, 6361, 6357)	675	___
2549W	Super O Military Set, *60* (2349, 3540, 6470, 6819, 6650, 3535)	1160	___
2551W	Super O GN Electric Freight Set, *60* (2358, 6828, 3512, 6827, 6736, 6812, 6427)	2300	___
2553WS	Super O Steam Freight Set, *60* (736, 2046W, 3830, 3435, 3419, 3672, 6357)	1615	___
2555W	Super O Santa Fe Freight Set with matching HO Set, *60* (2383P/T AA, 3434, 3366, 6414, 6464-900, 6357-50)	10000	___
2570	Super O Santa Fe Work Train Set, *61* (616, 6822, 6828, 6812, 6736, 6130)	800	___
2571	Super O Steam Freight Set, *61* (637, 736W, 3419, 6445, 6361, 6119-100)	550	___
2572	Super O B&M Diesel Freight Set, *61* (2359, 6544, 3830, 6448, 3519, 3535)	800	___
2573	Super O Steam Freight Set, *61* (736, 736W, 3545, 6416, 6475, 6440, 6357)	1400	___
2574	Super O Santa Fe Diesel Freight Set, *61* (2383P/T AA, 3665, 3419, 3830, 448, 6448, 6437)	1500	___
2575	Super O PRR Electric Freight Set, *61* (2360, 6530, 6828, 6464-900, 6827, 6736, 6560, 6437)	2500	___
2576	Super O Santa Fe Diesel Passenger Set, *61* (2383P/T AA, 2561, two 2562, 2563)	3030	___
4109WS	Electronic Control Set, *46* (671R, 4424W, 4452, 4454, 5459, 4457)	1085	___
4110WS	Electronic Control Set, *48–49* (671R, 4671W, 4452, 4454, 5459, 4357, 151, 97)	2500	___
11201	O27 Steam Freight Set, *62* (242, 1060T, 6042-75, 6502, 6047)	125	___
11011	O27 Diesel Freight Set, *62* (222, 3510, 6076, 6120)	145	___
11212	O27 Santa Fe Diesel Freight Set, *62* (633, 3349, 6825, 6057)	375	___
11222	O27 Steam Freight Set, *62* (236, 1050T, 3357, 6343, 6119-100)	195	___
11232	O27 NH Diesel Freight Set, *62* (232, 3410, 6062, 6413, 6057-50)	450	___
11242	O27 Steam Freight Set, *62* (233, 233W, 6465-100, 6476, 6162, 6017)	175	___
11252	O27 Texas Special Space Set, *62* 211P/T AA, 3509, 6448, 3349, 6463, 6057)	500	___

SETS

11268 027 C&O Diesel Freight Set, *62*
(2365, 3619, 3470, 3349, 6501, 6017) — 1425

11278 027 Steam Freight Set, *62*
(2037, 233W, 6473, 6162, 6050-110, 6825, 6017) — 260

11288 027 Space Set, *62*
(229P/C AB, 3413, 6512, 6413, 6463, 6059) — 1215

11298 027 Steam Freight Set, *62*
(2037, 233W, 6544, 3419, 6448, 3330, 6017) — 500

11308 027 Santa Fe Diesel Passenger Set, *62*
(218P/T AA, two 2412, 2414, 2416) — 730

11311 027 Steam Freight Set, *63*
(1062, 1061T, 6409-25, 6076-100, 6167-25) — 100

11321 027 Rio Grande Diesel Freight Set, *63*
(221, 3309, 6076-75, 6042-75, 6167-50) — 300

11331 027 Steam Freight Set, *63*
(242, 1060T, 6473, 6476-25, 6142, 6059-50) — 100

11341 027 Santa Fe Diesel Freight Set, *63*
(634, 3410, 6407, 6014-325, 6463, 6059-50) — 950

11351 027 Steam Freight Set, *63*
(237, 1060T, 6050-100, 6465-150, 6408, 6162,
6119-110) — 190

11361 027 Texas Special Space Set, *63*
(211P/T AA, 3665-100, 3413-150, 6470, 6413,
6257-100) — 750

11375 027 Steam Freight Set, *63*
(238, 234W, 6822-50, 6465-150, 6414-150,
6476-75, 6162, 6257-100) — 700

11385 027 Santa Fe Space Set, *63*
(223P/218C AB, 3619-100, 3470-100, 3349-100,
3830-75, 6407, 6257-100 or 6017-235) — 2000

11395 027 Steam Freight Set, *63*
(2037, 233W or 234W, 6464-725, 6469-50, 6536,
6440-50, 6560-50, 6119-100) — 600

11405 027 Santa Fe Diesel Passenger Set, *63*
(218P/T AA, two 2412, 2414, 2416) — 750

11420 027 Steam Freight Set, *64*
(1061, 1061T, 6042-250, 6167-25) — 200

11430 027 Steam Freight, *64*
(1062, 1061T, 6176, 6142, 6167-125) — 135

11440 027 Rio Grande Diesel Freight Set, *64*
(221, 3309, 6176-50, 6142-125, 6167-100) — 285

11450 027 Steam Freight Set, *64*
(242, 1060T, 6473, 6142-75, 6176-50, 6059-50) — 195

11460 027 Steam Freight Set, *64*
(238, 234W, 6014-335, 6465-150, 6142-100,
6176-75, 6119-100) — 150

11470 027 Steam Freight Set, *64*
(237, 1060T, 6014-335, 6465-150, 6142-100,
6176-75, 6119-100) — 150

11480 027 Diesel Freight Set, *64*
(213P/T AA, 6473, 6176-50, 6142-150, 6014-335,
6257-100 or 6059) — 560

11490 027 Diesel Passenger Set, *64–65*
(212P/T AA, 2404, 2405, 2406) — 360

11500 027 Steam Freight Set, *64*
(2029, 234W, 6465-150, 6402-50, 6176-75,
6014-335, 6257-100 or 6059) — 275

SETS

		Exc
11500	027 Steam Freight Set, *65* (2029, 234W, 6465-150, 6402-50, 6076, 6014-335, 6257-100 or 6059)	275 ___
11500	027 Steam Freight Set, *66* (2029, 234W, 6465-150, 6402-50, 6176-75, 6014-335, 6059)	275 ___
11510	027 Steam Freight Set, *64* (2029, 1060T, 6465-150, 6402-50, 6176-75, 6014-335, 6257-100 or 6059)	300 ___
11520	027 Steam Freight Set, *65–66* (242, 1062T, 6176, 3362/64, 6142, 6059)	165 ___
11530	027 Santa Fe Diesel Freight, *65–66* (634, 6014, 6142, 6402, 6130)	155 ___
11540	027 Steam Freight Set, *65–66* (239, 242T, 6473, 6465, 6176, 6119-100)	155 ___
11550	027 Steam Freight Set, *65–66* (239, 234W, 6473, 6465, 6176, 6119)	225 ___
11560	027 Texas Special Freight Set, *65–66* (211P/T AA, 6473, 6076, 6142, 6465, 6059)	210 ___
11590	027 Santa Fe Diesel Passenger Set, *66* (212P/T AA, 2408, 2409, 2410)	640 ___
11600	027 Steam Freight Set, *68* (2029, 234W, 6014, 6476, 6315, 6560, 6130)	1280 ___
11710	027 Steam Freight Set, *69* (1061, 1061T or 1062T, 6402, 6142, 6059)	170 ___
11720	Diesel Freight Set, *69* (2024, 6142, 6402, 6176, 6057)	240 ___
11730	027 UP Diesel Freight Set, *69* (645, 6402, 6014-85, 6176, 6142, 6167-85)	800 ___
11740	027 RI Diesel Freight Set, *69* (2041P/T AA, 6315, 6142, 6014-410, 6476, 6057)	310 ___
11750	027 Steam Freight Set, *69* (2029, 234T, 6014-85, 6476, 6473, 6315, 6130)	360 ___
11760	027 Steam Freight Set, *69* (2029, 234W, 6014-410, 6315, 6476, 3376, 6119)	355 ___
12502	Prairie-Rider Gift Pack, *62* (1862, 1862T, 3376, 1877 or 6473, 1866, 1865)	600 ___
12512	Enforcer Gift Pack, *62* (45, 3413, 3619, 3470, 3349, 6017)	1100 ___
12700	Steam Freight Set, *64* (736, 736W, 6464-725, 6162-100, 6414-75, 6476-125, 6437, no transformer)	1000 ___
12710	Steam Freight Set, *64–66* (736, 736W, 6464-725, 6162-100, 6414-75, 6476-125, 6437, LW transformer)	1150 ___
12720	Santa Fe Diesel Freight Set, *64* (2383P/T AA, 6464-725, 6162-100, 6414-75, 6476-125, 6437, no transformer)	1500 ___
12730	Santa Fe Diesel Freight Set, *64–66* (2383P/T AA, 6464-725, 6162-100, 6414-75, 6476-125, 6437, LW transformer)	895 ___
12740	Santa Fe Diesel Freight Set, *64* (2383P/T AA, 3662, 6361, 6436-110, 6315-60, 6464-525, 6822, 6437)	1500 ___
12760	Steam Freight Set, *64* (736, 736W, 3662, 6361, 6436-110, 6315-60, 6464-525, 6822, 6437)	1100 ___

12780	Santa Fe Diesel Passenger, *64–66* (2383P/T AA, 2521, 2522, two 2523)	1855
12800	B&M Diesel Freight Set, *65–66* (2346, 6428, 6436, 6464-475, 6415, 6017-100)	510
12820	Diesel Freight Set, *65* (2322, 3662, 6822, 6361, 6464-725, 6436, 6315, 6437)	1525
12840	Steam Freight Set, *66* (665, 736W, 6464-375, 6464-450, 6431, 6415, 6437)	925
12850	Diesel Freight Set, *66* (2322, 3662, 6822, 6361, 6464-725, 6436, 6315, 6437)	1700
13008	Super O Steam Freight Set, *62* (637, 736W, 3349, 6448, 6501, 6119-100)	500
13018	Super O Santa Fe Diesel Freight Set, *62* (616, 6500, 6650, 3519, 6448, 6017-235)	1200
13028	Super O Space Set, *62* (2359, 3665, 3349, 3820, 3470, 6017-100)	1000
13036	Super O General Set, *62* (1872, 1872T, 6445, 3370, 1876, 1875W)	980
13048	Super O Steam Freight Set, *62* (736, 736W, 6822, 6414, 3362, 6440, 6437)	720
13058	Super O Space Set, *62* (2383P/T AA, 3619, 3413, 6512, 470, 6470, 6437)	1600
13068	Super O PRR Electric Freight Set, *62* (2360, 6464-725, 6828, 6416, 6827, 6530, 6475, 6437)	3200
13078	Super O PRR Electric Passenger Set, *62* (2360, 2521, two 2522, 2523)	3500
13088	Super O Santa Fe Diesel Passenger Set, *62* (2383P/T AA, 2521, two 2522, 2523)	2500
13098	Super O Steam Freight Set, *63* (637, 736W, 6469, 6464-900, 6414, 6446, 6447)	2000
13108	Super O Santa Fe Space Set, *63* (617, 3665, 3419, 6448, 3830, 3470, 6119-100)	1000
13118	Super O Steam Freight Set, *63* (736, 736W, 6446-60, 6827, 3362, 6315-60, 6560, 6429)	1500
13128	Super O Santa Fe Space Set, *63* (2383P/T AA, 3619, 3413, 6512, 448, 6448, 64337)	1750
13138	Super O PRR Electric Freight Set, *63* (2360, 6464-725, 6828, 6416, 6827, 6315-60, 6436-110, 6437)	3800
13148	Super O Santa Fe Diesel Passenger Set, *63* (2383P/T AA, 2521, 2522, two 2523)	2500
13150	Super O Hudson Steam Freight Set, *64* (773, 736W or 773W, 3434, 6361, 3662, 6415, 3356, 6436-110, 6437)	2500

ABBREVIATIONS

Descriptions

AAR	Association of American Railroads (truck type)
AEC	Atomic Energy Commission
AF	American Flyer
CC	Command Control
DD	Double-door
EMD	Electro-Motive Division
ETD	End-of-train device
FARR	Famous American Railroad Series
FF	Fallen Flag Series
FM	Fairbanks-Morse
GE	General Electric
LL	Lionel Lines
MOW	Maintenance-of-way
MU	Multiple unit (commuter cars)
O	Lionel gauge (1¼" between outside rails)
OO	Lionel gauge (¾" between outside rails)
PFE	Pacific Fruit Express
REA	Railway Express Agency
SSS	Service Station Special
std	Standard gauge (2⅛" between outside rails)
std O	Standard O (scale length and dimension)
TMCC	TrainMaster Command Control
USMC	United States Marine Corps
1-D	One dome
2-D	Two dome
3-D	Three dome

ABBREVIATIONS

Railroad names

ACL	Atlantic Coast Line
ATSF	Atchison, Topeka & Santa Fe
B&A	Boston & Albany
BAR	Bangor & Aroostook
B&LE	Bessemer & Lake Erie
B&M	Boston & Maine
BN	Burlington Northern
BNSF	Burlington Northern Santa Fe
B&O	Baltimore & Ohio
C&IM	Chicago & Illinois Midland
C&EI	Chicago & Eastern Illinois
CB&Q	Chicago, Burlington & Quincy
CMStP&P	Chicago, Milwaukee, St. Paul & Pacific
CN	Canadian National
CNJ	Central of New Jersey
C&IM	Chicago & Illinois Midland
C&NW	Chicago & North Western
C&O	Chesapeake & Ohio
CP	Canadian Pacific
D&H	Delaware & Hudson
DL&W	Delaware, Lackawanna & Western
DM&IR	Duluth, Missabe & Iron Range
D&RGW	Denver & Rio Grande Western
D&TS	Detroit & Toledo Shore Line
DT&I	Detroit, Toledo & Ironton
EJ&E	Elgin, Joliet & Eastern
Erie-Lack.	Erie-Lackawanna
FEC	Florida East Coast
GM&O	Gulf, Mobile & Ohio
GN	Great Northern
GTW	Grand Trunk Western
IC	Illinois Central
ICG	Illinois Central Gulf
KCS	Kansas City Southern
L&N	Louisville & Nashville
LIRR	Long Island Railroad
LNAC	Louisville, New Albany & Corydon

Build Your Toy Train Library

Railroad names

LV	Lehigh Valley
MD&W	Minnesota, Dakota & Western
MKT	Missouri-Kansas-Texas
MN&S	Minneapolis, Northfield & Southern
MP	Missouri Pacific
MPA	Maryland & Pennsylvania
MILW	Milwaukee Road
M&StL	Minneapolis & St. Louis
NC&StL	Nashville, Chattanooga & St. Louis
NdeM	Nacionales de Mexico Railway
NH	New Haven
NKP	Nickel Plate Road
NP	Northern Pacific
NS	Norfolk Southern
N&W	Norfolk & Western
NYC	New York Central
NYNH&H	New York, New Haven & Hartford
NYO&W	New York, Ontario & Western
PC	Penn Central
P&E	Peoria & Eastern
P&LE	Pittsburgh & Lake Erie
PRR	Pennsylvania Railroad
RF&P	Richmond, Fredericksburg & Potomac
RI	Rock Island
SMARRCO	San Manuel Arizona Railroad Company
SP	Southern Pacific
SP&S	Spokane, Portland & Seattle
TA&G	Tennessee, Alabama & Georgia
TH&B	Toronto, Hamilton & Buffalo
T&P	Texas & Pacific
TP&W	Toledo, Peoria & Western
UP	Union Pacific
V&TRR	Virginia & Truckee Railroad
W&ARR	Western & Atlantic Railroad
WM	Western Maryland
WP	Western Pacific